Ford
Tempo and
Mercury
Topaz
Automotive
Repair
Manual

by Mark Christman
and John H Haynes
Member of the Guild of Motoring Writers

Models covered:
All Ford Tempo and Mercury Topaz models
with a gasoline engine
1984 through 1994

(7E12 - 36078)

(1418)

ABCDE
FGHIJ
KL

2

Haynes Publishing Group
Sparkford Nr Yeovil
Somerset BA22 7JJ England

Haynes North America, Inc
861 Lawrence Drive
Newbury Park
California 91320 USA

D0479012

Acknowledgements

We are grateful to the Ford Motor Company for assistance with technical information, certain illustrations and vehicle photos.

A book in the Haynes Automotive Repair Manual Series

Printed in the U.S.A.

ISBN 1 56392 128 6

Library of Congress Catalog Card Number 94-78742

While every attempt is made to ensure that the information in this manual is correct, no liability can be accepted by the authors or publishers for loss, damage or injury caused by any errors in, or omissions from, the information given.

98-352

Contents

Haynes mechanic, author and photographer with Ford Tempo

About this manual

Its purpose

The purpose of this manual is to help you get the best value from your vehicle. It can do so in several ways. It can help you decide what work must be done, even if you choose to have it done by a dealer service department or a repair shop; it provides information and procedures for routine maintenance and servicing; and it offers diagnostic and repair procedures to follow when trouble occurs.

We hope you use the manual to tackle the work yourself. For many simpler jobs, doing it yourself may be quicker than arranging an appointment to get the vehicle into a shop and making the trips to leave it and pick it up. More importantly, a lot of money can be saved by avoiding the expense the shop must pass on to you to cover its labor and overhead costs. An added benefit is the sense of satisfaction and accomplishment that you feel after doing the job yourself.

Using the manual

The manual is divided into Chapters. Each Chapter is divided into numbered Sections, which are headed in bold type between horizontal lines. Each Section consists of consecutively numbered paragraphs.

At the beginning of each numbered Section you will be referred to any illustrations which apply to the procedures in that Section. The reference numbers used in illustration captions pinpoint the pertinent Section and the Step within that Section. That is, illustration 3.2 means the illustration refers to Section 3 and Step (or paragraph) 2 within that Section.

Procedures, once described in the text, are not normally repeated. When it's necessary to refer to another Chapter, the reference will be given as Chapter and Section number. Cross references given without use of the word "Chapter" apply to Sections and/or paragraphs in the same Chapter. For example, "see Section 8" means in the same Chapter.

References to the left or right side of the vehicle assume you are sitting in the driver's seat, facing forward.

Even though we have prepared this manual with extreme care, neither the publisher nor the author can accept responsibility for any errors in, or omissions from, the information given.

NOTE

A **Note** provides information necessary to properly complete a procedure or information which will make the procedure easier to understand.

CAUTION

A **Caution** provides a special procedure or special steps which must be taken while completing the procedure where the Caution is found. Not heeding a Caution can result in damage to the assembly being worked on.

WARNING

A **Warning** provides a special procedure or special steps which must be taken while completing the procedure where the Warning is found. Not heeding a Warning can result in personal injury.

Introduction to the Ford Tempo/Mercury Topaz

The Ford Tempo and Mercury Topaz were introduced in 1984. The compact, front-wheel-drive sedans are available in either two- or four-door models.

Four-cylinder models are powered by Ford's 2.3L overhead valve, High Swirl Combustion (HSC) engine. Ford's 3.0L overhead valve V6 engine is used in other models. The 1984 HSC engine is equipped with an electronic feedback carburetor (50 states). In 1985, the carburetor was replaced by a Central Fuel Injection (CFI) system. All Canadian four-cylinder vehicles are equipped with a non-feedback carburetor. Later four-cylinder models and all V6 models are equipped with a multiport Electronic Fuel Injection (EFI) system.

Available transaxles are a four- or five-speed manual and an automatic transaxle in 1984 and 1985. After the 1985 model year, the four speed was no longer available.

The front suspension is a conventional front-wheel-drive MacPherson strut design. The rear suspension is also a MacPherson strut design, each side consisting of a shock absorber strut assembly and two parallel control arms.

Vehicle identification numbers

Modifications are a continuing and unpublicized process in automotive manufacturing. Because spare parts manuals and lists are compiled on a numerical basis, the individual vehicle numbers are essential to correctly identify the component required

Vehicle identification number (VIN)

The VIN number is very important because it is used for title and registration purposes. The VIN number is stamped on a metal plate fastened to the instrument panel close to the windshield on the driver's side (see illustration). It is visible from outside the vehicle, looking through the windshield on the driver's side.

Vehicle Certification Label

The Vehicle Certification Label (VC Label) is affixed to the left front door lock panel or door pillar (see illustrations). The upper half of the label contains the name of the manufacturer, the month and year of manufacture, the Gross Vehicle Weight Rating (GVWR), the Gross Axle Weight Rating (GAWR) and the certification statement.

The VC label also contains a Vehicle Identification Number which is used for warranty identification of the vehicle and indicates such things as manufacturer, type of restraint system, line, series, body type, engine model year and consecutive unit number.

Engine identification number

For quick engine identification, refer to the VIN, which lists the engine code as the eighth digit of the VIN. Four-cylinder engines will normally have an R, S, X or T in this position. V6 engines will be identified by a U. Also, there's usually an engine identification number stamped into a machined pad on the engine block.

Transaxle ratio number

The transaxle ratio code is listed on the Vehicle Certification label on the door pillar under AX.

Transaxle identification number

The transaxle identification number is located on a tag (see illustration) attached to the transaxle housing.

The Vehicle Identification Number (VIN), stamped on a metal plate fastened to the top of the dashboard on the driver's side, is clearly visible through the windshield

The Vehicle Certification label (VC label) is on the left front door lock panel or the door pillar

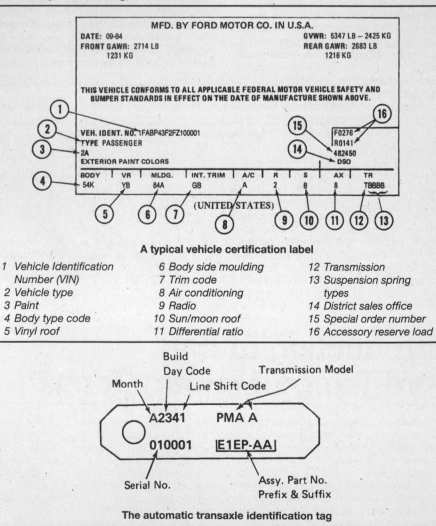

A typical vehicle certification label

1. Vehicle Identification Number (VIN)
2. Vehicle type
3. Paint
4. Body type code
5. Vinyl roof
6. Body side moulding
7. Trim code
8. Air conditioning
9. Radio
10. Sun/moon roof
11. Differential ratio
12. Transmission
13. Suspension spring types
14. District sales office
15. Special order number
16. Accessory reserve load

The automatic transaxle identification tag

Buying parts

Replacement parts are available from many sources, which generally fall into one of two categories - authorized dealer parts departments and independent retail auto parts stores. Our advice concerning these parts is as follows:

Retail auto parts stores: Good auto parts stores will stock frequently needed components which wear out relatively fast, such as clutch components, exhaust systems, brake parts, tune-up parts, etc. These stores often supply new or reconditioned parts on an exchange basis, which can save a considerable amount of money. Discount auto parts stores are often very good places to buy materials and parts needed for general vehicle maintenance such as oil, grease, filters, spark plugs, belts, touch-up paint, bulbs, etc. They also usually sell tools and general accessories, have convenient hours, charge lower prices and can often be found not far from home.

Authorized dealer parts department: This is the best source for parts which are unique to the vehicle and not generally available elsewhere (such as major engine parts, transmission parts, trim pieces, etc.).

Warranty information: If the vehicle is still covered under warranty, be sure that any replacement parts purchased - regardless of the source - do not invalidate the warranty!

To be sure of obtaining the correct parts, have engine and chassis numbers available and, if possible, take the old parts along for positive identification.

Maintenance techniques, tools and working facilities

Maintenance techniques

There are a number of techniques involved in maintenance and repair that will be referred to throughout this manual. Application of these techniques will enable the home mechanic to be more efficient, better organized and capable of performing the various tasks properly, which will ensure that the repair job is thorough and complete.

Fasteners

Fasteners are nuts, bolts, studs and screws used to hold two or more parts together. There are a few things to keep in mind when working with fasteners. Almost all of them use a locking device of some type, either a lockwasher, locknut, locking tab or thread adhesive. All threaded fasteners should be clean and straight, with undamaged threads and undamaged corners on the hex head where the wrench fits. Develop the habit of replacing all damaged nuts and bolts with new ones. Special locknuts with nylon or fiber inserts can only be used once. If they are removed, they lose their locking ability and must be replaced with new ones.

Rusted nuts and bolts should be treated with a penetrating fluid to ease removal and prevent breakage. Some mechanics use turpentine in a spout-type oil can, which works quite well. After applying the rust penetrant, let it work for a few minutes before trying to loosen the nut or bolt. Badly rusted fasteners may have to be chiseled or sawed off or removed with a special nut breaker, available at tool stores.

If a bolt or stud breaks off in an assembly, it can be drilled and removed with a special tool commonly available for this purpose. Most automotive machine shops can perform this task, as well as other repair procedures, such as the repair of threaded holes that have been stripped out.

Flat washers and lockwashers, when removed from an assembly, should always be replaced exactly as removed. Replace any damaged washers with new ones. Never use a lockwasher on any soft metal surface (such as aluminum), thin sheet metal or plastic.

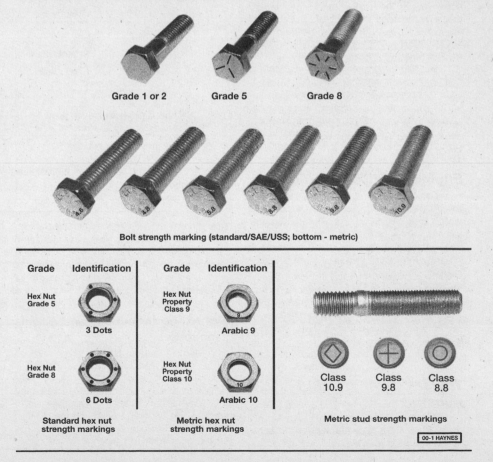

Grade 1 or 2   Grade 5   Grade 8

Bolt strength marking (standard/SAE/USS; bottom - metric)

Grade	Identification	Grade	Identification
Hex Nut Grade 5	3 Dots	Hex Nut Property Class 9	Arabic 9
Hex Nut Grade 8	6 Dots	Hex Nut Property Class 10	Arabic 10

Standard hex nut strength markings

Metric hex nut strength markings

Class 10.9   Class 9.8   Class 8.8

Metric stud strength markings

00-1 HAYNES

Fastener sizes

For a number of reasons, automobile manufacturers are making wider and wider use of metric fasteners. Therefore, it is important to be able to tell the difference between standard (sometimes called U.S. or SAE) and metric hardware, since they cannot be interchanged.

All bolts, whether standard or metric, are sized according to diameter, thread pitch and length. For example, a standard 1/2 - 13 x 1 bolt is 1/2 inch in diameter, has 13 threads per inch and is 1 inch long. An M12 - 1.75 x 25 metric bolt is 12 mm in diameter, has a thread pitch of 1.75 mm (the distance between threads) and is 25 mm long. The two bolts are nearly identical, and easily confused, but they are not interchangeable.

In addition to the differences in diameter, thread pitch and length, metric and standard bolts can also be distinguished by examining the bolt heads. To begin with, the distance across the flats on a standard bolt head is measured in inches, while the same dimension on a metric bolt is sized in millimeters (the same is true for nuts). As a result, a standard wrench should not be used on a metric bolt and a metric wrench should not be used on a standard bolt. Also, most standard bolts have slashes radiating out from the center of the head to denote the grade or strength of the bolt, which is an indication of the amount of torque that can be applied to it. The greater the number of slashes, the greater the strength of the bolt. Grades 0 through 5 are commonly used on automobiles. Metric bolts have a property class (grade) number, rather than a slash, molded into their heads to indicate bolt strength. In this case, the higher the number, the stronger the bolt. Property class numbers 8.8, 9.8 and 10.9 are commonly used on automobiles.

Strength markings can also be used to distinguish standard hex nuts from metric hex nuts. Many standard nuts have dots stamped into one side, while metric nuts are marked with a number. The greater the number of dots, or the higher the number, the greater the strength of the nut.

Metric studs are also marked on their ends according to property class (grade). Larger studs are numbered (the same as metric bolts), while smaller studs carry a geometric code to denote grade.

It should be noted that many fasteners, especially Grades 0 through 2, have no distinguishing marks on them. When such is the case, the only way to determine whether it is standard or metric is to measure the thread pitch or compare it to a known fastener of the same size.

Standard fasteners are often referred to as SAE, as opposed to metric. However, it should be noted that SAE technically refers to a non-metric fine thread fastener only. Coarse thread non-metric fasteners are referred to as USS sizes.

Since fasteners of the same size (both standard and metric) may have different

Metric thread sizes	Ft-lbs	Nm
M-6	6 to 9	9 to 12
M-8	14 to 21	19 to 28
M-10	28 to 40	38 to 54
M-12	50 to 71	68 to 96
M-14	80 to 140	109 to 154

Pipe thread sizes		
1/8	5 to 8	7 to 10
1/4	12 to 18	17 to 24
3/8	22 to 33	30 to 44
1/2	25 to 35	34 to 47

U.S. thread sizes		
1/4 - 20	6 to 9	9 to 12
5/16 - 18	12 to 18	17 to 24
5/16 - 24	14 to 20	19 to 27
3/8 - 16	22 to 32	30 to 43
3/8 - 24	27 to 38	37 to 51
7/16 - 14	40 to 55	55 to 74
7/16 - 20	40 to 60	55 to 81
1/2 - 13	55 to 80	75 to 108

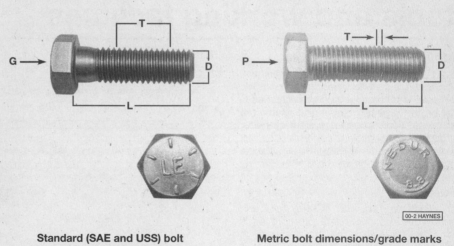

Standard (SAE and USS) bolt dimensions/grade marks

G   Grade marks (bolt strength)
L   Length (in inches)
T   Thread pitch (number of threads per inch)
D   Nominal diameter (in inches)

Metric bolt dimensions/grade marks

P   Property class (bolt strength)
L   Length (in millimeters)
T   Thread pitch (distance between threads in millimeters)
D   Diameter

strength ratings, be sure to reinstall any bolts, studs or nuts removed from your vehicle in their original locations. Also, when replacing a fastener with a new one, make sure that the new one has a strength rating equal to or greater than the original.

Tightening sequences and procedures

Most threaded fasteners should be tightened to a specific torque value (torque is the twisting force applied to a threaded component such as a nut or bolt). Overtightening the fastener can weaken it and cause it to break, while undertightening can cause it to eventually come loose. Bolts, screws and studs, depending on the material they are

made of and their thread diameters, have specific torque values, many of which are noted in the Specifications at the beginning of each Chapter. Be sure to follow the torque recommendations closely. For fasteners not assigned a specific torque, a general torque value chart is presented here as a guide. These torque values are for dry (unlubricated) fasteners threaded into steel or cast iron (not aluminum). As was previously mentioned, the size and grade of a fastener determine the amount of torque that can safely be applied to it. The figures listed here are approximate for Grade 2 and Grade 3 fasteners. Higher grades can tolerate higher torque values.

Fasteners laid out in a pattern, such as cylinder head bolts, oil pan bolts, differential cover bolts, etc., must be loosened or tight-

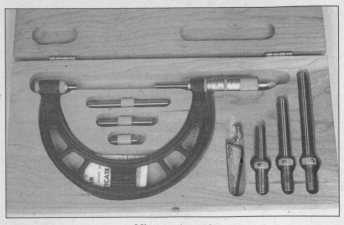

Micrometer set

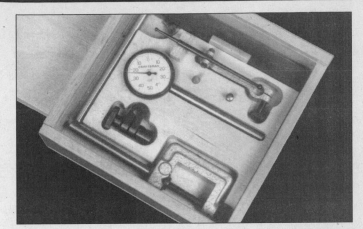

Dial indicator set

ened in sequence to avoid warping the component. This sequence will normally be shown in the appropriate Chapter. If a specific pattern is not given, the following procedures can be used to prevent warping.

Initially, the bolts or nuts should be assembled finger-tight only. Next, they should be tightened one full turn each, in a criss-cross or diagonal pattern. After each one has been tightened one full turn, return to the first one and tighten them all one-half turn, following the same pattern. Finally, tighten each of them one-quarter turn at a time until each fastener has been tightened to the proper torque. To loosen and remove the fasteners, the procedure would be reversed.

Component disassembly

Component disassembly should be done with care and purpose to help ensure that the parts go back together properly. Always keep track of the sequence in which parts are removed. Make note of special characteristics or marks on parts that can be installed more than one way, such as a grooved thrust washer on a shaft. It is a good idea to lay the disassembled parts out on a clean surface in the order that they were removed. It may also be helpful to make sketches or take instant photos of components before removal.

When removing fasteners from a component, keep track of their locations. Sometimes threading a bolt back in a part, or putting the washers and nut back on a stud, can prevent mix-ups later. If nuts and bolts cannot be returned to their original locations, they should be kept in a compartmented box or a series of small boxes. A cupcake or muffin tin is ideal for this purpose, since each cavity can hold the bolts and nuts from a particular area (i.e. oil pan bolts, valve cover bolts, engine mount bolts, etc.). A pan of this type is especially helpful when working on assemblies with very small parts, such as the carburetor, alternator, valve train or interior dash and trim pieces. The cavities can be marked with paint or tape to identify the contents.

Whenever wiring looms, harnesses or connectors are separated, it is a good idea to identify the two halves with numbered pieces of masking tape so they can be easily reconnected.

Gasket sealing surfaces

Throughout any vehicle, gaskets are used to seal the mating surfaces between two parts and keep lubricants, fluids, vacuum or pressure contained in an assembly.

Many times these gaskets are coated with a liquid or paste-type gasket sealing compound before assembly. Age, heat and pressure can sometimes cause the two parts to stick together so tightly that they are very difficult to separate. Often, the assembly can be loosened by striking it with a soft-face hammer near the mating surfaces. A regular hammer can be used if a block of wood is placed between the hammer and the part. Do not hammer on cast parts or parts that could be easily damaged. With any particularly stubborn part, always recheck to make sure that every fastener has been removed.

Avoid using a screwdriver or bar to pry apart an assembly, as they can easily mar the gasket sealing surfaces of the parts, which must remain smooth. If prying is absolutely necessary, use an old broom handle, but keep in mind that extra clean up will be necessary if the wood splinters.

After the parts are separated, the old gasket must be carefully scraped off and the gasket surfaces cleaned. Stubborn gasket material can be soaked with rust penetrant or treated with a special chemical to soften it so it can be easily scraped off. A scraper can be fashioned from a piece of copper tubing by flattening and sharpening one end. Copper is recommended because it is usually softer than the surfaces to be scraped, which reduces the chance of gouging the part. Some gaskets can be removed with a wire brush, but regardless of the method used, the mating surfaces must be left clean and smooth. If for some reason the gasket surface is gouged, then a gasket sealer thick enough to fill scratches will have to be used during reassembly of the components. For most applications, a non-drying (or semi-drying) gasket sealer should be used.

Hose removal tips

Warning: *If the vehicle is equipped with air conditioning, do not disconnect any of the A/C hoses without first having the system depressurized by a dealer service department or a service station.*

Hose removal precautions closely parallel gasket removal precautions. Avoid scratching or gouging the surface that the hose mates against or the connection may leak. This is especially true for radiator hoses. Because of various chemical reactions, the rubber in hoses can bond itself to the metal spigot that the hose fits over. To remove a hose, first loosen the hose clamps that secure it to the spigot. Then, with slip-joint pliers, grab the hose at the clamp and rotate it around the spigot. Work it back and forth until it is completely free, then pull it off. Silicone or other lubricants will ease removal if they can be applied between the hose and the outside of the spigot. Apply the same lubricant to the inside of the hose and the outside of the spigot to simplify installation.

As a last resort (and if the hose is to be replaced with a new one anyway), the rubber can be slit with a knife and the hose peeled from the spigot. If this must be done, be careful that the metal connection is not damaged.

If a hose clamp is broken or damaged, do not reuse it. Wire-type clamps usually weaken with age, so it is a good idea to replace them with screw-type clamps whenever a hose is removed.

Tools

A selection of good tools is a basic requirement for anyone who plans to maintain and repair his or her own vehicle. For the owner who has few tools, the initial investment might seem high, but when compared to the spiraling costs of professional auto maintenance and repair, it is a wise one.

To help the owner decide which tools are needed to perform the tasks detailed in this manual, the following tool lists are offered: *Maintenance and minor repair, Repair/overhaul* and *Special.*

The newcomer to practical mechanics

Dial caliper

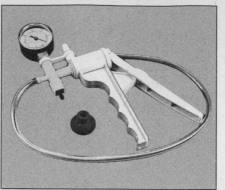

Hand-operated vacuum pump

Timing light

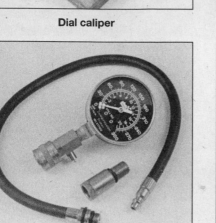

Compression gauge with spark plug hole adapter

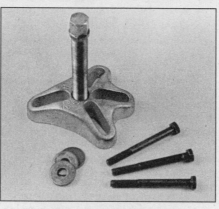

Damper/steering wheel puller

General purpose puller

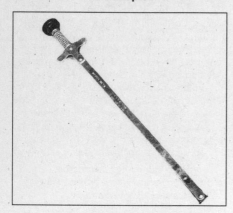

Hydraulic lifter removal tool

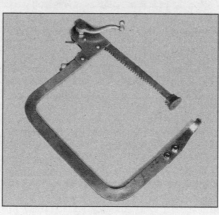

Valve spring compressor

Valve spring compressor

Ridge reamer

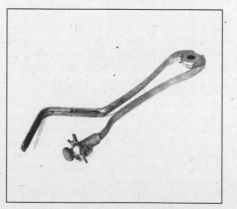

Piston ring groove cleaning tool

Ring removal/installation tool

Ring compressor

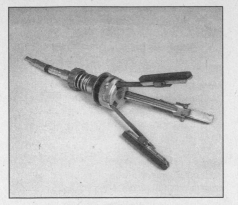
Cylinder hone

Brake hold-down spring tool

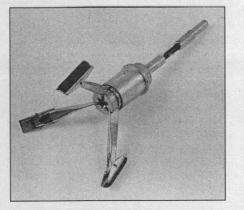
Brake cylinder hone

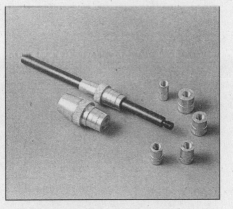
Clutch plate alignment tool

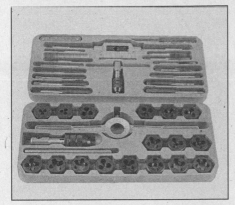
Tap and die set

should start off with the *maintenance and minor repair* tool kit, which is adequate for the simpler jobs performed on a vehicle. Then, as confidence and experience grow, the owner can tackle more difficult tasks, buying additional tools as they are needed. Eventually the basic kit will be expanded into the *repair and overhaul* tool set. Over a period of time, the experienced do-it-yourselfer will assemble a tool set complete enough for most repair and overhaul procedures and will add tools from the special category when it is felt that the expense is justified by the frequency of use.

Maintenance and minor repair tool kit

The tools in this list should be considered the minimum required for performance of routine maintenance, servicing and minor repair work. We recommend the purchase of combination wrenches (box-end and open-end combined in one wrench). While more expensive than open end wrenches, they offer the advantages of both types of wrench.

Combination wrench set (1/4-inch to 1 inch or 6 mm to 19 mm)
Adjustable wrench, 8 inch
Spark plug wrench with rubber insert
Spark plug gap adjusting tool
Feeler gauge set
Brake bleeder wrench
Standard screwdriver (5/16-inch x 6 inch)

Phillips screwdriver (No. 2 x 6 inch)
Combination pliers - 6 inch
Hacksaw and assortment of blades
Tire pressure gauge
Grease gun
Oil can
Fine emery cloth
Wire brush
Battery post and cable cleaning tool
Oil filter wrench
Funnel (medium size)
Safety goggles
Jackstands (2)
Drain pan

Note: *If basic tune-ups are going to be part of routine maintenance, it will be necessary to purchase a good quality stroboscopic timing light and combination tachometer/dwell meter. Although they are included in the list of special tools, it is mentioned here because they are absolutely necessary for tuning most vehicles properly.*

Repair and overhaul tool set

These tools are essential for anyone who plans to perform major repairs and are in addition to those in the maintenance and minor repair tool kit. Included is a comprehensive set of sockets which, though expensive, are invaluable because of their versatility, especially when various extensions and drives are available. We recommend the 1/2-inch drive over the 3/8-inch drive. Although the larger drive is bulky and more expensive,

it has the capacity of accepting a very wide range of large sockets. Ideally, however, the mechanic should have a 3/8-inch drive set and a 1/2-inch drive set.

Socket set(s)
Reversible ratchet
Extension - 10 inch
Universal joint
Torque wrench (same size drive as sockets)
Ball peen hammer - 8 ounce
Soft-face hammer (plastic/rubber)
Standard screwdriver (1/4-inch x 6 inch)
Standard screwdriver (stubby - 5/16-inch)
Phillips screwdriver (No. 3 x 8 inch)
Phillips screwdriver (stubby - No. 2)
Pliers - vise grip
Pliers - lineman's
Pliers - needle nose
Pliers - snap-ring (internal and external)
Cold chisel - 1/2-inch
Scribe
Scraper (made from flattened copper tubing)
Centerpunch
Pin punches (1/16, 1/8, 3/16-inch)
Steel rule/straightedge - 12 inch
Allen wrench set (1/8 to 3/8-inch or 4 mm to 10 mm)
A selection of files
Wire brush (large)
Jackstands (second set)
Jack (scissor or hydraulic type)

Note: *Another tool which is often useful is an electric drill with a chuck capacity of 3/8-inch and a set of good quality drill bits.*

Special tools

The tools in this list include those which are not used regularly, are expensive to buy, or which need to be used in accordance with their manufacturer's instructions. Unless these tools will be used frequently, it is not very economical to purchase many of them. A consideration would be to split the cost and use between yourself and a friend or friends. In addition, most of these tools can be obtained from a tool rental shop on a temporary basis.

This list primarily contains only those tools and instruments widely available to the public, and not those special tools produced by the vehicle manufacturer for distribution to dealer service departments. Occasionally, references to the manufacturer's special tools are included in the text of this manual. Generally, an alternative method of doing the job without the special tool is offered. However, sometimes there is no alternative to their use. Where this is the case, and the tool cannot be purchased or borrowed, the work should be turned over to the dealer service department or an automotive repair shop.

Valve spring compressor
Piston ring groove cleaning tool
Piston ring compressor
Piston ring installation tool
Cylinder compression gauge
Cylinder ridge reamer
Cylinder surfacing hone
Cylinder bore gauge
Micrometers and/or dial calipers
Hydraulic lifter removal tool
Balljoint separator
Universal-type puller
Impact screwdriver
Dial indicator set
*Stroboscopic timing light (inductive
     pick-up)*
Hand operated vacuum/pressure pump
Tachometer/dwell meter
Universal electrical multimeter
Cable hoist
*Brake spring removal and installation
     tools*
Floor jack

Buying tools

For the do-it-yourselfer who is just starting to get involved in vehicle maintenance and repair, there are a number of options available when purchasing tools. If maintenance and minor repair is the extent of the work to be done, the purchase of individual tools is satisfactory. If, on the other hand, extensive work is planned, it would be a good idea to purchase a modest tool set from one of the large retail chain stores. A set can usually be bought at a substantial savings over the individual tool prices, and they often come with a tool box. As additional tools are

needed, add-on sets, individual tools and a larger tool box can be purchased to expand the tool selection. Building a tool set gradually allows the cost of the tools to be spread over a longer period of time and gives the mechanic the freedom to choose only those tools that will actually be used.

Tool stores will often be the only source of some of the special tools that are needed, but regardless of where tools are bought, try to avoid cheap ones, especially when buying screwdrivers and sockets, because they won't last very long. The expense involved in replacing cheap tools will eventually be greater than the initial cost of quality tools.

Care and maintenance of tools

Good tools are expensive, so it makes sense to treat them with respect. Keep them clean and in usable condition and store them properly when not in use. Always wipe off any dirt, grease or metal chips before putting them away. Never leave tools lying around in the work area. Upon completion of a job, always check closely under the hood for tools that may have been left there so they won't get lost during a test drive.

Some tools, such as screwdrivers, pliers, wrenches and sockets, can be hung on a panel mounted on the garage or workshop wall, while others should be kept in a tool box or tray. Measuring instruments, gauges, meters, etc. must be carefully stored where they cannot be damaged by weather or impact from other tools.

When tools are used with care and stored properly, they will last a very long time. Even with the best of care, though, tools will wear out if used frequently. When a tool is damaged or worn out, replace it. Subsequent jobs will be safer and more enjoyable if you do.

How to repair damaged threads

Sometimes, the internal threads of a nut or bolt hole can become stripped, usually from overtightening. Stripping threads is an all-too-common occurrence, especially when working with aluminum parts, because aluminum is so soft that it easily strips out.

Usually, external or internal threads are only partially stripped. After they've been cleaned up with a tap or die, they'll still work. Sometimes, however, threads are badly damaged. When this happens, you've got three choices:

1) *Drill and tap the hole to the next suitable oversize and install a larger diameter bolt, screw or stud.*
2) *Drill and tap the hole to accept a threaded plug, then drill and tap the plug to the original screw size. You can also buy a plug already threaded to the original size. Then you simply drill a hole to the specified size, then run the threaded plug into the hole with a bolt and jam*

nut. Once the plug is fully seated, remove the jam nut and bolt.
3) *The third method uses a patented thread repair kit like Heli-Coil or Slimsert. These easy-to-use kits are designed to repair damaged threads in straight-through holes and blind holes. Both are available as kits which can handle a variety of sizes and thread patterns. Drill the hole, then tap it with the special included tap. Install the Heli-Coil and the hole is back to its original diameter and thread pitch.*

Regardless of which method you use, be sure to proceed calmly and carefully. A little impatience or carelessness during one of these relatively simple procedures can ruin your whole day's work and cost you a bundle if you wreck an expensive part.

Working facilities

Not to be overlooked when discussing tools is the workshop. If anything more than routine maintenance is to be carried out, some sort of suitable work area is essential.

It is understood, and appreciated, that many home mechanics do not have a good workshop or garage available, and end up removing an engine or doing major repairs outside. It is recommended, however, that the overhaul or repair be completed under the cover of a roof.

A clean, flat workbench or table of comfortable working height is an absolute necessity. The workbench should be equipped with a vise that has a jaw opening of at least four inches.

As mentioned previously, some clean, dry storage space is also required for tools, as well as the lubricants, fluids, cleaning solvents, etc. which soon become necessary.

Sometimes waste oil and fluids, drained from the engine or cooling system during normal maintenance or repairs, present a disposal problem. To avoid pouring them on the ground or into a sewage system, pour the used fluids into large containers, seal them with caps and take them to an authorized disposal site or recycling center. Plastic jugs, such as old antifreeze containers, are ideal for this purpose.

Always keep a supply of old newspapers and clean rags available. Old towels are excellent for mopping up spills. Many mechanics use rolls of paper towels for most work because they are readily available and disposable. To help keep the area under the vehicle clean, a large cardboard box can be cut open and flattened to protect the garage or shop floor.

Whenever working over a painted surface, such as when leaning over a fender to service something under the hood, always cover it with an old blanket or bedspread to protect the finish. Vinyl covered pads, made especially for this purpose, are available at auto parts stores.

Booster battery (jump) starting

Observe these precautions when using a booster battery to start a vehicle:

a) Before connecting the booster battery, make sure the ignition switch is in the Off position.

b) Turn off the lights, heater and other electrical loads.

c) Your eyes should be shielded. Safety goggles are a good idea.

d) Make sure the booster battery is the same voltage as the dead one in the vehicle.

e) The two vehicles MUST NOT TOUCH each other!

f) Make sure the transaxle is in Neutral (manual) or Park (automatic).

g) If the booster battery is not a maintenance-free type, remove the vent caps and lay a cloth over the vent holes.

Connect the red jumper cable to the positive (+) terminals of each battery **(see illustration)**.

Connect one end of the black jumper cable to the negative (-) terminal of the booster battery. The other end of this cable should be connected to a good ground on the vehicle to be started, such as a bolt or bracket on the body.

Start the engine using the booster battery, then, with the engine running at idle speed, disconnect the jumper cables in the reverse order of connection.

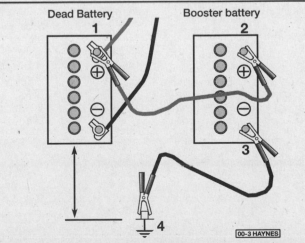

Dead Battery   Booster battery

Make the booster battery cable connections in the numerical order shown (note that the negative cable of the booster battery is NOT attached to the negative terminal of the dead battery)

Jacking and towing

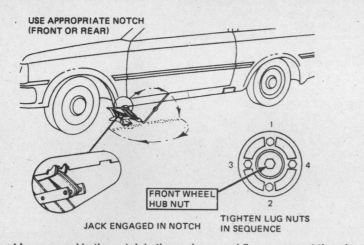

The jack must be engaged in the notch in the rocker panel flange nearest the wheel to be changed - there is a front and rear jacking notch on each side of the vehicle

To remove or install the anti-theft lug nut, insert the key into the slot in the lug nut, then place the lug nut wrench on the key and remove or install the lug nut

Jacking

Warning: *The jack supplied with this vehicle should only be used for raising the vehicle when changing a tire or placing jackstands under the frame. Never work under the vehicle or start the engine while this jack is being used as the only means of support.*

The vehicle should be on level ground. Place the shift lever in Park, if you have an automatic transaxle, or First gear if you have a manual transaxle. Block the wheel diagonally opposite the wheel being changed. Set the parking brake. **Warning:** *When one front wheel is lifted off the ground, neither the automatic nor the manual transaxle will prevent the vehicle from moving and possibly slipping off the jack, even if they have been placed in gear as described above. To prevent inadvertent movement of the vehicle while changing a tire, always set the parking brake and block the wheel diagonally opposite the wheel being changed.*

Remove the spare tire and jack from stowage. Remove the wheel cover (if so equipped) with the tapered end of the lug nut wrench by inserting and twisting the handle and then prying against the inner wheel cover flange. Loosen, but do not remove, the lug nuts (one-half turn is sufficient). **Caution:** *If you're removing the front wheel, don't loosen the front wheel hub nut.*

Place the scissors-type jack under the side of the vehicle and adjust the jack height with the jack handle so it fits in the notch in the vertical rocker panel flange nearest the wheel to be changed. There is a front and rear jacking notch on each side of the vehicle **(see illustration)**. When lifting the vehicle by any other means, special care must exercised to avoid damage to the fuel tank, filler neck, exhaust system or underbody. **Caution:** *Do not raise the vehicle with a bumper jack. The bumper system could be damaged. Also, jack slippage may occur, causing personal injury.*

Turn the jack handle clockwise until the wheel clears the ground. Remove the lug nuts and the wheel. Mark the location of the anti-theft lug nut on the wheel before removing it. Pull the wheel off and immediately replace it with the spare.

Replace the lug nuts with the beveled edges facing in. Tighten them snugly and carefully. Don't attempt to tighten them completely until the vehicle is lowered or it could slip off the jack.

Turn the jack handle counterclockwise to lower the vehicle. Remove the jack and tighten the lug nuts in a crisscross pattern.

Align the wheel cover with the valve stem extension matching the hole in the cover. Install the cover and be sure that it's snapped in place all the way around.

Stow the tire, jack and wrench. Unblock the wheels.

Anti-theft wheel lug nuts

If you have aluminum wheels, they are equipped with anti-theft wheel lug nuts (one per wheel). The key and your registration card are attached to the lug wrench stowed with the spare tire. Don't lose the registration card. You must send it to the manufacturer, not the dealer to get a replacement key if yours is lost.

To remove or install the anti-theft lug nut, insert the key into the slot in the lug nut **(see illustration)**. Place the lug nut wrench on the key and, while applying pressure on the key, remove or install the lug nut. Mark the anti-theft lug nut location on the wheel before removing it.

Towing

It equipped with an automatic transaxle, the vehicle may be towed on all four wheels at speeds less than 35 mph for distances up to 50 miles. Vehicles equipped with a manual transaxle are not limited in distance or speed of towing.

Towing equipment specifically designed for this purpose should be used and should be attached to the main structural members of the vehicle and not the bumper or brackets.

Safety is a major consideration when towing and all applicable state and local laws must be obeyed. A safety chain system must be used for all towings.

While towing, the parking brake should be released and the transaxle should be in Neutral. The steering must be unlocked (ignition switch in the Off position). Remember that power brakes will not work with the engine off.

Automotive chemicals and lubricants

A number of automotive chemicals and lubricants are available for use during vehicle maintenance and repair. They include a wide variety of products ranging from cleaning solvents and degreasers to lubricants and protective sprays for rubber, plastic and vinyl.

Cleaners

Carburetor cleaner and choke cleaner is a strong solvent for gum, varnish and carbon. Most carburetor cleaners leave a dry-type lubricant film which will not harden or gum up. Because of this film it is not recommended for use on electrical components.

Brake system cleaner is used to remove grease and brake fluid from the brake system, where clean surfaces are absolutely necessary. It leaves no residue and often eliminates brake squeal caused by contaminants.

Electrical cleaner removes oxidation, corrosion and carbon deposits from electrical contacts, restoring full current flow. It can also be used to clean spark plugs, carburetor jets, voltage regulators and other parts where an oil-free surface is desired.

Demoisturants remove water and moisture from electrical components such as alternators, voltage regulators, electrical connectors and fuse blocks. They are non-conductive, non-corrosive and non-flammable.

Degreasers are heavy-duty solvents used to remove grease from the outside of the engine and from chassis components. They can be sprayed or brushed on and, depending on the type, are rinsed off either with water or solvent.

Lubricants

Motor oil is the lubricant formulated for use in engines. It normally contains a wide variety of additives to prevent corrosion and reduce foaming and wear. Motor oil comes in various weights (viscosity ratings) from 0 to 50. The recommended weight of the oil depends on the season, temperature and the demands on the engine. Light oil is used in cold climates and under light load conditions. Heavy oil is used in hot climates and where high loads are encountered. Multi-viscosity oils are designed to have characteristics of both light and heavy oils and are available in a number of weights from 5W-20 to 20W-50.

Gear oil is designed to be used in differentials, manual transmissions and other areas where high-temperature lubrication is required.

Chassis and wheel bearing grease is a heavy grease used where increased loads and friction are encountered, such as for wheel bearings, balljoints, tie-rod ends and universal joints.

High-temperature wheel bearing grease is designed to withstand the extreme temperatures encountered by wheel bearings in disc brake equipped vehicles. It usually contains molybdenum disulfide (moly), which is a dry-type lubricant.

White grease is a heavy grease for metal-to-metal applications where water is a problem. White grease stays soft under both low and high temperatures (usually from -100 to +190-degrees F), and will not wash off or dilute in the presence of water.

Assembly lube is a special extreme pressure lubricant, usually containing moly, used to lubricate high-load parts (such as main and rod bearings and cam lobes) for initial start-up of a new engine. The assembly lube lubricates the parts without being squeezed out or washed away until the engine oiling system begins to function.

Silicone lubricants are used to protect rubber, plastic, vinyl and nylon parts.

Graphite lubricants are used where oils cannot be used due to contamination problems, such as in locks. The dry graphite will lubricate metal parts while remaining uncontaminated by dirt, water, oil or acids. It is electrically conductive and will not foul electrical contacts in locks such as the ignition switch.

Moly penetrants loosen and lubricate frozen, rusted and corroded fasteners and prevent future rusting or freezing.

Heat-sink grease is a special electrically non-conductive grease that is used for mounting electronic ignition modules where it is essential that heat is transferred away from the module.

Sealants

RTV sealant is one of the most widely used gasket compounds. Made from silicone, RTV is air curing, it seals, bonds, waterproofs, fills surface irregularities, remains flexible, doesn't shrink, is relatively easy to remove, and is used as a supplementary sealer with almost all low and medium temperature gaskets.

Anaerobic sealant is much like RTV in that it can be used either to seal gaskets or to form gaskets by itself. It remains flexible, is solvent resistant and fills surface imperfections. The difference between an anaerobic sealant and an RTV-type sealant is in the curing. RTV cures when exposed to air, while an anaerobic sealant cures only in the absence of air. This means that an anaerobic sealant cures only after the assembly of parts, sealing them together.

Thread and pipe sealant is used for sealing hydraulic and pneumatic fittings and vacuum lines. It is usually made from a Teflon compound, and comes in a spray, a paint-on liquid and as a wrap-around tape.

Chemicals

Anti-seize compound prevents seizing, galling, cold welding, rust and corrosion in fasteners. High-temperature anti-seize, usually made with copper and graphite lubricants, is used for exhaust system and exhaust manifold bolts.

Anaerobic locking compounds are used to keep fasteners from vibrating or working loose and cure only after installation, in the absence of air. Medium strength locking compound is used for small nuts, bolts and screws that may be removed later. High-strength locking compound is for large nuts, bolts and studs which aren't removed on a regular basis.

Oil additives range from viscosity index improvers to chemical treatments that claim to reduce internal engine friction. It should be noted that most oil manufacturers caution against using additives with their oils.

Gas additives perform several functions, depending on their chemical makeup. They usually contain solvents that help dissolve gum and varnish that build up on carburetor, fuel injection and intake parts. They also serve to break down carbon deposits that form on the inside surfaces of the combustion chambers. Some additives contain upper cylinder lubricants for valves and piston rings, and others contain chemicals to remove condensation from the gas tank.

Miscellaneous

Brake fluid is specially formulated hydraulic fluid that can withstand the heat and pressure encountered in brake systems. Care must be taken so this fluid does not come in contact with painted surfaces or plastics. An opened container should always be resealed to prevent contamination by water or dirt.

Weatherstrip adhesive is used to bond weatherstripping around doors, windows and trunk lids. It is sometimes used to attach trim pieces.

Undercoating is a petroleum-based, tar-like substance that is designed to protect metal surfaces on the underside of the vehicle from corrosion. It also acts as a sound-deadening agent by insulating the bottom of the vehicle.

Waxes and polishes are used to help protect painted and plated surfaces from the weather. Different types of paint may require the use of different types of wax and polish. Some polishes utilize a chemical or abrasive cleaner to help remove the top layer of oxidized (dull) paint on older vehicles. In recent years many non-wax polishes that contain a wide variety of chemicals such as polymers and silicones have been introduced. These non-wax polishes are usually easier to apply and last longer than conventional waxes and polishes.

Conversion factors

Length (distance)

Inches (in)	X	25.4	= Millimetres (mm)	X 0.0394	= Inches (in)
Feet (ft)	X	0.305	= Metres (m)	X 3.281	= Feet (ft)
Miles	X	1.609	= Kilometres (km)	X 0.621	= Miles

Volume (capacity)

Cubic inches (cu in; in^3)	X	16.387	= Cubic centimetres (cc; cm^3)	X 0.061	= Cubic inches (cu in; in^3)
Imperial pints (Imp pt)	X	0.568	= Litres (l)	X 1.76	= Imperial pints (Imp pt)
Imperial quarts (Imp qt)	X	1.137	= Litres (l)	X 0.88	= Imperial quarts (Imp qt)
Imperial quarts (Imp qt)	X	1.201	= US quarts (US qt)	X 0.833	= Imperial quarts (Imp qt)
US quarts (US qt)	X	0.946	= Litres (l)	X 1.057	= US quarts (US qt)
Imperial gallons (Imp gal)	X	4.546	= Litres (l)	X 0.22	= Imperial gallons (Imp gal)
Imperial gallons (Imp gal)	X	1.201	= US gallons (US gal)	X 0.833	= Imperial gallons (Imp gal)
US gallons (US gal)	X	3.785	= Litres (l)	X 0.264	= US gallons (US gal)

Mass (weight)

Ounces (oz)	X	28.35	= Grams (g)	X 0.035	= Ounces (oz)
Pounds (lb)	X	0.454	= Kilograms (kg)	X 2.205	= Pounds (lb)

Force

Ounces-force (ozf; oz)	X	0.278	= Newtons (N)	X 3.6	= Ounces-force (ozf; oz)
Pounds-force (lbf; lb)	X	4.448	= Newtons (N)	X 0.225	= Pounds-force (lbf; lb)
Newtons (N)	X	0.1	= Kilograms-force (kgf; kg)	X 9.81	= Newtons (N)

Pressure

Pounds-force per square inch (psi; lbf/in^2; lb/in^2)	X	0.070	= Kilograms-force per square centimetre (kgf/cm^2; kg/cm^2)	X 14.223	= Pounds-force per square inch (psi; lbf/in^2; lb/in^2)
Pounds-force per square inch (psi; lbf/in^2; lb/in^2)	X	0.068	= Atmospheres (atm)	X 14.696	= Pounds-force per square inch (psi; lbf/in^2; lb/in^2)
Pounds-force per square inch (psi; lbf/in^2; lb/in^2)	X	0.069	= Bars	X 14.5	= Pounds-force per square inch (psi; lbf/in^2; lb/in^2)
Pounds-force per square inch (psi; lbf/in^2; lb/in^2)	X	6.895	= Kilopascals (kPa)	X 0.145	= Pounds-force per square inch (psi; lbf/in^2; lb/in^2)
Kilopascals (kPa)	X	0.01	= Kilograms-force per square centimetre (kgf/cm^2; kg/cm^2)	X 98.1	= Kilopascals (kPa)

Torque (moment of force)

Pounds-force inches (lbf in; lb in)	X	1.152	= Kilograms-force centimetre (kgf cm; kg cm)	X 0.868	= Pounds-force inches (lbf in; lb in)
Pounds-force inches (lbf in; lb in)	X	0.113	= Newton metres (Nm)	X 8.85	= Pounds-force inches (lbf in; lb in)
Pounds-force inches (lbf in; lb in)	X	0.083	= Pounds-force feet (lbf ft; lb ft)	X 12	= Pounds-force inches (lbf in; lb in)
Pounds-force feet (lbf ft; lb ft)	X	0.138	= Kilograms-force metres (kgf m; kg m)	X 7.233	= Pounds-force feet (lbf ft; lb ft)
Pounds-force feet (lbf ft; lb ft)	X	1.356	= Newton metres (Nm)	X 0.738	= Pounds-force feet (lbf ft; lb ft)
Newton metres (Nm)	X	0.102	= Kilograms-force metres (kgf m; kg m)	X 9.804	= Newton metres (Nm)

Vacuum

Inches mercury (in. Hg)	X	3.377	= Kilopascals (kPa)	X 0.2961	= Inches mercury
Inches mercury (in. Hg)	X	25.4	= Millimeters mercury (mm Hg)	X 0.0394	= Inches mercury

Power

Horsepower (hp)	X	745.7	= Watts (W)	X 0.0013	= Horsepower (hp)

Velocity (speed)

Miles per hour (miles/hr; mph)	X	1.609	= Kilometres per hour (km/hr; kph)	X 0.621	= Miles per hour (miles/hr; mph)

Fuel consumption*

Miles per gallon, Imperial (mpg)	X	0.354	= Kilometres per litre (km/l)	X 2.825	= Miles per gallon, Imperial (mpg)
Miles per gallon, US (mpg)	X	0.425	= Kilometres per litre (km/l)	X 2.352	= Miles per gallon, US (mpg)

Temperature

Degrees Fahrenheit = (°C x 1.8) + 32

Degrees Celsius (Degrees Centigrade; °C) = (°F - 32) x 0.56

*It is common practice to convert from miles per gallon (mpg) to litres/100 kilometres (l/100km), where mpg (Imperial) x l/100 km = 282 and mpg (US) x l/100 km = 235

Safety first!

Regardless of how enthusiastic you may be about getting on with the job at hand, take the time to ensure that your safety is not jeopardized. A moment's lack of attention can result in an accident, as can failure to observe certain simple safety precautions. The possibility of an accident will always exist, and the following points should not be considered a comprehensive list of all dangers. Rather, they are intended to make you aware of the risks and to encourage a safety conscious approach to all work you carry out on your vehicle.

Essential DOs and DON'Ts

DON'T rely on a jack when working under the vehicle. Always use approved jackstands to support the weight of the vehicle and place them under the recommended lift or support points.

DON'T attempt to loosen extremely tight fasteners (i.e. wheel lug nuts) while the vehicle is on a jack - it may fall.

DON'T start the engine without first making sure that the transmission is in Neutral (or Park where applicable) and the parking brake is set.

DON'T remove the radiator cap from a hot cooling system - let it cool or cover it with a cloth and release the pressure gradually.

DON'T attempt to drain the engine oil until you are sure it has cooled to the point that it will not burn you.

DON'T touch any part of the engine or exhaust system until it has cooled sufficiently to avoid burns.

DON'T siphon toxic liquids such as gasoline, antifreeze and brake fluid by mouth, or allow them to remain on your skin.

DON'T inhale brake lining dust - it is potentially hazardous (see *Asbestos* below).

DON'T allow spilled oil or grease to remain on the floor - wipe it up before someone slips on it.

DON'T use loose fitting wrenches or other tools which may slip and cause injury.

DON'T push on wrenches when loosening or tightening nuts or bolts. Always try to pull the wrench toward you. If the situation calls for pushing the wrench away, push with an open hand to avoid scraped knuckles if the wrench should slip.

DON'T attempt to lift a heavy component alone - get someone to help you.

DON'T rush or take unsafe shortcuts to finish a job.

DON'T allow children or animals in or around the vehicle while you are working on it.

DO wear eye protection when using power tools such as a drill, sander, bench grinder, etc. and when working under a vehicle.

DO keep loose clothing and long hair well out of the way of moving parts.

DO make sure that any hoist used has a safe working load rating adequate for the job.

DO get someone to check on you periodically when working alone on a vehicle.

DO carry out work in a logical sequence and make sure that everything is correctly assembled and tightened.

DO keep chemicals and fluids tightly capped and out of the reach of children and pets.

DO remember that your vehicle's safety affects that of yourself and others. If in doubt on any point, get professional advice.

Asbestos

Certain friction, insulating, sealing, and other products - such as brake linings, brake bands, clutch linings, torque converters, gaskets, etc. - may contain asbestos. Extreme care must be taken to avoid inhalation of dust from such products, since it is hazardous to health. If in doubt, assume that they do contain asbestos.

Fire

Remember at all times that gasoline is highly flammable. Never smoke or have any kind of open flame around when working on a vehicle. But the risk does not end there. A spark caused by an electrical short circuit, by two metal surfaces contacting each other, or even by static electricity built up in your body under certain conditions, can ignite gasoline vapors, which in a confined space are highly explosive. Do not, under any circumstances, use gasoline for cleaning parts. Use an approved safety solvent.

Always disconnect the battery ground (-) cable at the battery before working on any part of the fuel system or electrical system. Never risk spilling fuel on a hot engine or exhaust component. It is strongly recommended that a fire extinguisher suitable for use on fuel and electrical fires be kept handy in the garage or workshop at all times. Never try to extinguish a fuel or electrical fire with water.

Fumes

Certain fumes are highly toxic and can quickly cause unconsciousness and even death if inhaled to any extent. Gasoline vapor falls into this category, as do the vapors from some cleaning solvents. Any draining or pouring of such volatile fluids should be done in a well ventilated area.

When using cleaning fluids and solvents, read the instructions on the container carefully. Never use materials from unmarked containers.

Never run the engine in an enclosed space, such as a garage. Exhaust fumes contain carbon monoxide, which is extremely poisonous. If you need to run the engine, always do so in the open air, or at least have the rear of the vehicle outside the work area.

If you are fortunate enough to have the use of an inspection pit, never drain or pour gasoline and never run the engine while the vehicle is over the pit. The fumes, being heavier than air, will concentrate in the pit with possibly lethal results.

The battery

Never create a spark or allow a bare light bulb near a battery. They normally give off a certain amount of hydrogen gas, which is highly explosive.

Always disconnect the battery ground (-) cable at the battery before working on the fuel or electrical systems.

If possible, loosen the filler caps or cover when charging the battery from an external source (this does not apply to sealed or maintenance-free batteries). Do not charge at an excessive rate or the battery may burst.

Take care when adding water to a non maintenance-free battery and when carrying a battery. The electrolyte, even when diluted, is very corrosive and should not be allowed to contact clothing or skin.

Always wear eye protection when cleaning the battery to prevent the caustic deposits from entering your eyes.

Household current

When using an electric power tool, inspection light, etc., which operates on household current, always make sure that the tool is correctly connected to its plug and that, where necessary, it is properly grounded. Do not use such items in damp conditions and, again, do not create a spark or apply excessive heat in the vicinity of fuel or fuel vapor.

Secondary ignition system voltage

A severe electric shock can result from touching certain parts of the ignition system (such as the spark plug wires) when the engine is running or being cranked, particularly if components are damp or the insulation is defective. In the case of an electronic ignition system, the secondary system voltage is much higher and could prove fatal.

Troubleshooting

Contents

This section provides an easy reference guide to the more common problems which may occur during the operation of your vehicle. These problems and possible causes are grouped under various components or systems; i.e. Engine, Cooling System, etc., and also refer to the Chapter and/or Section which deals with the problem.

Remember that successful troubleshooting is not a mysterious black art practiced only by professional mechanics.

It's simply the result of a bit of knowledge combined with an intelligent, systematic approach to the problem. Always work by a process of elimination, starting with the simplest solution and working through to the most complex - and never overlook the obvious. Anyone can forget to fill the gas tank or leave the lights on overnight, so don't assume that you are above such oversights.

Finally, always get clear in your mind why a problem has occurred and take steps to ensure that it doesn't happen again. If the electrical system fails because of a poor connection, check all other connections in the system to make sure that they don't fail as well. If a particular fuse continue to blow, find out why - don t just go on replacing fuses. Remember, failure of a small component can often be indicative of potential failure or incorrect functioning of a more important component or system.

Engine

1 Engine will not rotate when attempting to start

1 Battery terminal connections loose or corroded. Check the cable terminals at the battery, Tighten the cable or remove corrosion as necessary.
2 Battery discharged or faulty. If the cable connections are clean and tight on the battery posts, turn the key to the On position and switch on the headlights and/or windshield wipers. If they fail to function, the battery is discharged.
3 Automatic transaxle not completely engaged in Park or Neutral or clutch pedal not completely depressed.
4 Broken, loose or disconnected wiring in the starting circuit.
Inspect all wiring and connectors at the battery, starter solenoid and ignition switch.
5 Starter motor pinion jammed in flywheel ring gear. If manual transaxle, place transaxle in gear and rock the vehicle to manually turn the engine. Remove starter and inspect pinion and flywheel at earliest convenience (Chapter 5).
6 Starter solenoid faulty (Chapter 5).
7 Starter motor faulty (Chapter 5).
8 Ignition switch faulty (Chapter 12).

2 Engine rotates but will not start

1 Fuel tank empty.
2 Fault in the carburetor or fuel injection system (Chapters 4 and 5).
3 Battery discharged (engine rotates slowly). Check the operation of electrical components as described in the previous Section.
4 Battery terminal connections loose or corroded (see previous Section).
5 Fuel injector or fuel pump faulty (Chapter 4).
6 Excessive moisture on, or damage to, ignition components (Chapter 6).
7 Worn, faulty or incorrectly gapped spark plugs (Chapter 1).
8 Broken, loose or disconnected wiring in the starting circuit (see previous Section).
9 Distributor loose, causing ignition timing to change. Turn the distributor as necessary to start the engine, then set the ignition timing as soon as possible (Chapter 1).
10 Broken, loose or disconnected wires at the ignition coil or faulty coil (Chapter 5).

3 Starter motor operates without rotating engine

1 Starter pinion sticking. Remove the starter (Chapter 5) and inspect.
2 Starter pinion or flywheel teeth worn or broken.
3 Remove the flywheel/driveplate access cover from the oil pan and inspect.

4 Engine hard to start when cold

1 Battery discharged or low. Check as described in Section 1.
2 Fault in the fuel injection system (Chapters 4 and 5).
3 Fuel injection system in need of overhaul (Chapter 4).
4 Distributor rotor carbon tracked and/or damaged (Chapters 1 and 5).

5 Engine hard to start when hot

1 Air filter clogged (Chapter 1).
2 Fault in the fuel injection system (Chapters 4 and 5).
3 Fuel not reaching the fuel injection system (see Section 2).

6 Starter motor noisy or excessively rough in engagement

1 Pinion or flywheel gear teeth worn or broken. Remove the cover at the rear of the engine (if so equipped) and inspect.
2 Starter motor mounting bolts loose or missing.

7 Engine starts but stops immediately

1 Loose or faulty electrical connections at distributor, coil or alternator.
2 Fault in the fuel injection system (Chapters 4 and 5).
3 Insufficient fuel reaching the fuel injector. Check the fuel pressure (Chapter 5) or have the fuel injection pressure checked by your dealer or a properly equipped shop.
4 Vacuum leak at the gasket surfaces of the intake manifold, fuel charging assembly or throttle body. Make sure that all mounting bolts/nuts are tightened securely and that all vacuum hoses connected to the fuel injection assembly and manifold are positioned properly and in good condition.

8 Engine lopes while idling or idles erratically

1 Vacuum leakage. Check the mounting bolts/nuts at the fuel injection unit and intake manifold for tightness. Make sure that all vacuum hoses are connected and in good condition. Use a stethoscope or a length of fuel hose held against your ear to listen for vacuum leaks while the engine is running. A hissing sound will be heard. A soapy water solution will also detect leaks. Check the fuel injector and intake manifold gasket surfaces.
2 Fault in the fuel injection system (Chapters 4 and 5).

3 Leaking EGR valve or plugged PCV valve (see Chapters 1 and 6).
4 Air filter clogged (Chapter 1).
5 Fuel pump not delivering sufficient fuel to the fuel injector (see Chapter 4).
6 Fuel injection system out of adjustment (Chapter 4).
7 Leaking head gasket. If this is suspected, take the vehicle to a repair shop or dealer where the engine can be pressure checked.
8 Timing chain or sprockets worn (Chapter 2).
9 Camshaft lobes worn (Chapter 2).

9 Engine misses at idle speed

1 Spark plugs worn or not gapped properly (Chapter 1).
2 Fault in the fuel injection system (Chapters 4 and 5).
3 Faulty spark plug wires (Chapter 1).

10 Engine misses throughout driving speed range

1 Fuel filter clogged and/or impurities in the fuel system (Chapter 1).
2 Faulty or incorrectly gapped spark plugs (Chapter 1).
3 Fault in the fuel injection system (Chapters 4 and 5).
4 Incorrect ignition timing (Chapter 5).
5 Check for cracked distributor cap, disconnected distributor wires and damaged distributor components (Chapter 1).
6 Leaking spark plug wires (Chapter 1).
7 Faulty emissions system components (Chapter 6).
8 Low or uneven cylinder compression pressures. Remove the spark plugs and test the compression with a gauge (Chapter 2).
9 Weak or faulty ignition system (Chapter 5).
10 Vacuum leaks at the fuel injection unit, intake manifold or vacuum hoses (see Section 8).

11 Engine stalls

1 Idle speed incorrect. Refer to the VECI label and Chapter 5, then take the vehicle to a dealer (idle speed is not adjustable).
2 Fuel filter clogged and/or water and impurities in the fuel system (Chapter 1).
3 Distributor components damp or damaged (Chapter 5).
4 Fault in the fuel injection system or sensors (Chapters 4 and 6).
5 Faulty emissions system components (Chapter 6).
6 Faulty or incorrectly gapped spark plugs (Chapter 1). Also check the spark plug wires (Chapter 1).
7 Vacuum leak at the fuel injection unit, intake manifold or vacuum hoses. Check as described in Section 8.

12 Engine lacks power

1   Incorrect ignition timing (Chapter 5).
2   Fault in the fuel injection system (Chapters 4 and 6).
3   Excessive play in the distributor shaft. At the same time, check for a damaged rotor, faulty distributor cap, wires, etc. (Chapters 1 and 5).
4   Faulty or incorrectly gapped spark plugs (Chapter 1).
5   Fuel injection unit not adjusted properly or excessively worn (Chapter 4).
6   Faulty coil (Chapter 5).
7   Brakes binding (Chapter 1).
8   Automatic transaxle fluid level incorrect (Chapter 1).
9   Clutch slipping (Chapter 8).
10   Fuel filter clogged and/or impurities in the fuel system (Chapter 1).
11   Emissions control system not functioning properly (Chapter 6).
12   Use of substandard fuel. Fill the tank with the proper octane fuel.
13   Low or uneven cylinder compression pressures. Test with a compression tester, which will detect leaking valves and/or a blown head gasket (Chapter 2).

13 Engine backfires

1   Emissions systems not functioning properly (Chapter 6).
2   Fault in the fuel injection system (Chapters 4 and 6).
3   Ignition timing incorrect (Chapter 5).
4   Faulty secondary ignition system (cracked spark plug insulator, faulty plug wires, distributor cap and/or rotor) (Chapters 1 and 5).
5   Fuel injection unit in need of adjustment or worn excessively (Chapter 4).
6   Vacuum leak at the fuel injection unit, intake manifold or vacuum hoses. Check as described in Section 8.
7   Valves sticking (Chapter 2).

14 Pinging or knocking engine sounds during acceleration or uphill

1   Incorrect grade of fuel. Fill the tank with fuel of the proper octane rating.
2   Fault in the fuel injection system (Chapters 4 and 6).
3   Ignition timing incorrect (Chapter 5).
4   Fuel injection unit in need of adjustment (Chapter 4).
5   Improper spark plugs. Check the plug type against the VECI label located in the engine compartment. Also check the plugs and wires for damage (Chapter 1).
6   Worn or damaged distributor components (Chapter 5).
7   Faulty emissions system (Chapter 6).
8   Vacuum leak. Check as described in Section 8.

15 Engine continues running after switching off

1   Idle speed too high. Refer to Ignition timing section in Chapter 5; take vehicle to a dealer.
2   Fault in the fuel injection system (Chapters 4 and 5).
3   Ignition timing incorrectly adjusted (Chapter 5).
4   Inlet air temperature control system heat valve not operating properly (Chapter 6).
5   Excessive engine operating temperature. Probable causes of this are a malfunctioning thermostat, clogged radiator, faulty water pump (Chapter 3).

Engine electrical system

16 Battery will not hold a charge

1   Alternator drivebelt defective or not adjusted properly (Chapter 1).
2   Electrolyte level low or battery discharged (Chapter 1).
3   Battery terminals loose or corroded (Chapter 1).
4   Alternator not charging properly (Chapter 5).
5   Loose, broken or faulty wiring in the charging circuit (Chapter 5).
6   Short in the vehicle)e wiring causing a continual drain on battery (refer to Chapter 12 and the Wiring Diagrams).
7   Battery defective internally.

17 Ignition light fails to go out

1   Fault in the alternator or charging circuit (Chapter 5).
2   Alternator drivebelt defective or not properly adjusted (Chapter 1).

18 Ignition light falls to come on when key is turned on

1   Instrument cluster warning light bulb defective (Chapter 12).
2   Alternator faulty (Chapter 5).
3   Fault in the instrument cluster printed circuit, dashboard wiring or bulb holder (Chapter 12).

Fuel system

19 Excessive fuel consumption

1   Dirty or clogged air filter element (Chapter 1).
2   Incorrectly set ignition timing (Chapter 5).

3   Choke sticking or improperly adjusted (Chapter 1).
4   Emissions system not functioning properly (Chapter 6).
5   Fault in the fuel injection system (Chapters 4 and 5).
6   Fuel injection system internal parts excessively worn or damaged (Chapter 4).
7   Low tire pressure or incorrect tire size (Chapter 1).

20 Fuel leakage and/or fuel odor

1   Leak in a fuel feed or vent line (Chapter 4).
2   Tank overfilled. Fill only to automatic shut-off.
3   Evaporative emissions system filter clogged (Chapter 6).
4   Vapor leaks from system lines (Chapter 4).
5   Fuel injection internal ports excessively worn or out of adjustment clutch (Chapter 4).

Cooling system

21 Overheating

1   Insufficient coolant in the system (Chapter 1).
2   Water pump drivebelt defective or not adjusted properly (Chapter 1).
3   Radiator core blocked or radiator grille dirty and restricted (Chapter 3).
4   Thermostat faulty (Chapter 3).
5   Fan blades broken or cracked (Chapter 3).
6   Radiator cap not maintaining proper pressure. Have the cap pressure tested by gas station or repair shop.
7   Ignition timing incorrect (Chapter 5).

22 Overcooling

Thermostat faulty (Chapter 3).

23 External coolant leakage

1   Deteriorated or damaged hoses or loose clamps. Replace hoses and/or tighten the clamps at the hose connections (Chapter 1).
2   Water pump seals defective. If this is the case, water will drip from the weep hole in the water pump body (Chapter 3).
3   Leakage from radiator core or header tank. This will require the radiator to be professionally repaired (see Chapter 3 for removal procedures).
4   Engine drain plug leaking (Chapter 1) or water jacket core plugs leaking (see Chapter 2).

24 Internal coolant leakage

Note: *Internal coolant leaks can usually be detected by examining the oil. Check the dipstick end inside of the rocker arm cover for water deposits and an oil consistency like that of a milkshake.*

1   Leaking cylinder head gasket. Have the cooling system pressure tested.
2   Cracked cylinder bore or cylinder head. Dismantle the engine and inspect (Chapter 2).

25 Coolant loss

1   Too much coolant in the system (Chapter 1)
2   Coolant boiling away due to overheating (see Section 15)
3   External or internal leakage (see Sections 23 and 24)
4   Faulty radiator cap. Have the cap pressure tested.

26 Poor coolant circulation

1   Inoperative water pump. A quick test is to pinch the top radiator hose closed with your hand while the engine is idling, then let it loose. You should feel the surge of coolant if the pump is working properly (Chapter 1).
2   Restriction in the cooling system. Drain, flush and refill the system (Chapter 1). If necessary, remove the radiator (Chapter 3) and have it revere flushed.
3   Water pump drivebelt defective or not adjusted properly (Chapter 1).
4   Thermostat sticking (Chapter 3).

Clutch

27 Fails to release (pedal pressed to the floor - shift lever does not move freely in and out of Reverse)

1   Worn cable (Chapter 8).
2   Clutch plate warped or damaged (Chapter 8).
3   Worn or dry clutch release shaft bushing (Chapter 8).

28 Clutch slips (engine speed increases with no increase in vehicle speed)

1   Linkage out of adjustment (Chapter 8).
2   Clutch plate oil soaked or lining worn. Remove clutch (Chapter 8) and inspect.
3   Clutch plate not seated. It may take 30 or 40 normal starts for a new one to seat.

29 Grabbing (chattering) as clutch is engaged

1   Oil on clutch plate lining. Remove (Chapter 8) and inspect. Correct any leakage source.
2   Worn or loose engine or transaxle mounts. These units mow slightly when the clutch is released. Inspect the mounts and bolts (Chapter 2).
3   Worn splines on clutch plate hub. Remove the clutch components (Chapter 8) and inspect.
4   Warped pressure plate or flywheel. Remove the clutch components and inspect.

30 Squeal or rumble with clutch fully disengaged (pedal depressed)

1   Worn, defective or broken release bearing (Chapter 8).
2   Worn or broken pressure plate springs (or diaphragm fingers) (Chapter 8).

31 Clutch pedal stays on floor when disengaged

Linkage or release bearing binding. Inspect the linkage or remove the clutch component as necessary.

Manual transaxle

32 Noisy in Neutral with engine running

1   Input shaft bearing worn.
2   Damaged main drive gear bearing.
3   Worn countershaft bearings.
4   Worn or damaged countershaft endplay shim.

33 Noisy in all gears

1   Any of the above causes, and/or:
2   Insufficient lubricant (see the checking procedures in Chapter 1).

34 Noisy in one particular gear

1   Worn, damaged or chipped gear teeth for that particular gear.
2   Worn or damaged synchronizer for that particular gear.

35 Slips out of high gear

1   Transaxle loose on clutch housing (Chapter 7).
2   Shift rods interfering with the engine mounts or clutch lever (Chapter 7).
3   Shift rods not working freely (Chapter 7).
4   Dirt between the transaxle case and engine or misalignment of the transaxle (Chapter 7).
5   Worn or improperly adjusted linkage Chapter 7).

36 Difficulty In engaging gears

1   Clutch not releasing completely (see clutch adjustment in Chapter 8).
2   Loose, damaged or out-of-adjustment shift linkage. Make a thorough inspection, replacing parts as necessary (Chapter 7).

37 Oil leakage

1   Excessive amount of lubricant in the transaxle (see Chapter 1 for correct checking procedures). Drain lubricant as required.
2   Driveaxle oil seal (Chapter 8) or speedometer oil seal in need of replacement (Chapter 7).

Automatic transaxle

Note: *Due to the complexity of the automatic transaxle, it's difficult for, the home mechanic to properly diagnose and service this component. For problems other than the following, the vehicle should be taken to a dealer or reputable mechanic.*

38 General shift mechanism problems

1   Chapter 7 deals with checking and adjusting the shift linkage on automatic transaxles. Common problems which may be attributed to poorly adjusted linkage are:

Engine starting In gears other than Park or Neutral
Indicator on shifter pointing to a gear other than the one actually being used
Vehicle moves when in Park

2   Refer to Chapter 7 to adjust the linkage.

39 Transaxle will not downshift with accelerator pedal pressed to the floor

Chapter 7 deals with adjusting the throttle cable to enable the transaxle to downshift properly.

40 Transaxle slips, shifts rough, is noisy or has no drive in forward or reverse gears

1   There are many probable causes for the above problems, but the home mechanic should be concerned with only one possibility: fluid level.

2   Before taking the vehicle to a repair shop, check the level and condition of the fluid as described in Chapter 1. Correct fluid level as necessary or change the fluid and filter if needed. If the problem persists have a professional diagnose the probable cause.

41 Fluid leakage

1   Automatic transaxle fluid is a deep red color. Fluid leaks should not be confused with engine oil, which can easily be blown by air flow to the transaxle.

2   To pinpoint a leak, first remove all built-up dirt and grime from around the transaxle. Degreasing agents and/or steam cleaning will achieve this. With the underside clean, drive the vehicle at low speeds so air flow will not blow the leak far from its source. Raise the vehicle and determine where the leak is coming from. Common areas of leakage are:

a) *Pan: Tighten the mounting bolts and/or replace the pan gasket as necessary (see Chapter 7).*

b) *Filler pipe: Replace the rubber seal where the pipe enters the transaxle case.*

c) *Transaxle oil lines: Tighten the connectors where the lines enter the transaxle case and/or replace the lines.*

d) *Vent pipe: Transaxle overfilled and/or water in fluid (see checking procedures, Chapter 1).*

e) *Speedometer connector: Replace the O-ring where the speedometer cable enters the transaxle case (Chapter 7).*

Driveaxles

42 Clicking noise in turns

Worn or damaged outer joint. Check for cut or damaged seals. Repair as necessary (Chapter 8).

43 Knock or clunk when accelerating after coasting

Worn or damaged inner joint. Check for cut or damaged seals. Repair as necessary (Chapter 8).

44 Shudder or vibration during acceleration

1   Excessive joint angle. Have checked and correct as necessary (Chapter 8).

2   Worn or damaged CV joints. Repair or replace as necessary (Chapter 8).

3   Sticking CV joint assembly. Correct or replace as necessary (Chapter 8).

Rear axle

45 Noise

1   Road noise. No corrective procedures available.

2   Tire noise. Inspect tires and check tire pressures (Chapter 1).

3   Rear wheel bearings loose, worn or damaged (Chapter 10).

Brakes

Note: *Before assuming that a brake problem exists, make sure that the tires are in good condition and inflated properly (see Chapter 1), that the front end alignment is correct and that the vehicle is not loaded with weight in an unequal manner.*

46 Vehicle pulls to one side during braking

1   Defective, damaged or oil contaminated disc brake pads on one side. Inspect as described in Chapter 9.

2   Excessive wear of brake pad material or disc on one side. Inspect and correct as necessary.

3   Loose or disconnected front suspension components. Inspect and tighten all bolts to the specified torque (Chapter 10).

4   Defective caliper assembly. Remove the caliper and inspect for a stuck piston or other damage (Chapter 9).

47 Noise (high-pitched squeal with brakes applied)

Disc brake pads worn out. The noise comes from the wear sensor rubbing against the disc (does not apply to all vehicles) or the actual pad backing plate itself if the material is completely worn away. Replace the pads with new ones immediately (Chapter 9). If the pad material has worn completely away, the brake rotors should be inspected for damage as described in Chapter 9.

48 Excessive brake pedal travel

1   Partial brake system failure. Inspect the entire system (Chapter 9) and correct as required.

2   Insufficient fluid in the master cylinder. Check (Chapter 1), add fluid and bleed the system if necessary (Chapter 9).

3   Rear brakes not adjusting properly. Make a series of starts and stops while the vehicle is in Reverse. If this does not correct the situation, remove the drums and inspect the self-adjusters (Chapter 9).

49 Brake pedal feels spongy when depressed

1   Air in the hydraulic lines. Bleed the brake system (Chapter 9).

2   Faulty flexible hoses. Inspect all system hoses and lines. Replace parts as necessary.

3   Master cylinder mounting bolts/nuts loose.

4   Master cylinder defective (Chapter 9).

50 Excessive effort required to stop vehicle

1   Power brake booster not operating properly (Chapter 9).

2   Excessively worn linings or pads. Inspect and replace if necessary (Chapter 9).

3   One or more caliper pistons or wheel cylinders seized or sticking. Inspect and rebuild as required (Chapter 9).

4   Brake linings or pads contaminated with oil or grease. Inspect and replace as required (Chapter 9).

5   New pads or shoes installed and not yet seated. It will take a while for the new material to seat against the drum (or rotor).

51 Pedal travels to the floor with little resistance

Little or no fluid in the master cylinder reservoir caused by leaking wheel cylinder(s), leaking caliper piston(s), loose, damaged or disconnected brake lines. Inspect the entire system and correct as necessary.

52 Brake pedal pulsates when brakes are applied

1   Caliper improperly installed. Remove and inspect (Chapter 9).

2   Rotor defective. Remove the rotor (Chapter 9) and check for excessive lateral runout and parallelism. Have the rotor resurfaced or replace it with a new one.

Suspension and steering systems

53 Vehicle pulls to one side

1   Tire pressures uneven (Chapter 1).
2   Defective tire (Chapter 1).
3   Excessive wear in suspension or steering components (Chapter 10).
4   Front end in need of alignment.
5   Front brakes dragging. Inspect the brakes as described in Chapter 9.

54 Shimmy, shake or vibration

1   Tire or wheel out-of-balance or out-of-round. Have professionally balanced.
2   Loose, worn or out-of-adjustment wheel bearings (Chapter 10).
3   Shock absorbers and/or suspension components worn or damaged (Chapter 10).

55 Excessive pitching and/or rolling around corners or during braking

1   Defective shock absorbers. Replace as a set (Chapter 10).
2   Broken or weak springs and/or suspension components. Inspect as described in Chapter 10.

56 Excessively stiff steering

1   Lack of fluid in power steering fluid reservoir (Chapter 1).
2   Incorrect tire pressures (Chapter 1).
3   Front end out of alignment.

57 Excessive play in steering

1   Excessive wear in suspension or steering components (Chapter 10).
2   Steering gear damaged (Chapter 10).

58 Lack of power assistance

1   Steering pump drivebelt faulty or not adjusted properly (Chapter 1).
2   Fluid level low (Chapter 1).
3   Hoses or lines restricted. Inspect and replace parts as necessary.
4   Air in power steering system. Bleed the system (Chapter 10).

59 Excessive tire wear (not specific to one area)

1   Incorrect tire pressures (Chapter 1).
2   Tires out-of-balance. Have professionally balanced.

3   Wheels damaged. Inspect and replace as necessary.
4   Suspension or steering components excessively worn (Chapter 10).

60 Excessive tire wear on outside edge

1   Inflation pressures incorrect (Chapter 1).
2   Excessive speed in turns.
3   Front end alignment incorrect (excessive toe-in). Have profession- ally aligned.
4   Suspension arm bent or twisted (Chapter 10).

61 Excessive tire wear on inside edge

1   Inflation pressures incorrect (Chapter 1).
2   Front end alignment incorrect. Have professionally aligned.
3   Loose or damaged steering components (Chapter 10).

62 Tire tread worn in one place

1   Tires out-of-balance.
2   Damaged or buckled wheel. Inspect and replace if necessary.
3   Defective tire (Chapter 1).

Notes

Chapter 1
Tune-up and routine maintenance

Contents

Specifications

Recommended lubricants and fluids

Note: *Listed here are manufacturer recommendations at the time this manual was written. Manufacturers occasionally upgrade their fluid and lubricant specifications, so check with your local auto parts store for current recommendations.*

Engine oil type .... API category SG
Engine oil viscosity .... See accompanying chart

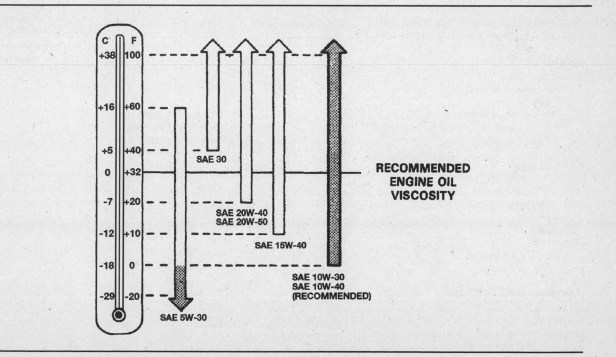

RECOMMENDED ENGINE OIL VISCOSITY

Recommended lubricants and fluids (continued)

Note: *Listed here are manufacturer recommendations at the time this manual was written. Manufacturers occasionally upgrade their fluid and lubricant specifications, so check with your local auto parts store for current recommendations.*

Engine oil capacity
  Four-cylinder engine
    With filter.. 5.0 qts
    Without filter... 4.0 qts
  V6 engine
    With filter.. 5.0 qts
    Without filter... 4.0 qts
Brake fluid type... DOT 3 heavy-duty brake fluid
Power steering fluid type... Motorcraft **Type F** ATF* (part no. XT-1-QF)
Automatic transaxle
  Fluid type... Motorcraft **MERCON** ATF* (part no. XT-2-QDX)
  Fluid capacity .... 8.3 qts
Manual transaxle
  Lubricant type
    1984 through 1991.. Motorcraft **Type F** ATF* (part no. XT-1-QF) or
      Motorcraft **DEXRON II** ATF*
    1992 and later... Motorcraft **MERCON** ATF* (part no. XT-2-QDX)
  Lubricant capacity
    1984 through 1992 MTX II and MTX III .... 6.1 pts
    1993 MTX III five-speed .... 6.4 pts
    1992 and later MTX IV five-speed (V6 only)...... 6.4 pts
Coolant type .... Ethylene glycol-based
antifreeze and water, 50/50 mixture

    * *ATF = Automatic Transmission Fluid*

General

Drivebelt tension (with tool no. T63L-8620-A)
  Alternator/power steering/air conditioning
    New belt... 150 to 190 lbs
    Used belt.. 140 to 160 lbs
  Water pump new belt
    New belt... 50 to 90 lbs
    Used belt.. 40 to 60 lbs
Radiator cap pressure
  Standard.. 16 psi
  Lower limit (must hold pressure) .... 13 psi
  Upper limit (must relieve pressure)........................ 18 psi

Brakes

Front disc brake pad thickness (minimum).................. 1/8 inch
Rear drum brake shoe lining thickness (minimum)...... 1/16 inch

Ignition system

Spark plug type
  Four-cylinder engine
    1987 and earlier
      Standard engine .... Motorcraft AWSF52C
      HO engine.. Motorcraft AWSF32C
    1988 and later... Motorcraft AWSF42C
  V6 engine.. Motorcraft AWSF32P
Spark plug gap
  Four-cylinder engine
    1988 and earlier .... 0.044 inch
    1989 and later... 0.054 inch
  V6 engine.. 0.044 inch
Idle speed .... Refer to the *Vehicle Emission Control Information* label
Firing order
  Four cylinder engine.. 1-3-4-2
  V6 engine 1-4-2-5-3-6

Torque specifications   **Ft-lbs**

Wheel lug nuts .... 80 to 105
Spark plugs... 6 to 10
Oil pan drain plug .... 15 to 25
Engine block drain plug .... 5 to 8

FOUR-CYLINDER ENGINE

Front of vehicle

V6 ENGINE

Front of vehicle

The blackened terminal shown on the distributor cap indicates the Number One spark plug wire position

Cylinder location and distributor rotation

1   Introduction to routine maintenance

This Chapter is designed to help the home mechanic maintain the Ford Tempo/Mercury Topaz with the goals of maximum performance, economy, safety and reliability in mind.

On the following pages is a master maintenance schedule, followed by procedures dealing specifically with each item on the schedule. Visual checks, adjustments, component replacement and other helpful items are included. Refer to the accompanying illustrations of the engine compartment and the underside of the vehicle for the locations of various components.

Servicing your Tempo/Topaz in accordance with the mileage/time maintenance schedule and the step-by-step procedures will result in a planned maintenance program that should produce a long and reliable service life. Keep in mind that it is a comprehensive plan, so maintaining some items but not others at the specified intervals will not produce the same results.

As you service your Tempo/Topaz, you will discover that many of the procedures can and should be grouped together because of the nature of the particular procedure you're performing or because of the close proximity of two otherwise unrelated components to one another.

For example, if the vehicle is raised for chassis lubrication, you should inspect the exhaust, suspension, steering and fuel systems while you're under the vehicle. When you're rotating the tires, it makes good sense to check the brakes since the wheels are already removed. Finally, let's suppose you have to borrow or rent a torque wrench. Even if you only need it to tighten the spark plugs, you might as well check the torque of as many critical fasteners as time allows.

The first step in this maintenance program is to prepare yourself before the actual work begins. Read through all the procedures you're planning to do, then gather up all the parts and tools needed. If it looks like you might run into problems during a particular job, seek advice from a mechanic or an experienced do-it-yourselfer.

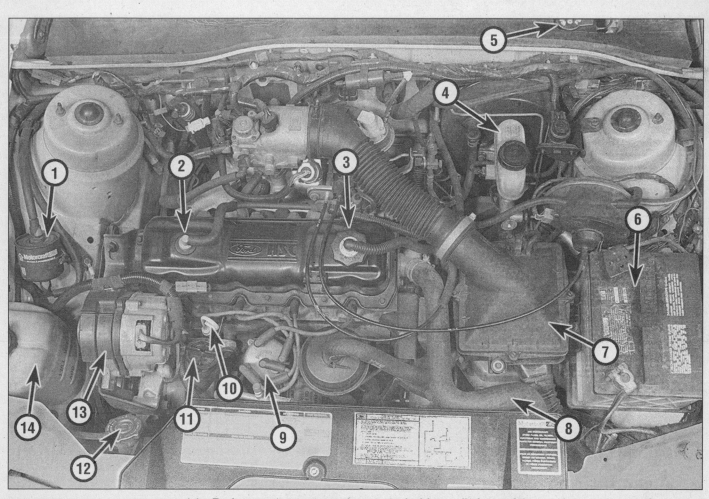

1.1a Engine compartment components, typical four-cylinder model

1 Fuel filter	6 Battery	11 Power steering fluid reservoir
2 PCV valve	7 Air cleaner assembly	12 Radiator cap
3 Engine oil filler cap	8 Upper radiator hose	13 Alternator
4 Brake fluid reservoir	9 Distributor	14 Coolant reservoir
5 Windshield washer fluid reservoir	10 Engine oil dipstick	

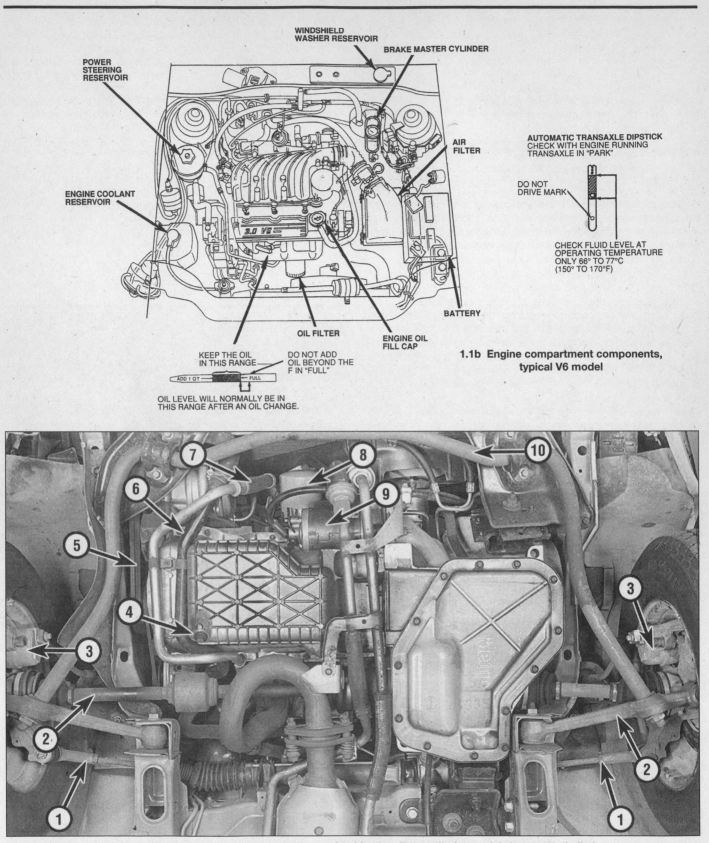

POWER
STEERING
RESERVOIR

WINDSHIELD
WASHER RESERVOIR

BRAKE MASTER CYLINDER

AIR
FILTER

ENGINE COOLANT
RESERVOIR

3.0 V6

OIL FILTER

ENGINE OIL
FILL CAP

BATTERY

AUTOMATIC TRANSAXLE DIPSTICK
CHECK WITH ENGINE RUNNING
TRANSAXLE IN "PARK"

DO NOT
DRIVE MARK

CHECK FLUID LEVEL AT
OPERATING TEMPERATURE
ONLY 66° TO 77°C
(150° TO 170°F)

**1.1b Engine compartment components,
typical V6 model**

KEEP THE OIL
IN THIS RANGE

DO NOT ADD
OIL BEYOND THE
F IN "FULL"

ADD 1 QT   FULL

OIL LEVEL WILL NORMALLY BE IN
THIS RANGE AFTER AN OIL CHANGE.

1.1c Engine compartment components - underside view (four-cylinder model shown, V6 similar)

1	Tie rod	5	Power steering/air conditioning	8	Engine oil filter
2	Driveaxle		compressor drivebelt	9	Starter motor
3	Front brake caliper	6	Engine coolant tube	10	Stabilizer bar
4	Engine oil drain plug	7	Air conditioning line		

2 Ford Tempo & Mercury Topaz Maintenance schedule

The following maintenance intervals are based on the assumption that the vehicle owner will be doing the maintenance or service work, as opposed to having a dealer service department do the work. Although the time/mileage intervals are loosely based on factory recommendations, most have been shortened to ensure, for example, that such items as lubricants and fluids are checked/ changed at intervals that promote maximum engine/driveline service life. Also, subject to the preference of the individual owner interested in keeping his or her vehicle in peak condition at all times, and with the vehicle's ultimate resale in mind, many of the maintenance procedures may be performed more often than recommended in the following schedule. We encourage such owner initiative. If only a minimum maintenance schedule is preferred, consult the owner's manual provided with your model for requirements.

When the vehicle is new it should be serviced initially by a factory authorized dealer service department to protect the factory warranty. In many cases the initial maintenance check is done at no cost to the owner.

Every 250 miles or weekly whichever comes first

Check the engine oil level (Section 4)
Check the engine coolant level (Section 4)
Check the windshield washer fluid level (Section 4)
Check the brake fluid level (Section 4)
Check the tires and tire pressures (Section 5)

Every 3000 miles or 3 months, whichever comes first

All items listed above plus . . .
Check the power steering fluid level (Section 6)
Check the automatic transaxle fluid level (Section 7)
Change the engine oil and oil filter (Section 8)

Every 6000 miles or 6 months, whichever comes first

All items listed above plus . . .
Inspect/replace the underhood hoses (Section 9)

Check/adjust the drivebelts (Section 10)
Check/service the battery (Section 11)

Every 12,000 miles or 12 months, whichever comes first

All items listed above plus . . .
Inspect/replace the windshield wiper blades (Section 12)
Replace the air filter (Section 13)
Check the PCV valve and filter (Section 14)
Check the fuel system (Section 15)
Replace the fuel filter (Section 16)
Inspect the cooling system (Section 17)
Inspect the exhaust system (Section 18)
Rotate the tires (Section 19)
Inspect the steering and suspension components (Section 20)
Inspect the brake system (Section 21)
Lubricate the parking brake cable (Section 21)
Lubricate the automatic transaxle control linkage (Section 22)
Check/replenish the manual transaxle lubricant (Section 23)

Every 24,000 miles or 24 months, whichever comes first

All items listed above plus . . .
Replace the spark plugs (Section 24)
Check/replace the spark plug wires distributor cap and rotor (Section 25)
Check the choke and lubricate the linkage - carbureted models only - (Section 26)
Service the cooling system (drain flush and refill) (Section 27)

3   Tune-up sequence

The term *tune-up* is used in this manual to represent a combination of individual operations rather than one specific procedure. If from the time the vehicle is new the routine maintenance schedule is followed closely and frequent checks are made of fluid levels and high wear items as suggested throughout this manual the engine will be kept in relatively good running condition and the need for additional work will be minimized.

More likely than not however there will be times when the engine is running poorly due to lack of regular maintenance. This is even more likely if a used vehicle which has not received regular and frequent maintenance checks is purchased. In such cases an engine tune-up will be needed outside of the regular routine maintenance intervals.

The first step in any tune-up or diagnostic procedure to help correct a poor running engine is a cylinder compression check. A compression check (see Chapter 2) will help determine the condition of internal engine components and should be used as a guide for tune-up and repair procedures. If for instance a compression check indicates serious internal engine wear a conventional tune-up will not improve the performance of the engine and would be a waste of time and money. Because of its importance the compression check should be done by someone with the right equipment and the knowledge to use it properly.

The following procedures are those most often needed to bring a generally poor running engine back into a proper state of tune.

Minor tune-up

Clean, inspect and test the battery (Section 11)
Check all engine related fluids (Section 4)
Check and adjust the drivebelts (Section 10)
Replace the spark plugs (Section 24)
Inspect the distributor cap and rotor (Section 25)

Inspect the spark plug and coil wires (Section 25)
Check and adjust (if adjustable) the idle speed (Chapter 4)
Check the PCV valve (Section 14)
Check the air filter (Section 13)
Check the cooling system (Section 17)
Check all underhood hoses (Section 9)

Major tune-up

All items listed under Minor tune-up, plus . . .
Check the EGR system (Chapter 6)
Check the ignition system (Chapter 5)
Check the charging system (Chapter 5)
Check the fuel system (Section 15)
Replace the air and PCV filters (Sections 13 and 14)
Replace the distributor cap and rotor (Section 25)
Replace the spark plug wires (Section 25)

4   Fluid level checks (Every 250 miles or weekly)

Refer to illustrations 4.4, 4.9, 4.15 and 4.22
1   Fluids are an essential part of the lubrication, cooling, brake and windshield washer systems. Because the fluids gradually become depleted and/or contaminated during normal operation of the vehicle they must be periodically replenished. See Recommended lubricants fluids and capacities at the beginning of this Chapter before adding fluid to any of the following components. **Note**: *The vehicle must be on level ground when fluid levels are checked.*

Engine oil

2   The oil level is checked with a dipstick which is located on the front of the engine near the alternator. The dipstick extends through a metal tube down into the oil pan.
3   The oil level should be checked before the vehicle has been driven or about 15 minutes after the engine has been shut off. If the oil is checked immediately after driving the vehicle some of the oil will remain in the upper part of the engine, resulting in an inaccurate reading on the dipstick.

4   Pull the dipstick from the tube and wipe all the oil from the end with a clean rag or paper towel. Insert the clean dipstick all the way back into the tube and pull it out again. Note the oil at the end of the dipstick. At its highest point the level should be above the Add mark in the SAFE or crosshatched range **(see illustration)**.
5   It takes one quart of oil to raise the level from the Add mark to the circle on the dipstick. Do not allow the level to drop below the Add mark or oil starvation may cause engine damage. Conversely, overfilling the engine (adding oil above the circle) may cause oil fouled spark plugs, oil leaks or oil seal failures.
6   To add oil, remove the filler cap located on the valve cover. After adding oil, wait a few minutes to allow the level to stabilize, then pull out the dipstick and check the level again. Add more oil if required. Install the filler cap and tighten it by hand only.
7   Checking the oil level is an important preventive maintenance step. A consistently low oil level indicates oil leakage through damaged seals, defective gaskets or past worn rings or valve guides. If the oil looks milky in color or has water droplets in it, the cylinder head gasket may be blown or the head or block may be cracked. The engine should be checked immediately. The condition of the oil should also be checked. Whenever you check the oil level, slide your thumb and index finger up the dipstick before wiping off the oil. If you see small dirt or metal particles clinging to the dipstick, the oil should be changed (refer to Section 8).

Engine coolant

Warning: *Do not allow antifreeze to come in contact with your skin or painted surfaces of the vehicle. Flush contaminated areas immediately with plenty of water. Do not store new coolant or leave old coolant lying around where it's accessible to children or pets. They are attracted by its sweet smell. Ingestion of even a small amount of coolant can be fatal! Wipe up garage floor and drip pan coolant spills immediately. Keep antifreeze containers covered and repair leaks in your cooling system immediately.*
8   All vehicles covered by this manual are equipped with a pressurized coolant recovery system. A white plastic coolant reservoir located in the right front corner of the engine compartment is connected by a hose to the radiator filler neck. If the engine overheats, coolant escapes through a valve in the radiator cap and travels through the hose into the reservoir. As the engine cools, the coolant is automatically drawn back into the cooling system to maintain the correct level.
9   The coolant level in the reservoir should be checked regularly. **Warning:** *Do not remove the radiator cap to check the coolant level when the engine is warm.* The level in the reservoir varies with the temperature of the engine. When the engine is cold, the coolant level should be at or slightly above the Add mark on the reservoir. Once the engine has warmed up, the level should be at or near the Full Hot mark **(see illustration)**. If

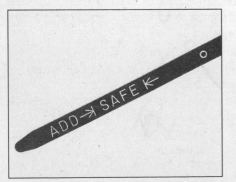

4.4 The oil level should be in the SAFE range - if it's below the ADD line, add enough oil to bring the level into the SAFE range (if the level is between the SAFE range and the circle DO NOT add more oil)

4.9 The coolant level in the reservoir should be at the ADD line when it's cool and between the FULL HOT and ADD lines when the engine is at operating temperature

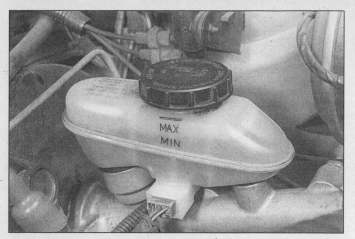

4.15 The brake fluid level should be between the MAX and MIN lines on the master cylinder reservoir

4.22 The windshield washer fluid reservoir is located in the left rear corner of the engine compartment - in cold climates, never fill it more than 2/3-full and DO NOT use cooling system antifreeze!

it isn't, allow the engine to cool, then remove the cap from the reservoir and add a 50/50 mixture of ethylene glycol based antifreeze and water.

10   Drive the vehicle and recheck the coolant level. Do not use rust inhibitors or additives. If only a small amount of coolant is required to bring the system up to the proper level, water can be used. However, repeated additions of water will dilute the antifreeze and water solution. In order to maintain the proper ratio of antifreeze and water, always top up the coolant level with the correct mixture. An empty plastic milk jug or bleach bottle makes an excellent container for mixing coolant.

11   If the coolant level drops consistently, there may be a leak in the system. Inspect the radiator, hoses, filler cap, drain plugs and water pump (see Section 17). If no leaks are noted, have the radiator cap pressure tested by a service station.

12   If you have to remove the radiator cap, wait until the engine has cooled completely, then wrap a thick cloth around the cap and turn it to the first stop. If coolant or steam escapes, let the engine cool down longer, then remove the cap.

13   Check the condition of the coolant as well. It should be relatively clear. If it is brown or rust colored, the system should be drained, flushed and refilled. Even if the coolant appears to be normal, the corrosion inhibitors wear out, so it must be replaced at the specified intervals.

Brake fluid

14   The brake fluid level is checked by looking through the plastic reservoir mounted on the master cylinder. The master cylinder is mounted on the front of the power booster unit in the left rear corner of the engine compartment.

15   The fluid level should be between the Max and Min lines on the side of the reservoir **(see illustration)**.

16   If the fluid level is low, wipe the top of the reservoir and the cap with a clean rag to prevent contamination of the system as the cap is unscrewed.

17   Add only the specified brake fluid to the reservoir (refer to *Recommended lubricants and fluids* at the front of this Chapter or to your owner's manual). Mixing different types of brake fluid can damage the system. Fill the reservoir to the Max line. **Warning:** *Brake fluid can harm your eyes and damage painted surfaces, so use extreme caution when handling or pouring it. Do not use brake fluid that has been standing open or is more than one year old. Brake fluid absorbs moisture from the air. Excess moisture can cause a dangerous loss of braking effectiveness.*

18   While the reservoir cap is off, check the master cylinder reservoir for contamination. If rust deposits, dirt particles or water droplets are present, the system should be drained and refilled by a dealer service department or repair shop.

19   After filling the reservoir to the proper level, make sure the cap is seated to prevent fluid leakage and/or contamination.

20   The fluid level in the master cylinder will drop slightly as the brake shoes or pads at each wheel wear down during normal operation. If the brake fluid level drops consistently, check the entire system for leaks immediately. Examine all brake lines, hoses and connections, along with the calipers, wheel cylinders and master cylinder (see Section 21).

21   When checking the fluid level, if you discover one or both reservoirs empty or nearly empty, the brake system should be bled (Chapter 9).

Windshield washer fluid

22   Fluid for the windshield washer system is stored in a plastic reservoir located at the left rear corner of the engine compartment, immediately behind the brake master cylinder **(see illustration)**.

23   In milder climates, plain water can be used in the reservoir, but it should be kept no more than 2/3 full to allow for expansion if the water freezes. In colder climates, use windshield washer system antifreeze, available at any auto parts store, to lower the freezing point of the fluid. Mix the antifreeze with water in accordance with the manufacturer's directions on the container. **Caution:** *Do not use cooling system antifreeze. It will damage the vehicle's paint.*

5   Tire and tire pressure checks (every 250 miles or weekly)

Refer to illustrations 5.2, 5.3, 5.4a, 5.4b and 5.8

1   Periodic inspection of the tires may spare you the inconvenience of being stranded with a flat tire. It can also provide you with vital information regarding possible problems in the steering and suspension systems before major damage occurs.

2   The original tires on this vehicle are equipped with 1/2-inch side bands that will appear when tread depth reaches 1/16-inch, but they don't appear until the tires are worn out. Tread wear can be monitored with a simple, inexpensive device known as a tread depth indicator **(see illustration)**.

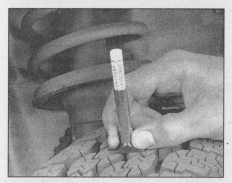

5.2 Until the tires wear down to a tread depth of 1/16-inch, the wear bars will not appear - in the meantime, monitor wear with a tread depth indicator by inserting the screwdriver-like tip between two tread blocks, pushing it down until it bottoms, then simply reading the indicated depth on the calibrated barrel

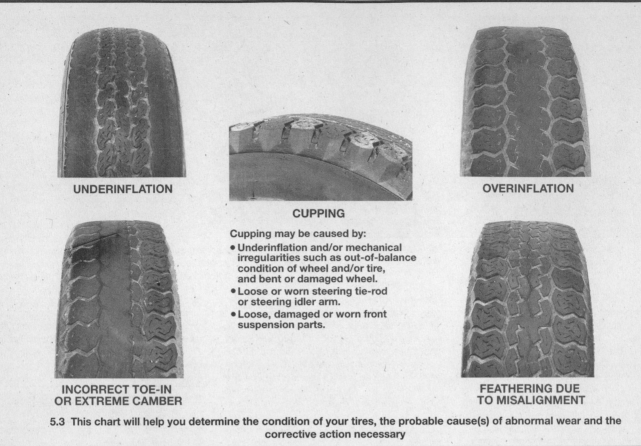

UNDERINFLATION

CUPPING

OVERINFLATION

Cupping may be caused by:
- Underinflation and/or mechanical irregularities such as out-of-balance condition of wheel and/or tire, and bent or damaged wheel.
- Loose or worn steering tie-rod or steering idler arm.
- Loose, damaged or worn front suspension parts.

INCORRECT TOE-IN
OR EXTREME CAMBER

FEATHERING DUE
TO MISALIGNMENT

5.3 This chart will help you determine the condition of your tires, the probable cause(s) of abnormal wear and the corrective action necessary

3   Note any abnormal tread wear **(see illustration)**. Tread pattern irregularities such as cupping, flat spots and more wear on one side than the other are indications of front end alignment and/or balance problems. If any of these conditions are noted, take the vehicle to a tire shop or service station to correct the problem.

4   Look closely for cuts, punctures and embedded nails or tacks. Sometimes a tire will hold air pressure for a short time or leak down very slowly after a nail has embedded itself in the tread. If a slow leak persists, check the valve stem core to make sure it is tight **(see illustration)**. Examine the tread for an object that may have embedded itself in the tire or for a "plug" that may have begun to leak (radial tire punctures are repaired with a plug that is installed in a puncture). If a puncture is suspected, it can be easily verified by spraying a solution of soapy water onto the puncture area **(see illustration)**. The soapy solution will bubble if there is a leak. Unless the puncture is unusually large, a tire shop or service station can usually repair the tire.

5   Carefully inspect the inner sidewall of each tire for evidence of brake fluid leakage. If you see any, inspect the brakes immediately.

6   Correct air pressure adds miles to the life span of the tires, improves mileage and enhances overall ride quality. Tire pressure cannot be accurately estimated by looking at a tire, especially if it's a radial. A tire pressure gauge is essential. Keep an accurate gauge in the glove box. The pressure gauges attached to the nozzles of air hoses at gas stations are often inaccurate.

7   Always check tire pressure when the tires are cold. Cold, in this case, means the vehicle has not been driven over a mile in the three hours preceding a tire pressure check. A pressure rise of four to eight pounds is not uncommon once the tires are warm.

8   Unscrew the valve cap protruding from the wheel or hubcap and push the gauge firmly onto the valve stem **(see illustration)**.

5.4a If a tire continually loses pressure over and over again at a slow rate, check the valve stem core first to make sure that it's snug

5.4b If the valve stem core is tight, raise the corner of the vehicle with the low tire and spray the tire with a solution of soapy water - slow leaks will cause small bubbles to appear

5.8 Check the pressure of all four tires at least once a week with an accurate tire pressure gauge

6.2 The power steering fluid filler cap/dipstick is located right in front of the engine oil dipstick

Note the reading on the gauge and compare the figure to the recommended tire pressure shown on the tire placard on the driver's side door. Be sure to reinstall the valve cap to keep dirt and moisture out of the valve stem mechanism. Check all four tires and, if necessary, add enough air to bring them up to the recommended pressure.

9   Don't forget to keep the spare tire inflated to the specified pressure (refer to your owner's manual or the tire sidewall). Note that the pressure recommended for the compact spare is higher than for the tires on the vehicle.

6   Power steering fluid level check (every 3000 miles or 3 months)

Refer to illustrations 6.2 and 6.5
1   Check the power steering fluid level periodically to avoid steering system problems, such as damage to the pump. **Caution:** *DO NOT hold the steering wheel against either stop (extreme left or right turn) for more than five seconds. If you do, the power steering pump could be damaged* .
2   On 1984 through 1991 models, the power steering pump, located at the right front corner of the engine, utilizes a built-in reservoir and is equipped with a twist-off cap with an integral fluid level dipstick for verifying fluid level **(see illustration)**. 1992 and later models use a remote reservoir mounted next to the right hand strut tower. On remote reservoirs, fluid level is checked by looking through the plastic reservoir and verifying that the fluid is between the Max and Min lines.
3   Park the vehicle on level ground and apply the parking brake.
4   Run the engine until it has reached normal operating temperature. With the engine at idle, turn the steering wheel back-and-forth several times to get any air out of the steering system. Shut the engine off.
5   On 1984 through 1991 models, remove the cap and wipe the dipstick. Install, then remove the cap again and note the fluid level. It must be between the two lines designating the Full Hot range **(see illustration)** (be sure to use the proper temperature range on the

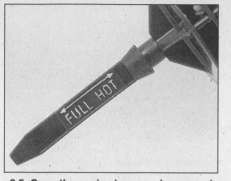

6.5 Once the engine is properly warmed up and the wheel has been turned back-and-forth a few times to rid the system of air bubbles, pull the dipstick out and wipe it off, reinsert it and verify that the fluid level is in the FULL HOT range - if it isn't, add enough fluid to bring the level between the two lines

dipstick when checking the fluid level. The Full Cold lines on the reverse side of the dipstick are only usable when the engine is cold). On 1992 and later models, simply verify the fluid level is between the level marks on the remote reservoir.
6   Add small amounts of fluid until the level is correct. **Caution:** *Do not overfill. If too much fluid is added, remove the excess with a clean syringe or suction pump.*
7   Check the power steering hoses and connections for leaks and wear (see Section 9).
8   Check the condition and tension of the power steering pump drivebelt (see Section 10).

7   Automatic transaxle fluid level check (every 3000 miles or 3 months)

Refer to illustrations 7.4 and 7.6
1   The automatic transaxle fluid level should be carefully maintained. Low fluid level can lead to slipping or loss of drive, while overfilling can cause foaming and loss

7.4 The automatic transaxle dipstick is located at the left front corner of the engine compartment, just in front of the air cleaner housing

of fluid. Either condition can cause transaxle damage.
2   Since transaxle fluid expands as it heats up, the fluid level should only be checked when the transaxle is warm (at normal operating temperature). If the vehicle has just been driven over 20 miles (32 km), the transaxle can be considered warm. **Caution:** *If the vehicle has just been driven for a long time at high speed or in city traffic in hot weather, or if it has been pulling a trailer, an accurate fluid level reading cannot be obtained. Allow the transaxle to cool down for about 30 minutes.* You can also check the transaxle fluid level when the transaxle is cold. If the vehicle has not been driven for over five hours and the fluid is about room temperature (70 to 95 degrees F), the transaxle is cold. However, the fluid level is normally checked with the transaxle warm to ensure accurate results.
3   Immediately after driving the vehicle, park it on a level surface, set the parking brake and start the engine. While the engine is idling, depress the brake pedal and move the selector lever through all the gear ranges, beginning and ending in Park.
4   Locate the automatic transaxle dipstick tube at the left front corner of the engine compartment, in front of the air cleaner housing **(see illustration)** .
5   With the engine still idling, pull the dipstick from the tube, wipe it off with a clean rag, push it all the way back into the tube and withdraw it again, then note the fluid level.
6   If the transaxle is cold, the level should be in the room temperature range on the dipstick (between the two circles); if it's warm, the fluid level should be in the operating temperature range (between the two lines) **(see illustration)**. If the level is low, add the specified automatic transmission fluid through the dipstick tube. Use a funnel to prevent spills.
7   Add just enough of the recommended fluid to fill the transaxle to the proper level. It takes about one pint to raise the level from the low mark to the high mark when the fluid is hot, so add the fluid a little at a time and keep checking the level until it's correct.
8   The condition of the fluid should also be checked along with the level. If the fluid is

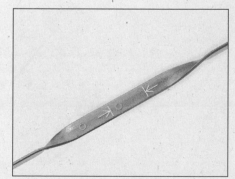

7.6 If the automatic transaxle fluid is cold, the level should be between the two circles - if it's at operating temperature, the level should be between the two lines

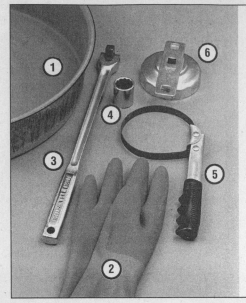

1 **Drain pan** - It should be fairly shallow in depth, but wide in order to prevent spills

2 **Rubber gloves** - When removing the drain plug and filter, it is inevitable that you will get oil on your hands - the gloves will prevent burns!

3 **Breaker bar** - Sometimes the oil drain plug is pretty tight and a long breaker bar is needed to loosen it

4 **Socket** - To be used with the breaker bar or a ratchet (must be the correct size to fit the drain plug)

5 **Filter wrench** - This is a metal band-type wrench, which requires clearance around the filter to be effective

6 **Filter wrench** - This type fits on the bottom of the filter and can be turned with a ratchet or breaker bar - different size wrenches are available for different types of filters

8.2 These tools are required when changing the engine oil and filter

black or a dark reddish-brown color, or if it smells burned, it should be changed (see Chapter 7). If you are in doubt about its condition, purchase some new fluid and compare the two for color and smell.

8 Engine oil and filter change (every 3000 miles or 3 months)

Refer to illustrations 8.2. 8.4a, 8.4b and 8.12

1 Frequent oil changes are the most important preventive maintenance procedures that can be done by the home mechanic. As engine oil ages, it becomes diluted and contaminated, which leads to premature engine wear.

2 Make sure that you have all the necessary tools before you begin this procedure **(see illustration).** You should also have plenty of rags or newspapers handy for mopping up oil spills.

3 Access to the oil drain plug and filter will be improved if the vehicle can be lifted on a hoist, driven onto ramps or supported by jackstands. **Warning:** *Do not work under a vehicle supported only by a bumper, hydraulic or scissors-type jack, always use jackstands!*

4 If you haven't changed the oil on this vehicle before, get under it and locate the oil drain plug **(see illustrations)** and the oil filter. The exhaust components will be warm as you work, so note how they are routed to avoid touching them when you are under the vehicle.

5 Start the engine and allow it to reach normal operating temperature, oil and sludge will flow out more easily when warm. If new oil, a filter or tools are needed. use the vehicle to go get them and warm up the engine/oil at the same time. Park on a level surface and shut off the engine when it's warmed up. Remove the oil filler cap from the rocker arm cover.

6 Raise the vehicle and support it on jackstands. Make sure it is safely supported !

7 Being careful not to touch the hot exhaust components, position a drain pan under the plug in the bottom of the engine, then remove the plug. **Caution:** *It's a good*

idea to wear an old glove while unscrewing the plug the final few turns to avoid being scalded by hot oil. **Note:** *Do not mistake the oil level sensor for the oil drain plug on vehicles so equipped. The sensor is mounted higher and has a wire attached* **(see illustration 8.4b).**

8 It may be necessary to move the drain pan slightly as oil flow slows to a trickle. Inspect the old oil for the presence of metal particles.

9 After all the oil has drained, wipe off the drain plug with a clean rag. Any small metal particles clinging to the plug would immediately contaminate the new oil.

10 Clean the area around the drain plug opening, reinstall the plug and tighten it securely, but don't strip the threads.

11 Move the drain pan into position under the oil filter, located on the front radiator side of the engine.

12 Loosen the oil filter by turning it counter-clockwise with a filter wrench **(see illustration).** Any standard filter wrench will work.

13 Sometimes the oil filter is screwed on so tightly that it cannot be loosened. If it is, punch a metal bar or long screwdriver directly through it, as close to the engine as possible, and use it as a T-bar to turn the filter. Be prepared for oil to spurt out of the canister as it is punctured.

14 Once the filter is loose, use your hands to unscrew it from the block. Just as the filter is detached from the block, immediately tilt the open end up to prevent the oil inside the filter from spilling out. **Warning:** *The engine exhaust manifold may still be hot, so be careful.*

15 Using a clean rag, wipe off the mounting surface on the block. Also, make sure that none of the old gasket remains stuck to the mounting surface. It can be removed with a scraper if necessary.

16 Compare the old filter with the new one to make sure they are the same type. Smear some engine oil on the rubber gasket of the new filter and screw it into place. Over tightening the filter will damage the gasket, so don't use a filter wrench. Most filter manufacturers recommend tightening the filter by hand only. Normally they should be tightened

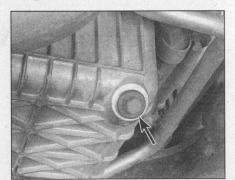

8.4a On four-cylinder engines, the oil drain plug is located at the right rear corner of the pan - it's usually in very tight, so use a six-point socket to avoid rounding off the hex

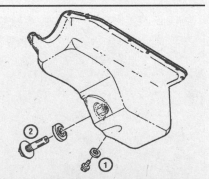

8.4b On V6 engines, the oil drain plug (1) is also located at the right rear of the pan - don't confuse the oil level sensor (2) with the drain plug.

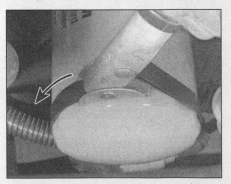

8.12 The oil filter is usually on very tight and will require a special wrench for removal - Do not use the wrench to tighten the new filter

3/4-turn after the gasket contacts the block, but be sure to follow the directions on the filter or container.

17   Remove all tools and materials from under the vehicle, being careful not to spill the oil in the drain pan, then lower the vehicle.

18   Add new oil to the engine through the oil filler cap in the rocker arm cover. Use a funnel to prevent oil from spilling onto the top of the engine. Pour four quarts of fresh oil into the engine. Wait a few minutes to allow the oil to drain into the pan, then check the level on the dipstick (see Section 4 if necessary). If the oil level is in the Safe range, install the filler cap.

19   Start the engine and run it for about a minute. **Warning:** *Observe the oil warning or pressure gauge; it should indicate normal oil pressure a few seconds after start-up. While the engine is running, look under the vehicle and check for leaks at the oil pan drain plug and around the oil filter. If either one is leaking, stop the engine and tighten the plug or filter slightly.*

20   Wait a few minutes, turn off the engine, then recheck the level on the dipstick. Add oil as necessary to bring the level into the Safe range.

21   During the first few trips after an oil change, make it a point to check frequently for leaks and proper oil level.

22   The old oil drained from the engine cannot be reused in its present state and should be discarded. Oil reclamation centers, auto repair shops and gas stations will normally accept the oil, which can be recycled. After the oil has cooled, it can be drained into a container (plastic jugs, bottles, milk cartons, etc.) for transport to a disposal site.

---

9   Underhood hose check and replacement (every 6000 miles or 6 months)

Refer to illustration 9.5

Warning: *Replacement of air conditioning hoses must be left to a dealer service department or air conditioning shop that has the equipment to depressurize the system safely. Never remove air conditioning components or hoses until the system has been depressurized.*

General

1   High temperatures under the hood can cause the deterioration of the rubber and plastic hoses used for engine, accessory and emission systems operation. Periodic inspection should be made for cracks, loose clamps, material hardening and leaks.

2   Information specific to the cooling system hoses can be found in Section 17.

3   Most (but not all) hoses are secured to the fittings with clamps. Where clamps are used, check to be sure they haven't lost their tension, allowing the hose to leak. If clamps aren't used, make sure the hose has not expanded and/or hardened where it slips over the fitting, allowing it to leak.

PCV system hose

4   To reduce hydrocarbon emissions, crankcase blow-by gas must be vented into the intake manifold for combustion. This is accomplished through the PCV system. Air flow is introduced into the crankcase through a hose between the air cleaner housing and the valve cover. A small filter, either in the air cleaner housing or in the valve cover provides the crankcase with clean air. Engine vacuum from the Intake manifold through a rubber hose to the rocker arm cover mounted PCV valve draws this air and the blow-by gasses into the intake manifold. The blow-by gas mix with in-coming air before being burned in the combustion chambers.

5   Check the PCV hose for cracks, leaks and other damage. Disconnect it from the valve cover **(see illustration)** and the intake manifold and check the inside for obstructions. If it's clogged, replace it.

Vacuum hoses

6   It is quite common for vacuum hoses, especially those in the emissions system, to be color coded or identified by colored stripes molded into each hose. Various systems require hoses with different wall thicknesses, collapse resistance and temperature resistance. When replacing hoses, be sure the new ones are made of the same material.

7   Often the only effective way to check a hose is to remove it completely from the vehicle. If more than one hose is removed, be sure to label the hoses and fittings to ensure correct installation.

8   When checking vacuum hoses, be sure to include any plastic fittings in the check. Inspect the fittings for cracks and the hose where it fits over each fitting for distortion, which could cause leakage.

9   A small piece of vacuum hose (1/4-inch inside diameter) can be used as a stethoscope to detect vacuum leaks. Hold one end of the hose to your ear and probe around vacuum hoses and fittings, listening for the "hissing" sound characteristic of a vacuum leak. **Warning:** *When probing with the vacuum hose stethoscope, be careful not to*

9.5 The hose between the PCV valve (arrow) and the intake manifold should be periodically inspected and cleaned (early four-cylinder engine shown)

allow your body or the hose to come into contact with moving engine components such as drivebelts, the cooling fan, etc.

Fuel hose

Warning: *Gasoline is extremely flammable, so take extra precautions when you work on any part of the fuel system. Don't smoke or allow open flames or bare light bulbs near the work area, and don't work in a garage where a natural gas-type appliance (such as a water heater or clothes dryer) with a pilot light is present. If you spill any fuel on your skin, rinse it off immediately with soap and water. When you perform any kind of work on the fuel system, wear safety glasses and have a Class B type fire extinguisher on hand.*

10   The fuel lines are usually under a small amount of pressure, so if any fuel lines are to be disconnected be prepared to catch spilled fuel. **Warning:** *If your vehicle is equipped with fuel injection you must relieve the fuel system pressure before servicing the fuel lines. Refer to Chapter 4 for the fuel system pressure relief procedure.*

11   Check all rubber fuel lines for deterioration and chafing. Check especially for cracks in areas where the hose bends and just before fittings, such as where a hose attaches to the fuel pump, fuel filter and carburetor or fuel injection unit.

12   High quality fuel line, usually identified by the word Fluroelastomer printed on the hose, should be used for fuel line replacement. Never, under any circumstances, use unreinforced vacuum line, clear plastic tubing or water hose for fuel lines. **Warning:** *When replacing hose on fuel-injected models, make sure it is designed to be used with the fuel-injection system installed on your vehicle, since fuel injection system operating pressures are much higher than those on carbureted models.*

13   Spring-type clamps are commonly used on fuel lines. These clamps often lose their tension over a period of time, and can be "sprung" during the removal process. As a result, it is recommended that all spring-type clamps be replaced with screw clamps whenever a hose is replaced.

Metal lines

14   Sections of metal line are often used for fuel line between the fuel pump and carburetor or fuel injection unit. Check carefully to be sure the line has not been bent and crimped and that cracks have not started in the line, particularly where bends occur.

15   If a section of metal fuel line must be replaced, use seamless steel tubing only, since copper and aluminum tubing do not have the strength necessary to withstand vibration caused by the engine.

16   Check the metal brake lines where they enter the master cylinder and brake proportioning unit (if used) for cracks in the lines and loose fittings. Any sign of brake fluid leakage calls for an immediate thorough inspection of the brake system.

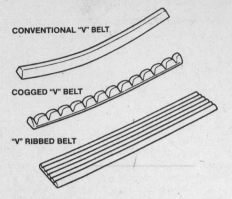

10.1 Different types of drivebelts are used to power the various accessories mounted on the engine

10 Drivebelt check, adjustment and replacement (every 6000 miles or 6 months)

Refer to illustrations 10.1, 10.2a, 10.2b, 10.2c, 10.2d, 10.4, 10.5, 10.6, 10.7, 10.8, 10.9, 10.10, 10.13 and 10.15

Description

1   The accessory drivebelts, also referred to as V-belts or simply fan belts **(see illustration)**, are located at the right end of the engine. The condition and tension of the drivebelts are critical to the operation of the engine and accessories. Excessive tension causes bearing wear, while insufficient tension produces slippage, noise, component vibration and belt failure. Because of their composition and the high stresses to which they are subjected, drivebelts stretch and deteriorate as they get older. As a result, they must be periodically checked and adjusted.

Four-cylinder models

2   The number and type of belts used on a particular vehicle depends on the accessories installed. On models prior to 1992, a conventional V-belt transmits power from the crankshaft to the water pump. On vehicles equipped with an air pump, another V-belt driven by the water pump pulley turns the air pump. Manual adjustment is required for both **(see illustration)**. If your vehicle is equipped

with air conditioning and/or power steering, these accessories are driven by a second crankshaft-driven V-ribbed belt. This belt required manual adjustment until 1988 when an automatic tensioner was incorporated. The alternator is driven via a cogged V-belt off the power steering pump pulley and, prior to 1992, required manual adjustment **(see illustrations)**. 1992 and later models utilize one V-ribbed belt to operate all systems and an automatic tensioner to eliminate all manual belt adjustments **(see illustration)**.

V6 models

3   The V6 models are equipped with 2 V-ribbed belts. The first belt is routed over the alternator, power steering pump, air conditioning compressor and the crankshaft pulley. The belt is non-adjustable and utilizes an automatic tensioner. The second V-ribbed belt drives the water pump and also features an automatic tensioner. Therefore, all manual belt adjustments are eliminated.

Check

4   With the engine off, open the hood and locate the drivebelts at the right end of the engine. With a flashlight, check each belt for

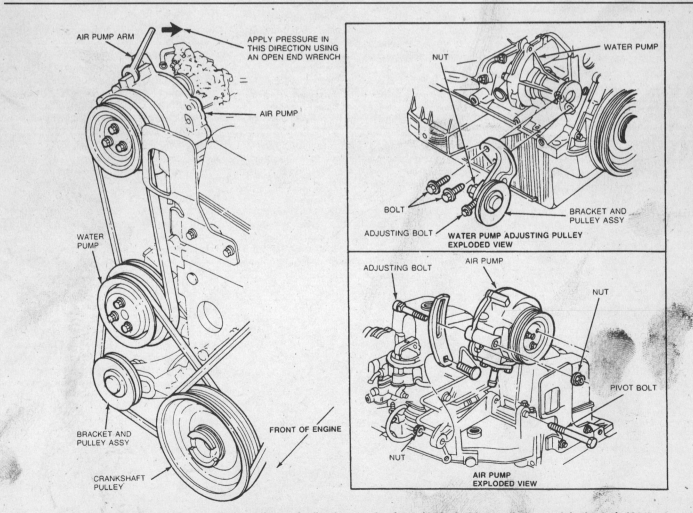

10.2a Water pump and air pump belt routing and adjusting mechanisms (typical of four-cylinder models through 1991)

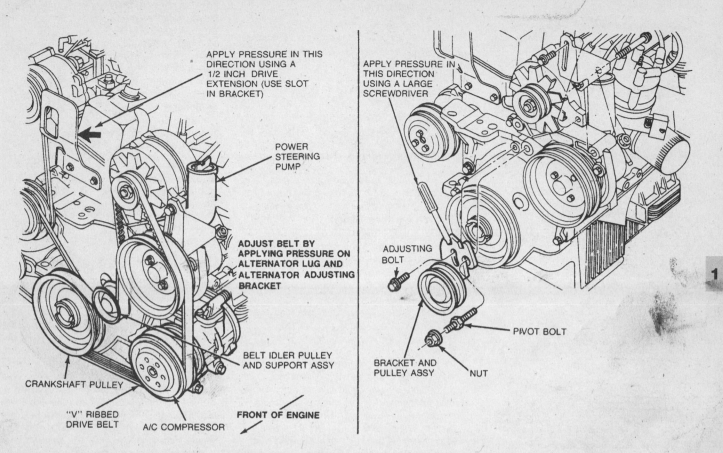

APPLY PRESSURE IN THIS DIRECTION USING A 1/2 INCH DRIVE EXTENSION (USE SLOT IN BRACKET)

POWER STEERING PUMP

ADJUST BELT BY APPLYING PRESSURE ON ALTERNATOR LUG AND ALTERNATOR ADJUSTING BRACKET

BELT IDLER PULLEY AND SUPPORT ASSY

CRANKSHAFT PULLEY

"V" RIBBED DRIVE BELT   A/C COMPRESSOR   FRONT OF ENGINE

APPLY PRESSURE IN THIS DIRECTION USING A LARGE SCREWDRIVER

ADJUSTING BOLT

PIVOT BOLT

BRACKET AND PULLEY ASSY   NUT

10.2b Alternator, power steering and air conditioning compressor belt routing and adjusting mechanism (typical of four-cylinder models through 1987)

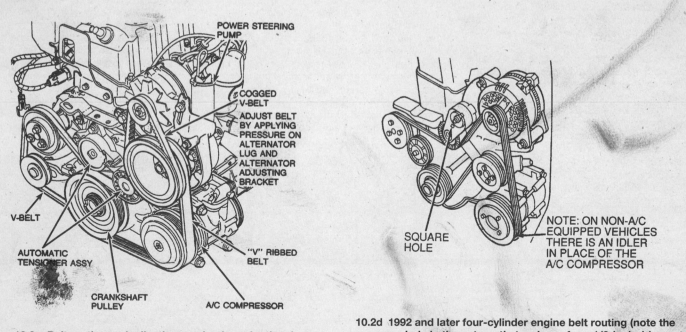

POWER STEERING PUMP

COGGED V-BELT

ADJUST BELT BY APPLYING PRESSURE ON ALTERNATOR LUG AND ALTERNATOR ADJUSTING BRACKET

V-BELT

AUTOMATIC TENSIONER ASSY

CRANKSHAFT PULLEY   A/C COMPRESSOR   "V" RIBBED BELT

SQUARE HOLE

NOTE: ON NON-A/C EQUIPPED VEHICLES THERE IS AN IDLER IN PLACE OF THE A/C COMPRESSOR

10.2c Belt routing and adjusting mechanisms for the air conditioning compressor, alternator and power steering units on 1988 through 1991 four-cylinder models

10.2d 1992 and later four-cylinder engine belt routing (note the square hole in the automatic tensioner for a 1/2-inch drive breaker bar)

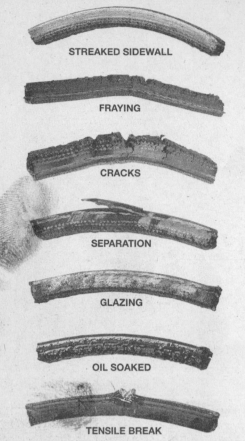

STREAKED SIDEWALL

FRAYING

CRACKS

SEPARATION

GLAZING

OIL SOAKED

TENSILE BREAK

10.4 Here are some of the more common problems associated with drivebelts (check the belts very carefully to prevent an untimely breakdown)

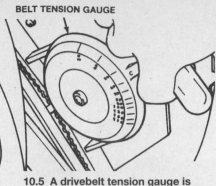

BELT TENSION GAUGE

10.5 A drivebelt tension gauge is recommended for checking the belts (the unit illustrated is a Burroughs model - follow the manufacturer's instructions)

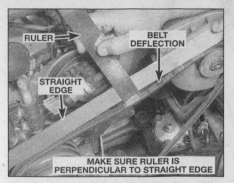

RULER   BELT DEFLECTION

STRAIGHT EDGE

MAKE SURE RULER IS PERPENDICULAR TO STRAIGHT EDGE

10.6 Measuring drivebelt deflection with a straightedge and ruler

separation of the rubber plies from each side of the core, a severed core, separation of the ribs from the rubber, cracks, torn or worn ribs and cracks in the inner ridges of the ribs. Also check for fraying and glazing, which gives the belt a shiny appearance **(see illustration)**. Both sides of each belt should be inspected, which means you'll have to twist them to check the undersides. Use your fingers to feel a belt where you can't see it. If any of the above conditions are evident, replace the belt as described below.

5   To check the tension on manually adjustable belts in accordance with factory recommendations, install a drivebelt tension

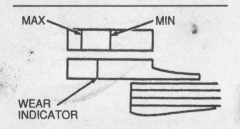

MAX   MIN

WEAR
INDICATOR

10.7 Keep the wear indicator of automatic tensioners between the MAX and MIN marks - if it's outside the marks, the belt is worn out or the wrong size

gauge, available at most auto parts stores, **(see illustration)**. Measure the tension in accordance with the tension gauge instructions and compare your measurement to the specified drivebelt tension for either a used or new belt. **Note**: *A "new" belt is defined as any belt which has not been run, while a "used" belt is one that has been run for more than ten minutes.*

6   The special gauge is the most accurate way to check belt tension. However, if you don't have a gauge, and cannot borrow one, the following "rule-of-thumb" method is recommended as an alternative. Lay a straightedge across the longest free span (the distance between two pulleys) of the belt. Push down firmly on the belt at a point half way between the pulleys and see how much the belt moves (deflects). Measure the deflection with a ruler **(see illustration)**. The belt should deflect 1/8 to 1 /4-inch if the distance from pulley center-to-pulley center is less than 12-inches; it should deflect from 1/8 to 3/8-inch if the distance from pulley center to-pulley center is over 12 inches.

7   On models with automatic tensioner, belt stretch is determined by inspecting the wear indicator marks on the tensioner assembly **(see illustration)**. If the indicator mark is beyond the MAX mark, the belt is worn and must be replaced. **Note:** *To inspect*

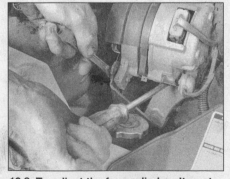

10.8 To adjust the four-cylinder alternator drivebelt, loosen the pivot and adjustment bolts and pry the alternator up to tighten the belt (be sure to retighten the bolts)

the water pump tensioner mark on V6 models, you must look from the underside of the vehicle.

Adjustment (belts without automatic tensioner)

8   If the alternator drivebelt must be adjusted, first loosen the pivot bolt, then loosen the adjustment bolt that secures the alternator to the slotted bracket. Pivot the alternator up to tighten the belt or down to loosen the belt. Use a large screwdriver or pry bar to lever the alternator into position as the bolts are retightened **(see illustration)**. Be very careful not to damage the aluminum housing of the alternator (pry against the front half of the alternator). Recheck the belt tension using one of the above methods. Repeat this Step until the alternator drivebelt tension is correct.

9   If the power steering/air conditioner compressor drivebelt must be adjusted, locate the idler pulley on the right front corner of the block. Loosen the idler pulley bracket bolts slightly **(see illustration)** and turn the adjuster bolt (clockwise to tighten the belt and counterclockwise to loosen it). Be sure to tighten the bracket bolts after the belt is tensioned. Check the belt tension as described earlier in this Section.

10   The water pump belt tension can be changed by moving the idler pulley in the slotted bracket located just below the pump on the right rear corner of the engine. Raise

10.9 The four-cylinder model serpentine drivebelt is adjusted by turning the adjusting bolt (arrow) after the idler pulley bracket bolts have been loosened slightly (arrows)

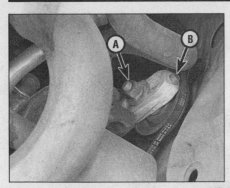

10.10 To adjust the four-cylinder model water pump drivebelt, loosen the locknut (arrow A) and turn the adjuster bolt (arrow B) until the belt is the correct tension, then tighten the locknut

the vehicle and support it on jackstands. Loosen the locknut, then turn the adjusting bolt to change the belt tension **(see illustration)**. When the belt tension is correct, tighten the locknut securely.

11 If your vehicle is equipped with an air pump loosen the pivot and adjustment bolts, then move the pump up or down as required to change the belt tension. The air pump has a cast-in lug designed to accept an open-end wrench, which can be used as a lever to tension the belt **(see illustration 10.2a)**. Be sure to tighten the bolts when the belt tension is correct.

Replacement (all belts)

12 On non auto-tensioned applications, to replace a belt, follow the above procedures for drivebelt adjustment but slip the belt off the pulleys and remove it. If you're replacing the water pump, air pump or alternator drivebelts, the power steering pump/air conditioning compressor belt must come off first. Since belts tend to wear out more or less at the same time, it is a good idea to replace all of them at the same time. Mark each belt and the corresponding pulley grooves so the replacement belts can be installed properly.

13 On belts with automatic tensioners, to remove the belt, rotate the tensioner against the spring tension, simultaneously remove the belt from the tensioner idler pulley and remove the belt from the remaining pulleys. On 1989 and earlier models insert a 1/2-inch breaker bar into the square hole provided in the tensioner arm **(see illustration)**. On 1990 and later models, a special tool (available at most auto parts stores) is required to rotate the tensioner. **Note:** *If the belt is not to be replaced, mark the direction of rotation on the belt to make sure the belt is installed the same way.*

14 Take the old belts with you when purchasing new ones in order to make a direct comparison for length, width and design.

15 When replacing a V-ribbed drivebelt, make sure that it fits properly into the pulley grooves. It must be completely engaged **(see illustration)**. **Note:** *Due to the unusual*

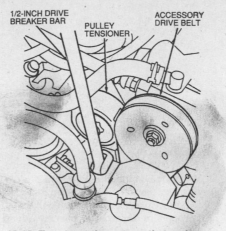

10.13 To retract the automatic tensioner and remove the belt, insert a breaker bar into the slot or square hole provided in the tensioner's arm and rotate it against spring tension (1989 and earlier)

routing necessary to reduce the number of belts on 1992 and later models, the power steering pump pulley must be driven from the back (non-V-ribbed) side of the belt and consequently does not have a grooved pulley.

16 Installation is the reverse of removal.

17 Adjust the belts, if necessary, as described earlier in this Section.

11 Battery check, maintenance and charging (every 6000 miles or 6 months)

Check and maintenance

Refer to illustrations 11.1, 11.8a, 11.8b, 11.8c and 11.8d

Warning: *Certain precautions must be followed when checking and servicing the battery. Hydrogen gas, which is highly flammable, is always present in the battery cells, so keep lighted tobacco and all other open flames and sparks away from the battery. The electrolyte inside the battery is actually dilute sulfuric acid, which will cause injury if splashed on your skin or in your eyes. It will also ruin clothes and painted surfaces. When removing the battery cables, always detach the negative cable first and hook it up last!*

1 Battery maintenance is an important procedure which will help ensure that you are not stranded because of a dead battery. Several tools are required for this procedure **(see illustration)**.

2 Before servicing the battery, always turn the engine and all accessories off and disconnect the cable from the negative terminal of the battery.

3 A sealed (sometimes called maintenance-free) battery is standard equipment on the Ford Tempo/Mercury Topaz. The cell caps cannot be removed. No electrolyte checks are required and water cannot be added to the cells. However, if an aftermarket battery has been installed and it is a type that

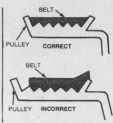

10.15 On V-ribbed belts, make sure the belt is properly seated into the pulleys, as shown

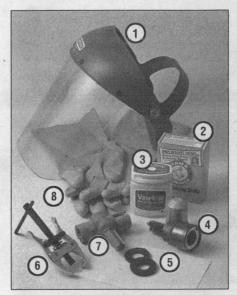

11.1 Tools and materials required for battery maintenance

1 **Face shield/safety goggles** - *When removing corrosion with a brush, the acidic particles can easily fly up into your eyes*

2 **Baking soda** - *A solution of baking soda and water can be used to neutralize corrosion*

3 **Petroleum jelly** - *A layer of this on the battery posts will help prevent corrosion*

4 **Battery post/cable cleaner** - *This wire brush cleaning tool will remove all traces of corrosion from the battery posts and cable clamps*

5 **Treated felt washers** - *Placing one of these on each post, directly under the cable clamps, will help prevent corrosion*

6 **Puller** - *Sometimes the cable clamps are very difficult to pull off the posts, even after the nut/bolt has been completely loosened. This tool pulls the clamp straight up and off the post without damage*

7 **Battery post/cable cleaner** - *Here is another cleaning tool which is a slightly different version of number 4 above, but it does the same thing*

8 **Rubber gloves** - *Another safety item to consider when servicing the battery; remember that's acid inside the battery!*

11.8a Battery terminal corrosion usually appears as light, fluffy powder

11.8b Removing the cable from a battery post with a wrench - sometimes a special battery pliers is required for this procedure if corrosion has caused deterioration of the nut hex (always remove the ground cable first and hook it up last!)

11.8c Regardless of the type of tool used to clean the battery posts, a clean, shiny surface should be the result

11.8d When cleaning the cable clamps, all corrosion must be removed (the inside of the clamp is tapered to match the taper on the post, so don't remove too much material)

requires regular maintenance, the following procedure can be used.

4   Check the electrolyte level in each of the battery cells. It must be above the plates. There's usually a split-ring indicator in each cell to indicate the correct level. If the level is low, add distilled water only, then install the cell caps. **Caution:** *Overfilling the cells may cause electrolyte to spill over during periods of heavy charging, causing corrosion and damage to nearby components.*

5   If the positive terminal and cable clamp on your vehicle's battery is equipped with a rubber protector, make sure that it's not torn or damaged. It should completely cover the terminal.

6   The external condition of the battery should be checked periodically. Look for damage such as a cracked case.

7   Check the tightness of the battery cable clamps to ensure good electrical connections and inspect the entire length of each cable, looking for cracked or abraded insulation and frayed conductors.

8   If corrosion (visible as white, fluffy deposits) is evident, remove the cables from the terminals, clean them with a battery brush and reinstall them **(see illustrations).** Corrosion can be kept to a minimum by installing specially treated washers (available at auto parts stores) or by applying a layer of petroleum jelly or grease to the terminals and cable clamps after they are assembled.

9   Make sure that the battery carrier is in good condition and that the hold-down clamp bolt is tight. If the battery is removed (see Chapter 5 for the removal and installation procedure), make sure that no parts remain in the bottom of the carrier when it's reinstalled. When reinstalling the hold-down clamp, don't overtighten the bolt.

10   Corrosion on the carrier, battery case and surrounding areas can be removed with a solution of water and baking soda. Apply the mixture with a small brush, let it work, then rinse it off with plenty of clean water.

11   Any metal parts of the vehicle damaged by corrosion should be coated with a zinc-based primer, then painted.

12   Additional information on the battery, charging and jump starting can be found in Chapter 5 and at the front of this manual.

Charging

13   Remove all of the cell caps (if equipped) and cover the holes with a clean cloth to prevent spattering electrolyte. Disconnect the negative battery cable and hook up the battery charger leads to the battery posts (positive to positive, negative to negative), then plug in the charger. Make sure it is set at 12-volts if it has a selector switch.

14   If you're using a charger with a rate higher than two amps, check the battery regularly during charging to make sure it doesn't overheat. If you're using a trickle charger, you can safely let the battery charge overnight after you've checked it regularly for the first couple of hours.

15   If the battery has removable cell caps, measure the specific gravity with a hydrometer every hour during the last few hours of the charging cycle. Hydrometers are available inexpensively from auto parts stores - follow the instructions that come with the hydrometer. Consider the battery charged when there's no change in the specific gravity reading for two hours and the electrolyte in the cells is gassing (bubbling) freely. The specific gravity reading from each cell should

be very close to the others. If not, the battery probably has a bad cell(s).

16   Some batteries with sealed tops have built-in hydrometers on the top that indicate the state of charge by the color displayed in the hydrometer window. Normally, a bright-colored hydrometer indicates a full charge and a dark hydrometer indicates the battery still needs charging. Check the battery manufacturer's instructions to be sure you know what the colors mean.

17   If the battery has a sealed top and no built-in hydrometer, you can hook up a digital voltmeter across the battery terminals to check the charge. A fully charged battery should read 12.6 volts or higher.

18   Further information on the battery and jump starting can be found in Chapter 5 and at the front of this manual.

12   Windshield wiper blade check and replacement (every 12000 miles or 12 months)

Refer to illustrations 12.5 and 12.14

Check

1   Road film can build up on the wiper blades and affect their efficiency, so they should be washed regularly with a mild detergent solution.

2   The windshield wiper and blade assembly should be inspected periodically. Even if you do not use your wipers, the sun and elements will dry out the rubber portions, causing them to crack and break apart. If inspection reveals hardened or cracked rubber, replace the wiper blades. If inspection reveals nothing unusual, wet the windshield, turn the wipers on, allow them to cycle several times, then shut them off. An uneven wiper pattern across the glass or streaks over clean glass indicate that the blades should be replaced.

3   The operation of the wiper mechanism can loosen the fasteners, so they should be checked and tightened, as necessary, at the same time the wiper blades are checked (see Chapter 12 for further information regarding the wiper mechanism).

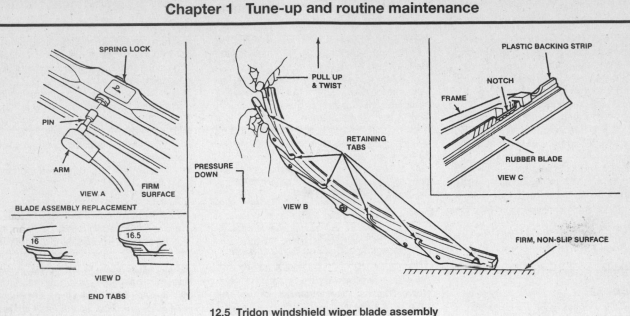

12.5 Tridon windshield wiper blade assembly

1

Tridon blade assembly replacement

4   Cycle the arm and blade assembly to a position on the windshield where removal of the blade assembly can be performed without difficulty. Turn the ignition key off at the desired position.

5   To remove the blade assembly from the wiper arm, press on the spring lock and pull the blade assembly from the pin (see illustration). **Caution:** *To prevent distortion of the spring lock, do not use excessive force.*

6   To install the blade assembly, push it onto the pin until the spring lock engages the pin. Be sure that the blade assembly is securely attached to the pin.

Tridon blade element replacement

7   On the plastic backing strip, which is part of the rubber blade element, locate either 7/16-inch long notch. The notches are approximately one inch from either end of the blade.

8   Place the wiper blade assembly on a workbench with either notched end of the backing strip visible.

9   Grasp the frame portion of the wiper blade assembly and push down until the blade assembly is tightly bowed.

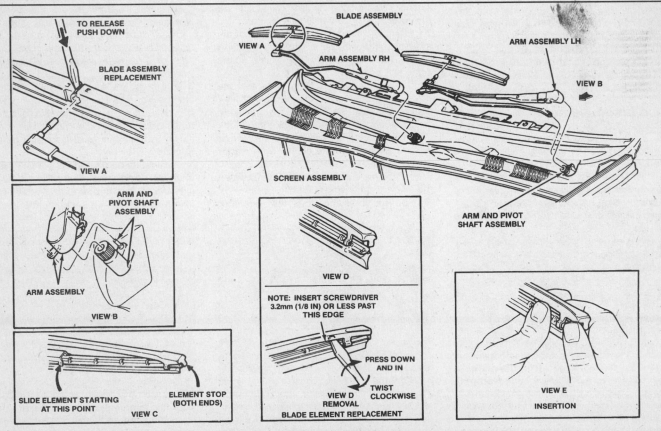

12.14 Trico windshield wiper blade assembly

10   With the blade assembly in the bowed position, grasp the tip of the backing strip firmly, pulling up and twisting counter-clockwise at the same time. The backing strip will then snap out of the retaining tab on the end of the frame **(see illustration 12.5)**.

11   Slide the backing strip down the frame until the notch lines up with the next retaining tab. Twist slightly and the backing strip will snap out.

12   Continue this operation with the remaining tabs until the blade element is completely detached from the frame.

13   To install the blade element, reverse the above procedure, making sure that all six tabs are locked to the backing strip before installing the blade on the wiper arm.

Trico blade assembly replacement

Note: *The Trico brand blade assembly has a rectangular hole located directly above the wiper arm mounting pin with no apparent provision for release. The hole serves for removal, since the release is internal.*

14   Cycle the wiper assembly to a position on the windshield where removal of the blade assembly can be performed without difficulty. Turn the ignition key off at the desired position. With the blade assembly resting on the windshield, insert a small standard screwdriver into the rectangular hole on top of the blade and push down on the coil spring inside the hole. While pressing down with the screwdriver, pull the wiper blade from the wiper arm pin **(see illustration on previous page)**.

15   To install the blade assembly, push it onto the pin until it snaps into place. Be sure that the blade assembly is securely attached to the wiper arm.

Trico blade element replacement

16   At one end of the rubber blade element, insert a standard screwdriver between the blade and the metal backing strip **(view D in**

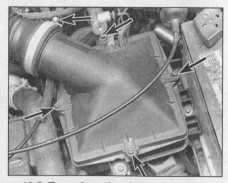

13.2 To replace the air filter element, loosen the air intake duct hose clamp (arrow), slip the duct off the air cleaner housing cover, remove the four screws (arrows) and lift off the cover (early model shown; later models use quick-release wire clamps)

illustration 12.14). Press down and in, then twist the screwdriver clockwise to release the element from the retaining tab.

17   Slide the blade element out of the remaining tabs until the element is completely detached from the frame.

18   To install the element, slide the metal backing strip into four of the retaining tabs (View C), then twist the backing strip into the fifth and end tab.

19   Make sure that all the tabs are locked onto the metal backing strip before installing the blade on the wiper arm.

13   Air filter replacement (every 12000 miles or 12 months)

Refer to illustration 13.2
Note: *The air filter element cannot be cleaned. If inspection reveals that the element is dirty, install a new one.*

1   On carbureted, CFI, and early multiport EFI engines, loosen the hose clamp and disconnect the clean air duct at the air cleaner housing. On 1992 and later four-cylinder and V6 multiport engines, remove the clean air tube at the air-housing-mounted MAF sensor (refer to Chapter 4, if necessary).

2   On 1984 through 1991 models, remove the four air cleaner housing cover screws and lift the cover off **(see illustration)**. On 1992 and later models, disconnect the MAF sensor electrical connector and release the air cleaner housing cover hold-down clamps. Lift the cover to expose the air filter element.

3   Remove the filter element. Note that the creases in the paper element are facing down. The new element must be installed the same way or it won't fit.

4   Check the inner sealing surface of the cover for evidence of leakage past the air cleaner element. Place a light on the inside "clean side" of the filter and look through the filter at the light. If the light cannot be seen or if there are holes in the element, no matter how small, replace it with a new one.

5   Clean the inner sealing surface between the air cleaner housing and cover.

6   Before installing the new air filter

14.2a To check the PCV valve, remove it from the valve cover (V6 model shown) . . .

element, check it for deformed seals and holes in the paper. If the element is marked **TOP**, be sure the marked side faces up. The paper creases must face down.

7 ' Position the cover on the housing and make sure it is seated all the way around. On 1992 and later housings, insert the cover tabs first, then position the cover.

8   The remaining installation is the reverse of removal.

9   Reconnect the duct and tighten the hose clamp securely.

14   PCV valve and filter check (every 12000 miles or 12 months)

Refer to illustrations 14.2a, 14.2b and 14.4
Note: *To maintain efficient operation of the PCV system, clean the hoses and check the PCV valve and filter at the intervals recommended in the maintenance schedule. For additional information on the PCV system, refer to Chapter 6.*

1   Locate the PCV valve on the valve cover. **Note**: On V6 models, the PCV valve is located on the rear cover towards the front of the engine.

2   To check the valve, first pull it out of the valve cover **(see illustrations)** and shake it - if it rattles, reinstall it in the cover. If the valve *doesn't rattle, it is probably clogged with deposits; install a new PCV valve.* **Note:** *A new PCV valve will not include the elbow. The original must be transferred to the new valve. If a new elbow is purchased, it may be necessary to soak it in warm water for up to an hour to slip it onto the new valve. Do not attempt to force the elbow onto the valve or it will break.*

3   If the valve is clogged, the hoses can also be plugged. Remove the hose between the valve and the intake manifold and the hose between the rocker arm cover and the air cleaner housing and inspect it (refer to Section 9).

4   Remove and check the PCV system filter. On some vehicles, the filter is integral with the oil filler cap; on other vehicles, the filter assembly is in a separate housing **(see**

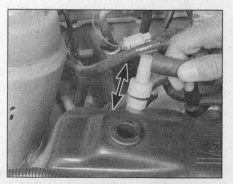

14.2b . . . and shake it - if a clicking or rattling sound is heard, the valve is probably working properly (early four-cylinder model shown)

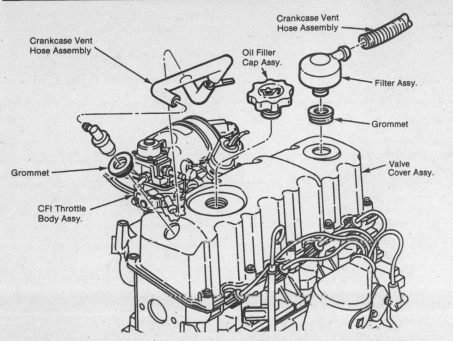

14.4 Some vehicles are equipped with a PCV filter that is integral with the oil filler cap: on others, like this one, the PCV filter is a separate assembly - to remove it, detach the plastic hose and pull straight up (be sure to replace the rubber grommet if it's cracked or distorted)

illustration); still others have both. If filter (or filter assembly) appears to be restrictive or dirty, replace it. Reinstall the hoses to the system.

5   Start the engine and verify vacuum at PCV valve. If no vacuum is felt, the hose from the intake manifold to the PCV valve must be kinked or leaking. Reinstall the PCV valve after proper vacuum is obtained.

6   With engine running at idle, disconnect the crankcase vent hose from the air cleaner housing and feel for vacuum at the hose. If vacuum is felt, the PCV valve/system is working properly. If no vacuum is felt, disconnect the evaporative emission system hose (if so equipped) and plug the fitting. If vacuum is now felt, the evaporative emission system is malfunctioning, but the PCV system is working (see Chapter 6).

7   If no vacuum is felt or if your vehicle doesn't have an evaporative system hose attached to the PCV hose, the oil filler cap, hoses or rocker arm cover gasket may be leaking or the PCV valve may be bad. Check for vacuum leaks at the valve, filler cap, filter assembly (if used) and all hoses.

8   Check the PCV valve rubber grommet in the rocker arm cover for cracks and distortion. If it's damaged, replace it.

15   Fuel system check (every 12000 miles or 12 months)

Warning: *Gasoline is extremely flammable, so take extra precautions when you work on any part of the fuel system. Don't smoke or allow open flames or bare light bulbs near the work area, and don't work in a garage where a natural gas-type appliance (such as a water heater or clothes dryer) with a pilot light is present. If you spill any fuel on your skin, rinse it off immediately with soap and water. When you perform any kind of work on the fuel system, wear safety glasses and have a Class B type fire extinguisher on hand.*

1   If you smell gasoline while driving or after the vehicle has been sitting in the sun, inspect the fuel system immediately.

2   Remove the gas filler cap and inspect it for damage and corrosion. The gasket should have an unbroken sealing imprint. If the gasket is damaged or corroded, install a new cap.

3   Inspect the fuel feed and return lines for cracks. Make sure that the connections between the fuel lines and the carburetor or fuel injection system and between the fuel lines and the in-line fuel filter are tight. **Warning:** *If your vehicle is fuel injected, you must relieve the fuel system pressure before servicing fuel system components. The fuel system pressure relief procedure is outlined in Chapter 4.*

4   Since some components of the fuel system, the fuel tank and part of the fuel feed and return lines, for example, are underneath the vehicle, they can be inspected more easily with the vehicle raised on a hoist. If that's not possible, raise the vehicle and support it on jackstands.

5   With the vehicle raised and safely supported, inspect the gas tank and filler neck for punctures, cracks and other damage. The connection between the filler neck and the tank is particularly critical. Sometimes a rubber filler neck will leak

because of loose clamps or deteriorated rubber. Inspect all fuel tank mounting brackets and straps to be sure that the tank is securely attached to the vehicle. **Warning:** *Do not, under any circumstances, try to repair a fuel tank (except rubber components). A welding torch or any open flame can easily cause fuel vapors inside the tank to explode.*

6   Carefully check all rubber hoses and metal lines leading away from the fuel tank. Check for loose connections, deteriorated hoses, crimped lines and other damage. Repair or replace damaged sections as necessary (refer to Chapter 4).

16   Fuel filter replacement (every 12000 miles or 12 months)

Refer to illustrations 16.3 and 16.12
Warning: *Gasoline is extremely flammable, so take extra precautions when you work on any part of the fuel system. Don't smoke or allow open flames or bare light bulbs near the work area, and don't work in a garage where a natural gas-type appliance (such as a water heater or clothes dryer) with a pilot light is present. If you spill any fuel on your skin, rinse it off immediately with soap and water. When you perform any kind of work on the fuel system, wear safety glasses and have a Class B type fire extinguisher on hand.*

Fuel-injected vehicles

Warning: *Before removing the fuel filter, the fuel system pressure must be relieved.*

1   Relieve fuel system pressure (refer to Chapter 4)

2   Locate the fuel filter on the right side of the engine compartment. Inspect the fittings at both ends of the filter to see if they are clean. If more than a light coating of dust is present, clean the fittings before proceeding.

3   Removal of the hairpin clip from each fitting is a two-stage procedure. First, spread the two clip legs apart about 1/8-inch to disengage them, then push in on them. Pull on the other end of the clip to detach it from the fitting **(see illustration). Caution:** *Do not use any tools or you may damage the plastic clips or fittings.*

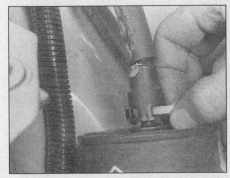

16.3 Before disengaging the hoses from either end of the fuel filter, pull on the triangular tab and slide the nylon clip out to unlock the fittings

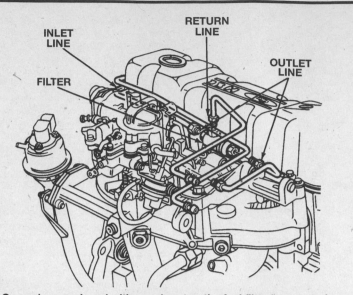

16.12 On engines equipped with a carburetor, the fuel filter is mounted on top of the engine, adjacent to the carburetor and has three lines attached to it

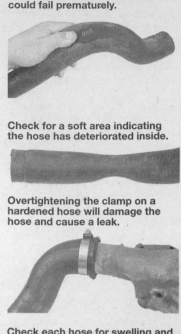

Check for a chafed area that could fail prematurely.

Check for a soft area indicating the hose has deteriorated inside.

Overtightening the clamp on a hardened hose will damage the hose and cause a leak.

Check each hose for swelling and oil-soaked ends. Cracks and breaks can be located by squeezing the hose.

17.4 Hoses, like drivebelts, have a habit of failing at the worst possible time - to prevent the inconvenience of a blown radiator or heater hose, inspect them carefully as shown here

4   Once both hairpin clips are released, grasp the fuel hoses, one at a time, and pull them straight off the filter.

5   After the hoses have been detached, check the clips for damage and distortion. If they were damaged in any way during removal, new ones must be used when the hoses are reattached to the new filter (if new clips are packaged with the filter, be sure to use them in place of the originals).

6   Note which way the fuel flow arrow on the filter is pointing. The new filter must be installed in the same way. Loosen the filter retaining clamp and remove the filter.

7   Clean the fittings on the new filter and check for burrs (dirt or burrs on the fittings could damage the hose fitting O-rings and fuel leaks could result).

8   Install the new filter and tighten the clamp securely. Make sure the arrow is pointing in the right direction.

9   Carefully push each hose onto the filter until it is seated against the collar on the fitting, then install the hairpin clips. The triangular shaped side of each clip must point away from the filter. Make sure the clips are securely attached to the hose fittings if they come off, the hoses could back off the filter and a fire could result!

10   Press the button on the inertia switch to close the fuel pump circuit. Install the switch and tighten the nuts securely.

11   Start the engine and check for fuel leaks.

Carburetor-equipped vehicles

12   Remove the air cleaner duct from the top of the carburetor to gain access to the filter (see illustration).

13   Place a rag under the filter, then remove the fuel return line from the top of the filter while holding the fitting with a back-up wrench. A flare nut wrench should be used if available it will prevent rounding off the fuel line fitting hex.

14   Remove the inlet and outlet lines and detach the filter from the engine. Be sure to use a back-up wrench to keep the fittings on the filter from turning.

15   Position the new filter and thread the lines into the fittings by hand. Be very careful not to cross thread the fittings. Make sure the fuel flow arrow on the filter is pointing toward the carburetor fuel line.

16   Tighten the fuel return line fitting first (the one on top of the filter), followed by the outlet line (to the carburetor) and finally the inlet line (from the pump).

17   Start the engine and check for fuel leaks at the fittings while the engine idles for two minutes. If fuel leaks are noted, tighten the appropriate fitting(s) slightly.

18   Reinstall the air cleaner duct.

17 Cooling system check (every 12000 miles or 12 months)

Refer to illustration 17.4

1   Many major engine failures can be attributed to a faulty cooling system. If the vehicle is equipped with an automatic transaxle, the cooling system also plays an important role in prolonging transmission life because it cools the transaxle fluid.

2   The engine should be cold for the cooling system check, so perform the following procedure before the vehicle is driven for the day or after it has been shut off for at least three hours.

3   Remove the radiator cap and clean it thoroughly, inside and out, with clean water. Also clean the filler neck on the radiator. The presence of rust or corrosion in the filler neck means the coolant should be changed (Section 27). The coolant inside the radiator should be relatively clean and transparent. If it's rust colored, drain the system and refill it with new coolant.

4   Carefully check the radiator hoses and the smaller diameter heater hoses (see illustration). Inspect each coolant hose along its entire length, replacing any hose which is cracked, swollen or deteriorated. Cracks will show up better if the hose is squeezed. Pay close attention to hose clamps that secure the hoses to cooling system components. Hose clamps can pinch and puncture hoses, resulting in coolant leaks.

5   Make sure that all hose connections are tight. A leak in the cooling system will usually show up as white or rust colored deposits on the area adjoining the leak. If wire-type clamps are used on the hoses, it may be a good idea to replace them with screw-type clamps.

6   Clean the front of the radiator and air conditioning condenser with compressed air, if available, or a soft brush. Remove all bugs, leaves, etc. embedded in the radiator fins. Be extremely careful not to damage the cooling fins or cut your fingers on them.

7   If the coolant level has been dropping consistently and no leaks are detectable, have the radiator cap and cooling system pressure checked at a service station.

18 Exhaust system check (every 12000 miles or 12 months)

1 With the engine cold (at least three hours after the vehicle has been driven), check the complete exhaust system from the engine to the end of the tailpipe. Ideally, the inspection should be done with the vehicle on a hoist to permit unrestricted access. If a hoist is not available, raise the vehicle and support it securely on jackstands.

2 Check the exhaust pipes and connections for evidence of leaks, severe corrosion and damage. Make sure that all brackets and hangers are in good condition and tight.

3 At the same time, inspect the underside of the body for holes, corrosion, open seams, etc. which may allow exhaust gases to enter the passenger compartment. Seal all body openings with silicone or body putty .

4 Rattles and other noises can often be traced to the exhaust system, especially the mounts and hangers. Try to move the pipes, muffler and catalytic converter. If the components can come in contact with the body or suspension parts, secure the exhaust system with new mounts.

5 Check the running condition of the engine by inspecting inside the end of the tailpipe. The exhaust deposits here are an indication of engine state-of-tune. If the pipe is black and sooty or coated with white deposits, the engine is in need of a tune-up, including a thorough fuel system inspection and adjustment.

19 Tire rotation (every 12000 miles or 12 months)

Refer to illustration 19.2

1 The tires should be rotated at the specified intervals and whenever uneven wear is noticed. Since the vehicle will be raised and the tires removed anyway, check the brakes also (Section 21).

2 Radial tires must be rotated in a specific pattern **(see illustration)**. Note: *Do not include special space saver or temporary spare tires in the rotation schedule; they are for emergency use only. Consult your owner's manual if further clarification is necessary.*

3 Refer to the information in *Jacking and towing* at the front of this manual for the proper procedure to follow when raising the vehicle and changing a tire. If the brakes are to be checked, do not apply the parking brake as stated.

4 The vehicle must be raised on a hoist or supported on jackstands to get all four wheels off the ground. Make sure the vehicle is safely supported !

5 After the rotation procedure is finished, check and adjust the tire pressures as necessary and be sure to check the lug nut tightness.

20 Steering and suspension check (every 12000 miles or 12 months)

Refer to illustrations 20.10a, 20.10b, 20.11 and 20.12

Note: *The steering linkage and suspension components should be checked periodically. Worn or damaged suspension and steering linkage components can result in excessive and abnormal tire wear, poor ride quality and vehicle handling and reduced fuel economy. For detailed illustrations of the steering and suspension components, refer to Chapter 10.*

Strut check

1 Park the vehicle on level ground, turn the engine off and set the parking brake. Check the tire pressures.

2 Push down at one corner of the vehicle, then release it while noting the movement of the body. It should stop moving and come to rest in a level position within one or two bounces.

3 If the vehicle continues to move up-and-down or if it fails to return to its original position, a worn or weak strut is probably the reason.

4 Repeat the above check at each of the three remaining corners of the vehicle.

5 Raise the vehicle and support it on jackstands.

6 Check the shock struts for evidence of fluid leakage. A light film of fluid is no cause for concern. Make sure that any fluid noted is from the shocks and not from some other source. If leakage is noted, replace the struts as a set.

7 Check the struts to be sure that they are securely mounted and undamaged. Check the upper mounts for damage and wear. If damage or wear is noted, replace the struts as a set.

8 If struts must be replaced, refer to Chapter 10 for the procedure.

Steering and suspension check

9 Visually inspect the steering system components for damage and distortion. Look for leaks and damaged seals, boots and fittings.

10 Wipe the lower end of the steering knuckle and control arm. Have an assistant grasp the lower edge of the tire and move the wheel in and-out **(see illustration)** while you look for movement at the steering knuckle-to-control arm joint **(see illustration)**. If there is any movement, the suspension balljoint must be replaced.

11 Grasp each front tire at the front and rear edges, push in at the rear, pull out at the front and feel for play in the steering system

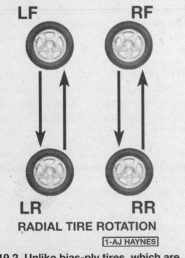

LF   **RF**

LR   **RR**

RADIAL TIRE ROTATION

1-AJ HAYNES

19.2 Unlike bias-ply tires, which are rotated in a criss-cross pattern, radial tires must be rotated as shown here

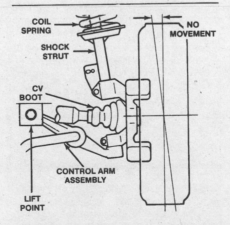

COIL SPRING
SHOCK STRUT
NO MOVEMENT
CV BOOT
CONTROL ARM ASSEMBLY
LIFT POINT

20.10a To check the suspension balljoints, try to move the lower edge of each front tire in-and-out while watching/feeling for movement at the top of the tire . . .

20.10b . . . and at the balljoint-to-steering knuckle joint (arrow)

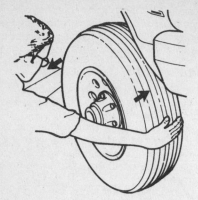

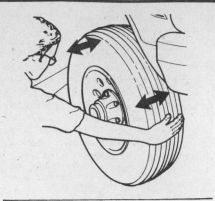

20.11 To check the steering gear mounts and tie-rod connections for play, grasp each front tire like this and try to move it back-and-forth - if play is noted, check the steering gear mounts and make sure that they're tight; if either tie-rod is worn or bent, replace it

components **(see illustration)**. If any free play is noted, check the steering gear mounts and the tie-rod balljoints for looseness. If the steering gear mounts are loose, tighten them. If the tie-rods are loose, the balljoints may be worn (check to make sure the nuts are tight). Additional steering and suspension system information and illustrations can be found in Chapter 10.

Front wheel bearing check

Note: *The front wheel bearings are a "cartridge" design and are permanently lubricated and sealed at the factory. They require no scheduled maintenance or adjustment. They can, however, be checked for excessive play. If the following check indicates that either of the front bearings is faulty, replace both bearings.*

12   Grasp each front tire at the front and rear edges, then push in-and-out on the wheel and feel for play **(see illustration)**. There should be no noticeable movement. Turn the wheel and listen for noise from the bearings. If any of these conditions are noted, refer to Chapter 10 for the bearing replacement procedure.

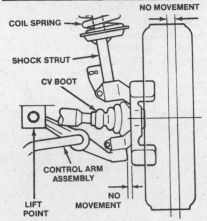

20.12 To check the wheel bearings, try to move the tire in-and-out - if any play is noted, or if the bearings feel rough or sound noisy when the tire is rotated, replace the wheel bearings

21   Brake system check (every 12000 miles or 12 months)

Refer to illustrations 21.7, 21.11, 21.15, 21.16. 21.17 and 21.22
Note: *In addition to the specified intervals, the brake system should be inspected each time the wheels are removed or a malfunction is indicated. Because of the obvious safety considerations, the following brake system checks are some of the most important*

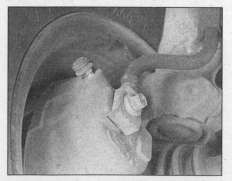

21.7 Check the flexible rubber brake hoses at all four wheels for cracks, swelling, leaks and chafing

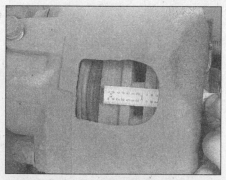

21.11 The front disc brake pads can be checked easily through the inspection hole in each caliper - position a six-inch steel rule against the pads and measure the lining thickness

maintenance procedures you can perform on your vehicle.

Symptoms of brake system problems

1   If the brakes make a high-pitched squealing or scraping noise when applied, the brake pads are probably worn, damaged, contaminated or misaligned. When you hear this noise, replace the pads immediately and carefully inspect the calipers and brake system or expensive damage to the rotors could result.
2   Any of the following symptoms could indicate a potential brake system defect. The vehicle pulls to one side when the brake pedal is depressed, the brakes make squealing or dragging noises when applied, brake travel is excessive, the pedal pulsates and brake fluid leaks are noted (usually on the inner side of the tire or wheel). If any of these conditions are noted, inspect the brake system immediately.

Brake lines and hoses

Note: *Steel tubing is used throughout the brake system, with the exception of flexible, reinforced hoses at the front wheels and as connectors at the rear axle. Periodic inspection of these lines is very important.*
3   Park the vehicle on level ground and turn the engine off.
4   Remove the wheel covers. Loosen, but do not remove, the lug nuts on all four wheels.
5   Raise the vehicle and support it securely on jackstands.
6   Remove the wheels (see *Jacking and towing* at the front of this book, or refer to your owner's manual, if necessary).
7   Check all brake hoses and lines for cracks, chafing of the outer cover, leaks, blisters and distortion. Check all threaded fittings for leaks and make sure the brake hose mounting bolts and clips are secure **(see illustration)**.
8   If leaks or damage are discovered, they must be fixed immediately. Refer to Chapter 9 for detailed information on brake system repair procedures.

Front disc brakes

9   If it hasn't already been done, raise the front of the vehicle and support it securely on jackstands. Apply the parking brake and remove the front wheels.
10   The disc brake calipers, which contain the pads, are now visible. Each caliper has an outer and an inner pad; all pads should be checked.
11   Note the pad thickness by looking through the inspection hole in the caliper **(see illustration)**. If the lining material is 1/8-inch thick or less, or if it is tapered from end to-end, the pads should be replaced (see Chapter 9). Keep in mind that the lining material is riveted or bonded to a metal plate or shoe. The metal portion is not included in this measurement.

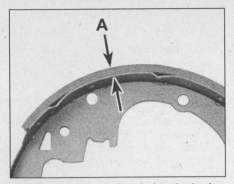

21.15 If the lining is bonded to the brake shoe, measure the lining thickness from the outer surface to the metal shoe, as shown here; if the lining is riveted to the shoe, measure from the lining outer surface to the rivet head

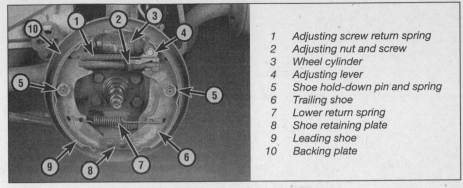

1	Adjusting screw return spring
2	Adjusting nut and screw
3	Wheel cylinder
4	Adjusting lever
5	Shoe hold-down pin and spring
6	Trailing shoe
7	Lower return spring
8	Shoe retaining plate
9	Leading shoe
10	Backing plate

21.16 Rear drum brake components

12 Check the condition of the brake disc. Look for score marks, deep scratches and overheated areas (they will appear blue or discolored). If damage or wear is noted, the disc can be removed and resurfaced by an automotive machine shop or replaced with a new one. Refer to Chapter 9 for more detailed inspection and repair procedures.

Rear drum brakes

13 Refer to Chapter 9 and remove the rear brake drums.

14 **Warning:** *Brake dust produced by lining wear and deposited on brake components may contain asbestos, which is hazardous to your health. DO NOT blow it out with compressed air and DO NOT inhale it! DO NOT use gasoline or solvents to remove the dust. Brake system cleaner should be used to flush the dust into a drain pan. After the brake components are wiped clean with a damp rag, dispose of the contaminated rags and solvent in a covered and labeled container. Try to use non-asbestos replacement parts whenever possible.*

15 Note the thickness of the lining material on the rear brake shoes **(see illustration)** and look for signs of contamination by brake fluid and grease. If the lining material is within

21.17 Carefully peel back the rubber boots on each end of the wheel cylinder - if the exposed area is covered with brake fluid, the wheel cylinder is leaking and must be replaced

1/16-inch of the recessed rivets or metal shoes, replace the brake shoes with new ones. The shoes should also be replaced if they are cracked, glazed (shiny lining surfaces) or contaminated with brake fluid or grease. See Chapter 9 for the replacement procedure.

16 Check the shoe return and hold-down springs and the adjusting mechanism to make sure they are installed correctly and in good condition **(see illustration)**. Deteriorated or distorted springs, if not replaced, could allow the linings to drag and wear prematurely.

17 Check the wheel cylinders for leakage by carefully peeling back the rubber boots **(see illustration)**. If brake fluid is noted behind the boots, the wheel cylinders must be replaced (see Chapter 9).

18 Check the drums for cracks, score marks, deep scratches and hard spots, which will appear as small discolored areas. If imperfections cannot be removed with emery cloth, the drums must be resurfaced by an

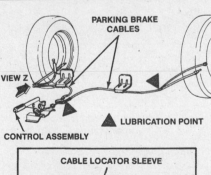

21.22 Lubricate the parking brake cable linkage, adjuster assembly, connectors and the areas of the parking brake cable that come in contact with other parts of the vehicle, as shown here

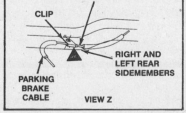

automotive machine shop (see Chapter 9 for more detailed information).

19 Refer to Chapter 9 and install the brake drums.

20 Install the wheels, but do not lower the vehicle yet.

Parking brake

Note: *The parking brake cable and linkage should be periodically checked and lubricated. This maintenance procedure helps prevent the parking brake cable adjuster or the linkage from binding and adversely affecting the operation or adjustment of the parking brake.*

Lubrication

21 Set the parking brake

22 Apply multi-purpose grease to the parking brake linkage, adjuster assembly, connectors and the areas of the parking brake cable that come in contact with the other parts of the vehicle **(see illustration)**.

23 Release the parking brake and repeat the lubrication procedure.

24 Remove the jackstands and lower the vehicle.

25 Tighten the wheel lug nuts to the specified torque and install the wheel covers.

Check

26 The easiest, and perhaps most obvious, method of checking the parking brake is to park the vehicle on a steep hill with the parking brake set and the transmission in Neutral. If the parking brake cannot prevent the vehicle from rolling, refer to Chapter 9 and adjust it.

22 Automatic transaxle control linkage lubrication (every 12000 miles or 12 months)

Refer to illustration 22.3

1 Open the hood and locate the shift cable running up the backside of the transaxle on the left side.

2 Clean the linkage and pivot points at the upper end of the cable.

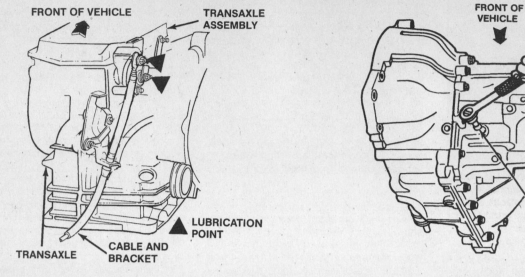

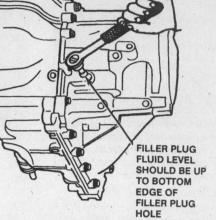

22.3 Lubricate the shift linkage and pivot points of the automatic transaxle shift cable with multi-purpose grease

23.1 The manual transaxle lubricant filler plug is located on the side of the transaxle housing - remove it with a socket and ratchet

3   Lubricate the shift linkage and pivot points with multi-purpose grease **(see illustration)**.

23 Manual transaxle lubricant level check (every 12000 miles or 12 months)

Refer to illustration 23.1
Note: *The transaxle lubricant level and quality should not deteriorate under normal driving conditions. However, it is recommended that you check the level occasionally. The most convenient time would be when your vehicle is raised for another reason, such as an engine oil change.*
1   The transaxle has an inspection and filler plug which must be removed to check the lubricant level **(see illustration)**. If the vehicle is raised to gain access to the plug, be sure to support it safely on jackstands do not crawl under a vehicle which is supported only by a jack!
2   Remove the plug from the transmission and use your little finger to reach inside the housing and feel the lubricant level. It should be at or very near the bottom of the plug hole.
3   If it isn't, add the recommended lubricant through the plug hole with a syringe or squeeze bottle.
4   Install and tighten the plug securely and check for leaks after the first few miles of driving.

24 Spark plug replacement (every 24000 miles or 24 months)

Refer to illustrations 24.2, 24.5a, 24.5b, 24.6 and 24.10
1   The spark plugs are located on the front (radiator) side of the engine and also (on V6 engines) on the rear side of the engine.

2   In most cases, the tools necessary for spark plug replacement include a spark plug socket which fits onto a ratchet (spark plug sockets are padded inside to prevent damage to the porcelain insulators on the new plugs), various extensions and a gap gauge to check and adjust the gaps on the new plugs **(see illustration)**. A special plug wire removal tool is available for separating the wire boots from the spark plugs, but it

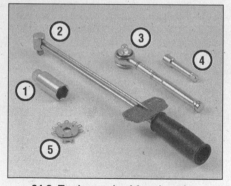

24.2 Tools required for changing spark plugs

1   **Spark plug socket -** *This will have special padding inside to protect the spark plug porcelain insulator*
2   **Torque wrench -** *Although not mandatory, use of this tool is the best way to ensure that the plugs are tightened properly*
3   **Ratchet -** *Standard hand tool to fit the plug socket*
4   **Extension -** *Depending on model and accessories, you may need special extensions and universal joints to reach one or more of the plugs*
5   **Spark plug gap gauge -** *This gauge for checking the gap comes in a variety of styles - Make sure the gap for your engine is included*

isn't absolutely necessary. A torque wrench should be used to tighten the new plugs.
3   The best approach when replacing the spark plugs is to purchase the new ones in advance, adjust them to the proper gap and replace the plugs one at a time. When buying the new spark plugs, be sure to obtain the correct plug type for your particular engine. This information can be found on the *Vehicle Emission Control Information* label located under the hood and in the factory owner's manual. If differences exist between the plug specified on the emissions label and in the owner's manual, assume that the emissions label is correct.
4   Allow the engine to cool completely before attempting to remove any of the plugs. While you are waiting for the engine to cool, check the new plugs for defects and adjust the gaps.
5   The gap is checked by inserting the proper thickness gauge between the electrodes at the tip of the plug **(see illustration)**. The gap between the electrodes should be the same as the one specified on

24.5a Spark plug manufacturers recommend using a wire-type gauge when checking the gap - if the wire does not slide between the electrodes with a slight drag, adjustment is required

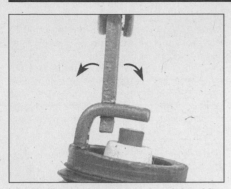

24.5b To change the gap, bend the side electrode only, as indicated by the arrows and be very careful not to crack or chip the porcelain insulator surrounding the center electrode

the Vehicle Emissions Control Information label. The wire should just slide between the electrodes with a slight amount of drag. If the gap is incorrect, use the adjuster on the gauge body to bend the curved side electrode slightly until the proper gap is obtained **(see illustration)**. If the side electrode is not exactly over the center electrode, bend it with the adjuster until it is. Check for cracks in the porcelain insulator (if any are found. the plug should not be used).

6   With the engine cool, remove the spark plug wire from one spark plug. Pull only on the boot at the end of the wire, do not pull on the wire. A plug wire removal tool should be used if available **(see illustration)** .

7   If compressed air is available, use it to blow any dirt or foreign material away from the spark plug hole. A common bicycle pump will also work. The idea here is to eliminate the possibility of debris falling into the cylinder as the spark plug is removed.

8   Place the spark plug socket over the plug and remove it from the engine by turning it in a counterclockwise direction.

9   Compare the spark plug to those shown in the accompanying photos to get an indication of the general running condition of the engine .

10   Thread one of the new plugs into the hole until you can no longer turn it with your fingers, then tighten it with a torque wrench (if available) or the ratchet. It might be a good idea to slip a short length of rubber hose over the end of the plug to use as a tool to thread it into place **(see illustration)**. The hose will grip the plug well enough to turn it, but will start to slip if the plug begins to cross-thread in the hole this will prevent damaged threads and the accompanying repair costs.

11   Before pushing the spark plug wire onto the end of the plug, inspect it following the procedures outlined in Section 25.

12   Attach the plug wire to the new spark plug, again using a twisting motion on the boot until it is seated on the spark plug.

13   Repeat the procedure for the remaining spark plugs, replacing them one at a time to prevent mixing up the spark plug wires.

---

25 Spark plug wire, distributor cap and rotor check and replacement (every 24000 miles or 24 months)

Refer to illustrations 25.11, 25.12, 25.13a and 25.13b

Spark plug wires

Note: *Every time a spark plug wire is detached from a spark plug, the distributor cap or the coil, silicone dielectric compound (white grease available at auto parts stores) must be applied to the inside of each boot before reconnection. Use a small standard screwdriver to coat the entire inside surface of each boot with a thin layer of the compound.*

1   The spark plug wires should be checked and, if necessary, replaced at the same time new spark plugs are installed.

2   The easiest way to identify bad wires is to make a visual check while the engine is running. In a dark, well-ventilated garage, start the engine and look at each plug wire. Be careful not to come into contact with any moving engine parts. If there is a break in the wire, you will see arcing or a small spark at the damaged area. If arcing is noticed, make a note to obtain new wires.

3   The spark plug wires should be inspected one at a time, beginning with the spark plug for the number one cylinder to prevent confusion. Clearly label each original plug wire with a piece of tape marked with the correct number. The plug wires must be reinstalled in the correct order to ensure proper engine operation.

4   Disconnect the plug wire from the first spark plug. A removal tool can be used **(see illustration 24.6)**, or you can grab the wire boot, twist it slightly and pull the wire free. Do not pull on the wire itself, only on the rubber boot.

5   Push the wire and boot back onto the end of the spark plug. It should fit snugly. If it doesn't, detach the wire and boot once more and use a pair of pliers to carefully crimp the metal connector inside the wire boot until it does.

6   Using a clean rag, wipe the entire length of the wire to remove built-up dirt and grease.

7   Once the wire is clean, check for burns, cracks and other damage. Do not bend the wire sharply or you might break the conductor.

8   Disconnect the wire from the distributor. Again, pull only on the rubber boot. Check for corrosion and a tight fit. Replace the wire in the distributor.

9   Inspect each of the remaining spark plug wires, making sure that each one is securely fastened at the distributor and spark plug when the check is complete.

10   If new spark plug wires are required, purchase a set for your specific engine model. Pre-cut wire sets with the boots already installed are available. Remove and replace the wires one at a time to avoid mix-ups in the firing order.

Distributor cap and rotor

Note: *It is common practice to install a new distributor cap and rotor each time new spark plug wires are installed. If you're planning to install new wires, install a new cap and rotor also. But if you are planning to reuse the existing wires, be sure to inspect the cap and rotor to make sure that they are in good condition.*

11   Remove the mounting screws and detach the cap from the distributor. Check it

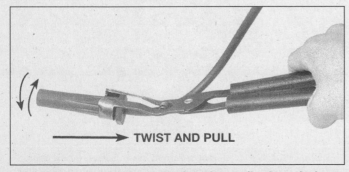

24.6 When removing the spark plug wires, pull only on the boot and use a twisting/pulling motion

TWIST AND PULL

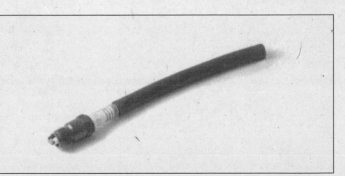

24.10 A length of 3/16-inch ID rubber hose will save time and prevent damaged threads when installing the spark plugs

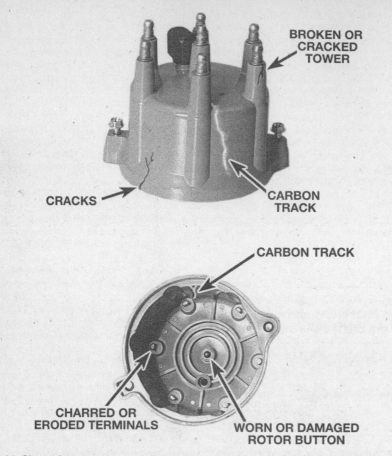

25.11 **Shown here are some of the common defects to look for when inspecting the distributor cap (if in doubt about its condition, install a new one)**

for cracks, carbon tracks and worn, burned or loose terminals **(see illustration)**

12   Check the rotor for cracks and carbon tracks. Make sure the center terminal spring tension is adequate and look for corrosion and wear on the rotor tip **(see illustration).**

13   Replace the cap and rotor if damage or defects are found. On early year models, note that the rotor is held on the shaft by two screws and is indexed so it can only be installed one way **(see illustration).** Later model rotors slide and engage into the

slotted distributor shaft. Before installing the cap, apply silicone dielectric compound to the rotor tip **(see illustration) (see Note at beginning of this Section)**.

14   When installing a new cap, remove the wires from the old cap one at a time and attach them to the new cap in the exact same location. Do not simultaneously remove all the wires from the old cap or firing order mix-ups may occur.

26   Carburetor choke check (every 24000 miles or 24 months)

Refer to illustrations 26.8a and 26.8b

1   The choke only operates when the engine is cold, so this check should be performed before the engine has been started for the day.

2   Open the hood and remove the metal duct from the top of the carburetor.

3   Locate the choke plate (the flat plate attached by small screws to a pivot shaft) in the carburetor throat.

4   Operate the throttle linkage and make sure the plate closes completely. Start the engine and watch the plate when the engine starts, the choke plate should open slightly.

5   Allow the engine to continue running at idle speed. As the engine warms up to operating temperature, the plate should slowly open.

6   After a few minutes, the choke plate should be fully open to the vertical position.

7   Note that the engine speed corresponds to the plate opening angle. With the plate closed, the engine should run at a fast idle speed. As the plate opens, the engine speed will decrease. The fast idle speed is controlled by the fast idle cam, and even though the choke plate is open completely, the idle speed will remain high until the throttle is opened. releasing the fast idle cam. Check the drop in idle speed as the choke

25.12 **Check the rotor for cracks and carbon tracks and make sure the center terminal spring tension is adequate - if the rotor tip is burned or corroded, a new rotor should be installed (early four-cylinder model shown; other models may differ somewhat)**

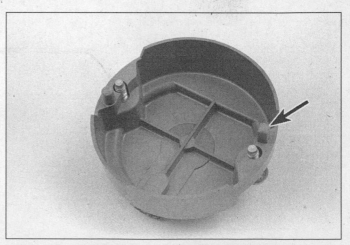

25.13a **On early models, be sure to align the square peg on the rotor (arrow) with the square hole in the distributor shaft mount when installing the new rotor (later models use a slotted distributor shaft and rotor)**

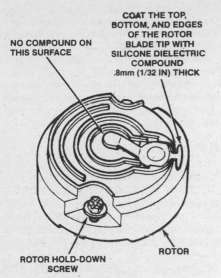

NO COMPOUND ON THIS SURFACE

COAT THE TOP, BOTTOM, AND EDGES OF THE ROTOR BLADE TIP WITH SILICONE DIELECTRIC COMPOUND .8mm (1/32 IN) THICK

ROTOR HOLD-DOWN SCREW

ROTOR

25.13b Apply silicone dielectric compound (grease) to the rotor as shown here before installing the distributor cap (early model shown - later models slightly different, but the same general procedure applies)

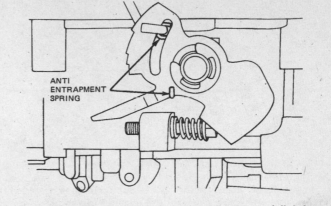

ANTI ENTRAPMENT SPRING

26.8a If the choke is sticking, lubricate the fast idle cam and link (arrows) . . .

plate opens by occasionally tapping the accelerator.

8   If the choke doesn't work as described, shut off the engine and check the shaft and linkage for deposits which could cause binding. Use a spray-on choke cleaning solvent to remove the deposits as you operate the linkage **(see illustrations).** This should loosen up the linkage and the shaft and allow the choke to work properly. If the choke still fails to function correctly, the choke bimetal assembly is malfunctioning and the carburetor may have to be overhauled. Refer to Chapter 4 for further information regarding carburetor overhaul.

9   At regular intervals, clean and lubricate the choke shaft. the fast idle cam and linkage and the vacuum diaphragm pulldown rod to ensure good choke performance.

27 Cooling system servicing, draining, flushing and refilling (every 24000 miles or 24 months)

Refer to illustrations 27.4 and 27.5

Warning: *Antifreeze is a corrosive and poisonous solution, so be careful not to spill any of the coolant mixture on the vehicle's paint or your skin. If this happens, rinse immediately with plenty of clean water. Consult local authorities regarding proper disposal procedures for antifreeze before draining the cooling system. In many areas, reclamation centers have been established to collect used oil and coolant mixtures.*

1   Periodically, the cooling system should be drained, flushed and refilled to replenish the antifreeze mixture and prevent formation of rust and corrosion, which can impair the performance of the cooling system and cause engine damage. When the cooling system is serviced, all hoses and the radiator cap should be checked and replaced if necessary.

Draining

2   Apply the parking brake and block the wheels. If the vehicle has just been driven, wait several hours to allow the engine to cool down before beginning this procedure.

3   Once the engine is completely cool, remove the radiator cap.

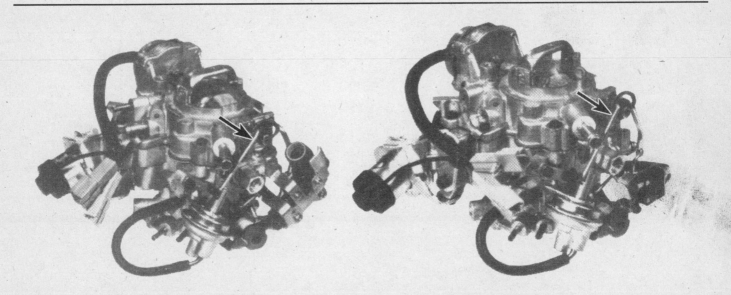

MODEL 6149 FEEDBACK CARBURETOR

MODEL 1949 CARBURETOR

26.8b . . . and the vacuum diaphragm pulldown rod (arrows)

27.4 The radiator drain fitting (arrow) is located at the lower left rear corner of the radiator - before opening the valve, push a short section of 3/8-inch diameter rubber hose onto the plastic fitting to prevent the coolant from splashing as it drains

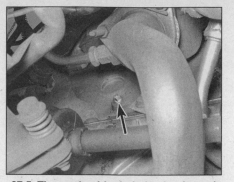

27.5 The engine block drain plug (arrow) is located on the backside of the block on four-cylinder models - V6 engines have two plugs - one on each side of the block

4   Move a large container under the radiator drain to catch the coolant **(see illustration)**. Attach a 3/8-inch diameter hose to the drain fitting to direct the coolant into the container, then open the drain fitting (a pair of pliers may be required to turn it).

5   After the coolant stops flowing out of the radiator, move the container under the engine block drain plug if equipped **(see illustration)**. Remove the plug and allow the coolant in the block to drain.

6   While the coolant is draining, check the condition of the radiator hoses, heater hoses and clamps (refer to Section 17 if necessary).

7   Replace any damaged clamps or hoses (refer to Chapter 3 for detailed replacement procedures).

Flushing

8   Once the system is completely drained, flush the radiator with fresh water from a garden hose until water runs clear at the drain. The flushing action of the water will remove sediments from the radiator but will not remove rust and scale from the engine and cooling tube surfaces.

9   These deposits can be removed by the chemical action of a cleaner such as Ford

Cooling System Fast Flush. Follow the procedure outlined in the manufacturer's instructions. If the radiator is severely corroded, damaged or leaking, it should be removed (Chapter 3) and taken to a radiator repair shop.

10   Remove the overflow hose from the coolant recovery reservoir. Drain the reservoir and flush it with clean water, then reconnect the hose.

Refilling

11   Close and tighten the radiator drain. Install and tighten the block drain plug.

12   Place the heater temperature control in the maximum heat position.

13   Slowly add new coolant (a 50/50 mixture of water and antifreeze) to the radiator until it is full. Add coolant to the reservoir up to the lower mark.

14   Leave the radiator cap off and run the engine in a well-ventilated area until the thermostat opens (coolant will begin flowing through the radiator and the upper radiator hose will become hot).

15   Turn the engine off and let it cool. Add more coolant mixture to bring the level back up to the lip on the radiator filler neck.

16   Squeeze the upper radiator hose to expel air, then add more coolant mixture if necessary. Replace the radiator cap.

17   Start the engine, allow it to reach normal operating temperature and check for leaks.

Chapter 2 Part A
Four-cylinder engine

Contents

Specifications

General

Valve clearance (nominal)	0.072 to 0.174 inch
Cylinder numbers (drivebelt end-to-transaxle end)	1-2-3-4
Firing order	1-3-4-2
Cylinder compression pressure	Lowest-reading cylinder must be within 75% of highest-reading cylinder (see chart below)

Camshaft lobe lift

Base engine	
Intake	0.249 inch
Exhaust	0.239 inch
Allowable lift loss	0.004 inch
High Output (HO) engine	
Intake	0.262 inch
Exhaust	0.262 inch
Allowable lift loss	0.004 inch

①②③④

Front

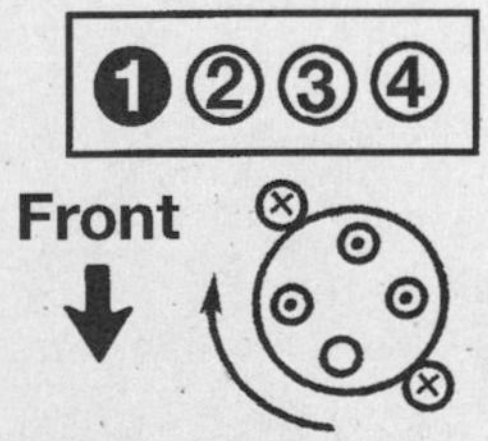

Four-cylinder engine

Cylinder location and distributor rotation

Maximum PSI	Minimum PSI	Maximum PSI	Minimum PSI
134	101	164	123
136	102	166	124
138	104	168	126
140	105	170	127
142	107	172	129
144	108	174	131
146	110	176	132
148	111	178	133
150	113	180	135
152	114	182	136
154	115	184	138
156	117	186	140
158	118	188	141
160	120	190	142
162	121	192	144

Cylinder compression pressure chart

2A

Torque specifications

	Ft-lbs (unless otherwise indicated)
Cylinder head bolts	
Step 1	52 to 59
Step 2	70 to 76
Engine mounts	
Left front	26 to 36
Left rear	73 to 97
Left center	65 to 87
Exhaust manifold bolts	
Step 1	5 to 7
Step 2	20 to 30
Flywheel/driveplate bolts	54 to 64
Intake manifold bolts	
Step 1	5 to 7
Step 2	15 to 22
Oil pan-to-engine bolts	6 to 9
Oil pan-to-transaxle bolts	30 to 39
Oil pump bolts	15 to 23
Valve cover bolts	7 to 10
Rocker arm fulcrum bolts	
Step 1	4 to 7
Step 2	20 to 26
Rear main oil seal retainer bolts	71 to 106 in-lbs

1   General information

This Part of Chapter 2 is devoted to in-vehicle repair procedures for the four-cylinder engine. All information concerning engine removal and installation and engine block and cylinder head overhaul can be found in Part C of this Chapter.

The following repair procedures are based on the assumption that the engine is installed in the vehicle. If the engine has been removed from the vehicle and mounted on a stand, many of the steps outlined in this Part of Chapter 2 will not apply.

The Specifications included in this Part of Chapter 2 apply only to the procedures contained in this Part. Part C of Chapter 2 contains the Specifications necessary for cylinder head and engine block rebuilding.

2   Repair operations possible with the engine in the vehicle

Many major repair operations can be accomplished without removing the engine from the vehicle.

Clean the engine compartment and the exterior of the engine with some type of pressure washer before any work is done. A clean engine will make the job easier and will help keep dirt out of the internal areas of the engine.

Depending on the components involved, it may be a good idea to remove the hood to improve access to the engine as repairs are performed (refer to Chapter 11 if necessary).

If vacuum, exhaust, oil or coolant leaks develop. indicating a need for gasket or seal replacement, the repairs can generally be made with the engine in the vehicle. The intake and exhaust manifold gaskets, oil pan gasket and cylinder head gasket are all accessible with the engine in place.

Exterior engine components such as the intake and exhaust manifolds, the oil pan (and the oil pump), the water pump, the starter motor, the alternator, the distributor and the fuel injection system can be removed for repair with the engine in place. For starter and alternator procedures refer to Chapter 5.

Since the cylinder head can be removed without pulling the engine, valve component servicing can also be accomplished with the engine in the vehicle.

In extreme cases caused by a lack of necessary equipment, repair or replacement of piston rings, pistons, connecting rods and rod bearings is possible with the engine in the vehicle. However, this practice is not recommended because of the cleaning and preparation work that must be done to the components involved.

3   Cylinder compression check

Refer to illustration 3.4

1   A compression check will tell you what mechanical condition the upper end (pistons, rings, valves, head gasket) of your engine is in. Specifically, it can tell you if the compression is low due to leakage caused by worn piston rings, defective valves and seats or a blown head gasket. **Note:** *The engine must be at normal operating temperature, the oil must be at the proper level and the battery must be fully charged during this check. Also, if the engine is equipped with a carburetor, the choke valve must be open all the way to get an accurate compression reading (if the engine is warm, the choke should be open).*

2   Begin by cleaning the area around the spark plugs before you remove them (compressed air should be used, if available; otherwise, a small brush or even a bicycle tire pump will work). The idea is to prevent dirt from getting into the cylinders as the compression check is done. Remove all of the spark plugs from the engine. Be careful not to burn yourself.

3   Disable the ignition system by detaching the primary (low voltage) wires from the coil (see Chapter 5). Also, if you're working on a fuel-injected model, disable the fuel pump (see Chapter 4, Section 2).

4   With the compression gauge in the number one spark plug hole **(see illustration),** depress the accelerator pedal all the way to the floor to open the throttle valve. Crank the engine over at least four compression strokes while watching the gauge. The compression should build up quickly in a healthy engine. Low compression on the first stroke, followed by gradually increasing pressure on successive strokes. indicates worn piston rings. A low

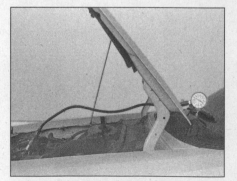

3.4 Use a compression gauge with a fitting that threads into the spark plug holes (position the gauge so it can be seen through the windshield as you open the throttle by depressing the accelerator and use the ignition key to crank the engine over)

compression reading on the first stroke, which does not build up during successive strokes, indicates leaking valves or a blown head gasket (a cracked head could also be the cause). Record the highest gauge reading obtained.

5 Repeat the procedure for the remaining cylinders and compare the results to the Specifications.

6 Add some engine oil (about three squirts from a plunger-type oil can) to each cylinder, through the spark plug hole, and repeat the test.

7 If the compression increases after the oil is added, the piston rings are definitely worn. If the compression does not increase significantly, the leakage is occurring at the valves or head gasket. Leakage past the valves may be caused by burned valve seats and/or faces or warped, cracked or bent valves.

8 If two adjacent cylinders have equally low compression, there is a strong possibility that the head gasket between them is blown. The appearance of coolant in the combustion chambers or the crankcase would verify this condition.

9 If the compression is unusually high, the combustion chambers are probably coated with carbon deposits. If that's the case, the cylinder head should be removed and decarbonized.

10 If compression is way down or varies greatly between cylinders, it would be a good idea to have a leak-down test performed by an automotive repair shop. This test will pinpoint exactly where the leakage is occurring and how severe it is.

4 Top Dead Center (TDC) for number 1 piston - locating

Refer to illustrations 4.6 and 4.8

1 Top Dead Center (TDC) is the highest point in the cylinder that each piston reaches as it travels up-and-down when the crankshaft turns. Each piston reaches TDC on the compression stroke and again on the exhaust stroke, but TDC generally refers to piston position on the compression stroke. The timing marks on the flywheel (models with manual transaxle) or the driveplate (models with automatic transaxle) are referenced to the number one piston at TDC on the compression stroke.

2 Positioning the piston(s) at TDC is an essential part of many procedures such as rocker arm removal, timing chain and sprocket replacement and distributor removal.

3 Before beginning this procedure, be sure to disconnect the coil primary wires (see Chapter 5).

4 In order to bring any piston to TDC, the crankshaft must be turned using one of the methods outlined below. When looking at the front of the engine (on the passenger side of the vehicle), normal crankshaft rotation is *clockwise*. **Warning:** *Before beginning this procedure, be sure to place the transaxle in Neutral or Park.*

a) *The preferred method is to turn the crankshaft with a large socket and breaker bar attached to the pulley bolt threaded into the front of the crankshaft.*

b) *A remote starter switch, which may save some time, can also be used. Attach the switch leads to the small ignition switch terminal and the positive (red) battery cable terminal on the starter solenoid (mounted near the battery). Once the piston is close to TDC, use a socket and breaker bar as described above.*

c) *If an assistant is available to turn the ignition switch to the Start position in short bursts, you can get the piston close to TDC without a remote starter switch. Use a socket and breaker bar as described in Paragraph a) to complete the procedure.*

5 Note the position of the terminal for the number one spark plug wire on the distributor cap (it's marked with a 1). Use a scribe or chalk to make a mark on the distributor directly under the terminal. Remove the screws, detach the cap from the distributor and set it aside.

6 On early models, turn the crankshaft (see Paragraph 4 above) until the triangular notch on the flywheel/driveplate is aligned with the stationary pointer in the bellhousing inspection window **(see illustration)**.

Note: *Although the 5° BTDC mark on the flywheel (manual transaxle) and the triangular notch (5° BTDC mark) on the driveplate (automatic transaxle) are really intended for initial engine timing, they're close enough for any procedure which requires that the number one piston be set at TDC.*

7 On later models, the timing marks are located on the front pulley and upper right side of the timing chain cover while facing the

2A

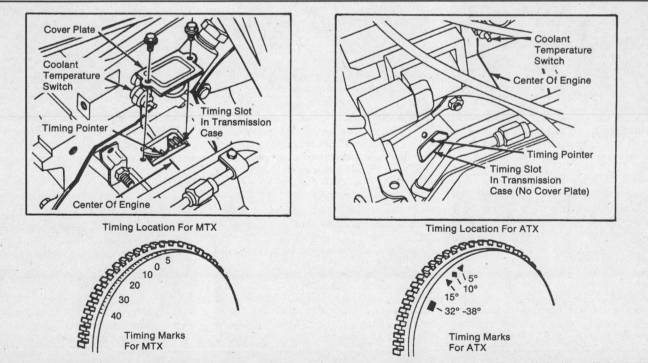

Timing Location For MTX

Timing Location For ATX

Timing Marks For MTX

Timing Marks For ATX

4.6 On early models, to bring the number one piston to TDC on the compression stroke, turn the crankshaft clockwise until the 5° BTDC mark on the flywheel (left - manual transaxle) or the triangle pointing toward the crankshaft (right - automatic transaxle) is aligned with the stationary pointer in the inspection window . . .

4.8 . . . then see if the rotor is pointing at the mark on the distributor body as shown here (the mark corresponds to the location of the number one spark plug wire terminal on the distributor cap)

pulley. The marks are similar to illustration 4.7 in Chapter 2, Part B).

8   Look at the distributor rotor, it should be pointing directly at the mark you made on the distributor body **(see illustration)**. If the rotor is pointing at the terminal for the number four spark plug (toward the engine), the number one piston is at TDC on the exhaust stroke.

9   To get the piston to TDC on the compression stroke, turn the crankshaft one complete turn (360-degrees) clockwise. The rotor should now be pointing at the mark on

the distributor. When the rotor is pointing at the number one spark plug wire terminal in the distributor cap and the timing marks are aligned, the number one piston is at TDC on the compression stroke.

10   After the number one piston has been positioned at TDC on the compression stroke, TDC for any of the remaining cylinders can be located by turning the crankshaft 180° at a time and following the firing order (1-3-4-2).

5   Intake manifold - removal and installation

Refer to illustrations 5.5a, 5.5b, 5.6, 5.8a, 5.8b, 5.9, 5.10, 5.11 and 5.20

Warning: *Allow the engine to cool completely before beginning this procedure.*

Removal

1   Refer to Chapter 4 and relieve the fuel system pressure (fuel-injected models only).

2   Disconnect the cable from the negative terminal of the battery.

3   On carbureted and central fuel-injected models, drain the cooling system (see Chapter 1).

4   On fuel-injected models, loosen the hose clamp and detach the air intake duct from the fuel charging assembly or throttle body. On carbureted models, remove the wing nuts and detach the metal duct from the carburetor.

5   Pop the throttle cable and speed control cable, if so equipped, off the throttle linkage with a screwdriver, remove the bracket bolts and set the cable and bracket assembly aside **(see illustrations)**.

6   On central fuel injected models, clearly label the electrical connectors, then unplug them from the fuel injector, the throttle position sensor, the throttle actuator, the temperature sensor, the EGR valve and the oxygen sensor **(see illustration)**.

7   On multi-port systems, disconnect the fuel charging system electrical connector from the main vehicle harness connector.

8   If your vehicle is equipped with an automatic transaxle, use a screwdriver to pry the downshift rod loose from the linkage, detach the return spring and position it to one side **(see illustrations)**.

9   Label and detach the power brake vacuum hose, the cruise control vacuum hose, the EGR valve vacuum hose, the PCV hose and all other vacuum hoses and electrical connectors attached to the carburetor/throttle body or the intake manifold **(see illustration)**.

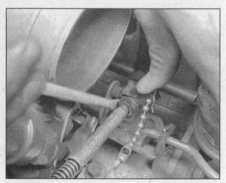

5.5a Pop the throttle cable off the throttle shaft with a screwdriver (central fuel injection is shown, others are similar). . .

5.5b . . . then remove the throttle cable/cruise control bracket bolts (arrows) and set the cable bracket assembly aside

5.6 Before removing the intake manifold, the electrical connectors (arrows) must be unplugged (central fuel injection shown)

5.8a Disconnect the throttle shaft and the automatic transaxle downshift rod by prying them apart with a screwdriver . . .

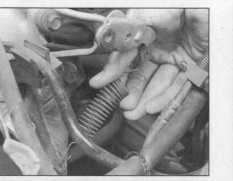

5.8b . . . then unhook the return spring from the throttle lever

5.9 Label and detach all vacuum hoses (arrows) (central fuel injection shown)

5.10 Disconnect the pipe from the EGR valve by unscrewing the threaded fitting (arrow) with a wrench

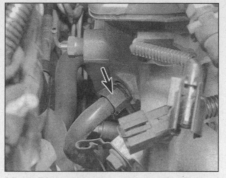

5.11 Disconnect the coolant tube fitting (arrow) from the backside of the intake manifold

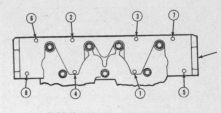

5.20 Intake manifold bolt TIGHTENING sequence

10   Disconnect the pipe from the EGR valve **(see illustration).**

11   On carbureted and central fuel injected models, remove the coolant inlet tube fitting from the intake manifold **(see illustration).**

12   On multi-port fuel-injected systems, remove the fuel pressure regulator shield located at the front of the intake manifold by removing the two attaching bolts, then remove the upper intake manifold (see Chapter 4).

13   Disconnect the fuel hose from the carburetor, the fuel supply and return lines from the fuel charging assembly or, on multi-port fuel-injection systems, the fuel supply and return lines from the fuel rail (see Chapter 4, if necessary).

14   Remove the eight manifold-to-cylinder head fasteners (noting the locations of any studded bolts) and remove the intake manifold assembly. It may be necessary to gently tap the upper manifold with a rubber mallet to break the mating surfaces free.

15   Place clean shop rags into the cylinder head intake ports to prevent dirt/debris from entering the engine.

Installation

Note: *The mating surfaces of the cylinder head and manifold must be perfectly clean when the manifold is installed. Gasket removal solvents in aerosol cans are available at most auto parts stores and may be helpful when removing old gasket material that is stuck to the head and manifold (since the manifold is made of aluminum, aggressive scraping can cause damage). Be sure to*
follow the directions printed on the container.

16   Use a gasket scraper to remove all traces of sealant and old gasket material, then wipe the mating surfaces with a cloth saturated with lacquer thinner or acetone. If there is old sealant or oil on the mating surfaces when the manifold is installed, vacuum leaks may develop.

17   Use a tap of the correct size to chase the threads in the bolt holes, then use compressed air (if available) to remove the debris from the holes. **Warning:** *Wear safety glasses or a face shield to protect your eyes when using compressed air.*

18   If present, remove the shop rags from the cylinder head ports.

19   Apply a thin, uniform layer of RTV sealant to the manifold mating surfaces and to the cylinder head side of the gasket. Slip one bolt into place at each end of the manifold and hang the new gasket over the bolts, verifying proper orientation of the gasket (all bolt holes and port passages should match the gasket). **Note:** *Assembly must be completed within several minutes. Don't allow the RTV sealant to dry.*

20   Position the manifold on the head and thread the bolts into place. Install the remaining bolts, then tighten them to the torque listed in this Chapter's Specifications in the recommended sequence **(see illustration).** Work up to the final torque in two steps.

21   The rest of installation is the reverse of removal.

22   After reassembly, reset /reconnect the fuel pump inertia switch if disabled during fuel pressure relief operations.

23   Refill the radiator with coolant (see Chapter 1).

23   Run the engine and check for vacuum, oil and coolant leaks.

---

6   Exhaust manifold - removal and installation

Refer to illustrations 6.3, 6.6, 6.7, 6.8 and 6.15

Warning: *Allow the engine to cool completely before beginning this procedure.*

Removal

1   Disconnect the negative battery cable from the battery.

2   Remove the intake manifold (see Section 5).

3   Unplug the oxygen sensor wire connector **(see illustration).**

4   Loosen the clamp and detach the heated air intake duct from the manifold shield, if so equipped.

5   Raise the vehicle and support it on jackstands.

6   Locate the elbow-shaped section of exhaust pipe between the exhaust manifold and the catalytic converter. Remove the nuts from the three exhaust manifold-to-exhaust pipe studs **(see illustration).** It may be a good idea to apply penetrating oil to the threads and allow it to soak in before attempting to loosen the nuts.

7   At the lower end of the elbow section **(see illustration),** remove the single bolt from

6.3 Disconnect the oxygen sensor electrical connector

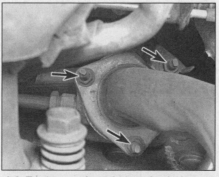

6.6 To remove the exhaust pipe between the manifold and the catalytic converter, remove all three of the flange nuts at the manifold (arrows) . . .

6.7 . . . and the two bolt and spring assemblies that attach the pipe to the catalytic converter - the bracket bolt must be removed as well

2A

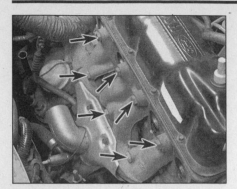

6.8 The exhaust manifold is attached to the head with seven bolts (four short ones and three long ones)

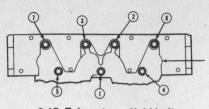

6.15 Exhaust manifold bolt TIGHTENING sequence

the small pipe support bracket and the two bolts from the flange between the elbow and the catalytic converter.

8   Remove the seven exhaust manifold bolts **(see illustration)**. Note that the bolts are not all the same length - keep track of where they are installed.

9   Detach the exhaust manifold from the head.

Installation

10   Clean and thoroughly inspect the manifold for cracks and damage. Check the fasteners and bolt holes for stripped or damaged threads. Use a tap of the correct size to chase the threads in the bolt holes, then use compressed air (if available) to remove the debris from the holes. **Warning:** *Wear safety glasses or a face shield to protect your eyes when using compressed air.*

11   The manifold and cylinder head mating surfaces must be clean before the manifold is reinstalled. Use a gasket scraper to remove all traces of carbon deposits.

12   Lightly oil all bolts prior to installation.

13   Slip one bolt into place at each end of the manifold and hang the new gasket over the bolts verifying proper orientation of the gasket (all bolt holes and port passages should match the gasket).

8.4 To measure cam lobe lift, secure a dial indicator to the head next to each valve (one at a time) and position the dial indicator plunger tip against the rocker arm, directly above and in line with the pushrod

14   Hold the manifold in place and install the bolts.

15   When tightening the bolts, follow the recommended sequence **(see illustration)**. Tighten the bolts in two steps until the torque listed in this Chapter's Specifications is reached.

16   The remaining installation steps are the reverse of removal.

17   After reassembly, reset /reconnect fuel pump inertia switch if disabled during fuel pressure relief operations.

18   Recheck/refill the radiator with coolant.

19   Run the engine and check for vacuum, oil and coolant leaks.

7   Valve cover - removal and installation

Removal

1   Remove the oil filler cap and set it aside.

2   Disconnect the PCV valve and hose assembly from the valve cover.

3   Detach the throttle linkage cable from the top of the valve cover, if so attached.

4   Disconnect the cruise control cable, if equipped, from the top of the valve cover, if so attached.

5   Remove the mounting bolts and detach the cover from the engine. If the cover is stuck, tap it with a soft-face hammer to break it loose. **Note:** *Later models use an integral (built-in) gasket which should last the life of the vehicle if not damaged. Therefore, avoid using sharp-bladed instruments in removing the cover. After removal, verify that the integral gasket is positioned in the cover and not stuck to the cylinder head.*

6   Clean the cylinder head and valve cover mating surfaces. Use a cloth saturated with lacquer thinner or acetone to remove all traces of oil. Aerosol gasket removal solvents are available at auto parts stores and may prove helpful.

Installation

7   Before installing the valve cover, refer to Section 11 and make sure the cylinder head bolts are tight.

8   On pre-integral (non molded-in) gaskets, lay the new gasket in place. Make sure the holes are lined up. **Note**: *No sealant is required when installing the valve cover.*

However, in order to prevent the gasket from sticking to the head and cover the next time removal is required, a very thin layer of RTV sealant can be applied to both sides of the gasket.

9   On later models a with molded-in valve cover gasket, first verify that the gasket is not nicked or cut. **Note:** *Small cuts/nicks of 1/8-inch or less can be filled in using RTV sealant. However, larger or numerous cuts/nicks can result in oil leakage, at which point the entire valve cover must be replaced.*

10   Apply one drop of thread locking compound to each cover bolt.

11   Lower the cover onto the head. Make sure the holes are lined up, then install the bolts finger-tight.

12   Tighten the bolts to the torque listed in this Chapter's Specifications in a criss-cross pattern.

13   The rest of installation is the reverse of removal.

14   Start the engine and check for oil leaks.

8   Camshaft lobe lift measurement

Refer to illustration 8.4

1   In order to determine the extent of cam lobe wear, the lobe lift should be checked prior to camshaft removal. Since the camshaft cannot be removed with the engine in the vehicle, the procedure is covered in Part C.

2   Remove the valve cover (see Section 7).

3   Position the number one piston at TDC on the compression stroke (see Section 4).

4   Beginning with the valves for the number one cylinder, mount a dial indicator on the engine and position the plunger against the top surface of the first rocker arm. The plunger should be directly above and in line with the pushrod **(see illustration)**.

5   Zero the dial indicator, then very slowly turn the crankshaft in the normal direction of rotation until the indicator needle stops and begins to move in the opposite direction. The point at which it stops indicates maximum cam lobe lift.

6   Record this figure for future reference, then reposition the piston at TDC on the compression stroke.

7   Move the dial indicator to the other number one cylinder rocker arm and repeat the check. Be sure to record the results for each valve.

8   Repeat the same check for the remaining valves. Since each piston must be at TDC on the compression stroke for this procedure, work from cylinder-to-cylinder following the firing order sequence.

9   After the check is complete, compare the results to the Specifications. If camshaft lobe lift is less than specified, cam lobe wear has occurred and a new camshaft should be installed (see Chapter 2C).

9.2 Loosen the bolt (arrow) and pivot the rocker arm to the side to remove the pushrod

9 Rocker arms and pushrods - removal, inspection, installation and adjustment

Refer to illustrations 9.2, 9.3, 9.5a, 9.5b, 9.5c and 9.19

Removal

1   Remove the valve cover (see Section 7).
2   Loosen the rocker arm fulcrum bolt until you can pivot the rocker arm to one side and pull the pushrod out of the valve lifter **(see illustration)**.
3   If you are removing more than one pushrod, store them in a holder made from a cardboard box **(see illustration)** so they can be returned to their original locations.

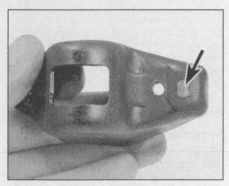

9.5a Check the rocker arm surfaces that contact the valve stem and pushrod (arrow), . . .

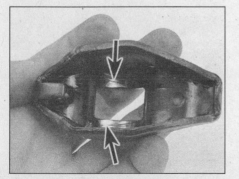

9.5b . . . the fulcrum seats in the rocker arms . . .

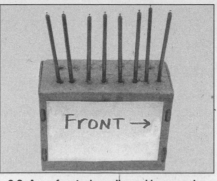

9.3 A perforated cardboard box can be used to store the pushrods to ensure that they are reinstalled in their original locations - note the label indicating the front of the engine

4   If you are going to remove more than one of the rocker arms, mark the rockers with their original fulcrums and store them so they can be returned to their original locations - don't mix them up!

Inspection

5   Check each rocker arm for wear, cracks and other damage, especially where the pushrods and valve stems contact the rocker arm faces **(see illustration)**. Check the fulcrum seat in each rocker arm and the fulcrum faces **(see illustrations)**. Look for galling, stress cracks and unusual wear patterns. If the rocker arms are worn or damaged, replace them with new ones and install new fulcrums as well.
6   Make sure the oil hole at the pushrod end of each rocker arm is open.
7   Inspect the pushrods for cracks and excessive wear at the ends. Roll each pushrod across a piece of plate glass to see if it's bent (if it wobbles, it's bent).

Installation

8   Lubricate the lower end of each pushrod with clean engine oil or moly-base grease and install it in its original location. Make sure each pushrod seats completely in the lifter socket.
9   Bring the number one piston to top dead center on the compression stroke (see Section 4).
10   Apply moly-base grease to the ends of

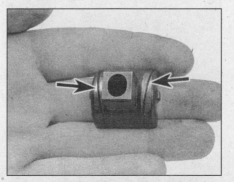

9.5c . . . and the fulcrums themselves for wear and galling

the valve stems and the upper ends of the pushrods before placing the rocker arms in position.
11   Set both number one cylinder rocker arms, the number two cylinder intake rocker arm and the number three cylinder exhaust rocker arm in place, then install the fulcrums and the bolts. Apply moly-base grease to the fulcrums to prevent damage to the mating surfaces before engine oil pressure builds up. Tighten the bolts to the torque listed in this Chapter's Specifications.
12   Turn the crankshaft 180-degrees in the normal direction of rotation until the number four piston is at TDC on the compression stroke. The distributor rotor should be pointing in the direction of terminal number four on the cap (if the cap is removed, the rotor should be pointing toward the engine block).
13   Install the remaining rocker arms and fulcrums and tighten the bolts to the torque listed in this Chapter's Specifications.
14   If any parts have been replaced, check the valve adjustment, as described below.
15   Install the valve cover (see Section 7).
16   Start the engine, listen for unusual valvetrain noises and check for oil leaks at the valve cover joint.

Adjustment

Note: *Adjustment is only needed when valve train parts have been replaced or valves and/or seats have been ground a considerable amount.*

17   Set the number one piston at Top Dead Center (TDC) on the compression stroke (see Section 4). This is position 1.
18   In this position you can check the following cylinder valves:

   Intake - Cylinders 1 and 2
   Exhaust - Cylinders 1 and 3

Note: *The arrangement of intake (I) and exhaust (E) valves, starting at the front (drivebelt) end of the engine, is as follows:*

   I-E-I-E-I-E-I

19   Using a lifter bleed-down tool **(see illustration)**, press on the rocker arm until the

9.19 Checking valve clearance with a lifter bleed-down tool and feeler gauge

2A

lifter leaks down completely. Check the clearance between the valve stem and rocker arm with a feeler gauge. Compare it to the Specifications in this Chapter and write it down. Repeat this procedure for each valve listed above.

20   Rotate the crankshaft one complete revolution (360-degrees) clockwise (this is position 2) and check the following valves:

      Intake - Cylinders 3 and 4
      Exhaust - Cylinders 2 and 4

If the clearances are within specification, install the valve covers.

21   If there is not enough clearance, use a shorter pushrod; too much clearance, use a longer one (available from your dealer).

---

10   Valve springs, retainers and seals - replacement

Refer to illustrations 10.8a, 10.8b, 10.9, 10.14 and 10.16

Note: *Broken valve springs and defective valve stem seals can be replaced without removing the cylinder head. Two special tools and a compressed air source are normally required to perform this operation, so read through this Section carefully and rent or buy the tools before beginning the job. If compressed air is not available, a length of nylon rope can be used to keep the valves from falling into the cylinder during this procedure.*

Removal

1   Remove the valve cover from the cylinder head (refer to Section 7).

2   Remove the spark plug from the cylinder with the defective valve component. If all of the valve stem seals are being replaced, remove all of the spark plugs.

3   Turn the crankshaft until the piston in the affected cylinder is at top dead center on the compression stroke (refer to Section 4 for the TDC locating procedure). If you're replacing all of the valve stem seals, begin with cylinder number one and work on the valves for one cylinder at a time. Move from cylinder-to-cylinder following the firing order sequence (1-3-4-2).

4   Thread an adapter into the spark plug hole and connect an air hose from a compressed air source to it. Most auto parts stores can supply the air hose adapter. **Note:** *Many cylinder compression gauges utilize a screw-in fitting that may work with your air hose quick-disconnect fitting.*

5   Remove the rocker arm mounting bolt, the rocker arm/fulcrum and the pushrod for the valve with the defective part. If all of the valve stem seals are being replaced, all of the rocker arms and pushrods should be removed (see Section 9).

6   Apply compressed air to the cylinder. The valves should be held in place by the air pressure. If the valve faces or seats are in poor condition, leaks may prevent the air pressure from retaining the valves refer to the

10.8a Once the spring is depressed . . .

alternative procedure below.

7   If you don't have access to compressed air, an alternative method can be used. Position the piston at a point approximately 45-degrees before TDC on the compression stroke, then feed a long piece of nylon rope through the spark plug hole until it fills the combustion chamber. Be sure to leave the end of the rope hanging out of the engine so it can be removed easily. Use a large breaker bar and socket to turn the crankshaft in the normal direction of rotation until *slight* resistance is felt.

8   Stuff shop rags into the cylinder head oil return holes to prevent parts from falling into the engine, then use a valve spring compressor to compress the spring/damper assembly. Remove the keepers with a small pair of needle-nose pliers, a magnet or a tweezers **(see illustrations)**. **Note:** *A couple of different types of tools are available for compressing the valve springs with the head in place. One type grips the lower spring coils and presses on the retainer as the knob is turned. The other type, shown here, utilizes the rocker arm mounting bolt for leverage. Both types work very well, although the lever type is usually less expensive.*

9   Remove the spring retainer and valve spring/damper assembly and set them aside. Using a pair of pliers, remove the valve stem seal **(see illustration)** and discard it. **Note:** *If air pressure fails to hold the valve in the*

10.9 It doesn't really matter how you remove the old valve stem seals. since they will be discarded, but be sure that you don't scratch, nick or otherwise damage the valve stems

closed position during this operation, the valve face or seat is probably damaged. If so, the cylinder head will have to be removed for additional repair operations.

10   Wrap a rubber band or tape around the top of the valve stem so the valve won't fall into the combustion chamber, then release the air pressure. **Note:** *If a rope was used instead of air pressure, turn the crankshaft slightly in the direction opposite normal rotation.*

11   Inspect the valve stem for damage. Rotate the valve in the guide and check the end for eccentric movement, which would indicate that the valve is bent.

12   Move the valve up-and-down in the guide and make sure it doesn't bind. If the valve stem binds, the valve is bent or the guide is damaged. In either case, the head will have to be removed for repair.

13   Reapply air pressure to the cylinder to retain the valve in the closed position, then remove the tape or rubber band from the valve stem. If a rope was used instead of air pressure. rotate the crankshaft in the normal direction of rotation until slight resistance is felt.

Installation

14   Lubricate the valve stem with engine oil and install a new valve stem seal. Use a deep socket of the appropriate diameter and a hammer to seat the seal squarely on the valve guide **(see illustration)**.

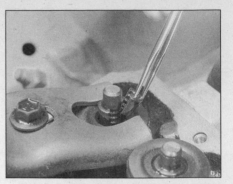

10.8b . . . the keepers can be removed with a small magnet or a pair of needle-nose pliers or tweezers

10.14 A deep socket and hammer can be used to seat the new seals on the valve guides

10.16 Keepers don't always want to stay in place, so apply a small dab of grease to each one as shown here before installation - it will hold them in place on the valve stem as the spring is released

11.4 Detach the wire harness connectors (arrows), remove the nut and disconnect the ground wire (arrow)

11.6 Remove the dipstick tube bracket bolt (arrow) from the radiator side . . .

15   Place the valve spring/damper assembly in position, then install the retainer.

16   Compress the valve spring assembly and carefully install the keepers in the grooves in the valve stem. Apply a small dab of grease to the inside of each keeper to hold it in place, if necessary **(see illustration).**

17   Remove the pressure from the spring tool and make sure the keepers are seated.

18   Disconnect the air hose and remove the adapter from the spark plug hole. If a rope was used in place of air pressure, pull it out of the cylinder.

19   Refer to Section 9 and install the rocker arm and pushrod.

20   If you are replacing all of the seals, repeat the procedure for each valve assembly. Remember, the piston for each cylinder must be positioned at TDC before removing the valve keepers.

21   Install the spark plug(s) and hook up the wire(s).

22   Install the valve cover (see Section 7).

23   Start and run the engine, then check for oil leaks and unusual sounds coming from the valve cover area.

11   Cylinder head - removal and installation

Refer to illustrations 11.4, 11.6, 11.7, 11.10 and 11.17

Removal

1   Remove the intake manifold (see Section 5)

2   Remove the exhaust manifold (see Section 6).

3   Refer to Section 7 and remove the valve cover.

4   Detach the heater hoses and radiator hose from the thermostat housing on the left end of the engine. Disconnect the coolant temperature sensor wire, remove the nut that secures the ground wire to the thermostat housing and unplug the wire from the electric cooling fan temperature switch (located in the head directly below the thermostat housing) **(see illustration).**

5   Remove the ignition coil bracket-to-head bolt, loosen the bracket to-block bolt and pivot the bracket forward (see Chapter 5 if necessary).

6   Remove the engine oil dipstick tube bracket bolt **(see illustration).**

7   Remove the ground strap and bracket bolts from the front end (drivebelt end) of the cylinder head **(see illustration).**

8   Remove the rocker arms and pushrods (see Section 9).

9   Loosen the head bolts in 1/4-turn increments until they can be removed by hand. Work from bolt-to-bolt in a pattern that's the reverse of the tightening sequence shown in illustration 11.17. Note that the rear bolts are longer than the front ones - they must be installed in their original locations.

10   Separate the head from the block. If it's stuck, carefully pry upon the right end of the head, using the engine mount as a fulcrum **(see illustration). Caution:** *DO NOT attempt to pry the head free anywhere else or damage may occur.*

Installation

11   The mating surfaces of the cylinder head and block must be perfectly clean when the head is installed. Use a gasket scraper to remove all traces of carbon and old gasket material, then wipe the mating surfaces with a cloth saturated with lacquer thinner or

11.7 . . . and the ground strap and bracket bolts (arrows) from the front (drivebelt) end of the cylinder head

acetone. If there is oil on the mating surfaces when the head is installed, the gasket may not seal correctly and leaks could develop. When working on the block, stuff the cylinders with clean shop rags to keep out debris. Use a vacuum cleaner to remove any debris that falls into the cylinders.

12   Check the block and head mating surfaces for nicks, deep scratches and other damage. If damage is slight, it can be removed with a file; if it's excessive, machining may be the only alternative.

13   Use a tap of the correct size to chase the threads in the head bolt holes. Mount each bolt in a vise and run a die down the threads to remove corrosion and restore the threads. Dirt, corrosion, sealant and damaged threads will affect torque readings.

14   If valves have been reground or new valves installed, check installed spring height and shim to specification if required (see Chapter 2, Part C).

15   Since there are no cylinder head alignment dowels, make sure the gasket is properly aligned after setting the head in place. Use Permatex High Tack or a similar adhesive to ensure that the head gasket doesn't move while the head is being lowered onto the block.

16   After applying a few dabs of Permatex to the side of the new gasket that faces the block, set it in place.

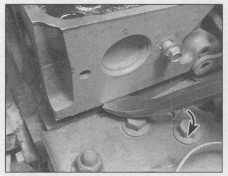

11.10 If you must pry the cylinder head loose from the block, do it at the front end of the head like this, using the right side engine mount as a fulcrum - if you attempt to pry the head loose from the block anywhere else, you will damage it!

2A

17　Lower the cylinder head onto the block. Install the cylinder head bolts in their original locations and tighten them finger tight. Following the recommended sequence **(see illustration),** tighten the bolts in two steps to the torque listed in this Chapter's Specifications.

18　The remaining installation steps are the reverse of removal.

12　Valve lifters - removal, inspection and installation

Refer to illustrations 12.4, 12.6a, 12.6b and 12.6c

1　Remove the cylinder head and related parts (see Section 11).

2　Before removing the lifters, arrange to store them in a clearly labeled box or in individually labeled plastic bags to ensure that they are reinstalled in their original locations.

3　There are several ways to extract lifters from the bores. On newer engines without a lot of varnish build-up, the lifters can often be removed with a small magnet. A machinist's scribe with a bent end can also be used to pull lifters out by positioning the point under the retainer ring in the top of each lifter.

12.4 The lifters in an engine that has accumulated many miles may have to be removed with a special tool - be sure to store the lifters in an organized manner to make sure they're reinstalled in their original locations

12.6b The foot of each lifter should be slightly convex - the side of another lifter can be used as a straightedge to check it; if it appears flat, it is worn and must not be reused

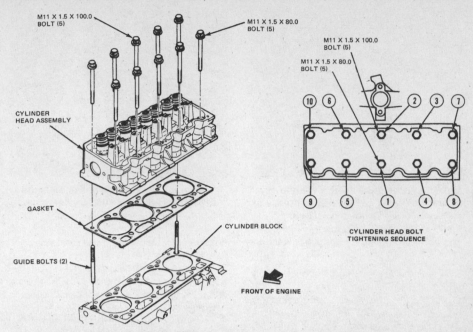

11.17 Cylinder head bolt TIGHTENING sequence - note that the bolts at the front of the head are shorter than the bolts at the rear

Caution: *Do not use pliers to remove the lifters unless you intend to replace them with new ones (along with the camshaft). The pliers may damage the precision machined and hardened lifters, rendering them useless.*

4　Special tools designed to grip and remove stubborn lifters are manufactured by several tool companies **(see illustration).** On engines with considerable gum and varnish, work the lifters up and down, using carburetor cleaner spray to loosen the deposits.

5　Once the lifters have been removed, clean them with solvent and dry them thoroughly without mixing them up. Remember that the lifters must be reinstalled in their original bores in the block.

6　Check each lifter wall, pushrod seat and foot for scuffing, score marks and uneven wear **(see illustration).** Each lifter foot (the surface that rides on the cam lobe) must be slightly convex, although this can be difficult to determine by eye **(see illustration).** If the base of the lifter is concave **(see illustration),** the lifters and camshaft must be replaced. If the lifter walls are damaged or worn, inspect the lifter bores in the engine block as well. If the pushrod seats **(see illustration)** are worn, check the pushrod ends.

7　If new lifters are being installed, a new camshaft must also be installed. If a new camshaft is installed, then use new lifters as well. Never install used lifters unless the

12.6a If the lifters are pitted or rough, they shouldn't be reused

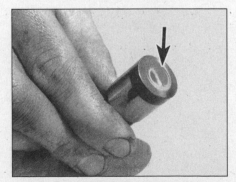

12.6c If the bottom of any lifter is worn concave, scratched or galled, replace the entire set with new lifters

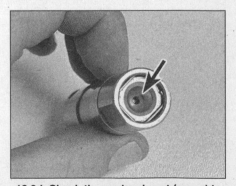

12.6d Check the pushrod seat (arrow) in the top of each lifter for wear

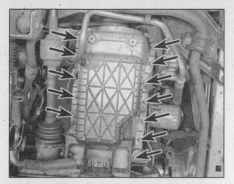

13.11a The oil pan is held in place with several small bolts along the flanges (arrows) . . .

13.11b . . . and two large bolts (arrows) on either side of the flywheel/driveplate access plate

13.12 To break the oil pan loose, carefully tap it with a large rubber hammer - don't attempt to pry the pan loose or you'll damage the sealing flanges on the pan and/or the mating surfaces of the block and oil leaks will result

2A

original camshaft is used and the lifters can be installed in their original locations.

8   Coat each lifter foot with assembly lube or moly-based grease before reinstalling it in the block.

9   The remaining installation steps are the reverse of removal.

---

13 Oil pan - removal and installation

Refer to illustrations 13.11a, 13.11b, 13.12 and 13.17

Removal

1   Disconnect the cable from the negative terminal of the battery.

2   Raise the vehicle and place it securely on jackstands.

3   Drain the oil (see Chapter 1 if necessary).

4   Drain the coolant (see Chapter 1 if necessary).

5   If your vehicle is a 1991 or earlier model equipped with a manual transaxle, remove the roll restrictor (refer to the engine removal Section in Chapter 2, Part C).

6   Disconnect all four hoses (two at the front and two at the rear) from the thermactor pipe assembly, then remove the pipe assembly (see Chapter 6).

7   Remove the starter motor (see Chapter 5).

8   Remove the elbow-shaped exhaust pipe section between the exhaust manifold and the catalytic converter (see Section 6).

9   Detach the coolant tube which is fastened to the lower radiator hose, the water pump and the tabs on the oil pan (see Chapter 4). **Warning:** *To avoid the possibility of splashing coolant into your eyes, don 't stand or lie directly under the junction between the coolant tube and the lower radiator hose. When the coolant tube is detached from the lower radiator hose, residual coolant may spill out.*

10   If the vehicle is equipped with air conditioning and/or power steering, remove the compressor/steering pump drivebelt, detach the compressor from the bracket and detach

the bracket from the block (see Chapter 3). Push the air conditioning low pressure line off to the side. Tie it out of the way, if necessary, but don't disconnect the hoses from the compressor.

11   Remove the oil pan bolts **(see illustrations).** Note that two of the bolts, located in the recess for the access cover, are larger than the others.

12   Because of the sealant used, the oil pan may be difficult to remove. Do not attempt to pry it loose from the block. Use a large rubber hammer to dislodge it, then remove it from the engine **(see illustration).**

Installation

13   Use a gasket scraper to remove all traces of old gasket material and sealant from the pan and block. Wipe the sealing surfaces with a cloth saturated with lacquer thinner or acetone. Aerosol gasket removal solvents are available at auto parts stores and may prove helpful.

14   Make sure the holes in the block are clean (use a tap to remove any sealant or corrosion from the threads).

15   It's also a good idea to remove and clean the oil pump pick-up tube and screen assembly. After cleaning both parts, install them (see the next Section).

16   Before proceeding, a trial mating of the pan to the block must be done to ensure that the sealant isn't smeared as the pan is installed. Check again for any residual oil that may have leaked down (particularly at the rear of the engine) and reclean as necessary.

17   Apply a continuous 3/16-inch diameter bead of RTV sealant to the groove in the oil pan flange **(see illustration).** Increase the bead width to 5/8-inch on the front cover and the rear seal retainer. The sealant must not protrude past the rear of the oil pan.

18   Immediately position the pan against the block and transaxle before the sealant "skins" over (approximately two minutes).

19   Install the oil pan flange bolts and tighten them enough to compress the sealant until the oil pan holes are aligned with the two tapped holes in the transaxle, but loose enough to allow the pan to move relative to the block.

20   Install the two oil pan-to-transaxle bolts and tighten them to the torque listed in this Chapter's Specifications to align the oil pan with the transaxle, then loosen the bolts 1/2-turn.

21   Tighten all oil pan flange bolts to the torque listed in this Chapter's Specifications.

22   Tighten the two oil pan-to-transaxle bolts to the torque listed in this Chapter's Specifications.

23   The remainder of installation is the reverse of removal.

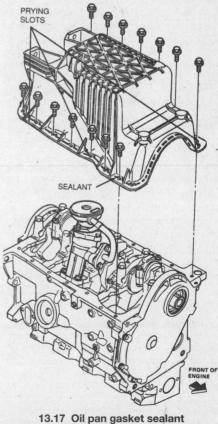

PRYING SLOTS

SEALANT

FRONT OF ENGINE

13.17 Oil pan gasket sealant application details

14.2 To separate the oil pump from the block, remove the two mounting bolts (arrows)

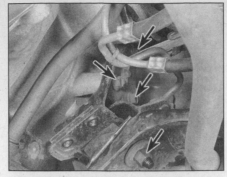

15.9 To remove the left front mount, raise the engine enough to clear the mount, then remove the mount-to-bracket nut and the three bolts (arrows)

15.15 To remove the rear mount, raise the engine enough to unload the mount, then remove the three mount-to-bracket nuts and the two mount-to-transaxle bolts - if you are replacing the bracket itself, also remove the three bracket-to-chassis bolts

14   Oil pump - removal and installation

Refer to illustration 14.2

Removal

1   Remove the oil pan as described in Section 13.
2   Remove the oil pump mounting bolts and detach the oil pump and intermediate driveshaft **(see illustration).**

Installation

3   Prime the oil pump by filling the inlet port with engine oil. Rotate the pump shaft until oil flows from the outlet port.
4   Insert the intermediate driveshaft into the oil pump. Install the pump and driveshaft as an assembly. **Caution:** *Don't attempt to force the pump into position if it won't seat. The driveshaft may not be aligned with the distributor shaft. To align the end of the drive-shaft with the distributor socket, remove the oil pump, rotate the intermediate driveshaft a few degrees and try again.*
5   Tighten the two oil pump mounting bolts to the torque listed in this Chapter's Specifi-cations.
6   Refer to Section 13 and install the oil pan.
7   Fill the crankcase to the proper level with the recommended engine oil (refer to Chapter 1 if necessary).
8   Operate the engine at fast idle and check for oil leaks.

15   Engine mounts - check and replacement

Refer to illustrations 15.9, 15.15, 15.26 and 15.29

1   Engine mounts seldom require attention, but broken or deteriorated mounts should be replaced immediately or the added strain placed on the driveline components may cause damage.

Check

2   During the check, the engine must be raised slightly to remove the weight from the mounts.

3   Raise the vehicle and support it securely on jackstands, then position the jack under the engine oil pan. Place a large block of wood between the jack head and the oil pan, then carefully raise the engine just enough to take the weight off the mounts.
4   Check the mounts to see if the rubber is cracked, hardened or separated from the metal plates. Sometimes the rubber will split right down the center. Rubber preservative should be applied to the mounts to slow deterioration.
5   Check for relative movement between the mount plates and the engine, transaxle or frame/body (use a large screwdriver or prybar to attempt to move the mounts). If movement is noted, lower the engine and tighten the mount fasteners.

Replacement

Left front mount

6   Raise the vehicle and place it securely on jackstands.
7   Place a wood block and a jack under the transaxle.
8   Raise the transaxle just enough to unload the mount no more than 1/2-inch.
9   Remove the mount-to-bracket nut **(see illustration). Note:** *1992 and later models use two nuts.*
10   Remove the lower three mount-to-transaxle bolts and detach the mount from the vehicle.
11   Position the new mount between the support bracket and the transaxle.
12   Install the three mount-to-transaxle bolts and tighten them securely.
13   Lower the jack enough for the mount to contact the bracket. Install the mount-to-bracket nut(s) and tighten it(them) securely.

Left rear mount

14   Raise the transaxle as described in Steps 6, 7 and 8 above.
15   Remove all three nuts from the lower mount bracket **(see illustration).**
16   Pull out the two mount-to-transaxle through bolts and detach the mount from the transaxle.
17   Install the mount over the left rear transaxle housing and bracket studs.
18   Install the two mount-to-transaxle through bolts and tighten the nuts securely.

19   Install the mount-to-bracket nut and tighten it securely.

Left rear bracket

20   Remove the rear mount as outlined above.
21   Remove the three bracket to chassis mounting bolts **(see illustration 15.15).**
22   Place the bracket in position.
23   Install the three bracket-to-chassis mounting bolts and tighten them securely.
24   Install the rear mount as outlined above.

Right engine center mount

Note: *The mount on 1992 and later models differs slightly from the previous models. Earlier models required that the engine side of the mount be removed from the chassis (rubber insulator) side to facilitate removal of the insulator. Later models do not require this step.*
25   Place a floor jack and a wood block under the engine oil pan. Raise the engine enough to unload the mount no more than 1/2-inch.
26   Remove the one mount-to-engine bracket attaching nut from the bottom of the double-ended stud and the two attaching bolts on the top of the bracket **(see illus-tration).** Do not remove the nut on top of the double-ended stud.

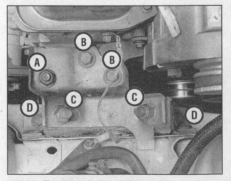

15.26 To detach the right mount, remove the nut(s) from the bottom end of the double-ended stud (A), the bracket-to-mount bolts (B) and the mount-to-insulator bracket nuts (C), then remove the two mount-to-body bolts (D) . . .

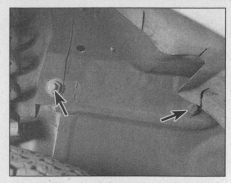

15.29 . . . and the mount-to-body nuts (arrows)

16.3 Mark the relative position of the flywheel/driveplate to the crankshaft before removing the bolts

27 On 1991 and earlier models, remove the two mount-to-insulator nuts and remove the engine-to-insulator mount bracket from the vehicle **(see illustration 15.26)**.

28 Remove two of the four insulator mount-to-chassis fasteners by removing the bolts accessible from within the engine compartment **(see illustration 15.26)**.

29 Remove the remaining two insulator-to-chassis nuts by working through the right front wheel opening **(see illustration)**.

30 Work the insulator mount out of position and remove it from the vehicle.

31 Work the new mount into the body opening. **Note:** *On 1991 and earlier mounts, It may be necessary to separate the engine support bracket from the insulator in order to facilitate installation.*

32 Loosely install the four insulator-to-chassis mounting nuts and bolts (two each). Tighten the nuts securely. Tighten the bolts securely.

33 On 1991 and earlier models, install the engine support bracket on top of the insulator and tighten the two nuts securely. On all models, make sure that the double-ended stud is aligned with the hole in the engine bracket.

34 Loosely install the mount-to-engine support nut on the double-ended stud and two bolts.

35 Tighten the mount support bracket nuts and bolts securely.

36 Lower the engine and remove the jack and wood block.

37 Remove the jackstands and lower the vehicle.

16 Flywheel/driveplate - removal and installation

Refer to illustrations 16.3 and 16.5

1 Raise the vehicle and support it securely on jackstands, then refer to Chapter 7 and remove the transaxle.

2 Remove the pressure plate and clutch disc (see Chapter 8 - manual transaxle equipped models).

3 If there is no dowel pin, make some marks on the flywheel/driveplate and crankshaft to ensure correct alignment during installation **(see illustration)**.

4 Remove the bolts that secure the flywheel/driveplate to the crankshaft. If the crankshaft turns, wedge a screwdriver

through the openings in the driveplate (automatic transaxle) or against the flywheel ring gear teeth (manual transaxle). Since the flywheel is fairly heavy, be sure to support it while removing the last bolt.

5 Remove the flywheel/driveplate from the crankshaft. On automatic transaxle models, there is a plate on the torque converter side of the driveplate **(see illustration)**.

6 Clean the flywheel to remove grease and oil. Inspect the friction surface for cracks, rivet grooves, burned areas and score marks. Light scoring can be removed with emery cloth. Check for cracked and broken ring gear teeth. Lay the flywheel on a flat surface and use a straightedge to check for warpage.

7 Clean and inspect the mating surfaces of the flywheel/driveplate and the crankshaft. If the crankshaft rear seal is leaking, replace it before reinstalling the flywheel/driveplate (see Section 16).

8 Position the flywheel/driveplate against the crankshaft. Be sure to align the marks made during removal. Before installing the bolts, apply thread locking compound to the threads.

9 Keep the flywheel/driveplate from turning as described above while you tighten the bolts to the torque listed in this Chapter's Specifications.

10 The remainder of installation is the reverse of the removal process.

17 Rear main oil seal - replacement

Refer to illustrations 17.3, 17.6, 17.7, 17.9, 17.10a and 17.10b

1 Remove transaxle, referring to Chapter 7A or 7B.

2 Remove flywheel/driveplate, referring to Section 16. **Note:** *The seal can be replaced without dropping the oil pan or removing the seal retainer. However, this method is more difficult because the lip of the seal is quite stiff and it's possible to cock the seal in the retainer bore or damage it during installation.*

3 If you want to take the chance, pry out the old seal with a screwdriver **(see illustration)**. Apply engine oil to the crankshaft

2A

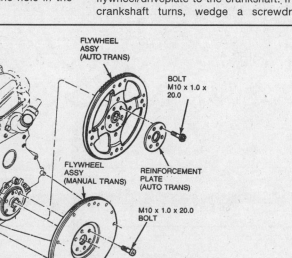

16.5 An exploded view of the flywheel/driveplate components

FLYWHEEL
ASSY
(AUTO TRANS)

BOLT
M10 x 1.0 x
20.0

FLYWHEEL
ASSY
(MANUAL TRANS)

REINFORCEMENT
PLATE
(AUTO TRANS)

M10 x 1.0 x 20.0
BOLT

DOWEL PIN MUST
BE BOTTOMED
INTO FLYWHEEL

FRONT OF VEHICLE

17.3 The quick way to replace the rear main oil seal is to simply pry the old one out with a screwdriver, lubricate the crankshaft journal and the lip of the new seal with oil and push the new seal into place

17.6 After removing the retainer assembly from the block, support it on a couple of wood blocks and drive out the old seal with a punch and hammer

17.7 Drive the new seal into the retainer with a block of wood or a section of pipe, if you have one large enough - make sure that you don't cock the seal in the retainer bore

17.9 Because the seal lip is quite stiff, it won't slide over the end of the crankshaft easily - carefully work the seal over the journal with a smooth, blunt object

seal journal and the lip of the new seal and carefully push the new seal into place. The lip is stiff, so carefully work it onto the seal journal of the crankshaft with a smooth object like the end of an extension **(see illustration 17.10a)** as you tap the seal into place. Don't rush it or you may damage the seal. The remaining Steps are the reverse of removal.
Note: *The following method is recommended but requires removal of the oil pan and the seal retainer*
4   Remove the oil pan (see Section 13).
5   Remove the seal retainer bolts, detach the seal retainer and peel off all the old gasket material.
6   Position the seal and retainer assembly on a couple of wood blocks on a workbench and drive the old seal out with a punch **(see illustration)**.
7   Drive the new seal into the retainer with a block of wood **(see illustration)** or a

section of pipe slightly smaller in diameter than the outside diameter of the seal.
8   Lubricate the crankshaft seal journal and the lip of the new seal with engine oil.
9   Slowly and carefully push the seal onto the crankshaft. The seal lip is stiff, so work it onto the crankshaft with a smooth object such as the end of a socket extension **(see illustration)** as you push the retainer against the block.

10   Slide the new gasket into place between the retainer and the block **(see illustration)**, then install and tighten all the retainer bolts to the torque listed in this Chapter's Specifications. The bottom sealing flange of the retainer must not extend below the bottom sealing flange (oil pan rail) of the block **(see illustration)**
11   The remaining steps are the reverse of removal.

17.10a Since it might be damaged during installation of the retainer assembly, leave the gasket off until the seal lip has been worked onto the crankshaft, then drop it into place and position it with a couple of retainer bolts

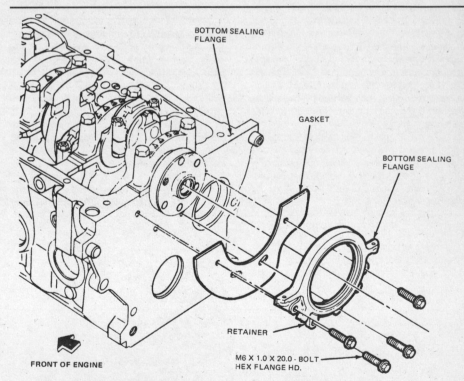

BOTTOM SEALING FLANGE

GASKET

BOTTOM SEALING FLANGE

RETAINER

M6 X 1.0 X 20.0 - BOLT HEX FLANGE HD.

FRONT OF ENGINE

17.10b The oil seal retainer bottom sealing flange must be even with the sealing flange on the block (there are no dowel pins to locate the retainer)

Chapter 2 Part B
V6 engine

Contents

Specifications

General

Valve clearance (lifter collapsed)	0.085 to 0.185 inch
Cylinder numbering (drivebelt end-to-transaxle end)	
Rear bank	1-2-3
Front bank	4-5-6
Firing order	1-4-2-5-3-6
Cylinder compression pressure	See Chapter 2, Part A
Camshaft lobe lift (intake and exhaust)	0.260 inch
Allowable camshaft lobe lift loss	0.005 inch

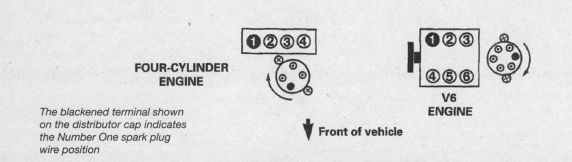

FOUR-CYLINDER ENGINE

V6 ENGINE

The blackened terminal shown on the distributor cap indicates the Number One spark plug wire position

Front of vehicle

Cylinder location and distributor rotation

Torque specifications

	Ft-lbs (unless otherwise noted)
Cylinder head bolts (follow the tightening sequence shown in Section 12)	
Step one	52 to 66
Step two	Back-off 360-degrees
Step three	33 to 41
Step four	63 to 73
Exhaust manifold bolts	15 to 22
Flywheel/driveplate bolts	54 to 64
Intake manifold-to-cylinder head bolts	
Step one	15 to 22
Step two	19 to 24
Oil pump mounting bolt	30 to 40
Oil pan bolts	84 to 120 in-lbs
Oil filter adapter-to-block bolts	18 to 22
Valve cover bolts/studs	84 to 120 in-lbs
Rocker arm fulcrum bolts	
Step one	5 to 11
Step two	20 to 28
Valve lifter guide plate retainer bolts	96 to 120 in-lbs

1   General information

This Part of Chapter 2 is devoted to in-vehicle repair procedures for the V6 engine. All information concerning engine removal and installation, repairs which require engine removal and engine block and cylinder head overhaul can be found in Part C of this Chapter.

The following repair procedures are based on the assumption that the engine is installed in the vehicle. If the engine has been removed from the vehicle and mounted on a stand, many of the steps outlined in this Part of Chapter 2 will not apply.

The specifications included in this Part of Chapter 2 apply only to the procedures contained in this Part. Part C of Chapter 2 contains the specifications necessary for cylinder head and engine block rebuilding.

2   Repair operations possible with the engine in the vehicle

Many major repair operations can be accomplished without removing the engine from the vehicle. Clean the engine compartment and the exterior of the engine with some type of pressure washer before any work is done. A clean engine will make the job easier and will help keep dirt out of the internal areas of the engine.

Depending on the components involved, it may be a good idea to remove the hood to improve access to the engine as repairs are performed (see Chapter 11 if necessary).

If vacuum, exhaust, oil or coolant leaks develop, indicating a need for gasket or seal replacement, the repairs can generally be made with the engine in the vehicle. The intake and exhaust manifold gaskets, oil pan gasket and cylinder head gaskets are all accessible with the engine in place.

Exterior engine components such as the intake and exhaust manifolds, the oil pan (and the oil pump), the water pump, the starter motor, the alternator, the distributor and the fuel injection system components can be removed for repair with the engine in place.

Since the cylinder heads can be removed without pulling the engine, valve component servicing can also be accomplished with the engine in the vehicle.

In extreme cases caused by a lack of necessary equipment, repair or replacement of piston rings, pistons, connecting rods and rod bearings is possible with the engine in the vehicle. However, this practice is not recommended because of the cleaning and preparation work that must be done to the components involved.

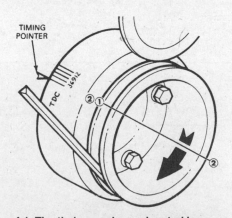

4.1 The timing marks are located low on the drivebelt end of the engine - positions 1 and 2 are for checking valve clearance (see Section 8)

3   Cylinder compression check

This procedure is the same as for the four-cylinder engine. Use the procedure and Specifications in Part A of this Chapter.

4   Top Dead Center (TDC) for number one piston - locating

Refer to illustration 4.1

This procedure is the same as for the four-cylinder engine. Follow the procedure in Part A of this Chapter, but refer to the illustration here for the location of the timing marks.

5   Valve covers - removal and installation

Removal

Refer to illustrations 5.3 and 5.4

1   Disconnect the negative cable from the battery.
2   Disconnect the spark plug wires from the spark plugs on the side(s) you are disassembling. If they are not numbered, tag them so they won't get mixed up on reassembly.
3   Note the location of the wire routing clips and studs **(see illustration)** and pull the clips off the studs.
4   If the front cover is being removed, disconnect the crankcase breather hose and move the wiring harnesses aside **(see illustration)**.
5   If the rear cover is being removed, remove the PCV valve (see Chapter 1) and the air intake throttle body (plenum) as described in Chapter 4.

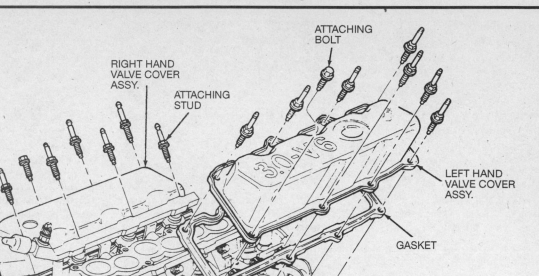

5.3 Valve cover mounting details

6   Remove the valve cover attaching bolts and studs. Use a deep socket to remove the studs.

7   Carefully remove the cover. If the cover is stuck, tap it with a soft-face hammer to break it loose. **Caution:** *The valve cover uses an integral (built in) gasket which should last the life of the vehicle if not damaged; therefore, do not use sharp-bladed instruments in removing cover. After removal, verify that the integral gasket is positioned in the cover and not stuck to the cylinder head.*

8   Using a gasket scraper or putty knife, remove all traces of gasket material (or sealer) from the cylinder head. Clean off all oil or dirt on the cover or head with acetone or lacquer thinner and a cloth.

Installation

9   Lightly oil all bolt and stud threads prior to installation.

10   Apply a bead of RTV sealant at the cylinder head-to-intake manifold rail step (two places per rail where they mate).

11   Verify that the cover integral gasket is not nicked or cut. **Note:** *small cuts/nicks of 1/8-inch or less can be filled in using RTV sealant. However, larger or numerous cuts/nicks can result in oil leakage, at which point the valve cover gasket must be replaced.*

12   Lower the cover onto the head, make sure the holes are lined up, then install the bolts finger tight.

13   Tighten the bolts to the torque listed in this Chapter's Specifications in a criss-cross pattern.

14   The rest of installation is the reverse of removal.

15   Start the engine and check for oil leaks.

6   Camshaft lobe lift measurement

This procedure is the same as for the four-cylinder engine. Refer to Part A of this Chapter and follow the procedure there, but use the Specifications listed in this Part.

7   Timing chain wear check

Note: *If a performance-related problem occurs or if planning for a possible future timing chain replacement, the extent of timing chain stretch wear can be determined with the engine still in the vehicle by following this procedure.*

1   Remove the front valve cover (see Section 5).

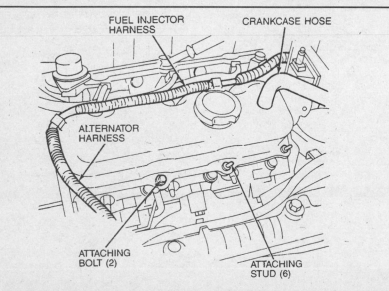

5.4 Remove the wiring harnesses and crankcase breather hose from the front valve cover

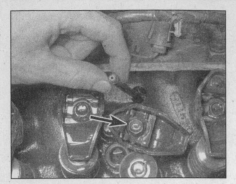

8.2 Loosen the bolt (arrow) and pivot the rocker arm to one side to remove the pushrod

8.3 A perforated cardboard box can be used to store the pushrods to ensure installation in their original locations

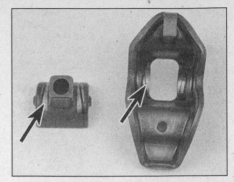

8.5 Check the rocker arm and fulcrum for wear and galling (arrows)

2   Install a dial indicator on the exhaust rocker arm for cylinder number 5 (see the *Camshaft lobe lift measurement* procedure in Part A of this Chapter).

3   Turn the crankshaft clockwise until the number one cylinder TDC position is reached (see Section 4). This will take up the slack on the right side of the chain.

4   Zero the dial indicator.

5   Slowly turn the crankshaft counterclockwise until the first movement is seen on the dial indicator. Stop and observe the timing marks to determine the number of degrees from TDC.

6   If the reading exceeds six-degrees, replace the timing chain and sprockets (see Chapter 2C).

7   Reinstall the components in reverse order of removal.

---

8   Rocker arms and pushrods - removal, inspection, installation and adjustment

---

Refer to illustrations 8.2, 8.3, 8.5 and 8.19

Removal

1   Remove the valve cover(s) (see Section 5).

2   Loosen the rocker arm fulcrum bolt until you can pivot the rocker arm to one side and pull the pushrod out of the valve lifter **(see illustration)**.

3   If you are removing more than one pushrod, store them in a holder made from a cardboard box **(see illustration)** so they can be returned to their original locations.

4   If you are going to remove more than one of the rocker arms, keep the rockers with their original fulcrums and store them so they can be returned to their original locations - don't mix them up!

Inspection

5   Check each rocker arm for wear, cracks and other damage, especially where the pushrods and valve stems contact the rocker arm faces. Check the fulcrum seat in each rocker arm and the fulcrum faces **(see illustration)**. Look for galling, stress cracks and

unusual wear patterns. If the rocker arms are worn or damaged, replace them with new ones and install new fulcrums as well.

6   Make sure the oil hole at the pushrod end of each rocker arm is open.

7   Inspect the pushrods for cracks and excessive wear at the ends. Roll each pushrod across a piece of plate glass to see if it's bent (if it wobbles, it's bent).

Installation

8   Lubricate the lower end of each pushrod with clean engine oil or moly-base grease and install it in its original location. Make sure each pushrod seats completely in the lifter socket.

9   Bring the number one piston to top dead center on the compression stroke (see Section 4).

10   Apply moly-base grease to the ends of the valve stems and the upper ends of the pushrods before placing the rocker arms in position.

11   Set both number one cylinder rocker arms, the number 3 and 6 cylinder intake rocker arms and the number 2 and 4 cylinder exhaust rocker arms in place, then install the fulcrums and the bolts. Apply moly-base grease to the fulcrums to prevent damage to the mating surfaces before engine oil pressure builds up. Tighten the bolts to the torque listed in this Chapter's Specifications.

12   Turn the crankshaft 360-degrees in the normal direction of rotation until the number five piston is at TDC on the compression stroke. The distributor rotor should be pointing in the direction of terminal number five on the cap.

13   Install the remaining rocker arms and fulcrums and tighten the bolts to the torque listed in this Chapter's Specifications.

14   If any parts have been replaced, check the valve adjustment, as described below.

15   Install the valve covers (see Section 5).

16   Start the engine, listen for unusual valvetrain noises and check for oil leaks at the valve cover joint.

Adjustment

Note: *Adjustment is only needed when valve train parts have been replaced or valves and/or seats have been ground.*

17   Set the number one piston at Top Dead Center (TDC) on the compression stroke (see Section 4). This is position 1 **(see illustration 4.1)**.

18   In this position you can check the following valves:

   Intake - Cylinders 1, 3 and 6
   Exhaust - Cylinders 1, 2 and 4

Note: *The arrangement of intake (I) and exhaust (E) valves, starting at the front (drivebelt) end of the engine is as follows:*

   Front cylinder bank
      I-E-I-E-I-E
   Rear cylinder bank
      E-I-E-I-E-I

19   Using a lifter bleed-down tool, available at most auto parts stores **(see illustration)**, press on the rocker arm until the lifter leaks down completely. Check the clearance between the valve stem and rocker arm with a feeler gauge. Compare it to the Specifications in this Chapter and write it down. Repeat this procedure for each valve listed above.

20   Rotate the crankshaft 360-degrees to position 2 and check the following valves:

   Intake - Cylinders 2, 4 and 5
   Exhaust - Cylinders 3, 5 and 6

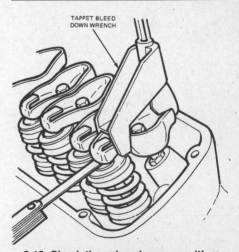

8.19 Check the valve clearance with a lifter bleed-down wrench and a feeler gauge

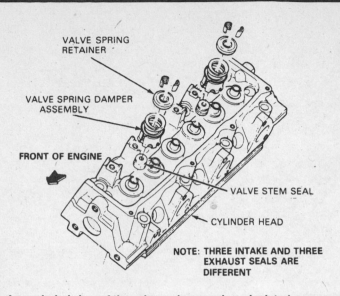

VALVE SPRING RETAINER

VALVE SPRING DAMPER ASSEMBLY

FRONT OF ENGINE

VALVE STEM SEAL

CYLINDER HEAD

NOTE: THREE INTAKE AND THREE EXHAUST SEALS ARE DIFFERENT

9.1 An exploded view of the valve springs, seals and related components

10.9 Use a scraper to remove the intake manifold gaskets

2B

If the clearances are within specification, install the valve covers.

21 If there is not enough clearance, use a shorter pushrod; too much clearance, use a longer one (available from your dealer).

9 Valve springs, retainers and seals - replacement

Refer to illustration 9.1

This procedure is the same as for the four-cylinder engine. Remove the valve cover(s) (see Section 5), refer to the accompanying illustration and follow the procedure in Part A of this Chapter.

10 Intake manifold - removal and installation

Refer to illustrations 10.9, 10.12, 10.13a, 10.13b and 10.15

Warning: *Relieve the fuel system pressure before following this procedure (see Chapter 4).*

Removal

1 Drain the coolant and disconnect the negative cable from the battery (see Chapter 1).

2 Disconnect the EGR tube nut from the EGR valve (if equipped). Loosen the tube nut and rotate the tube away from the valve. Remove the upper intake manifold and throttle body assembly (see Chapter 4) and valve covers as described in Section 5.

3 Label and disconnect all wiring, vacuum and coolant hoses from the intake manifold.

4 Disconnect the fuel lines from the fuel rail and cap the fittings (see Chapter 4). **Note:** *The injectors and fuel rail and harness may be removed with the intake manifold as an assembly.*

5 Remove the distributor and coil with the bracket (see Chapter 5) and remove the number 3 cylinder intake valve pushrod (see Section 8).

6 Remove the intake manifold mounting bolts/studs (this requires a Torx T-50 driver bit), noting the locations of the studs for reinstallation.

7 Remove the intake manifold. It may be

necessary to pry on the transaxle end of the manifold with a screwdriver to break the RTV seal. Use care to avoid damaging the machined surfaces.

8 Install clean shop rags in the lifter valley and intake manifold ports to prevent debris from entering the engine.

9 Clean away all traces of old gasket material **(see illustration)**. Remove oil and dirt with a cloth and solvent, such as acetone or lacquer thinner.

Installation

10 Lightly oil all bolts and studs prior to assembly.

11 If present, remove shop rags from the lifter valley and intake ports.

12 Apply a 1/4-inch bead of RTV sealant at each corner where the head joins the engine block **(see illustration)**.

13 Position the new gaskets and end seals on the engine with adhesive. Be sure the locating pins/tabs fit properly **(see illustrations)**. **Note:** *Assembly must be completed within several minutes. Don't allow the RTV sealant to dry.*

14 Carefully set the lower manifold into place. Be sure the gaskets don't shift out of place. Install the bolts and studs in their original locations.

15 Tighten the bolts/studs in numerical

10.12 Put extra sealant in the four corners before installing the new gaskets

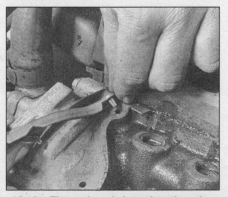

10.13a The end seals have locating pins which must be pressed into place

10.13b Be sure the locking tabs on the gaskets are engaged

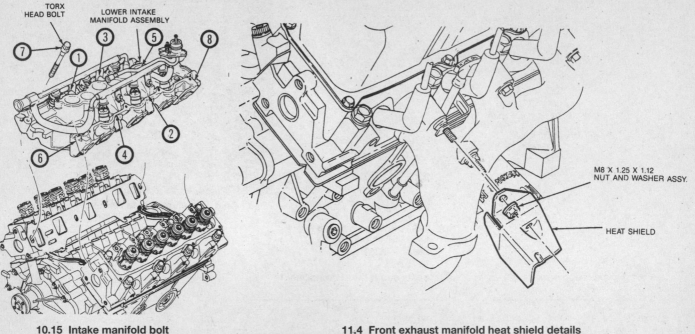

10.15 Intake manifold bolt tightening sequence

11.4 Front exhaust manifold heat shield details

sequence **(see illustration)**, reaching the torque listed in this Chapter's Specifications in two steps.

16   Reinstall all parts removed for access in the reverse order of removal.

17   Refill the cooling system and run the engine. Check the ignition timing.

18   Run the engine and check for fuel, vacuum and coolant leaks.

11   Exhaust manifolds - removal and installation

Warning: *Allow the engine to cool completely before following this procedure.*

Removal

Refer to illustrations 11.4, 11.6, 11.10 and 11.14

Front manifold

1   Raise the vehicle and support it securely on jack stands. Disconnect the exhaust pipe from the manifold. **Note:** *To ease removal of the manifold-to-pipe nuts, apply penetrating oil to the threads and allow it to soak in about 10 minutes.*

2   Remove the spark plugs from the front bank of cylinders (see Chapter 1).

3   Unbolt the oil dipstick tube and bracket and carefully rotate or remove the dipstick tube away from the manifold.

4   Remove the heat shield retaining nuts and remove heat shield **(see illustration)**. Penetrating oil will make the nuts easier to remove.

5   Remove the exhaust pipe-to-exhaust manifold stud nuts to free the exhaust pipe. Again, penetrating oil will make the nuts easier to remove.

6   Unbolt and remove the exhaust manifold from the vehicle **(see illustration)**.

Rear manifold

7   If not already done, raise the vehicle and support it securely on jack stands. Disconnect the exhaust pipe from the manifold being removed. **Note:** *To ease removal of the manifold-to-pipe nuts, apply penetrating oil to the threads and allow it to soak in about 10 minutes.*

8   Remove the spark plugs from the rear bank of cylinders (see Chapter 1).

9   Disconnect the EGR tube from the manifold (see Chapter 6). Be sure to use a back-up wrench on the lower fitting adapter.

10   Remove the heat shield retaining nuts and remove the shield **(see illustration)**.

11   Remove the exhaust pipe-to-exhaust manifold stud nuts to free the exhaust pipe. Penetrating oil will make the nuts easier to remove.

12   Drain the cooling system (see Chapter 1).

13   Remove the water pump (see Chapter 3).

14   Unbolt and remove the exhaust manifold from the vehicle **(see illustration)**.

Installation

15   Clean all gasket surfaces thoroughly and inspect the manifold(s) for cracks and

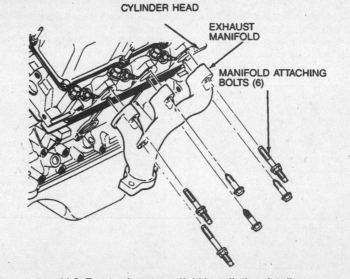

11.6 Front exhaust manifold installation details

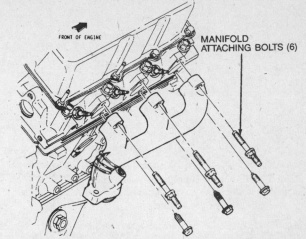

11.14 Rear exhaust manifold installation details

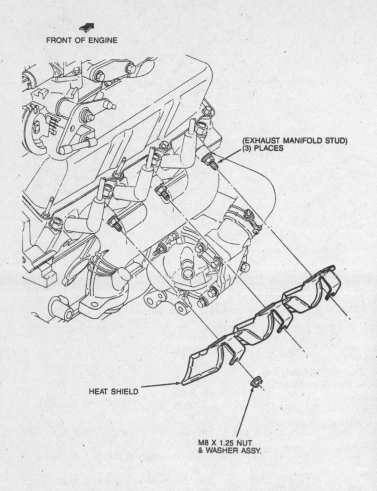

11.10 Rear exhaust manifold heat shield details

12.17 Once the bolts are removed, pry the head loose at a point where the gasket surfaces won't be damaged

damage. Check the fasteners and bolt holes for stripped or damaged threads.

16 Lightly oil all bolts prior to installation.

17 Position a new gasket and the manifold in place on the cylinder head.

18 Install the bolts and studs finger tight in their correct locations, then tighten them to the torque listed in this Chapter's Specifications.

19 Reinstall the remaining parts in the reverse order of removal.

20 Run the engine and check for exhaust leaks, and, if the rear manifold was removed, coolant leaks as well.

12 Cylinder heads - removal and installation

Refer to illustrations 12.17, 12.22 and 12.24

1 Drain the cooling system (see Chapter 1).

2 Disconnect the negative cable from the battery.

3 Remove the air cleaner duct.

4 Remove the drivebelts (see Chapter 1).

Removal

Front head

5 Remove power steering pump pulley shield and automatic belt tensioner mechanism.

6 Remove the power steering pump mounting nuts, leaving the hoses connected.

7 Remove the brace between the air conditioning compressor and upper alternator support.

8 Remove the three alternator support bracket-to-cylinder head bolts.

9 Move the alternator/power steering pump assembly away from the head to facilitate head removal. Be careful not to spill any power steering fluid.

10 Remove the oil dipstick and tube.

11 Remove the ignition coil and bracket (see Chapter 5).

Both heads

12 Remove the valve cover(s) (see Section 5).

13 Loosen the rocker arm fulcrum bolts enough to allow the rocker arms to be lifted off the pushrods and rotate them to one side.

14 Remove the pushrods (see Section 8).

Store them so they can be reinstalled in the same location.

15 Remove the intake manifold (see Section 10).

16 Remove the exhaust manifold(s) (see Section 11). **Note:** *Removal of the water pump is necessary to remove the rear exhaust manifold (see Section 7). However, the rear head can be removed with the manifold attached, eliminating the need to remove the water pump.*

17 Remove the cylinder head bolts and lift the head(s) off the engine **(see illustration)**. When removing the front head, lift the head clear of the locating dowels. Place the power steering pump aside in such a way that the fluid won't leak out.

18 Thoroughly remove all traces of gasket material with a gasket scraper and clean all parts with solvent. Use a rag and acetone or lacquer thinner to remove any traces of oil. See Chapter 2 Part C for cylinder head inspection procedures. Lightly coat cylinder walls with oil to prevent rusting.

19 Use a tap of the correct size to chase the threads in the head bolt holes. Run a rethreading die along the threads of the head

12.22 Position the new gasket over the dowels - make sure the UP (shown) or TOP mark is visible

bolts. Lightly oil the threads of the bolts except as noted below.

20   Recheck all head bolt holes and cylinder bores for any traces of coolant, oil or other foreign matter.

Installation

21   If the valves have been reground or new valves installed, check the installed spring height and shim to specification, if required (see Chapter 2, Part C).

22   Position the new gasket over the two hollow dowel pins on the block with the "V" cut towards the front of block. The top of the gasket should be stamped TOP or UP to ensure correct installation **(see illustration)**.

23   Install the head bolts finger tight.

24   Following the sequence shown **(see illustration)**, tighten the head bolts in two steps to the torque listed in this Chapter's Specifications. **Note:** *When cylinder head bolts have been tightened using the above procedure, it is not necessary to retighten the bolts after extended engine operation. However, bolts may be rechecked for tightness if desired.*

25   Reinstall the parts removed in the reverse order of removal. Lubricate the rocker arm components with engine assembly lube.

26   Install the pushrods in their original

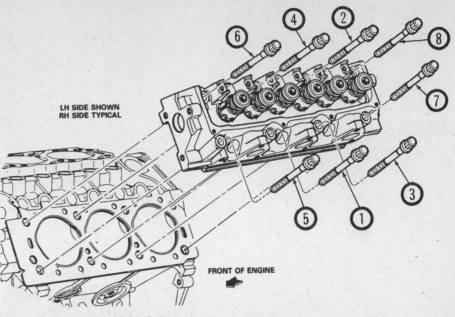

LH SIDE SHOWN
RH SIDE TYPICAL

FRONT OF ENGINE

12.24 Cylinder head bolt tightening sequence

locations. For each valve, rotate the crankshaft until the valve lifter is at its lowest position. Install the rocker arms, fulcrums and bolts. Tighten them to the torque listed in this Chapter's Specifications.

27   If a component has been replaced or the valves ground, check valve clearance as described in Section 8.

28   The remaining steps are reverse of removal.

29   Refill the cooling system, change the oil and filter (see Chapter 1) and run the engine. Check the ignition timing and inspect for any leaks.

---

13   Valve lifters - removal, inspection and installation

Refer to illustrations 13.5, 13.7a, 13.7b, 13.8, 13.9a and 13.9b

Removal

1   Remove the valve covers (see Section 5)

2   Remove the rocker arms and pushrods (see Section 8).

3   Remove the intake manifold (see Section 10).

4   Before removing the lifters and lifter parts, arrange to store them in a clearly labeled box to ensure that they are reinstalled in their original location.

5   Remove the two roller lifter guide plate retainer bolts and remove guide plate retainer **(see illustration)**. Check to see if the lifters are marked to indicate which side faces the drivebelt end of the engine. If not, mark the lifters before removal; they must be reinstalled in the same orientation so the rollers roll in the same direction.

6   Remove the six roller lifter guide plates by lifting straight out **(see illustration 13.5)**.

7   There are several ways to extract the lifters from the bores. Special tools designed to grip and remove lifters are manufactured by several tool companies and are widely available **(see illustration)**, but may not be needed in every case. On newer engines

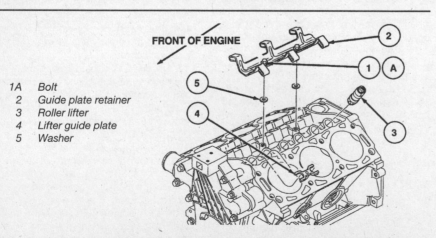

FRONT OF ENGINE

1A   Bolt
2   Guide plate retainer
3   Roller lifter
4   Lifter guide plate
5   Washer

13.5 Remove the two roller lifter guide plate retainer bolts and remove the guide plate retainer

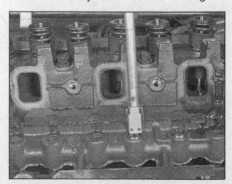

13.7a Stuck lifters can be removed with a special tool

13.7b You may be able to remove the lifters with a magnet

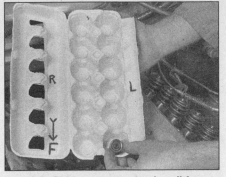

13.8 Old egg cartons work well for lifter storage

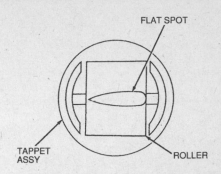

13.9a Check lifter rollers for score marks, ease of rotation and flat spots

without a lot of varnish buildup, the lifters can often be removed with a small magnet **(see illustration)** or even with your fingers. A machinist's scribe with a bent end can be used to pull the lifters out by positioning the point under the retainer ring in the top of each lifter. **Caution:** *Do not use pliers to remove the lifters unless you intend to replace them with new ones. The pliers may damage the precision machined and hardened lifters, rendering them useless.* On engines with considerable gum and varnish, work the lifters up and down, using carburetor cleaner spray to loosen the deposits. Excessive amounts of cleaner can contaminate the oil in the pan; replace it if this condition exists.

Inspection

8   Clean the lifters with solvent and dry them thoroughly while still keeping them in order **(see illustration)**.
9   Check each lifter wall and pushrod seat for scuffing, score marks, and uneven wear. Check rollers for score marks, ease of rotation and flat spots **(see illustration)**. If the lifters show signs of excessive wear, they must be replaced. If the rollers show signs of wear, the lifters and the camshaft must be replaced. If the lifter walls are damaged or worn (which is not very likely), inspect the lifter bores in the engine block as well. If the push-rod seats **(see illustration)** are worn, check the pushrod ends.
10   If a new camshaft is installed, use new lifters as well. Never install used lifters unless the original camshaft is used and the lifters can be installed in their original locations.

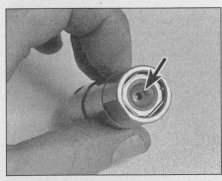

13.9b Check the pushrod seat (arrow) in the top of each lifter for wear

Installation

11   Lubricate the roller lifters with engine assembly lube.
12   Install the lifters in their original locations, align the flats on each pair of lifters and install the guide plates between them with the word "up" and the buttons visible.
13   Install the guide plate retainer and tighten the bolts securely.
14   Install the remaining parts in the reverse order of removal.
15   Refill the engine with coolant, check the oil level and start the engine. Check for oil and coolant leaks.

14   Oil pan - removal and installation

Removal

Refer to illustrations 14.10a and 14.10b

1   Disconnect the negative cable from the battery.
2   Remove the oil dipstick.
3   Raise the vehicle and support it securely on jackstands. Drain the coolant and oil and remove the oil filter (see Chapter 1).
4   Remove the retainer clip from the oil pan sensor and unplug the electrical connector from the sensor (if equipped).

2B

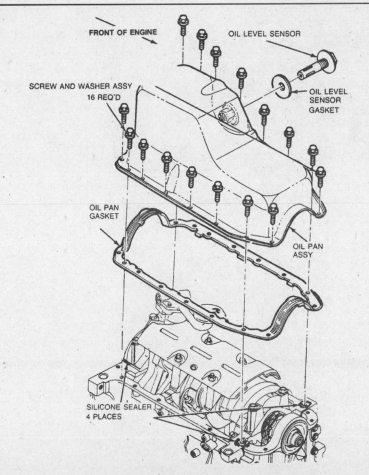

14.10a An exploded view of the oil pan components

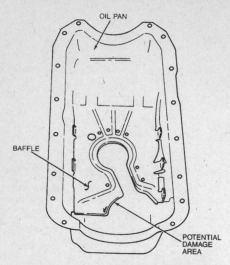

14.10b The oil pan must be pulled straight down without turning or prying or the baffle may be damaged near the oil pump

5   Disconnect the exhaust gas oxygen sensors at the header-to-pipe junction.
6   Remove the front exhaust pipe assembly and catalyst assembly (see Chapter 4).
7   Remove the starter motor (see Chap-

15.2 Oil pump mounting bolt and locating dowel (arrows)

ter 5).
8   On vehicles equipped with an automatic transaxle, remove the torque converter access plate.
9   On vehicles equipped with a manual transaxle, remove the left and right transaxle support plates.
10   Unbolt the oil pan and remove it from the vehicle **(see illustration on previous page)**. If the pan is difficult to break loose, tap on it with a rubber mallet. **Caution:** *The oil pan must be pulled straight down or possible damage to the baffle may result* **(see illustration)**.

Installation

11   Remove all traces of old gasket material from the mating surfaces and clean the oil pan with solvent. Clean the block and pan mating surfaces with acetone or lacquer thinner to remove any traces of oil.
12   Install a new gasket on the oil pan using a thin film of RTV sealant.
13   Apply a 1/4-inch bead of RTV sealant to the junctions of the block and rear main bearing cap and also the junction of the timing chain cover and block for a total of four places. **Note:** *Follow the gasket manufacturer's instructions. Don't allow the sealant to dry before installing the pan.*
14   Position the oil pan on the engine block and install the bolts, tightening them to the torque listed in this Chapter's Specifications.
15   Reinstall the remaining parts in the reverse order of removal.
16   Install a new oil filter, add coolant and oil (see Chapter 1). Run the engine and check for oil, coolant and exhaust leaks.

15   Oil pump and pickup tube - removal and installation

Removal

Refer to illustrations 15.2 and 15.3
1   Remove the oil pan (see Section 14).
2   Remove the oil pump mounting bolt **(see illustration)**.
3   Lower the oil pump assembly and intermediate shaft from the block **(see illustration)**.

Installation

4   Prime the pump by pouring oil into the oil pickup and turning the pump shaft by hand.
5   Fit the oil pump intermediate shaft into the pump **(see illustration 15.3)**, taking care that the shaft seats completely in the pump. Do not try to force it. If it does not align, turn the pump slightly and try again.
6   Install the oil pump assembly into the block, engaging the intermediate shaft into the distributor shaft. Take care to position the locating dowel and tighten the bolt to the torque listed in this Chapter's Specifications.
7   Reinstall the oil pan (see Section 14), add oil and a new filter (see Chapter 1). Run the engine and check for leaks.

16   Rear main oil seal - replacement

Refer to illustrations 16.3, 16.5, 16.7 and 16.8.
1   Remove the transaxle (see Chapter 7).
2   Remove the flywheel or driveplate (see Section 18).
3   Using a sharp awl, carefully punch one

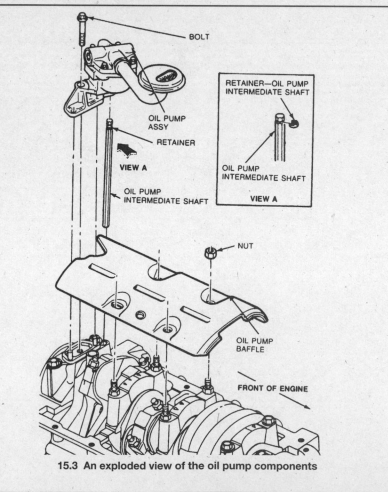

15.3 An exploded view of the oil pump components

hole into the seal between the seal lip and the engine block **(see illustration)**.

4   Screw in the threaded end of the seal installer. Use the tool to remove the seal. If you don't have the special tool, you may be able to thread a sheet-metal screw into the hole in the seal and pull on the screw with a pair of locking pliers.

5   If the special tool is unavailable, and the procedure above doesn't work, you may be able to pry the seal out with a screwdriver **(see illustration)**.

6   Thoroughly clean the seal bore and crankshaft sealing surface and lubricate the new seal with engine oil.

7   Place the new seal in position. Position the tool and seal on the crankshaft **(see illustration)**. Alternate bolt tightening to properly seat the seal. **Note:** *Flywheel/driveplate bolts may be used if necessary.*

8   If the special tool is not available, carefully work the seal lip over the end of the crankshaft and tap the seal in with a hammer and blunt drift until it's properly seated in the bore **(see illustration)**. **Note:** *The rear face of this seal must be within 0.005-inch of the rear face of the block.*

9   Reinstall the remaining components in the reverse order of removal.

10   Start the engine and check for oil leaks.

17 Engine mounts - check and replacement

This procedure is the same as for the four-cylinder engine (see Part A of this Chapter), except for the following:

Right front mount replacement

Refer to illustration 17.2

1   Remove the load from the engine mount by placing a wood block between a floor jack and the oil pan and raising the engine approximately 1/2-inch. **Warning:** *Do not place any part of your body under the engine when it is supported only by a jack!*

2   Remove insulator lower nut **(see illustration)**.

3   Remove insulator-to-air conditioning bracket bolt.

16.8 If the special tool is not available, tap around the seal, slowly working it into position

16.3 Do not scratch the crankshaft when punching a hole in the seal

16.5 You may be able to gently pry the seal out, but don't scratch the bore or the crankshaft

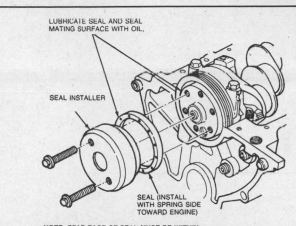

LUBRICATE SEAL AND SEAL MATING SURFACE WITH OIL.

SEAL INSTALLER

SEAL (INSTALL WITH SPRING SIDE TOWARD ENGINE)

NOTE: REAR FACE OF SEAL MUST BE WITHIN 0.127mm (0.005-INCH) OF THE REAR FACE OF THE BLOCK

16.7 A special Ford tool is recommended to install the seal

4   Remove insulator from vehicle. **Note:** *raising the engine further or removing the stabilizing bar bracket may be necessary for the insulator stud to clear the hole in the bracket.*

5   Install the new insulator into position between the stabilizer bar bracket and air conditioning bracket.

6   Loosely install the upper bolt/nut and lower nut, then lower the engine slightly to load insulator.

7   Tighten the insulator fasteners securely.

8   Remove the floor jack from under the engine and take the vehicle off the jackstands.

18 Flywheel/driveplate - removal and installation

Refer to illustrations 18.3 and 18.5

1   Raise the vehicle and support it securely on jackstands, then refer to Chapter 7 and remove the transaxle.

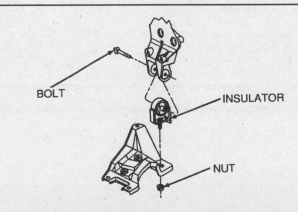

BOLT

INSULATOR

NUT

17.2 An exploded view of right-hand front mount

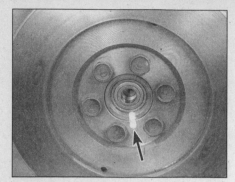

18.3 Mark the relative position of the flywheel/driveplate to the crankshaft before removing the bolts

2   Remove the pressure plate and clutch disc (see Chapter 8 - manual transaxle equipped models).

3   If there is no dowel pin, make some marks on the flywheel/driveplate and crankshaft to ensure correct alignment during installation **(see illustration)**.

4   Remove the bolts that secure the flywheel/driveplate to the crankshaft. If the crankshaft turns, wedge a screwdriver through the openings in the driveplate (automatic transaxle) or against the flywheel ring gear teeth (manual transaxle). Since the flywheel is fairly heavy, be sure to support it while removing the last bolt.

5   Remove the flywheel/driveplate from the crankshaft. On automatic transaxle models, there is a plate on the torque converter side of the driveplate **(see illustration)**.

6   Clean the flywheel to remove grease and oil. Inspect the friction surface for cracks, rivet grooves, burned areas and score marks. Light scoring can be removed with emery cloth. Check for cracked and broken ring gear teeth. Lay the flywheel on a flat surface and use a straightedge to check for warpage.

7   Clean and inspect the mating surfaces of the flywheel/driveplate and the crankshaft. If the crankshaft rear seal is leaking, replace it before reinstalling the flywheel/driveplate (see Section 16).

8   Position the flywheel/driveplate against the crankshaft. Be sure to align the marks made during removal. Before installing the bolts, apply thread-locking compound to the threads.

9   Keep the flywheel/driveplate from turning as described above while you tighten the bolts to the torque listed in this Chapter's Specifications.

10   The remainder of installation is the reverse of the removal Steps.

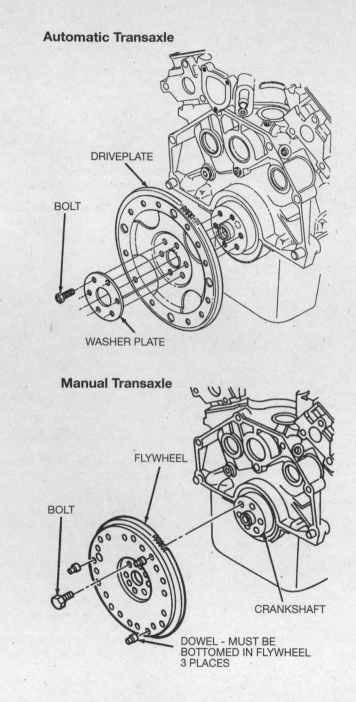

18.5 An exploded view of the flywheel/driveplate components

Chapter 2 Part C
General engine overhaul procedures

Contents

Specifications

Four-cylinder engine

General

Bore and stroke	3.68 x 3.30 inches
Compression pressure	See Chapter 2, Part A
Displacement	2.3 liters (140 cubic inches)
Oil pressure	55 to 70 psi at 2000 rpm

Cylinder head and valves

Valve seats	
Width	
Intake	0.080 inch
Exhaust	0.090 inch
Angle	45-degrees
Valve face angle	44 to 45-degrees
Valve margin width (minimum)	1/32 inch
Valve guide bore diameter (intake and exhaust)	0.3433 inch
Cylinder head warpage limit	0.003 inch per 6 inch span
Valve stem diameter	
Standard	
Intake	0.3415 to 0.3422 inch
Exhaust	0.3411 to 0.3418 inch
First oversize	
Intake	0.3566 to 0.3572 inch
Exhaust	0.3561 to 0.3568 inch
Second oversize	
Intake	0.3716 to 0.3722 inch
Exhaust	0.3561 to 0.3568 inch
Valve stem-to-guide clearance	
Intake	0.0018 inch
Exhaust	0.0023 inch
Valve springs	
Free length (approximate)	1.76 inches
Installed height	1.49 inches
Valve lifter diameter	0.874 inch
Lifter-to-bore clearance	0.001 to 0.002 inch

Engine block

Cylinder bore
  Diameter .... 3.679 to 3.683 inches
  Out-of-round
    Standard .... 0.001 inch
    Service limit.. 0.004 inch
  Taper service limit .... 0.010 inch
Camshaft bore inside diameter
  No. 1 .... 2.205 to 2.204 inches
  No. 2 .... 2.189 to 2.188 inches
  No. 3 .... 2.189 to 2.188 inches
  No. 4 .... 2.205 to 2.204 inches
Camshaft bearings
  Inside diameter .... 2.010 to 2.009 inches
  Runout/out-of-round limit .... 0.005 inch

Camshaft

Bearing oil clearance .... 0.001 to 0.003 inch
Endplay .... 0.009 inch
Timing chain deflection... 1/4 inch
Camshaft lobe lift.. See Chapter 2 Part A

Pistons and rings

Piston diameter
  Coded red .... 3.6784 to 3.6790 inches
  Coded blue.. 3.6796 to 3.6802 inches
  Coded yellow .... 3.6808 to 3.6814 inches
Piston-to-cylinder bore clearance .... 0.0012 to 0.0022 inch
Ring groove width
  Compression .... 0.080 to 0.081 inch
  Oil control .... 0.188 to 0.189 inch
Piston pin
  Length .... 3.01 to 3.04 inches
  Diameter .... 0.9119 to 0.9124 inch
Pin bore diameter .... 0.9124 to 0.9127 inch
Pin-to-piston clearance .... 0.0002 to 0.0005 inch
Pin-to-rod clearance... Interference fit
Piston rings
  End gap
    Compression... 0.008 to 0.016 inch
    Oil control (steel rail) .... 0.015 to 0.055 inch
  Side clearance
    Compression (both)
      Standard... 0.002 to 0.004 inch
      Service limit.. 0.006 inch
    Oil control .... Snug fit

Crankshaft and connecting rods

Main bearing journal
  Diameter... 2.2489 to 2.2490 inches
  Out-of-round limit.. 0.0004 inch
  Taper limit... 0.0003 inch
  Runout limit .... 0.0002 inch
Thrust bearing journal length... 1.275 to 1.277 inches
Crankshaft journal thrust face runout limit .... 0.001 inch
Connecting rod journal
  Diameter... 2.124 to 2.125 inches
  Out-of-round limit.. 0.0002 inch
  Taper limit... 0.0003 inch
Main bearing oil clearance
  Desired .... 0.0008 to 0.0015 inch
  Allowable .... 0.0008 to 0.0024 inch
Connecting rod bearing oil clearance
  Desired .... 0.0008 to 0.0015 inch
  Allowable .... 0.0008 to 0.0024 inch
Connecting rod endplay (side clearance)
  Standard... 0.0035 to 0.0105 inch
  Service limit.. 0.014 inch
Crankshaft endplay... 0.004 to 0.008 inch

Torque specifications   **Ft-lbs** (unless otherwise indicated)

Camshaft sprocket bolt	41 to 56
Camshaft tensioner bolts	72 to 108 in-lbs
Camshaft thrust plate bolts	72 to 108 in-lbs
Connecting rod cap nuts	21 to 26
Crankshaft pulley bolt	140 to 170
Crankshaft rear oil seal retainer bolts	72 to 108 in-lbs
Front cover bolts	72 to 108 in-lbs
Main bearing cap bolts	51 to 66

V6 engine

General

Bore and stroke	3.5 x 3.14 inches
Cylinder compression pressure	101 psi minimum (see text)
Displacement	3.0 liters (182 cubic inches)
Oil pressure (at 2500 rpm, engine warm)	40 to 60 psi

Cylinder head and valves

Cylinder head warpage limit	0.003 inch per 6 inch span
Valve seat angle	45-degrees
Valve seat width	
Intake	0.06 to 0.08 inch
Exhaust	0.08 to 0.10 inch
Valve guide bore diameter (intake and exhaust)	0.315 to 0.314 inch
Valve stem-to-guide clearance	
Intake	0.0010 to 0.0028 inch
Exhaust	0.0015 to 0.0033 inch
Minimum valve margin width	1/32 inch
Valve face angle	44-degrees
Valve stem diameter	
Standard	
Intake	0.3134 to 0.3126 inch
Exhaust	0.3129 to 0.3121 inch
First oversize	
Intake	0.3283 to 0.3276 inch
Exhaust	0.3279 to 0.3271 inch
Second oversize	
Intake	0.3433 to 0.3425 inch
Exhaust	0.3428 to 0.3420 inch
Valve spring	
Free length	1.84 inches
Installed height	1.58 inches
Valve lifter diameter	0.874 inch
Lifter-to-bore clearance	
Standard	0.0007 to 0.0027 inch
Service limit	0.005 inch

Crankshaft and connecting rods

Connecting rod journal	
Diameter	2.1253 to 2.1261 inches
Out-of-round limit	0.0003 inch
Taper limit	0.0003 inch
Connecting rod bearing oil clearance	
Desired	0.0010 to 0.0014 inch
Allowable	0.0008 to 0.0027 inch
Connecting rod side clearance (endplay)	0.006 to 0.014 inch
Main bearing journal	
Diameter	2.5190 to 2.5198 inches
Out-of-round limit	0.0003 inch
Taper limit	0.0006 inch
Runout limit	0.002 inch
Main bearing oil clearance	
Desired	0.0010 to 0.0014 inch
Allowable	0.0005 to 0.0023 inch
Crankshaft endplay	0.004 to 0.008 inch

2C

Cylinder bore

Diameter	3.5043 to 3.5053 inches
Out-of-round limit	
Standard	0.0006 inch
Maximum	0.0002 inch
Taper (maximum)	0.002 inch

Pistons and rings

Piston diameter	
Coded red	3.5024 to 3.5031 inches
Coded blue	3.5035 to 3.5041 inches
Coded yellow	3.5045 to 3.5051 inches
Piston-to-bore clearance	
Standard	0.0014 to 0.0022 inch
Service limit	0.0032 inch
Piston pin	
Length	2.728 to 2.760 inches
Diameter	0.9119 to 0.9124 inch
Pin-to-piston clearance	0.0002 to 0.0005 inch
Pin to rod clearance	Press fit
Piston rings	
End gap	
Compression (both)	0.010 to 0.020 inch
Oil control (steel rail)	0.010 to 0.049 inch
Side clearance	
Compression (both)	0.0012 to 0.0031 inch
Oil control	Snug fit in piston

Camshaft

Endplay	0.001 to 0.005 inch
Journal-to-bearing (oil) clearance	0.001 to 0.003 inch
Journal diameter (all)	2.0074 to 2.0084 inches
Bearing inside diameter	2.0094 to 2.0104 inches
Bearing out-of-round limit	0.004 inch
Bearing inside diameter	
Nos. 1 and 4	2.1531 to 2.1541 inches
Nos. 2 and 3	2.1334 to 2.1344 inches
Camshaft lobe lift	See Chapter 2 Part B

Torque specifications

	Ft-lbs (unless otherwise indicated)
Camshaft sprocket bolt	37 to 51
Camshaft thrust plate bolts	84 in-lbs
Connecting rod cap nuts	26
Crankshaft damper bolt	93 to 121
Front cover bolts	19
Main bearing cap bolts	55 to 63

1   General information

Included in this portion of Chapter 2 are the general overhaul procedures for the cylinder head and internal engine components. The information ranges from advice concerning preparation for an overhaul and the purchase of replacement parts to detailed, step-by-step procedures covering removal and installation of internal engine components and the inspection of parts.

The following Sections have been written based on the assumption that the engine has been removed from the vehicle. For information concerning in-vehicle engine repair, as well as removal and installation of the external components necessary for the overhaul, see Part A or B of this Chapter and Section 6 of this Part.

The Specifications included here in Part C are only those necessary for the inspection and overhaul procedures which follow. Refer to Part A or B for additional Specifications.

Warning: *On models so equipped, whenever working in the vicinity of the front grille/bumper, steering wheel, steering column or other components of the airbag system, the system should be disarmed. To do this, perform the following steps:*

a) *Turn the ignition switch to Off.*
b) *Detach the cable from the negative battery terminal, then detach the positive cable. Wait two minutes for the electronic module backup power supply to be depleted.*

To enable the system

a) *Turn the ignition switch to the Off position.*

b) *Connect the positive battery cable first, then connect the negative cable.*

2   Engine removal - methods and precautions

If you have decided that the engine must be removed for overhaul or major repair work, several preliminary steps should be taken.

Locating a suitable work area is extremely important. A shop is, of course, the most desirable place to work. Adequate work space, along with storage space for the vehicle, will be needed. If a shop or garage is not available, at the very least a flat, level, clean work surface made of concrete or asphalt is required.

Cleaning the engine compartment and engine before beginning the removal procedure will help keep tools clean and organized.

An engine hoist or A-frame will also be necessary. Make sure that the equipment is rated in excess of the combined weight of the engine and transaxle. Safety is of primary importance, considering the potential hazards involved in lifting the engine out of the vehicle.

If the engine is being removed by a novice, a helper should be available. Advice and aid from someone more experienced would also be helpful. There are many instances when one person cannot simultaneously perform all of the operations required when lifting the engine out of the vehicle.

Plan the operation ahead of time. Arrange for or obtain all of the tools and equipment you will need prior to beginning the job.

Some of the equipment necessary to perform engine removal and installation safely and with relative ease are (in addition to an engine hoist) a heavy duty floor jack, complete sets of wrenches and sockets as described in the front of this manual, wooden blocks and plenty of rags and cleaning solvent for mopping up spilled oil, coolant and gasoline. If the hoist is to be rented, make sure that you arrange for it in advance and perform beforehand all of the operations possible without it. This will save you money and time.

Plan for the vehicle to be out of use for a considerable amount of time. A machine shop will be required to perform some of the work which the do-it-yourselfer cannot accomplish due to a lack of special equipment. These shops often have a busy schedule, so it would be wise to consult them before removing the engine in order to accurately estimate the amount of time required to rebuild or repair components that may need work.

Always use extreme caution when removing and installing the engine. Serious injury can result from careless actions. Plan ahead, take your time and a job of this nature, although major, can be accomplished successfully.

3 Engine overhaul - general information

Refer to illustration 3.1

It's not always easy to determine when, or if, an engine should be completely overhauled, as a number of factors must be considered.

High mileage is not necessarily an indication that an overhaul is needed, while low mileage does not preclude the need for an overhaul. Frequency of servicing is probably the most important consideration. An engine that has had regular and frequent oil and filter changes, as well as other required maintenance, will most likely give many thousands of miles of reliable service. Conversely, a neglected engine may require an overhaul very early in its life.

Excessive oil consumption is an indication that piston rings and/or valve guides are in need of attention. Make sure that oil leaks are not responsible before deciding that the rings and/or guides are bad.

If the engine is making obvious knocking or rumbling noises, the connecting rod and/or main bearings are probably at fault. Check the oil pressure with a gauge installed in place of the oil pressure sending unit **(see illustration)** and compare it to the Specifications. If it's extremely low, the bearings and/or oil pump are probably worn out. The sending unit is located above the oil filter on four-cylinder engines and adjacent to the distributor on V6 engines.

Loss of power, rough running, excessive valve train noise and high fuel consumption rates may also point to the need for an overhaul, especially if they are all present at the same time. If a complete tune-up doesn't remedy the situation, major mechanical work is the only solution.

An engine overhaul involves restoring the internal parts to the specifications of a new engine. During an overhaul, the piston rings are replaced and the cylinder walls are reconditioned (rebored and/or honed). If a rebore is done, new pistons are required. The main bearings, connecting rod bearings and camshaft bearings are generally replaced with new ones and, if necessary, the crankshaft may be reground to restore the journals. Generally, the valves are serviced as well, since they are usually in less-than-perfect condition at this point. While the engine is being overhauled, other components, such as the distributor, starter and alternator, can be rebuilt as well. The end result should be a like new engine that will give many trouble free miles. **Note:** *Critical cooling system components such as the hoses, the drivebelts, the thermostat and the water pump MUST be replaced with new parts when an engine is overhauled. The radiator should be checked carefully to ensure that it isn't clogged or leaking; if in doubt, replace it with a new one. Also, we do not recommend overhauling the*

3.1 The oil pressure can be checked by removing the sending unit (arrow) and installing a pressure gauge - on four-cylinder models, it's located on the oil filter mount, next to the distributor

oil pump - always install a new one when an engine is rebuilt.

Before beginning the engine overhaul, read through the entire procedure to familiarize yourself with the scope and requirements of the job. Overhauling an engine is not difficult, but it is time consuming. Plan on the vehicle being tied up for a minimum of two weeks, especially if parts must be taken to an automotive machine shop for repair or reconditioning. Check on availability of parts and make sure that any necessary special tools and equipment are obtained in advance. Most work can be done with typical hand tools, although a number of precision measuring tools are required for inspecting parts to determine if they must be replaced. Often an automotive machine shop will handle the inspection of parts and offer advice concerning reconditioning and replacement. **Note:** *Always wait until the engine has been completely disassembled and all components, especially the engine block, have been inspected before deciding what service and repair operations must be performed by an automotive machine shop. Since the block's condition will be the major factor to consider when determining whether to overhaul the original engine or buy a rebuilt one, never purchase parts or have machine work done on other components until the block has been thoroughly inspected. As a general rule, time is the primary cost of an overhaul, so it doesn't pay to install worn or substandard parts.*

As a final note, to ensure maximum life and minimum trouble from a rebuilt engine, everything must be assembled with care in a spotlessly clean environment.

4 Engine rebuilding alternatives

The do-it-yourselfer is faced with a number of options when performing an engine overhaul. The decision to replace the engine block, piston/connecting rod assemblies and crankshaft depends on a number of factors, with the number one consideration being the condition of the block. Other considerations are cost, access to machine shop facilities, parts availability, time required to complete the project and the extent of prior mechanical experience on the part of the do-it-yourselfer.

Some of the rebuilding alternatives include:

Individual parts - If the inspection procedures reveal that the engine block and most engine components are in reusable condition, purchasing individual parts may be the most economical alternative. The block, crankshaft and piston/connecting rod assemblies should all be inspected carefully. Even if the block shows little wear, the cylinder bores should be surface honed.

Crankshaft kit - This rebuild package consists of a reground crankshaft and a matched set of pistons and connecting rods. The pistons will already be installed on the

5.7 The battery ground strap is attached to a stud at the top of the transaxle - remove the nut, detach the ground strap and set it aside (four-cylinder model shown)

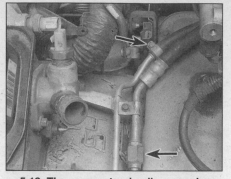

5.19 The power steering lines can be disconnected at the fittings on top of the transaxle - be sure to use a backup wrench when loosening the pressure line fitting (arrow) to prevent damage to the line (four-cylinder model shown)

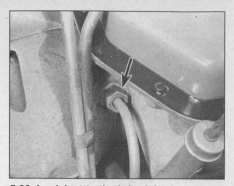

5.20 Look just to the left of the two power steering lines routed up the front of the bellhousing and you'll see the upper transmission fluid cooler line (arrow) - unscrew the threaded fitting and pull the line away from the bellhousing

connecting rods. Piston rings and the necessary bearings will be included in the kit. These kits are commonly available for standard cylinder bores, as well as for engine blocks which have been bored to a regular oversize.

Short block - A short block consists of an engine block with a crankshaft, camshaft/timing chain and piston/connecting rod assemblies already installed. All new bearings are incorporated and all clearances will be correct. The existing valve train components, cylinder head and external parts can be bolted to the short block with little or no machine shop work necessary.

Long block - A long block consists of a short block plus an oil pump, oil pan, cylinder head, valve cover(s) and front cover. All components are installed with new bearings, seals and gaskets incorporated throughout. The installation of manifolds and external parts is all that is necessary.

Give careful thought to which alternative is best for you and discuss the situation with local automotive machine shops, auto parts dealers and experienced rebuilders before ordering or purchasing replacement parts.

5   Engine - removal and installation

Refer to illustrations 5.7, 5.19, 5.20, 5.22, 5.25, 5.27, 5.28, 5.29a, 5.29b, 5.34, 5.35a, 5.35b, 5.37 and 5.39

Note 1: *This procedure requires the vehicle to be raised and securely supported at least 25-inches off the floor in order to clear the engine/transaxle assembly. A vehicle hoist is the recommended method in which to accomplish this, but large, sturdy jackstands will also work.*

Note 2: *If your vehicle is equipped with air conditioning, have the system discharged by a dealer service department or an automotive air conditioning shop before starting this procedure.*

Warning: *If vehicle is equipped with airbags, refer to Chapter 12, to disarm the airbag system prior to performing any work described below.*

Removal

1   Refer to Chapter 11 and remove the hood.
2   Disconnect the cable from the negative terminal of the battery.
3   Drain the cooling system (see Chapter 1).
4   Remove the air intake duct and the air cleaner assembly (see Chapter 4).
5   Remove the protective shield from the upper crossmember. Remove the upper radiator hose and disconnect the lower hose from the radiator. Catch the coolant in a drain pan (see Chapter 3).
6   Remove the ignition coil from the engine (see Chapter 5).
7   Detach the electrical connector from the oil pressure switch and remove the ground straps from the bellhousing and the right end of the cylinder head **(see illustration)**.
8   Detach the wire harness connector from the distributor and set the harness aside (see Chapter 5 if necessary).
9   If your vehicle is equipped with an automatic transaxle, detach the transmission fluid cooler lines from the radiator (see Chapter 3).
10   Remove the radiator shroud/cooling fan assembly and the radiator (see Chapter 3).
11   If your vehicle is equipped with air conditioning, detach the lines from the air conditioning compressor (see Chapter 3).
12   Label and disconnect all wires that would interfere with engine removal (see Chapters 2A, 2B, 3, 4 and 5, if necessary).
13   Label and disconnect all vacuum hoses that would interfere with engine removal (refer to Chapters 2A or 2B and 4, if necessary).
14   On earlier four-cylinder models, disconnect the coolant tube by unscrewing the threaded fitting at the back side of the intake manifold (see Chapter 2A).
15   Disconnect the accelerator and (if equipped) the cruise control cable and bracket and set them aside (see Chapter 4).
16   If your vehicle is equipped with an automatic transaxle, detach the select cable from the select lever and remove the throttle valve cable (V6) or linkage (four-cylinder) (see Chapter 7B).

17   If your vehicle is equipped with a manual transaxle, disconnect the clutch cable from the lever on the transaxle (see Chapter 7A).
18   Disconnect the fuel lines from the fuel injection unit, fuel rail or carburetor. On models with multiport fuel injection, be sure to relieve the fuel pressure first (see Chapter 4).
19   If your vehicle is equipped with power steering, locate the power steering lines on top of the transaxle **(see illustration)**. Disconnect the lines (one has a threaded fitting and the other is held in place with a hose clamp). Be sure to cap both lines to prevent leaks and contamination of the system.
20   If your vehicle is equipped with an automatic transaxle, detach the upper fluid cooler line threaded fitting from the transaxle **(see illustration)**. Plug the line to prevent leakage.
21   Raise the vehicle and place it securely on jackstands. Note: The jackstands must be high enough to support the vehicle at least 25-inches off the floor in order to clear the engine/transaxle assembly. A vehicle hoist is recommended.
22   If your vehicle is equipped with an automatic transaxle, detach the lower cooler line threaded fitting from the transaxle **(see illustration)**. Plug the line to prevent leakage.

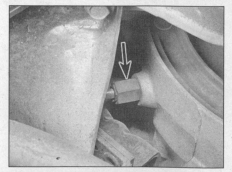

5.22 Looking at the front of the transaxle housing from underneath the left wheel well, you'll see the lower transmission fluid cooler line fitting just above and behind the left stabilizer bar mounting bracket - unscrew the threaded fitting (arrow) and pull it away from the transaxle

5.25 It's easier to remove the torque converter nuts while the engine is installed in the vehicle (four-cylinder model shown)

23 On four-cylinder models, remove the elbow shaped section of exhaust pipe between the exhaust manifold and the catalytic converter. On V6 models, remove the exhaust "Y" pipe and catalytic converter (see Chapter 4).

24 On four-cylinder models, disconnect the hoses and remove the thermactor pipe assembly (see Chapter 6).

25 If your vehicle is equipped with an automatic transaxle, rotate the engine by hand to expose each torque converter nut (see illustration) and remove them.

26 Disconnect the large cable from the starter motor (see Chapter 5 if necessary). Disconnect the starter cable brackets from the upper starter motor-to-transaxle stud and from the front mount and position the starter motor wire harness aside.

27 On models with a manual transaxle, remove the roll restrictor, if equipped (see illustration).

28 Disconnect the speedometer cable (see illustration).

29 Disconnect the coolant hose from the water pump (see Chapter 3), then disconnect the two air conditioning line brackets from the bottom of the oil pan and the back side of the block (see illustrations).

30 On four-cylinder models, remove the lower control arm through bolts and detach the inner ends of the lower control arms from the body (see Chapter 10).

31 On V6 models, disconnect the lower balljoints and pull down on the control arms to disengage them from the spindle (see Chapter 10).

32 On four-cylinder models, refer to Chapter 10 and remove the stabilizer bar.

33 Remove the driveaxles (see Chapter 8).

34 If your vehicle is equipped with an automatic transaxle, remove the shift linkage bracket bolts from the transaxle and detach the bracket (see illustration).

35 On four-cylinder models, attach an engine hoist chain to the left front corner of the block and the right rear corner of the cylinder head (see illustrations). On V6 models, attach the hoist chain at the right front and left rear corners of the cylinder

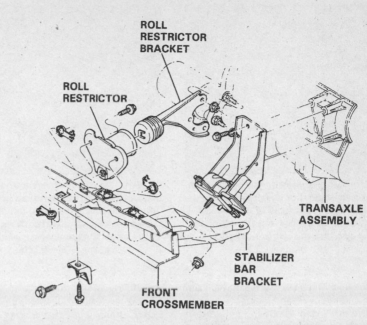

5.27 To remove the roll restrictor (used on models with a manual transaxle), remove the bolts and U-nuts that attach it to the front crossmember, remove the nuts that attach the bracket to the starter motor-to-transaxle mounting studs and pull the restrictor and bracket out as an assembly

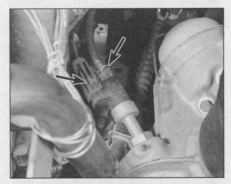

5.28 To detach the speedometer cable from the transaxle, unplug the electrical connector, remove the hairpin wire clip (arrows) and pull the cable out

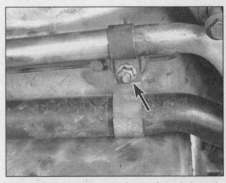

5.29a Remove the nut (arrow) and detach the A/C line bracket from the oil pan (the other, darker line is the coolant tube (it can remain in place during engine removal), then . . .

5.29b . . . detach the remaining bracket (arrow) from the back side of the block and tie up the A/C line with a piece of wire someplace out of the way so it won't hang up during engine removal (four-cylinder model shown)

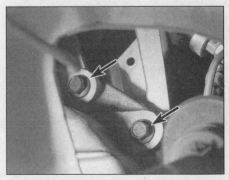

5.34 The manual shift linkage bracket bolts are accessible through the driveaxle tunnel in the inner wheel well

2C

5.35a Your engine may have lifting hooks to attach a chain, but if it doesn't, you'll have to obtain a couple of grade 5 or stronger bolts of the correct thread pitch - screw one into the left front corner of the block . . .

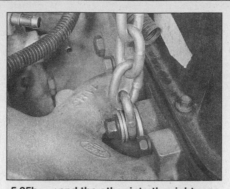

5.35b . . . and the other into the right rear corner of the cylinder head (make sure that each bolt is long enough to screw at least 3/4-inch into the block or head with the chain and washers in place) (four-cylinder model shown)

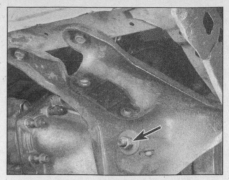

5.37 Both the left and right stabilizer bar mounting brackets must be disconnected from the front crossmember and removed - also disconnect the left bracket (shown) from the front mount by removing the single large nut (arrow) in the middle of the bracket

head. Warning: The bolts must thread at least 3/4-inch into the block and head.

36 Raise the engine about 1/2-inch to take the load off the rear mount, then detach the left rear mount from the body bracket by removing both nuts. The actual rubber mount should remain attached to the transaxle (see Chapter 2A or 2B).

37 Remove the one (1991 and earlier) or two (1992 and later) left front mount-to-stabilizer bar bracket nut(s). Next, remove the three left front stabilizer bar bracket-to-crossmember bolts from the vehicle and remove the stabilizer bar bracket **(see illustration)**. The actual rubber mount should remain attached to the transaxle. Refer to Chapter 2A or 2B.

38 Remove the two bolts and the nut attaching the right engine center rubber mount assembly to the engine-mounted bracket. The actual rubber mount should remain attached to the vehicle body (see Chapter 2A or 2B).

39 On V6 models, remove the one right front mount-to-stabilizer bar bracket nut. Next, remove the three right front stabilizer bar bracket-to-crossmember bolts from the vehicle and remove the stabilizer bar bracket. **(see illustration)**. The actual rubber mount

5.39 Before LOWERING the engine/ transaxle assembly from the engine compartment, double check your work to make sure that all wires, vacuum hoses, etc. are disconnected and out of the way, then carefully lower the assembly to the floor

should remain attached to the air conditioning bracket (see Chapter 2B).

40 Carefully LOWER the engine/transaxle assembly down through the engine compartment **(see illustration 5.39)**. Detach the hoist and slide the engine out from underneath the vehicle.

41 Reattach the hoist to the chain on the engine and raise the hoist slightly to remove the slack from the chain - do not raise the engine.

42 Remove the engine-to-transaxle bolts and separate the engine from the transaxle. When you pull the transaxle away from the engine, the engine will tilt as the center of gravity shifts. Adjust the hoist as needed to keep the engine level. **Note 1:** *On four-cylinder models, be sure to first remove the oil pan-to-transaxle bolts (see Chapter 2A).* **Note 2:** *On automatic transaxle models, be careful not to allow the torque converter to fall out of the transaxle bellhousing when the engine and transaxle are separated. After the engine is free, secure the torque converter in the transaxle.*

Installation

43 Attach the engine to the transaxle, referring to Chapter 7 (and 2A on four-cylinder models) for the torque specifications. Position the engine and transaxle under the engine compartment and attach the hoist to the chain on the engine.

44 Before proceeding, verify that the two transaxle rubber mounts and the engine's center mount bracket are installed and tightened securely. Verify that the engine's right center rubber mount is installed on the vehicle's body and tightened securely. On V6 engines, also verify the right front rubber mount is installed onto the engine's air conditioning bracket.

45 Carefully raise the engine/transaxle into the engine compartment.

46 Position a jack underneath the transaxle pan to take the weight off the mount. Be sure to place a block of wood between the jack head and the pan to prevent damage to the pan.

47 Install but do not tighten the right engine center mount bracket bolts and nut (see Chapter 2A or 2B).

48 Install but do not tighten the left rear mount bracket nuts (see Chapter 2A or 2B).

49 Attach the stabilizer bar bracket to the left front transaxle mount and the chassis crossmember. On V6 models, also attach the right front stabilizer bar bracket to the crossmember and to the transaxle mount. Tighten the nut(s) that attach the mount(s) to the bracket(s) and the three bolts that attach the bracket (s) to the crossmember to the torque listed in this Chapter's Specifications (see Chapter 2A or 2B and 10).

50 Tighten the right engine center mount and the right rear mount nuts to the torque listed in this Chapter's Specifications, then detach the chain from the engine.

51 The remainder of installation is the reverse of removal.

52 Refer to Section 26 for the initial start-up procedure.

53 Set the ignition timing (see Chapter 5).

54 Test drive the vehicle and check for leaks.

6 Engine overhaul - disassembly sequence

1 It's much easier to disassemble and work on the engine if it's mounted on a portable engine stand. These stands can often be rented quite cheaply from an equipment rental yard. Before the engine is mounted on a stand, the flywheel/driveplate should be removed from the crankshaft.

2 If a stand is not available, it's possible to disassemble the engine with it blocked up on a sturdy workbench or on the floor. Be extra careful not to tip or drop the engine when working without a stand.

3 If you are going to obtain a rebuilt engine, all external components must come off first, to be transferred to the replacement engine, just as they will if you are doing a

complete engine overhaul yourself. These include:

    Alternator and brackets
    Emissions control components
    Distributor, spark plug wires and spark
        plugs
    Thermostat and housing cover
    Water pump
    Fuel system components
    Intake/exhaust manifolds
    Oil filter
    Engine mounts
    Clutch and flywheel/driveplate

Note: When removing the external components from the engine, pay close attention to details that may be helpful or important during installation. Note the installed position of gaskets, seals, spacers, pins, washers, bolts and other small items.

4   If you are obtaining a short block, which consists of the engine block, crankshaft, pistons and connecting rods all assembled, then the cylinder head, oil pan and oil pump will have to be removed as well. See *Engine rebuilding alternatives* for additional information regarding the different possibilities to be considered.

5   If you are planning a complete overhaul, the engine should be disassembled in the following order:

Four-cylinder engine

    Flywheel/driveplate (including dowel
        pins and plate)
    Oil filler cap and tube assembly
    Crankcase vent hose
    PCV vent valve
    Carburetor or fuel injection components
    Distributor cap, spark plug wires and
        spark plugs
    EGR tube/EGR valve
    Crankshaft pulley
    Accelerator shaft bracket
    Fuel pump and pushrod (carbureted
        models)
    Water pump
    Oil pan
    Oil pump and intermediate driveshaft
    Oil filter
    Front cover and timing chain damper
    Valve cover

    Rocker arms, fulcrums and pushrods
    Thermostat
    Dipstick tube and dipstick
    Distributor
    Intake manifold
    Exhaust manifold
    Cylinder head
    Valve lifters
    Timing chain, sprockets and tensioner
    Camshaft
    Rear oil seal retainer
    Piston/connecting rod assemblies
    Crankshaft and main bearings

V6 engine

    Flywheel/driveplate (including dowel
        pins and plate)
    Oil filler cap and tube assembly
    Crankcase vent hose
    PCV vent valve
    Upper intake manifold assembly
    Valve covers
    Rocker arms and pushrods
    Intake and exhaust manifolds
    Valve lifters
    Cylinder heads
    Timing chain cover
    Timing chain and sprockets
    Camshaft
    Oil pan
    Oil pump
    Piston/connecting rod assemblies
    Crankshaft and main bearings

6   Critical cooling system components such as the hoses, the drivebelts, the thermostat and the water pump MUST be replaced with new parts when an engine is overhauled. Also, we do not recommend overhauling the oil pump - always install a new one when an engine is rebuilt.

7   Before beginning the disassembly and overhaul procedures, make sure the following items are available:

    Crankshaft damper removal/installation
        tool (V6 only)
    Common hand tools
    Small cardboard boxes or plastic bags
        for storing parts
    Gasket scraper
    Ridge reamer
    Micrometers

    Telescoping gauges
    Dial indicator set
    Valve spring compressor
    Cylinder surfacing hone
    Piston ring groove cleaning tool
    Electric drill motor
    Tap and die set
    Wire brushes
    Oil gallery brushes
    Cleaning solvent

7   Cylinder head - disassembly

Refer to illustrations 7.2, 7.3a and 7.3b
Note: New and rebuilt cylinder heads are commonly available for most engines at auto parts stores. Due to the fact that some specialized tools are necessary for the disassembly and inspection procedures, and replacement parts may not be readily available, it may be more practical and economical for the home mechanic to purchase a replacement head rather than taking the time to disassemble, inspect and recondition the original.

1   Cylinder head disassembly involves removal of the intake and exhaust valves and related components. Remove the rocker arms and fulcrums from the cylinder heads. Label the parts and store them separately so they can be reinstalled in their original locations.

2   Before the valves are removed, arrange to label and store them, along with their related components, so they can be kept separate and reinstalled in the same valve guides they are removed from **(see illustration)**.

3   Compress the springs on the first valve with a spring compressor and remove the keepers **(see illustration)**. Carefully release the valve spring compressor and remove the retainer, the valve spring, the valve spring damper, the valve stem seal and the valve. Store the components together and discard the seal. If the valve binds in the guide (won't pull through), push it back into the head and deburr the area around the keeper groove with a fine file or whetstone **(see illustration)**.

4   Repeat the above procedure for the remaining valves. Remember to keep all the

7.2 A small plastic bag, with an appropriate label, can be used to store the valve train components so they can be kept together and reinstalled in the original position

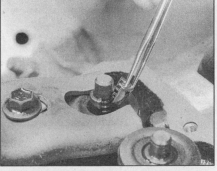

7.3a Use a valve spring compressor to compress the spring, then remove the keepers from the valve stem

7.3b If the valve won't pull through the guide, deburr the edge of the stem end and the area around the top of the keeper groove with a file or whetstone

2C

8.12 Check the cylinder head gasket surface for warpage by trying to slip a feeler gauge under the straightedge (see the Specifications for the maximum warpage allowed and use a feeler gauge of that thickness)

8.14 A dial indicator can be used to determine the valve stem-to-guide clearance (move the valve stem as indicated by the arrows)

parts for each valve together so they can be reinstalled in the same locations.

5 Once the valves and related components have been removed and stored in an organized manner, the head should be thoroughly cleaned and inspected. If a complete engine overhaul is being done, finish the engine disassembly procedures before beginning the cylinder head cleaning and inspection process.

8 Cylinder head - cleaning and inspection

Refer to illustrations 8.12, 8.14, 8.15, 8.16, 8.17 and 8.18

1 Thorough cleaning of the cylinder head and related valve train components, followed by a detailed inspection, will enable you to decide how much valve service work must be done during the engine overhaul.

Cleaning

2 Scrape away all traces of old gasket material and sealing compound from the head gasket, intake manifold and exhaust manifold sealing surfaces. Be very careful not to gouge the cylinder head. Special gasket removal solvents, which soften gaskets and make removal much easier, are available at auto parts stores.

3 Remove any built up scale from the coolant passages.

4 Run a stiff wire brush through the various holes to remove any deposits that may have formed in them.

5 Run an appropriate size tap into each of the threaded holes to remove any corrosion and thread sealant that may be present. If compressed air is available, use it to clear the holes of debris produced by this operation.

6 Clean the rocker arm bolt threads with a wire brush.

7 Clean the cylinder head with solvent and dry it thoroughly. Compressed air will speed the drying process and ensure that all holes and recessed areas are clean.

Note: Decarbonizing chemicals are available and may prove very useful when cleaning the cylinder head and valve train components. They are very caustic and should be used with caution. Be sure to follow the instructions on the container.

8 Clean the rocker arms, fulcrums and pushrods with solvent and dry them thoroughly (don't mix them up during cleaning). Compressed air will speed the drying process and can be used to clean out the oil passages.

9 Clean all the valve springs, keepers and retainers with solvent and dry them thoroughly. Do the components from one valve at a time to avoid mixing up the parts.

10 Scrape off any heavy deposits that may have formed on the valves, then use a motorized wire brush to remove deposits from the valve heads and stems. Again, make sure the valves do not get mixed up.

Inspection

Cylinder head

11 Inspect the head very carefully for cracks, evidence of coolant leakage and other damage. If cracks are found, a new cylinder head should be obtained.

12 Using a straightedge and feeler gauge, check the head gasket mating surface for warpage **(see illustration)**. If the warpage exceeds the specified limit, the head can be resurfaced at an automotive machine shop.

13 Examine the valve seats in each of the combustion chambers. If they are pitted, cracked or burned, the head will require valve service that is beyond the scope of the home mechanic.

14 Check the valve stem-to-guide clearance by measuring the lateral movement of the valve stem with a dial indicator attached securely to the head **(see illustration)**. The valve must be in the guide and approximately 1/16-inch off the seat. The total valve stem movement indicated by the gauge needle must be divided by two to obtain the actual clearance. After this is done, if there is still some doubt regarding the

condition of the valve guides they should be checked by an automotive machine shop (the cost should be minimal).

Valves

15 Carefully inspect each valve face for uneven wear, deformation, cracks, pits and burned spots. Check the valve stem for scuffing and galling and the neck for cracks. Rotate the valve and check for any obvious indication that it's bent. Look for pits and excessive wear on the end of the stem. The presence of any of these conditions indicates the need for valve service by an automotive machine shop. Also measure the valve stem diameter with a micrometer in the most-worn areas and compare your measurements to this Chapter's Specifications **(see illustration)**. Replace any valves with excessive stem wear.

16 Measure the margin width on each valve **(see illustration)**. Any valve with a margin narrower than 1 /32-inch will have to be replaced with a new one.

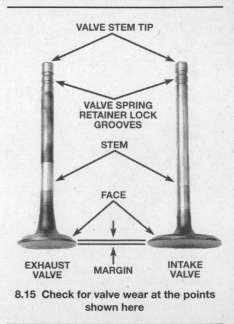

VALVE STEM TIP

VALVE SPRING RETAINER LOCK GROOVES

STEM

FACE

EXHAUST VALVE   MARGIN   INTAKE VALVE

8.15 Check for valve wear at the points shown here

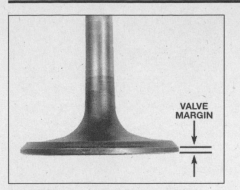

8.16 The margin width on each valve must be as specified (if no margin exists, the valve cannot be reused)

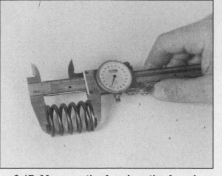

8.17 Measure the free length of each valve spring with a dial or vernier caliper

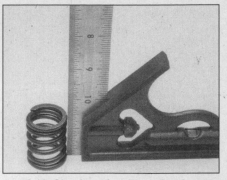

8.18 Check each valve spring for squareness

Valve components

17　Check each valve spring for wear (on the ends) and pits. Measure the free length and compare it to the Specifications **(see illustration)**. Any springs that are shorter than specified have sagged and should not be reused. The tension of all springs should be checked with a special fixture before deciding that they are suitable for use in a rebuilt engine (take the springs to an automotive machine shop for this check).

18　Stand each spring on a flat surface and check it for squareness **(see illustration)**. If any of the springs are distorted or sagged, replace all of them with new parts.

19　Check the spring retainers and keepers for obvious wear and cracks. Any questionable parts should be replaced with new ones, as extensive damage will occur if they fail during engine operation.

Rocker arm components

20　Check the rocker arm faces (the areas that contact the pushrod ends and valve stems) for pits, wear, galling, score marks and rough spots. Check the rocker arm fulcrum contact areas and fulcrums as well. Look for cracks in each rocker arm.

21　Inspect the pushrod ends for scuffing and excessive wear. Roll each pushrod on a flat surface, such as a piece of plate glass, to determine if it's bent.

22　Check the rocker arm bolts for damaged threads.

23　Any damaged or excessively worn parts must be replaced with new ones.

24　If the inspection process indicates that the valve components are in generally poor condition and worn beyond the limits specified, which is usually the case in an engine that is being overhauled, reassemble the valves in the cylinder head and refer to Section 9 for valve servicing recommendations.

25　If the inspection turns up no excessively worn parts, and if the valve faces and seats are in good condition, the valve train components can be reinstalled in the cylinder head without major servicing. Refer to the appropriate Section for the cylinder head reassembly procedure.

9　Valves - servicing

1　Because of the complex nature of the job and the special tools and equipment needed, servicing of the valves, the valve seats and the valve guides, commonly known as a valve job, is best left to a professional.

2　The home mechanic can remove and disassemble the head, do the initial cleaning and inspection, then reassemble and deliver the head to a dealer service department or an automotive machine shop for the actual valve servicing.

3　The dealer service department, or automotive machine shop, will remove the valves and springs, recondition or replace the valves and valve seats, recondition the valve guides, check and replace the valve springs, spring retainers and keepers as required, replace the valve seals with new ones, reassemble the valve components and make sure the installed spring height is correct. The cylinder head gasket surface will also be resurfaced if it's warped.

4　After the valve job has been performed by a professional. the head will be in like new condition. When the head is returned, be sure to clean it again before installation on the engine to remove any metal particles and abrasive grit that may still be present from the valve service or head resurfacing operations. Use compressed air, if available, to blow out all the oil holes and passages. Caution: *Wear eye protection.*

10　Cylinder head - reassembly

Refer to illustrations 10.6 and 10.8

1　Regardless of whether or not the head was sent to an automotive repair shop for valve servicing, make sure it's clean before beginning reassembly .

2　If the head was sent out for valve servicing, the valves and related components will already be in place. Refer to Step 8.

3　Beginning at one end of the head, lubricate and install the first valve. Apply moly-base grease or clean engine oil to the valve stem.

4　Slide a new valve stem seal over the valve and seat it on the guide with a deep socket and hammer (gently tap the seal until it's completely seated on the guide). Be very careful not to deform or cock the seal during installation. **Note:** *Intake and exhaust valve seals are different. On four cylinder models, the intake seals normally have a wide band near the base and a ring at the top, while exhaust seals have two rings. On the V6 engine, the intake seals have a silver band and the exhaust seals have a red band - DO NOT mix them up!*

5　Install valve spring seats or shims if any, then set the valve spring, damper and retainer in place.

6　Compress the springs with a valve spring compressor. Position the keepers in the valve stem grooves, then slowly release the compressor and make sure the keepers seat properly. Apply a small dab of grease to each keeper to hold it in place if necessary **(see illustration)**.

7　Repeat the same procedure for each valve. Be sure to return the components to their original locations - don't mix them up!

8　Check the installed valve spring height with a dial caliper or a ruler graduated in 1/64-inch increments. If the head was sent out for service work, the installed height should be correct (but don't automatically assume that it is). The measurement is taken from the underside of the spring retainer to the top of the spring

10.6 Apply a small dab of grease to each keeper as shown here before installation - it'll hold them in place on the valve stem as the spring is released

2C

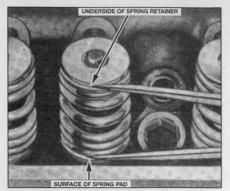

10.8 Be sure to check the valve spring installed height (the distance from the bottom of the spring retainer to the upper surface of the spring seat or shim)

11.1a To keep the crankshaft from turning, thread a couple of flywheel or driveplate bolts into the crankshaft and have an assistant wedge a large screwdriver between them . . .

11.1b . . . while you loosen the crankshaft pulley bolt with a breaker bar and socket

seat or shim **(see illustration)**. If the height is greater than specified, shims can be added under the springs to correct it. **Caution:** *Do not, under any circumstances, shim the springs to the point where the installed height is less than specified.*

9   Reinstall the rocker arms and fulcrums (see part A or B of this Chapter).

11   Crankshaft front oil seal - replacement

Refer to illustrations 11.1a, 11.1b, 11.2, 11.3, 11.4, 11.5 and 11.7

1   With the engine out of the vehicle and the crankshaft immobilized **(see illustration)**, remove the pulley mounting bolt with a breaker bar **(see illustration)**.
2   On four-cylinder models, remove the pulley from the crankshaft with a puller **(see illustration)**.
3   On V6 engines, use a bolt-type damper puller to remove the damper. **Caution:** *Do not use gear puller as it will damage the damper. Use a puller with bolts that thread into hub* **(see illustration)**.
4   Using a large screwdriver, carefully pry the oil seal out of the cover **(see illustration)**.
5   Clean the bore in the cover and coat the outer edge of the new seal with engine oil or

11.2 Though the pulley on some engines may slide off the crankshaft easily, a puller may be needed on some (four-cylinder engines only)

multi-purpose grease. Using a socket with an outside diameter slightly smaller than the outside diameter of the seal, carefully drive the new seal into place with a hammer **(see illustration)**. If a socket isn't available, a short section of large-diameter pipe will work. Check the seal after installation to be sure that the spring didn't pop out of place.
6   On four-cylinder models, apply multipurpose grease to the seal contact surface of the pulley hub, then slide the pulley onto the crankshaft. The keyway in the pulley hub must be aligned with the Woodruff key in the

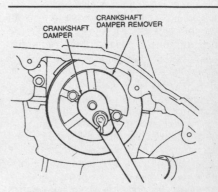

11.3 On V6 engines, when removing the crankshaft damper, use a standard bolt-type puller, available at most auto parts stores. DO NOT use a jaw-type puller!

crankshaft nose. Install the bolt and tighten it to the torque listed in this Chapter's Specifications.
7   On V6 engines, apply RTV sealant to the keyway in the damper and position the damper on the crankshaft. Be sure the keyway is aligned with the crankshaft key. Install the damper using an installation tool **(see illustration)**. If unavailable, start the damper with a soft-faced hammer and finish installation using the damper retaining bolt. Tighten the bolt to the torque listed in this Chapter's Specifications.

11.4 Carefully pry the front cover seal out with a screwdriver (be careful not to nick or gouge the seal bore walls)

11.5 Clean the bore, then apply grease or oil to the outer edge of the new seal and drive it squarely into the opening with a large socket and hammer - DO NOT damage the seal in the process!

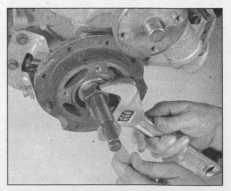

11.7 On V6 engines, press the crankshaft damper into place with a special installation tool like the one shown

12.4a Remove all six front cover bolts . . .

12.4b . . . then wedge a screwdriver between the right engine mount bracket bolt and the lug on the cover and gently pry the cover off (it's made of aluminum, so be very careful not to damage it)

12.5 Remove and inspect the timing chain damper assembly - if it's heavily worn, replace it

12 Front cover, timing chain and sprockets - removal, wear checks and installation

Four-cylinder engine

Refer to illustrations 12.4a, 12.4b, 12.5, 12.6, 12.11, 12.12, 12.14, 12.20a and 12.20b

Timing chain cover removal

1   The engine must be removed from the vehicle for this procedure (see Section 5).
2   Remove the oil pan (see Chapter 2A).
3   Remove the crankshaft pulley (see Section 11).
4   Remove the front cover mounting bolts **(see illustration)**. Pry the cover away from the block with a large screwdriver or pry bar **(see illustration)**. **Caution:** *Pry only at the point shown or damage to the gasket mating surfaces may result and oil leaks could develop.*
5   Remove the timing chain damper assembly from the cover **(see illustration)** and inspect it for wear. If it's excessively worn, replace it.
6   Remove the bolts and detach the timing chain tensioner **(see illustration)**. Check the tensioner slipper (the surface on which the chain rides). If grooves more than 0.060-inch deep are present, replace the tensioner.

Timing chain wear check

7   Turn the crankshaft in a counter-clockwise direction (viewed from the front of the engine) to take up the slack on the left side of the chain.
8   Make a reference mark on the block at the approximate mid-point of the left chain run, then measure from the point to the chain and record the distance.
9   Turn the crankshaft in the other direction to take up the slack on the right side of the chain. Force the left side of the chain out with your finger and take a second measurement from the reference mark on the block.
10   Subtract the first measurement from the second measurement to obtain the chain deflection. Compare it to this Chapter's Specifications. If chain deflection is excessive, replace the chain and both sprockets with new ones.

Timing chain and sprockets - removal

11   Turn the crankshaft until the timing marks on the sprockets are aligned **(see illustration)**. The marks are small dimples drilled near the outer edges.
12   Remove the camshaft sprocket mounting bolt and washer. If the crankshaft turns, install a couple of flywheel bolts in the rear end of the crankshaft and wedge a screwdriver between them. Slide both sprockets

and the timing chain forward **(see illustration)** and remove them as an assembly. **Note:** *If the camshaft or crankshaft are moved while the timing chain and sprockets are off the engine, they'll have to be repositioned to exactly where they were before removal or the timing marks will not line up on installation.*

Timing chain and sprockets - installation

13   Use a gasket scraper to remove all traces of old gasket material and sealant from the cover and engine block, then clean the mating surfaces with a cloth saturated with lacquer thinner or acetone. Clean the chain and sprockets with solvent.
14   Make sure the dowel pin in the camshaft and the Woodruff key in the crankshaft are in place, then slide both sprockets and the timing chain onto the shafts with the timing marks aligned **(see illustration overleaf)**. Each sprocket has a slot that must be aligned with the pin in the camshaft or the key in the crankshaft. Install the camshaft bolt and washer and tighten the bolt to the torque listed in this Chapter's Specifications. **Note:** *The washer on the camshaft sprocket bolt must be installed with the chamfer OUT, facing the bolt head (which means that the flat side of the washer must be next to the*

2C

12.6 To detach the timing chain tensioner, simply remove the two mounting bolts (arrows)

12.11 Rotate the crankshaft until the timing marks (arrows) on the sprockets are aligned opposite each other as shown here

12.12 Remove the camshaft sprocket, crankshaft sprocket and timing chain as an assembly - the chain doesn't have enough sideplay to allow for sprocket removal one at a time

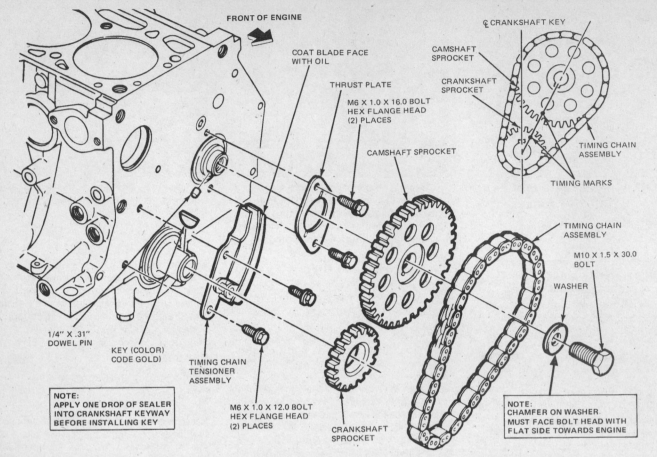

FRONT OF ENGINE

COAT BLADE FACE WITH OIL

THRUST PLATE

M6 X 1.0 X 16.0 BOLT HEX FLANGE HEAD (2) PLACES

CAMSHAFT SPROCKET

¢ CRANKSHAFT KEY

CAMSHAFT SPROCKET

CRANKSHAFT SPROCKET

TIMING CHAIN ASSEMBLY

TIMING MARKS

TIMING CHAIN ASSEMBLY

M10 X 1.5 X 30.0 BOLT

WASHER

1/4" X .31" DOWEL PIN

KEY (COLOR) CODE GOLD)

TIMING CHAIN TENSIONER ASSEMBLY

NOTE: APPLY ONE DROP OF SEALER INTO CRANKSHAFT KEYWAY BEFORE INSTALLING KEY

M6 X 1.0 X 12.0 BOLT HEX FLANGE HEAD (2) PLACES

CRANKSHAFT SPROCKET

NOTE: CHAMFER ON WASHER MUST FACE BOLT HEAD WITH FLAT SIDE TOWARDS ENGINE

12.14 Four-cylinder engine timing chain/sprockets and related components - exploded view (note the installed location of the chamfer on the camshaft sprocket washer)

sprocket). Install the tensioner and tighten the bolts to the torque listed in this Chapter's Specifications. Lubricate the timing chain, sprockets and tensioner with engine oil. Position the chain damper assembly in the front cover.

Front cover installation - factory method

Note: *The following method for front cover installation, which is recommended by the factory, requires that the new crankshaft oil seal be installed in the cover after the cover is installed on the engine. That's because the seal lip actually seals against the pulley hub rather than the crankshaft, which makes it difficult to align the cover precisely without the pulley in place on the crankshaft. However, the factory procedure also requires a special front cover alignment tool that slides onto the nose of the crankshaft. If you don 't have access to the tool and/or don't want to purchase it, the alternative procedure (steps 20 through 26) works just as well, IF YOU DO IT CAREFULLY!*

15   Apply a thin layer of RTV sealant to both sides of the new front cover gasket and position the gasket on the cover. Slip a couple of bolts through the holes in the cover to support the gasket.

16   Position the front cover on the engine

(remember, the seal will be installed after the cover is bolted in place).

17   Slide the special alignment tool onto the end of the crankshaft. Make sure that the crankshaft key is aligned with the keyway in the tool.

18   Install the cover bolts and tighten them in a criss-cross pattern. Work up to the final torque in three steps. Remove the alignment tool.

19   Install the new seal and the crankshaft pulley (see Section 11).

12.20a While supporting the cover near the seal bore, drive the old seal out from the inside with a punch and hammer

Front cover installation - alternative method

20   If not already done, remove the original seal from the cover and install a new one **(see illustrations).**

21   Apply a thin layer of RTV sealant to both sides of the new front cover gasket and position the gasket on the cover. Slip a couple of bolts through the holes in the cover to support the gasket.

22   Attach the front cover and gasket to the

12.20b Clean the bore, then apply a small amount of grease or oil to the outer edge of the new seal and drive it squarely into the opening with a large socket and a hammer - DO NOT damage the seal in the process!

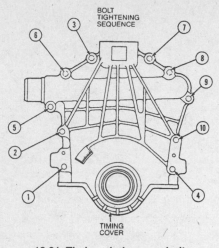

12.31 Timing chain cover bolt identification and tightening sequence (V6 engine)

12.33 Scrape away all gasket material, then clean the mating surfaces with lacquer thinner or acetone

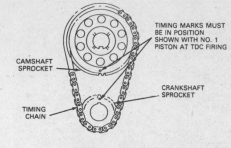

12.35 Aligning the timing marks (V6 engine)

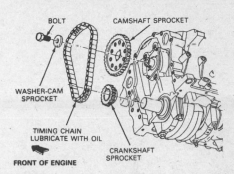

12.36 An exploded view of the timing chain components (V6 engine)

engine. Install, but do not tighten, the cover mounting bolts.

23 Lubricate the pulley hub seal contact surface with moly-base grease and slide the pulley onto the crankshaft with one hand while supporting the front cover with the other hand. Make sure the Woodruff key in the crankshaft is aligned with the keyway in the pulley hub. If the cover is slightly misaligned, it will center itself when the pulley hub is pushed through the seal lip.

24 Tighten the front cover mounting bolts in a criss-cross pattern. Work up to the final torque in listed in this Chapter's Specifications in three steps.

25 Install the pulley, pulley bolt and washer and tighten the bolt to the torque listed in this Chapter's Specifications (see Section 11).

26 Install the oil pan (see Chapter 2A).

V6 engine

Refer to illustrations 12.31, 12.33, 12.35, 12.36, 12.39 and 12.42

Timing chain wear check

27 This procedure is described in Chapter 2, Part B.

Timing chain cover removal

28 Remove the engine from the vehicle (refer to Section 5) and remove the oil pan (see Chapter 2B).

29 Remove the crankshaft damper (see Section 11).

30 Remove the water pump from the timing chain cover (see Chapter 3). **Note:** *The water pump may be removed with the front cover as an assembly, if desired.*

31 Remove the ten timing chain cover attaching bolts **(see illustration).**

32 Tap the cover loose with a soft-face hammer or carefully pry it loose with a flat-bladed screwdriver and remove it from the engine. **Caution:** *Do not use excessive force or you may crack the cover. If the cover is*

difficult to remove, recheck for remaining bolts.

33 Thoroughly clean and inspect all parts and remove all traces of gasket material **(see illustration).** Remove oil film with a solvent such as lacquer thinner or acetone.

Timing chain and sprockets - removal

34 Position the number one piston at Top Dead Center (see Chapter 2B).

35 Check that the upper and lower timing chain sprocket marks are aligned **(see illustration).** If they are not, temporarily install the crankshaft damper bolt and use it to turn the crankshaft clockwise until the two marks are adjacent to each other.

36 Remove the camshaft sprocket retaining bolt and washer **(see illustration)**

37 Pull the camshaft sprocket away from the engine and move it down slightly to release the chain from the crankshaft sprocket.

38 If the crankshaft sprocket won't come off by hand, carefully pry it off with two screwdrivers.

Timing chain and sprockets - installation

39 Reinstall the crankshaft sprocket **(see illustration),** making sure the keyway and timing mark are at the top (12 o'clock position).

40 If the sprocket is difficult to install, slip a

length of pipe over the crankshaft and tap the sprocket into place with a small hammer. Make sure the key does not slip out of place.

41 Place the chain around the camshaft sprocket with the timing mark facing down (six o'clock position). Slip the chain over the crankshaft sprocket and position the camshaft sprocket on the camshaft. Tighten the bolt to the torque listed in this Chapter's Specifications. **Note:** *Inspect the cam bolt for blockage in its oil holes prior to installing.* **Caution:** *This bolt transmits pressurized oil and should never be replaced with a standard bolt or severe engine damage will result.*

42 At this point, the timing marks should be adjacent (camshaft sprocket mark at six o'clock and crankshaft sprocket mark at 12 o'clock) **(see illustration). Caution:** *Severe engine damage could result from improper timing. Rotate the engine very slowly*

12.39 The crankshaft sprocket should have the keyway at the top (12 o'clock) (V6 engine)

12.42 The timing marks (arrows) should be directly across from each other (V6 engine)

2C

13.8 The lifters in an engine that has accumulated many miles may have to be removed with a special tool - be sure to store lifters in an organized manner to make sure they are reinstalled in their original locations

13.13 After removing the thrust plate, thread a bolt into the end of the camshaft to use as a handle during removal and installation

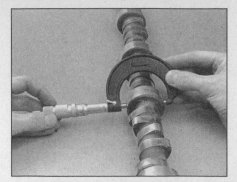

13.16 The camshaft bearing journal diameters are checked to pinpoint excessive wear and out-of-round conditions

clockwise, through two revolutions, using a wrench on the crankshaft bolt. If anything hits, do not force the engine to turn; back up and recheck the timing procedure.

Front cover installation

43   Install the new gasket on the engine over the dowels. Use RTV sealant to hold it in place. Position the cover on the engine.

44   Apply pipe sealant to the threads of bolts 2 and 5 in the tightening sequence. Tighten the bolts to the torque listed in this Chapter's Specifications in the sequence shown **(see illustration 12.31)**.

45   Reinstall the remaining parts in the reverse order of removal.

---

13 Camshaft and bearings - removal, inspection and installation

Refer to illustrations 13.8, 13.13, 13.16, 13.18 and 13.22

Removal

1   The camshaft cannot be removed with the engine in the vehicle. If camshaft replacement is required, the engine must be removed before proceeding

2   Remove the drivebelts (refer to Chapter 1).

3   Remove the crankshaft pulley/damper (see Section 11) and the oil pan (see Chapter 2A or 2B).

4   Remove the front cover, timing chain and sprockets. On four-cylinder engines remove the chain tensioner (see Section 12).

5   On four-cylinder models, remove the valve cover, pushrods and the cylinder head with intake and exhaust manifold assemblies attached (see Chapter 2A).

6   On V6 engines, remove the valve covers, pushrods, distributor, intake manifold and roller lifter guide retainer and guides (see Chapter 2B).

7   Before removing the lifters, arrange to store them in a clearly labeled box or in individually labeled plastic bags to ensure that they are reinstalled in their original

locations. If the roller lifters are not marked to indicate which side faces the front of the engine, be sure to mark them so they can be reinstalled exactly as they were (the roller must turn the same direction).

8   There are several ways to extract the lifters from the bores. A special tool designed to grip and remove lifters **(see illustration)** is manufactured by many tool companies and is widely available, but it may not be required in every case. On newer engines without a lot of varnish buildup, the lifters can often be removed with a small magnet. A machinist's scribe with a bent end can also be used to pull the lifters out by positioning the point under the retainer ring in the top of each lifter. DO NOT attempt to withdraw the camshaft from the block with the lifters in place!

9   Once the lifters have been removed, store them where they won't get dirty.

10   Mount a dial indicator on the engine, check the camshaft endplay and compare it to the Specifications. If it's excessive, a new thrust plate should correct it.

11   If your four-cylinder engine is equipped with a carburetor, remove the fuel pump, gasket and pump pushrod (see Chapter 4 if necessary).

12   Remove the two bolts and detach the camshaft thrust plate from the block.

13   Thread a bolt into the end of the camshaft to use as a handle when removing the camshaft from the block **(see illustration)**.

14   Carefully pull the camshaft out. Support it near the block so the lobes don't nick or gouge the bearings as it is withdrawn.

Inspection

Camshaft and bearings

15   After the camshaft has been removed from the engine, cleaned with solvent and dried, inspect the bearing journals for uneven wear, pitting and evidence of seizure. If the journals are damaged, the bearing inserts in the block are probably damaged as well. Both the camshaft and the bearings will have to be replaced.

16   If they're in good condition, measure the bearing journals with a micrometer **(see illustration)** to determine their size and whether

or not they're out-of-round. The inside diameter of each bearing can be measured with a telescoping gauge and micrometer. Subtract each cam journal diameter from the corresponding bearing inside diameter to obtain the bearing oil clearance. Compare the clearance for each bearing to the Specifications. If it's excessive for any of the bearings, have new bearings installed by an automotive machine shop.

17   Check the camshaft lobes for heat discoloration, score marks, chipped areas, pitting and uneven wear. If the lobes are in good condition and the lobe lift measurements are within the specified limits, the camshaft can be reinstalled (assuming that the bearing journals are in acceptable condition).

18   Camshaft lobe lift can be checked with the camshaft installed in the engine (refer to Chapter 2A or 2B) or after it has been removed using the following procedure. Measure the major (A) and minor (B) diameters of each lobe with a vernier caliper or a micrometer and record the results **(see**

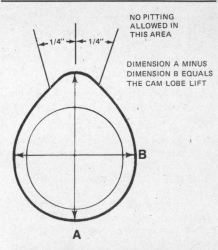

NO PITTING ALLOWED IN THIS AREA

1/4"   1/4"

DIMENSION A MINUS DIMENSION B EQUALS THE CAM LOBE LIFT

B

A

13.18 To determine camshaft lobe lift, measure the major (A) and minor (B) diameters of each lobe with a micrometer or vernier caliper - subtract each minor diameter from the major diameter to arrive at the lobe lift

13.22 Be sure to apply moly-base grease or engine assembly lube to the cam lobes and bearing journals before installing the camshaft

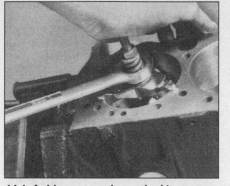

14.1 A ridge reamer is required to remove the ridge from the top of each cylinder - do this before removing the pistons!

14.3 Check the connecting rod side clearance with a feeler gauge as shown

illustration). The difference between the two is the lobe lift. If the measured lift for any lobe is less than specified, replace the camshaft.

Lifters

19   For lifter inspection criteria, refer to the appropriate section in Chapter 2A or 2B.
20   Never install used lifters unless the original camshaft is used and the lifters can be installed in their original locations.

Bearing replacement

21   Camshaft bearing replacement requires special tools and expertise that place it outside the scope of the home mechanic. Take the block to an automotive machine shop to ensure that the job is done correctly.

Installation

22   Lubricate the camshaft lobes and journals with moly-base grease or engine assembly lube **(see illustration)**.
23   Slide the camshaft into the engine. Support the cam near the block and be very careful not to scrape or nick the bearings.
24   Apply moly-base grease to the rear of the thrust plate, then install it on the block and tighten the mounting bolts to the torque listed in this Chapter's Specifications.

14.5 To prevent damage to the crankshaft journals and cylinder walls, slip sections of hose over the rod bolts before removing the pistons

25   If installing a new camshaft, mount a dial indicator on the engine, check the camshaft endplay and compare it to the Specifications. If it's excessive, a new thrust plate should correct it.
26   Install the timing chain, sprockets, timing chain tensioner (four-cylinder only), front cover, oil seal and crankshaft pulley (see Sections 11 and 12).
27   The remaining installation steps are the reverse of removal (see Chapter 2A or 2B).

14   Piston/connecting rod assembly - removal

Refer to Illustrations 14.1, 14.3 and 14.5
Note: *Prior to removing the piston/connecting rod assemblies, remove the cylinder head, the oil pan and the oil pump by referring to the appropriate Sections in Chapter 2, Part A or B.*
1   Completely remove the ridge at the top of each cylinder with a ridge reaming tool **(see illustration)**. Follow the manufacturer's instructions provided with the tool. Failure to remove the ridges before attempting to remove the piston/connecting rod assemblies will result in piston breakage.
2   After the cylinder ridges have been removed, turn the engine upside-down so the crankshaft is facing up.
3   Before the connecting rods are removed, check the endplay (side clearance) with feeler gauges. Slide them between the first connecting rod and the crankshaft throw until the play is removed **(see illustration)**. The endplay is equal to the thickness of the feeler gauge(s). If the endplay exceeds the service limit, new connecting rods will be required. If new rods (or a new crankshaft) are installed, the endplay may fall under the specified minimum (if it does, the rods will have to be machined to restore it - consult an automotive machine shop for advice, if necessary). Repeat the procedure for the remaining connecting rods.
4   Check the connecting rods and caps for identification marks. If they aren't plainly marked, use a small center punch

to make the appropriate number of indentations on each rod and cap (1, 2 ,3, etc., depending on the cylinder they are associated with).
5   Loosen each of the connecting rod cap nuts 1/2-turn at a time until they can be removed by hand. Remove the number one connecting rod cap and bearing insert. Don't drop the bearing insert out of the cap. While supporting connector rod, slip a short length of plastic or rubber hose over each connecting rod cap bolt to protect the crankshaft journal and cylinder wall when the piston is removed **(see illustration)**. Push the connecting rod/piston assembly out through the top of the engine. Use a wooden hammer handle to push on the upper bearing insert in the connecting rod. If resistance is felt, double-check to make sure that all of the ridge was removed from the cylinder.
6   Repeat the procedure for the remaining cylinders. After removal, reassemble the connecting rod caps and bearing inserts in their respective connecting rods and install the cap nuts finger tight. Leaving the old bearing inserts in place until reassembly will help prevent the connecting rod bearing surfaces from being accidentally nicked or gouged.

15   Crankshaft - removal

Refer to illustrations 15.1, 15.3, 15.4a, 15.4b and 15.4c
Note: *The crankshaft can be removed only after the engine has been removed from the vehicle. It is assumed that the flywheel or driveplate, front crankshaft pulley, timing chain and sprockets, oil pan, oil pump and piston/connecting rod assemblies have already been removed. On four-cylinder engines, the rear main oil seal housing must also be unbolted and separated from the block before proceeding with crankshaft removal.*
1   Before the crankshaft is removed, check the endplay. Mount a dial indicator with the stem in line with and just touching one of the

2C

15.1 Checking crankshaft endplay with a dial indicator

crank throws **(see illustration)**.

2   Push the crankshaft all the way to the rear and zero the dial indicator. Next, pry the crankshaft to the front as far as possible and note the reading on the dial indicator. The distance that it moves is the end play. If it's greater than specified, check the crankshaft thrust surfaces for wear. If no wear is evident, a new thrust bearing should correct the end play. If the end play is less than the minimum, check the thrust bearing surfaces for deep scratches, burrs, nicks and dirt.

3   If a dial indicator is not available, feeler gauges can be used. Gently pry or push the crankshaft all the way to the front of the

15.4a Use a center-punch or number stamping dies to mark the main bearing caps to ensure installation in their original locations on the block (make the punch marks near one of the bolt heads)

15.4c The arrow on the main bearing cap indicates the front of the engine

15.3 Checking crankshaft endplay with a feeler gauge

engine. Slip feeler gauges between the crankshaft and the front face of the thrust main bearing to determine the clearance **(see illustration)**. The thrust bearing is the upper main bearing (in the block) on the center journal (four-cylinder engines) or the number three bearing from the front of the engine (V6 engines).

4   Check the main bearing caps to see if they are marked to indicate their locations. They should be numbered consecutively from the front of the engine to the rear. If they aren't, mark them with number stamping dies or a center punch **(see illustration)**. Main bearing caps generally have a cast-in arrow, which points to the front of the engine **(see illustrations)**. Loosen the main bearing cap bolts 1/4-turn at a time each, until they can be removed by hand.

15.4b The arrow on the main bearing cap indicates the front of the engine

16.1a A hammer and a large punch can be used to knock the core plugs sideways in their bores

5   Gently tap the caps with a soft-face hammer, then separate them from the engine block. If necessary, use the bolts as levers to remove the caps. Try not to drop the bearing inserts if they come out with the caps.

6   Carefully lift the crankshaft out of the engine. It's a good idea to have an assistant available. since the crankshaft is quite heavy. With the bearing inserts in place in the engine block and main bearing caps, return the caps to their respective locations on the block and tighten the bolts finger tight.

7   Remove the Woodruff key from the crankshaft nose so it doesn't get lost. If it's hard to remove, just leave it in place.

16   Engine block - cleaning

Refer to illustrations 16.1a, 16.1b, 16.8 and 16.10

1   Use a hammer and punch to drive one edge of each core plug into the block, then use pliers to remove it **(see illustrations)**.

2   Using a gasket scraper, remove all traces of gasket material from the engine block. Be very careful not to nick or gouge the gasket sealing surfaces.

3   Remove the main bearing caps and separate the bearing inserts from the caps and the engine block. Tag the bearings, indicating which cylinder they were removed from and whether they were in the cap or the block. then set them aside.

4   Remove all of the threaded oil gallery plugs from the block. Discard the plugs and use new ones when the engine is reassembled.

5   If the engine is extremely dirty it should be taken to an automotive machine shop to be steam cleaned or hot tanked.

6   After the block is returned, clean all oil holes and oil galleries one more time. Brushes specifically designed for this purpose are available at most auto parts stores. Flush the passages with warm water until the water runs clear, dry the block thoroughly and wipe all machined surfaces with a light, rust-preventive oil. If you have access to compressed air, use it to speed the drying process and to blow out all the oil holes and galleries.

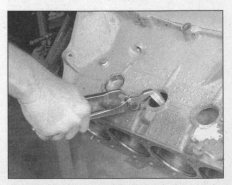

16.1b Pull the core plugs from the block with pliers

16.8 All bolt holes in the block - particularly the main bearing cap and head bolt holes - should be cleaned and restored with a tap (be sure to remove debris from the holes after this is done)

16.10 A large socket on an extension can be used to drive the new core plugs into the bores

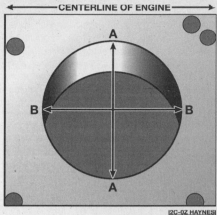

17.4a Measure the diameter of each cylinder just under the wear ridge (A), at the center (B) and at the bottom

7   If the block isn't extremely dirty or sludged up, you can do an adequate cleaning job with warm soapy water and a stiff brush. Take plenty of time and do a thorough job. Regardless of the cleaning method used, be sure to clean all oil holes and galleries very thoroughly, dry the block completely and coat all machined surfaces with light oil.

8   The threaded holes in the block must be clean to ensure accurate torque readings during reassembly. Run the proper size tap into each of the holes to remove any rust, corrosion, thread sealant or sludge and to restore any damaged threads **(see illustration)**. If possible, use compressed air to clear the holes of debris produced by this operation. Now is a good time to clean the threads on the head bolts and the main bearing cap bolts as well.

9   Reinstall the main bearing caps and tighten the bolts finger tight.

10   After coating the sealing surfaces of the new core plugs with a non-hardening sealant (such as Permatex number 2), install them in the engine block **(see illustration)**. Make sure they are driven in straight and seated properly or leakage could result. Special tools are available for this purpose, but a large socket, with an outside diameter that will just slip into the soft plug, and a hammer will work just as well.

11   Apply non-hardening sealant (such as Permatex number 2 or Teflon tape) to the new oil gallery plugs and thread them into the holes in the block. Make sure they're tightened securely.

12   If the engine isn't going to be reassembled right away, cover it with a large plastic trash bag to keep it clean.

17   Engine block- inspection

Refer to illustrations 17.4a, 17.4b and 17.4c

1   Before the block is inspected, it should be cleaned as described in Section 16. Double-check to make sure that the ridge at the top of each cylinder has been completely removed.

2   Visually check the block for cracks, rust

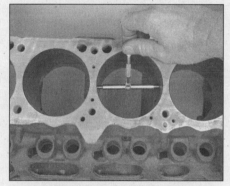

17.4b The ability to "feel" when the telescoping gauge is at the correct point will be developed over time, so work slowly and repeat the check until you're satisfied the bore measurement is accurate

and corrosion. Look for stripped threads in the threaded holes. It's also a good idea to have the block checked for hidden cracks by an automotive machine shop that has the special equipment to do this type of work. If defects are found, have the block repaired, if possible, or replaced.

3   Check the cylinder bores for scuffing and scoring.

4   Measure the diameter of each cylinder at the top (just under the ridge area), center and bottom of the cylinder bore, parallel to the crankshaft axis **(see illustrations)**.

5   Next, measure each cylinder's diameter at the same three locations across the crankshaft axis. Compare the results to this Chapter's Specifications.

6   Bore service limit is equal to the average of the two "B" measurements.

7   Taper is equal to the difference of the "A" and "C" measurements across the crankshaft axis.

8   Out-of-round is equal to the difference between the two "B" measurements.

9   If the required precision measuring tools aren't available, the piston-to-cylinder clearances can be obtained, though not quite as accurately, using feeler gauge stock. Feeler gauge stock comes in 12-inch lengths and various thicknesses and is generally available at auto parts stores.

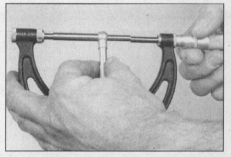

17.4c The gauge is then measured with a micrometer to determine the bore size

10   To check the clearance, select a feeler gauge and slip it into the cylinder along with the matching piston. The piston must be positioned exactly as it normally would be. The feeler gauge must be between the piston and cylinder on one of the thrust faces (90-degrees to the piston pin bore).

11   The piston should slip through the cylinder (with the feeler gauge in place) with moderate pressure.

12   If it falls through or slides through easily, the clearance is excessive and a new piston will be required. If the piston binds at the lower end of the cylinder and is loose toward the top, the cylinder is tapered. If tight spots are encountered as the piston/feeler gauge is rotated in the cylinder, the cylinder is out-of-round.

13   Repeat the procedure for the remaining pistons and cylinders.

14   If the cylinder walls are badly scuffed or scored, or if they're out-of- round or tapered beyond the limits given in this Chapter's Specifications, have the engine block rebored and honed at an automotive machine shop. If a rebore is done, oversize pistons and rings will be required.

15   If the cylinders are in reasonably good condition and not worn to the outside of the limits, and if the piston-to-cylinder clearances can be maintained properly, they don't have to be rebored. Honing is all that's necessary (see Section 18). If a rebore is done,

oversize pistons and rings will be required. **Note:** *Ford recommends that if the bore diameter is in the lower 1/3 of the specified range, a red piston should be used. If the bore diameter is in the middle of the specified range, a blue piston should be used and if the bore diameter is in the upper 1/3 of the range, a yellow piston should be used.*

18 Cylinder honing

Refer to illustrations 18.3a and 18.3b

1   Prior to engine reassembly, the cylinder bores must be honed so the new piston rings will seat correctly and provide the best possible combustion chamber seal. **Note:** *If you don't have the tools or don't want to tackle the honing operation, most automotive machine shops will do it for a reasonable fee.*
2   Before honing the cylinders, install the main bearing caps and tighten the bolts to the specified torque.
3   Two types of cylinder hones are commonly available - the flex hone or ''bottle brush'' type and the more traditional surfacing hone with spring-loaded stones. Both will do the job, but for the less experienced mechanic the "bottle brush" hone will probably be easier to use. You'll also need plenty of light oil or honing oil, some rags and an electric drill motor. Proceed as follows:

a) *Mount the hone in the drill motor, compress the stones and slip it into the first cylinder* **(see illustration).**
b) *Lubricate the cylinder with plenty of oil, turn on the drill and move the hone up-and-down in the cylinder at a pace which will produce a fine crosshatch pattern on the cylinder walls. Ideally, the crosshatch lines should intersect at approximately a 60° angle* **(see illustration).** *Be sure to use plenty of lubricant and don't take off any more material than is absolutely necessary to produce the desired finish.* **Note:** *Piston ring manufacturers may specify a smaller crosshatch angle than the traditional 60-degrees - read and follow any instructions printed on the piston ring packages.*
c) *Don't withdraw the hone from the cylinder while it's running. Instead, shut off the drill and continue moving the hone up-and down in the cylinder until it comes to a complete stop, then compress the stones and withdraw the hone. If you're using a "bottle brush'' type hone, stop the drill motor, then turn the chuck in the normal direction of rotation while withdrawing the hone from the cylinder.*
d) *Wipe the oil out of the cylinder and repeat the procedure for the remaining cylinders.*

4   After the honing job is complete, chamfer the top edges of the cylinder bores with a small file so the rings won't catch when the pistons are installed. Be very careful not to nick the cylinder walls with the end of the file.

18.3a A "bottle brush" hone will produce better results if you've never honed cylinders before

5   The entire engine block must be washed again very thoroughly with warm, soapy water to remove all traces of the abrasive grit produced during the honing operation. **Note:** *The bores can be considered clean when a white cloth - dampened with clean engine oil - used to wipe down the bores doesn't pick up any more honing residue, which will show up as gray areas on the cloth. Be sure to run a brush through all oil holes and galleries and flush them with running water.*
6   After rinsing, dry the block and apply a coat of light rust preventive oil to all machined surfaces. Wrap the block in a plastic trash bag to keep it clean and set it aside until reassembly.

19 Piston/connecting rod assembly - inspection

Refer to illustrations 19.4a, 19.4b, 19.10 and 19.11

1   Before the inspection process can be carried out, the piston/connecting rod assemblies must be cleaned and the original piston rings removed from the pistons. **Note:** *Always use new piston rings when the engine is reassembled.*
2   Using a piston ring installation tool, carefully remove the rings from the pistons. Be careful not to nick or gouge the pistons in the process.
3   Scrape all traces of carbon from the crown (top) of the piston. A hand-held wire brush or a piece of fine emery cloth can be

19.4a The piston ring grooves can be cleaned with a special tool, as shown here . . .

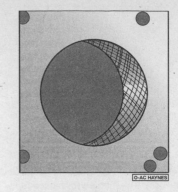

18.3b The cylinder hone should leave a smooth, crosshatch pattern with the lines intersecting at approximately a 60-degree angle

used once the majority of the deposits have been scraped away. Do not, under any circumstances, use a wire brush mounted in a drill motor to remove deposits from the pistons. The piston material is soft and will be eroded away by the wire brush.
4   Use a piston ring groove cleaning tool to remove carbon deposits from the ring grooves **(see illustration).** If a ring groove cleaning tool isn't available, use a broken piece from one of the old rings **(see illustration).** Be very careful to remove only the carbon deposits - don't remove any metal and do not nick or scratch the sides of the ring grooves.
5   Once the deposits have been removed, clean the piston/rod assemblies with solvent and dry them with compressed air (if available). Make sure that the oil return holes in the back sides of the ring grooves are clear.
6   If the pistons aren't damaged or worn excessively, and if the engine block isn't rebored, new pistons won't be necessary. Normal piston wear appears as even vertical wear on the piston thrust surfaces and slight looseness of the top ring in its groove. New piston rings, on the other hand, should always be used when an engine is rebuilt.
7   Carefully inspect each piston for cracks around the skirt, at the pin bosses and at the ring lands.
8   Look for scoring and scuffing on the

19.4b . . . or a section of a broken ring

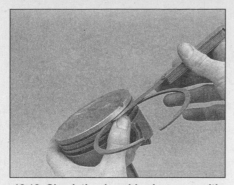

19.10 Check the ring side clearance with a feeler gauge at several points around the groove

19.11 Measure the piston diameter at a 90-degree angle to the piston pin and in line with it

20.2 Measure the diameter of each crankshaft journal at several points to detect taper and out-of-round conditions

2C

thrust faces of the skirt, holes in the piston crown and burned areas at the edge of the crown. If the skirt is scored or scuffed, the engine may have been suffering from overheating and/or abnormal combustion, which caused excessively high operating temperatures. The cooling and lubrication systems should be checked thoroughly. A hole in the piston crown is an indication that abnormal combustion (pre-ignition) was occurring. Burned areas at the edge of the piston crown are usually evidence of spark knock (detonation). If any of the above conditions are noted, the causes must be corrected or the damage will occur again.

9   Corrosion of the piston, in the form of small pits, indicates that coolant is leaking into the combustion chamber and/or the crankcase. Again, the cause must be corrected or the problem may persist in the rebuilt engine.

10   Measure the piston ring side clearance by laying a new piston ring in each ring groove and slipping a feeler gauge in beside it **(see illustration)**. Check the clearance at three or four locations around each groove. Be sure to use the correct ring for each groove - they are different. If the side clearance is greater than specified, new pistons will have to be used.

11   Check the piston-to-bore clearance by measuring the bore (see Section 17) and the piston diameter. Make sure that the pistons and bores are correctly matched. Measure the piston across the skirt, at a 90-degree angle to and in line with the piston pin **(see illustration)**. Subtract the piston diameter from the bore diameter to obtain the clearance. If it's greater than specified, the block will have to be rebored and new pistons and rings installed.

12   Check the piston-to-rod clearance by twisting the piston and rod in opposite directions. Any noticeable play indicates that there is excessive wear, which must be corrected. The piston/connecting rod assemblies should be taken to an automotive machine shop to have the pistons and rods rebored and new pins installed.

13   If the pistons must be removed from the connecting rods for any reason, they should be taken to an automotive machine shop.

While they are there, have the connecting rods checked for bend and twist, since automotive machine shops have special equipment for this purpose. **Note:** *Unless new pistons and/or connecting rods must be installed, do not disassemble the pistons and connecting rods.*

14   Check the connecting rods for cracks and other damage. Temporarily remove the rod caps, lift out the old bearing inserts, wipe the rod and cap bearing surfaces clean and inspect them for nicks, gouges and scratches. After checking the rods, replace the old bearings, slip the caps into place and tighten the nuts finger tight.

20   Crankshaft - inspection

Refer to illustration 20.2

1   Clean the crankshaft with solvent and dry it with compressed air (if available). Be sure to clean the oil holes with a stiff brush and flush them with solvent. Check the main and connecting rod bearing journals for uneven wear, scoring, pits and cracks. Check the rest of the crankshaft for cracks and other damage.

2   Using a micrometer, measure the diameter of the main and connecting rod journals and compare the results to the Specifications **(see illustration)**. By measuring the

diameter at a number of points around each journal's circumference, you'll be able to determine whether or not the journal is out-of-round. Take the measurement at each end of the journal, near the crank throws, to determine if the journal is tapered.

3   If the crankshaft journals are damaged, tapered, out-of-round or worn beyond the limits given in the Specifications, have the crankshaft reground by an automotive machine shop. Be sure to use the correct size bearing inserts if the crankshaft is reconditioned.

4   Check the oil seal journals at the rear of the crankshaft and on the front pulley/damper for wear and damage. If the seal has worn a groove in the journal, or if it is nicked or scratched, the new seal may leak. Small nicks and scratches can be dressed with crocus cloth. However, major grooves or dings are best left for a machine shop to repair. If repair is not feasible, a replacement crankshaft or damper should be installed.

5   Refer to Section 21 and examine the main and rod bearing inserts.

21   Main and connecting rod bearings - inspection

Refer to illustration 21.1

1   Even though the main and connecting rod bearings should be replaced with new

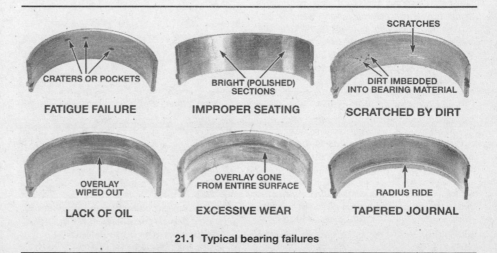

21.1 Typical bearing failures

ones during the engine overhaul, the old bearings should be retained for close examination, as they may reveal valuable information about the condition of the engine **(see illustration)**.

2   Bearing failure occurs because of lack of lubrication, the presence of dirt or other foreign particles, overloading the engine and corrosion. Regardless of the cause of bearing failure, it must be corrected before the engine is reassembled to prevent it from happening again.

3   When examining the bearings, remove them from the engine block, the main bearing caps, the connecting rods and the rod caps and lay them out on a clean surface in the same general position as their location in the engine. This will enable you to match any bearing problems with the corresponding crankshaft journal.

4   Dirt and other foreign particles get into the engine in a variety of ways. If may be left in the engine during assembly, or it may pass through filters or the PCV system. It may get into the oil, and from there into the bearings. Metal chips from machining operations and normal engine wear are often present. Abrasives are sometimes left in engine components after reconditioning, especially when parts are not thoroughly cleaned using the proper cleaning methods. Whatever the source, these foreign objects often end up embedded in the soft bearing material and are easily recognized. Large particles will not embed in the bearing and will score or gouge the bearing and journal. The best prevention for this cause of bearing failure is to clean all parts thoroughly and keep everything spotlessly clean during engine assembly. Frequent and regular engine oil and filter changes are also recommended.

5   Lack of lubrication (or lubrication breakdown) has a number of interrelated causes. Excessive heat (which thins the oil), overloading (which squeezes the oil from the bearing face) and oil leakage or throw off (from excessive bearing clearances, worn oil pump or high engine speeds) all contribute to lubrication breakdown. Blocked oil passages, which usually are the result of misaligned oil holes in a bearing shell, will also oil starve a bearing and destroy it. When lack of lubrication is the cause of bearing failure, the bearing material is wiped or extruded from the steel backing of the bearing. Temperatures may increase to the point where the steel backing turns blue from overheating.

6   Driving habits can have a definite effect on bearing life. Full throttle, low speed operation (lugging the engine) puts very high loads on bearings, which tends to squeeze out the oil film. These loads cause the bearings to flex, which produces fine cracks in the bearing face (fatigue failure). Eventually the bearing material will loosen in pieces and tear away from the steel backing. Short trip driving leads to corrosion of bearings because insufficient engine heat is produced to drive off the condensed water and corrosive gases. These products collect in the engine oil,

forming acid and sludge. As the oil is carried to the engine bearings, the acid attacks and corrodes the bearing material.

7   Incorrect bearing installation during engine assembly will lead to bearing failure as well. Tight fitting bearings leave insufficient bearing oil clearance and will result in oil starvation. Dirt or foreign particles trapped behind a bearing insert result in high spots on the bearing which lead to failure.

22   Engine overhaul - reassembly sequence

1   Before beginning engine reassembly, make sure you have all the necessary new parts, gaskets and seals as well as the following items on hand:

> Common hand tools
> Crankshaft damper removal/installation tool (V6 only)
> 1/2-inch drive torque wrench
> Piston ring installation tool
> Piston ring compressor
> Short lengths of rubber or plastic hose to fit over connecting rod bolts
> Plastigage
> Feeler gauges
> A fine-tooth file
> New engine oil
> Engine assembly lube or moly-base grease
> RTV gasket sealant
> Thread locking compound

2   In order to save time and avoid problems, engine reassembly must be done in the following general order:

Four cylinder engine

> New camshaft bearings (must be done by automotive machine shop)
> Camshaft
> Crankshaft and main bearings
> Piston rings
> Piston/connecting rod assemblies
> Rear main oil seal retainer
> Timing chain and sprockets
> Front cover
> Oil pump
> Oil pan
> Lifters

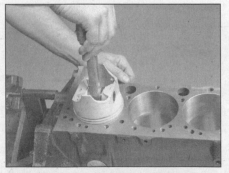

23.3 When checking piston ring end gap, the ring must be square in the cylinder bore (this is done by pushing the ring down with the top of a piston as shown)

> Cylinder head
> Rocker arms and pushrods
> Valve cover
> Intake and exhaust manifolds
> Water pump
> Fuel pump (carburetor equipped vehicles)
> Flywheel/driveplate

V6 engine

> Crankshaft and main bearings
> Piston/connecting rod assemblies
> Oil pump
> Oil pan
> Camshaft
> Timing chain and sprockets
> Timing chain cover
> Cylinder heads
> Valve lifters
> Intake manifold
> Rocker arms and pushrods
> Exhaust manifolds
> Valve covers
> Intake manifold assembly
> Rear main oil seal
> Flywheel/driveplate

23   Piston rings - installation

Refer to illustrations 23.3, 23.4, 23.5, 23.9a, 23.9b and 23.12

1   Before installing the new piston rings, the ring end gaps must be checked. It's assumed that the piston ring side clearance has been checked and verified correct (see Section 19).

2   Lay out the piston/connecting rod assemblies and the new rings so the ring sets will be matched with the same piston and cylinder during the end gap measurement and engine assembly.

3   Insert the top (number one) ring into the first cylinder and square it up with the cylinder walls by pushing it in with the top of the piston **(see illustration)**. The ring should be near the bottom of the cylinder, at the lower limit of ring travel.

4   To measure the end gap, slip feeler gauges between the ends of the ring until a gauge equal to the gap width is found **(see illustration)**. The feeler gauge should slide

23.4 With the ring square in the cylinder, measure the end gap with a feeler gauge

23.5 If the end gap is too small, clamp a file in a vise and file the ring ends (from the outside in only) to enlarge the gap slightly

23.9a Installing the spacer/expander in the oil control ring groove

23.9b DO NOT use a piston ring installation tool when installing the oil ring side rails

between the ring ends with a slight amount of drag. Compare the measurement to the Specifications. If the gap is larger or smaller than specified, double-check to make sure that you have the correct rings before proceeding.

5   If the gap is too small, it must be enlarged or the ring ends may come in contact with each other during engine operation, which can cause serious damage. The end gap can be increased by filing the ring ends very carefully with a fine file. Mount the file in a vise equipped with soft jaws, slip the ring over the file with the ends contacting the file face and slowly move the ring to remove material from the ends - file only from the outside in **(see illustration)**.

6   Excess end gap is not critical unless it's greater than listed in this Chapter's Specifications. Again, double-check to make sure you have the correct rings for your engine.

7   Repeat the procedure for each ring that will be installed in the first cylinder and for each ring in the remaining cylinders. Remember to keep rings, pistons and cylinders matched up.

8   Once the ring end gaps have been checked/corrected, the rings can be installed on the pistons.

9   The oil control ring (lowest one on the piston) is installed first. It's composed of three separate components. Slip the spacer/expander into the groove **(see illustration)**. Next, install the lower side rail. Don't

use a piston ring installation tool on the oil ring side rails, as they may be damaged. Instead, place one end of the side rail into the groove between the spacer/expander and the ring land, hold it firmly in place and slide a finger around the piston while pushing the rail into the groove **(see illustration)**. Next, install the upper side rail in the same manner.

10   After the three oil ring components have been installed, check to make sure that both the upper and lower side rails can be turned smoothly in the ring groove and stagger the gaps at least 1/2-inch apart.

11   The number two (middle) ring is installed next. It's stamped with a mark which must face up, toward the top of the piston. **Note:** *Always follow the instructions printed on the ring package or box - different manufacturers may require different approaches. Don 't mix up the top and middle rings, as they have different cross-sections.*

12   Use a piston ring installation tool and make sure that the identification mark is facing the top of the piston, then slip the ring into the middle groove on the piston **(see illustration)**. Don't expand the ring any more than necessary to slide it over the piston.

13   Install the number one (top) ring in the same manner. Make sure the mark is facing up. Be careful not to confuse the number one and number two rings.

14   Repeat the procedure for the remaining pistons and rings.

24   Crankshaft - installation and main bearing oil clearance check

Refer to illustrations 24.5a, 24.5b, 24.10 and 24.14

1   Crankshaft installation is the first step in engine reassembly. It's assumed at this point

23.12 Installing the compression rings with a ring expander - the mark (arrow) must face up

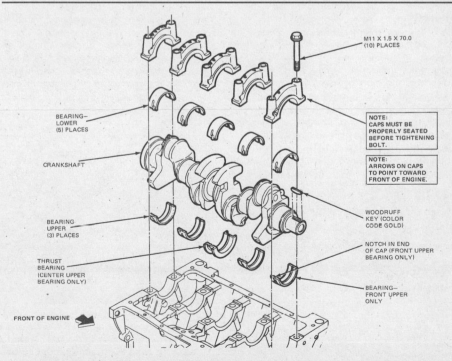

24.5a Typical four-cylinder engine crankshaft and main bearings - exploded view (note the location of the V-shaped notch in the front upper bearing shell)

2C

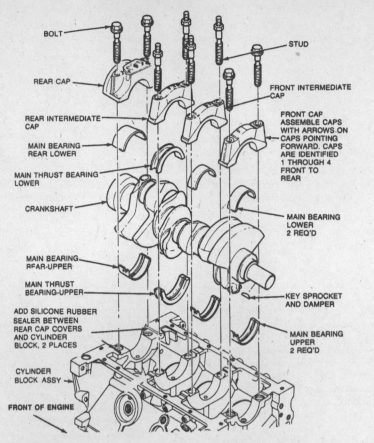

24.5b Typical V6 engine crankshaft and main bearings - exploded view

that the engine block and crankshaft have been cleaned, inspected and repaired or reconditioned.

2   Position the engine with the bottom facing up.

3   Remove the main bearing cap bolts and lift out the caps. Lay them out in the proper order to ensure that they are installed correctly.

4   If they're still in place, remove the old bearing inserts from the block and the main bearing caps. Wipe the main bearing surfaces of the block and caps with a clean, lint free cloth. They must be kept spotlessly clean.

5   Clean the back sides of the new main bearing inserts and lay one bearing half in each main bearing saddle in the block **(see illustrations)**. **Note:** *The front bearing insert on four-cylinder models has a small V-shaped notch in the parting line face.* Lay the other bearing half from each bearing set in the corresponding main bearing cap. Make sure the tab on the bearing insert fits into the recess in the block or cap. Also, the oil holes in the block must line up with the oil holes in the bearing insert. Do not hammer the bearing into place and don't nick or gouge the bearing faces. No lubrication should be used at this time.

24.14 Compare the width of the crushed Plastigage to the scale on the envelope to determine the main bearing oil clearance (always take the measurement at the widest point of the Plastigage); be sure to use the correct scale - standard and metric ones are included

6   The flanged thrust bearing must be installed in the center saddle in the block on four-cylinder engines and the number three bearing on V6 engines.

7   Clean the faces of the bearings in the block and the crankshaft main bearing journals with a clean, lint-free cloth. Check or clean the oil holes in the crankshaft, as any dirt here can only go one way - straight through the new bearings!

8   Once you're certain that the crankshaft is clean, carefully lay it in position (an assistant would be very helpful here) in the main bearings.

9   Before the crankshaft can be permanently installed, the main bearing oil clearance must be checked.

10   Trim several pieces of the appropriate size Plastigage - they must be slightly shorter than the width of the main bearings - and place one piece on each crankshaft main bearing journal, parallel with the journal axis **(see illustration)**.

11   Clean the faces of the bearings in the caps and install the caps in their respective positions - don't mix them up with the arrows pointing toward the front of the engine. Do not disturb the Plastigage!

12   Starting with the center main and working out toward the ends, tighten the main bearing cap bolts, in three steps, to the torque listed in this Chapter's Specifications. DO NOT rotate the crankshaft at any time during this operation!

13   Remove the bolts and carefully lift off the main bearing caps. Keep them in order. Don't disturb the Plastigage or rotate the crankshaft. If any of the main bearing caps are difficult to remove, tap them gently from side-to-side with a soft-face hammer to loosen them.

14   Compare the width of the crushed Plastigage on each journal to the scale printed on the Plastigage container to obtain the main bearing oil clearance **(see illustration)**. Check the Specifications to make sure it's correct.

15   If the clearance is not as specified. the bearing inserts may be the wrong size (which means different ones will be required). Before deciding that different inserts are needed, make sure that no dirt or oil was between the bearing inserts and the caps or block when the clearance was measured. If the Plastigage was wider at one end than the other, the journal may be tapered (see Section 20).

16   Carefully scrape all traces of the Plastigage material off the main bearing journals and/or the bearing faces. Don't nick or scratch the bearing faces.

17   Carefully lift the crankshaft out of the engine. Clean the bearing faces in the block, then apply a thin, uniform layer of clean moly-base grease or engine assembly lube to each of the bearing surfaces. Be sure to coat the thrust faces as well as the journal face of the center bearing .

18   Make sure the crankshaft journals are clean, then lay the crankshaft back in place in

24.10 Lay the Plastigage strips (arrow) on the main bearing journals, parallel to the crankshaft centerline

the block. Clean the faces of the bearings in the caps, then apply lubricant to them. Install the caps in their respective positions with the arrows pointing toward the front of the engine. On V6 engines, apply RTV sealant in a 1/8-inch bead to the rear main bearing cap-to-cylinder-block parting line. Oil the threads and install the bolts finger tight.

19 Tighten all except the thrust bearing to the torque listed in this Chapter's Specifications. Pry the crankshaft forward against the thrust surface of the bearing. Hold the crankshaft in this position, then pry the thrust bearing cap to the rear. Maintain the forward pressure on the crankshaft and tighten the center cap bolts to the torque listed in this Chapter's Specifications. Recheck the torque on all of the cap bolts.

20 Rotate the crankshaft a number of times by hand to check for any obvious binding. The torque required to turn the crankshaft should not exceed 4.5 ft-lbs (it can be measured by installing the bolt in the front of the crankshaft and turning the bolt with a socket attached to a torque wrench - read the torque just as the crankshaft starts to turn).

21 The final step is to check the crankshaft endplay with a feeler gauge or a dial indicator as described in Section 15. The endplay should be correct if the crankshaft thrust faces are not worn or damaged and new bearings have been installed.

22 Install a new rear main oil seal (see Chapter 2A or 2B), then bolt the housing to the block.

23 If it was removed, install the Woodruff key in the front of the crankshaft. Fill the keyway slot with LocTite 518, or equivalent, up to where the front face of the sprocket will fall.

25 Piston/connecting rod assembly - installation and rod bearing oil clearance check

Refer to illustrations 25.8, 25.9, 25.11 and 25.13

1 Before installing the piston/connecting rod assemblies, the cylinder walls must be perfectly clean, the top edge of each cylinder must be chamfered (to remove the sharp edge) and the crankshaft must be in place.

2 Remove the connecting rod cap from the end of the number one connecting rod. Remove the old bearing inserts and wipe the bearing surfaces of the connecting rod and cap with a clean, lint free cloth. They must be kept spotlessly clean.

3 Clean the back side of the new upper bearing half, then lay it in place in the connecting rod. Make sure that the tang on the bearing fits into the appropriate slot in the rod. Do not hammer the bearing insert into place and be very careful not to nick or gouge the bearing face. Do not lubricate the bearing at this time.

4 Clean the back side of the other bearing insert and install it in the rod cap. Again, make sure the tang on the bearing fits into

25.8 The notch in each piston must face the FRONT of the engine as the pistons are installed

the slot in the cap, and do not apply any lubricant. It is critically important that the mating surfaces of the bearing and connecting rod are perfectly clean and oil free when they are assembled.

5 Position the piston ring gaps at 120-degree intervals around the piston, then slip a section of plastic or rubber hose over each connecting rod cap bolt.

6 Lubricate the piston and rings with clean engine oil and attach a piston ring compressor to the piston. Leave the skirt protruding about 1/4-inch to guide the piston into the cylinder. The rings must be compressed until they are flush with the piston.

7 Rotate the crankshaft until the number one connecting rod journal is at BDC (bottom dead center) and apply a coat of engine oil to the cylinder walls.

8 With the notch on top of the piston facing the front of the engine **(see illustration)**, gently insert the piston/connecting rod assembly into the number one cylinder bore and rest the bottom edge of the ring compressor on the engine block. Tap the top edge of the ring compressor to make sure it's contacting the block around its entire circumference.

9 Carefully tap on the top of the piston with the end of a wooden hammer handle **(see illustration)** while guiding the end of the connecting rod into place on the crankshaft journal. The piston rings may try to pop out of the ring compressor just before entering the

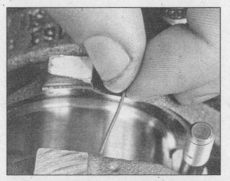

25.11 Lay the Plastigage strips on each rod bearing journal, parallel to the crankshaft centerline

25.9 Drive the piston gently into the cylinder bore with the end of a wooden or plastic hammer handle

cylinder bore, so keep some downward pressure on the ring compressor. Work slowly, and if any resistance is felt as the piston enters the cylinder, stop immediately! Find out what's hanging up and fix it before proceeding. DO NOT, for any reason, force the piston into the cylinder - you'll break a ring and/or the piston!

10 Once the piston/connecting rod assembly is installed, the connecting rod bearing oil clearance must be checked before the rod cap is permanently bolted in place.

11 Cut a piece of the appropriate size Plastigage slightly shorter than the width of the connecting rod bearing and lay it in place on the number one connecting rod journal, parallel with the journal axis **(see illustration)**.

12 Clean the connecting rod cap bearing face, remove the protective hoses from the connecting rod bolts and install the rod cap. Make sure the mating mark on the cap is on the same side as the mark on the connecting rod. Install the nuts and tighten them to the torque listed in this Chapter's Specifications, working up to it in three steps. **Note:** *Use a thin-wall socket to avoid erroneous torque readings that can result if the socket becomes wedged between the rod cap and nut. Do not rotate the crankshaft at any time during this operation.*

13 Remove the rod cap, being very careful not to disturb the Plastigage. Compare the width of the crushed Plastigage to the scale printed on the Plastigage container to obtain the oil clearance **(see illustration)**. Compare

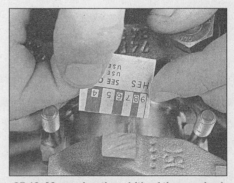

25.13 Measuring the width of the crushed Plastigage to determine the rod bearing oil clearance (be sure to use the correct scale - standard and metric ones are included)

2C

it to the Specifications to make sure the clearance is correct. If the clearance is not as specified, the bearing inserts may be the wrong size (which means different ones will be required). Before deciding that different inserts are needed, make sure that no dirt or oil was between the bearing inserts and the connecting rod or cap when the clearance was measured. Also, recheck the journal diameter. If the Plastigage was wider at one end than the other, the journal may be tapered (see Section 20).

14   Carefully scrape all traces of the Plastigage material off the rod journal and/or bearing face. Be very careful not to scratch the bearing - use your fingernail or a credit card. Make sure the bearing faces are perfectly clean, then apply a uniform layer of clean moly-base grease or engine assembly lube to both of them. You'll have to push the piston into the cylinder to expose the face of the bearing insert in the connecting rod - be sure to slip the protective hoses over the rod bolts first.

15   Slide the connecting rod back into place on the journal, remove the protective hoses from the rod cap bolts, install the rod cap and tighten the nuts to the torque listed in this Chapter's Specifications. Again, work up to the final torque in three steps.

16   Repeat the above procedure for each of the remaining piston/connecting rod assemblies. Keep the back sides of the bearing inserts and the inside of each connecting rod and cap perfectly clean during reassembly. Make sure that you have the correct piston for each cylinder and the notch on the piston faces the front (timing chain end) of the engine when the piston is installed.

Remember, use plenty of oil to lubricate the piston before installing the ring compressor. Also, when installing the rod caps for the final time, be sure to lubricate the bearing faces adequately.

17   After all the piston/connecting rod assemblies have been properly installed, rotate the crankshaft a number of times by hand to check for any obvious binding.

18   As a final step, the connecting rod endplay (side clearance) must be checked. Refer to Section 14 for this procedure. Compare the measured end play to the Specifications to make sure it's correct. If it was correct before disassembly and the original crankshaft and rods were reinstalled, it should still be right. If new rods or a new crankshaft were installed, the end play may be too small. If so, the rods will have to be removed and taken to an automotive machine shop for recessing.

26   Initial start-up and break-in after overhaul

Warning: *Have a fire extinguisher handy when starting the engine for the first time.*

1   Once the engine has been installed in the vehicle, double-check the engine oil and coolant levels.

2   With the spark plugs out of the engine, the fuel pump disabled (fuel-injected models only - see Chapter 4, Section 2) and the coil primary (low voltage) wire disconnected, crank the engine until oil pressure registers on the gauge or until the oil light goes out.

3   Install the spark plugs, hook up the plug wires and restore the fuel and ignition system functions.

4   Start the engine. It may take a few moments for the gasoline to reach the carburetor or injector, but the engine should start without a great deal of effort. **Note:** *If the engine keeps backfiring, recheck the ignition timing and spark plug wires.*

5   After the engine starts, it should be allowed to warm up to normal operating temperature. While the engine is warming up, make a thorough check for oil and coolant leaks.

6   Shut the engine off and recheck the engine oil and coolant levels.

7   Check the ignition timing and adjust it, if necessary (see Chapter 5).

8   Drive the vehicle to an area with minimum traffic, accelerate at full throttle from 30 to 50 mph, then allow the vehicle to slow to 30 mph with the throttle closed. Repeat the procedure 10 or 12 times. This will load the piston rings and cause them to seat properly against the cylinder walls. Check again for oil and coolant leaks.

9   Drive the vehicle gently for the first 500 miles (no sustained high speeds) and keep a constant check on the oil level. It's not unusual for an engine to use oil during the break-in period.

10   At approximately 500 to 600 miles, change the oil and filter.

11   For the next few hundred miles, drive the vehicle normally. Don't pamper it or abuse it.

12   After 2000 miles, change the oil and filter again and consider the engine fully broken in.

Chapter 3
Cooling, heating and air conditioning systems

Contents

Specifications

General

Drivebelt tension	See Chapter 1
Radiator cap pressure rating	16 psi
Cooling system capacity	See Chapter 1
Refrigerant capacity	35 to 37 ounces

Torque specifications

Ft-lbs (unless otherwise indicated)

Cooling fan temperature switch	96 to 144 in-lbs
Thermostat housing bolts	
Four-cylinder engine	12 to 18
V6 engine	96 to 120 in-lbs
Water pump bolts	15 to 22
Water pump pulley shield	84 to 120 in-lbs

3

1 General information

Engine cooling system

The Tempo and Topaz are equipped with a pressurized engine cooling system that's thermostatically controlled by a coolant temperature switch in the thermostat housing. A conventional water pump, mounted on the engine, moves coolant through the engine. The coolant flows around each cylinder and toward the rear of the engine. Cast-in passages direct coolant around the intake and exhaust ports, the spark plug areas and the exhaust valve guides.

The thermostat is located in a housing at the rear of the engine. During warm-up, the closed thermostat prevents coolant from circulating through the radiator. As the engine nears normal operating temperature, the thermostat opens and allows coolant to travel through the radiator, where it's cooled before returning to the engine.

The radiator is a cross-flow type with either a copper or aluminum core. The end tanks are made of molded, glass-filled nylon and have an oven-cured epoxy on the outside of the tanks. Because of its construction, the radiator cannot be serviced by the home mechanic. If it's damaged, it must be taken to a radiator shop.

Heating system

The heating system consists of a blower fan and heater core located inside the dashboard, the heater hoses connecting the heater core to the engine cooling system and the heater/air conditioning control assembly on the dashboard.

Hot engine coolant is circulated through the heater core at all times. When the heater is activated, a door opens to expose the heater box to the passenger compartment. A fan switch on the dash board activates the blower motor, which forces air through the core, heating the air.

Air conditioning system

The air conditioning system consists of a condenser mounted in front of the radiator, an evaporator mounted within the heater/air conditioner assembly inside the dashboard, a compressor mounted on the engine, an accumulator (filter-drier) containing a high-pressure relief valve, a control valve and the plumbing connecting all the components.

A blower fan forces the warmer air of the passenger compartment through the evaporator core, transferring the heat from the air to the refrigerant (sort of a radiator-in-reverse). The liquid refrigerant boils off into low pressure vapor, taking the heat with it when it leaves the evaporator.

Warning: *On models so equipped, whenever working in the vicinity of the front grille/bumper, steering wheel, steering column or other components of the airbag system, the system should be disarmed. To do this, perform the following steps:*

a) *Turn the ignition switch to Off.*
b) *Detach the cable from the negative battery terminal, then detach the positive cable. Wait two minutes for the electronic module backup power supply to be depleted.*

To enable the system

a) *Turn the ignition switch to the Off position.*
b) *Connect the positive battery cable first, then connect the negative cable.*

2 Antifreeze - general information

Warning: *Do not allow antifreeze to contact your skin or painted surfaces of the vehicle. Flush contacted areas immediately with plenty of water. Don't store new coolant or leave old coolant lying around where it's easily accessible to children and pets - they are attracted by its sweet smell and may drink it. Ingestion of even a small amount can be fatal. Wipe up garage floor and drip pan coolant spills immediately. Keep antifreeze containers covered and repair leaks in your cooling system as soon as they are discovered.*

The cooling system should be filled with a water/ethylene glycol-based antifreeze solution which will prevent freezing down to at least -20-degrees F. It also provides protection against corrosion and increases the coolant boiling point.

The cooling system should be drained, flushed and refilled at least every other year (see Chapter 1). The use of antifreeze solutions for periods longer than two years could result in damage from the formation of rust and scale in the system.

Before adding coolant to the system, check all hose connections and fittings - antifreeze can leak through very minute openings.

The ideal mixture of antifreeze to water which you should use depends on the relative weather conditions. The mixture should contain at least 50 percent antifreeze, but never more than 70 percent antifreeze.

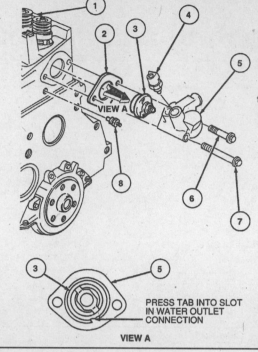

3.4a Four-cylinder engine thermostat installation details; this illustration shows the late-model tab-and-slot design housing; earlier model thermostats must be rotated to remove them from the housing

1 Cylinder head
2 Gasket
3 Thermostat
4 Coolant temperature sensor
5 Thermostat housing
6 Short bolt
7 Long bolt
8 Coolant temperature sending unit (for gauge or light)

3 Thermostat - replacement

Refer to illustrations 3.4a, 3.4b, 3.6, 3.8, 3.9, 3.11, 3.12, and 3.13.

Removal

1   Disconnect the cable from the negative terminal of the battery.

2   Position a drain pan below the radiator.

3   Remove the radiator cap, locate the draincock on the lower left hand side of the radiator and attach a section of rubber hose to the drain tube and open the fitting. Drain the radiator until the coolant level is below the thermostat housing. Close the fitting.

4   Locate thermostat housing **(see illustrations)** and, depending on the model, determine if the air intake duct and/or the PCV valve hose must be removed to increase access to thermostat housing (see Chapters 4 and 6).

5   Loosen the hose clamp and disconnect the upper radiator hose from the thermostat housing. On later V6 models, also remove the heater hose.

6   On four-cylinder models, unplug the coolant temperature sensor electrical

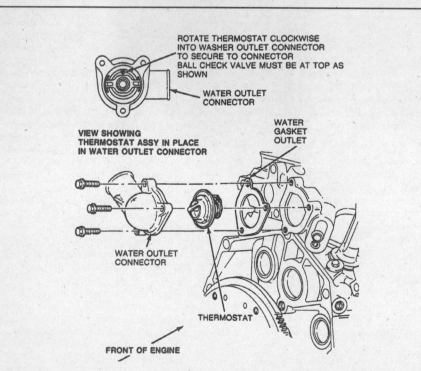

3.4b V6 engine thermostat installation details - note the location of the ball check valve

3.6 Before removing the thermostat housing on four-cylinder engines, unplug the temperature switch and/or coolant temperature sensor electrical connectors - if equipped, remove the nut that attaches the ground wire to the rear thermostat housing bolt (arrows)

3.8 If the thermostat housing is stuck, don't pry it loose or you may damage the gasket mating surfaces - use a soft-face hammer or a hammer and piece of wood to break the gasket seal

3.9 To unlock the thermostat from the housing, rotate it counterclockwise until it's free, then pull it straight out (all except tab-and-slot type housing)

3.11 To remove the thermostat from the engine, gently pry it loose with a small screwdriver

connector(s) **(see illustration)**. On multi-sensor-equipped thermostat housings, mark the connectors so that they can be installed back on the correct sensor.

7   On four-cylinder models, if equipped, remove the nut that secures the ground wire to the thermostat housing and detach the wire.

8   Remove the mounting bolts and detach the thermostat housing. **Note:** *If the housing is difficult to remove, tap it gently with a soft-face hammer or a piece of wood (see illustration). Don't try to pry the housing loose or damage to the gasket sealing surfaces may occur and leaks may develop.*

9   On V6 and earlier four-cylinder models, rotate the thermostat counterclockwise to remove it from the housing **(see illustration)**.

10   On later four-cylinder models equipped with a tab-and-slot design housing **(see illustration 3.4a)**, gently pry the thermostat straight out with a small screwdriver.

11   If the thermostat remains attached to the engine, carefully pry it out with a small screwdriver **(see illustration)**.

Installation

12   Remove all gasket material and old sealant from the mating surfaces of the housing and engine **(see illustration)**, then wipe them with a cloth saturated with lacquer thinner or acetone.

13   On V6 and earlier four-cylinder models, insert the thermostat into the housing cavity and rotate it clockwise to lock it in place. **Note:** *On V6 models, make sure the ball check valve is at the top of the housing* **(see illustration)**.

14   On later four-cylinder models with a tab-and-slot design housing **(see illustration 3.4a)**, align the tab on the thermostat with the notch in the thermostat housing and press the thermostat in to seat against the gasket.

15   Apply a thin layer of RTV sealant to both sides of the new gasket, then position it on the housing and use the bolts to hold it in place.

16   Place the thermostat housing and gasket in position on the cylinder head and thread the bolts into the holes. Tighten the bolts to the torque listed in this Chapter's Specifications.

17   The remainder of installation is the

reverse of removal.

18   Refill the cooling system, start engine and check for coolant leaks. Recheck coolant and top off after engine has cooled.

---

4   Cooling fan motor and circuit - description and check

Warning: *To avoid possible injury or damage, DO NOT operate the engine with the hood open until the fan has been examined for cracks or damage. Never attempt to repair a fan with damaged blades - replace it. In addition, The electric cooling fan is wired so that it operates only when the ignition switch is in the Run position. Unplug the cooling fan prior to performing any underhood service, since the fan could cycle if the ignition switch is left in the On position, even though the engine is not running.*

Description

Non-air-conditioned models

The fan motor on models through 1987 is controlled by a circuit from the ignition key to the cooling fan temperature switch located in the thermostat housing. When coolant temperature exceeded approximately

3.12 Make sure that all the old gasket material is removed from the mating surfaces of both the head and the thermostat housing (four-cylinder engine shown)

210-degrees F, the switch would close and complete the circuit from the ignition switch, through the fan temperature switch to the fan motor. In later models, this circuit was modified to include a fan motor relay. In this design, the cooling fan temperature switch controls the latching coil of the relay, which in turn, completes a separate circuit within the relay from battery to the fan motor.

Air-conditioned models

Because of the extra demands placed on the cooling system due to air conditioning, more sophisticated control over the fan motor was necessary. On models through 1991, additional fan motor control is accomplished by the Cooling Fan Control Module (a non-serviceable electronic device) while the air conditioning is in operation. In 1992, the Integrated Relay Control Module (IRCM) was introduced due to even higher demands for efficiency and fan control. The electronics and switches within the IRCM are controlled by the Electronic Engine Control module (EEC-IV), which controls the fan motor (and fan speed on V6 models) only if a pre-programmed set conditions are met. The IRCM has subsequently been replaced with the Constant Control Relay Module (CCRM), which operates in a similar fashion. The

3

3.13 When installing the thermostat on V6 and earlier four-cylinder engines, push the thermostat in, then turn it clockwise to lock it in place - make sure the ball check valve is at the top on the V6 engine thermostat housing

conditions in which the fan motor is energized are many; however, under most circumstances, the fan should be energized whenever the air conditioning system is cycling and/or whenever the coolant temperature exceeds 210-degrees F.

Check

1   Because the electric cooling fan motor circuit on air conditioned models is under computer control during some phases of operation, a complete test of this system requires special equipment not available to the home mechanic. However, there are several things you can check.
2   Locate the fan motor electrical connector on the back of the fan motor. Unplug it and inspect the electrical connector to make sure it's plugged in securely.
3   Depending on the model year, locate the cooling fan control module or the IRCM/CCRM (see Section 5) and make sure that the electrical connector of the control module is securely attached.
4   Examine the wires between the relay control module and the fan to make sure that they're in good condition. If they're frayed or broken, repair them.
5   On 1984 through 1991 models, disconnect the connector at the cooling fan temperature switch (see Section 5) and, using a continuity tester or ohmmeter, check the continuity between the terminals of the switch. Warm up the engine and allow the coolant temperature to exceed its normal operating range briefly. At this point, the resistance between the two terminals on the switch should be close to zero. **Caution:** *Do not allow the engine to overheat during this test.* **Note:** *1992 and later models do not use a separate fan switch. Fan circuit temperature sensing is done by the ECT (engine coolant temperature sensor).*

 a) *If the resistance across the temperature switch doesn't drop when exceeding normal coolant temperatures, the switch is bad. Replace it (see Section 5).*
 b) *If the resistance across the temperature switch does drop to nearly zero, the switch is operational and the problem is elsewhere.*

6   To test the fan motor, first unplug the fan motor connector (note the terminal location of the black ground wire on V6 models). Next, install a grounded jumper wire to the ground terminal on the motor. Finally, attach a fused jumper wire from the battery positive terminal to the remaining fan motor terminal. The motor should run. If not, replace it (see Section 6). **Note:** *V6 models use a two-speed fan and a three-terminal connector. Assuming the first test passed, test the second speed by moving the battery jumper wire to the other terminal. The motor must pass both test to be considered functional.*
7   If the fan does operate when jumped directly from the battery, two additional possibilities exist:

 a) *There is an open circuit somewhere between the temperature switch, the computer, the control relay and the motor, in which case you can troubleshoot the problem with a test light or continuity tester.*
 b) *If the circuits check out, there is a problem with either the cooling fan controller, the integrated relay control module or the ECC computer itself. Take the vehicle to a dealer service department or other repair shop and have the system repaired.* **Caution:** *Do not drive the vehicle if it is overheating; have it towed.*

---

5   Cooling fan temperature switch and controller - replacement

---

Refer to illustrations 5.11 and 5.12

Cooling fan temperature switch (all models, 1984 through 1991)

1   Locate the temperature switch on or near the thermostat housing. On 1988 through 1991 models, do not confuse the Engine Coolant Temperature (ECT) sensor with the fan temperature switch. **Note:** *1992 and later models do not utilize a fan temperature switch; however, four-cylinder models*

have the ECT sensor on the thermostat housing.
2   Unplug the electrical connector.
3   Wrap the threads of the new switch with Teflon tape to prevent leakage.
4   Unscrew the switch. Be prepared for coolant leakage. Install the new switch as quickly as possible.
5   Installation is the reverse of removal. Tighten the switch securely.
6   Top off radiator coolant (see Chapter 1), start the engine and check for coolant leaks around the sensor and verify the fan is operational.

Cooling fan motor relay (all air-conditioned models through 1991, 1988 and later non-air-conditioned models)

7   Locate the fan motor relay in the engine compartment, next to the left side headlight.
8   Unplug the electrical connector and remove the attaching screw.
9   Installation is reverse of removal. Start the engine and verify the fan is operational.

Cooling fan controller (air-conditioned models through 1991)

10   Empty the glove compartment.
11   Push the sides of the glove compartment liner in **(see illustration),** swing the liner down from the opening and let it hang on the hinges.
12   Working through the glove compartment opening, remove the bolt attaching the cooling fan controller mounting bracket to the cowl top panel **(see illustration).**
13   Pull the controller down, unplug the electrical connector and remove the controller.
14   Installation is the reverse of removal. Start the engine and verify the fan and air conditioning system is operational.

IRCM/CCRM (1992 and later air-conditioned models)

15   Locate the IRCM/CCRM in the engine compartment on the left side strut tower.
16   Unplug the electrical connector and remove the screws.
17   Installation is the reverse of removal. Start the engine and verify the fan and air conditioning system are operational.

---

6   Cooling fan and motor - replacement

Refer to illustrations 6.4 and 6.5
Caution: *The cooling fan motors for the four-cylinder and V6 engines are similar, but cannot be interchanged. Improper application will result in fan motor failure and vehicle overheating.*

1   Disconnect the cable from the negative terminal of the battery.

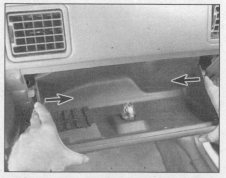

5.11 To gain access to the cooling fan controller (and the heater blower motor and resistor as well), push in on the sides of the glove compartment and swing it down out of the way

5.12 The cooling fan controller is attached to the cowl top panel by a small bracket (arrow) - to replace it, remove the bracket bolt, pull the controller down and unplug the electrical connector

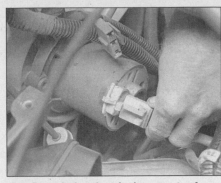

6.4 Detach the electrical connector from the cooling fan motor

2   If required for access, remove the coil assembly (see Chapter 5).

3   If required for access, remove the "sight shield" (the plastic protector attached to the radiator support).

4   Unplug the electrical connector from the fan motor **(see illustration)**. Disconnect the wire harness from the clip on the cooling fan shroud.

5   Remove the nut and bolt, then detach the fan motor/shroud assembly from the radiator **(see illustration).**

6   Remove the fan retainer clip from the motor shaft and detach the fan. **Note:** *If a metal burr is noted on the motor shaft after the retainer clip is removed, file off the burr before removing the fan.*

7   Remove the three nuts and washers and withdraw the fan motor from the shroud.

8   Installation is the reverse of removal. Start the engine, allow it to warm up, and verify fan is operational.

7   Radiator - removal and installation

Refer to illustrations 7.8a, 7.8b and 7.10
Note: *Refer to the exploded view of the radiator and electric cooling fan/shroud assemblies in Section 6 if necessary.*
Warning: *If vehicle is equipped with airbags, refer to Chapter 12, to disarm the airbag system prior to performing any work described below.*

Removal

1   Disconnect the cable from the negative terminal of the battery.

2   Drain the coolant from the radiator (see Chapter 1 if necessary).

3   If required for access, remove the "sight shield" (the plastic protector attached to the radiator support).

4   Loosen the hose clamp and detach the upper hose from the radiator.

5   Detach the overflow hose from the radiator filler neck.

6   Remove the electric cooling fan and shroud assembly (see Section 6).

7   Loosen the hose clamp and detach the lower hose from the radiator.

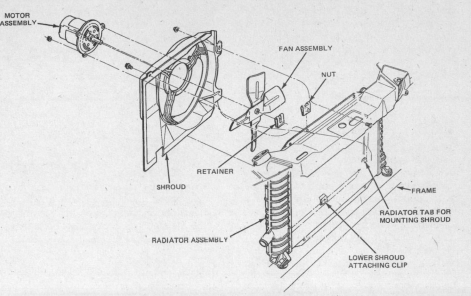

6.5 Cooling fan motor and shroud assembly - exploded view

8   If your vehicle is equipped with an automatic transaxle, disconnect the upper and lower oil cooler line threaded fittings **(see illustrations).** Cap the fittings and the lines to prevent leakage.

9   Remove the two nuts attaching the top

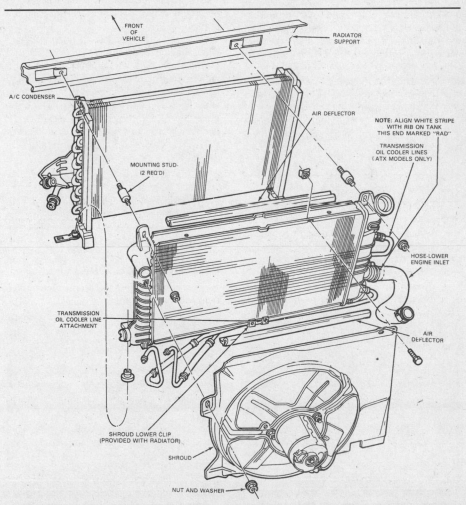

7.8a Air conditioning condenser, radiator and electric cooling fan/shroud components - exploded view

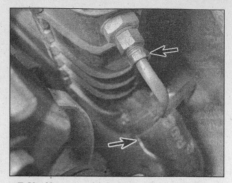

7.8b If your vehicle is equipped with an automatic transaxle, detach the upper and lower oil cooler line threaded fittings (arrows) - cap the fittings and lines to prevent leakage

7.10 Before installing the radiator, make sure that both rubber mounts (the right one is shown here) are properly installed on the stabilizer bar bracket bolts that stick up through the lower crossmember

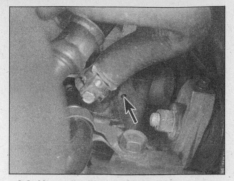

8.3 Use a flashlight to check the "weep hole" (arrow) in the underside of the water pump - if coolant is dripping out of the hole, the pump will have to be replaced

of the radiator to the radiator support. If either stud loosens, be sure to tighten it before reinstalling the radiator. Tip the top of the radiator to the rear far enough to clear the mounting studs and lift the radiator from the vehicle.

Installation

10   Make sure that the radiator rubber mounts aren't stuck to the lower mounting brackets. They must be properly installed on the stabilizer bar bracket mounting bolts that protrude through the lower crossmember **(see illustration)**.

11   Installation is the reverse of removal.

12   When installation is complete, add coolant to the system (see Chapter 1).

13   Start vehicle and check for coolant leaks. Check automatic transaxle fluid level and top off if required.

8   Water pump - check

Refer to illustration 8.3

1   A failure in the water pump can cause overheating and serious engine damage because a defective pump will not circulate coolant through the engine.

2   There are two ways to check the operation of the water pump while it's in

place on the engine. If either check indicates that the pump is defective, replace it with a new or rebuilt unit.

3   The water pump body has a "weep" hole in the underside **(see illustration)**. If the pump seal fails, coolant will leak out of the hole. You'll need to get underneath the water pump to see the hole, so raise the vehicle and place it on jackstands. Use a flashlight to help determine if coolant is leaking from the pump.

4   If the water pump shaft bearing fails it will usually make a squealing sound (don't confuse drivebelt slippage, which makes a similar sound, with water pump bearing failure). Even before the bearing actually fails, shaft wear can be detected by grasping the pulley firmly and moving it up-and-down. If excessive play is noted, the shaft and/or bearing are worn and the pump should be replaced.

9   Water pump - removal and installation

Refer to illustrations 9.6a, 9.6b, 9.8 and 9.21.

Four-cylinder engine

1   Disconnect the cable from the negative terminal of the battery.

2   Drain the engine coolant (see Chapter 1 if necessary).

3   If your vehicle is equipped with an air pump, loosen the adjusting bolt and remove the belt (see Chapter 1).

4   If your vehicle is equipped with an air pump, slide the thermactor pump hose clamp, located below the pump, out of the way, remove the three pump bracket bolts and detach the pump and bracket as an assembly.

5   On models not equipped with automatic belt tensioner, loosen the idler pulley and remove the water pump drivebelt. On later models with an automatic tensioner, use a 1/2 inch breaker bar to engage the tensioner and rotate it against the spring tension to relieve belt tension. Remove the belt from the water pump pulley (see Chapter 1).

6   Remove the coolant tube bracket bolts from the underside of the oil pan and the back side of the block and detach the brackets from the engine **(see illustrations)**.

7   Pull the coolant tube straight down far enough to detach it from the water pump.

8   Remove the three mounting bolts **(see illustration)** and detach the water pump.

9   Remove all traces of old gasket material and sealant from the mating surfaces of the engine block, then clean the new pump and the block with a cloth saturated with lacquer thinner or acetone.

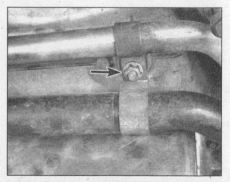

9.6a Before removing the water pump, disconnect the coolant tube bracket (arrow) from the underside of the pan, then . . .

9.6b . . . remove the bracket bolt (arrow) from the rear of the block and pull the coolant tube straight down far enough to detach it from the water pump housing

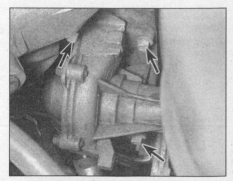

9.8 The water pump is retained by three bolts

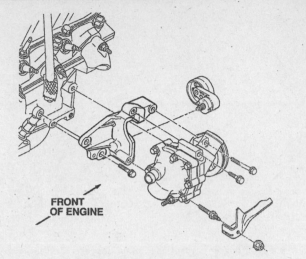

9.21 V6 engine water pump mounting details - exploded view

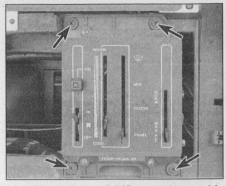

10.2 The heater and A/C control assembly is attached to the dashboard with four screws (arrows)

10   Apply a thin layer of RTV sealant to both sides of the new gasket and position the gasket on the engine block.

11   Install the new pump and tighten the three bolts to the torque listed in this Chapter's Specifications.

12   The remainder of installation is the reverse of removal. **Note:** *Install a new O-ring on the water pump inlet tube and apply silicone lubricant prior to installation to prevent leaks.*

13   Refill the cooling system, start engine and check for coolant leaks. Recheck the coolant level and top off after the engine has cooled.

V6 engine

14   Disconnect the cable from the negative terminal of the battery.

15   Drain the engine coolant (see Chapter 1 if necessary).

16   Using a 1/2-inch breaker bar, engage the tensioner and rotate against the spring tension to relieve belt tension. Remove the belt from the water pump pulley (see Chapter 1).

17   Remove the water pump-to-front cover hose.

18   Remove the coolant tube upper and lower bracket bolts from the underside of the engine and pull the tube out of the water pump. **Note:** *It may be necessary to raise the front of the vehicle and place it securely on jackstands before you can remove the tube.*

19   Remove the heater hose from the back of the water pump.

20   Remove the water pump pulley shield and note the location of the studded bolt for reassembly.

21   Remove the three mounting bolts **(see illustration)** and detach the water pump.

22   Install the new pump and tighten the bolts to the torque listed in this Chapter's Specifications.

23   The remainder of installation is the reverse of removal. **Note:** *Install a new O-ring on the water pump inlet tube and apply silicone lubricant prior to installation to prevent leaks.*

24   Refill the cooling system, start the engine and check for coolant leaks. Recheck the coolant and top it off after the engine has cooled.

10   Heater and air conditioning control assembly - removal and installation

Refer to illustrations 10.2, 10.4, 10.8, 10.9, 10.11 and 10.14

Control assembly (early models)

1   Remove the cluster opening finish panel (see Chapter 11).

2   Remove all four screws from the heater and air conditioning control assembly and pull the control assembly out of the register housing **(see illustration)**.

3   Move all three control levers all the way down.

4   Detach the temperature control cable end retainer by squeezing the two tabs together and pushing the retainer out of the bracket. Detach the right-angle tip of the cable from the temperature control selector lever **(see illustration)**.

5   Detach the other two cables from the function control and air inlet selector levers,

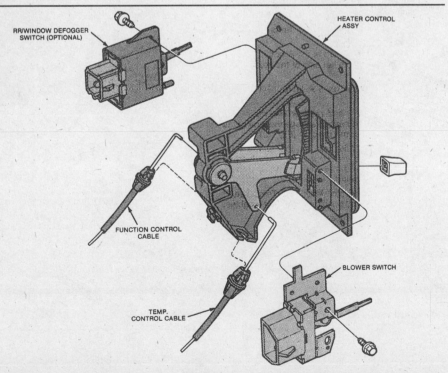

10.4 An exploded view of the heater and A/C control assembly from the back side - note that the control cables are easily detached from the levers once the retainers are popped out of the brackets

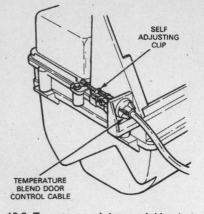

10.8 To remove a later model heater control assembly, the control cable must be disconnected at the blend door lever arm

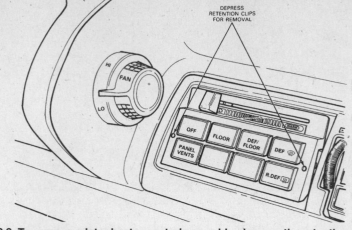

10.9 To remove a later heater control assembly, depress the retention clips with two small Phillips screwdrivers

respectively, in the same manner.

6   Unplug all electrical connectors from the heater control assembly and remove the heater and A/C control assembly from the dashboard.

7   Installation is the reverse of removal.

Control assembly (late models)

8   Move the temperature control lever to COOL and disconnect the temperature control cable housing from mounting bracket on the heater case **(see illustration)**.

9   Insert the ends of two small Phillips screwdrivers into the holes provided in the control assembly bezel. Lightly push on the screwdrivers to release the internal spring clips and release the control assembly from the register housing **(see illustration)**.

10   Pull the control assembly out of the register housing and disconnect the temperature control cable from the mounting bracket and the lever arm.

11   Identify and unplug electrical connectors and vacuum hoses and remove the control assembly **(see illustration)**.

12   Installation is the reverse of removal.

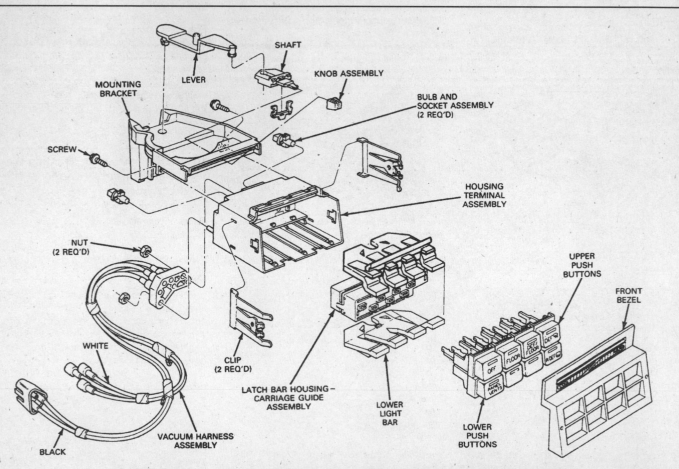

10.11 Exploded view of later model heater/air conditioning control assembly components

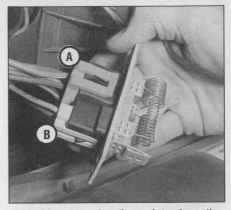

10.14 To remove the blower switch assembly, unplug the connectors at the blower switch and the A/C push button switch, then remove the two mounting screws (arrows)

11.3 To remove the heater blower resistor, located on the heater box behind the glove compartment, take out the two mounting screws (arrows)

11.4 After removing the resistor from the recess in the heater box, unplug the two electrical connectors (A and B). If you're removing the blower motor assembly, unplug connector B only

Blower switch (early models)

13   Remove the blower switch knob from the lever (simply pull it straight off).
14   Remove the heater and A/C control assembly (see Steps 1 and 2) and pull it out from the dashboard far enough to gain access to the electrical connectors for the A/C push button and blower switches (see illustration).
15   Remove the two blower switch assembly mounting screws and detach the switch from the heater and A/C control assembly.
16   When installing the blower switch, make sure that the alignment pin on the switch is engaged with the hole in the switch mounting bracket.
17   Installation is otherwise the reverse of removal.

Blower switch (late models)

18   Insert the end of a small pocket screwdriver into the slot provided in the blower switch bezel.
19   Apply a light upward force to the bezel to depress the internal spring clips and remove the switch from the instrument panel.
20   Pull blower switch out of instrument panel and disconnect electrical connectors from the control assembly.
21   Installation is otherwise the reverse of removal.

11   Heater blower motor and resistor - removal and installation

Refer to illustrations 11.3, 11.4 and 11.9
Warning: If vehicle is equipped with airbags, refer to Chapter 12, to disarm the airbag system prior to performing any work described below.

Heater blower resistor

1   Disconnect the cable from the negative terminal of the battery.
2   Push the sides of the glove compartment liner in and pull the liner from the opening (see illustration 5.11). Allow the glove compartment and door to hang on the hinges.
3   Remove the screws that secure the resistor to the heater box (see illustration)
4   Pull the resistor assembly down far enough to disconnect the two electrical connectors (see illustration) and remove it.
5   Installation is the reverse of removal.

Heater blower motor assembly

6   Disconnect the cable from the negative terminal of the battery.
7   Push the sides of the glove compartment liner in and pull the liner from the opening (see illustration 5.7, if necessary). Allow the glove compartment and door to hang on the hinges.
8   Unplug the blower assembly electrical connector from the smaller terminal on top of the blower resistor (see illustrations 11.3 and 11.4).
9   Remove the mounting screws (see illustration) and detach the blower assembly.
10   Installation is the reverse of removal.

12   Air conditioning system - check and maintenance

Refer to illustration 12.9
Warning: The air conditioning system is under high pressure. DO NOT loosen any hose or line fittings or remove any components until after the system has been discharged. Air conditioning refrigerant should be properly discharged into an EPA-approved container at a dealer service department or an automotive air-conditioning repair facility. Always wear eye protection when disconnecting air conditioning system fittings.
1   The following maintenance steps should be performed on a regular basis to ensure that the air conditioner continues to operate at peak efficiency.

11.9 The blower motor assembly is held in place with four mounting screws (arrows)

a) Check the tension of the drivebelt and adjust if necessary (see Chapter 1).
b) Check the condition of the hoses. Look for cracks, hardening and deterioration.
c) Check the fins of the condenser for leaves, bugs and any other foreign material. A soft brush and compressed air can be used to remove them.

2   The system should be run for about 10 minutes at least once a month. This is particularly important during the winter months because long term non-use can cause hardening and failure of the seals.
3   The most common cause of poor cooling is low refrigerant charge. If a noticeable drop in system cooling ability occurs, the following procedure will help pinpoint the cause.
4   Warm the engine to normal operating temperature.
5   The hood and doors should be open.
6   Press the A/C mode button.
7   Slide the temperature selector lever all the way down to the coolest position.
8   Turn the fan switch selector to the Hi position.
9   With the compressor engaged, feel the evaporator inlet pipe between the orifice and

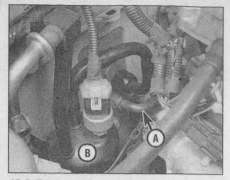

12.9 To determine whether the refrigerant level is adequate, feel the evaporator inlet pipe (A) with one hand and the surface of the accumulator (B) with the other and note the temperature of each

13.2 Before raising the vehicle, unplug the electrical connector, unscrew the suction line from the threaded fitting and disconnect the discharge line spring coupling (arrows)

the evaporator. Put your other hand on the surface of the accumulator can (see illustration).

10   If both surfaces feel about the same temperature and if both feel a little cooler than the surrounding air, the refrigerant level is probably okay. The problem is elsewhere.

11   If the inlet pipe has frost accumulation or feels cooler than the accumulator surface, the refrigerant charge is probably low.

13   Air conditioning compressor - removal and installation

Refer to illustrations 13.2, 13.4 and 13.9
Warning: *Have the air conditioning system discharged by a dealer service department or an automotive air conditioning shop before beginning this procedure. While you're at the dealer or repair shop, ask where you can obtain a 1/2-inch spring lock coupling tool. This tool is inexpensive but absolutely essential for servicing air conditioning components because the system lines cannot be disconnected or reattached without it.* **Note:** *Ford recommends that whenever a compressor must be replaced, it is necessary to replace the accumulator/drier. Also, if the compressor is damaged due to a mechanical failure, a complete system flushing must be*

done and a retrofit filtering system must be added to prevent reoccurrence and other system problems. A filtering kit is available from your dealer; however, the flushing must be left to a certified repair facility.

1   Disconnect the cable from the negative terminal of the battery.
2   Unplug the electrical connector from the compressor (see illustration).
3   On earlier four-cylinder and V6 engines using a compressor with top-mounted manifold fittings, disconnect the suction line threaded fitting from the compressor (use a backup wrench) and, using a 1/2-inch spring lock coupling tool, disconnect the discharge tube at the spring lock coupling (see Chapter 4, Section 3.26). Plug all open fittings to prevent debris and moisture from entering the system. **Note:** *Some V6 models may be equipped with spring lock couplings at both lines.*
4   On later model four-cylinder engines using a compressor with a rear-mounted combination manifold, remove the bolt retaining the manifold/tube assembly to the compressor rear head (see illustration) or remove the two spring lock coupling connectors. Plug all open fittings to prevent debris and moisture from entering the system.
5   If required to gain access to compressor, remove the electric cooling fan and shroud assembly (see Section 6).

6   If required to gain additional access to the compressor, remove the radiator (see Section 7).
7   Depending on the model, assess the best way to get compressor out of engine compartment. If removal from below is chosen, raise the vehicle and place it securely on jackstands.
8   Remove the air conditioning drivebelt (see Chapter 1).
9   Remove the four bolts attaching the compressor to the mounting bracket (see illustration).
10   Remove the compressor from the vehicle.
11   If a new compressor id being installed, follow the directions with the compressor regarding the draining of excess oil prior to installation.
12   Installation is the reverse of removal. Make sure to use new air conditioning O-rings at all connections and lubricate them with refrigerant oil.
13   The system must be evacuated, recharged and leak tested by a dealer service department or an automotive air conditioning shop.

14   Air conditioning condenser - removal and installation

Refer to illustrations 14.4 and 14.5
Warning: *If vehicle is equipped with airbags, refer to Chapter 12, to disarm the airbag system prior to performing any work described below.*
Warning: *Have the air conditioning system discharged by a dealer service department or an automotive air conditioning shop before beginning this procedure. While you're at the dealer or repair shop, ask where you can obtain a 1/2-inch spring lock coupling tool. This tool is inexpensive but absolutely essential for servicing air conditioning components because the system lines cannot be disconnected or reattached without it.*

1   Drain the cooling system (see Chapter 1).
2   Remove the electric cooling fan and shroud assembly (see Section 6).
3   Remove the radiator (see Section 7).
4   Using a 1/2-inch spring lock coupling

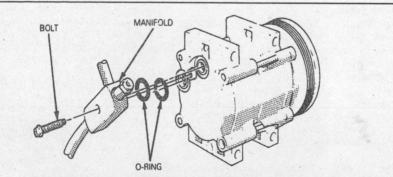

13.4 To remove the refrigerant lines from the rear-mounted manifold-type compressor, remove the center bolt and detach the assembly

13.9 Remove the four bolts to detach the compressor from the mounting bracket (four-cylinder engine shown, V6 similar)

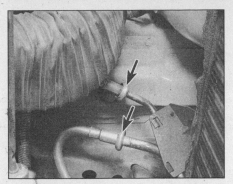

14.4 The liquid (suction) line and compressor discharge line are both attached to the condenser lines with spring couplings that can only be disconnected with a special tool

14.5 The condenser is suspended from the radiator support by two mounting bracket screws (this is the left one)

tool (see Section 13), disconnect the lines from the condenser **(see illustration)**.

5   Remove the condenser upper mounting bracket bolts **(see illustration)** and remove the condenser from the vehicle.

6   Installation is the reverse of removal.

7   The system must be recharged by a dealer service department or an automotive air conditioning shop.

---

15 Air conditioning accumulator and pressure switch - removal and installation

Refer to illustrations 15.2 and 15.13

Warning: *Have the air conditioning system discharged by a dealer service department or an automotive air conditioning shop before beginning this procedure. While you're at the dealer or repair shop, ask where you can obtain a 1/2-inch spring lock coupling tool. This tool is inexpensive but absolutely essential for servicing air conditioning components because the system lines cannot be disconnected or reattached without it.*

Pressure switch

1   Disconnect the cable from the negative terminal of the battery.

2   Unplug the electrical connector from the clutch cycling pressure switch **(see illustration)**.

3   Unscrew the pressure switch from the accumulator.

4   Lubricate the O-ring on the pressure switch fitting with clean refrigerant oil.

5   Screw the pressure switch onto the accumulator nipple. If the threaded fitting is plastic, tighten the switch finger tight. If the threaded fitting is metal, tighten the switch with a wrench.

6   Reattach the electrical connector to the switch.

7   Have the system recharged and the pressure switch checked for proper operation and refrigerant leakage by a dealer service department or an automotive air conditioning shop.

Accumulator

8   Disconnect the cable from the negative terminal of the battery.

9   If your vehicle is equipped with an air pump, remove it from the engine (see

Chapter 6).

10   Unplug the wire harness connector from the pressure switch on top of the accumulator **(see illustration 15.2)**.

11   Disconnect the suction hose from the accumulator at the spring coupling **(see illustrations 13.3 and 15.2)**.

12   Disconnect the accumulator line from the evaporator core **(see illustration 15.2)**. Use a backup wrench to prevent component damage.

13   Loosen the clamp screw **(see illustration)** and remove the accumulator.

14   Installation is the reverse of removal. Have the system recharged by a dealer service department or an automotive air conditioning shop.

---

16 Heater core - removal and installation

Refer to illustrations 16.7, 16.9 and 16.16

Warning: *If vehicle is equipped with airbags, refer to Chapter 12, to disarm the airbag system prior to performing any work described below.*

1987 and earlier models without air conditioning

1   Drain the engine coolant (see Chapter 1).

2   Loosen the heater hose clamps at the heater core tubes and detach the heater hoses from the tubes.

3   Cap the heater core tubes to prevent spilling coolant into the passenger compartment.

4   Remove the glove compartment door and liner.

5   Move the temperature control lever to the Warm position.

6   Remove the screws attaching the heater core cover to the heater assembly and detach the cover.

7   Working in the engine compartment,

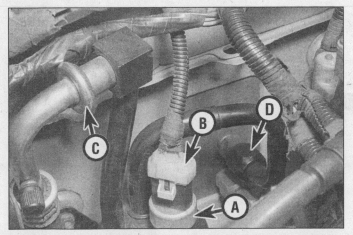

15.2 If you are simply replacing the clutch cycling pressure switch (A), unplug the electrical connector (B) and unscrew the switch - if you're replacing or removing the entire accumulator assembly, unplug the switch and disconnect both the outlet line (C) to the compressor and the inlet line (D) from the evaporator

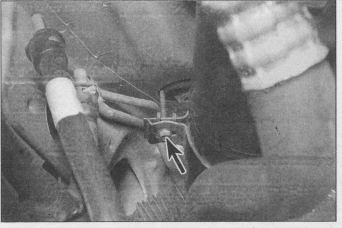

15.13 Loosen the accumulator clamp screw (arrow) and lift the accumulator straight up to remove it from the engine compartment

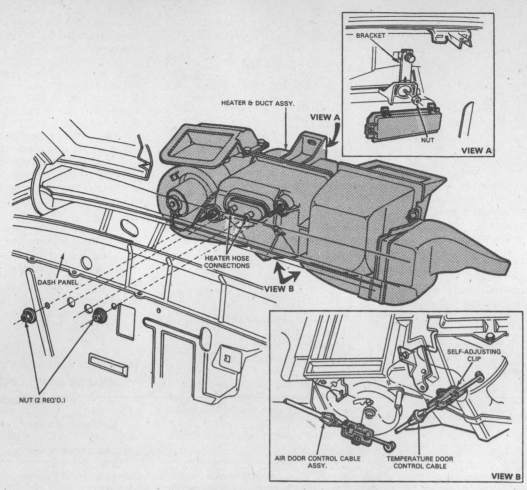

16.7 Heater case assembly mounting details (1989 and earlier models)

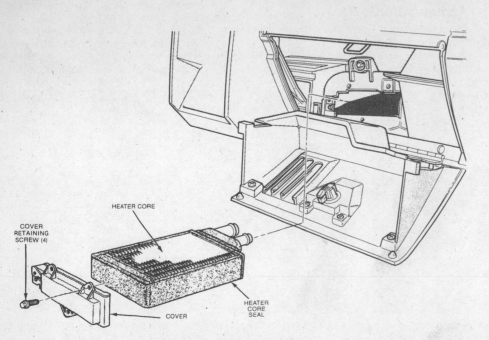

16.9 Heater core mounting details (1987 and earlier models without air conditioning)

loosen the two nuts attaching the heater case assembly to the dash panel **(see illustration)**.

8   Push the heater core tubes into the passenger compartment to loosen the heater core from the heater case assembly.

9   Pull the heater core out of the heater case assembly and remove it through the glove compartment opening **(see illustration)**.

10   Installation is the reverse of removal.

11   Fill the cooling system to the proper level with the correct mixture of coolant and water (see Chapter 1).

12   Start the engine and check for coolant leaks and proper operation of the heater. When the engine cools, recheck the coolant level.

All models with air conditioning

13   Later models may be equipped with either an aluminum or copper/brass heater core. All replacement cores sold by the dealer parts department are made of copper/brass. Be sure to install the correct seal. Identify the type of core by removing the heater hoses and checking the tube. An aluminum core will

have a gray-colored tube while a brass/copper core will have a brass-colored tube. If the vehicle is equipped with an aluminum core, be sure to replace the original seal with a new part. If the vehicle is equipped with a copper/ brass core, it is not necessary to replace the seal if it is in good shape.

14   Perform Steps 1 through 3.

15   Working inside the vehicle, remove the two screws that retain the floor duct to the plenum. Next, remove the screw that retains the floor duct to the instrument panel and remove the floor duct.

16   Remove the screws that retain the heater core cover to the case assembly **(see illustration).**

17   Remove the heater core cover and heater core.

18   Installation is the reverse of removal.

19   Refill the cooling system (see Chapter 1), start the engine and check for coolant leaks and proper operation of the heater. When the engine cools, recheck the coolant level.

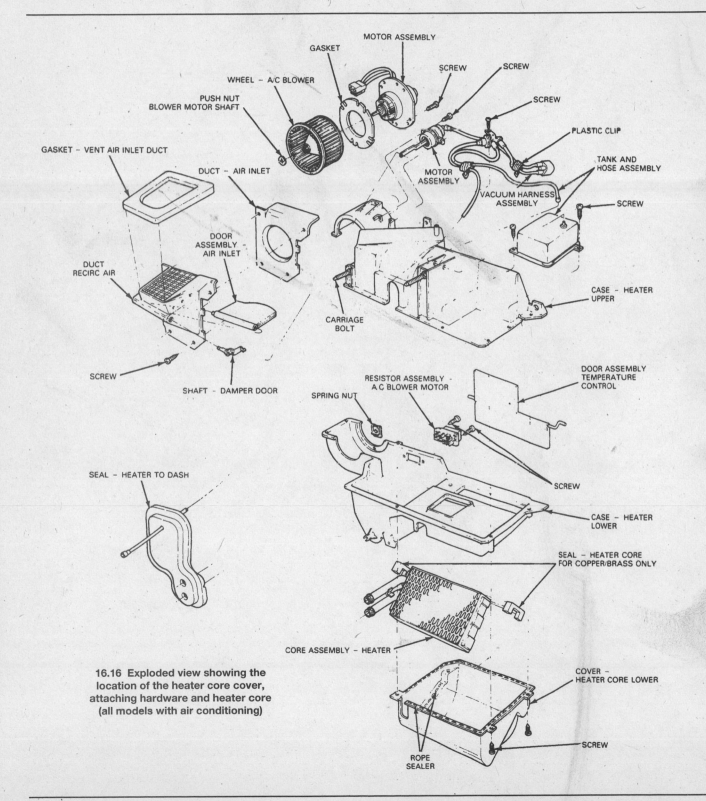

16.16 Exploded view showing the location of the heater core cover, attaching hardware and heater core (all models with air conditioning)

Notes

Chapter 4
Fuel and exhaust systems

Contents

Specifications

Carbureted vehicles

Main system feedback adjustment screw depth (below top of air horn screw boss)	
Carburetors with S on screw boss	0.250 ± 0.010 inch
All other carburetors	0.180 ± 0.010 inch
Auxiliary main jet/pullover valve adjustment	0.345 ± 0.010 inch (must protrude through the back side of the throttle pickup lever [side opposite adjustment screw head])
Fuel bowl vent adjustment clearance	
Off vehicle	0.120 ± 0.010 inch
On vehicle	0.020 to 0.040 inch
Accelerator pump stroke	2.15 ± 0.010 inch
Fuel pressure (at idle)	4.5 to 6.5 psi
Fuel pump pushrod length	2.43 inch (minimum)

Fuel-Injected vehicles

Central Fuel Injection pressure	14.5 psi
Multi-port EFI system pressure	
Four-cylinder engine	45 to 60 psi
V6 engine	30 to 45 psi

Torque specifications

Ft-lbs (unless otherwise indicated)

Carbureted vehicles

Fuel filter	
Return line nut	6 to 9
Filter inlet/outlet line nuts	15 to 18
Fuel pump	
Bolts	11 to 19
Outlet nut	15 to 18
Carburetor mounting nuts	20

Central fuel injection (CFI) system

Fuel charging assembly-to-intake manifold nuts	14 to 16 in-lbs
Injector retainer screw	18 to 22 in-lbs
Cover mounting screws	28 to 32 in-lbs
Throttle body	
ISC motor-to-bracket screws	44 to 50 in-lbs
ISC motor-to-throttle body screws	38 to 44 in-lbs
TPS sensor screws	14 to 16 in-lbs
Throttle body-to-main body screws	38 to 44 in-lbs

4

Torque specifications (continued)

Ft-lbs (unless otherwise indicated)

Multi-port fuel Injection

Air bypass valve-to-throttle body bolts	71 to 97 in-lbs
Fuel rail mounting bolts	
Four-cylinder engine	
1988 through 1993	15 to 22
1994	71 to 106 in-lbs
V6 engine	7 to 10
Fuel pressure regulator-to-injector manifold screws	27 to 40 in-lbs
Throttle body-to-upper intake manifold bolts	12 to 15
Upper and lower manifold support bracket bolts	15 to 22
Upper-to-lower intake manifold bolts	15 to 22
Accelerator cable	
Mounting bracket bolts	10 to 15
Accelerator pedal pivot bolt	6 to 9
Throttle valve bracket bolts	10 to 15

1   General information

Fuel system

The fuel system consists of the fuel tank, the fuel pump, an air cleaner assembly, either a carburetor or a fuel injection system and the various steel, plastic and/or nylon lines and fittings connecting everything together. In 1984, all US vehicles were equipped with a one-barrel Holley 6149 feedback carburetor. 1985 through 1987 US vehicles are equipped with a central fuel injection (CFI) system. The Electronic Fuel Injection (EFI) system used on 1988 to present US vehicles is known as multi-point (or multi-port) fuel injection, since there is an injector in the intake manifold at each cylinder's intake port.

The fuel pump on carburetor-equipped vehicles is a mechanical type mounted on the block and driven off the camshaft by a pushrod. The pump on fuel-injected vehicles is electric and is mounted inside the fuel tank.

Exhaust system

All vehicles are equipped with either a single exhaust manifold (four-cylinder) or pair of manifolds (V6), a catalytic converter, an exhaust pipe and a muffler. Any component of the exhaust system can be replaced. The "dual brick underbody" type converter utilizes both a three-way catalyst and a conventional oxidation catalyst (refer to Chapter 6 for further details regarding the catalytic converter).

The engine is equipped at the factory with a single-pipe exhaust system. Replacement systems differ from the production system in the number of basic pieces used. The factory-installed exhaust system has a one-piece converter. The converter assembly is a bolt-on catalyst installed between the inlet pipe and the muffler. A slip joint is used between the converter and muffler on underbody converter systems and the muffler is secured with a U-bolt. The exhaust system is usually serviced in four pieces. The rear section of the muffler inlet pipe (intermediate muffler inlet) is furnished separately from the muffler.

2   Fuel pressure relief procedure

Refer to illustrations 2.2 and 2.5
Warning: *Gasoline is extremely flammable, so take extra precautions when you work on any part of the fuel system. Don't smoke or allow open flames or bare light bulbs near the work area, and don't work in a garage where a natural gas-type appliance (such as a water heater or clothes dryer) with a pilot light is present. If you spill any fuel on your skin, rinse it off immediately with soap and water. When you perform any kind of work on the fuel system, wear safety glasses and have a Class B type fire extinguisher on hand.*

All fuel-injected models

1   Open the trunk lid and peel back the carpet from the left side of the trunk.
2   Locate the two nuts with the electrical wire running between them **(see illustration).** Remove the two nuts and pull out the fuel system inertia switch.

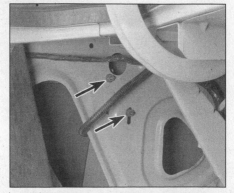

2.2   To detach the inertia switch when relieving the fuel system pressure, remove the two nuts (arrows) in the left bulkhead of the trunk

3   There are two ways to open the fuel pump electrical circuit. Either unplug the inertia switch electrical connector or shake the switch vigorously (tapping it on the floor of the trunk will also work).
4   Start the engine and allow it to run until it stops, then crank the engine for a few seconds with the starter.
5   The fuel system pressure is now relieved. When finished working on the fuel system, simply plug the electrical connector back into the switch or, if you tapped the switch on the trunk to open the circuit, reset the inertia switch by depressing the square button **(see illustration).**
6   Reinstall the inertia switch and tighten the two mounting nuts securely.

3   Fuel lines and fittings

Refer to illustrations 3.5, 3.9, 3.10, 3.13, 3.14, 3.26a, 3.26b and 3.26c
Warning: *The fuel system pressure must be relieved before disconnecting fuel lines and fittings (Section 2). Gasoline is extremely flammable, so take extra precautions when you work on any part of the fuel system. Don't smoke or allow open flames or bare light*

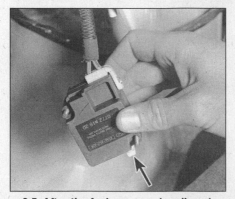

2.5   After the fuel pressure is relieved, depress the button (arrow) on the switch to reset it

bulbs near the work area, and don't work in a garage where a natural gas-type appliance (such as a water heater or clothes dryer) with a pilot light is present. If you spill any fuel on your skin, rinse it off immediately with soap and water. When you perform any kind of work on the fuel system, wear safety glasses and have a Class B type fire extinguisher on hand.

Push connect fittings - disassembly and reassembly

1   Ford uses two different push connect fitting designs. Fittings used with 3/8 and 5/16-inch diameter lines have a "hairpin" type clip; fittings used with 1/4-inch diameter lines have a "duck bill" type clip. The procedure used for releasing each type of fitting is different. The clips should be replaced whenever a connector is disassembled.

2   Disconnect all push connect fittings from fuel system components such as the fuel filter, the carburetor/fuel charging assembly, the fuel tank, etc. before removing the assembly.

3/8 and 5/16-inch fittings (hairpin clip)

3   Inspect the internal portion of the fitting for accumulations of dirt. If more than a light coating of dust is present, clean the fitting before disassembly.

4   Some adhesion between the seals in the fitting and the line will occur over a period of time. Twist the fitting on the line, then push and pull the fitting until it moves freely.

5   Remove the hairpin clip from the fitting by bending the shipping tab down until it clears the body **(see illustration)**. Then, using nothing but your hands, spread each leg about 1/8-inch to disengage the body and push the legs through the fitting. Finally, pull lightly on the triangular end of the clip and work it clear of the line and fitting. Remember, don't use any tools to perform this part of the procedure.

6   Grasp the fitting and hose and pull it straight off the line.

7   Do not reuse the original clip in the fitting. A new clip must be used.

8   Before reinstalling the fitting on the line, wipe the line end with a clean cloth. Inspect the inside of the fitting to ensure that it's free of dirt and/or obstructions.

9   To reinstall the fitting on the line, align

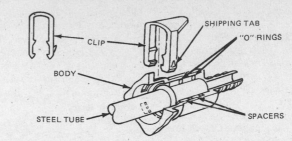

3.5 An exploded view of the hairpin clip type push connect fitting

them and push the fitting into place. When the fitting is engaged, a definite click will be heard. Pull on the fitting to ensure that it's completely engaged **(see illustration).** To install the new clip, insert it into any two adjacent openings in the fitting with the triangular portion of the clip pointing away from the fitting opening. Using your index finger, push the clip in until the legs are locked on the outside of the fitting.

1/4-inch fittings (duck bill clip)

10   The duck bill clip type fitting consists of a body, spacers, O-rings and the retaining clip **(see illustration)**. The clip holds the fitting securely in place on the line. One of the two following methods must be used to disconnect this type of fitting.

11   Before attempting to disconnect the fitting, check the visible internal portion of the fitting for accumulations of dirt. If more than a light coating of dust is evident, clean the fitting before disassembly.

12   Some adhesion between the seals in the fitting and line will occur over a period of time. Twist the fitting on the line, then push and pull the fitting until it moves freely.

13   The preferred method used to disconnect the fitting requires a special tool. To disengage the line from the fitting, align the slot in the push connect disassembly tool with either tab on the clip (90 degrees from the slots on the side of the fitting) and insert the tool **(see illustration)**. This disengages the duck bill from the line. **Note:** *Some fuel lines have a secondary bead which aligns with the outer surface of the clip. The bead can make tool insertion difficult. If necessary, use the alternative disassembly method described in Step 16.*

14   Holding the tool and the line with one hand, pull the fitting off **(see illustration).**

3.9 Connecting push connect fittings

4

Note: *Only moderate effort is necessary if the clip is properly disengaged. The use of anything other than your hands should not be required.*

15   After disassembly, inspect and clean the line sealing surface. Also inspect the inside of the fitting and the line for any internal parts that may have been dislodged from the fitting. Any loose internal parts should be immediately reinstalled (use the line to insert the parts).

16   The alternative disassembly procedure requires a pair of small Channelock pliers. The pliers must have a jaw width of 3/16-inch or less.

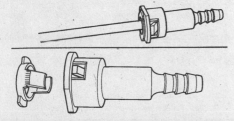

3.10 A push-connect fitting with a duck bill clip

3.13 Duck bill clip fitting removal using the special Ford disassembly tool

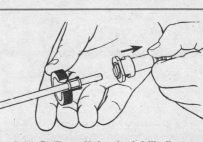

3.14 Pulling off the duck bill clip type push connect fitting

17   Align the jaws of the pliers with the openings in the side of the fitting and compress the portion of the retaining clip that engages the body. This disengages the retaining clip from the body (often one side of the clip will disengage before the other-both sides must be disengaged).

18   Pull the fitting off the line. **Note:** *Only moderate effort is required if the retaining clip has been properly disengaged. Do not use any tools for this procedure.*

19   Once the fitting is removed from the line end, check the fitting and line for any internal parts that may have been dislodged from the fitting. Any loose internal parts should be immediately reinstalled (use the line to insert the parts).

20   The retaining clip will remain on the line. Disengage the clip from the line bead to remove it. Do not reuse the retaining clip - install a new one!

21   Before reinstalling the fitting, wipe the line end with a clean cloth. Check the inside of the fitting to make sure that it's free of dirt and/or obstructions.

22   To reinstall the fitting, align it with the line and push it into place. When the fitting is engaged, a definite click will be heard. Pull on the fitting to ensure that it's fully engaged.

23   Install the new replacement clip by inserting one of the serrated edges on the duck bill portion into one of the openings. Push on the other side until the clip snaps into place.

Spring lock couplings - disassembly and reassembly

24   The fuel supply and return lines used on some engines utilize spring lock couplings instead of plastic push connect fittings at the engine fuel rail end. The male end of the spring lock coupling, which is girded by two O-rings, is inserted into a female flared end engine fitting. The coupling is secured by a garter spring which prevents disengagement by gripping the flared end of the female fitting.

25   Note that the fuel feed and return line fittings are not of the same diameter. The fuel feed line is 1/2-inch in diameter, the return fitting is 3/8-inch diameter, and associated lines are 5/8-inch diameter. Each of these lines requires a special spring lock coupling tool of the proper size, available in kit form at most automotive parts stores which carry speciality tools.

26   Study the accompanying illustrations carefully before detaching either spring lock coupling fitting **(see illustrations)**.

---

4   Fuel pump and fuel pressure - check

Refer to illustrations 4.18, 4.21 and 4.22

Mechanical fuel pump (carburetor equipped vehicles)

1   If a problem occurs in the fuel pump itself, it will normally either deliver no fuel at all or not enough to sustain high engine speeds or loads.

2   When an engine develops a lean (fuel starved) condition, the fuel pump is often to blame, but the same symptoms will be evident if the carburetor float bowl filter is clogged. A lean condition will also occur if the carburetor is malfunctioning, the fuel lines and hoses are leaking, kinked or restricted or the electrical system is shorting out or malfunctioning.

General check

3   If the fuel pump is noisy:
a) *Check for loose fuel pump mounting bolts and, if necessary, tighten them to the specified torque. Replace the gasket if necessary.*
b) *Check for loose or missing fuel line mounting clips. Loose or missing clips will sound louder when you are sitting inside the vehicle than when standing outside of it. Tighten the clips on the fuel lines if necessary.*

c) *Check for a worn, short or sticking fuel pump pushrod. Refer to the specifications for fuel pump pushrod length.*

4   Before removing a potentially defective fuel pump:
a) *Be sure the tank has fuel in it.*
b) *Be sure the fuel filter is not plugged. If it hasn't been changed recently, install a new one.*
c) *Inspect all rubber hoses from the fuel pump to the fuel tank for kinks and cracks. With the engine idling, check all fuel lines and rubber hoses and connections from the fuel pump to the fuel tank for fuel leaks. Tighten any loose connections and replace kinked, cracked or leaking fuel lines or hoses as required. Leaking or kinked lines or hoses will severely affect fuel pump performance.*
d) *Inspect the fuel pump inlet and outlet connections for fuel leaks. Tighten them if necessary.*
e) *Inspect the fuel pump diaphragm crimp (the area where the stamped steel section is attached to the casting) and the breather hole(s) in the casting for evidence of fuel or oil leakage. Replace the pump if it's leaking.*

Output (capacity) test

Warning: *Gasoline is extremely flammable, so take extra precautions when you work on any part of the fuel system. Don't smoke or allow open flames or bare light bulbs near the work area, and don't work in a garage where a natural gas-type appliance (such as a water heater or clothes dryer) with a pilot light is present. If you spill any fuel on your skin, rinse it off immediately with soap and water. When you perform any kind of work on the fuel system, wear safety glasses and have a Class B type fire extinguisher on hand.*

5   Remove the air cleaner assembly.

6   Carefully disconnect the fuel line at the fuel filter inlet. The fuel line is pressurized so it's a good idea to shield your eyes with goggles or wrap a shop rag around the fitting when breaking it loose. Use a 5/8-inch backup wrench on the filter hex to prevent damage.

3.26a If the spring lock couplings are equipped with safety clips, pry them off with a small screwdriver

3.26b Open the spring-loaded halves of the spring lock coupling tool and place it in position around the coupling, then close it

3.26c To disconnect the coupling, push the tool into the cage opening to expand the garter spring and release the female fitting, then pull the male and female fittings apart

7   Attach a section of rubber fuel hose to the end of the disconnected line with hose clamps and route the end of the hose into an approved gasoline container. Disconnect the high tension wire from the coil and ground it on the engine with a jumper wire. Crank the engine over for ten seconds. The fuel pump should deliver 1/3-pint of fuel in ten seconds.

8   If the output is as specified, perform the pressure test below.

9   If the output is less than specified, repeat the test with a remote fuel supply. Detach the hose from the fuel pump inlet line and attach a separate section of fuel hose to the line with a hose clamp. Route the end of the hose into the remote fuel supply (an approved gasoline container at least half full of fuel) and repeat the procedure in Step 7. If the output is now as specified, the problem is either a plugged intake filter or a kinked or leaking fuel hose. Make the necessary repairs.

10   If the output is still low, remove the fuel pump and pushrod (refer to the next Section). Make sure that the pushrod length is within the specified limits. If it is, replace the fuel pump.

Pressure test

11   Connect a fuel pressure gauge (0 to 15 psi) to the fuel filter end of the line.

12   Start the engine - it should be able to run for over 30 seconds on the fuel in the carburetor bowl - and read the pressure after ten seconds. Compare your reading to the specified pressure.

13   If pump pressure is not as specified, install a new fuel pump (refer to the next Section), after the fuel pump pushrod length has been verified correct.

14   Reconnect the fuel lines and install the air cleaner.

Electric fuel pump (fuel-injected vehicles)

Circuit check

Note: *The electric fuel pump and circuit are an integral part of the EEC-IV system, so a complete diagnosis must determine whether the pump and the circuit are operating properly. Such a procedure is beyond the scope of the average home mechanic; However, a loss of fuel flow and/or pressure, usually indicated by a partial or complete loss of performance, is often a sign that the fuel pump has malfunctioned. Therefore, perform the following rudimentary check of the pump if the above symptoms occur. Further investigation of the fuel pump circuit, however, should be left to a qualified professional at a dealer service department or other repair shop.*

15   Always verify that there is fuel in the tank and that none of the lines and fittings are leaking fuel before starting this procedure. The easiest way to determine whether the electric in-tank fuel pump is working is to have an assistant turn the ignition key to Start while you put you ear to the filler neck and

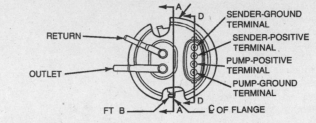

4.18 The electrical terminals at the fuel pump/sending unit flange

listen for the telltale whirring sound that indicates the pump is operating. If the pump is silent, proceed to the next Steps.

16   Locate the inertia switch in the trunk (refer to Section 2).

17   Unplug the wire harness from the inertia switch and connect a continuity tester between one of the wires and ground.

18   If no continuity exists, switch to the other wire and recheck for continuity. If continuity is not indicated at either wire, the fuel tank must be removed from the vehicle (Section 5) and continuity must be checked between the wiring harness and the switch wires. If the wires check out OK, check continuity across the pump terminals **(see illustration)**. If no continuity exists across the terminals, replace the fuel pump and sender assembly (Section 7). If continuity exists across the pump terminals, check the ground circuit or the connections to the pump from the body connector.

19   Reconnect the wire harness to the inertia switch and attach a voltmeter to the wiring harness on the pump side of the switch (the side that indicated continuity).

20   Turn the ignition switch to On while monitoring the voltage to the fuel pump. The meter should read 10-volts or more for one second, then return to zero.

21   If voltage is not as specified, check the inertia switch to make sure it's not open **(see illustration)**, then check the electrical circuit to find the fault.

Pressure check

Warning: *Gasoline is extremely flammable, so take extra precautions when you work on any part of the fuel system. Don't smoke or allow open flames or bare light bulbs near the work area, and don't work in a garage where a natural gas-type appliance (such as a water heater or clothes dryer) with a pilot light is present. If you spill any fuel on your skin, rinse it off immediately with soap and water. When you perform any kind of work on the fuel system, wear safety glasses and have a Class B type fire extinguisher on hand.*

Central fuel injection (CFI) systems

22   The CFI fuel charging assembly is equipped with either hairpin clip type fittings (utilized on earlier systems) or spring lock coupling type fittings (used on later CFI systems). In either case, you will need to fabricate a special adapter setup for your standard fuel pressure gauge before you can attach it in line between the fuel feed line and the fuel charging assembly **(see illustration)**.

23   Relieve the system fuel pressure (see Section 2).

24   Disconnect the fuel feed line hairpin clip type or spring lock type coupling and detach the fuel feed line (the bigger one) from the fuel charging assembly (see Section 3).

25   Install the fuel pressure gauge and adapter between the disconnected fuel line and the fuel charging assembly.

4

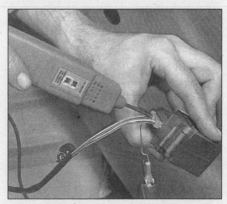

4.21 With the ignition switch off, check the inertia switch for continuity by attaching a paper clip to the alligator clip and poking it into the back side of one of the connector terminals, then pushing the probe of the continuity tester/test light into the other terminal

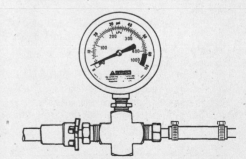

4.22 To adapt a standard fuel injection system pressure gauge for use with the CFI system, obtain a T-fitting (which will accept the gauge threaded fitting), two threaded male adapters - with male ends having an OD equal to the ID of a Ford hairpin clip type push connect fuel fitting (see Section 2) - to screw into the T-fitting and assemble as shown

26   Reset the inertia switch (see Section 2).

27   Start the engine, check the fuel system pressure at idle and compare it to the specified fuel pressure. Accelerate the engine. The pressure should remain stable regardless of engine rpm.

28   If the indicated pressure is higher than specified, either the fuel pressure regulator is stuck closed or there is an obstruction in the fuel return line.

29   If the indicated pressure is less than specified, either the fuel pump is malfunctioning, the injector is leaking, the fuel feed line is blocked or there is a leak somewhere in either the fuel feed or the fuel return line. Refer to whichever of the following sections that applies to the fuel injection system in your vehicle.

30   Relieve the system fuel pressure again, remove the gauge and re-attach the line to the fuel charging assembly.

31   Reset the inertia switch, start the engine and check for leaks.

Multi-point fuel injection models

32   With a fuel pressure gauge and adapter, the fuel pressure of all EFI equipped engines can be measured easily and quickly. These models are equipped with Schrader valves, so it is not necessary to detach any fuel lines to read the fuel pressure.

33   The special fuel pressure gauge/adapter assembly specified above is designed to relieve fuel pressure, as well as measure it, through the Schrader valve. If you have this gauge, you can use this method as an alternative to the fuel pressure relief procedure outlined in Section 2. **Warning:** *Never, however, attempt to relieve fuel pressure through the Schrader valve without this special setup.*

34   To attach the gauge, simply remove the valve cap, screw on the adapter and attach the gauge to the adapter.

35   Start the engine and allow it to reach a steady idle. Note the indicated fuel pressure reading and compare it to the specified pressure.

36   If the indicated fuel pressure is lower than specified, the problem is probably either a leaking fuel line, a malfunctioning fuel pump or a leaking injector.

37   If the indicated pressure is higher than specified, the cause could be a blocked fuel line or a stuck fuel pressure regulator.

38   Remove the special gauge, start the engine and check for fuel leaks.

---

5   Fuel tank - removal and installation

Refer to illustrations 5.5, 5.6, 5.7, 5.10 and 5.11

Note: *Don't begin this procedure until the gauge indicates that the tank is empty or nearly empty. If the tank must be removed when it's full (for example, if the fuel pump malfunctions), siphon any remaining fuel from*

5.5 Loosen the fuel filler and breather hose clamps, then detach both hoses

the tank prior to removal.

Warning: *Gasoline is extremely flammable, so take extra precautions when you work on any part of the fuel system. Don't smoke or allow open flames or bare light bulbs near the work area, and don't work in a garage where a natural gas-type appliance (such as a water heater or clothes dryer) with a pilot light is present. If you spill any fuel on your skin, rinse it off immediately with soap and water. When you perform any kind of work on the fuel system, wear safety glasses and have a Class B type fire extinguisher on hand.*

1   On fuel-injected vehicles, relieve the fuel pressure (refer to Section 2).

2   Detach the cable from the negative terminal of the battery.

3   Raise the vehicle and support it securely on jackstands.

4   Unless the vehicle has been driven far enough to completely empty the tank, it's a good idea to siphon the residual fuel out before removing the tank from the vehicle. Siphon or pump the fuel out through the fuel filler pipe and into an approved gasoline container. On US vehicles, a small-diameter hose may be necessary because of the small trap door installed in the fuel filler pipe to prevent vapors from escaping during refueling. Fuel-injected vehicles have reservoirs inside the tank to maintain fuel near the pump pick-up during vehicle cornering maneuvers and when the fuel level is low.

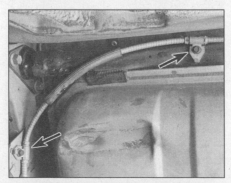

5.7 Remove the right side parking brake cable bracket bolts and pull the cable down so it will clear the right end of the fuel tank

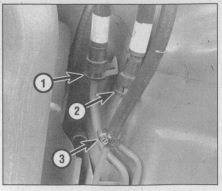

5.6 Release the hairpin clip at the fuel delivery hose (1), remove the duck bill clip from the fuel return line (2) and loosen the vapor recovery line hose clamp (3), then detach all three hoses

The reservoirs could prevent siphon tubes or hoses from reaching the bottom of the fuel tank. This situation can be overcome by repositioning the siphon hose several times.

5   Loosen the hose clamps securing the fuel filler neck hose and the breather hose to the fuel tank **(see illustration)** and detach both hoses.

6   Disconnect the fuel hose, the return hose and the vapor hose **(see illustration)** .

7   Remove both right side parking brake cable bracket bolts **(see illustration)** and lower the cable out of the way.

8   If possible, disconnect the wire harness from the fuel level sender unit before detaching the tank. On some vehicles, the harness connector is on top of the tank and inaccessible. Since no intermediate connection point is provided, the harness must be disconnected from the fuel sender with the tank suspended under the vehicle.

9   Place a floor jack under the tank and position a block of wood between the jack pad and the tank. Raise the jack until it's supporting the tank.

10   Remove the bolts or nuts from the front ends of the fuel tank straps **(see illustration)**. The straps are hinged at the other end so you can swing them out of the way.

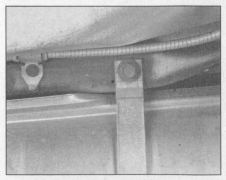

5.10 The two fuel tank retaining straps (this is the right side one) are hinged at the rear and bolted to the body at the front - after supporting the tank with a floor jack. remove the bolts and swing both straps down and to the rear

5.11 Lower the tank far enough to get at the sender unit (carburetor-equipped vehicles) or fuel pump/sending unit (fuel injected vehicles) and unplug the wire harness connector

11   Lower the tank far enough to unplug the wiring harness **(see illustration)**.

12   Remove the tank from the vehicle.

13   If you're replacing the tank, or having it cleaned or repaired, refer to Section 7 and remove the sender unit (carburetor-equipped vehicles) or fuel pump/sending unit (fuel-injected vehicles). For information regarding tank cleaning and repair, refer to Section 6.

14   Refer to Section 7 and install the fuel pump/sending unit.

15   Installation is the reverse of removal.

---

6   Fuel tank - cleaning and repair

1   Repairs to the fuel tank or filler neck should be performed by a professional with the proper training to carry out this critical and potentially dangerous work. Even after cleaning and flushing, explosive fumes can remain and could explode during repair of the tank.

2   If the fuel tank is removed from the vehicle, it should not be placed in an area where sparks or open flames could ignite the fumes coming out of the tank. Be especially careful inside garages where a natural gas appliance is located because the pilot light could cause an explosion.

---

7   Fuel pump - removal and installation

Refer to illustrations 7.2, 7.13 and 7.16
Warning: *Gasoline is extremely flammable, so take extra precautions when you work on any part of the fuel system. Don't smoke or allow open flames or bare light bulbs near the work area, and don't work in a garage where a natural gas-type appliance (such as a water heater or clothes dryer) with a pilot light is present. If you spill any fuel on your skin, rinse it off immediately with soap and water. When you perform any kind of work on the fuel system, wear safety glasses and have a Class B type fire extinguisher on hand.*

Mechanical fuel pump (carburetor equipped vehicles)

1   Loosen the threaded fuel line fittings (at the pump) with the proper size wrench (a flare nut wrench is recommended), then retighten them until they're just snug. Don't remove the lines at this time. The outlet line is pressurized, so protect your eyes with safety goggles or wrap the fitting with a shop rag, then loosen it carefully.

2   Loosen the mounting bolts two turns **(see illustration).** Use your hands only to loosen the fuel pump if it's stuck to the block. Have an assistant operate the starter while you keep one hand on the pump. As the camshaft turns, the pump pushrod will operate the pump - when the pump feels loose, stop turning the engine over.

3   Disconnect the lines from the pump.

4   Remove the fuel pump bolts and detach the pump and gasket. Discard the old gasket. Pull out the pushrod.

5   Measure the pushrod length and check it for wear. If it's shorter than specified or worn excessively, replace it.

6   Remove all old gasket material and sealant from the engine block. If you're installing the original pump, remove all the old gasket material from the pump mating surface as well. Wipe the mating surfaces of the block and pump with a cloth saturated with lacquer thinner or acetone.

7   Install the fuel pump pushrod. Insert the bolts through the pump (to use as a guides for the new gasket) and place the gasket in position on the fuel pump mounting flange. Position the fuel pump on the block (make sure the pump arm engages the pushrod properly). Tighten the bolts a little at a time until they're at the specified torque.

8   Attach the fuel lines to the pump. Start the threaded fitting by hand to avoid cross-threading it. Tighten the outlet nut securely. If any of the hoses are cracked, hardened or otherwise deteriorated, replace them at this time.

9   Start the engine and check for fuel leaks for two minutes.

10   Stop the engine and check the fuel line connections for leaks by running a finger under each fitting. Check for oil leaks at the fuel pump mounting gasket.

Electric fuel pump (fuel injected vehicles)

11   Relieve the fuel system pressure (refer to Section 2).

12   Remove the fuel tank (refer to Section 5).

13   Using a **brass** punch or wooden dowel only, tap the lock ring counterclockwise until it's loose **(see illustration).**

14   Carefully pull the fuel pump/sending unit assembly from the tank.

15   Remove the old lock ring gasket and discard it.

16   If you're planning to reinstall the original fuel pump/sending unit, remove the strainer by prying it off with a screwdriver **(see illustration),** wash it in clean solvent, then push it back onto the metal pipe on the end of the pump. If you're installing a new pump/sending unit, the assembly will include a new strainer.

17   Clean the fuel pump mounting flange

4

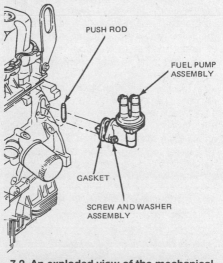

7.2 An exploded view of the mechanical type fuel pump used on carburetor equipped vehicles

7.13 Be sure to use a BRASS punch when loosening the lock ring on the electric fuel pump/sending unit (a spark from a steel punch or hammer could cause an explosion)

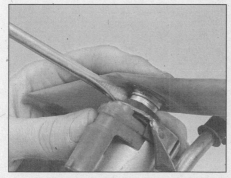

7.16 If you're replacing the pump, this step isn't necessary, but if you're going to reinstall the old pump, remove the strainer and clean it with solvent

8.4 To remove the air cleaner cover assembly, detach both vacuum hoses and remove all four cover bolts (arrows)

8.7 Depress the tang in the floor of the air cleaner housing with a screwdriver to disconnect the fresh air duct

8.8 To remove the air cleaner housing assembly, detach the thermactor hose clip (arrow), remove the hose and unscrew the bolts (arrows), then lift up the housing and disconnect the hose from the vacuum motor temperature sensor

and the tank mounting surface and seal ring groove.

18   Installation is the reverse of removal. Apply a thin coat of heavy grease to the new lock ring gasket to hold it in place during assembly.

8   Air cleaner housing - removal and installation

Refer to illustrations 8.4, 8.7 and 8.8

Carbureted and CFI engines

1   Open and secure the hood.
2   Disconnect the cable from the negative terminal of the battery.
3   Detach the PCV hose from the elbow fitting on the right rear lower corner of the air cleaner housing.
4   Label the vacuum hoses and fittings, then detach the hoses from the air cleaner housing cover **(see illustration)**.
5   Remove the screws **(see illustration 8.4)** and detach the cover.
6   Note how it's installed (flutes facing down), then remove the air filter.
7   Depress the tang **(see illustration)** that secures the fresh air duct to the air cleaner housing and detach the duct from the housing by pulling it forward.
8   Remove the hairpin clip that retains the thermactor hose to the right side of the housing **(see illustration)**.
9   Remove the two housing bolts **(see illustration 8.8)**.
10   Raise the air cleaner housing and detach the pre-heat tube (the bellows-like duct that attaches to the rear side of the housing) and the vacuum hose attached to the temperature sensor for the vacuum motor (for further information on the motor and the sensor (refer to Chapter 6).
11   Remove the air cleaner housing.
12   If you're planning to replace the housing, you'll have to remove both the vacuum motor and the temperature sensor and install them on the new housing. Refer to Chapter 6 for this procedure.
13   Installation is the reverse of removal.

Multiport fuel-injected engines

14   Remove the PCV tube from the lower rear of the air cleaner housing.
15   Remove the Pulse Air hose from the lower front of the air cleaner housing by rotating it 90-degrees clockwise.
16   On 1991 and earlier models, loosen the clamp and remove the clean air flex tube at the throttle body.
17   On 1991 and earlier models, remove the hot air tube from the air cleaner housing.
18   On 1991 and earlier models, loosen the clamp and disconnect the resonator tube at the air cleaner housing.
19   On 1992 and later models, loosen the clamp and remove the clean air flex tube at the MAF sensor.
20   On 1992 and later models, disconnect the MAF sensor electrical connector and, on four-cylinder models, the Intake Air Temperature (IAT) sensor wire from rear of the housing.
21   Remove the bracket-to-air cleaner housing retaining screw(s) from rear of housing.
22   Lift the air cleaner off the locating pins and the release tabs on air inlet tube. Remove the housing from the vehicle.
23   Installation is the reverse of removal.

9   Carburetor - removal and installation

Warning: *Gasoline is extremely flammable, so take extra precautions when you work on any part of the fuel system. Don't smoke or allow open flames or bare light bulbs near the work area, and don't work in a garage where a natural gas-type appliance (such as a water heater or clothes dryer) with a pilot light is present. If you spill any fuel on your skin, rinse it off immediately with soap and water. When you perform any kind of work on the fuel system, wear safety glasses and have a Class B type fire extinguisher on hand.*

Removal

1   Remove the air cleaner duct from the carburetor.
2   Disconnect the throttle cable from the throttle lever.

3   If your vehicle is equipped with an automatic transaxle, disconnect the TV rod from the throttle lever.
4   **Note:** *Label all vacuum hoses and fittings before removing them to simplify installation.* Disconnect all vacuum hoses and the fuel line from the carburetor. Use a back-up wrench on the fuel inlet fitting when removing the fuel line to avoid changing the float level.
5   Label the wires and terminals, then unplug all wire harness connectors.
6   Disconnect the canister vent hose at the bowl vent tube.
7   If your vehicle is equipped with a Model 6149 carburetor, remove the oxygen sensor wire from the clip on the pulldown diaphragm assembly mounting screw.
8   Remove the two mounting nuts and detach the carburetor from the intake manifold. Remove the carburetor mounting gasket.

Installation

9   Clean the gasket mating surfaces of the intake manifold and the carburetor to remove all traces of the old gasket. Place a new gasket on the intake manifold. Position the carburetor on the gasket and install the mounting nuts. To prevent distortion or damage to the carburetor body flange, tighten the nuts to the specified torque in several steps.
10   The remaining installation steps are the reverse of removal.
11   Check and adjust if necessary the curb idle speed, idle fuel mixture and fast idle speed (refer to Section 10).
12   Refer to Chapter 7B for the automatic transaxle TV rod adjustment procedure.

10   Carburetor - overhaul and adjustment

Refer to illustrations 10.6, 10.10, 10.11, 10.15, 10.18, 10.21, 10.30, 10.35a and 10.35b

Warning: *Gasoline is extremely flammable, so take extra precautions when you work on* *any part of the fuel system. Don't smoke or allow open flames or bare light bulbs near the work area, and don't work in a garage where a natural gas-type appliance (such as a water heater or clothes dryer) with a pilot light is present. If you spill any fuel on your skin, rinse it off immediately with soap and water. When you perform any kind of work on the fuel system, wear safety glasses and have a Class B type fire extinguisher on hand.*

Diagnosis

1   A thorough road test and check of carburetor adjustments should be done before any major carburetor service work. Specifications for some adjustments are listed on the Vehicle Emissions Control Information label found in the engine compartment.

2   Some performance complaints directed at the carburetor are actually a result of loose, out-of-adjustment or malfunctioning engine or electrical components. Others develop when vacuum hoses leak, are disconnected or are incorrectly routed. The proper approach to analyzing carburetor problems should include a routine check of the following items:

a)   Inspect all vacuum hoses and actuators for leaks and correct installation (see Chapter 6).
b)   Tighten the intake manifold nuts and carburetor mounting nuts evenly and securely.
c)   Perform a cylinder compression test.
d)   Clean or replace the spark plugs as necessary.
e)   Check the resistance of the spark plug wires.
f)   Inspect the ignition primary wires and check the vacuum advance operation. Replace any defective parts.
g)   Check the ignition timing according to the instructions printed on the Emissions Control Information label.
h)   Check the fuel pump pressure.
i)   Check the heat control valve in the air cleaner for proper operation (see Chapter 6).
j)   Check/replace the air filter element.
k)   Check PCV system (see Chapter 6).

3   Carburetor problems usually show up as flooding, hard starting, stalling, severe backfiring, poor acceleration and lack of response to idle mixture screw adjustments. A carburetor that is leaking fuel and/or

1   Choke linkage assembly
2   Mechanical fuel bowl vent assembly
3   Air cleaner bracket and screws
4   Air horn assembly and screw
5   Choke bimetal assembly
6   Choke pulldown lever, lock washer and retaining nut
7   Accelerator pump assembly and auxiliary main jet/pullover valve actuating rod
8   Accelerator pump actuator assembly
9a   Main feedback control assembly (model 6149)
9b   Vacuum gradient power enrichment assembly
10   Air horn gasket
11   Solekicker
12   Main metering jet
13   WOT enrichment pullover valve
14   Accelerator pump check ball and weight
15a Main system feedback metering valve assembly (model 6149)
15b Vacuum gradient power enrichment metering valve assembly (model 1949)
16   Float assembly
17   Fast idle cam assembly
18   Pulldown diaphragm and linkage assembly
19   Drop-in booster venturi and O-ring
20   Main body assembly
21   Fuel inlet fitting (needle and seat) and gasket
22   Hot idle compensator gasket, cover and screw

23   Throttle position sensor and mounting screw
24   Throttle body gasket
25   Curb idle RPM adjusting screw and spring
26   Idle mixture components
27   Fast idle RPM adjusting screw and spring
28   Throttle body assembly and screws
29   Idle channel restrictor and O-ring

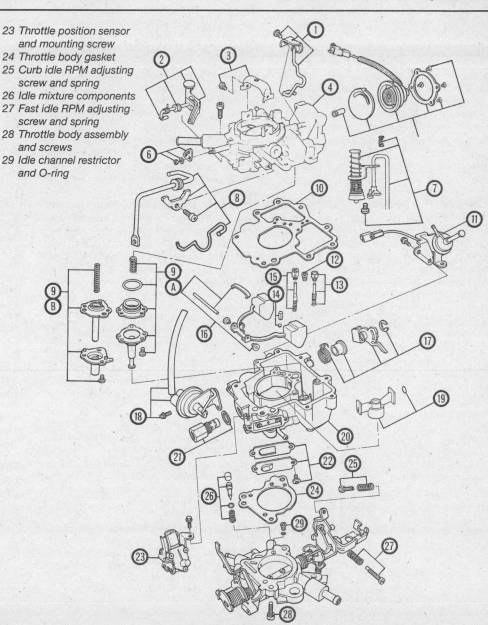

10.6 Model 1949 non-feedback (Canadian) and Model 6149 feedback (US) carburetor components - exploded view

covered with wet looking deposits definitely needs attention.

4   Diagnosing carburetor problems may require that the engine be started and run with the air cleaner off. While running the engine without the air cleaner, backfires are possible. This situation is likely to occur if the carburetor is malfunctioning, but just the removal of the air cleaner can lean the fuel/air mixture enough to produce an engine backfire. **Warning:** *Do not position any part of your body, especially your face, directly over the carburetor during inspection and servicing procedures while the engine is running.*

Overhaul

5   Once it's determined that the carburetor needs adjustment or an overhaul, several options are available. If you're going to attempt to overhaul the carburetor yourself, first obtain a good quality carburetor rebuild kit (which will include all necessary gaskets, internal parts, instructions and a parts list). You'll also need some special solvent and a means of blowing out the internal passages of the carburetor with air.

6   Because the vehicles covered by this book are primarily fuel injected (most Canadian vehicles and 1984 US models are equipped with carburetors) and because carburetor designs are constantly modified by the manufacturer in order to meet increasingly more stringent emissions regulations, it isn't feasible for us to do a step-by-step overhaul of each type. You'll receive a detailed, well illustrated set of instructions with any carburetor overhaul kit; they will apply in a more specific manner to the carburetor on your vehicle. An exploded view of a

10.10 With the air horn assembly removed, place a finger over the float hinge pin retainer and invert the main body, then catch the accelerator pump check ball and weight

typical Tempo/Topaz carburetor is included here **(see illustration on previous page)**.

7   Another alternative is to obtain a new or rebuilt carburetor. They are readily available from dealers and auto parts stores. Make absolutely sure the exchange carburetor is identical to the original. A tag is usually attached to the top of the carburetor. It will aid in determining the exact type of carburetor you have. When obtaining a rebuilt carburetor or a rebuild kit, take time to make sure that the kit or carburetor matches your application exactly. Seemingly insignificant differences can make a large difference in the performance of your engine.

8   If you choose to overhaul your own carburetor, allow enough time to disassemble the carburetor carefully, soak the necessary parts in the cleaning solvent (usually for at least one-half day or according to the instructions listed on the carburetor cleaner) and

10.11 Using a straightedge, check the position of the floats (they should be flush with the surface of the main body casting)

reassemble it, which will usually take much longer than disassembly. When disassembling the carburetor, match each part with the illustration in the carburetor kit and lay the parts out in order on a clean work surface. Overhauls by inexperienced mechanics can result in an engine which runs poorly or not at all. To avoid this, use care and patience when disassembling the carburetor so you can reassemble it correctly.

Adjustments

Float adjustment - dry

9   Remove the carburetor air horn.

10   Place a finger over the float hinge pin retainer and invert the main body. Catch the accelerator pump check ball and weight **(see illustration)**.

11   Using a straightedge, check the position of the floats **(see illustration)**. The dry float setting is correct when the outboard edge of both pontoons is flush with the surface of the main body casting (without a gasket). If adjustment is required, carefully bend the float tabs to raise or lower the float level.

12   Once the adjustment is correct, turn the main body right side up and check the float alignment. The float should move freely without contacting the float bowl walls. If the float pontoons are misaligned, straighten them by bending the float arms. Recheck the float level.

13   Before installing the air horn, insert the check ball first and then the weight.

Diaphragm adjustment (model 6149 carburetor only)

14   Remove the main system feedback diaphragm adjustment screw lead sealing disc from the air horn by drilling a 3/32-inch hole through the disc. Then insert a small punch to pry the disc out.

15   Turn the main system feedback adjustment screw as required to position the top of the screw 0.180 ± 0.010-inch below the top of the air horn **(see illustration)**. **Note:** *On carburetors stamped with an "S" on the top of the air horn adjustment screw boss, adjust the screw until it's 0.250 ± 0.010-inch down.*

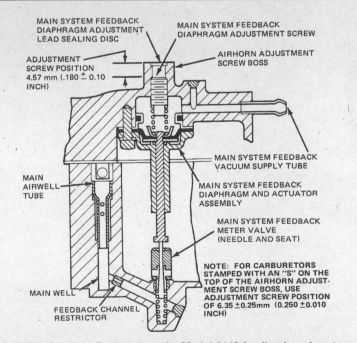

MAIN SYSTEM FEEDBACK DIAPHRAGM ADJUSTMENT LEAD SEALING DISC

MAIN SYSTEM FEEDBACK DIAPHRAGM ADJUSTMENT SCREW

ADJUSTMENT SCREW POSITION 4.57 mm (.180 ± 0.10 INCH)

AIRHORN ADJUSTMENT SCREW BOSS

MAIN AIRWELL TUBE

MAIN SYSTEM FEEDBACK VACUUM SUPPLY TUBE

MAIN SYSTEM FEEDBACK DIAPHRAGM AND ACTUATOR ASSEMBLY

MAIN SYSTEM FEEDBACK METER VALVE (NEEDLE AND SEAT)

NOTE: FOR CARBURETORS STAMPED WITH AN "S" ON THE TOP OF THE AIRHORN ADJUSTMENT SCREW BOSS, USE ADJUSTMENT SCREW POSITION OF 6.35 ±0.25mm (0.250 ±0.010 INCH)

MAIN WELL

FEEDBACK CHANNEL RESTRICTOR

10.15 Diaphragm adjustment on the Model 6149 feedback carburetor

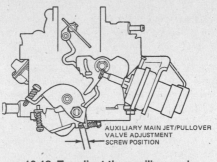

10.18 To adjust the auxiliary main jet/pullover valve adjustment screw, turn it in or out as required

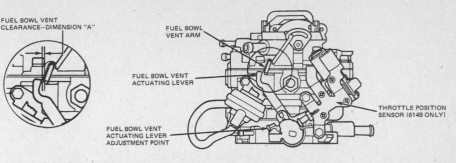

10.21 Lever clearance adjustment for the mechanical fuel bowl vent lever

16 Install a new lead sealing disc and stake it with a 1/4-inch pin punch.

17 Apply a 10-inches of mercury vacuum to the diaphragm and check for leaks. The diaphragm should hold vacuum.

Auxiliary main jet/pullover valve timing adjustment

18 The length of the auxiliary main jet/pullover valve adjustment screw which protrudes through the back side (the side opposite the adjustment screw head) of the throttle pick-up lever must be 0.345 ± 0.010-inch. To adjust it, turn the screw in or out as required **(see illustration)** .

Mechanical fuel bowl vent lever clearance adjustment

Note: *The lever clearance can be adjusted with the carburetor either on or off the vehicle. If it's done on the vehicle, wait until after the curb idle speed is correctly set.*

19 To adjust it on the vehicle, secure the choke plate in the wide open position.

20 Turn the ignition key to the On position to activate the TSP (engine not running). Open the throttle so the TSP plunger extends.

21 Verify that the throttle is in the idle set position (contacting the TSP plunger). Measure the clearance between the fuel bowl vent arm and the bowl vent actuating lever **(see illustration)**.

22 Fuel bowl vent clearance (dimension A) should be as specified (note that there is a difference between the on and off-vehicle specifications).

23 If adjustment is required, bend the bowl vent actuator lever at the adjustment point to obtain the required clearance.

24 When making the adjustment with the carburetor removed, secure the choke plate in the wide open position.

25 Set the throttle at the TSP off position.

26 Turn the TSP off idle adjustment screw counterclockwise until the throttle plate is closed in the throttle bore.

27 Fuel bowl vent clearance (dimension A) should be as specified.

28 If adjustment is required, bend the bowl vent actuator lever at the adjustment point to

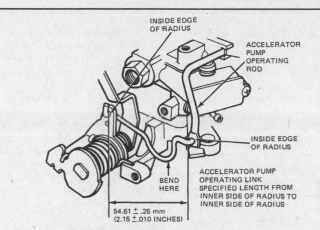

10.30 Accelerator pump stroke adjustment

obtain the required clearance. **Caution:** *Do not bend the fuel bowl vent arm and/or the adjacent portion of the actuator lever. TSP Off rpm must be set after carburetor installation.*

Accelerator pump stroke adjustment

29 Check the length of the accelerator pump operating link from the inside edge at the pump rod to the inside edge at the throttle lever hole. The dimension should be as specified.

30 Adjust it by bending the loop in the operating link **(see illustration)**.

Throttle position sensor adjustment (model 6149 carburetor only)

31 This adjustment is required if the throttle position sensor, housing or actuating pin assembly is replaced. If it's required, it must be done by a dealer service department because a specialized tool that is both

expensive and unavailable to the home mechanic is required.

Wide open throttle (WOT) A/C cut-off switch adjustment

Note: *The WOT A/C cut-off switch is a normally closed switch that allows current to flow at any throttle position other than wide open.*

32 Disconnect the wiring harness at the switch connector.

33 Connect a self-powered test light to the switch terminals. With the throttle at curb idle, TSP Off idle or fast idle position, the test light must be on. If the test light is not on, replace the switch assembly.

34 Rotate the throttle to the wide open position. The test light must go off, indicating an open circuit.

35 If the light remains on, insert a 0.165-inch drill bit shank (a 5/32-inch bit should work fine) between the throttle lever stop and the WOT stop boss on the carburetor main body casting **(see illustration)**. Hold the

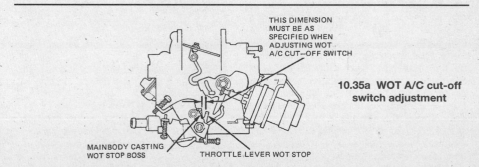

10.35a WOT A/C cut-off switch adjustment

4

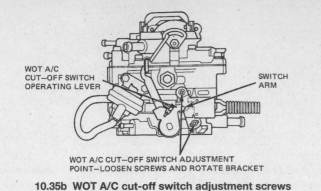

WOT A/C
CUT—OFF SWITCH
OPERATING LEVER

SWITCH
ARM

WOT A/C CUT—OFF SWITCH ADJUSTMENT
POINT—LOOSEN SCREWS AND ROTATE BRACKET

10.35b WOT A/C cut-off switch adjustment screws

throttle open as far as possible against the bit. Loosen the two switch mounting screws enough to allow the switch to pivot **(see illustration)**. Rotate the switch assembly until the test light just goes out. If the light doesn't go out within the adjustment range, replace the switch. If the light goes out, tighten the two switch bracket-to carburetor screws and remove the drill bit. Repeat Step 34.

11 Central fuel injection (CFI) system - general information

The central fuel injection (CFI) system is a single-point, pulse-time-modulated injection system. Fuel is metered into the air intake stream in accordance with engine demands by a single solenoid injection valve mounted in a throttle body on the intake manifold.

Fuel is supplied from the fuel tank by a low pressure, electric fuel pump mounted in the fuel tank. The fuel is filtered and sent to the fuel charging assembly injector fuel cavity and then to the regulator where the fuel delivery pressure is maintained at a constant value of 39 psi. A single injector nozzle is mounted vertically above the throttle plates and connected in series with the fuel pressure regulator. Excess fuel supplied by the pump but not needed by the engine is returned to the fuel tank by a steel fuel return line.

The fuel charging assembly consists of five individual components which perform the fuel and air metering function. The throttle body assembly is attached to the conventional carburetor mounting pad on the intake manifold and houses the air control system, fuel injector nozzle, fuel pressure regulator, fuel pressure diagnostic valve, cold engine speed control and throttle position sensor.

Air flow to the engine is controlled by a single butterfly valve mounted in a two piece, die-cast aluminum housing called a throttle body. The butterfly valve is identical in configuration to the throttle plates of a conventional carburetor and is actuated by a similar pedal and linkage arrangement.

The fuel injector nozzle is mounted vertically above the throttle plate and is an electro-mechanical device which meters and atomizes the fuel delivered to the engine. The injector valve body consists of a solenoid actuated ball and seat valve assembly.

An electrical control signal from the EEC electronic processor activates the solenoid, causing the ball to move off the seat and allows fuel to flow. The injector flow orifice is fixed and the fuel supply is constant. Therefore, fuel flow to the engine is controlled by how long the solenoid is energized.

The pressure regulator is integral to the fuel charging main body near the rear of the air horn surface. The regulator is located so as to nullify the effects of the supply line pressure drops. Its design is such that it is not sensitive to back pressure in the return line to the tank.

A second function of the pressure regulator is to maintain fuel supply pressure upon fuel pump shutdown. The regulator functions as a downstream check valve and traps the fuel between itself and the fuel pump. The constant fuel pressure level after engine shutdown precludes fuel line vapor formation and allows for rapid restarts and stable idle operation immediately thereafter.

The throttle actuator controls idle speed by modulating the throttle lever for the required air flow to maintain the desired engine rpm for any operating condition, from an idling cold engine to a warm engine at normal operating temperature. An idle tracking switch (ITS) determines when the throttle lever has contacted the actuator, signaling the need to control engine rpm. The DC motor extends or retracts a linear shaft through a gear reduction system. The motor direction is determined by the polarity of the applied voltage.

12.2 Before removing the fuel injector from the fuel charging assembly main body, unplug the electrical connector and set it aside, then remove the screw (arrow) and the retainer

A throttle position sensor (non-adjustable) is mounted to the throttle shaft on the choke side of the fuel charging assembly and is used to supply a voltage output proportional to the change in the throttle position. The TP sensor is used by the computer (EEC) to determine the operation mode (closed throttle, part throttle and wide open throttle) for selection of the proper fuel mixture, spark and EGR at all engine speeds and loads.

12 Central fuel injection (CFI) system - component replacement

Refer to illustrations 12.2, 12.3, 12.4, 12.5a, 12.5b, 12.10, 12.12, 12.13, 12.14a, 12.14b, 12.15, 12.19a, 12.19b, 12.20 and 12.23
Warning: *Gasoline is extremely flammable, so take extra precautions when you work on any part of the fuel system. Don't smoke or allow open flames or bare light bulbs near the work area, and don't work in a garage where a natural gas-type appliance (such as a water heater or clothes dryer) with a pilot light is present. If you spill any fuel on your skin, rinse it off immediately with soap and water. When you perform any kind of work on the fuel system, wear safety glasses and have a Class B type fire extinguisher on hand.*

Fuel Injector

Note: *If you're replacing the fuel injector, it isn't necessary to remove the fuel charging assembly from the intake manifold. If, however, you need to replace the base gasket, the spacer gasket between the main body and the throttle body or the idle speed control (ISC) throttle actuator, the fuel charging assembly must be removed from the intake manifold. Other than the components specifically mentioned here, we do not recommend further disassembly of the fuel charging assembly.*

1   Detach the cable from the negative terminal of the battery and relieve the fuel system pressure (refer to Section 2).
2   Unplug the fuel injector wire harness connector and remove the screw and retainer **(see illustration)**.
3   Using a screwdriver, carefully pry the fuel injector out of the fuel charging assembly **(see illustration)**.

12.3 Carefully pry the injector from the bore in the fuel charging assembly main body with a screwdriver

12.4 The small O-ring which seals the lower end of the injector will often come off the injector during removal and stick to the walls of the injector bore - be sure to remove it

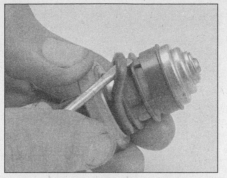

12.5a If you're planning to reinstall the old injector, be sure to peel off the old injector O-rings with a small screwdriver and discard them

12.5b Note the position of the large (upper) O-ring and the small (lower) one - they must be attached properly before installing the injector

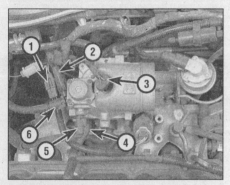

12.10 Disconnect the following items before removing the fuel charging assembly:

1 ISC connector	4 PCV valve
2 TPS connector	vacuum hose
3 Fuel injector	5 Fuel line fitting
connector	6 Fuel line fitting

4   The injector has two O-rings - a large, upper O-ring and a small, lower one. The lower O-ring may stick to the wall of the fuel injector bore **(see illustration)**. Be sure to remove and discard it.

5   Whether you're replacing the injector or reinstalling the original, do not reuse the old O-rings. Carefully peel the O-rings off the old injector **(see illustration)**. Position the new O-rings as shown **(see illustration)** and lubricate them with clean engine oil.

6   Installation of the injector is the reverse of removal.

12.12 To disconnect either fuel line fitting, spread the tangs of the hairpin clip apart far enough to disengage them from the fitting body, then pull the clip out - the fitting can then be pulled off

Base gasket

7   Relieve the fuel system pressure (refer to Section 2).

8   Detach the cable from the negative terminal of the battery.

9   Remove the air intake duct (refer to Section 8).

10   Clearly label the wires and terminals on the throttle body, then unplug and set aside all wires **(see illustration)**.

11   Detach the PCV hose from the throttle body **(see illustration 12.10)**.

12   Detach the fuel pressure and return lines from the fuel charging assembly **(see illus-**

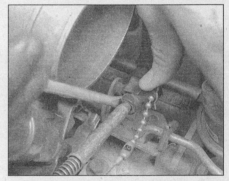

12.13 Using a screwdriver, pry the accelerator cable and, if equipped, the cruise control cable, from the throttle shaft linkage

tration). If necessary, refer to Section 3 for a detailed description of fuel line fitting removal.

13   Detach the throttle cable and (if equipped) cruise control cable assembly from the throttle rod **(see illustration)**.

14   If your vehicle is equipped with an automatic transaxle, remove the C-clip **(see illustration)** and detach the transmission downshift rod from the throttle shaft. Push down on the rod to detach it **(see illustration)**.

15   Remove the two fuel charging assembly mounting nuts **(see illustration)** and detach the assembly and gasket from the intake manifold.

4

12.14a If your vehicle is equipped with an automatic transaxle, pop the C-clip loose with a screwdriver...

12.14b ... then disengage the downshift rod from the throttle shaft linkage

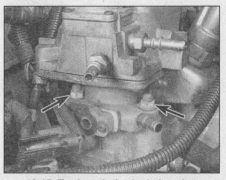

12.15 To detach the fuel charging assembly from the intake manifold, remove both mounting nuts (arrows)

12.19a To remove the ISC bracket, lay the fuel charging assembly upside down on a workbench and remove these two screws . . .

12.19b . . . followed by this one

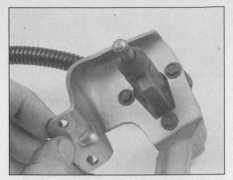

12.20 To detach the ISC motor from the bracket, remove the three mounting screws

16   If the gasket was leaking, position a new gasket on the manifold, install the fuel charging assembly and tighten the mounting nuts to the specified torque.

17   The remainder of the installation procedure is the reverse of removal.

Idle speed control (ISC) throttle actuator

Note: *Handle the fuel charging assembly carefully when servicing it on the bench to avoid damage to the throttle plates.*

18   Remove the fuel charging assembly (see Steps 7 through 15).

19   Remove the three ISC bracket screws **(see illustrations)** and detach the ISC and bracket assembly from the fuel charging assembly.

20   Remove the three ISC mounting screws **(see illustration)** and separate the ISC from the mounting bracket.

21   Installation is the reverse of removal.

Fuel charging body gasket

22   Remove the fuel charging assembly and ISC (Steps 7 through 15 and Step 19).

23   Turn the fuel charging assembly over and remove the four screws attaching the throttle body to the main body, then separate the two halves **(see illustration)**.

24   Remove and discard the old gasket. If it's necessary to use a gasket scraper, don't damage the mating surface.

12.23 To separate the throttle body from the main body of the fuel charging assembly, remove the four screws (arrows)

25   With the main body resting upside down on the bench, place the new gasket in position, attach the throttle body, install the four screws and tighten them evenly and securely.

26   Install the ISC and fuel charging assembly.

13   Multi-point fuel Injection system - general information

The Electronic Fuel Injection (EFI) system used on the four-cylinder engine since 1988 and as introduced on the V6 engine in 1992 is known as a multi-point, pulse time, speed density control design. Fuel is metered into the intake air stream in accordance with engine demand through multiple injectors (one for each cylinder) mounted on a tuned intake manifold.

An on-board Electronic Engine Control (EEC-IV) computer accepts inputs from various engine sensors to compute the required fuel flow rate necessary to maintain a prescribed air/fuel ratio throughout the entire engine operational range. The computer then outputs a command to the fuel injectors to meter the correct quantity of fuel. The period of time that the injectors are energized (known as "on time" or "pulse width") is controlled by the EEC computer. Air entering the engine is sensed by speed, pressure and temperature sensors. The outputs of these sensors are processed by the EEC-IV computer. The computer determines the needed injector pulse width and outputs a command to the injector to meter the exact quantity of fuel.

The EEC-IV engine control system also determines and compensates for the age of the vehicle and its uniqueness and it even senses and compensates for changes in altitude.

An electric in-tank fuel pump forces pressurized fuel through a series of metal and plastic lines and an in line fuel filter/reservoir to the fuel charging manifold assembly.

The fuel supply manifold assembly incorporates electrically actuated fuel injectors directly above each intake port.

When energized, the injectors spray a metered quantity of fuel into the intake air stream. A constant fuel pressure drop is maintained across the injector nozzles by a pressure regulator. The regulator is connected in series with the fuel injectors and is positioned downstream from them. Excess fuel passes through the regulator and returns to the fuel tank through a fuel return line.

The air throttle body assembly controls air flow to the engine through two circuits. A single large bore with a conventional throttle cable actuated butterfly-type valve controls air flow during most conditions. An air bypass channel around the throttle plate, through which both cold and warm engine idle airflow, is regulated by an air bypass valve assembly mounted on the intake manifold. The valve assembly is an electro-mechanical device controlled by the EEC computer. The air throttle body assembly also has an adjustment screw for setting the throttle plate at a minimum idle air flow position, an idle speed control motor and a throttle position sensor.

The air intake manifold is a two-piece aluminum casting which provides mounting flanges for the air throttle body assembly, fuel rail, accelerator control cable brackets, EGR valve and air bypass valve. Vacuum taps are provided to support various engine accessories and crankcase ventilation. Machined pockets in the lower intake manifold angle the injectors so they spray fuel immediately in front of each intake valve.

14   Multi-point Fuel Injection system - component checks and replacement

Refer to illustrations 14.2a, 14.2b, 14.10a, 14.10b, 14.19, 14.21a, 14.21b, 14.49, 14.50, 14.53, 14.70, 14.71 14.73, 14.75, 14.77a, 14.77b, 14.91a, 14.91b, 14.111, 14.112 and 14.114

Warning: *Gasoline is extremely flammable, so take extra precautions when you work on any part of the fuel system. Don't smoke or allow open flames or bare light bulbs near the work area, and don't work in a garage where a natural gas-type appliance (such as a water*

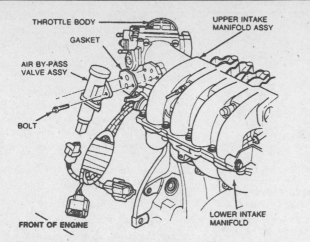

14.2a Exploded view of the air bypass assembly components - four-cylinder shown, V6 similar

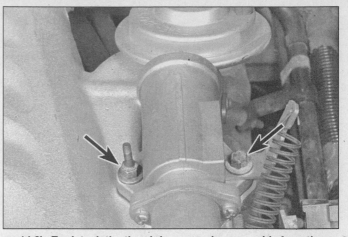

14.2b To detach the the air bypass valve assembly from the intake/throttle body assembly, remove the two screws (arrows) - V6 shown, four-cylinder similar

heater or clothes dryer) with a pilot light is present. If you spill any fuel on your skin, rinse it off immediately with soap and water. When you perform any kind of work on the fuel system, wear safety glasses and have a Class B type fire extinguisher on hand.

Note: It usually isn't necessary to disassemble the entire EFI systems to replace most components. To determine what must be removed, carefully read each section which applies to the component(s) you wish to replace.

Air bypass valve assembly - check, removal and installation

Check

1   Disconnect the electrical connector from the valve and, using a digital ohmmeter connected across the valve's terminals, measure the resistance - it should be about 7 to 13 ohms. If not, the valve should be replaced.

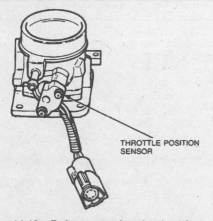

14.10a Before removing the throttle position sensor from the throttle body, be sure to scribe a mark across the sensor and the throttle body as shown - four-cylinder shown, V6 similar

Removal

2   Unplug the electrical connector from the air bypass valve. Remove the two air bypass valve retaining screws **(see illustrations)**.
3   Remove the air bypass valve and gasket. Discard the old gasket.

Installation

4   Make sure that both the throttle body and the air bypass valve gasket surfaces are clean.
5   Install the gasket on the throttle body surface and place the air bypass valve assembly in position. Install the mounting screws and tighten them securely.
6   The remainder of installation is the reverse of removal.
7   Start engine and check for vacuum leaks around gasket.

Throttle position sensor - check, removal and installation

Check

8   Disconnect the sensor electrical connector and, using a digital ohmmeter, connect the positive lead to the sensor's center terminal and the negative lead to one of the sensor's other terminals. Slowly move

14.10b To remove the throttle position sensor, verify alignment marks have been made, unplug the electrical connector, then remove the two screws (arrows) (V6 shown, four-cylinder similar)

the throttle lever until it is at the wide-open position; the ohmmeter's resistance should increase or decrease steadily. Release the throttle lever slowly and verify the reading again increases or decreases steadily (it will do the opposite of what it did when opened). If the resistance increases or decreases irregularly, or does not increase or decrease at all, the sensor is faulty.

Removal

9   Detach the cable from the negative battery terminal. Unplug the throttle position sensor electrical connector from the wiring harness, if not already done.
10   Scribe marks on the throttle body and the throttle position sensor to indicate proper alignment during installation **(see illustrations)**.
11   Remove the two mounting screws.
12   Detach the throttle position sensor.

Installation

13   Install the throttle position sensor. Make sure the rotary tangs on the sensor are in proper alignment and the wires are pointing down. Slide the tangs in to position over the throttle shaft blade, then rotate the sensor clockwise only to the installed position. **Caution:** If you attempt to install the throttle position sensor any other way, excessive idle speeds may result.
14   Align the scribe marks on the throttle body and the throttle position sensor. Secure the sensor to the throttle body assembly with the two screws and tighten the screws securely. **Note:** The sensor isn't adjustable.
15   Plug in the throttle position sensor electrical connector to the harness.
16   Attach the cable to the negative battery terminal.

Fuel pressure regulator - check, removal and installation

Check

17   Refer to Section 4 and check the fuel pressure at the fuel rail, then check the pressure again with the vacuum line from the

4

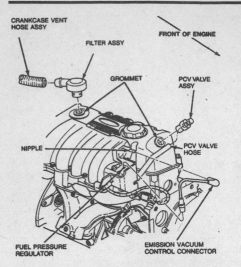

14.19 An exploded view showing locations of various four-cylinder engine components - note the fuel pressure regulator shield directly in front of the intake manifold

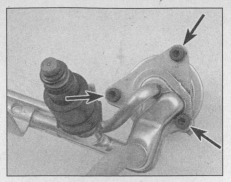

14.21a To remove the fuel pressure regulator from the fuel rail, remove the three allen screws (arrows) and detach regulator (fuel rail removed for clarity - V6 shown, four-cylinder similar)

pressure regulator disconnected and plugged. The pressure should be higher when the vacuum line is disconnected from the regulator. If not, the regulator is faulty or there is not sufficient vacuum reaching the regulator.

Removal

18   Remove the fuel tank cap to relieve the tank pressure. Relieve the system pressure (see Section 2).
19   On four-cylinder engines, remove the three bolts and detach the fuel rail shield (see illustration).
20   Detach the vacuum line from the regulator.
21   Remove the three Allen screws from the fuel pressure regulator and detach the regulator, gasket and O-ring (see illustrations). Discard the gasket and inspect the O-ring. If the O-ring is cracked or otherwise deteriorated, discard it.

Installation

22   Make sure the gasket surfaces of the fuel pressure regulator and fuel rail are clean. If you have to scrape away any old gasket material, be careful not to damage the gasket surfaces.

23   Lubricate the fuel pressure regulator O-ring with light oil.
24   Install the O-ring and gasket on the regulator.
25   Install the fuel pressure regulator on the fuel rail and tighten the screws to the specified torque.
26   Attach the vacuum line to the fuel pressure regulator.
27   On four-cylinder engines, install the fuel rail shield and tighten the bolts securely.
28   Reset fuel pump inertia switch if necessary.
29   Start engine and check for fuel leaks (don't forget your gas cap).

Air intake throttle body - removal and installation (four-cylinder engine)

Removal

30   Detach the cable from the negative battery terminal.
31   Detach and remove the air cleaner outlet tube.
32   Unplug the throttle position sensor connector from the harness.
33   Detach the air bypass hose.
34   Detach the throttle cable and, if equipped, the cruise control cable and/or TV control rod (see Section 15 this Chapter and Chapter 7, Part B).
35   Detach the throttle cable bracket.

36   Remove the four mounting bolts and detach the throttle body from the upper intake manifold. Remove and discard the throttle body gasket.

Installation

37   Make sure both the throttle body and upper intake manifold gasket surfaces are clean. If you have to scrape off any old gasket material, be careful not to damage the gasket surfaces or allow any gasket material to drop into the manifold.
38   Using a new gasket, install the throttle body on the upper intake manifold and tighten the mounting bolts to the specified torque.
39   Install the throttle cable bracket and tighten the mounting nuts securely.
40   Connect the throttle cable and, if equipped, the cruise control cable and/or TV control rod. Adjust TV control rod as required (see Chapter 7, Part B).
41   Attach the air bypass hose.
42   Plug in the throttle position sensor connector to the harness.
43   Install the air cleaner outlet tube between the air cleaner and throttle body. Tighten the clamps securely.
44   Attach the cable to the negative battery terminal.
45   Start the engine and check for vacuum leaks around the gasket.

Upper intake manifold - removal and installation (four-cylinder engine)

Removal

46   Detach the cable from the negative battery terminal.
47   Detach the air cleaner outlet tube from the throttle body.
48   Unplug the throttle position sensor from the wiring harness.
49   Detach the vacuum lines from the upper manifold (see illustration).

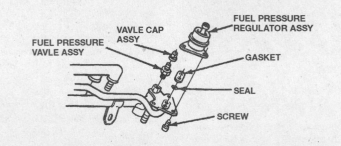

14.21b An exploded view of a typical fuel pressure regulator

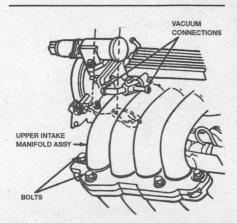

14.49 Detach the vacuum line from the fittings on the upper manifold

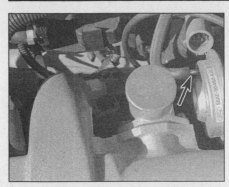

14.50 Detach the vacuum hose from the EGR valve (arrow), then reach underneath the valve and unscrew the threaded connector that attaches the EGR tube to the valve

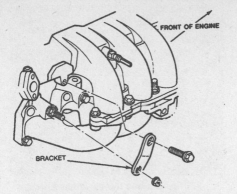

14.53 Detach the upper manifold support bracket by removing the top bolt only - leave the bottom bolt attached

14.70 Loosen the clamps (arrows) and detach the air intake duct

14.71 Remove the cover fasteners (arrows) for throttle cable access

50   Detach the EGR tube at the manifold connection **(see illustration)**.
51   Unplug the air bypass valve connector.
52   Remove the accelerator cable and, if equipped, the cruise control cable and/or TV control rod (see Section 15 of this Chapter and Chapter 7, Part B)
53   Remove the manifold upper support bracket top bolt **(see illustration)**.
54   Remove the fuel pressure regulator shield **(see illustration 14.19)**.
55   Remove the four upper manifold retaining bolts and one retaining shoulder nut.

56   Remove the upper manifold assembly and set it aside.
57   Remove and discard the gasket from the lower manifold assembly. **Caution:** *If you find it necessary to scrape off old gasket material, be careful not to damage the gasket surfaces or allow material to drop into the lower manifold.*

Installation

58   Make sure the gasket surfaces of the upper and lower intake manifolds are clean.
59   Place a new gasket on the lower

manifold and position the upper intake manifold on the lower manifold. Attach them with the four retaining bolts and nut and tighten them securely.
60   Reattach the manifold upper support bracket and tighten the bolt to the specified torque.
61   Coat the compression nut with anti-seize compound and reattach the EGR tube. Tighten the nut securely.
62   Attach the electrical connectors to the air bypass valve and throttle position sensor.
63   Attach the vacuum hoses to the upper manifold.
64   Install the fuel pressure regulator shield and tighten bolts securely.
65   Install throttle cable and if equipped, cruse control cable and/or TV control rod. Adjust TV control rod if required (see Section 15 this Chapter and Chapter 7B)
66   Attach the air cleaner outlet tube to the throttle body and secure it with the hose clamp.
67   Attach the cable to the negative battery terminal.
68   Start engine and check for vacuum leaks.

Air intake/throttle body assembly - removal and installation (V6 engine)

Removal

69   Detach the cable from the negative terminal of the battery.
70   Loosen the clamps and remove the air intake duct between the air cleaner housing and the throttle body **(see illustration)**.
71   Remove the Idle Air Bypass valve solenoid shield **(see illustration)**.
72   Detach the EGR supply tube and EVR vacuum line.
73   Label and then unplug the electrical connectors from the Throttle Position Sensor (TPS), the Idle Air Bypass valve and the Air Charge Temperature (ACT) sensor **(see illustration)**.
74   Remove the alternator to throttle body brace.
75   Clearly label, then disconnect all other wires and vacuum hoses from the throttle body **(see illustration)**.
76   Detach the throttle cable and if equipped, the cruse control cable and TV

4

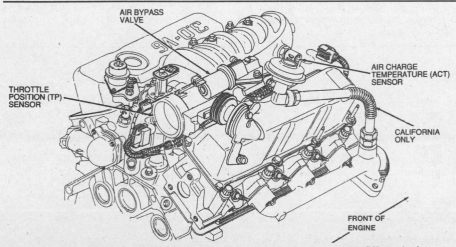

14.73 Locations of various sensor connectors and components (V6 engine)

14.75 Label and disconnect all wires and hoses (arrows)

control cable. (see Section 15 this Chapter and Chapter 7B).

77 Remove the six air intake/throttle body mounting bolts and lift off the throttle body assembly **(see illustrations)**.

Installation

78 Place a new gasket on the lower manifold and position the upper throttle body assembly on the lower manifold. Attach them with the six retaining bolts and nut and tighten them to the specified torque.

79 Reattach the alternator to throttle body assembly support bracket and tighten the bolts to the specified torque.

80 Coat the compression nut with anti-seize compound and reattach the EGR tube. Tighten the nut to the specified torque.

81 Attach the electrical connectors to the air bypass valve, throttle position sensor and air temperature sensor.

82 Attach the vacuum hoses to the throttle body assembly.

83 Connect throttle cable and if equipped, the TV cable to throttle body linkages. Adjust TV cable if required (see Section 15 this Chapter and Chapter 7B).

84 Attach the air cleaner outlet tube to the throttle body and secure it with the hose clamp.

85 Attach the cable to the negative battery terminal.

86 Start engine and check for vacuum leaks.

Fuel rail - removal and installation

Removal

87 Remove the fuel tank cap to relieve the tank pressure.

88 Relieve the system pressure (see Section 2).

89 Detach the cable from the negative battery terminal.

90 On four-cylinder engines, remove the three bolts and detach the fuel rail shield **(see illustration 14.19)**.

91 Detach the fuel supply and return lines **(see illustrations)**. Refer to Section 3 for fuel line fitting details.

92 On four-cylinder engines remove the upper intake manifold (see Steps 46

14.77a To remove the air intake/throttle body assembly, remove all six mounting bolts (arrows) - note that there are three different bolt lengths

through 57). On V6 engines, remove the air intake throttle body assembly (see Steps 69 through 77).

93 Unplug the wiring harness from the fuel injectors.

94 Detach the vacuum line from the fuel pressure regulator.

95 Remove the fuel rail mounting bolts and carefully separate the fuel rail from the fuel injectors.

Installation

96 Make sure the injector caps are clean.

97 Make sure the injectors are seated properly in the lower intake manifold, then carefully seat the fuel rail assembly over the four injectors.

98 Install the fuel rail bolts and tighten them to the specified torque.

99 Attach the vacuum line to the fuel pressure regulator.

100 Attach the fuel supply and return lines (see Section 3).

101 Connect the fuel injector wiring harness to the injectors.

102 On four-cylinder engines install the upper intake manifold (see Steps 58 through 66). On V6 engines install the air intake throttle body assembly (see Steps 78 through 84).

103 On four-cylinder engines, install the fuel rail shield and tighten the bolt securely.

104 Attach the cable to the negative battery cable.

14.77b Lift the air intake/throttle body assembly out of the vehicle very carefully to avoid damage to the TPS, air bypass valve, EGR valve, etc

105 Reset fuel pump inertia switch if necessary.

106 Start engine and check for vacuum and fuel leaks (don't forget your gas cap).

Fuel injectors - check, removal and installation

Check

Note: *The following checks will not detect dirty deposits in the injectors, which is one of the most common causes of injector failure. Fuel additives designed to clean the injectors are available inexpensively from auto parts stores - they may help. Complete injector cleaning must be performed by a dealer service department or other qualified shop that has the special equipment necessary for this procedure.*

107 With the engine running, listen to the sound of each injector with a mechanic's stethoscope (a long screwdriver will also work if you hold the handle end against your ear). The injectors should click rapidly. An injector that does not click is not functioning. **Caution:** Be careful of moving engine components when listening to the injectors.

108 With the engine off, disconnect the electrical connector from each injector, one at a time, and check the resistance across the two injector terminals with an ohmmeter. The resistance should be approximately 10 to 18 ohms. If not, the injector is probably faulty.

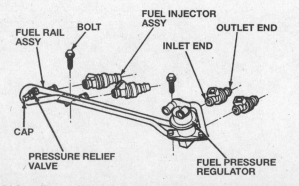

14.91a Four-cylinder fuel rail components - exploded view

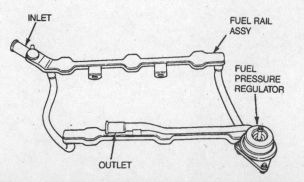

14.91b A view of the V6 fuel rail showing the locations of the fuel line inlet and return fitting connections

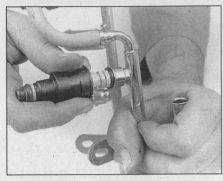

14.111 When pulling on an injector to remove it, use a gentle side-to-side rocking motion

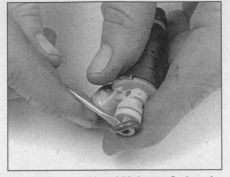

14.112 Remove the old injector O-rings by carefully peeling them off with a small screwdriver

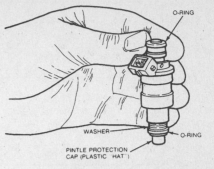

14.114 Inspect the plastic injector "hat" and washer and replace them if they're deteriorated

Removal

109 Remove the fuel tank cap to relieve the tank pressure, then relieve the system pressure (see Section 2). Detach the cable from the negative battery terminal.

110 Remove the fuel rail and injector assembly from the lower intake manifold (see Steps 87 through 95).

111 To remove each injector from the fuel rail, grasp the body and pull on it while gently rocking it from side-to-side **(see illustration)**.

112 Remove the old O-rings by carefully peeling them off with a small screwdriver **(see illustration). Caution:** *Handle the injectors with extreme care to prevent damage to sealing areas and sensitive fuel metering orifices.*

113 Ford recommends inspecting the injector O-rings (one on each end of each injector) for deterioration and replacing them as necessary. We recommend replacing all O-rings, regardless of their condition.

114 Inspect the plastic injector "hat" covering the pintle and the washer **(see illustration)** for deterioration. If cracked or missing, replace the injector. If the hat is missing look for it in the intake manifold.

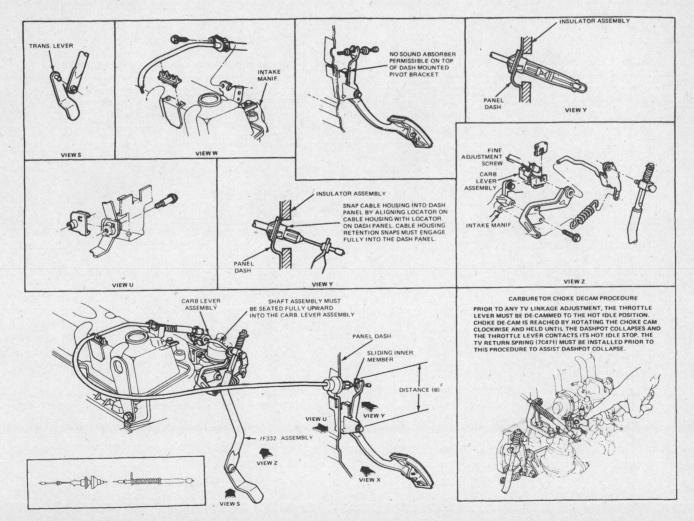

15.3a Accelerator cable throttle linkage and pedal assemblies for carburetor and CFI vehicles with an automatic transaxle

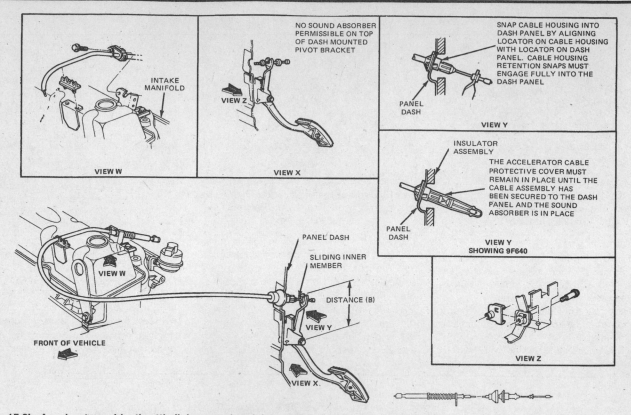

15.3b Accelerator cable, throttle linkage and pedal assemblies for carburetor and CFI vehicles with a manual transaxle

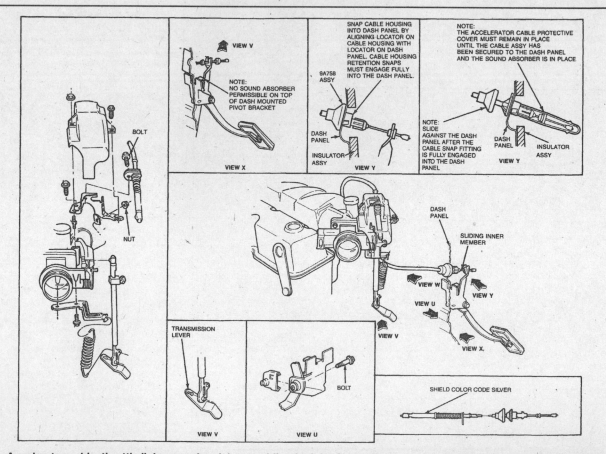

15.3c Accelerator cable, throttle linkage and pedal assemblies for later four-cylinder models (automatic transaxle shown, manual transaxle similar)

Installation

115 Lubricate the new O-rings with light oil and install two on each injector.
116 Using a gentle twisting motion, install the injectors in the lower intake manifold.
117 Install the fuel rail (see Steps 96 through 104).
118 Check the entire assembly for proper alignment and seating.
119 Reset fuel pump inertia switch if necessary.
120 Start engine and check for vacuum and fuel leaks (don't forget your gas cap).

Mass Air Flow (MAF) sensor (1992 and later models only)

Removal

121 Loosen the clamp and remove the clean air flex tube from the MAF sensor.
122 Disconnect the electrical connector from the MAF sensor.
123 Loosen the four screws retaining the MAF sensor to the air cleaner housing and remove the sensor. Discard the old gasket.

Installation

124 Clean the sensor flange and the air cleaner housing mating surfaces.
125 Align the sensor flange and the new gasket to the air cleaner housing and tighten the screws securely.
126 Install the clean air flex tube and electrical connector to MAF sensor.
127 Start the engine and check for vacuum leaks and proper operation of the sensor.

15 Throttle linkage components - removal and installation

Refer to illustrations 15.3a, 15.3b, 15.3c, 15.7 and 15.8

Accelerator cable

Removal

1 Remove the air intake duct.
2 On later models, remove the accelerator cable shield by removing the retaining bolt and nut.
3 Detach the cable snap-in nylon bushing from the accelerator pedal arm **(see illustrations)**.
4 Remove the cable housing from the dash panel by depressing the two tabs and pushing them out from inside the passenger compartment.
5 On earlier models, remove the cable from the retainer on the rocker arm cover.
6 Remove the speed control cable from the accelerator cable, if so equipped.
7 On V6 engines, disconnect the cable at the throttle lever by inserting a screwdriver between the cable and the throttle lever and twisting the screwdriver. On V6 engines, remove the cable end slug from the cam slug hole **(see illustration)**.
8 Remove the screw attaching the cable

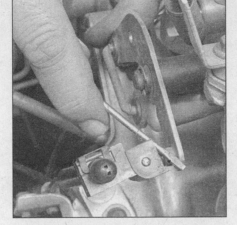

15.7 To detach the throttle cable from the throttle lever arm, insert a small screwdriver between the cable and the stud on the lever arm, then twist the screwdriver and the cable will pop off

15.8 To detach the cable from the bracket, remove the retainer bolt (arrow) and slide the cable from its slot in the bracket

housing to the engine mounting bracket and detach the cable from the bracket slot **(see illustration)**.

Installation

9 To install the cable, insert the pedal end of the cable with the cover in place through the dash panel and snap the cable housing into the dash panel. Make sure the cable housing retention tabs have engaged in the dash panel.
10 Push the cable sound absorber against the firewall.
11 Position the cable housing in the engine mounting bracket. Install the screw.
12 Connect the cable to the throttle lever (four-cylinder engine) or cam (V6 engine).
13 Install the speed control cable, if so equipped.
14 On earlier models, snap the cable into the retainer on the rocker arm cover.
15 Remove the cable protective cover and snap the nylon bushing into the accelerator pedal arm.
16 Check to make sure that the body insulation is properly positioned and not in contact with the moving part of the accelerator cable.
17 If so equipped, reinstall the accelerator cable shield and tighten securely.
18 Start engine and check for proper accelerator pedal/cable operation.

Mounting bracket

19 Remove the air duct assembly.
20 On later year models, remove accelerator cable shield by removing the retaining bolt and nut.
21 Disconnect the accelerator cable (see Step 6).
22 Remove the screw attaching the cable housing to the bracket.
23 Remove the speed control cable from the bracket, if so equipped.

24 Remove the bolts securing the mounting bracket to the engine.
25 Position the bracket on the engine, install the bolts and tighten them securely.
26 Position the cable housing in the bracket. Install the screw.
27 Install the speed control cable in the bracket, if so equipped.
28 Connect the cable to the throttle lever.
29 If so equipped, reinstall the accelerator cable shield and tighten securely.
30 Start engine and check for proper accelerator pedal/cable operation.

Accelerator pedal assembly

31 Remove the snap-in nylon bushing from the pedal arm.
32 Remove the pivot bolt attaching the pedal arm assembly to the dash bracket.
33 Position the pedal arm assembly in the dash bracket and install the pivot bolt.
34 Check to be sure that the carpeting and/or body insulation is properly positioned.
35 Snap the cable nylon bushing into the pedal arm.
36 Check the pedal assembly for free operation.

16 Exhaust system components - replacement

Refer to illustrations 16.2, 16.3a, 16.3b and 16.3c

Warning: *Never attempt to service any part of the exhaust system until it has cooled. Be especially careful when working around the catalytic converter. The temperature of the converter rises to a high level after only a few minutes of engine operation and, once the engine reaches its operating temperature, can remain high enough to cause burns for a long time after the engine is shut off.*
1 Raise the vehicle and support it securely on jackstands.

4

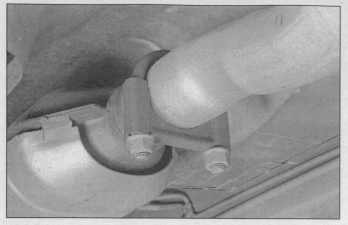

16.2 Prior to removing the exhaust hanger insulators, remove the U-bolt assembly to disconnect the forward end of the exhaust pipe from the catalytic converter

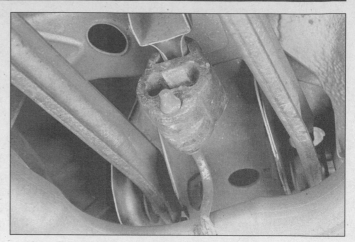

16.3a To detach the exhaust pipe/muffler assembly from the vehicle, remove the front rubber insulator . . .

2   Remove the U-bolt assembly immediately behind the catalytic converter **(see illustration)**.

3   Remove all three rubber insulators from the hanger brackets **(see illustrations)**, slide the muffler assembly to the rear to disconnect it from the catalytic converter and remove it.

4   Place the muffler assembly in position and slide it onto the converter outlet pipe. Check to make sure that the slot in the muffler and the tab on the converter are fully engaged.

5   Installation is otherwise the reverse of removal.

6   Lower the vehicle.

7   Start the engine and check for leaks.

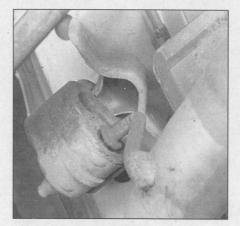

16.3b . . . the middle insulator . . .

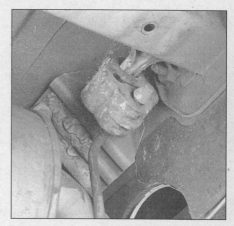

16.3c . . . and the rear insulator, then pull the exhaust pipe/muffler assembly to the rear and remove it from the vehicle

Chapter 5
Engine electrical systems

Contents

Specifications

Drivebelt deflection	See Chapter 1
Battery voltage	
Engine off	12-volts
Engine running	14-to-15 volts
Ignition coil-to-distributor cap wire resistance	
Duraspark II system	5000 ohms per inch
TFI-IV system	5000 ohms per foot
Ignition coil resistance	
Duraspark II system	
Primary resistance	0.8 to 1.6 ohms
Secondary resistance	7.7 to 10.5 K-ohms
Ballast resistor	0.8 to 1.6 ohms
TFI-IV system	
Primary resistance	0.3 to 1.0 ohms
Secondary resistance	8.0 to 11.5 K-ohms
Distributor component resistance (Duraspark II system)	
Stator assembly and wiring harness	400 to 1300 ohms
Stator assembly	400 to 1000 ohms

5

1 General information

The engine electrical systems include all ignition, charging and starting components. Because of their engine-related functions, these components are considered separately from chassis electrical devices like the lights, instruments, etc.

Be very careful when working on the engine electrical components. They are easily damaged if checked, connected or handled improperly. The alternator is driven by an engine drivebelt which could cause serious injury if your hands, hair or clothes become entangled in it with the engine running. Both the starter and alternator are connected directly to the battery and could arc or even cause a fire if mishandled, over-loaded or shorted out.

Never leave the ignition switch on for long periods of time with the engine off. Don't disconnect the battery cables while the engine is running. Correct polarity must be maintained when connecting battery cables from another source, such as another vehicle, during jump starting. Always disconnect the negative cable first and hook it up last or the battery may be shorted by the tool being used to loosen the cable clamps.

Additional safety related information on the engine electrical systems can be found in *Safety first* near the front of this manual. It should be referred to before beginning any operation included in this Chapter.

2 Battery - removal and installation

Refer to illustration 2.2

1 Disconnect both cables from the battery terminals. **Caution:** *Always disconnect the negative cable first and hook it up last or the battery may be shorted by the tool being used to loosen the cable clamps.*

2 Locate the battery hold down clamp between the battery and the air cleaner

2.2 The battery hold-down clamp and bolt (arrow) are located at the lower right side of the battery, next to the air cleaner housing assembly

housing **(see illustration).** Remove the bolt and the hold down clamp.

3   Lift out the battery. Special straps that attach to the battery posts are available - lifting and moving the battery is much easier if you use one. Be careful - it's heavy.

4   While the battery is out, inspect the battery tray for corrosion.

5   If you are replacing the battery, make sure you get one that's identical, with the same dimensions, amperage rating, cold cranking power, etc.

6   Installation is the reverse of removal.

3   Battery - emergency jump starting

Refer to the *Booster battery (jump) starting* procedure at the front of this manual.

4   Battery cables - check and replacement

1   Periodically inspect the entire length of each battery cable for damage, cracked or burned insulation and corrosion. Poor battery cable connections can cause starting problems and decreased engine perfor-mance.

2   Check the cable-to-terminal connec-tions at the ends of the cables for cracks, loose wire strands and corrosion. The presence of white, fluffy deposits under the insulation at the cable terminal connection is a sign that the cable is corroded and should be replaced. Check the terminals for distortion, missing mounting bolts and corrosion.

3   When replacing the cables, always disconnect the negative cable first and hook it up last or the battery may be shorted by the tool used to loosen the cable clamps. Even if only the positive cable is being replaced, be sure to disconnect the negative cable from the battery first. (see Chapter 1 for further information regarding battery removal).

4   Disconnect the old cables from the battery, then trace each of them to their opposite ends and detach them from the starter solenoid and ground terminals. Note the routing of each cable to ensure correct installation.

5   If you are replacing one or both cables, take them with you when buying new cables. It is very important that you replace the cables with identical parts. Cables have characteristics that make them easy to identify: positive cables are usually red, larger in cross-section and have a larger diameter battery post clamp; ground cables are usually black, smaller in cross-section and have a smaller diameter clamp for the negative post.

6   Clean the threads of the relay or ground connection with a wire brush to remove rust and corrosion. Apply a light coat of corrosion inhibitor or petroleum jelly, to the threads to prevent future corrosion.

7   Attach the cable to the relay or ground

connection and tighten the mounting nut/bolt securely.

8   Before connecting the new cable to the battery, make sure that it reaches the battery post without having to be stretched.

9   Connect the positive cable first, followed by the negative cable.

5   Ignition system - general information

TFI-IV or Distributor Ignition (DI) system (all US models and Canadian models from 1988)

The operation of the TFI-IV distributor (also known as DI for Distributor Ignition) is accomplished through the Hall Effect vane switch stator assembly. The vane switch unit consists of a distributor shaft-mounted rotary vane with a stationary Hall sensor on one side of the vane and a magnet on the other. The vane is made of ferrous material with small, symmetrically positioned windows cut out. Each window represents a cylinder in the engine; therefore, a four-cylinder engine will have four windows. When a vane passes through the gap between the Hall sensor and the magnet, the magnetic field produced by the magnet is shunted (magnetically shorted), and increases the strength of the magnet many times. The Hall device is very sensitive to magnetic fields and senses this increase and produces an induced voltage of it's own. This voltage is constantly being monitored by the PCM (Powertrain Control Module). When a window appears (as when the distributor turns the rotary vane) the magnetic field diminishes because the magnet is no longer shunted. The collapsing field produces a corresponding voltage drop in the Hall sensor output. Assuming the original timing was set correctly, this voltage drop signals the PCM of the relative position of the crankshaft so the PCM can determine proper spark advance based on engine demand and calibration. In effect, the Hall effect sensor (or PIP sensor) acts as a electronic crankshaft position sensor by producing a (PIP) Profile Ignition Pick-up signal. The PCM returns a Spark Output (SPOUT) signal to the TFI-IV module on the distributor which handles the primary coil voltage switching duties electronically. The high voltage distribution from the coil is accomplished through a conventional rotor, cap and ignition wires.

In addition to providing data for ignition timing, the PIP is also used for fuel injection system management. On later models, one slightly wider window on the rotating vane representing the number one cylinder results in a different "Halls Effect" pulse which new circuitry in the PCM recognizes as being the number one cylinder. The PCM uses this information to synchronize the fuel injectors in newer Sequential Fuel Injected (SFI) vehicles. SFI systems distinguish this additional feature by re-naming the PIP sensor to the Camshaft Position (CMP) sensor.

All TFI-IV distributors are equipped with a gear-driven distributor with a die cast base housing, a "Hall Effect" vane switch stator assembly and a device for fixed octane adjustment. The Thick Film Integrated IV (TFI-IV) ignition module is housed in a molded thermoplastic box mounted on the base of the distributor. In addition, the TFI-IV/EEC-IV type distributor has neither a centrifugal nor a vacuum advance mechanism (advance is handled by the computer instead).

Prior to 1993, the TFI-IV module allowed push starting of the vehicle if necessary. However, With the advent of the new Computer Controlled Dwell (CCD) design in 1993, the standard TFI-IV module has been replaced with the Ignition Control Module (ICM). The ICM module does not incorporate a push start feature. This is the only real difference between the TFI and ICM modules. Also during this time, the entire system was re-named to Distributor Ignition (DI) to distin-guish it from the new distributorless ignition systems currently being introduced by Ford. All Vehicles use the "E-core" type ignition coil.

Duraspark II ignition system (Canadian models through 1987)

The operation of the Duraspark system is electrically similar to the US models but is mechanically different. Mechanically, the system uses an armature assembly with "spokes" instead of the rotary vane windows and a different magnetic pickup unit (although the "Hall effect" is still an operating premise). In this case, when the distributor's armature "teeth" or "spokes" approach the magnetic coil assembly, a voltage is induced which signals a remotely mounted "ignition module" to turn off the coil primary current as in a conventional breakerless ignition system. The important difference between the two is that the TFI-IV module is controlled by the Electronic Engine Control IV (EEC-IV), while the Duraspark II module is not.

Because this system lacks the computa-tional ability of the PCM to determine spark advance, the distributors on Canadian vehicles are equipped with centrifugal and vacuum advance mechanisms which control the actual point of ignition based on engine speed and load. As engine speed increases, two weights move out and alter the position of the armature in relation to the distributor shaft, advancing the ignition timing. As engine load increases (when climbing hills or acceler-ating, for example), a drop in intake manifold vacuum causes the base plate to move slightly in the opposite direction (clockwise) under the action of the spring in the vacuum unit, retarding the timing and counteracting the centrifugal advance. Under light loads (moderate steady speeds, for example), the comparatively high intake manifold vacuum acting on the vacuum advance diaphragm causes the base plate assembly to move in a counterclockwise direction to provide a greater amount of timing advance.

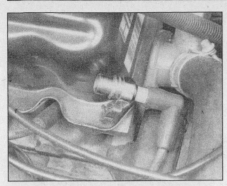

6.6 To use a calibrated ignition tester (available at most auto parts stores), simply disconnect a spark plug wire, attach the wire to the tester, clip the tester to a convenient ground (like a valve cover bolt) and operate the starter - if there's enough power to fire the plug, sparks will be visible between the electrode tip and the tester body

Canadian vehicles are equipped with either the standard Duraspark II ignition module, or the universal ignition module (UIM). Although both modules are similar in appearance, they can be distinguished by the number of electrical connectors and the color of the rubber grommets used to seal the holes where the wires enter each module. The Duraspark II module has two connectors and a blue grommet while the UIM module has three connectors with a yellow grommet **(see illustration 10.51)**.

Duraspark II distributors have a two piece cap. When removing the cap to change a stator, for example, the upper half is removed, then the rotor is removed, then the lower half of the cap is removed. Vehicles equipped with the Duraspark II ignition module have an oil filled coil.

6   Ignition system - check

Refer to illustration 6.6
Warning: *Because of the very high secondary (spark plug) voltage generated by the ignition system, extreme care should be taken when this check is done. This not only includes the distributor, coil, control module and spark plug wires, but related items that are connected to the system as well, such as the plug connectors, tachometer and testing equipment.*

General checks

1   Check all ignition wiring connections for tightness, cuts, corrosion or any signs of bad connections. Repair as needed.
2   Check for poor spark plug wire connections at plugs and distributor cap, and for carbon deposits inside the spark plug boots.
3   If necessary, remove the spark plug wires and measure their resistance, each should be less than 30,000 ohms. Refer to Chapter 1 on spark plug wire removal.

Replace bad wires as required.
4   If necessary, remove and check the coil to distributor wire and compare it to the Specifications in this Chapter. Replace the wire if required.

Checking with calibrated ignition tester

5   If the engine turns over but won't start, disconnect the spark plug lead from any spark plug and attach it to a calibrated ignition tester (available at most auto parts stores). Make sure the tester is designed for Ford ignition systems if a universal tester isn't available.
6   Connect the clip on the tester to a bolt or metal bracket on the engine **(see illustration)**, crank the engine and watch the end of the tester to see if bright blue, well-defined sparks occur.
7   If sparks occur, sufficient voltage is reaching the plug to fire it (repeat the check at the remaining plug wires to verify that the distributor cap and rotor are OK). However, the plugs themselves may be fouled, so remove and check them as described in Chapter 1 or install new ones.
8   If no sparks or intermittent sparks occur, remove the distributor cap and check the cap and rotor as described in Chapter 1. If moisture is present, dry out the cap and rotor, then reinstall the cap and repeat the spark test.
9   If there's still no spark, detach the secondary coil wire from the distributor cap and hook it up to the tester (reattach the plug wire to the spark plug), then repeat the spark check.
10   If sparks now occur, the distributor cap, rotor, plug wire(s) or spark plug(s) or any combination may be defective.

11   If no sparks occur, check the primary (small) wire connections at the coil to make sure they're clean and tight. Refer to Section 7 and check the ignition coil supply voltage circuit. Make any necessary repairs, then repeat the check again.
12   If there's still no spark, and the spark plug and coil wires test good, the ignition coil, module or other internal components may be defective.

7   Ignition coil and circuits - check and coil replacement

Duraspark II system (Canadian models through 1987)

Refer to illustrations 7.2, 7.6, 7.12, 7.19, 7.24, 7.28, 7.38, 7.42, 7.49, 7.52, 7.59, 7.69a, 7.69b, 7.78 and 7.86

Supply voltage circuits

1   If you've been referred to this Section from the preliminary ignition system check in Section 6, remove the spark tester if you have not already done so and reconnect the coil wire to the distributor cap.
2   If the starter relay has a terminal labeled 1, detach the cable from the starter relay to the starter motor **(see illustration)**.
3   If the starter relay doesn't have a terminal labeled 1, detach the wire to the 5 terminal of the relay **(see illustration 19.2)**.
4   Carefully insert small straight pins into the red and white module wires. **Caution:** *Don't allow the pins to ground on anything.*
5   Check the battery voltage with a voltmeter and record it for reference later.
6   Check the voltage at the points indicated with the ignition switch in various

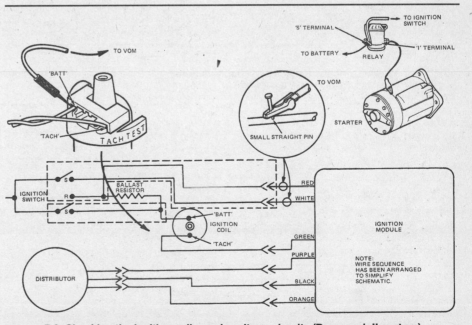

7.2 Checking the ignition coil supply voltage circuits (Duraspark II system)

5

WIRE/ TERMINAL	CIRCUIT	IGNITION SWITCH TEST POSITION
RED	RUN	RUN
WHITE	START	START
'BATT' TERMINAL IGNITION COIL	BALLAST RESISTOR BYPASS	START

7.6 Check the supply voltage circuit terminals with the switch in various positions (Duraspark II system)

positions **(see illustration). Note:** *Attach the negative lead of the VOM to the distributor base and wiggle the wires in the wiring harness when performing the voltage checks.*

7   If the indicated voltage readings are 90 percent or more of battery voltage, the supply voltage circuit is okay. Refer to Step 12.

8   If the indicated voltage readings are less than 90 percent of battery voltage, check the wiring harness and connector(s) (refer to the wiring diagrams at the end of this book). Inspect the ignition switch for wear and/or damage (refer to Chapter 12).

9   Turn the ignition switch to the Off position.

10   Remove the straight pins.

11   Reattach any cables/wires removed from the starter relay.

Ignition coil supply voltage

12   Attach the negative lead of a VOM to the distributor base **(see illustration)**.

13   Turn the ignition switch to the Run position.

14   Attach the positive lead of the VOM to the BATT terminal on the ignition coil.

15   If the indicated voltage is 6-to-8 volts, refer to the distributor stator assembly and wiring harness check in Section 11.

16   If the indicated voltage is less than 6 or more than 8-volts, refer to Step 23.

17   Turn the ignition switch to the Off position.

Ignition coil secondary resistance

18   Disconnect and inspect the ignition coil wires and connector.

19   Check the resistance between the BATT terminal and the center terminal of the coil **(see illustration)**.

20   If the resistance is as specified, the coil secondary circuit is normal. Refer to the ignition module check in Section 10.

21   If the indicated resistance is less or more than the specified resistance, replace the ignition coil (Step 89).

22   Reconnect the coil wires.

Ignition coil primary resistance

23   Detach the ignition coil wires.

24   Measure the primary resistance between the BATT and TACH terminals **(see illustration)**.

25   If the resistance is as specified, the ignition coil primary resistance is normal. Check the primary circuit continuity (Step 28).

26   If the indicated resistance is less or more than the specified resistance, replace the ignition coil (Step 89).

27   Reconnect the coil wire.

Primary circuit continuity

28   Carefully insert a small straight pin into the ignition module green wire **(see illustration)**. Refer to Section 10 for a more detailed illustration of the module terminals. **Caution:** *Don't allow the straight pin to ground against anything.*

29   Attach the negative lead of the VOM to the distributor base.

30   Turn the ignition switch to the Run position.

31   Measure the voltage at the green module wire.

32   If the indicated voltage is greater than 1.5-volts, check the module (Section 10).

33   If the indicated voltage is 1.5-volts or less, inspect the wiring harness and the connectors between the ignition module and the coil.

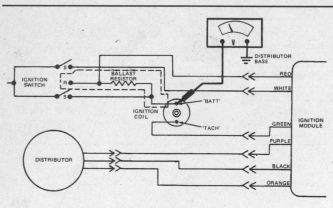

7.12 Checking the ignition coil supply voltage (Duraspark II system)

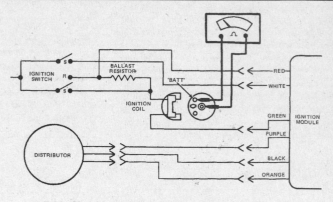

7.19 Checking ignition coil secondary resistance (Duraspark II system)

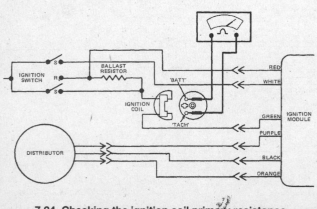

7.24 Checking the ignition coil primary resistance (Duraspark II system)

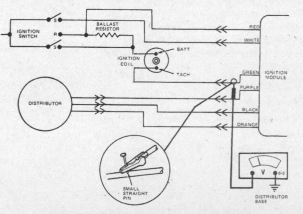

7.28 Checking primary circuit continuity (Duraspark II system)

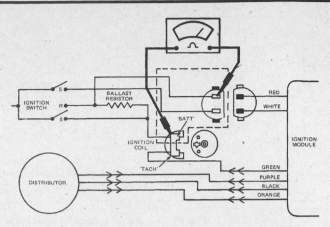

7.38 Checking the ballast resistor (Duraspark II system)

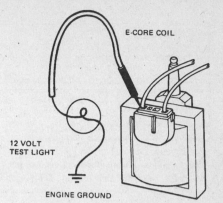

7.42 Checking ignition coil primary circuit switching (TFI-IV or DI system)

34   Turn the ignition switch to the Off position.
35   Remove the straight pin.

Ballast resistor

36   Separate and inspect the ignition module two-wire connector with the red and white wires.
37   Unplug and inspect the ignition coil connector.
38   Attach the leads from an ohmmeter to the BATT terminal of the ignition coil and the red wire in the module connector (see illustration).
39   If the indicated resistance is the same as the specified primary resistance, the problem is either intermittent or not in the ignition system.
40   If the indicated resistance is less or more than the specified primary resistance, replace the ballast resistor.

TFI-IV or DI system (all US models and Canadian models from 1988)

Ignition coil primary circuit

41   Unplug the wiring harness connector from the ignition module. Inspect it for dirt, corrosion and damage (refer to Section 10 for a detailed illustration of the connector terminals), then plug it back in.
42   Attach a 12-volt DC test light between the coil TACH terminal and a good engine ground (see illustration).
43   Crank the engine.
44   If the light flashes, or comes on but doesn't flash, refer to Step 47.
45   If the light stays off or is very dim, refer to Step 56.
46   Remove the test light.

Ignition coil primary resistance

47   Turn the ignition switch to Off.
48   Unplug the ignition coil wire harness connector. Inspect it for dirt, corrosion and damage.
49   Measure the resistance between the primary terminals of the ignition coil (see illustration).

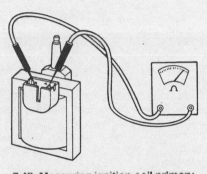

7.49 Measuring ignition coil primary resistance (TFI-IV or DI system)

50   If the indicated resistance is within the specified limits, proceed to Step 52.
51   If the indicated resistance is less or more than specified, replace the ignition coil (Step 89).

Ignition coil secondary resistance

52   Measure the resistance from the negative primary terminal to the secondary terminal of the ignition coil (see illustration).
53   If the indicated resistance is within the specified limits, proceed to Step 65.
54   If the indicated resistance is less or more than the specified resistance, replace the ignition coil (Step 89).
55   Reconnect the ignition coil wires.

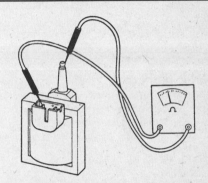

7.52 Measuring ignition coil secondary resistance (TFI-IV or DI system)

Primary circuit continuity

56   Unplug the wiring harness connector from the ignition module. Inspect it for dirt, corrosion and damage.
57   Attach the negative lead of a VOM to the distributor base.
58   Measure battery voltage and record it for future reference.
59   Attach the positive lead of the VOM to a small straight pin inserted into connector terminal 2 (see illustration). Caution: *Don't allow the straight pin to ground against anything.*
60   Turn the ignition switch to the Run position and measure the terminal 2 voltage.
61   If the measured voltage is 90 percent of

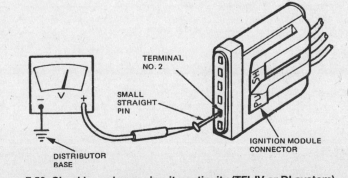

7.59 Checking primary circuit continuity (TFI-IV or DI system)

CONNECTOR TERMINAL	WIRE/CIRCUIT	IGNITION SWITCH TEST POSITION
#2	TO IGNITION COIL (–) TERMINAL	RUN
#3	RUN CIRCUIT	RUN AND START
#4	START CIRCUIT	START

7.69a Check the wire harness connector voltage with the switch in various positions (TFI-IV or DI system)

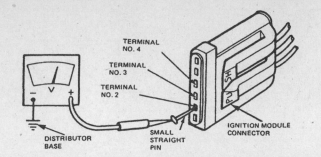

7.69b Check the wiring harness between the coil and the module (TFI-IV or DI system)

battery voltage, proceed to the wiring harness check (Step 65).

62   If the measured voltage is less than 90 percent of battery voltage, proceed to Step 75.

63   Turn the ignition switch to the Off position.

64   Remove the straight pin.

Wiring harness

65   Unplug the wiring harness connector from the ignition module. Inspect it for dirt, corrosion and damage.

66   Disconnect the wire at the S terminal of the starter relay.

67   Attach the negative lead of a VOM to the distributor base.

68   Measure battery voltage and record it for future reference.

69   Using the accompanying table **(see illustration)**, measure the connector terminal voltage by attaching the positive lead of the VOM to a small straight pin inserted into the connector terminals, one at a time, with the ignition switch in the indicated positions **(see illustration)**. Note: *1993 models with ICM module utilize pin number 4 for Ignition Diagnostic Monitoring (IDM) and not for push start. Therefore, no output is expected and any measurements taken will be meaningless.*

70   If the indicated voltage is 90 percent of battery voltage at all three terminals, refer to the EEC-IV/TFI-IV check in Section 10.

71   If the indicated voltage is less than 90 percent of battery voltage, inspect the wiring harness and the connectors (refer to the wiring diagrams at the end of this book for the appropriate circuits). Check the ignition

switch for damage or wear (refer to Chapter 12).

72   Turn the ignition switch to the Off position.

73   Remove the straight pin.

74   Reconnect the wire to the S terminal of the starter relay.

Ignition coil primary voltage

75   Attach the negative lead of a VOM to the distributor base.

76   Measure battery voltage and record it.

77   Turn the ignition switch to the Run position.

78   Measure the voltage at the negative terminal of the ignition coil **(see illustration)**.

79   If the indicated voltage is 90 percent of battery voltage, inspect the wiring harness between the ignition module and the coil negative terminal.

80   If the indicated voltage is less than 90 percent of battery voltage, then proceed to Step 82.

81   Turn the ignition switch to the Off position.

Ignition coil supply voltage

82   Unplug the ignition coil wire harness.

83   Attach the negative lead of a VOM to the distributor base.

84   Measure battery voltage.

85   Turn the ignition switch to the Run position.

86   Measure the voltage at the positive terminal of the ignition coil **(see illustration)**.

87   If the indicated voltage is 90 percent of

battery voltage, inspect the ignition coil connector and terminals for dirt, corrosion and damage. If both the connector and terminals are clean, replace the ignition coil (Step 89).

88   If the indicated voltage is less than 90 percent of battery voltage, inspect and repair the circuit between the ignition coil and the ignition switch (refer to the wiring diagrams at the end of the book). Check the ignition switch for damage and wear (refer to Chapter 12).

Ignition coil replacement

89   Detach the cable from the negative terminal of the battery.

90   Detach the wires from the primary terminals on the coil (some coils have a single connector for the primary wires).

91   Unplug the coil secondary lead.

92   Remove both bracket bolts and detach the coil.

93   Installation is the reverse of removal.

---

8   Distributor - removal and installation

Refer to illustrations 8.3, 8.4 and 8.5

Removal

1   Detach the cable from the negative terminal of the battery.

2   Detach the coil secondary lead from the coil and the wires from the plugs, then remove the distributor cap and wires as an assembly (refer to Chapter 1).

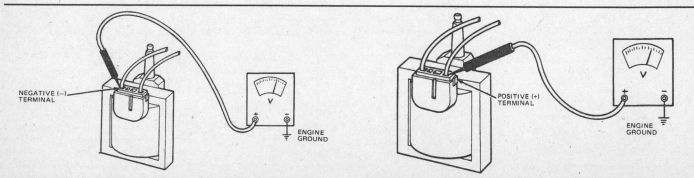

7.78 Measuring ignition coil primary voltage (TFI-IV or DI system)   **7.86 Measuring ignition coil supply voltage (TFI-IV or DI system)**

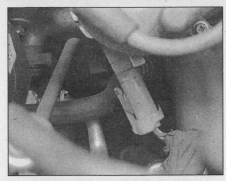

8.3 Unplug the module electrical connector from the base of the distributor

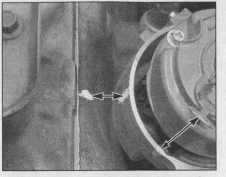

8.4 Mark the position of the rotor on the edge of the distributor base (arrow) and paint or scribe alignment marks on the distributor base and the block to ensure proper reinstallation

8.5 Remove the distributor hold-down bolt and clamp

3   Unplug the module electrical connector **(see illustration).**

4   Make a mark on the edge of the distributor base directly below the rotor tip and in line with it (if the rotor on your engine has more than one tip, use the center one for reference). Also, mark the distributor base and the engine block to ensure that the distributor is installed correctly **(see illustration).**

5   Remove the distributor hold down bolt and clamp **(see illustration),** then pull the distributor straight up to remove it. Be careful not to disturb the intermediate driveshaft. **Caution:** *If the crankshaft is turned while the distributor is removed, or if a new distributor is required, the alignment marks will be useless.*

Installation (crankshaft not turned after distributor removal)

6   Insert the distributor into the engine so that it's mark lines up with the corresponding engine block mark. Due to the helical gears involved, upon initial insertion it will be necessary to position the rotor in such a way that it leads it's alignment mark on the distributor base slightly. The distributor shaft will rotate as the gears mesh, bringing the rotor and base marks into alignment. This process may take several attempts until the correct "lead" is found.

7   If the distributor doesn't seat completely, the hex shaped recess in the lower end of the distributor shaft is not mating properly with the oil pump shaft. If this is the case, remove the distributor and use a long screwdriver (or special pump priming tool) to rotate the oil pump shaft. It shouldn't take much. Repeat step 6 until the distributor seats properly and both distributor to engine and rotor to distributor marks are correctly aligned. Proceed to Step 11 this Section.

Installation (crankshaft turned after distributor removal)

8   Refer to Chapter 2 and position the number one piston at TDC on the compression stroke.

9   Temporarily install the cap onto distributor and note the location of the number one spark plug wire (trace the correct wire back from the number one spark plug if necessary). Make a mark on the side of the distributor directly under the number one wire and as close to the cap as possible. Refer to the specification Section in Chapter 1 for a pictorial view showing the correct location for the number one cylinder wire.

10   Perform steps 6 and 7 above, except disregard the initial rotor to distributor base mark and use the mark indicated in step 9 to align rotor.

Final installation

11   With the distributor marks aligned, the rotor should be pointing at the alignment mark you made on the distributor housing and the distributor base to engine block marks should be in alignment as they were before removal.

12   Place the hold down clamp in position and loosely install the bolt.

13   Install the distributor cap and tighten the cap screws securely.

14   Plug in the module electrical connector.

15   Reattach the spark plug wires to the plugs.

16   Connect the cable to the negative terminal of the battery.

17   Check the ignition timing (refer to Section 9) and tighten the distributor hold down bolt securely.

9   Ignition timing - check and adjustment

Refer to illustrations 9.4, 9.6a and 9.6b

Note: *This procedure applies to both Canadian and US-specification vehicles. However, check the Vehicle Emission Control Information label on your vehicle to see if a different procedure is specified.*

1   Apply the parking brake and block the wheels. Place the transmission in Park (automatic) or Neutral (manual). Turn off all accessories (heater, air conditioner, etc.).

2   Start the engine and warm it up. Once it has reached operating temperature, turn it off.

3   if you have a 1987 or earlier Canadian vehicle, disconnect the vacuum hoses from the distributor vacuum advance unit and plug the hoses.

4   If you have a US vehicle or 1988 or later Canadian vehicle, unplug the single wire SPOUT (Spark Output) signal connector located immediately above the TFI-IV or ICM module harness connector **(see illustration).** Vehicles equipped with a double wire SPOUT connector incorporate a special shorting bar into the connector. If this is the case, remove the shorting bar. **Note:** *This operation disconnects the PCM's SPOUT signal to the number 5 terminal on the module. When no signal is received, the TFI-IV or ICM module reverts to a internal back-up timing mode. Accurate timing measurements can only be made in this mode.* **Caution:** *Don't confuse the CMP sensor connector with the SPOUT connector on 1992 and later four-cylinder engines, since erroneous timing measurements and possible damage to the engine will result.*

5   Connect an inductive timing light and a tachometer in accordance with the manufacturer's instructions. **Caution:** *Make sure that the timing light and TACH wires don't hang*

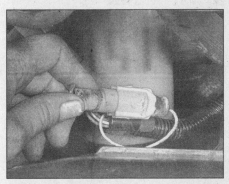

9.4 On all US and 1988 and later Canadian vehicles, unplug this single wire connector located above the ignition module plug before adjusting the ignition timing - some vehicles may be equipped with a special shorting bar connector; if so, remove the bar (four-cylinder engine shown, V6 similar)

5

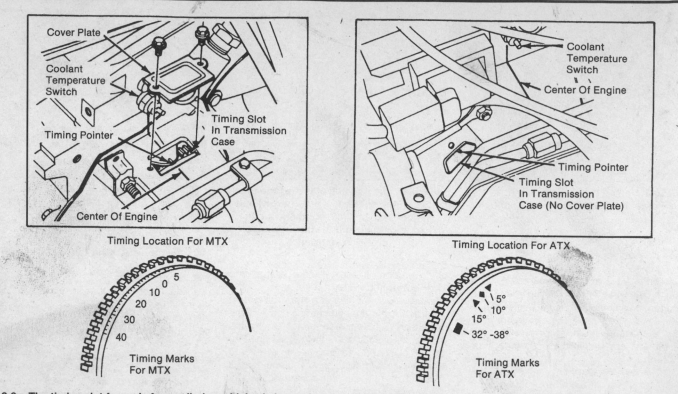

Timing Location For MTX

Timing Location For ATX

Timing Marks For MTX

Timing Marks For ATX

9.6a The timing slot for early four-cylinder vehicles is located on top of the bellhousing (note that manual transaxle equipped vehicles have a cover plate which must be removed) - but the marks themselves are different; numbers are stamped into the flywheel on vehicles with a manual transaxle, while small geometric shapes are punched out of the driveplate on vehicles with an automatic transaxle

anywhere near the electric cooling fan or they may become entangled in the fan blades when it comes on.

6   On early four-cylinder engines, locate the timing slot in the top of the bellhousing immediately below the thermostat housing in the left end of the cylinder head **(see illustration)**. If your vehicle is equipped with a manual transaxle, remove the screws and detach the cover plate. On later four-cylinder engines and on V6 engines, the timing marks are located on the front damper and timing chain cover **(see illustration)**.

7   Start the engine again.

8   On early four-cylinder engines, point the

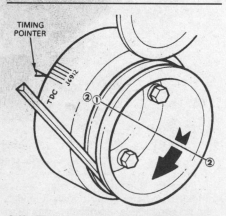

9.6b The V6 and later four-cylinder timing marks are on the front engine damper and timing chain cover

timing light through the slot at the flywheel (manual transaxle) or driveplate (automatic transaxle) and note whether the timing mark (the 10° mark on manual transaxle equipped vehicles or the triangle shaped mark on automatic transaxle equipped vehicles) is aligned with the timing pointer at the edge of the timing slot. On later four-cylinder and V6 engines, point the light down through the right hand (four-cylinder) or left hand (V6) side of the engine (facing front of engine) toward the pulley timing marks.

9   If the proper mark isn't aligned with the stationary pointer, loosen the distributor hold down bolt. Turn the distributor clockwise (to retard timing) or counterclockwise (to advance timing) until the correct timing mark on the flywheel/driveplate is aligned with the stationary pointer. Tighten the distributor hold down bolt securely when the timing is correct and recheck it to make sure it didn't change when the bolt was tightened.

10   Turn off the engine.

11   Plug in the single wire SPOUT connector, install the SPOUT shorting bar or attach the vacuum hoses depending on the vehicle.

12   Restart the engine and check the idle speed. Note that the specified rpm for automatic and manual transaxle equipped vehicles is different. Because the engine is equipped with automatic idle speed control, idle rpm is not adjustable. If the idle rpm is not within the specified range, take the vehicle to a dealer service department or repair shop. Adjustment requires specialized

test equipment and procedures that are beyond the scope of the home mechanic.

13   Turn off the engine.

14   Remove the timing light and tachometer.

10   Ignition module - check and replacement

Refer to illustrations 10.2, 10.11, 10.15, 10.20, 10.30, 10.45, 10.51, 10.55, 10.56 and 10.57

Caution: *The ignition module is a delicate and relatively expensive electronic component. The following tests must be done with the right equipment by someone that knows how to use it properly. Failure to follow the step-by-step procedures could result in damage to the module and/or other electronic devices, including the EEC-IV microprocessor itself (in US vehicles). Additionally, all devices under computer control are protected by a Federally mandated extended warranty. Check with your dealer before attempting to diagnose them yourself.*

Duraspark II system (Canadian models through 1987) - check

Ignition module voltage

1   Turn the ignition switch off.

2   Carefully insert a small straight pin into

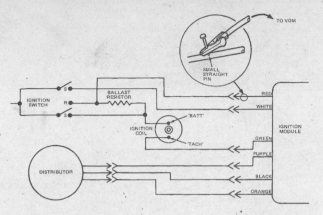

10.2 Checking ignition module voltage (Duraspark II system)

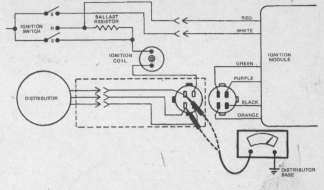

10.11 Measuring the resistance of the ignition module-to-stator assembly wiring harness (Duraspark II system)

the red module wire **(see illustration)**. **Caution:** *Don't allow the straight pin to ground against anything.*

3   Attach the negative lead of a VOM to the distributor base.

4   Measure battery voltage.

5   Attach the positive voltmeter lead to the pin in the red module wire with the ignition switch in the Run position.

6   If the measured voltage is 90 percent of battery voltage, check the ballast resistor (refer to Section 7).

7   If the measured voltage is less than 90 percent of the battery voltage, inspect the wiring harness between the module and the ignition switch (refer to the wiring diagrams at the end of the manual). Also inspect the ignition switch for wear and damage (refer to Chapter 12).

8   Turn the ignition switch to the Off position.

9   Detach the VOM and remove the straight pin.

Ignition module wiring harness

10   Attach one lead of an ohmmeter to the distributor base.

11   Check the resistance between the wiring harness terminals mating with the black and purple module wires and ground

by attaching the remaining ohmmeter lead to the wire terminals one at a time **(see illustration)**.

12   If the resistance is greater than 70,000 ohms, the ignition module to-distributor stator wiring harness resistance is normal. Check the ignition coil secondary resistance (refer to Section 7).

13   If the resistance is less than 70,000 ohms, inspect the wiring harness between the module connector and the distributor, including the distributor grommet.

Ignition module-to-coil wire

14   Unplug and inspect the four-wire ignition module electrical connector and the ignition coil connector.

15   Connect one lead of an ohmmeter to the distributor base and the other lead to the TACH terminal of the ignition coil connector **(see illustration)**.

16   Measure the resistance between the TACH terminal of the ignition coil connector and ground.

17   If the resistance is greater than 100 ohms, replace the ignition module (Step 43).

18   If the resistance is less than 100 ohms, inspect the wiring harness between the ignition module and the coil.

19   Reattach the ignition module and coil connectors.

Ground circuit

20   Carefully insert a small straight pin into the black module wire **(see illustration)**. **Caution:** *Don't allow the straight pin to ground against anything.*

21   Attach the negative lead of a VOM to the distributor base.

22   Turn the ignition switch to the Run position.

23   Measure the voltage at the black wire.

24   If the voltage is greater than 0.5-volt, check the distributor ground circuit (Step 28).

25   If the voltage is less than 0.5-volt, replace the ignition module (refer to Step 43).

26   Turn the ignition switch to the Off position.

27   Remove the straight pin and detach the VOM.

Distributor ground circuit

28   Unplug the distributor connector from the wiring harness and inspect it for dirt, corrosion and damage.

29   Attach one lead of an ohmmeter to the distributor base.

30   Attach the other lead to the black wire in

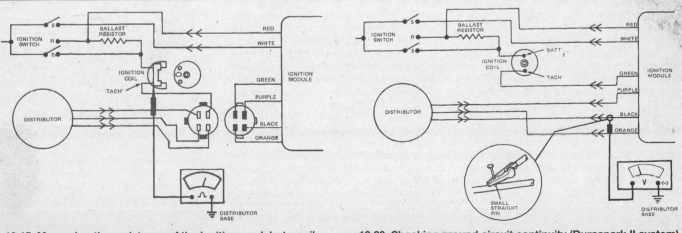

10.15 Measuring the resistance of the ignition module-to-coil wire (Duraspark II system)

10.20 Checking ground circuit continuity (Duraspark II system)

5

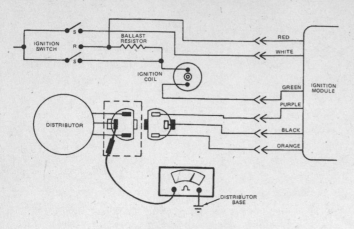

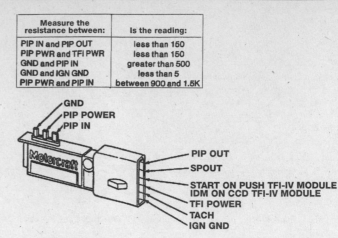

Measure the resistance between:	Is the reading:
PIP IN and PIP OUT	less than 150
PIP PWR and TFI PWR	less than 150
GND and PIP IN	greater than 500
GND and IGN GND	less than 5
PIP PWR and PIP IN	between 900 and 1.5K

10.30 Checking distributor ground circuit continuity (Duraspark II system)

10.45 To test the TFI or ICM module, perform the resistance measurements as shown - if out of specification, replace the module

the distributor connector (**see illustration**). Measure the resistance in the distributor ground circuit. **Note:** *Wiggle the distributor grommet when making this check.*

31   If the resistance is less than 1-ohm, the distributor ground circuit is okay. Inspect the wiring harness and the connectors between the distributor and the ignition module.

32   If the resistance is greater than 1-ohm, check the ground screw in the distributor.

TFI-I V or DI systems (all US models and Canadian models from 1988) - check

33   Perform the checks outlined in Section 6 and 7 of this Chapter. If the problem is not found, proceed with the TFI/ICM checks.

34   Disconnect the SPOUT signal wire as described in Section 9 Step 4 this Chapter to enable the TFI/ICM internal back-up timing mode.

35   Using a calibrated spark tester, check for spark (refer to Section 6 this Chapter if necessary).

36   If there is spark, the problem is probably within the PCM to module circuitry. Diagnosis beyond this point is best left to a dealer service department. If a no spark condition still exists, the problem could be the TFI/ICM module. Continue to next step.

37   **Note**: *Prior to 1988, no factory bench test procedure of the TFI/ICM module existed. The factory recommended replacement if a problem was suspected. Therefore, on these models, you must purchase a new ignition module before performing the following check. Since the check can result in only one of two possibilities (you will need a new module, or you won't), the odds are 50/50 that you'll be buying a new module that you may not need. Electronic components can't be returned once they're purchased, so if you're unwilling to invest in a new module that you may not need, stop here. Take the vehicle to a dealer and have the module checked out.*

38   Reconnect the SPOUT signal wire or shorting bar removed in Step 34.

39   Remove the TFI/ICM and module as described in Steps 54 through 56.

1984 through 1987 models

40   Install a new module on the distributor (see Step 57 and 58 this Section). Connect the body harness to the TFI-IV. Make sure the unit is grounded with a jumper lead from the distributor to the engine. Rotate the distributor shaft by hand and check for spark at the secondary coil wire with the ignition tester (see Section 6).

41   If there is spark, the old module has failed. Leave the new module on the distributor and install the distributor (refer to Section 8 this Chapter).

42   If there is no spark, the PIP/CMP sensor has failed. Your old module is okay but you need a new or rebuilt distributor.

43   Install the old module onto the new/rebuilt distributor (refer to Step 57 and 58) and reinstall the distributor (refer to Section 8 this Chapter). Put your new module on the shelf for another day!

44   Verify spark using ignition tester (refer to Section 6 this Chapter if necessary).

1988 and later models

45   Perform the module pin-to-pin resistance measurements as shown in the accompanying table (**see illustration**).

46   If the module fails any test, install a new module on the distributor (see Step 57 and 58). Connect the body harness to the TFI-IV. Make sure the unit is grounded with a jumper lead from the distributor to the engine. Rotate the distributor shaft by hand and check for spark at the secondary coil wire with the ignition tester (see Section 6).

47   If all readings are within specification, the PIP/CMP sensor has failed. Your module is okay but you need a new or rebuilt distributor.

48   Install the old module onto the new/rebuilt distributor (refer to Step 57 and 58 this Section) and reinstall the distributor (refer to Section 8 this Chapter).

49   Verify spark using ignition tester (refer to Section 6 this Chapter if necessary).

Duraspark II ignition module - replacement

50   Detach the cable from the negative terminal of the battery.

51   Vehicles equipped with a Duraspark II system may have either the standard Duraspark II module or the universal ignition module (**see illustration**). If your vehicle is equipped with the standard module, unplug both connectors; if your vehicle is equipped

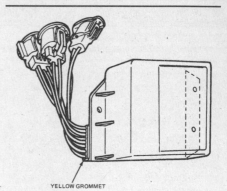

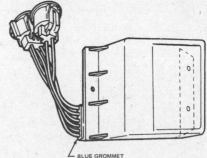

10.51 Duraspark II ignition systems will have one of two different ignition modules - the one on the top, known as a universal ignition module (UIM), has three electrical connectors and a yellow grommet - the one on the bottom is the standard Duraspark II module with two connectors and a blue grommet

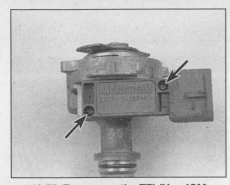

10.55 To remove the TFI-IV or ICM ignition module from the distributor base, remove the two screws (arrows) . . .

10.56 . . . then pull the module straight down to detach the spade terminals from the stator connector

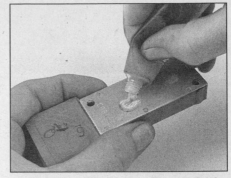

10.57 Be sure to wipe the back side of the module clean and apply a film of dielectric grease (essential for cool operation of the module) - DO NOT use any other type of grease!

with the UIM module, unplug all three connectors.
52 Remove the mounting screws and detach the module.
53 Installation is the reverse of removal.

TFI-IV or ICM ignition module - replacement

54 If necessary to get access to remove the TFI/ICM module, remove the distributor from the engine (refer to Section 8). **Note:** *On some models the distributor must be removed before the module can be detached because other components interfere with an on vehicle removal.*
55 Remove the two module mounting screws with a 1/4-inch drive 7/32-inch deep socket **(see illustration)**.
56 Pull straight down on the module to disconnect the spade connectors from the stator connector **(see illustration)**.
57 Whether you are installing the old module or a new one, wipe the back side of the module clean with a soft, clean shop rag and apply a film of silicone dielectric grease to the back side of the module **(see illustration)** .
58 Installation is the reverse of removal. When plugging in the module, make sure that the three terminals are inserted all the way into the stator connector.

11 Distributor stator assembly - check and replacement

Refer to illustrations 11.2, 11.7, 11.15, 11.19, 11.36, 11.38, 11.39, 11.40, 11.41, 11.42, 11.46, 11.55a and 11.55b

Duraspark II system (Canadian models through 1987) - check

Stator assembly and wiring harness

1 Unplug the ignition module four-wire connector. Inspect it for dirt, corrosion and/or damage.
2 Attach the leads of an ohmmeter to the wiring harness terminals of the black and purple wires **(see illustration)**.
3 Measure the resistance between the two wiring harness terminals. **Note:** *Wiggle the wires in the harness when making the check.*
4 If the resistance is as specified, the distributor stator assembly and wiring harness is okay. Measure the ignition module-to-distributor stator assembly wiring harness resistance (Section 10).
5 If the resistance is less or more than the specified resistance, measure the resistance of the distributor stator assembly itself (Step 6).

Stator assembly

Note: *This is not the same test as the one above.*
6 Unplug the distributor wire harness connector. Inspect it for dirt, corrosion and damage.
7 Attach the leads of an ohmmeter to the wiring harness terminals of the orange and purple wires **(see illustration)**.
8 If the resistance is as specified, the distributor stator is okay. Inspect the wiring harness between the distributor and the ignition module .
9 If the resistance is less or more than the specified resistance, replace the stator assembly (Step 12).
10 Detach the ohmmeter and reconnect the distributor and ignition module connectors.

TFI-I V or DI system (all US models and Canadian models from 1988) - check

11 The factory doesn't specify a check for the TFI-IV system stator (sensor). If the ignition module is good, but the system won't function normally, the distributor must be replaced with a new one, since the stator can't be replaced as a separate unit.

5

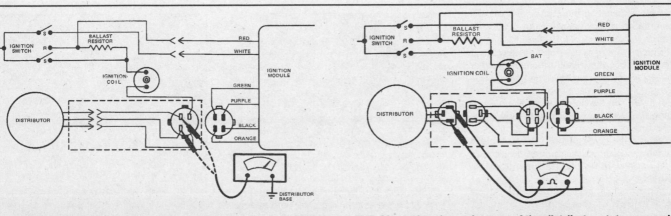

11.2 Measuring the resistance of the stator assembly and wiring harness (Duraspark II system)

11.7 Measuring the resistance of the distributor stator assembly (Duraspark II system)

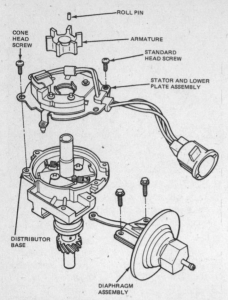

11.15 An exploded view of the Duraspark II distributor components

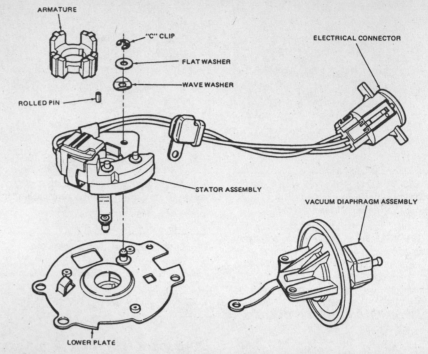

11.19 An exploded view of the Duraspark II distributor stator assembly

Duraspark II distributor stator - replacement

12   Disconnect the cable from the negative battery terminal.

13   Remove the distributor cap and set the cap and wires aside as an assembly .

14   Remove the rotor from the distributor shaft.

15   Unplug the distributor wiring harness connector **(see illustration)**.

16   Using a small gear puller or two screwdrivers as levers, remove the armature **(see illustration 11.15)**.

17   Remove the two screws retaining the lower plate and stator assembly to the distributor base. Note that there are two different size screws used.

18   Detach the lower plate assembly and stator assembly from the distributor.

19   Remove the C-clip, flat washer and wave washer securing the stator assembly to the lower plate assembly, then separate the stator assembly from the lower plate assembly **(see illustration)**.

20   Before installing the stator, remove any accumulated dirt or grease from parts that are to be reused.

21   Place the stator assembly on the lower plate assembly and install the wave washer (outer edge up), flat washer and C-clip.

22   Install the stator assembly/lower plate assembly in the distributor base. Be sure to engage the pin on the stator assembly in the diaphragm rod.

23   Attach the lower plate to the distributor base with the screws (remember, the screws are not the same size and are not interchangeable).

24   When installing the armature, note that there are two notches in it. Install the armature on the sleeve and plate assembly employing the unused notch and a new roll pin.

25   Reconnect the distributor wiring harness.

26   Reinstall the rotor and distributor cap. Make sure the ignition wires are securely connected to the cap and spark plugs.

27   Connect the cable to the negative battery terminal.

28   Check the ignition timing (refer to Section 9).

TFI-IV or DI distributor stator - replacement

29   Remove the distributor cap and position it out of the way with the wires attached.

30   Disconnect the TFI module from the wire harness.

31   Remove the distributor (refer to Section 8).

32   Remove the rotor (refer to Chapter 1 if necessary).

33   Although not absolutely necessary, it's a good idea to remove the ignition module (Section 10) to prevent possible damage to the module while the distributor is being disassembled.

34   Clamp the lower end of the distributor housing in a vise. Place a shop rag in the vise jaws to prevent damage to the distributor and don't overtighten the vise.

35   Before removing the drive gear, note that the roll pin is slightly offset. When the distributor is reassembled, the roll pin cannot be reinstalled through the drive gear and distributor shaft holes unless the holes are perfectly lined up.

36   With an assistant holding the distributor steady in the vise, use a 5/32-inch diameter pin punch to hammer the roll pin out of the shaft **(see illustration)**.

37   Loosen the vise and reposition the distributor with the drive gear facing up.

38   Remove the drive gear with a small puller **(see illustration)**.

11.36 With the distributor shaft housing locked securely in a vise lined with several shop rags to prevent damage to the housing, drive out the roll pin with a 5/32-inch pin punch

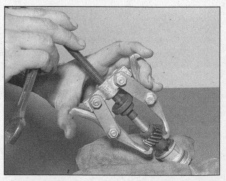

11.38 With the distributor shaft pointing up like this, use a small puller to separate the drive gear from the shaft

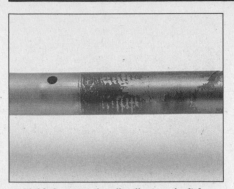

11.39 Inspect the distributor shaft for burrs or residue buildup like this in the vicinity of the hole for the drive gear roll pin (remove it with emery cloth to prevent damage to the distributor shaft bushing when removing and installing the shaft)

39 Before removing it from the distributor, check the shaft for burrs or built up residue, particularly around the drive gear roll pin hole **(see illustration)**. If burrs or residue are evident, polish the shaft with emery paper and wipe it clean to prevent damage to the lip seal and bushing in the distributor base.

40 After removing any burrs/residue, remove the shaft assembly by gently pulling on the plate. Note the relationship of the spacer washer to the distributor base before removing the washer **(see illustration)**.

41 Remove the octane rod retaining screw **(see illustration)**.

42 Lift the inner end of the rod off the stator retaining post **(see illustration)** and pull the octane rod from the distributor base. **Note:** *Don't lose the grommet installed in the octane rod hole. The grommet protects the electronic components of the distributor from moisture.*

43 Remove the two stator screws **(see illustration 11.42)**.

44 Gently lift it straight up and remove the stator assembly from the distributor.

45 Check the shaft bushing in the distributor base for wear or signs of excessive heat buildup. If signs of wear and/or damage are evident, replace the complete distributor assembly.

11.40 As soon as you remove the distributor shaft, note how the washer is installed before removing it (it could easily fall out and get lost)

46 Inspect the O-ring at the base of the distributor. If it s damaged or worn, remove it and install a new one **(see illustration)**.

47 Inspect the base casting for cracks and wear. If any damage is evident, replace the distributor assembly.

48 Place the stator assembly in position over the shaft bushing and press it down onto the distributor base until it's completely seated on the posts.

49 Install the stator screws and tighten them securely.

50 Insert the octane rod through the hole in the distributor base and push the inner end of the rod onto the post. **Note:** *Make sure that the octane rod hole is properly sealed by the grommet.*

51 Reinstall the octane rod screw and tighten it securely.

52 Apply a light coat of engine oil to the distributor shaft and insert the shaft through the bushing.

53 Mount the distributor in the vise with the lower end up. Be sure to line the vise jaws with a few clean shop rags to protect the distributor base. Place a block of wood under the distributor shaft to support it and prevent it from falling out while the drive gear is being installed.

54 Since the holes in the drive gear and distributor shaft are drilled off center, the gear can only be installed one way with the holes lined up.

11.41 To detach the octane rod from the distributor, remove the retaining screw - note the condition of the small square rubber grommet that seals the octane rod hole when you pull the rod out (it seals the interior of the distributor to prevent moisture from damaging the electronics)

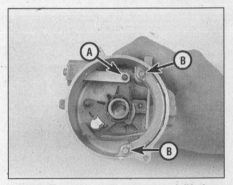

11.42 To remove the octane rod, lift the inner end of the rod off the stator assembly post (A) - to remove the stator assembly, remove both mounting screws (B) and lift the stator straight up off the posts

55 Using a deep socket and hammer, carefully tap the drive gear back onto the distributor shaft **(see illustration)**. Make sure the hole in the drive gear and the hole in the shaft are lined up. Because the holes were drilled off center by the factory, they must be perfectly aligned or you'll have to remove the gear, rotate it 180-degrees and reinstall it **(see illustration)**.

56 Once the drive gear is seated and the

11.46 If the O-ring at the base of the distributor is worn or damaged, replace it with a new one

11 55a After securing the distributor assembly upside down in a vise, "eyeball" the roll pin holes in the drive gear and the shaft, then tap the drive gear onto the shaft with a deep socket and hammer

11.55b If the drive gear and shaft roll pin holes are misaligned, the roll pin cannot be driven through the drive gear and shaft holes - the drive gear must now be pulled off the shaft and realigned

5

holes are lined up, turn the distributor sideways in the vise and, with an assistant steadying it, drive a new roll pin into the drive gear with a 5/32-inch pin punch. Make sure that neither end of the roll pin protrudes from the drive gear.

57   Check the distributor shaft for smooth rotation, then remove the distributor assembly from the vise.

58   Install the TFI-IV module (refer to Section 10).

59   Install the rotor (refer to Chapter 1 if necessary).

60   Install the distributor.

---

12   Charging system - general information and precautions

The charging system includes the alternator, either an internal or an external voltage regulator, a charge indicator, the battery, a fusible link and the wiring between all the components. The charging system supplies electrical power for the ignition system, the lights, the radio, etc. The purpose of the voltage regulator is to limit the alternator's voltage to a preset value. This prevents power surges, circuit overloads, etc., during peak voltage output. The fusible link is a short length of insulated wire integral with the engine compartment wiring harness. The link is four wire gauges smaller in diameter than the circuit it protects. The alternator is driven by a drivebelt at the front (right end) of the engine.

The Tempo/Topaz has had four different alternators utilized over the years (three for the four-cylinder engine, one for the V6) depending on the model and options installed.

Early models used a basic external fan Rear Terminal alternator in conjunction with an remote electronic voltage regulator. This alternator is recognizable by the three insulated post terminals on the back. The EVR (external voltage regulator) is mounted on the right fender apron of the vehicle. Because of it's limited application, it will not be addressed in this manual.

The new IAR (integral alternator/regulator) external fan design followed shortly. This alternator features a built-in (integral) modular electronic regulator and modular rectifier assembly. This type can be recognized by its rear externally mounted regulator module and two plug-in connectors (one into the regulator and one into the side of the alternator for the rectifier module).

In 1991, the second IAR alternator was introduced to handle the increased load of air conditioned vehicles with automatic transaxles. This four-cylinder alternator can be most easily recognized by it's internal fan design. Unfortunately, only the regulator and brush assembly can be serviced; further disassembly is not possible. Other problems (such as a diode failure) require that the entire alternator assembly be replaced. Due to this

constraint, the regulator and brush holder are easily accessible from the outside of the unit.

The release of the V6 engine version resulted in a fourth alternator type. The V6 model also uses an IAR, internal fan-type alternator. However, unlike the latest four-cylinder version, the V6 regulator/brush assembly is mounted internally to the unit along with the rectifier, necessitating a complete teardown to replace the regulator or brushes.

The charging system doesn't ordinarily require periodic maintenance. However, the drivebelt, battery and wires and connections should be inspected at the intervals outlined in Chapter 1.

Be very careful when making electrical circuit connections to a vehicle equipped with an alternator and note the following:

a) *When reconnecting wires to the alternator from the battery, be sure to note the polarity.*

b) *Before using arc welding equipment to repair any part of the vehicle, disconnect the wires from the alternator and the battery terminals.*

c) *Never start the engine with a battery charger connected.*

d) *Always disconnect both battery leads before using a battery charger.*

---

13   Charging system - check

Refer to illustrations 13.2, 13.6, 13.9, 13.23, 13.24 and 13.25

General Checks

1   If a malfunction occurs in the charging circuit, don't automatically assume that the alternator is causing the problem. First check the following items:

a) *The battery cables where they connect to the battery. Make sure the connections are clean and tight (refer to Chapter 1).*

b) *Check the external alternator wiring harness and the connectors at the alternator and voltage regulator. They must be in good condition, clean and tight.*

13.2 To measure battery voltage, hook the voltmeter leads to the battery terminals - to measure charging voltage, start the engine

c) *Check the drivebelt condition and tension (refer to Chapter 1).*

d) *Make sure the alternator mounting and adjustment bolts are tight.*

e) *Check the fusible link located between the starter relay (on the left inner fender well-refer to Section 19) and the alternator. If it's burned, determine the cause, repair the circuit and replace the link (refer to Chapter 12).*

f) *Run the engine and check the alternator for abnormal noise.*

Voltage Tests (four-cylinder engine alternators)

2   Using a voltmeter, check the battery voltage with the engine off. It should be approximately 12-volts (**see illustration**).

3   Start the engine and check the battery voltage again. It should now be approximately 14-to-15 volts.

4   If the voltage reading is less or more than the specified charging voltage proceed with the following steps.

5   Locate the regulator terminal (screw F) on the back of the alternator (the screw is under an insulating cap on the regulator module). **Note:** *Some later models may not have an F terminal, in which case the following test cannot be performed.*

6   With the ignition switch in the Off position, touch the F screw with the voltmeter positive lead while touching the alternator housing with the negative lead (**see illustration**).

7   The meter should indicate battery voltage if the system is operating normally.

8   If less than battery voltage is indicated, proceed to the next Steps 9 through 14 to determine the cause of the voltage drop. If battery voltage is indicated proceed to Step 15.

9   Disconnect the wire harness from the regulator and connect the voltmeter positive

13.6 The regulator F terminal screw is located on the voltage regulator - to perform a field circuit drain test, touch the positive lead of a voltmeter or VOM to the F terminal and the negative

lead to the alternator housing - alternator shown is IAR external fan type, F terminal location on other alternators; some later alternators do not have an F terminal

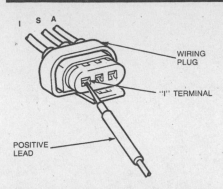

13.9 To check the voltage at the regulator wiring harness plug, touch the positive lead of a VOM to the I terminal, then the S terminal while touching the negative lead to the rear of the alternator housing (four-cylinder models)

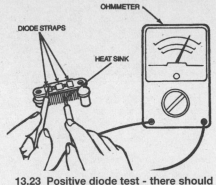

13.23 Positive diode test - there should be continuity from the diode to the heat sink only

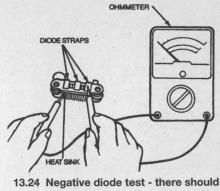

13.24 Negative diode test - there should be continuity from the heat sink to the diode only

lead to terminal I in the plug **(see illustration)**. No voltage should be indicated.

10   If voltage is indicated, check the I lead from the ignition switch to identify and eliminate the voltage source (refer to the wiring diagrams at the end of this book).

11   Reconnect the regulator harness and connect the voltmeter positive lead to terminal S. No voltage should be indicated.

12   If voltage is indicated, disconnect the wire harness from the alternator. Again, connect the positive voltmeter lead to terminal S in the wiring harness connector.

13   If voltage is still indicated, repair the S lead to the alternator plug to eliminate the voltage source.

14   If no voltage is indicated, the problem is with the rectifier. Replace the rectifier, refer to Section 15 this Chapter. **Note:** *The rectifier is not replaceable on four-cylinder internal fan-type alternator - if rectifier is bad, replace alternator (refer to Section 14 this Chapter).*

15   If battery voltage is seen at Step 6, touch the F screw with the volt meter positive lead while touching the negative lead to the alternator housing, turn key to RUN position. Voltage at F screw should now be less than two volts with key in RUN position indicating regulator is turned on and grounding field circuit.

16   If no drop in voltage is noticed, remove

regulator plug from alternator and check for battery voltage at I lead (regulator turn-on) with key in RUN position. If battery voltage is seen, replace regulator (See Section 15 this Chapter).

17   If battery voltage is not seen at alternator plug I lead, service I circuit from plug to ignition switch (refer to the wiring diagrams at the end of this book).

Voltage Tests (V6 engine alternator)

Note: *The V6 engine alternator does not incorporate screw F, A or S circuit for testing (field current is generated internally and stator-to-regulator connections are made internally); therefore, on-vehicle testing is limited. However, some basic input voltage tests can be made to verify that no external problems exist. Further diagnosis requires disassembly of the alternator.*

18   Disconnect the connector from the alternator and connect a jumper wire from the wiring connector I lead to the battery negative post cable clamp. Turn the ignition to the RUN position with the engine off. The indicator light in the instrument cluster should light up.

19   If the indicator does not light, check the indicator bulb for continuity and replace the bulb if it is burned out. If the bulb checks out good, service the open in the I lead circuit from the alternator plug to the ignition key (refer to the wiring diagrams at the end of this book).

20   If the indicator does light, remove the jumper wire and connect the negative lead of a voltmeter to the battery negative post cable clamp and connect the voltmeter positive lead to the alternator wiring connector 'A' lead. Battery voltage should be indicated.

21   If battery voltage is not indicated, check the 'A' lead circuit wiring from the plug to the battery.

22   If battery voltage is indicated, clean and tighten the ground connections to the engine and alternator. Turn the ignition to the RUN position with the engine off. If the indicator still does not light or if the alternator output voltage is low, remove and teardown the alternator for component testing or replace the complete alternator. Refer to Section 14 (replace alternator) or Section 15 (alternator teardown).

Rectifier assembly test (V6 engine alternator)

Note: *The only component test possible on the V6 engine alternator is the rectifier diode test. If test passes, replace the regulator.*

23   Check for continuity between the positive diode lead and the heat sink at the positive side, using an ohmmeter. There should be continuity only in the direction from the diode lead to the heat sink **(see illustration)**.

24   Check for continuity between the negative diode lead and the heat sink at the negative side, using an ohmmeter. There should be continuity only in the direction from the heat sink to the negative diode **(see illustration)**.

25   Check the diode trio for continuity using an ohmmeter. There should be continuity in one direction only **(see illustration)**.

26   If all tests pass, replace regulator (refer to Section 15 this Chapter).

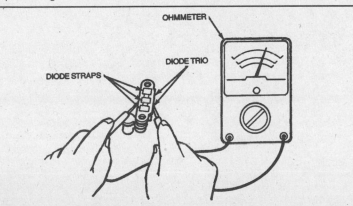

13.25 Diode trio test - there should be continuity in one direction only

---

14 Alternator - removal and installation

Refer to illustrations 14.2a, 14.2b, 14.4a and 14.4b

1   Detach the cable from the negative terminal of the battery.

14.2a To remove the alternator, unplug both the alternator and the voltage regulator wire harness connectors (arrows) - alternator shown is IAR external fan type, connections on other alternators vary slightly; for example, the others use a separate threaded post type B+ terminal instead of quick-connect plug as shown

14.2b To unplug the alternator wire harness connector, pry the tangs on each end of the plug open with a small screwdriver

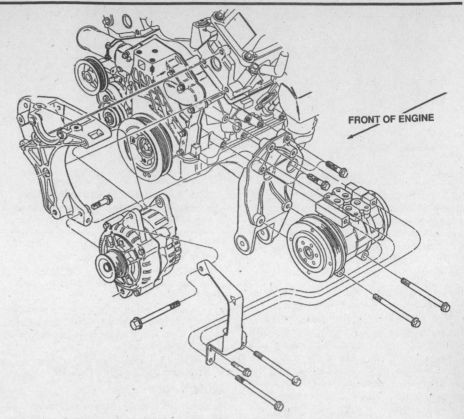

FRONT OF ENGINE

14.4a V6 engine alternator mounting details - exploded view

2   Unplug the electrical connectors from the alternator and the voltage regulator **(see illustrations)**.

3   Refer to Chapter 1, loosen the alternator adjustment and pivot bolts and detach the drivebelt.

4   Remove the adjustment and pivot bolts and separate the alternator from the engine **(see illustrations)**.

5   Installation is the reverse of removal.

6   After the alternator is installed, adjust the drivebelt tension (refer to Chapter 1).

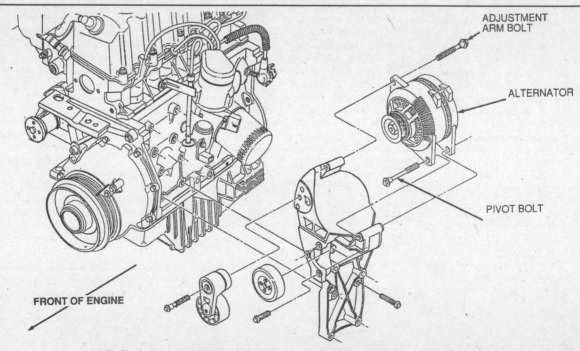

FRONT OF ENGINE

ADJUSTMENT ARM BOLT

ALTERNATOR

PIVOT BOLT

14.4b Typical four-cylinder engine alternator mounting details - exploded view

15.3 To detach the voltage regulator/brush holder assembly, remove the four screws (arrows) - alternator shown is IAR external fan type, regulator/brush holder removal on internal fan type is similar

15.5 To remove the brushes from the voltage regulator/brush holder assembly, detach the rubber plugs from the two brush lead wire screws and remove both screws (arrows)

15.9 Before installing the voltage regulator/brush holder assembly, insert a paper clip as shown to hold the brushes in place during installation - after installation, simply pull the paper clip out

15 Voltage regulator/rectifier and alternator brushes - replacement

Refer to illustrations 15.3, 15.5, 15.9, 15.12, 15.13, 15.14, 15.15, 15.29, 15.31, 15.33, 15.34, 15.36, 15.37, 15.38, 15.39, 15.41 and 15.43

Voltage regulator/rectifier/brush - replacement (external fan, integral regulator)

1   Remove the alternator (refer to Section 14).
2   Set the alternator on a clean workbench.
3   Remove the four voltage regulator mounting screws **(see illustration)** Note: *Screws have Torx heads and require a special screwdriver.*
4   Detach the voltage regulator. If only the rectifier is to be replaced, proceed to Step 10.
5   Detach the rubber plugs and remove the brush lead retaining screws and nuts to separate the brush leads from the holder **(see illustration). Note:** *Screws have Torx heads and require a special screwdriver.*
6   After noting the relationship of the brushes to the brush holder assembly, remove both brushes. Don't lose the springs.
7   If you're installing a new voltage regulator, insert the old brushes into the brush holder of the new regulator. If you're installing new brushes, insert them into the brush holder of the old regulator. Make sure the springs are properly compressed and the brushes are properly inserted into the recesses in the brush holder.
8   Install the brush lead retaining screws and nuts.
9   Insert a short section of wire, like a paper clip, through the hole in the voltage regulator **(see illustration)** to hold the brushes in the retracted position during regulator installation. If only the voltage

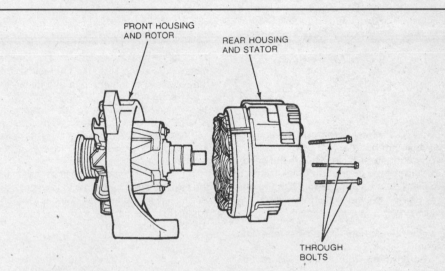

15.12 After the regulator has been detached, remove the three through bolts and separate the front housing with rotor from the rear housing with the stator assembly attached - it may be necessary to gently tap the front cover with a plastic hammer to part the two halves

regulator is to be replaced, proceed to Step 19. If rectifier needs replacing, continue.
10 Scribe a line across the end housings and stator laminated core for alignment reference during reassembly.
11 Remove the three through bolts.
12 Separate the front housing rotor assembly from the stator and rear housing. It may be necessary to gently tap the front housing with a plastic mallet to aid in parting the assemblies **(see illustration)**.
13 Using a soldering iron, remove the solder from the rectifier and the stator leads **(see illustration). Caution:** *If the rectifier is to be reused, do not place the soldering iron on an individual lead for no more than five seconds at a time - otherwise, the rectifier may be damaged if it's overheated.*
14 Some rectifier/stator assemblies use a spade type connector block instead of solder. if this is the case, carefully pry the

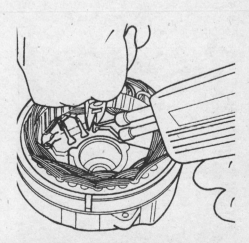

15.13 On most alternators, you will have to de-solder the three stator wires from the rectifier as shown - don't overheat the rectifier if you intend on using it again!

5

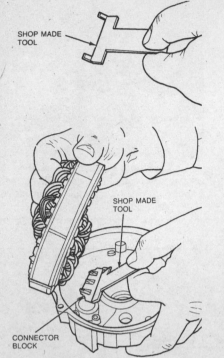

SHOP MADE TOOL

SHOP MADE TOOL

CONNECTOR BLOCK

15.14 On some alternators, the stator wires might be attached using a spade type connector block; if this is the case, carefully pry the connector block from the rectifier leads - a special tool like the one shown will make the job easier

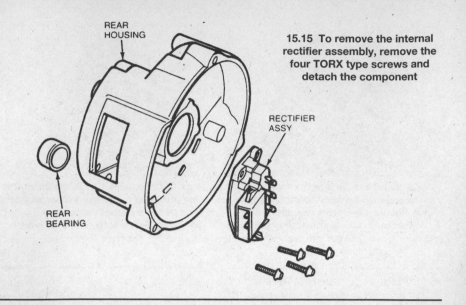

REAR HOUSING

REAR BEARING

RECTIFIER ASSY

15.15 To remove the internal rectifier assembly, remove the four TORX type screws and detach the component

connector block from the rectifier **(see illustration)**.
15 Remove the four TORX-type rectifier attach screws and remove the rectifier from the rear housing **(see illustration)**.
16 Wipe the rear housing rectifier location with a clean cloth and apply a 3/32-inch wide by 3/4-inch long strip of compound across the base plate. **Warning:** *Failure to apply heat sink compound will result in premature component failure.*

17 Clean the replacement rectifier mounting surface and seat the rectifier into the recessed mounting area and install the attach screws.
18 Reassembly up to regulator installation is reverse of removal. **Note:** *Remember to line up the scribe marks, use good electrical solder and don't overheat the rectifier leads.*
19 Carefully install the regulator. Make sure the brushes don't hang up on the rotor.
20 Install the voltage regulator screws and tighten them securely.
21 Remove the wire or paper clip.
22 Install the alternator (refer to Section 14).

Voltage regulator/brush - replacement (internal fan, integral regulator)

23 Remove the alternator (refer to Section 14).
24 Remove the four voltage regulator mounting screws **(see illustration 15.3)**.

Note: *The screws have Torx heads and require a special screwdriver.*
25 Detach the voltage regulator.
26 Pry the insulating caps off of the countersunk holes containing the two regulator to brush block attach screws and remove the screws **(see illustration 15.5)**. **Note:** *The screws have Torx heads and require a special screwdriver.*
27 Install a new brush holder assembly to the regulator (or new regulator to the original brush holder). Tighten the screw securely. **Note:** *According to the factory manual, individual brushes are not available for this alternator.*
28 The remaining reassembly is the reverse of disassembly.

Voltage regulator/rectifier/brush - replacement (V6 only)

29 Remove the alternator, then mark the alternator halves with paint or a scribe **(see illustration)** to ensure proper reassembly.
30 Remove the three through bolts. Don't attempt to pull the alternator apart until you've read the next Step.
31 The rear bearing is pressed into the rear end frame. Place a 200 watt soldering iron on the rear end frame for three or four minutes **(see illustration)**. If you're using an iron with less output, keep it in contact a few minutes longer.
32 Pull the alternator halves apart. Pry them apart with a screwdriver if necessary, but don't use excessive force. If the two halves don't come apart fairly easily, the bearing is still stuck in the bore in the end frame housing. You'll damage the bearing or the end frame housing if you use excessive force. Put the soldering iron back on the end frame for a few more minutes.
33 Remove the B+ (battery) terminal nut and insulation bush from the outside of the

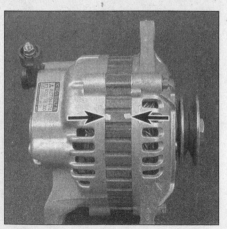

15.29 Mark the alternator halves with paint or a scribe to ensure they're properly aligned when reassembled

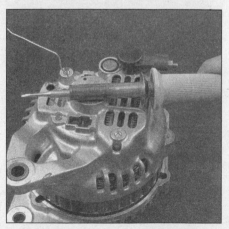

15.31 Heat the rear end frame with a 200W soldering iron to expand it enough to pull the bearing loose

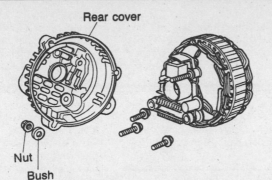

Rear cover

Nut

Bush

15.33 Exploded view of the rear housing (end frame), the B terminal nut, its insulation bush and the three internal regulator/rectifier attach screws - the stator core with the combined regulator and rectifier can be removed from the rear housing as an assembly, as shown, once the above hardware is removed

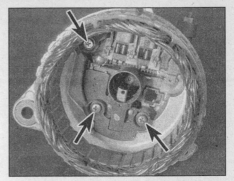

15.34 Remove the three rectifier and brush holder mounting screws (arrows)

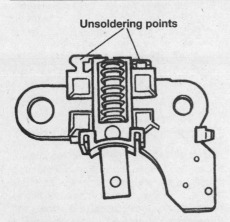

Unsoldering points

15.36 To replace the brushes, de-solder the brush pigtail at the indicated points and remove them from the brush holder assembly

Wear limit (the ⚙ mark)

2 ~ 3 mm
(0.08 ~ 0.12 in)

Brush holder end line

15.37 Solder the pigtail for the new brush so the wear limit line of the brush projects 0.080 to 0.120-inch (2 to 3mm) out of the brush holder

alternator **(see illustration)**.

34   Remove the rectifier and brush holder mounting screws from inside the alternator **(see illustration)**.

35   Remove the stator core with the rectifier and regulator attached from the rear housing. **Note:** *it may be necessary to gently tap on*

the B+ terminal to dislodge the regulator from the rear housing. If the purpose of the teardown was regulator or rectifier replacement and brush wear is acceptable, proceed to Step 38. If brush replacement is in order, continue.

36   Remove the solder from the brush pigtail **(see illustration)**, then detach the brush from the holder.

37   Solder the pigtail for the new brush so the wear limit line of the brush projects 0.080 to 0.120-inch (2 to 3mm) out from the end of the brush holder **(see illustration)**. If the purpose of the tear down was for brush replacement only, proceed to Step 41. For rectifier/regulator replacement, continue.

38   Using a soldering iron, remove the

solder from the rectifier and the stator leads **(see illustration). Caution:** *Use the soldering iron for no more than five seconds at a time - otherwise, the rectifier may be damaged if it's overheated.*

39   Using a soldering iron, remove the solder from the lead between the voltage regulator and the rectifier **(see illustration)**.

40   Resolder the replacement component(s). **Note:** *Use good electrical solder and don't overheat the rectifier leads.*

41   Reassembly is otherwise the reverse of removal **except** before installing the front housing and rotor into the rear housing, push the brushes into the brush holder and insert a paper clip through the hole in the end frame to secure the brushes in position **(see illustration). Note:** *Remember to line up the scribe marks.*

5

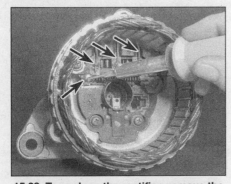

15.38 To replace the rectifier, remove the solder from the rectifier leads (arrows) and from between the regulator and rectifier (shown) - if you're only replacing the regulator/brush holder assembly, it's not necessary to de-solder the rectifier leads, but you'll still have to de-solder the lead between the two components

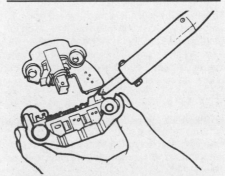

15.39 You may find it easier to remove the entire regulator/brush holder assembly, then de-solder the leads between the rectifier and the regulator/brush holder assembly to separate them

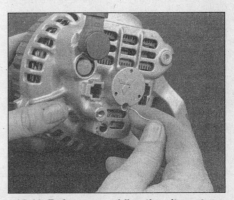

15.41 Before assembling the alternator, push each brush into the holder and insert a paper clip through the indicated hole

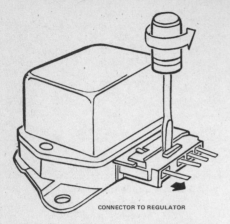

CONNECTOR TO REGULATOR

15.43 To detach the wire harness from the remote voltage regulator, position the tip of a screwdriver as shown and twist it - the screwdriver will push the connector off the regulator

42   Remove the wire securing the brush when you've completed reassembly.

Remote regulator

43   Remove the negative cable from the battery terminal, then disconnect the wire harness from the regulator. Use a screwdriver to unplug the harness connector-do not pull on the wires **(see illustration)**.
44   Remove the mounting bolts and detach the regulator.
45   Installation is the reverse of removal.

16   Starting system - general information

The function of the starting system is to crank the engine to start it. The system is composed of the starter motor, starter relay, battery, switch and connecting wires.

Early model starters used a positive engagement drive mechanism and moveable pole shoe activated by the field coils of the motor to engage the drive. Turning the ignition key to the Start position actuates a fender mounted high amperage starter relay through the starter control circuit. The starter relay then connects the battery to the starter. The battery supplies the electrical energy to the starter motor, which does the actual work of cranking the engine.

Later models followed with the industry standard by incorporating the high amperage relay into a more conventional starter motor solenoid/relay design. Although the remote relay is retained, it acts only as 1) a simple relay connecting battery voltage to the starter solenoid when the key is turned to Start, and 2) as a terminal block for various connectors. Once actuated, the starter motor solenoid physically drives the high-amperage relay contacts together and completes the starter motor circuit as well as engage the drive.

Vehicles equipped with an automatic transaxle have a Neutral start switch in the starter control circuit, which prevents operation of the starter unless the shift lever is in Neutral or Park. The circuit on vehicles with a manual transaxle prevents operation of the starter motor unless the clutch pedal is depressed.

Never operate the starter motor for more than 30 seconds at a time without pausing to allow it to cool for at least two minutes. Excessive cranking can cause overheating, which can seriously damage the starter.

17   Starfter motor and circuit - in-vehicle check

Refer to illustrations 17.14 and 17.17
Note: *Before diagnosing starter problems, make sure the battery is fully charged.*

General check (all vehicles)

1   If the starter motor doesn't turn at all when the switch is operated, make sure the shift lever is in Neutral or Park (automatic transaxle) or the clutch pedal is depressed (manual transaxle).
2   Make sure the battery is charged and that all cables at the battery and starter relay terminals are secure.
3   If the starter motor spins but the engine doesn't turn over, then the drive assembly in the starter motor is slipping and the starter motor must be replaced (refer to Section 18).
4   If, when the switch is actuated, the starter motor doesn't operate at all but the starter relay operates (clicks), then the problem lies with either the battery, the starter relay contacts or the starter motor connections.
5   If the starter relay doesn't click when the ignition switch is actuated, either the starter relay circuit is open or the relay itself is defective. Check the starter relay circuit (refer to the wiring diagrams at the end of this book) or replace the relay (refer to Section 19).
6   To check the starter relay circuit, remove the push-on connector from the fender mounted relay (the red one with a blue stripe). Make sure that the connection is clean and secure and the relay bracket is grounded. If the connections are good, check the operation of the relay with a jumper wire. To do this, place the transaxle in Park (automatic) or Neutral (manual). Remove the push-on connector from the relay. Connect a jumper wire between the battery positive terminal and the exposed terminal on the relay. If the starter motor now operates, the starter relay is okay. The problem is in the ignition switch, neutral start switch or in the starting circuit wiring (look for open or loose connections).
7   If the starter motor still doesn't operate, replace the starter relay (refer to Section 19).
8   If the starter motor cranks the engine at an abnormally slow speed, first make sure the battery is fully charged and all terminal connections are clean and tight. Also check the connections at the starter relay and battery ground. Eyelet terminals should not be easily rotated by hand. Also check for a short to ground. If the engine is partially seized, or has the wrong viscosity oil in it, it will crank slowly.
9   Run the engine until normal operating temperature is reached, then disconnect the coil wire from the distributor cap and ground it on the engine.
10   Connect a voltmeter positive lead to the positive battery terminal and then connect the negative lead to the negative terminal.
11   Crank the engine and take the voltmeter readings as soon as a steady figure is indicated. Do not allow the starter motor to turn for more than 30 seconds at a time. A reading of 9 volts or more, with the starter motor turning at normal cranking speed is normal. If the reading is 9 volts or more but the cranking speed is slow the solenoid contacts are probably burned or there is high resistance somewhere in the starter motor circuit. If the reading is less than 9 volts and the cranking speed is slow the motor is faulty or there is very low resistance (short) in the circuit.

Starter cranking circuit test (early remote relay type)

Note: *To recognize an early remote relay starter make the following observations: Follow the large diameter positive battery cable (red) from the battery to it's cable end. If the cable terminates at one of the large terminal posts at the fender mounted starter relay **and** a second large diameter cable (red) is attached to the second terminal post and continues to the starter motor, yours is an early system. To determine the location of excessive resistance in the starter circuit, perform the following simple series of tests.*
12   Disconnect the ignition coil wire from the distributor cap and ground it on the engine.
13   Connect a remote control starter switch from the battery terminal of the starter relay to the S terminal of the relay.
14   Make the test connections as shown **(see illustration)**. Refer to this illustration as you perform the following tests.
15   Operate the ignition switch and take the voltmeter readings as soon as a steady figure is indicated. Don't allow the starter motor to turn for more than 30 seconds at a time.
16   The voltage drop in the circuit will be indicated by the voltmeter (put the voltmeter on the 0-to-2 volt range). The maximum allowable voltage drop should be a maximum of:
a)   0.5-volt with the voltmeter negative lead connected to the starter terminal and the positive lead connected to the battery positive terminal (Connection 1 in illustration 17.14). This tests the entire positive side of the starter circuit for high resistance. On early models, Steps b through d should determine on which side of the remote relay the bad cable or connection is, or if the relay is bad.

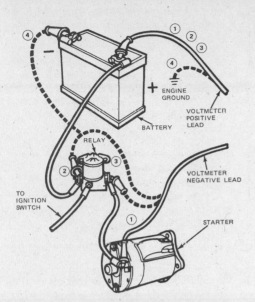

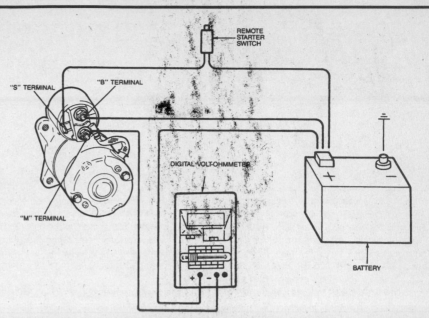

17.14 The test lead connections for the starter cranking circuit test on early model starters

17.17 Connections for testing the starter cranking circuit on later starters

b) *0.1-volt with the voltmeter negative lead connected to the starter relay (battery side) and the positive lead connected to the positive terminal of the battery (Connection 2). If it fails, check connections from battery to relay and/or replace cable from same.*

c) *0.3-volt with the voltmeter negative lead connected to the starter relay (starter side) and the positive lead connected to the positive terminal of the battery (Connection 3). If it fails, replace relay.*

d) *0.1-volt with the voltmeter negative lead connected to the starter terminal and the positive lead connected to the relay (starter side). If it fails, check connections from relay to starter and/or replace cable from same.*

e) *0.3-volt with the voltmeter negative lead connected to the negative terminal of the battery and the positive lead connected to the engine ground (Connection 4). If it fails, check ground cable connections and/or replace same*

Starter cranking circuit test (later starter solenoid/relay type)

Note: *To recognize a later integrated solenoid/relay starter, make the following observations: Follow the large-diameter positive battery cable (red) from the battery to its cable end. If the cable goes directly to starter motor-mounted solenoid **or** terminates at one of the large-terminal posts at the fender-mounted starter relay **and** the second large-diameter cable (red) is attached to the **same** terminal and continues to the starter motor, yours is a later system. To determine the location of excessive resistance in the*

starter circuit, perform the following simple series of tests.

17 Make the test connections as shown **(see illustration).** Refer to this illustration as you perform the following tests.

18 Disconnect the ignition coil wire from the distributor cap and ground it on the engine.

19 Operate the ignition switch (or use a remote starter switch) and take the voltmeter readings as soon as a steady figure is indicated. Don't allow the starter motor to turn for more than 30 seconds at a time.

20 The voltage drop in the circuit will be indicated by the voltmeter (put the voltmeter on the O-to-2 volt range).

a) *With the positive voltmeter lead on the positive battery post and the negative lead on the solenoid terminal "M," operate the starter motor. The voltmeter should read 0.5 volt or less.*

b) *If the voltage at terminal "M" is greater than 0.5 volt, move the negative lead of the voltmeter to the solenoid terminal "B" and repeat the test. If the voltage at terminal "B" reads less than 0.5 volts, the problem is either in the solenoid connections or the contacts. Clean the solenoid terminals "B," "S" and "M". Repeat test.*

c) *If the voltmeter still reads higher than 0.5 volts at terminal "M" and lower than 0.5 volt at terminal "B", the problem is in the solenoid contacts. Remove the starter for repair.*

d) *If the voltmeter reads more than 0.5 volt at terminal "B", clean the cables and the connections at the solenoid. If the voltmeter still reads more than 0.5 volt, the problem is either a bad positive battery connection or cable. Repair as necessary.*

e) *To locate the excessive voltage drop, move the voltmeter negative lead toward the battery and check each connection point. When the high voltmeter reading disappears, the last connection point checked is the problem.*

18 Starter motor - removal and installation

Refer to illustrations 18.3 and 18.6

1 Detach the cable from the negative terminal of the battery.

2 Raise the vehicle and support it securely on jackstands.

3 Disconnect the large cable from the terminal on the starter motor. On solenoid starters, also remove the small-diameter starter solenoid wire **(see illustration)**.

4 On four-cylinder engines, remove the two bolts attaching the rear support bracket **(see illustration 18.3)** and detach the bracket.

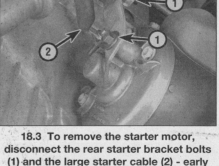

18.3 To remove the starter motor, disconnect the rear starter bracket bolts (1) and the large starter cable (2) - early starter motor shown, later starter similar . . .

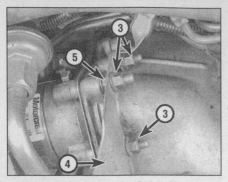

18.6 . . . then remove the Pulse Air system bracket nuts (3) and bracket, if equipped (4) then the starter motor stud nuts (5) - if your vehicle is an early model equipped with a manual transaxle, the roll restrictor brace is also bolted to the three studs and must be detached before you can get at the bracket or the starter motor stud nuts

5   If your four-cylinder vehicle is equipped with a roll restrictor (manual transaxle equipped vehicles only), remove the three

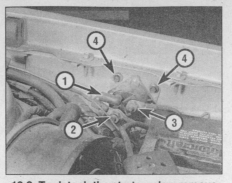

19.2 To detach the starter relay, remove the start switch wire (1) the battery positive lead and fusible link (2), the starter motor lead (3) and the relay mounting bracket bolts (4) - early model relay shown, later models similar

nuts that attach the brace to the transmission housing and remove the brace.

6   On four-cylinder engines, remove the three nuts that attach the Pulse Air check valve bracket to the starter motor studs **(see illustration)** and pull the bracket off the

studs. **Note:** *Later models use one stud for the negative battery cable; remove the cable, if equipped.*

7   On early four-cylinder engines, remove the three nuts that secure the starter motor studs **(see illustration 18.6)** and remove the starter.

8   On V6 engine, remove the three starter attach bolts and remove starter.

9   Installation is the reverse of removal.

---

19   Starter relay - removal and installation

Refer to illustration 19.2

1   Detach the cable from the negative terminal of the battery.

2   Label the wires and the terminals then disconnect the Neutral safety switch wire (automatics only), the battery cable, the fusible link and the starter cable from the relay terminals **(see illustration)**.

3   Remove the mounting bolts and detach the relay.

4   Installation is the reverse of removal.

Chapter 6
Emissions control systems

Contents

1   General information

Refer to illustration 1.7

1   To prevent pollution of the atmosphere from incompletely burned and evaporating gases, and to maintain good driveability and fuel economy, a number of emission control systems are incorporated. They include the:

    Electronic Engine Control (EEC-IV) system
    Exhaust Gas Recirculation (EGR) system
    Thermactor systems (secondary air injection)
    Fuel evaporative emission control system
    Positive Crankcase Ventilation (PCV) system
    Inlet air temperature control system
    Catalytic converter

2   All of these systems are linked, directly or indirectly, to the EEC-IV system.

3   The Sections in this Chapter include general descriptions, checking procedures within the scope of the home mechanic and component replacement procedures (when possible) for each of the systems listed above.

4   Before assuming that an emissions control system is malfunctioning, check the fuel and ignition systems carefully. The diagnosis of some emission control devices requires specialized tools, equipment and training. If checking and servicing become too difficult or if a procedure is beyond your ability. consult a dealer service department.

5   This doesn't mean, however, that emission control systems are particularly difficult to maintain and repair. You can quickly and easily perform many checks and do most (if not all) of the regular maintenance at home with common tune-up and hand tools. **Note:** *The most frequent cause of emissions problems is simply a loose or broken vacuum hose or wire, so always check the hose and wiring connections first.*

6   Pay close attention to any special precautions outlined in this Chapter. It should be noted that the illustrations of the various systems may not exactly match the system installed on your vehicle because of changes made by the manufacturer during production or from year-to-year.

7   A *Vehicle Emissions Control Information* label is located in the engine compartment **(see illustration)**. This label contains important emissions specifications and adjustment information, as well as a vacuum hose schematic with emissions components identified. When servicing the engine or emissions systems, the VECI label in your particular vehicle should always be checked for up-to-date information.

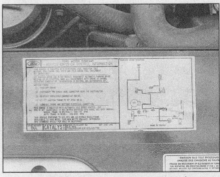

1.7 The Vehicle Emission Control Information (VECI) label located in the engine compartment contains essential information (like the spark plug type, the ignition timing procedure and a vacuum hose routing diagram)

2.5a On early carbureted and CFI models the Air Charge Temperature (ACT) sensor is screwed into the left (driver's) side of the intake manifold (early four-cylinder multiport models had the sensor screwed into the opposite (right) side)

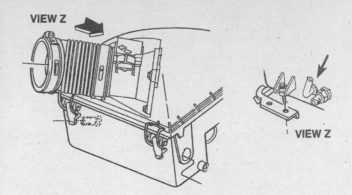

2.5b On later four-cylinder models, the ACT (arrow in view Z) is mounted in the air cleaner housing as shown - the air box must be removed to get access to the sensor

2   Electronic Engine Control (EEC-IV) system - component descriptions and trouble codes

Note: *If the "SERVICE ENGINE SOON" light on the dashboard is lit, proceed to Step 37 and check for trouble codes.*

General description

1   The Electronic Engine Control (EEC-IV) system consists of an onboard computer. Early EEC-IV computers were known as the Electronic Control Assembly (ECA) and later was re-named the Powertrain Control Module (PCM). Regardless of name, they both perform the same function. In this chapter, PCM will always be used when in reference to the EEC-IV computer.

2   The PCM, located inside the dashboard to the left of the steering column, is the "brain" of the EEC-IV system. Information sensors which monitor various functions of the engine and other electronic components (switches, relays, etc.) send data to the PCM. Based on the data and the information programmed into the computer's memory, the PCM generates output signals to control critical engine functions, various relays, solenoids and other actuators (see below). In general, the PCM and it's sensors complete a closed-loop system which influences the air/fuel mixture, ignition timing, EGR, thermactor, evaporative control, and other engine management operations. The PCM is specifically calibrated to optimize the emissions, fuel economy and driveability of your vehicle.

3   Because of a Federally-mandated 5 year/50,000 mile extended warranty which covers the PCM, the information sensors, and all components under its control, any operator-induced damage to these items may void the warranty. Therefore, during warranty periods, it isn't a good idea to attempt diagnosis or replacement of the PCM at home. Take your vehicle to a dealer service department if the PCM or a system component malfunctions.

Information input sensors

Refer to illustrations 2.5a, 2.5b, 2.5c, 2.6, 2.7a, 2.7b, 2.8, 2.9, 2.13, 2.15 and 2.16

Note: *The dates given are applicable to most models; however, California models may differ.*

Air conditioning pressure cycle switch

4   When battery voltage is applied to the compressor clutch through the cycle switch, a signal is sent to the PCM, which interprets the signal as an added load created by the air conditioner compressor and increases engine idle speed accordingly to compensate. The switch is located on top of the accumulator. For more information, refer to Chapter 3.

Air Charge Temperature (ACT) sensor (all models)

5   The ACT sensor provides the PCM with information on the temperature of the air within the intake manifold. The PCM translates the sensor signal and adjusts the air/fuel mixture and other system functions accordingly. On carbureted and CFI engines, the ACT sensor is threaded into the number four intake manifold runner **(see illustration)**. On four-cylinder multiport engines from 1988 through 1991, the ACT sensor is threaded into the number one intake manifold runner. The ACT sensor on 1992 and later four-cylinder models is mounted into the air cleaner housing and provides data on incoming ambient air temperature **(see illustration)**. On V6 engines, the ACT sensor is installed in the intake plenum **(see illustration)**. **Note:** *On 1993 models, the sensor has been re-named the Intake Air Temperature (IAT) sensor.*

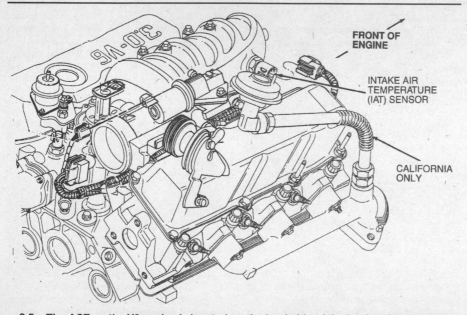

FRONT OF ENGINE

INTAKE AIR TEMPERATURE (IAT) SENSOR

CALIFORNIA ONLY

2.5c The ACT on the V6 engine is located on the backside of the intake plenum when viewed from the front of the vehicle - note that the ACT sensor was re-named the Intake Air Temperature (IAT) sensor on 1993 models

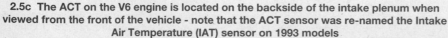

2.6 The EGR Valve Position (EVP) sensor is located on top of the EGR valve - to replace it, simply unplug the connector and remove the mounting bolts

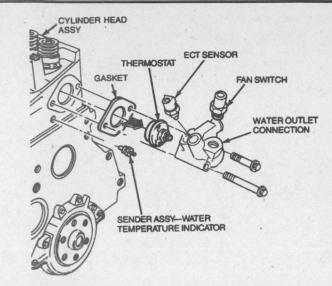

2.7a On four-cylinder multiport EFI models, the Engine Coolant Temperature (ECT) sensor is threaded into the thermostat housing next to the fan switch - do not confuse them - on carbureted and CFI models, the ECT is threaded into the intake manifold

EGR Valve Position (EVP) Sensor (1984 through 1987 models)

6   Located on the EGR valve (see illustration), the EVP feeds back information to the PCM on the position of the EGR valve. The PCM translates this signal and uses this information to optimize EGR valve operation.

Engine Coolant Temperature (ECT) sensor (all models)

7   The ECT sends the PCM a constantly varying voltage signal proportional to the engine coolant temperature. The PCM translates this signal and adjusts the air/fuel mixture and other system functions accordingly. On carbureted and CFI models utilizing coolant-heated intake manifolds, the sensor is threaded into the intake manifold. On multiport fuel-injected models, the sensor was moved to the thermostat housing on four-cylinder models (see illustration) and is located in the intake manifold on V6 models (see illustration).

Manifold Absolute Pressure (MAP) sensor (1984 through 1991 models)

8   The MAP sensor sends a signal to the PCM that is proportional to absolute pressure in the intake manifold. The output signal is used by the PCM to control the fuel injectors and air/fuel mixture. The MAP sensor is mounted on the firewall (see illustration). Note: *The MAP sensor was replaced with the MAF sensor in 1992.*

Oxygen (EGO) sensor (all models)

9   The EGO sensor constantly monitors the oxygen content of the exhaust gases. A voltage signal which varies in accordance with the difference between the oxygen content of the exhaust gases and the surrounding atmosphere is sent to the PCM. The PCM translates this signal and adjusts the air/fuel mixture and other system functions accordingly. The EGO (or HEGO) sensor(s) is threaded into the exhaust manifold on four-cylinder models and in both front and rear exhaust header pipes on V6 models (see illustration).

Profile Ignition Pickup (PIP) sensor (all models)

10   Integral with the distributor, the PIP informs the PCM of crankshaft position and speed. The PIP assembly consists of an armature with windows and metal tabs corresponding to the number of cylinders that rotate past a stator assembly generating an electrical pulse (the Hall Effect switch). These pulses are processed by the PCM to obtain the required crankshaft information. For more information on the TFI-IV/DI distributor refer to the appropriate Section in Chapter 5.

Throttle Position Sensor (TPS) (all models)

11   The TPS senses throttle movement and position, then transmits an electrical signal to the PCM. This signal enables the PCM to determine when the throttle is closed, in its normal cruise condition or wide open. The TPS is mounted on the side of the throttle body and connected directly to the throttle shaft. For more information on the TPS, refer to the appropriate Section in Chapter 4.

Vehicle Speed Sensor (VSS) (1988 and later models)

12   The speed sensor generates a signal waveform proportional to vehicle speed and supplies it to the PCM for processing. The

6

2.7b Location of the V6 Engine Coolant Temperature (ECT) sensor (arrow)

2.8 The Manifold Absolute Pressure (MAP) sensor is mounted on the firewall - to replace it, unplug the electrical connector, detach the vacuum hose and remove both mounting bolts

2.9 The Exhaust Gas Oxygen (EGO) sensor(s) (arrow) is screwed into the exhaust manifold (four-cylinder models) or the exhaust header pipes (V6 models)

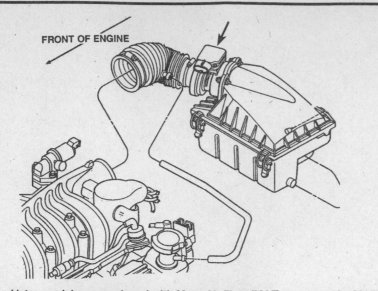

2.13 1992 and later models are equipped with Mass Air Flow (MAF) sensors - the MAF is mounted in the air cleaner housing - arrow - (V6 MAF sensor shown, four-cylinder similar)

PCM uses VSS input to control the fuel injectors, ignition timing and transaxle shift points. It also supplies information for the cruse control system if equipped. The sensor is located on the transaxle as part of the speedometer drive mechanism. For more information on the VSS, refer to the appropriate Section in Chapter 7A.

Mass Air Flow (MAF) sensor (1992 and later models)

13   The MAF sensor uses a hot wire sensing element to measure the volume of air entering the engine. A reference voltage warms the wire and incoming air cools the wire, changing it's resistance in proportion to the amount of air passing by the wire. The

output signal is used by the PCM to control the fuel injectors and air/fuel mixture. The MAF sensor is mounted in the air cleaner housing to isolate it from unwanted heat and vibration **(see illustration)**. **Note:** *The MAF replaces the MAP sensor used on vehicles until 1991.* For more information on the MAF sensor, refer to the appropriate Section in Chapter 4.

Camshaft Position (CMP) Sensor (1992 and later models)

14   The CMP informs the PCM of number one cylinder piston location (cylinder identification). On V6 engines, the CMP is located inside the distributor and mechanically is simply a slightly wider window on the rotating

vane (see PIP sensor above) representing the number one cylinder. This results in a different "Hall Effect" pulse which new circuitry in the PCM recognizes as being number one cylinder. The four-cylinder engine uses a separate variable reluctance type sensor mounted in the block next to the distributor. The PCM uses this information to synchronize the fuel injectors in newer Sequential Fuel Injected (SFI) systems. For further information on the distributor type CMP, refer to the appropriate Section in Chapter 5.

Pressure Feedback EGR (PFE) sensor (1988 and later models)

15   The PFE determines the EGR flow rate by monitoring the pressure across a fixed orifice located between the exhaust manifold and EGR valve. The PCM uses this information to optimize the operation of a conventional EGR valve. The PFE sensor is located on the rear firewall **(see illustration)**. **Note:** *The PFE sensor replaces the EVP sensor used through 1988.*

Power Steering Pressure (PSP) switch (1987 and later models)

16   A normally open switch closes when power steering pressure increases above a set level (as when the wheels are being turned hard). When closed, a signal is sent to the PCM. The PCM then adjust idle speed to compensate for the extra load on the engine due to the power steering pump. The switch is located on the steering gear assembly **(see illustration)**.

Output devices

Refer to illustrations 2.20, 2.21, 2.22 and 2.27
Note: *The dates given are applicable for most*

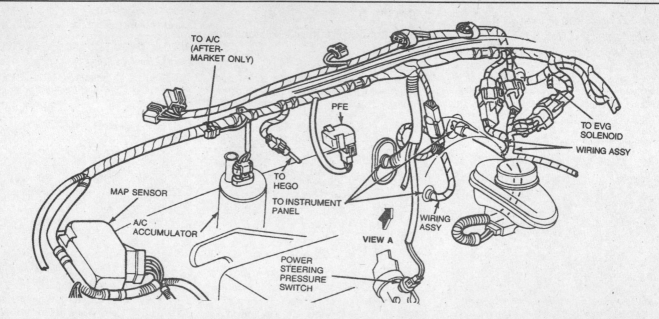

2.15 The Pressure Feedback EGR (PFE) sensor is usually located on the rear firewall in the engine compartment

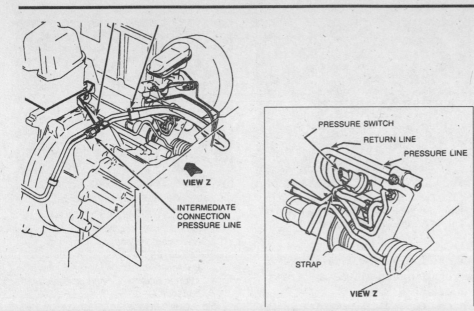

2.16 **The Power Steering Pressure (PSP) switch is located on the steering gear assembly behind the transaxle**

2.20 **The canister purge solenoid valve is located on the left side of the engine compartment, next to the left wheel well**

models; however, California models may differ.

A/C and cooling fan controller module (1984 through 1991 models)

17   The controller is operated by the PCM, the coolant temperature switch and the brake light switch. The controller module provides an output signal which controls operation of the A/C compressor clutch and the engine cooling fan. For more information on the controller, refer to the appropriate Section in Chapter 3.

EEC power relay (1984 through 1991 models)

18   When activated by the ignition switch, this relay supplies battery voltage to the PCM when the switch is on. **Note:** *The EEC relay was incorporated into the IRCM/CCRM after 1991.*

Integrated Relay Control Module (IRCM) (1992 and later models)

19   The IRCM interfaces with the PCM to provide control for the cooling fan, air conditioning clutch, fuel pump and ECC power. The module was re-named in 1993 to the

Constant Control Relay Module (CCRM). For more information, refer to the appropriate Section in Chapter 3.

Canister purge (CANP) solenoid (1984 and later models)

20   located on the left fender well **(see illustration)**, the CANP solenoid switches manifold vacuum to operate the canister purge valve when a signal is received from the PCM. Vacuum opens the purge valve when the solenoid is energized.

EGR Control (EGRC) and EGR Vent (EGRV) solenoid (1984 US models only)

21   The EGRC and EGRV solenoids work in conjunction to switch (EGRC) or bleed (EGRV) manifold vacuum to the EGR valve on command from the PCM (based in part on input from the EVP sensor). The solenoids are located on the rear firewall **(see illustration)**.

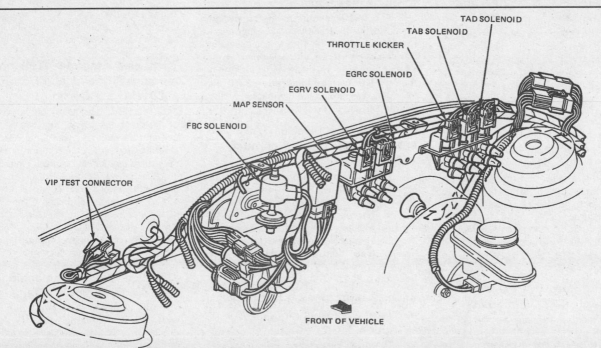

2.21 **The combined EGRC and EGRV solenoid, along with the TAB and TAD control solenoids, are all mounted against the rear firewall on most early vehicles equipped with these systems**

Note: *The EGRC/EGRV solenoids were replaced with the EVR solenoid on all CFI models. For more information, refer to Section 4 in this Chapter.*

EGR Vacuum Regulator (EVR) solenoid (1985 and later US, 1988 and later Canada)

22   The EVR control solenoid switches manifold vacuum to operate a conventional EGR valve on command from the PCM (based in part on input from the PFE sensor). The solenoid is located on the left fender apron **(see illustration)**. Vacuum opens the EGR valve when the solenoid is energized. For more information, refer to Section 4 in this Chapter.

Feedback control (FBC) solenoid (1984 only US, through 1987 Canada)

23   On early feedback carbureted engines, the FBC solenoid regulates the idle, off idle and main system fuel/air ratios in accordance with signals from the PCM. For more information on the FBC solenoid, refer to the appropriate Section in Chapter 4.

CFI Injector Solenoid (1985 through 1987 CFI models)

24   The CFI systems utilizes a single solenoid operated fuel injector located in the fuel charging assembly. The PCM controls the length of time the injector is open. The "open" time of the injector determines the amount of fuel delivered. For information regarding injector replacement, refer to the appropriate Section in Chapter 4.

Multiport Fuel Injectors (1988 and later models)

25   Multiport EFI systems utilize injectors at every intake port. The PCM controls the length of time the injector is open. The "open" time of the injectors determines the amount of fuel delivered to each cylinder. For information regarding injector replacement, refer to the appropriate Section in Chapter 4.

Fuel pump relay (1985 through 1991 fuel-injected models only)

26   The fuel pump relay is activated by the PCM with the ignition switch in the On position. When the ignition switch is turned to the On position, the relay is activated to supply initial line pressure to the system. For information regarding fuel pump check and replacement, refer to Chapter 4. **Note:** *The fuel pump relay was incorporated into the CCRM/IRCM in 1992.*

Idle Speed Control (ISC) solenoid (1985 through 1987 CFI models)

27   The solenoid motor changes idle speed in accordance with signals from the PCM and is located on the charging assembly **(see illustration)**. For information regarding ISC replacement, refer to the appropriate Section in Chapter 4.

2.22 On CFI systems, the EGR Vacuum Regulator solenoid valve can be found on the left strut tower

Idle Air Control (IAC) valve (1988 and later multiport fuel-injected models)

28   The IAC valve (better known as the air bypass valve) allows additional air to bypass the throttle plate and control idle speed as commanded by the PCM. For information regarding air bypass valve replacement, refer to the appropriate Section in Chapter 4.

Shift indicator light (1988 and later models)

29   The shift indicator tells the driver when to shift gears for optimum fuel economy. The PCM signals it to light up in accordance with the information it receives regarding engine speed and manifold vacuum level.

Thermactor Air By-Pass (TAB) solenoid (1984 only US, 1984 through 1987 Canada)

30   The TAB solenoid provides a vacuum signal to the By-Pass valve in response to signals from the PCM. The bypass valve then by-passes the thermactor air pump to the atmosphere. The TAB solenoid is located on the rear firewall **(see illustration 2.21)**. For information regarding the thermactor system, refer to Section 5 in this Chapter.

Thermactor Air Diverter (TAD) solenoid (1984 only US, through 1987 Canada)

31   The TAD solenoid provides a vacuum signal to the diverter valve in response to signals from the PCM. The diverter valve then diverts thermactor pump air to either the exhaust manifold or the catalytic converter. The TAD solenoid is located on the rear firewall **(see illustration 2.21)**. For more information regarding the thermactor system, refer to Section 5 in this Chapter.

Air Diverter (AIRD) solenoid (1990 and later California models, four-cylinder only)

32   The AIRD solenoid provides a vacuum signal to the AIRD air control valve under direction of the PCM. The AIRD air control valve regulates the flow of pulsed air in

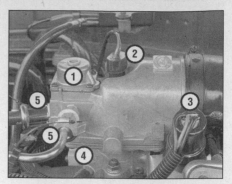

2.27 CFI fuel charging assembly components

1   *Fuel pressure regulator*
2   *Fuel injector electrical connector*
3   *Idle Speed Control (ISC) motor electrical connector*
4   *Throttle Position (TP) sensor electrical connector*
5   *Fuel line fittings*

Pulsed Secondary Air Injection system. The AIRD solenoid is located on the left hand fender apron. For information regarding the pulsed air injection, refer to Section 5 in this Chapter.

(AIRD) air control valve (1990 and later California models, four-cylinder only)

33   The AIRD air control valve is the actual control device which regulates the flow of air into the pulse air injection system **(see illustration 5.43b)**. A vacuum valve within the control valve housing opens and shuts the air flow passage in response to the vacuum signal provided by the AIRD solenoid. For information regarding the pulsed air injection, refer to Section 5 in this Chapter.

Thick Film Integrated (TFI) ignition module (1984 and later US models, 1988 and later Canada)

34   The TFI-IV module, mounted on the side of the distributor base, triggers the ignition coil and determines dwell. The PCM uses a signal from the Profile Ignition Pick-Up to determine crankshaft position. Ignition timing is determined by the PCM, which then signals the module to fire the coil. In 1993 the TFI was re-named to Ignition Control Module (ICM) when Ford switched to the Computer Controlled Dwell (CCD) design . For further information regarding the TFI-IV/ICM module, refer to the appropriate Section in Chapter 5.

Throttle kicker (TK) solenoid (1984 only US, through 1987 Canada)

35   The kicker solenoid is a two-port valve with an atmospheric vent. A vacuum diaphragm (throttle kicker) is used to maintain nominal idle speed on command from the PCM. For further information regarding the throttle kicker, refer to the appropriate Section in Chapter 4.

Wide Open Throttle (WOT) A/C cut-out

36   This circuit is energized by the PCM when a WOT condition is detected. During WOT, power to the A/C compressor clutch is disconnected until sometime after partial throttle operation resumes. For further information regarding the WOT A/C cut-out, refer to the appropriate Section in Chapter 3.

EEC-IV system trouble codes

Refer to illustration 2.39

37   The EEC-IV engine management system has a self-diagnosis capability that stores trouble codes in the PCM (computer) that identify problem areas in the system. You can retrieve these codes and use them as an aid to diagnosing problems in the engine management system. Often, when a code is stored in the PCM, the "SERVICE ENGINE SOON" light on the instrument panel will illuminate.

38   In the engine compartment, find the "Self-Test" connector. Usually, the connector has two parts: a large one with six output terminals and a single input terminal. The connector is located on the right (passenger's) side of the firewall, near the strut tower.

39   With the engine off, connect the positive probe of an analog voltmeter to the battery positive post. Unplug the "Self-Test" connector. Connect a jumper wire between the input to pin 2 on the larger connector and connect the voltmeter negative probe to pin 4

(see illustration). Set the voltmeter on a 15 or 20-volt scale, then connect a timing light to the engine. The three types of codes this test will provide are:

*O - **Key On Engine Off (KOEO)** (on-demand codes with the engine off)*

*C - **Continuous Memory** (codes stored when the engine was running)*

*R - **Engine Running** (ER) (codes produced as the engine is running)*

O (KOEO)

40   Turn on the ignition and watch the voltmeter needle. It will display the codes as sweeps of the needle. For example, two sweeps followed by three sweeps is code 23, with a four-second delay between codes. Write the codes down for reference. The codes will appear in numerical order, repeating once.

C (Continuous Memory)

41   After the KOEO codes are reported, there will be a short pause and any stored Continuous Memory codes will appear in order. Remember that the "Pass" code is 11, or sweep, two-second pause, sweep.

R (Engine Running)

42   Start the engine. The first part of this test makes sure the system can advance the ignition timing. Check the ignition timing. It should be advanced about 20-degrees above base timing (check the VECI label for the base timing specification).

43   Shut off the engine, restart it and run it

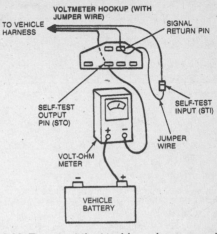

2.39 To output the trouble codes, connect a voltmeter as shown and, using a jumper wire, bridge the self-test input connector to the signal return pin (terminal number 2)

for two minutes, then turn it off for ten seconds before restarting it. The voltmeter needle should make some quick sweeps, then show an engine code (two sweeps for a four-cylinder engine, three for a V6). After another pause will be one sweep, the signal to tap the accelerator so the system can check throttle component operation (this is called the "throttle goose test"). After this there will be a pause, followed by the Engine Running codes, which will appear in the same manner as before, repeating twice.

Trouble code chart

Code	Test condition	Probable cause
11	O,R,C	System OK, testing complete
12	R	Idle speed control out of specified range
13	O,R,C	Normal idle not within specified range
14	O,C	Ignition profile pickup erratic
15	O	ROM test failure
15	C	Power interrupt to computer memory
16	R	Erratic idle, oxygen sensor out of range or throttle not closing
17	R	Curb idle out of specified range
18	R	SPOUT circuit open
19	O	No power to processor
19	R	Erratic idle speed or signal
21	O,R,	Coolant temperature out of specified range
21	O,R,C	Coolant temperature sensor out of specified range
22	O,R,C	MAP sensor out of specified range
23	O,R,C	Throttle position signal out of specified range
24	O,R	Air charge temperature low
26	O,R	Mass Air Flow sensor or circuit
27	C	Vehicle Speed Sensor or circuit
28	O,R	Vane air temperature sensor or circuit
29	C	No continuity in Vehicle Speed Sensor circuit
31	O,R,C	Canister or EGR valve control system
32	O,R,C	Canister or EGR valve control system
33	R,C	Canister or EGR valve not operating properly
34	O,R,C	Canister or EGR valve control circuit
35	O,R,C	EGR pressure feedback, regulator circuit
38	C	Idle control circuit
39	C	Automatic overdrive circuit
41	C	Oxygen sensor signal

6

Trouble code chart (continued)

Code	Test condition	Probable cause
41	R	Lean fuel mixture
42	R,C	Fuel mixture rich
43	C	Lean fuel mixture at wide open throttle
43	R	Engine too warm for test
44	R	Air management system inoperative
45	R	Thermactor air diverter circuit
46	R	Thermactor air bypass circuit
47	R	Low flow of unmetered air at idle
48	R	High flow of unmetered air at idle
49	C	SPOUT signal defaulted to 10-degrees
51	O,C	Coolant temperature sensor out of specified range
52	O,R	Power steering pressure switch out of specified range
53	O,C	Throttle Position Sensor input out of specified range
54	O,C	Vane air flow sensor or air charge temperature sensor
55	R	Charging system under specified voltage (1984 through 1988)
55	R	Open ignition key power circuit (1984 through 1988)
56	O,R,C	Mass Air Flow sensor or circuit
57	C	Transmission neutral pressure switch circuit
58	O	CFI - idle control circuit; EFI - vane air flow circuit
58	R	Idle speed control motor or circuit
58	C	Vane air temperature sensor or circuit
59	O,C	Transmission throttle pressure switch circuit
61	O,C	Coolant temperature switch out of specified range
62	O	Transmission circuit fault
63	O,C	Throttle Position Sensor or circuit
64	O,C	Air Charge Temperature (ACT) sensor
65	C	Fuel control system not switching to closed loop
66	O,C	No Mass Air Flow sensor signal
67	O,R,C	Neutral drive switch or circuit
67	C	Air conditioner clutch switch circuit
69	O,C	Vehicle Speed Sensor or circuit
72	C	System power circuit, electrical interference
72	R	No Manifold Absolute Pressure or Mass Air Flow sensor signal fluctuation
73	O,R	Throttle Position Sensor or circuit
74	R	Brake on/off ground circuit fault
75	R	Brake on/off power circuit fault
76	R	No vane airflow change
77	R	Throttle "goose" test not performed
78	C	Power circuit
79	O	Air conditioner clutch circuit
81	O	Thermactor air circuit
82	O	Thermactor air circuit, integrated controller circuit
83	O	EGR control circuit (four-cylinder models only)
83	O	Cooling fan circuit (V6 models only)
83	O,C	Low speed fuel pump relay (1984 through 1988 models)
83	O,C	EGR solenoid or circuit (1989 and later models)
84	O,R	EGR control circuit
85	O,R	Canister purge circuit or transmission shift control circuit
85	C	Excessive fuel pressure or flow
85	O	Canister purge circuit
86	C	Low fuel pressure or flow
87	O,R, C	Fuel pump circuit
88	O	Integrated controller
89	O	Lock-up solenoid
91	R,C	Oxygen sensor problem, fuel pressure out of specified range or injectors out of balance
92	R	Fuel mixture rich, fuel pressure high
93	O	Throttle Position Sensor or circuit
94	R	Secondary air system inoperative
95	O,C	Fuel pump circuit problem
95	R	Thermactor air diverter circuit
96	O,C	Fuel pump circuit
96	R	Thermactor air bypass circuit
98	R	Repeat test sequence
99	R	Repeat test sequence
99	R	System hasn't learned to control idle speed

3 Electronic Engine Control (EEC-IV) system - component replacement

Note: *Because of the Federally mandated extended warranty (5 years or 50,000 miles at the time this manual was written), which covers the PCM, the information sensors and the devices it controls, there's no point in replacing any of the following components yourself unless the warranty has expired.*

Air Charge Temperature (ACT) sensor

1   Detach the cable from the negative terminal of the battery.

2   Depending on the model and year, locate the ACT sensor in the intake manifold or air cleaner housing (**see illustrations 2.5a, 2.5b, and 2.5c**).

3   Unplug the electrical connector from the sensor.

4   Remove the sensor with a wrench.

5   Wrap the threads of the new sensor with teflon tape to prevent air leaks.

6   Installation is the reverse of removal.

EGR Valve Position (EVP) sensor

7   Detach the cable from the negative terminal of the battery.

8   Locate the EVP sensor on the EGR valve (**see illustration 2.6**).

9   Unplug the electrical connector from the sensor.

10   Remove the three mounting bolts and detach the sensor.

11   Installation is the reverse of removal.

Engine Coolant Temperature (ECT) sensor

12   Detach the cable from the negative terminal of the battery.

13   Depending on the model and year, locate the ECT sensor in the intake manifold or thermostat housing (**see illustrations 2.7a and 2.7b**).

14   Unplug the electrical connector from the sensor.

15   Remove the sensor with a wrench.

16   Wrap the threads of the new sensor with teflon tape to prevent coolant leakage.

17   Installation is the reverse of removal. Replace any lost coolant.

Manifold Absolute Pressure (MAP) sensor

18   Detach the cable from the negative terminal of the battery.

19   Locate the MAP sensor on the firewall (**see illustration 2.8**).

20   Unplug the electrical connector from the sensor.

21   Detach the vacuum line from the sensor.

22   Remove the two mounting bolts and detach the sensor.

23   Installation is the reverse of removal.

Exhaust Gas Oxygen (EGO) sensor

24   Detach the cable from the negative terminal of the battery.

25   Raise the vehicle and support it securely on jackstands.

26   Locate the EGO sensor(s) on the exhaust manifold (four-cylinder engines) or in both front and rear exhaust header pipes (V6 engines) (**see illustration 2.9**).

27   Unplug the electrical connector from the sensor(s).

28   Remove the sensor(s) with a wrench.

29   Coat the threads of the new sensor with anti-seize compound to prevent the threads from welding themselves to the manifold.

30   Install sensor(s) and tighten securely.

31   Installation is the reverse of removal.

Pressure Feedback (PFE) Sensor

32   Detach the cable from the negative terminal of the battery.

33   Locate the PFE sensor on the rear firewall (**see illustration 2.15**).

34   Remove the pressure feedback hose.

35   Detach the sensor harness connector.

36   Remove the sensor attach screw and remove sensor.

37   Installation is the reverse of removal.

Power Steering Pressure (PSP) switch

38   Detach the cable from the negative terminal of the battery.

39   Locate the pressure switch on the power steering gear assembly (**see illustration 2.16**)

40   Detach the switch electrical connector.

41   Remove the switch. **Note:** *Be prepared to quickly cap the hole with a plug or new switch to prevent loss of fluid.*

42   Installation is the reverse of removal.

43   Purge the power steering system of any air, referring to Chapter 10.

Camshaft position sensor (four-cylinder models only)

44   Locate the sensor in the engine block to the left side of the distributor (facing the engine).

45   Remove the electrical connector.

46   Remove the retaining screw and pull the sensor out of the block.

47   Installation is the reverse of removal.

Canister Purge Solenoid

48   Detach the cable from the negative terminal of the battery.

49   Locate the canister purge solenoid on the left side of the engine compartment, next to the left wheel well (**see illustration 2.20**).

50   Unplug the electrical connector from the solenoid.

51   Label the vacuum hoses and ports, then detach the hoses.

52   Remove the solenoid.

53   Installation is the reverse of removal.

EGR Control (EGRC) Solenoid or EGR Vent (EGRV) Solenoid

54   Detach the cable from the negative terminal of the battery.

55   Locate the vacuum control solenoid(s) on the firewall. (**see illustration 2.21**).

56   Unplug the electrical connector from the solenoid(s).

57   Label the vacuum hoses and ports, then detach the hoses.

58   Remove the solenoid/bracket screws and detach the solenoid(s).

59   Installation is the reverse of removal.

EGR Vacuum Regulator (EVR) solenoid

60   Detach the cable from the negative terminal of the battery.

61   Locate the EVR on the left side fender apron (**see illustration 2.22**).

62   Detach the sensor harness connector and vacuum hose.

63   Remove the sensor attach screw and remove solenoid.

64   Installation is the reverse of removal.

Thermactor Air By-Pass (TAB) solenoid or Thermactor Air Diverter (TAD) solenoid

65   Detach the cable from the negative terminal of the battery.

66   Locate the vacuum control solenoid(s) on the rear firewall (**see illustration 2.21**).

67   Unplug the electrical connector from the solenoid(s).

68   Label the vacuum hoses and ports, then detach the hoses.

69   Remove the solenoid/bracket screws and detach the solenoid(s).

70   Installation is the reverse of removal.

Air Diverter (AIRD) solenoid

71   Detach the cable from the negative terminal of the battery.

72   Locate the EVR on the left side fender apron.

73   Detach the sensor harness connector and vacuum hose.

74   Remove the sensor by unclipping it from the bracket.

75   Installation is the reverse of removal.

AIRD air control valve

76   Locate the AIRD air control valve on top of the pulse air silencer (**see illustration 5.43b**).

77   Remove the clean air tube from the air cleaner housing and the vacuum hose.

78   Remove the two attach screws and remove valve.

79   Installation is the reverse of removal.

6

4   Exhaust Gas Recirculation (EGR) system

Refer to illustrations 4.4, 4.24 and 4.25

General description

1   The EGR system is designed to reintroduce small amounts of exhaust gas into the combustion cycle, thus reducing the generation of nitrogen oxide emissions (NOx). The amount of exhaust gas reintroduced and the timing of the cycle is controlled by various factors such as engine speed, altitude, manifold vacuum, exhaust system backpressure, coolant temperature and throttle angle. All EGR valves are vacuum actuated and the vacuum diagram for your particular vehicle is shown on the *Vehicle Emissions Control Information* label in the engine compartment.

2   Three types of EGR valves are used on Tempo/Topaz vehicles: the ported valve type used on Canadian vehicles, and two electronically controlled types used on US vehicles. Of the two electronic systems, the first used was the Electronic EGR valve (EEGR) or (Sonic) system. Later models used the Pressure Feedback Electronic (PFE) system.

Ported valve

3   The ported EGR valve is operated by a vacuum signal from the carburetor EGR port, which actuates the valve diaphragm. As the vacuum increases sufficiently to overcome the spring, the valve is opened, allowing EGR flow. The amount of flow is contingent upon the tapered pintle or the poppet position, which is affected by the vacuum signal.

Electronic EGR (EEGR)

4   The electronic EGR valve used on US 1984 through 1987 EEC-IV systems controls EGR flow through a closed loop electronically controlled system. In operation, the EGR Valve Position (EVP) sensor (attached to the top of the valve) continuously signals the PCM of the position of the EGR valve. The PCM uses this data to indirectly calculate the flow through the EGR valve. This information, plus other sensor input is then processed in the PCM and if required, a more optimum EGR valve position is calculated. On feedback carburetor models, this new valve position is directed by the PCM to either the EGR Control (EGRC) or EGR Vent (EGRV). These solenoids provide vacuum control over the EGR valve, and supply or bleed vacuum to adjust the EGR valve to the position determined by the PCM **(see illustration)**. On CFI models, the new valve position is directed to the EGR Vacuum Regulator (EVR) which serves the same purpose. On either system, as supply vacuum overcomes the spring load, the EGR diaphragm is actuated, lifting the pintle off the seat and allowing exhaust gas to recalculate. The actual amount of flow is proportional to the pintle position, however, the EVP sensor responds to the new position by sending an updated position signal to the PCM and the process repeats, thus closing the loop.

Pressure Feedback Electronic (PFE)

5   The Pressure Feedback Electronic system (downstream sensing type) is used on all 1988 and later models. In principle, the operation of the PFE system is similar to the EEGR system. Both use electronics and vacuum in a closed loop control circuit to control the EGR valve. The major difference is in how the EGR valve position is determined. The PFE helps the PCM determine the EGR flow rate by monitoring the pressure differences generated as exhaust gases flow by a sensing tube located between the exhaust manifold and EGR valve inlet (the EGR tube).

A hose connects the sensing tube and the PFE sensor, allowing the remotely mounted sensor to experience the changes in pressure as engine operating conditions change. The PFE sensor converts the pressure into an electrical signal and sends it to the PCM. The PCM uses this data to indirectly calculate the flow through the EGR valve. This information, plus other sensor input is then processed in the PCM and if required, a more optimum EGR valve position is calculated. This new valve position is then converted into PCM output signals which are directed to the EGR Vacuum Regulator (EVR). The EVR provides vacuum control over the EGR valve, and supplies vacuum to adjust the EGR valve to the position determined by the PCM. The EVP sensor responds to the new pressure differential created by the change in EGR valve position/flow by sending an updated position signal to the PCM and the process repeats, thus closing the loop.

Checking

Ported EGR valve (1984 through 1987 Canadian vehicles)

6   Make sure that all vacuum lines are properly routed, secure and in good condition (not cracked, kinked or broken off).

7   When the engine is cold, there should be no vacuum to operate the EGR valve. If there is vacuum, check the ported vacuum switch (PVS) or temperature vacuum switch (TVS) and replace them as required.

8   There should be no vacuum to the valve at curb idle (engine warm).

9   There should be vacuum to the valve at 3000 rpm. If there is no vacuum, check the TVS and PVS and replace them as required.

10   With the engine at idle, apply 8 in-Hg vacuum to the valve. The valve stem should move, opening the valve, and the engine should stall or run roughly. If the valve stem

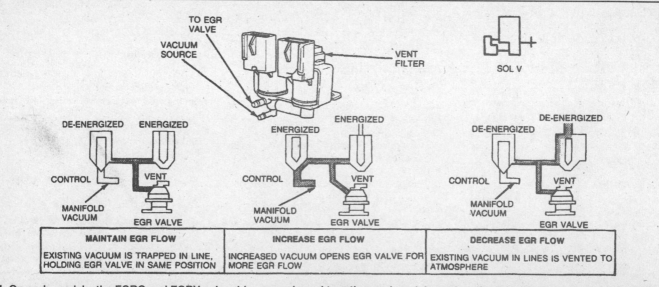

4.4   On early models, the EGRC and EGRV solenoids are packaged together and work in conjunction to control the vacuum supply to the EGR valve as shown

4.24 Unscrew the threaded fitting attaching the EGR pipe to the EGR valve - it's a good idea to use anti-seize compound on the threads when installing the new valve to prevent the threads from welding to the valve (V6 engine shown, four cylinder similar)

4.25 To detach the EGR valve from the intake manifold, remove the two mounting bolts (arrows)

moves but the engine doesn't respond, remove and clean the inlet and outlet ports with a wire brush. Do not sandblast or clean the valve with gasoline or damage will result!

11   With the engine at idle, trap 4 in-Hg vacuum in the valve. Vacuum shouldn't drop more than 1 in-Hg in 30 seconds. If it does, replace the valve.

12   When the valve is suspected of leaking (indicated by a rough idle or stalling) perform the following simple check:

a) *Insert a blocking gasket (no flow holes) between the valve and base and reinstall the valve.*

b) *If the engine idle improves, replace the valve and remove the blocking gasket. If the idle doesn't improve, take the vehicle to a dealer service department.*

Electronic EGR valve (1984 through 1987 US) and Pressure Feedback Electronic (1988 and later)

Note: *Aside from the following simple check and maintenance steps, the electronically controlled EGR valve systems cannot be diagnosed or serviced by the home mechanic. Additional checks must be done by a dealer service department.*

13   Make sure the vacuum hoses are in good condition and hooked up correctly.

14   Make sure there is no vacuum to the EGR valve at idle with the engine at normal operating temperatures.

15   To perform a leakage test, connect a vacuum pump to the EGR valve.

16   Apply 5-to-6 in-Hg of vacuum to the valve.

17   Trap the vacuum - it should not drop more than 1 in-Hg in 30 seconds.

18   If the specified conditions are not met, the EGR valve, O-ring or EVP must be replaced.

19   To perform a functional test, release the vacuum to the EGR valve but keep the pump connected. Restart the engine and allow it to idle. Note the idle speed.

20   Apply 5-to-10 in Hg vacuum to the EGR valve and observe the engine idle speed. If any of the following conditions occur when vacuum is applied to the EGR valve, replace the valve.

a) *The engine does not stall.*

b) *The idle speed does not drop more then 100 rpm.*

c) *The idle speed does not return to normal (plus or minus 25 rpm) after the vacuum is released.*

21   If all is well, reconnect the EGR vacuum line.

Component replacement

22   Detach the cable from negative terminal of the battery.

23   On US vehicles with EEGR, unplug the electrical connector from the EGR valve position sensor (refer to Section 3 if necessary).

24   Unscrew the threaded fitting that attaches the EGR pipe to the EGR valve **(see illustration).**

25   Remove the two mounting bolts and detach the valve **(see illustration).**

26   Remove the old gasket.

27   If you're replacing the EGR valve but not the position sensor, remove the sensor from the old valve (refer to Section 3) and install it on the new valve.

28   Installation is the reverse of removal.

29   For control device removal and installation, refer to Section 3 this Chapter.

---

5   Thermactor (air injection) systems (four-cylinder models only)

Refer to illustrations 5.2a, 5.2b, 5.3, 5.43a, 5.43b, 5.47a, 5.47b and 5.49

General description

1   The thermactor (secondary air injection)

exhaust emission control systems reduce carbon monoxide and hydrocarbon content in the exhaust gases by injecting fresh air into the hot exhaust gases leaving the exhaust ports. When fresh air is mixed with hot exhaust gases, oxidation is increased, reducing the concentration of hydrocarbons and carbon monoxide and converting them into harmless carbon dioxide and water. Two basic types of thermactor designs have been utilized, the application depending on the sophistication of the electronic engine control system and the state or country the vehicle is designated for. In general, because of their inability to effectively control the combustion process, feedback carbureted and some early CFI models required the more complicated Managed Thermactor Air (MTA) system. This design requires a crankshaft driven "air pump" and various electromechanical controls. Later models equipped with the more technically advanced CFI systems and all the multiport EFI models utilize the simpler Pulsed Air Injection (PAIR) system. This design does not require an "air pump" and is a relatively passive system.

Managed Thermactor Air (MTA) (1984 US models, 1984 through 1987 Canadian models)

2   Early Tempo/Topaz vehicles utilize the "managed air" thermactor system, which diverts air pump generated thermactor air either upstream to the exhaust manifold check valve or downstream to the rear section check valve and dual bed catalyst. An air control valve is used to direct the air upstream or downstream depending on a vacuum signal sent from the Thermactor Air Diverter solenoid (TAD). The TAD is ultimately controlled by the ECC-IV computer. In addition, an air bypass valve is used to dump air to the atmosphere during certain condi-

6

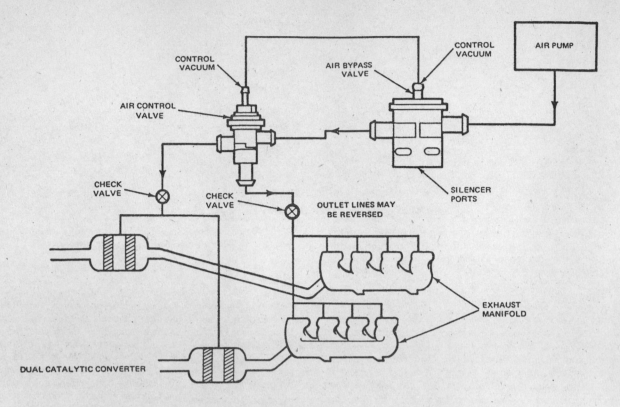

5.2a Typical Managed Air Thermactor system

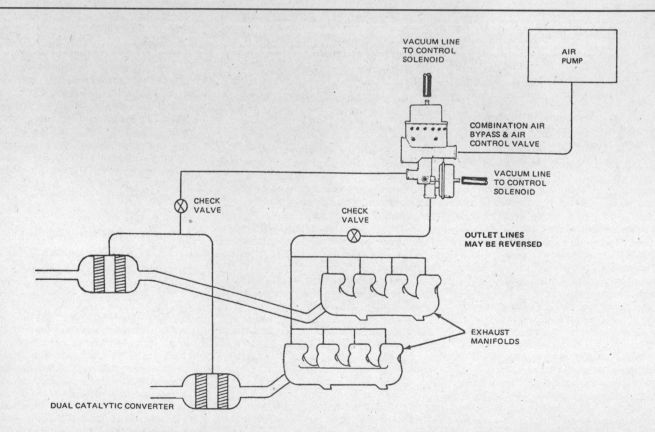

5.2b Typical Managed Air Thermactor system with combined bypass/control valve - electronically controlled

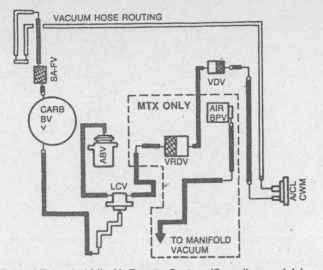

5.3 Typical Extended Idle Air Bypass System (Canadian models)

tions **(see illustration)**. The bypass valve is activated by a vacuum signal from the Thermactor Air Bypass solenoid (TAB) which is again controlled by the ECC-IV computer. In some applications, the two valves are combined into a single air bypass/control valve **(see illustration)**. Because of the overly rich fuel/air mixture at idle, injected air can raise temperatures within the exhaust system above desirable limits, therefore, an extended idle air bypass system in carburetor equipped vehicles also vents thermactor air to the atmosphere during extended idling.

Checking

Extended idle air bypass system - Canadian vehicles

3   With the engine at normal operating temperature, increase the speed momentarily, then allow it to return to idle. If, after 30 seconds, the thermactor bypass valve dumps secondary air through the vents, the system is okay. If it doesn't, check the routing and condition of the air hose and vacuum lines **(see illustration)**.

Extended idle air bypass system - US carburetor equipped vehicles

4   The normally closed idle tracking switch (ITS) opens when the throttle returns to idle, signaling the EEC-IV module to de-energize the normally closed solenoid. When this occurs, vacuum is removed from the normally closed bypass valve and causes the bypass valve to dump secondary thermactor air to the atmosphere.

5   With the engine warmed up and the transaxle in Neutral, momentarily increase engine speed, then allow it to return to idle. If, after 2-1/2 minutes, the thermactor bypass valve dumps secondary air through the vents, the system is okay. If it doesn't, check the routing and condition of the hoses. If the hoses are okay, check the bypass valve function. If the bypass valve is okay, check battery voltage to the ITS and continuity

through the (normally closed) ITS while manually cycling the switch. If the ITS is okay, verify that the solenoid functions properly (that it actually opens and closes). If the solenoid is okay, check the vacuum signal to the solenoid. If the vacuum signal is okay, the problem is with the PCM. Further checking of the system must be performed by a dealer service department.

Air supply pump

6   Check and adjust the drivebelt tension (refer to Chapter 1).
7   Disconnect the air supply hose at the air bypass valve inlet.
8   The pump is operating satisfactorily if air flow is felt at the pump outlet with the engine running at idle, increasing as the engine speed is increased.
9   If the air pump doesn't pass the above tests, replace it with a new or rebuilt unit.

Air bypass valve

10   With the engine running at idle, disconnect the hose from the valve outlet.
11   Remove the vacuum hose from the port and remove or bypass any restrictions or delay valves in the vacuum hose.
12   Verify that vacuum is present in the vacuum hose by putting your finger over the end.
13   Reconnect the vacuum hose to the port.
14   With the engine running at 1500 rpm, the air pump supply air should be felt or heard at the air bypass valve outlet.
15   With the engine running at 1500 rpm, disconnect the vacuum hose. Air at the valve outlet should be decreased or shut off and air pump supply air should be felt or heard at the silencer ports.
16   Reconnect all hoses.
17   If the normally closed air bypass valve doesn't successfully pass the above tests, check the air pump (refer to Steps 5 through 7).
18   If the air pump is operating satisfactorily, replace the air bypass valve with a new one.

Air supply control valve

19   With the engine running at 1500 rpm, disconnect the hose at the air supply control valve inlet and verify that air is flowing through the hose .
20   Reconnect the hose to the valve inlet.
21   Disconnect the hoses at the vacuum port and at outlets A and B **(see illustration 5.2a)**.
22   With the engine running at 1500 rpm, air flow should be felt at outlet B with little or no air flow at outlet A.
23   With the engine running at 1500 rpm, connect a line from any manifold vacuum fitting to the vacuum port.
24   Air flow should be present at outlet A with little or no air flow at outlet B.
25   Reconnect all hoses.
26   If all conditions above are not met, replace the air control valve with a new one.

Combination air bypass/air control valve

27   Disconnect the hoses from outlets A and B **(see illustration 5.2b)**.
28   Disconnect the vacuum hose at port D and plug the hose.
29   With the engine running at 1500 rpm, verify that air flows from the bypass vents.
30   Unplug and reconnect the vacuum hose at port D, then disconnect and plug the hose attached to port S.
31   Verify that vacuum is present in the hose to port D by momentarily disconnecting it.
32   Reconnect the vacuum hose to port D.
33   With the engine running at 1500 rpm, verify that air is flowing out of outlet B with no air flow present at outlet A.
34   Attach a length of hose to port S.
35   With the engine running at 1500 rpm, apply vacuum to the hose and verify that air is flowing out of outlet A.
36   Reconnect all hoses. Be sure to unplug the hose to Port S before reconnecting it.
37   If all conditions above are not met, replace the combination valve with a new one.

Check valve

38   Disconnect the hoses from both ends of the check valve.
39   Blow through both ends of the check valve, verifying that air flows in one direction only.
40   If air flows in both directions or not at all, replace the check valve with a new one.
41   When reconnecting the valve, make sure it is installed in the proper direction.

Thermactor system noise test

42   The thermactor system is not completely noiseless. Under normal conditions, noise rises in pitch as the engine speed increases. To determine if noise is the fault of the air injection system, detach the drivebelt (after verifying that the belt tension is correct) and operate the engine. If the noise disappears. proceed with the following checks.
Caution: *The pump must accumulate 500 miles (vehicle miles) before the following check is valid.*

6

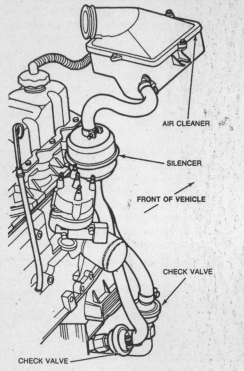

5.43a Typical unmanaged Pulse Air System (PAIR)

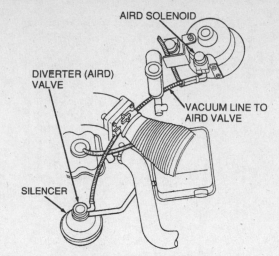

5.43b Managed Pulse Air System utilizing an Air Diverter (AIRD) control valve and AIRD vacuum solenoid (California only)

a) Check for seized pump and replace if required.

b) Check for loose or broken mounting brackets or bolts, replace and/or tighten securely if required.

c) Check for overtightened mounting bolts (may warp or bind pump).

d) Check for leaky, pinched, kinked, or damaged hoses and rework or replace as required.

e) Check that the bypass and diverter valves are operating correctly, reference this Section. Repair as required.

Pulsed Air Injection (PAIR) (1985 and later US, 1988 and later Canadian models)

43   All later models are equipped with an air injection system called Pulse Air or Thermactor II. This design uses natural pulses present in the exhaust system to pull air into the exhaust manifold and/or catalyst through pulse air check valves. The pulse air check valve is connected on one end to the exhaust manifold and/or catalytic converter with a long steel tube and to the air cleaner with a hose on the other end. A silencer is installed between the check valve and the air cleaner housing to help muffle the pulses **(see illustration)**. 1990 and later California models use a managed pulse air system for additional control by utilizing an Air Diverter (AIRD), also known as the air control valve, which is controlled by a vacuum signal from the (AIRD) solenoid valve **(see illustration)**. The vacuum signal allows the valve to either pass or block the flow of pulsed air. The (AIRD) solenoid valve is controlled by the

ECC-IV computer which opens or closes the solenoid depending on operating/driving conditions.

Checking

44   Visually inspect the Thermactor system hoses, tubes, check valves and control valve if equipped for leaks that may be due to backflow of hot exhaust gas. If holes are found and/or traces of exhaust gas products are evident, the check valve may be suspect. Replace any damaged hoses.

Functional test one

45   Remove the hose from the air cleaner at the inlet of the silencer or pulse air control valve if the vehicle has a managed system.

46   With engine at normal operating temperature and at idle in NEUTRAL air should be drawn into the silencer or air control valve.

47   If no flow is noted or if exhaust gas backflow is evident on non-managed system, wait for the engine to cool, remove the two check valves and bench test. The check valve should allow free flow of air in the direction of the arrow only **(see illustrations)**.

5.47a The check valves on a Pulse Air System (Thermactor II) are located below and in front of the starter motor - be sure to use a back-up wrench when detaching the pipe from either valve

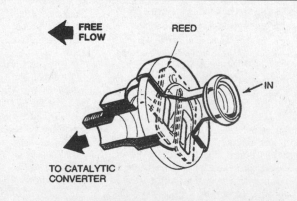

5.47b Verify that air flows freely through the Pulse Air Check Valve in the direction of the arrows and is blocked in the opposite direction

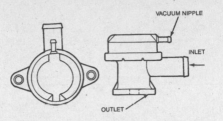

5.49 Verify that when vacuum is applied to Pulse Air Control Valve that air flows freely in the direction of the arrow and is blocked when the vacuum is released

The valve should check (or block) the free flow of exhaust gas in the opposite direction. If these conditions are met, valve is operating properly, if not, replace the check valves.

48   If no flow is noted on managed air system, pull the vacuum line off of the air control valve while the engine is running and verify that vacuum exists. If vacuum exists, the problem is either a malfunctioning air control valve or bad check valves.

49   To determine the cause, remove the air control valve from the top of the silencer. Start engine and again check for air being drawn into the silencer. If no flow is noted or if exhaust gas backflow is evident, remove the two check valves and bench test as described in step 47. Replace check valves if necessary. If flow appears normal, the problem is probably a malfunctioning air control valve. Bench test the control valve by applying a external vacuum source, it should allow free flow of air through the valve **(see illustration)**. If suspect, replace it.

50   If no vacuum is evident at the air control valve vacuum line while the engine is running, make sure the (AIRD) solenoid has manifold vacuum at it's inlet port and check for vacuum at its outlet port **(see illustration 2.22)**. If vacuum is present at the outlet port, the vacuum line between the solenoid valve and the air control valve is plugged, leaking or kinked. If vacuum is not present, either the solenoid is bad or the PCM circuit to the solenoid is malfunctioning. The solenoid can be removed and taken to a repair facility to be bench tested. If the solenoid is bad, replace it.

51   If the solenoid checks out, vacuum is present at the inlet and still no vacuum appears at the outlet, the ECC-IV circuitry is probably suspect. The repair of the ECC-IV systems are best left up to a professional repair facility.

Functional test two

52   Start engine and increase engine speed to slightly over 1500 RPM.

53   Remove vacuum line at air control valve and verify that **NO** vacuum is present. Reconnect vacuum line if test passes.

54   If vacuum is present at elevated RPM, the (AIRD) control solenoid is stuck or malfunctioning or the ECC-IV circuitry not operating properly. The repair of the ECC-IV systems are best left up to a professional repair facility.

Component replacement

55   On MTA systems, to replace the air bypass valve, air supply control valve, check valve, combination air bypass/air control valve or the silencer, label and disconnect the hoses leading to them, replace the faulty component and reattach the hoses to the proper ports. Make sure the hoses are in good condition. If not, replace them with new ones.

56   To replace the MTA air supply pump, first loosen the appropriate engine drivebelts (refer to Chapter 1), then remove the faulty pump from the mounting bracket. Label all hoses as they're removed to facilitate installation of the new unit.

57   After the new pump is installed, adjust the drivebelts to the specified tension (refer to Chapter 1.

58   If you're replacing either of the check valves on a Pulse Air System, be sure to use a back-up wrench **(see illustration 5.47a)**.

59   For control device removal and installation, refer to Section 3 of this Chapter.

6   Fuel evaporative emissions control system

Refer to illustrations 6.2a, 6.2b, 6.4, 6.5, 6.6, 6.7 and 6.21

General description

1   This system is designed to prevent hydrocarbons from being released into the atmosphere by trapping and storing fuel vapor from the fuel tank, the carburetor or the fuel injection system.

2   The serviceable parts of the system include a charcoal filled canister and the connecting lines between the fuel tank, fuel tank filler cap and the carburetor or fuel injection system **(see illustrations)**.

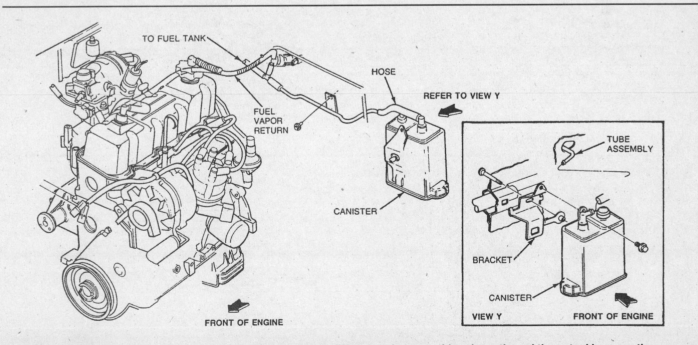

6.2a A typical canister venting system on a US vehicle (note any differences between this schematic and the actual hose routing on your vehicle by referring to the VECI label)

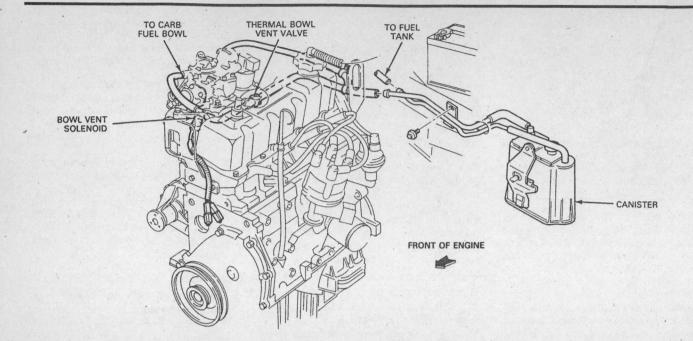

6.2b A typical canister venting system on a Canadian vehicle (note any differences between this schematic and the actual hose routing on your vehicle by referring to the VECI label)

3   Vapor trapped in the gas tank is vented through a valve in the top of the tank. The vapor leaves the valve through a single line and is routed to a carbon canister located between the left front wheel well and the front bumper, where it's stored until the next time the engine is started.

4   On all Canadian and 1984 US vehicles, a canister purge valve **(see illustration)** controls the flow of vapor from the canister to the intake manifold .

5   On all other US (EEC-IV) vehicles, the

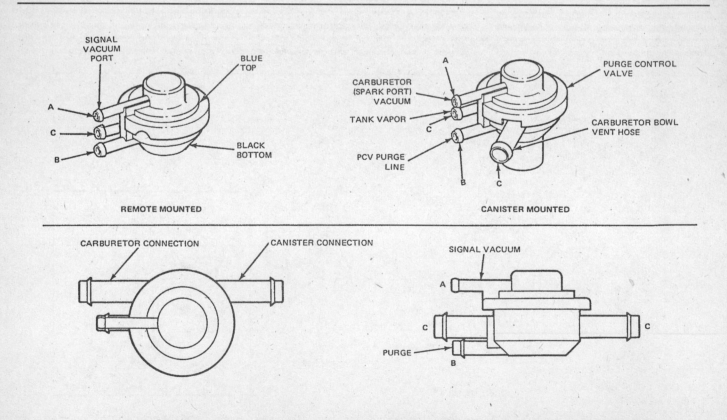

6.4 A typical inline canister purge valve used on Canadian vehicles and 1984 US vehicles

canister outlet is connected to an electrically actuated canister purge solenoid **(see illustration)** that is, in turn, connected to the air cleaner housing. The canister purge solenoid valve is normally closed. When the engine is started, the solenoid is energized by a signal from the PCM and allows intake vacuum to open the line between the canister and the air cleaner housing, which draws vapor stored in the canister through the air cleaner and into the engine where it's burned.

6   On all Canadian and 1984 US vehicles, vaporized fuel that would otherwise collect in the carburetor float bowl and pass directly into the atmosphere is also vented to the carbon canister when the engine is stopped. Vapor flow is controlled by a fuel bowl solenoid vent valve **(see illustration)**, which is normally open when the engine is off but closes the line to the canister when the engine is started. The valve returns to its normally open position when the engine is turned off. **Note:** *If the valve leaks or doesn't close, the fuel/air mixture will be leaned out. If a lean fuel mixture is suspected as the cause of a problem, check the bowl vent solenoid valve for proper closing during engine operation (refer to Step 16).*

7   The thermal vent valve **(see illustration)** is a temperature actuated off/on valve in the carburetor-to-canister vent line and is closed when the engine compartment is cold. This prevents fuel tank vapor (generated when the engine heats up before the engine compartment does) from being vented through the carburetor float bowl and forces it instead into the carbon canister. This effect can occur, for example, when sunlight strikes a vehicle that has been sitting out all night and begins to warm the fuel tank. With the thermal vent valve closed, the vapor cannot enter the carburetor float bowl vent valve, but is routed instead to the carbon canister. As the engine compartment warms up during normal engine operation, the thermal vent valve opens. When the engine is again turned off, the thermal vent valve (now open because underhood temperature is above 120-degrees F) allows fuel vapor generated in the carburetor float bowl to pass through the valve and be stored in the carbon canister. As the thermal vent valve cools, it closes and the cycle begins again.

Checking

Charcoal canister

8   There are no moving parts and nothing to wear in the canister. Check for loose, missing, cracked or broken fittings and inspect the canister for cracks and other damage. If the canister is damaged, replace it (refer to Step 20).

Canister purge valve (carburetor equipped vehicles)

9   Clearly label all vacuum hoses and ports, then detach the hoses from the valve.
10   Remove the valve.
11   Apply vacuum to port B **(see illustration 6.4).** The valve should be closed (no

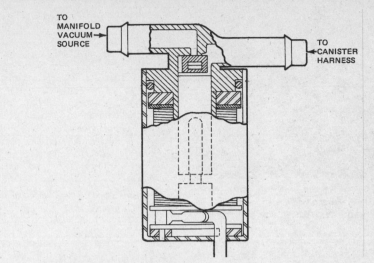

6.5 A typical canister purge solenoid used on all EEC-IV equipped vehicles

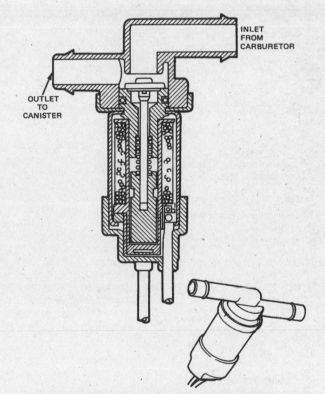

6.6 A typical carburetor fuel bowl solenoid vent valve

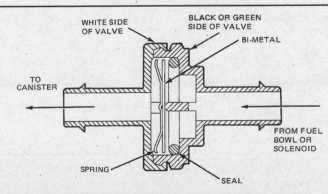

6.7 A typical carburetor fuel bowl thermal vent valve

6

6.21 To remove the charcoal canister, detach the vacuum hose and remove the mounting bolt (arrows)

air flows through it). If it does, the valve is open. Replace it with a new one.

12   After applying and maintaining 16 in-Hg vacuum to port A, apply vacuum to port B again. Air should pass through (the valve should open). If no air flows, the valve is closed. Replace it. **Caution:** *Never apply vacuum to port C. Doing so may dislodge the internal diaphragm and the valve will be permanently damaged.*

Canister purge solenoid valve (fuel injected vehicles)

13   Remove the valve (refer to Step 24).
14   With the valve de-energized, apply 5 in-Hg to the vacuum source port **(see illustration 6.5)**. The valve should not pass air. If it does, replace the valve.
15   Apply 9-to-14 volts to the valve electrical connector terminals with jumper wires. The valve should open and pass air. If it doesn't, replace the valve.

Carburetor fuel bowl solenoid vent valve

16   Remove the valve (refer to Step 24).
17   Apply 9-to-14 volts to the valve electrical connector terminals with jumper wires. The valve should close, preventing air from passing through. If the valve doesn't close, replace it.

Carburetor fuel bowl thermal vent valve

Note: *You'll need an oven and an accurate thermometer to test the fuel bowl thermal vent valve.*
18   Remove the valve (refer to Step 24).
19   The vent should be fully closed at 90-degrees F and below and at 120 degrees F and above. If it isn't, replace it.

Component replacement
Charcoal canister
20   Locate the canister in the engine compartment.
21   Reach up above the canister and remove the single mounting bolt **(see illustration)**.
22   Lower the canister, detach the hose

from the purge valve, or purge solenoid valve, and remove the canister.
23   Installation is the reverse of removal.

All other components
24   Referring to the appropriate vacuum hose and vacuum valve schematics in this Section and on the VECI label of your vehicle, locate the component to be replaced.
25   Label the hoses and fittings, then detach the hoses and remove the component.
26   Installation is the reverse of removal.

---

7   Positive Crankcase Ventilation (PCV) system

Refer to illustration 7.1

General description

1   The Positive Crankcase Ventilation (PCV) system **(see illustration)** cycles crankcase vapors back through the engine where they are burned. The valve regulates the amount of ventilating air and blow-by gas to the intake manifold and prevents backfire from traveling into the crankcase.
2   The PCV system consists of a replaceable PCV valve, a crankcase ventilation filter (integral with the oil filler cap on some vehicles, separate on others) and the connecting hoses.
3   The air source for the crankcase ventilation system is in the air cleaner. Air passes through the PCV filter (in the rocker arm cover or the oil filler cap) and through a hose connected to the air cleaner housing. On vehicles with a PCV filter integrated into the oil filler cap, the cap is sealed at the opening to prevent the entrance of outside air. From the oil filler cap, or separate PCV filter in the valve cover, the air flows into the rocker arm chamber and the crankcase, from which it circulates up into another section of the rocker arm chamber and finally enters a spring loaded regulator valve (PCV valve) that controls the amount of flow as operating conditions vary. The vapors are routed to the

intake manifold through the crankcase vent hose tube and fittings. This process goes on continuously while the engine is running.

Checking

4   Checking procedures for the PCV system components are included in Chapter 1.

Component replacement

5   Component replacement involves simply installing a new valve or hose in place of the one removed during the checking procedure.

---

8   Inlet air temperature control system (1984 through 1991 four-cylinder models only)

Refer to illustrations 8.3a, 8.3b, 8.3c, 8.4, 8.9, 8.20, 8.24 and 8.27

General description

1   The inlet air temperature control system provides heated intake air during warm-up, then maintains the inlet air temperature within a 70-degrees F to 105-degrees F operating range by mixing warm and cool air. This allows leaner fuel/air mixture settings which reduce emissions and improves driveability.
2   Two fresh air inlets - one warm and one cold - are used. The balance between the two is controlled by intake manifold vacuum, a temperature vacuum switch and a time delay valve. A vacuum motor, which operates a heat duct valve in the air cleaner, is controlled by the vacuum switch.
3   When the underhood temperature is cold, warm air radiating off the exhaust manifold is routed by a shroud which fits over the manifold up through a hot air inlet tube and into the air cleaner **(see illustrations)**. This provides warm air for the engine resulting in better driveability and faster warm-up. As the underhood temperature rises, a heat duct valve within the air cleaner

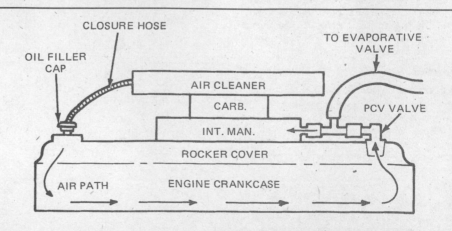

7.1 A typical Positive Crankcase Ventilation (PCV) system

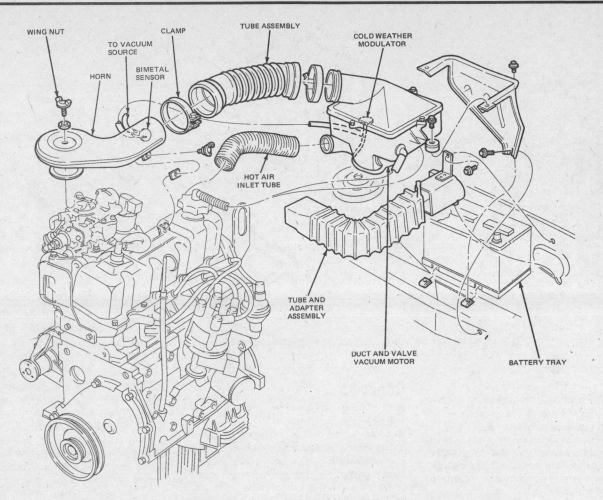

8.3a A typical air cleaner housing assembly and duct system on a carburetor-equipped vehicle

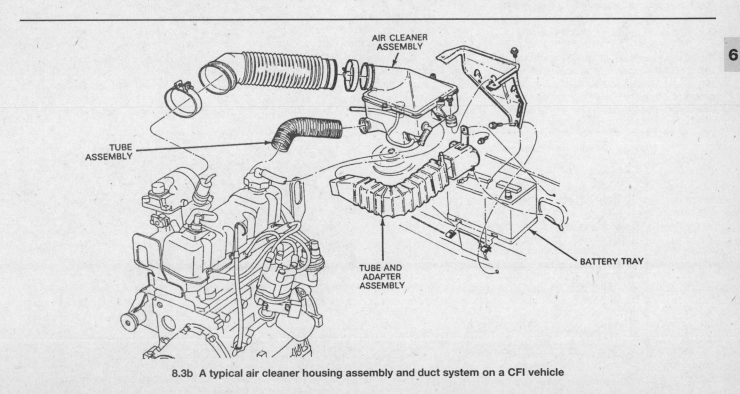

8.3b A typical air cleaner housing assembly and duct system on a CFI vehicle

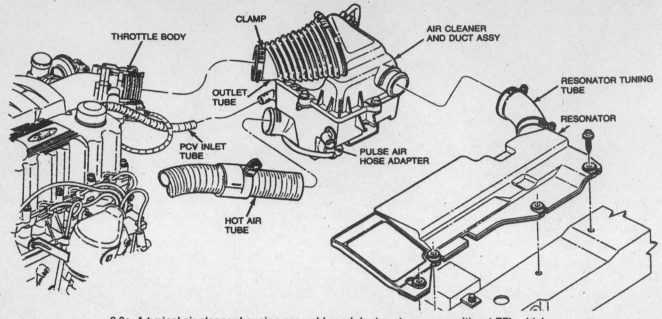

8.3c A typical air cleaner housing assembly and duct system on a multiport EFI vehicle

housing is gradually closed by a vacuum motor and the air cleaner draws air through a cold air duct instead. The result is a consistent intake air temperature.

4 A temperature vacuum switch **(see illustration)** mounted on the air cleaner housing monitors the temperature of the inlet air heated by the exhaust manifold. A bimetal disc in the temperature vacuum switch orients itself in one of two positions, depending on the temperature. One position allows vacuum through a hose to the motor; the other position blocks vacuum.

5 The vacuum motor itself is regulated by a cold weather modulator (CWM), mounted between the temperature vacuum switch and the motor, which provides the motor with a range of graduated positions between fully open and fully closed.

Checking

Note: *Make sure that the engine is cold before beginning this test.*

6 Always check the vacuum source and the integrity of all vacuum hoses between the source and the vacuum motor before beginning the following test. Do not proceed until they're okay.

7 Apply the parking brake and block the wheels.

8 Detach, but do not remove, the air cleaner housing and element (see Chapter 4).

9 Turn the air cleaner housing upside down so the vacuum motor door is visible **(see illustration)**. The door should be open. If it isn't, it may be binding or sticking. Make sure that it's not rusted in an open or closed position by attempting to move it by hand. If

it's rusted, it can usually be freed by cleaning and oiling the hinge. If it fails to work properly after servicing, replace it.

10 If the vacuum motor door is okay but the motor still fails to operate correctly, check carefully for a leak in the hose leading to it. Check the vacuum source to and from the bimetal sensor and the time delay valve as well. If no leak is found, replace the vacuum motor (refer to Step 26).

11 Start the engine. If the duct door has moved or moves to the "heat on" (closed to fresh air) position, go to Step 15.

12 If the door stays in the "heat off" (closed to warm air) position place a finger over the bimetal sensor bleed. The duct door must move rapidly to the "heat on" position. If the door doesn't move to the "heat on" position, stop the engine and replace the vacuum

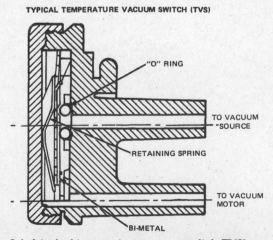

8.4 A typical temperature vacuum switch (TVS)

8.9 A typical air cleaner housing with the air filter removed, showing the hot air flapper valve system in the Cold Air position

8.20 To remove the TVS from the air cleaner housing cover, pry the retaining clip off with a small screwdriver

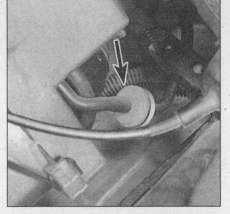

8.24 The Cold Weather Modulator (CWM) (arrow) is located in the vacuum line between the TVS and the vacuum motor underneath the air cleaner housing assembly - you'll have to detach the housing, lift it up and tilt it backward to gain access to the CWM

8.27 The vacuum motor is mounted on the underside of the air cleaner housing - to remove it, detach the housing, turn it upside down, detach the vacuum hose from the motor and remove both mounting screws

motor (refer to Step 26). Repeat this Step with the new vacuum motor.

13   With the engine off, cool the bimetal sensor and the cold weather modulator (CWM) by spraying them with compressed air.

14   Restart the engine. The duct door should move to the "heat on" position. If the door doesn't move or moves only partially, replace the TVS (refer to Step 18).

15   Start and run the engine briefly (less than 15 seconds). The duct door should move to the "heat on" position.

16   Shut off the engine and watch the duct door. It should stay in the "heat on" position for at least two minutes.

17   If it doesn't stay in the "heat on" position for at least two minutes replace the CWM (refer to Step 23) and repeat this Step after cooling the CVM and bimetal sensor again.

Component replacement

Temperature vacuum switch (TVS)

18   Clearly label, then detach both vacuum hoses from the TVS (one is coming from the vacuum source at the manifold and the other is going to the vacuum motor underneath the air cleaner housing).

19   Remove the air cleaner housing cover assembly (refer to Chapter 1 or 4 if necessary).

20   Pry the TVS retaining clip off with a screwdriver **(see illustration)**.

21   Remove the TVS.

22   Installation is the reverse of removal.

Cold weather modulator (CWM)

23   Detach the air cleaner housing assembly (refer to Chapter 1 or 4) and turn it upside down.

24   Locate the CWM **(see illustration)**, then detach both vacuum hoses and remove the CWM.

25   Installation is the reverse of removal.

Vacuum motor

26   Detach the air cleaner housing assembly

(refer to Chapter 1 or 4) and turn it upside down.

27   Locate the vacuum motor **(see illustration)**.

28   Detach the vacuum hose and remove both motor mounting screws.

29   Remove the motor.

30   Installation is the reverse of removal.

9   Catalytic converter

Refer to illustrations 9.1, 9.8, 9.9 and 9.10

General description

1   The catalytic converter **(see illustration)** is designed to reduce hydrocarbon, carbon monoxide and nitrogen oxide pollutants in the exhaust. The converter "oxidizes" these components (speeds up the heat producing chemical reaction between the exhaust gas constituents) and converts them to water and carbon dioxide.

2   The converter, which closely resembles a muffler, is located in the exhaust system immediately behind the short elbow shaped section of pipe below the exhaust manifold (you'll need to raise the vehicle to inspect or replace it).

3   **Warning:** *If large amounts of unburned gasoline enter the converter, it may overheat and cause a fire. Always observe the following precautions:*

   Use only unleaded gasoline
   Avoid prolonged idling
   Do not run the engine with a nearly empty fuel tank
   Avoid coasting with the ignition turned off

Checking

Note: *An infrared sensor is required to check the actual operation of the catalytic converter. Such a device is prohibitively expensive. Take*

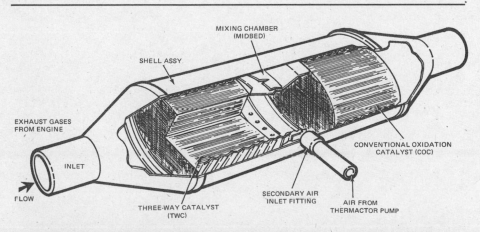

9.1 A typical Tempo/Topaz catalytic converter with a three-way catalyst (reduction of NOx) and conventional oxidation catalyst (reduction of HC and CO) - later models eliminated the oxidation catalyst and added a second stage three-way catalyst

MIXING CHAMBER (MIDBED)

SHELL ASSY

EXHAUST GASES FROM ENGINE

INLET

FLOW

THREE-WAY CATALYST (TWC)

SECONDARY AIR INLET FITTING

AIR FROM THERMACTOR PUMP

CONVENTIONAL OXIDATION CATALYST (COC)

6

9.8 To remove the catalytic converter, first remove the flange bolts . . .

9.9 . . . then loosen the hose clamps, detach both thermactor hoses from the inlet pipes . . .

9.10 . . . and loosen the nuts on the U-bolt at the rear of the converter

the vehicle to a dealer service department or a service station for this procedure. However, there are a few things you should check whenever the vehicle is raised for any reason.

4   Check the bolts at the flange between the exhaust pipe elbow section and the front end of the catalytic converter and the U-bolt that secures the rear end of the converter to the main exhaust pipe for a tight fit. On four-cylinder models, also check the hose clamps that seal the ends of both thermactor hoses to the catalytic converter for tightness.

5   Check the converter itself for dents (maximum 3/4-inch deep) and other damage which could affect its performance.

6   Inspect the heat insulator plates above and below the catalytic converter for damage and loose fasteners.

Component replacement

Warning: *Don't attempt to remove the catalytic converter until the complete exhaust system is cool.*

7   Raise the vehicle and support it securely on jackstands. Apply penetrating oil to the clamp bolts and allow it to soak in.

8   Remove the flange bolts **(see illustration)** from the flange between the elbow and exhaust pipe. Remove the old gaskets if they are stuck to the pipes.

9   On four-cylinder models, release the hose clamps **(see illustration)** and detach the hoses from the thermactor pipe inlets.

10   Remove the U-bolt **(see illustration)** from the rear joint between the catalytic converter and the main exhaust pipe assembly.

11   Remove the catalytic converter.

12   Installation of the converter is the reverse of removal. Be sure to use a new exhaust pipe gasket at the flange.

13   It's always a good idea to inspect and, if necessary, replace the rubber exhaust pipe hangers while the vehicle is raised (refer to Chapter 4).

14   Start the engine and check carefully for exhaust leaks.

Chapter 7 Part A
Manual transaxle

Contents

7A

Specifications

Torque specifications

	Ft-lbs
Shift housing-to-support assembly bolts	7 to 10
Shift lever-to-control assembly bolts	15 to 20
Shift rod cap-to-housing	7 to 10
Shift rod-to-transaxle shaft clamp	7 to 10
Shifter support assembly-to-mount bolts	23 to 29
Speedometer retainer screw	4 to 6
Transaxle stabilizer bar bolt	23 to 35
Transaxle-to-engine bolts	25 to 35

1 General information

The vehicles covered by this manual are equipped with either a four or five speed manual transaxle or a three speed automatic transaxle. Information on the manual transaxle is included in this Part of Chapter 7.

Service procedures for the automatic transaxle are contained in Chapter 7, Part B.

The manual transaxle is a compact, two piece, lightweight aluminum alloy housing containing both the transmission and differential assemblies.

Because of the complexity, unavailability of replacement parts and special tools necessary, internal repair procedures for the manual transaxle are not recommended for the home mechanic. For readers who wish to tackle a transaxle rebuild, exploded views and a brief *Transaxle overhaul - general information* Section are provided. The bulk of information in this Chapter is devoted to removal and installation procedures.

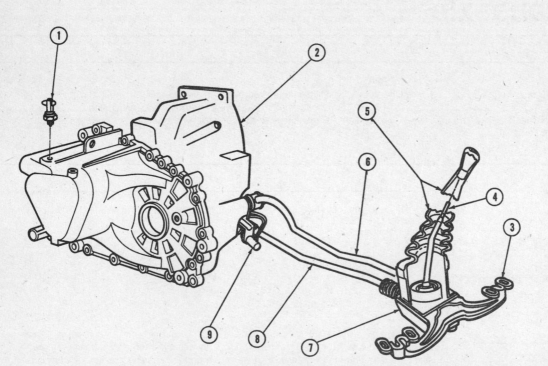

1　Transmission case
2　Clutch housing
3　Support assembly
　　(stabilizer rod)
4　Gearshift lever
　　assembly
5　Stabilizer
6　Control selector
　　housing
7　Shift rod and
　　clevis assembly
8　Switch and
　　bracket assembly
　　(control selector
　　indicator)

2.1a External shift linkage - four-speed manual transaxle

1　Backup light switch
2　Transmission case
3　Support assembly
4　Gearshift lever
　　assembly
5　Gearshift boot and
　　knob assembly
6　Stabilizer
7　Control selector
　　housing
8　Shift rod and clevis
　　assembly
9　Switch and bracket
　　assembly (control
　　selector indicator),
　　pre 1992 models only

2.1b External shift linkage - five-speed manual transaxle

2 Shift linkage - removal and installation

Refer to illustrations 2.1a, 2.1b, 2.2a and 2.2b

1 The external gearshift mechanism **(see illustrations)** consists of a shift lever, transmission shift rod, stabilizer rod and shift housing. The shift housing provides for shift lever mounting and connection to the shift rod. The housing is bolted to the stabilizer, which is rubber mounted and attached to the floor pan. On the transaxle end, the stabilizer rod is mounted through a rubber insulator to a boss on the clutch housing. The function of the stabilizer rod is to equalize the movement of the engine with the shift mechanism and prevent engine movement from pulling the transaxle out of gear. Rubber boots are provided for protection of the shafts and for sound insulation. Adjustment of the external linkage is not required.

Shift lever assembly

Removal

2 Loosen the shift knob locking nut located under the shift knob **(see illustrations)**.

3 Remove the shift knob by rotating it counterclockwise on the shift lever.

4 Remove the shift knob locking nut.

5 Remove the four screws that hold the boot assembly to the floor pan. Slide the boot up and over the shift lever.

6 Through the tunnel opening, remove the four bolts that hold the shift lever assembly to the control assembly mounting bracket. Lift the shift lever assembly out of the mounting bracket and tunnel opening.

Installation

7 Insert the shift lever assembly through the tunnel opening into the control assembly. Make sure the lower plastic pivot ball on the shift lever is inserted into the bushing on the end of the shift rod.

8 Fasten the shift lever to the control

1 Gearshift lever knob
2 Locking nut
3 Gearshift lever boot assembly
4 Bolt
5 Spring nut
6 Gearshift lever assembly
7 Bolt
8 Screw
9 Shift stabilizer bar support assembly
10 Screw
11 Shift rod to selector housing cap
12 Bushing
13 Bolt
14 Control selector housing
15 Shift rod and clevis assembly
16 Selector switch lever
17 Gearshift lever clamp
18 Nut
19 Gearshift rod sleeve
20 Gearshift stabilizer bar bushing
21 Bolt
22 Flat washer
23 Indicator switch and bracket assembly
24 Plug

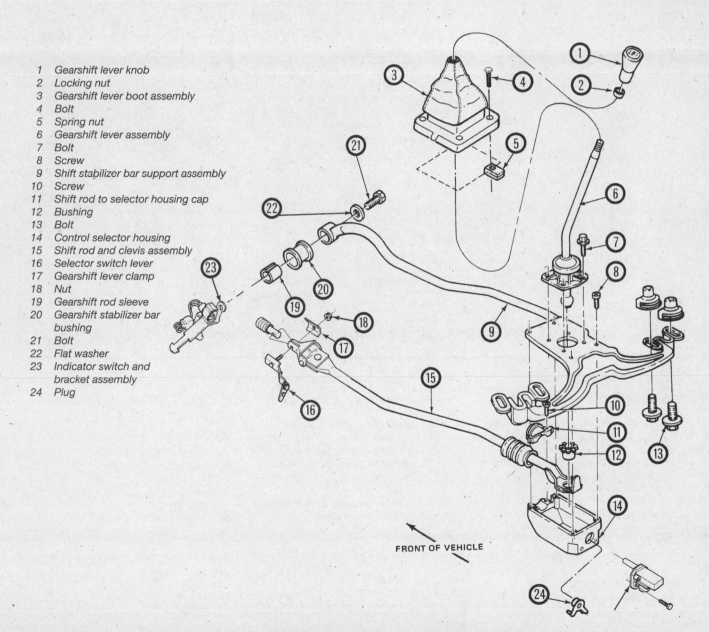

7A

FRONT OF VEHICLE

2.2a Exploded view of the four-speed manual transaxle shift linkage

1   *Gearshift lever boot/knob assembly*
2   *Gearshift lever assembly*
3   *Bolt*
4   *Spring nut*
5   *Bolt*
6   *Screw*
7   *Shift stabilizer bar support assembly*
8   *Screw*
9   *Shift rod to selector housing cap*
10 *Bushing*
11 *Bolt*
12 *Control selector housing*
13 *Shift rod and clevis assembly*
14 *Selector switch lever*
15 *Gearshift lever clamp*
16 *Nut*
17 *Gearshift rod sleeve*
18 *Gearshift stabilizer bar bushing*
19 *Bolt*
20 *Flat washer*
21 *Indicator switch and bracket assembly, (pre-1992 models)*

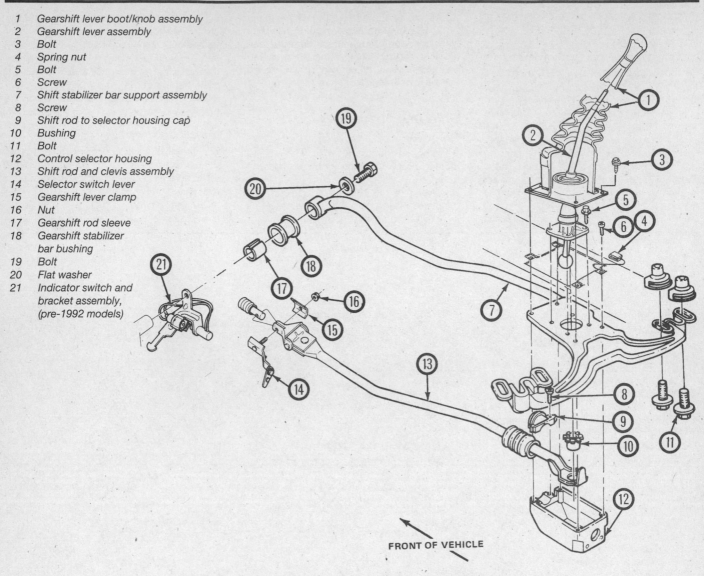

FRONT OF VEHICLE

2.2b Exploded view of five-speed manual transaxle shift linkage

assembly with the four bolts. Tighten the bolts to the specified torque.

9   Depress the clutch and operate the shift lever to check the function and tightness of all fasteners.

10 Slide the boot assembly down the shift lever and secure it to the floor pan.

11 Thread the locking nut down as far as it will go.

12 Thread the shift knob down until it reaches the locking nut and back it off to a readable position.

13 Tighten the locking nut against the shift knob.

Transmission gearshift stabilizer bar bushing
Removal

14 Raise the vehicle and support it securely on jackstands.

15 If equipped, detach the wiring harness

connector from the transmission control selector indicator switch.

16 Disconnect the stabilizer bar from the transaxle case by removing the bolt, the two washers and if equipped, the switch and bracket **(see illustrations 2.2a and 2.2b).**

17 Push the metal sleeve out of the center of the rubber bushing.

18 Pull the rubber bushing out of the stabilizer bar ring with a pair of pliers.

Installation

19 Grease the bushing and push it into the stabilizer bar ring with a pair of pliers.

20 Lubricate the metal sleeve and install it in the bushing (center it in the bushing).

21 Line up the stabilizer bar bushing with the boss on the transaxle case and attach it with the bolt, washer, and if equipped, the switch and bracket assembly. Tighten the bolts to the specified torque.

Support assembly and shift rod/clevis assembly
Removal

22 Remove the shift knob, locking nut, shift boots and shift lever assembly (refer to Steps 2 through 6 above).

23 Raise the vehicle and support it securely on jackstands.

24 Remove the bolt and washer which holds the stabilizer bar to the transaxle. If equipped, disconnect and remove the transaxle control selector indicator switch and bracket.

25 Loosen the shifter rod clamp nut and remove the clamp and lever assembly from the shift rod.

26 Remove the four bolts that hold the support assembly to the body. **Note**: *It may be necessary to lower the exhaust system (refer to Chapter 4) in order to remove the*

support assembly from between the exhaust pipe and the body.

27 Remove the four screws which hold the control selector housing and the shift rod assembly to the support assembly.

28 Remove the two screws that hold the shift rod retaining cap to the control selector housing.

29 Remove the shift rod/clevis assembly from the control selector housing.

Installation

30 Install the shift rod/clevis assembly in the control selector housing.

31 Fasten the shift rod retainer cap to the housing and slide the rubber boot over the mating surfaces. Tighten the bolts to the specified torque.

32 Fasten the control selector housing to the support assembly.

33 Position the support assembly under the vehicle so the mounting bracket slots line up with the body J-nuts and loosely attach the assembly with four bolts. Do not torque at this time.

34 Slide the shift rod over the transaxle input shaft and rotate the shift rod until the horizontal holes in the input shaft line up with the holes in the shift rod U-joint. Install and tighten the bolt/lever assembly, the clamp and the nut. Tighten the bolt to the specified torque.

35 Line up the stabilizer bar bushing and the transmission control selector indicator switch if equipped, with the boss on the transaxle case. Locate the washer on the passenger side of the stabilizer bar and if equipped, the switch and bracket on the driver's side of the stabilizer bar and tighten the bolt to the specified torque. Attach the connector to the switch if equipped.

36 Tighten the four nuts holding the support assembly to the body weld bolts to the specified torque.

37 Lower the vehicle.

38 Install the shift lever assembly, shift boot, locking nut and shift knob (refer to Steps 7 through 13 above).

3 Manual transaxle - removal and installation

1 Wedge a wood block approximately 7-inches long under the clutch pedal to hold it up slightly above its normal position.

2 Grasp the clutch cable and pull forward, disconnecting it from the clutch release shaft assembly.

3 Remove the clutch cable from the rib on the upper surface of the transaxle case. Remove the starter ground cable and wiring clip from the upper transaxle-to-stud bolt.

4 Remove the upper transaxle-to-engine mount bolt and stud bolt.

5 Remove the air cleaner.

6 Raise the vehicle and support it securely on jackstands.

7 Remove the front stabilizer bar mounting brackets. Discard the bolts .

8 Remove the nut and bolt securing the lower control arm balljoint to the steering knuckle assembly. Discard the nut and bolt. Repeat this procedure on the other side.

9 Using a large pry bar, pry the lower control arm away from the knuckle. **Caution:** *Do not pinch or cut the balljoint boot.* The pry bar must not contact the lower arm. Repeat this procedure on the other side.

10 Pry the left inner driveaxle CV joint assembly from the transaxle (refer to Chapter 8). **Note**: *Lubricant will drain from the opening. Install shipping plugs in each seal. If shipping plugs are not available, install 15/16-inch diameter dowels in each opening after each inner CV joint is removed to prevent the differential side gears from dropping.*

11 Remove the inboard CV joint from the transaxle (refer to Chapter 8) by grasping the left hand steering knuckle and swinging the knuckle and shaft out from the transaxle. Be very careful when using a prybar to remove the CV joint assembly. Carelessness can result in damage to the differential oil seal.

12 If the CV joint assembly cannot be pried from the transaxle, a special tool known as a differential rotator, must be inserted through the left side so the joint can be tapped out. The tool can be used from either side of the transaxle.

13 Wire the shaft assembly in a near level position to prevent damage during the remaining operations. Repeat this procedure on the opposite side.

14 Using a small screwdriver, remove the wire harness connector from the transaxle back-up light switch.

15 Remove the three nuts from the starter mounting studs which hold the engine roll restrictor bracket.

16 Remove the engine roll restrictor if equipped.

17 Remove the three starter stud bolts.

18 Remove the shift mechanism-to-shift shaft nut and bolt and if equipped, the control selector indicator switch arm. Remove the shift shaft.

19 Remove the shift mechanism stabilizer bar-to-transaxle mounting bolt. If equipped, remove the screw and detach the control selector indicator switch and bracket assembly.

20 Using a large crowfoot wrench, remove the speedometer cable from the transaxle (refer to Section 5).

21 Remove the two stiffener brace bolts from the oil pan and clutch housing .

22 Position a transmission jack under the transaxle.

23 Remove the two nuts that secure the rear insulator to the body bracket (refer to Chapter 2).

24 Remove the bolts that secure the front insulator to the body bracket.

25 Lower the transaxle jack until the transaxle clears the rear insulator. Support the engine with a jack under the oil pan.

Position a block of wood between the oil pan and the jack.

26 Remove the four engine-to-transaxle mounting bolts. One of the bolts holds the ground strap and the wiring loom stand off bracket.

27 Detach the transaxle from the rear of the engine and lower it. The transaxle casting may have sharp edges, so wear gloves when handling the transaxle assembly.

28 Installation is the reverse of removal. Refer to Chapter 2 for torque specifications.

4 Transaxle overhaul - general information

Refer to illustrations 4.4a, 4.4b, 4.4c and 4.4d

1 Overhauling a manual transaxle is a difficult job for the do-it-yourselfer. It involves the disassembly and reassembly of many small parts. Numerous clearances must be precisely measured and, if necessary, changed with select fit spacers and snap-rings. As a result, if transaxle problems arise, it can be removed and installed by a competent do-it-yourselfer, but overhaul should be left to a transmission repair shop. Rebuilt transaxles may be available - check with your dealer parts department and auto parts stores. At any rate, the time and money involved in an overhaul is almost sure to exceed the cost of a rebuilt unit.

2 Nevertheless, it s not impossible for an inexperienced mechanic to rebuild a transaxle if the special tools are available and the job is done in a deliberate step-by-step manner so nothing is overlooked.

3 The tools necessary for an overhaul include internal and external snap-ring pliers, a bearing puller, a slide hammer, a set of pin punches, a dial indicator and possibly a hydraulic press. In addition, a large, sturdy workbench and a vise or transaxle stand will be required.

4 During disassembly of the transaxle, make careful notes of how each piece comes off, where it fits in relation to other pieces and what holds it in place. Exploded views are included **(see illustrations overleaf)** to show where the parts go-but actually noting how they are installed when you remove the parts will make it much easier to get the transaxle back together.

5 Before taking the transaxle apart for repair, it will help if you have some idea what area of the transaxle is malfunctioning. Certain problems can be closely tied to specific areas in the transaxle, which can make component examination and replacement easier. Refer to the Troubleshooting section at the front of this manual for information regarding possible sources of trouble.

7A

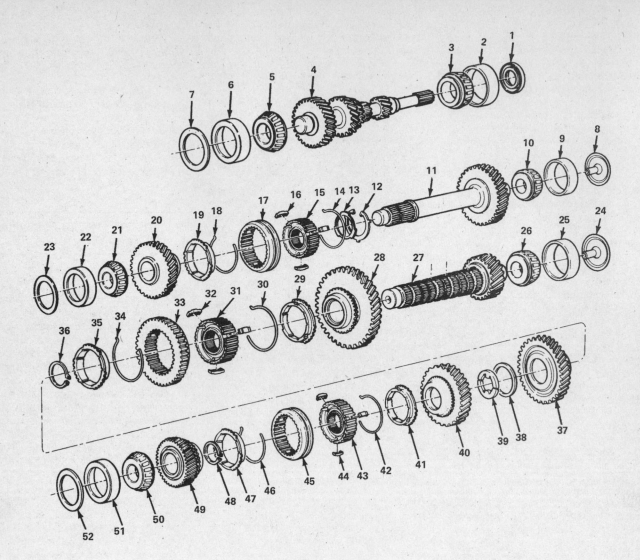

4.4a Five-speed manual transaxle shaft assemblies - exploded view

1 Input shaft seal assembly	19 Synchronizer blocking ring	36 Ist/2nd synchronizer retaining ring
2 Roller bearing race	20 5th speed gear	37 2nd speed gear
3 Input shaft front bearing retaining ring	21 5th gear shaft rear bearing	38 2nd/3rd thrust washer
4 Input cluster shaft	22 Roller bearing race	39 2nd/3rd gear
5 Input shaft rear bearing	23 Bearing preload shim	40 3rd speed gear thrust washer
6 Roller bearing race	24 Mainshaft funnel	41 Synchronizer blocking ring
7 Bearing preload shim	25 Roller bearing race	42 Synchronizer spring
8 5th gear funnel	26 Mainshaft front bearing	43 3rd/4th synchronizer hub
9 Roller bearing race	27 Mainshaft	44 Synchronizer hub 3rd/4th insert
10 5th gear shaft front bearing	28 Ist speed gear	45 3rd/4th synchronizer sleeve
11 5th gear drive shaft	29 Synchronizer blocking ring	46 Synchronizer spring
12 Synchronizer insert retainer	30 Synchronizer spring	47 Synchronizer blocking ring
13 Synchronizer retaining spacer	31 1st/2nd synchronizer hub	48 3rd/4th synchronizer ring
14 Synchronizer spring	32 Synchronizer hub Ist/2nd insert	49 4th speed gear
15 5th gear synchronizer hub	33 Reverse sliding gear	50 Mainshaft rear bearing
16 5th gear synchronizer hub Insert	34 Synchronizer spring	51 Roller bearing race
17 5th gear synchronizer sleeve	35 Synchronizer blocking ring	52 Bearing preload shim
18 Synchronizer spring		

4.4b Five-speed manual transaxle case and related components - exploded view

53   Clutch housing
54   Back-up light switch assembly
55   Reverse relay lever
56   Reverse relay lever pivot pin
57   External retaining ring
58   Reverse relay lever pin
59   Shift lever
60   Ball (10.319 mm)
61   5th/Reverse inhibitor spring
62   3rd/4th shift bias spring
63   Shift lever shaft
64   Shift lever pin
65   Shift lever shaft seal
66   Shift gate mounting bolts
67   Shift gate plate
68   Selector arm pin
69   Shift gate selector pin
70   Shift gate selector arm
71   Input shift shaft
72   Shift shaft detent plunger
73   Shift shaft detent spring
74   Shift shaft assembly seal
75   Shift shaft boot
76   Fork control shaft block
77   Reverse relay lever actuating pin
78   Main shift fork control shaft
79   Ist/2nd Fork
80   Fork interlock sleeve
81   Rollpin
82   Fork selector arm
83   3rd/4th Fork
84   5th shift relay lever
85   Reverse shift relay lever pin
86   5th relay lever pivot pin
87   External retaining ring
88   5th fork
89   5th fork retaining pin
90   5th fork control shaft
91   Reverse idle gear shaft
92   Reverse idle gear bushing
93   Reverse idle gear
94   Case magnet
95   Transaxle case
96   Vent assembly
97   Fill plug
98   Reverse shaft retaining bolt
99   Detent plunger retaining screw
100   Shift shaft detent plunger
101   Shift shaft detent spring
102   Fork interlock sleeve retaining pin
103   Transaxle case bolt
104   Seal assembly (LH) - differential
105   Shim - differential bearing preload
106   Differential bearing race
107   Differential bearing assembly
108   Side gear thrust washer
109   Sidegear

110   Pinion gear
111   Pinion gear thrust washer
112   Pinion gear shaft
113   Pinion gear shaft retaining pin
114   Final drive gear
115   Differential (LH) case
116   Differential (RH) case
117   Case and drive gear rivet
118   Speedometer drive gear
119   O-ring (5.16 x 1.6 mm)
120   Speedometer gear retainer
121   Speedometer retainer-to-case seal

122   Speedometer driven gear
123   Case-to-clutch housing dowel
124   Neutral switch
125   Shift gate pawl spring
126   Reverse shift relay lever support bracket
127   Reverse lockout pawl pivot pin
128   5th/Reverse kick down spring
129   Shift gate selector pin
130   Shift gate plate pawl
131   Ball
132   Bolt
133   C-clip

7A

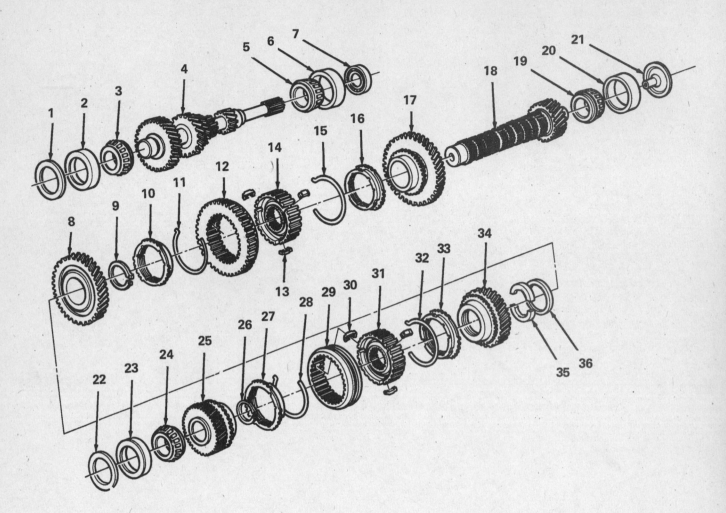

4.4c Four-speed manual transaxle shafts - exploded view

1	Bearing preload shim	13	Synchro hub lst/2nd insert	25	4th speed gear
2	Roller bearing race	14	lst/2nd synchro hub	26	3rd/4th synchro retaining ring
3	Input shaft rear bearing	15	Synchronizer spring	27	Synchro blocking ring
4	Input cluster shaft	16	Synchro blocking ring	28	Synchronizer spring
5	Input shaft front bearing	17	lst speed gear	29	3rd/4th synchro sleeve
6	Roller bearing race	18	Mainshaft	30	Synchro hub 3rd/4th insert
7	Input shaft seal assembly	19	Mainshaft front bearing	31	3rd/4th synchro
8	2nd speed gear	20	Roller bearing race	32	Synchronizer spring
9	lst/2nd synchro retaining ring	21	Main shaft funnel	33	Synchro blocking ring
10	Synchro blocking ring	22	Bearing preload shim	34	3rd speed gear
11	Synchronizer spring	23	Roller bearing race	35	2nd/3rd gear thrust washer
12	Reverse sliding gear	24	Mainshaft rear bearing	36	2nd/3rd thrust washer retaining ring

4.4d Four-speed manual transaxle case and related components - exploded view

37 Clutch housing
38 Transaxle-to-engine bolt
39 Dowel
40 Reverse relay lever pivot pin
41 Back-up light switch assembly
42 Back-up light switch
43 External retaining ring
44 Reverse inhibitor spring and retaining assembly
   A Pin
   B Washer
   C Spring
   D Ring
45 Reverse inhibitor plunger
46 Shift lever shaft
47 Selector plate mounting bolt
48 Selector plate
49 Shift lever
50 Shift lever shaft set screw
51 Roll pin
52 Input shift shaft selector plate arm
53 Expansion plug
54 Input shift shaft detent plunger
55 Input shift shaft detent spring
56 Ceramic case magnet
57 Input shift shaft
58 O-ring seal (5.16 x 1.6 mm)
59 Speedometer driven gear retainer
60 Speedometer retainer-to-case seal
61 Speedometer driven gear
62 Speedometer retaining screw
63 Right differential seal assembly
64 Dowel
65 Shift shaft oil seal assembly
66 input shift shaft boot
67 Differential bearing race
68 Transaxle identification tag
69 Case vent
70 3rd/4th fork
71 Fork selector arm
72 Spring pin
73 Fork interlock sleeve
74 lst/2nd fork
75 Reverse idler shaft
76 Reverse idler gear
77 Fill plug
78 Reverse shaft retaining bolt

79 Main shift shaft detent plunger
80 Main shift shaft detent spring
81 Detent plunger retaining screw
82 Fork interlock sleeve retaining pin
83 Driveaxle seal
84 Bolt
85 Case

86 Differential bearing preload shim
87 Differential bearing race
88 Main shift shaft
89 Reverse relay actuating lever pin
90 Differential and final drive ring gear
91 3rd/4th shift bias spring

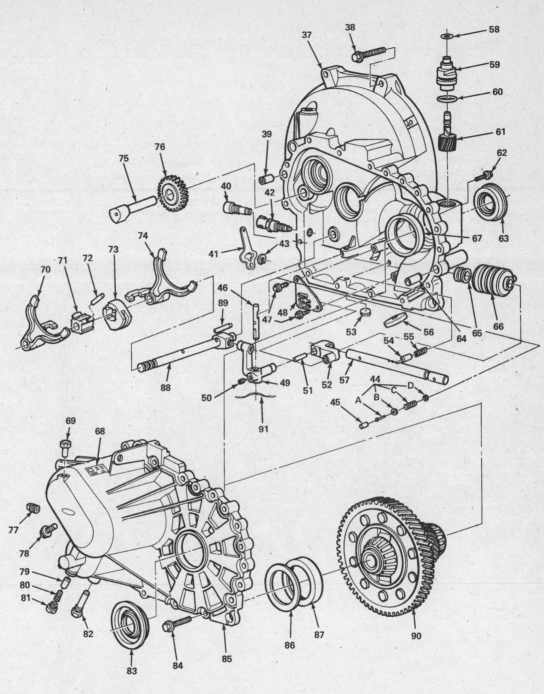

7A

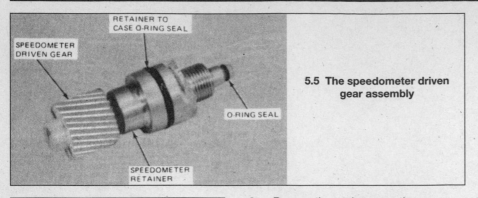

5.5 The speedometer driven gear assembly

5 Speedometer driven gear - removal and installation

Refer to illustration 5.5

1   Clean the top of the speedometer retainer.

2   Remove the retainer mounting screw.

3   carefully pull up on the cable to withdraw the speedometer retainer and the driven gear from the bore.

4   Unscrew the speedometer cable from the retainer.

5   Carefully remove the small O-ring from the stem end of the speedometer driven gear **(see illustration)**.

6   Slide the speedometer gear from the retainer.

7   Carefully remove the large O-ring from the retainer groove.

8   Replace the O-rings with new ones.

9   reassembly is the reverse of disassembly.

10   Lightly grease the O-ring on the retainer.

11   Using a 13/16-inch deep socket, gently tap the retainer and gear assembly into the bore while aligning the groove in the retainer with the screw hole in the side of the clutch housing case.

12   Install the screw and tighten it securely.

Chapter 7 Part B
Automatic transaxle

Contents

Specifications

Transaxle fluid type and capacity .... See Chapter 1

Torque specifications   **Ft-lbs**
Engine oil pan-to-transaxle case bolts .... 30 to 39
Fluid filter bolts .... 7 to 9
Manual lever-to-control cable nut .... 10 to 15
Shift lever-to-control assembly bolts .... 15 to 20
Shift cable bracket-to-retainer bolt .... 15 to 24
Shift cable retainer-to-transaxle bolt .... 15 to 24
Shift lever pivot bolt .... 14 to 19
Speedometer retainer screw .... 4 to 6
Transaxle pan bolts .... 15 to 19
TV control linkage trunnion bolt
   Carbureted and CFI engines .... 7 to 11
    Four-cylinder multiport fuel-injected engines .... 6 to 9
Transaxle-to-engine block bolts... 25 to 33

7B

1   General information

Due to its complexity and because of the special tools and skills required to overhaul an automatic transaxle, all major repairs should be done by a dealer service department or a transmission shop. Also, unlike a conventional automatic transaxle, the type used in the Tempo/Topaz is controlled by a microcomputer. The troubleshooting procedures are complex and well beyond the scope of the home mechanic. Therefore, the procedures in this Chapter are limited to general diagnosis, routine adjustments, on-vehicle replacement of a few components and transaxle removal and installation.

You can adjust the throttle valve linkage, shift control cable and Neutral start switch and replace a worn or damaged driveaxle oil seal or speed sensor. But if the transaxle requires internal repairs or an overhaul, take it to a dealer service department or a transmission repair shop.

2   Diagnosis - general

Note: *Automatic transmission malfunctions may be caused by five general conditions: poor engine performance, improper adjustment, hydraulic malfunctions, mechanical malfunctions or malfunctions in the computer or its signal network. Diagnosis of these problems should always begin with a check of the easily repaired items: fluid level and condition (Chapter 1), shift linkage adjustment and* *throttle linkage adjustment. Next, perform a road test to determine if the problem has been corrected or if more diagnosis is necessary. If the problem persists after the preliminary tests and corrections are completed, additional diagnosis should be done by a dealer service department or transmission repair shop.*

Preliminary checks

1   Drive the vehicle to warm the transaxle to normal operating temperature.

2   Check the fluid level as described in Chapter 1:
  a) *If the fluid level is unusually low, add enough fluid to bring the level within the crosshatched area of the dipstick, then check for external leaks.*
  b) *If the fluid level is abnormally high, drain off the excess, then check the drained fluid for contamination by coolant.*
  c) *If the fluid is foaming, drain it and refill the transaxle, then check for coolant in the fluid or a high fluid level.*

3   Check the engine idle speed. **Note:** *If the engine is malfunctioning, do not proceed with the preliminary checks until it has been repaired and runs normally.*

4   Check the throttle valve linkage for freedom of movement. Adjust it if necessary (Section 3). **Note**: *The throttle valve linkage may function properly when the engine is shut off and cold, but it may malfunction once the engine is hot. Check it cold and at normal engine operating temperature.*

5   Inspect the shift control cable (Section 4). Make sure that it s properly adjusted and that the linkage operates smoothly.

Fluid leak diagnosis

6   Most fluid leaks are easy to locate visually. Repair usually consists of replacing a seal or gasket. If a leak is difficult to find, the following procedure may help.

7   Identify the fluid. Make sure it s transaxle fluid and not engine oil or brake fluid.

8   Try to pinpoint the source of the leak. Drive the vehicle several miles, then park it over a large sheet of cardboard. After a minute or two, you should be able to locate the leak by determining the source of the fluid dripping onto the cardboard.

9   Make a careful visual inspection of the suspected component and the area immediately around it. Pay particular attention to gasket mating surfaces. A mirror is often helpful for finding leaks in areas that are hard to see.

10   If the leak still cannot be found, clean the suspected area thoroughly with a degreaser or solvent, then dry it.

11   Drive the vehicle for several miles at normal operating temperature and varying speeds. After driving the vehicle, visually inspect the suspected component again.

12   Once the leak has been located, the cause must be determined before it can be properly repaired. If a gasket is replaced but the sealing flange is bent, the new gasket will not stop the leak. The bent flange must be straightened.

13   Before attempting to repair a leak, check to make sure that the following conditions are corrected or they may cause another leak. **Note:** *Some of the following conditions (a leaking torque converter, for instance) cannot be fixed without highly specialized tools and expertise. Such problems must be referred to a transmission shop or a dealer service department.*

Gasket leaks

14   Check the pan periodically. Make sure the bolts are tight, no bolts are missing, the gasket is in good condition and the pan is flat (dents in the pan may indicate damage to the valve body inside).

15   If the pan gasket is leaking, the fluid level or the fluid pressure may be too high, the vent may be plugged, the pan bolts may be too tight, the pan sealing flange may be warped, the sealing surface of the transaxle housing may be damaged, the gasket may be damaged or the transaxle casting may be cracked or porous. If sealant instead of gasket material has been used to form a seal between the pan and the transaxle housing, it may be the wrong sealant.

Seal leaks

16   If a transaxle seal is leaking, the fluid level or pressure may be too high, the vent may be plugged, the seal bore may be damaged, the seal itself may be damaged or improperly installed, the surface of the shaft protruding through the seal may be damaged or a loose bearing may be causing excessive shaft movement.

17   Make sure the dipstick tube seal is in good condition and the tube is properly seated. Periodically check the area around the speed sensor for leakage. If transaxle fluid is evident, check the sensor O-ring for damage. Also inspect the side gear shaft oil seals for leakage.

Case leaks

18   If the case itself appears to be leaking, the casting is porous and will have to be repaired or replaced.

19   Make sure the oil cooler hose fittings are tight and in good condition.

Fluid comes out the vent pipe or fill tube

20   If this condition occurs, the transaxle is overfilled, there is coolant in the fluid, the case is porous, the dipstick is incorrect, the vent is plugged or the drain back holes are plugged.

---

3   Throttle valve (TV) control linkage - check and adjustment

Refer to illustrations 3.3, 3.4, 3.19, 3.21 and 3.23

General description

1   The TV control linkage on carburetor equipped engines consists of the coupling lever on the carburetor, the shaft assembly, the transaxle control rod assembly, the external control lever on the transaxle and a linkage return spring. The coupling lever follows the motion of the carburetor throttle lever. The TV linkage shaft and control rod transmits motion between the coupling lever on the carburetor and the TV control lever on the transaxle.

2   The TV control linkage on CFI fuel-injected engines consists of a coupling lever on the throttle body, the rod assembly, the bellcrank assembly, the transaxle control rod assembly, the external TV control lever on the transaxle and a linkage return spring. The coupling lever follows the motion of the throttle body shaft. The control rod, the bellcrank assembly and the control rod transmit motion between the coupling lever on the throttle body and the TV control lever on the transaxle.

3   The TV control linkage on four-cylinder multiport fuel-injected engines consists of an adjustable length TV control rod directly connecting the throttle cam to the transaxle TV lever arm. A spring from the TV control rod to a bracket on the throttle body provides the force required to overcome the internal transaxle lever force and returns the transaxle TV lever to the idle position **(see illustration).**

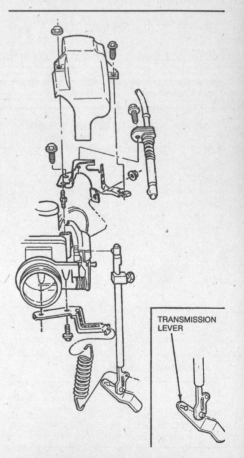

TRANSMISSION LEVER

3.3 An exploded view of the throttle valve components for the four-cylinder multiport fuel-injected engine

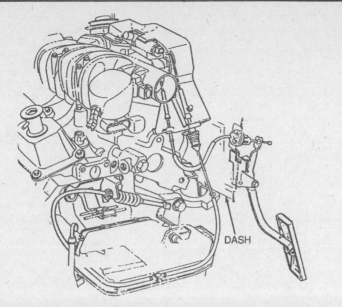

3.4 V6 engine throttle valve components and cable routing

4   The TV control linkage on V6 engines consists of an adjustable length cable connecting the throttle cam to the transaxle TV lever arm. A spring from the transaxle TV lever to a bracket on the transaxle provides the force required to overcome the internal transaxle lever force and returns the transaxle TV lever to the idle position **(see illustration)**.

5   On all engines, the control rod or cable assembly is adjusted to proper length during initial assembly. The transaxle's external TV control lever actuates an internal control mechanism which regulates the transaxle's control pressure, which in turn affects the shifting characteristics of the vehicle. The transaxle's external TV control lever motion is limited by internal transaxle stops at idle and slightly beyond wide open throttle. The linkage return spring must overcome the transaxle lever load (due to spring loading to WOT).

6   The TV control linkage is set to the proper length during initial assembly using the procedures as outlined under linkage check and adjustment. However, in general, when the linkage is properly adjusted, the TV control lever on the transaxle will just contact the internal idle stop (lever rotated clockwise as far as it will travel when viewed from the left side of the vehicle) when the throttle lever is in the closed throttle position. In addition, at wide open throttle, the TV control lever on the transaxle should fall slightly short of the internal wide open stop. The wide open throttle position must not be used as the reference point for adjusting the linkage.

Shift trouble diagnosis related to throttle linkage adjustment

7   If the transaxle shifts early and/or softly with or without a slip/bump feel, or if there is no forced downshift (kickdown) function at the appropriate speeds, the TV control linkage is set too short.

8   If shifts are extremely delayed, upshifts are harsh or idle engagement is harsh, the TV control linkage is set too long. Adjust linkage as described in this Section.

9   If idle engagement is harsh after engine warm-up, there's a shift clunk when the throttle is backed off after heavy acceleration, the coasting downshifts from 3rd to 2nd, or 2nd to 1st in the D range are harsh, or upshifts are delayed during light acceleration, either:

a) *The TV control rod or linkage shaft isn't returning properly. Remove the cause of the interference, then check and/or reset the linkage as described in this Section.*

b) *On carburetor and CFI models, excessive friction due to binding of the grommets or fittings is preventing the TV control linkage from returning. Check for bent/twisted rods and levers causing misalignment of the grommets. Repair or replace the defective components (replace the grommets if they're damaged). Reset the TV control linkage as described in this Section.*

10   If upshifts are erratic and/or delayed, there is no kickdown or engagements are harsh, the adjustment clamping mechanism on the control rod assembly or control cable might be loose. Check the integrity of the clamping mechanism and if necessary, reset the TV control linkage as described in this Section.

11   If there are no upshifts and/or engagements are harsh, either:

a) *The TV control rod or cable is disconnected (leaving the transaxle at maximum TV pressure). Reconnect the TV control rod or cable. If the disconnected rod is caused by defective grommets, replace the grommets.*

b) *The linkage return spring is broken or disconnected. Reconnect or replace the spring.*

Linkage check and adjustment
Manual linkage (all vehicles)

12   **Note:** *This is a critical adjustment and should be performed prior to TV related trouble shooting or adjustment.* Be sure that the D detent in the transaxle corresponds exactly with the stop in the console. Hydraulic leakage at the manual valve can cause delays in engagement and/or slipping if the linkage is not correctly adjusted.

Carburetor-equipped engines

13   Check for wide open carburetor and linkage travel at full throttle. The carburetor full throttle stop must be contacted by the carburetor throttle linkage and there must be a slight amount of movement left in the transaxle throttle linkage. Be sure that the throttle linkage return spring is connected and the carburetor throttle lever returns to the closed position.

14   Start the engine and warm it up to normal operating temperature. Turn off all accessories. Verify that the hot engine curb idle speed is correct (refer to Chapter 4). **Note**: *The linkage cannot be properly set if the throttle lever is on the choke fast idle cam. The following steps require working near the EGR system. Care must be taken to avoid contact with hot parts.*

15   Loosen the bolt on the sliding trunnion block on the TV control rod assembly at least one turn.

16   Remove any corrosion from the control rod and free up the trunnion block so it slides freely.

17   With the engine idling and the transaxle in Park, rotate the transaxle TV control lever up using one finger and a light force (about one pound) to make sure the TV control lever is against the internal stop. Without relaxing the force on the TV control lever, tighten the bolt on the trunnion block to the specified torque.

CFI fuel-injected four-cylinder engines

18   Simultaneously hold the throttle open to maintain 1000 rpm while pressing lightly on the ISC motor shaft. After the shaft retracts completely, release the throttle and quickly unplug the ISC motor connector (refer to Chapter 4 if necessary).

19   Loosen the bolt on the sliding trunnion block on the TV control rod assembly **(see illustration)** at least one turn.

7B

3.19 To adjust the TV control linkage, loosen the bolt on the sliding trunnion block at least one turn . . .

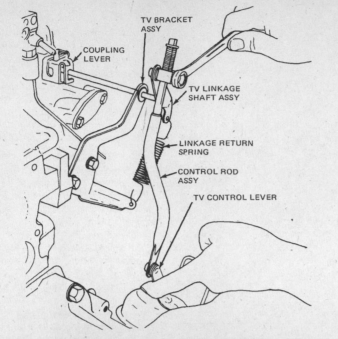

3.21 . . . then, using one finger, rotate the TV control lever at the transaxle up against the internal idle stop and tighten the bolt on the trunnion block

20   Remove any corrosion from the control rod and free up the trunnion block so it slides freely.

21   With the ISC plunger retracted and the trunnion block loosened, rotate the transaxle TV control lever up using one finger and a light force (about one pound) to make sure the TV control lever is against the internal idle stop **(see illustration)**. Without relaxing the force on the TV control lever, tighten the bolt on the trunnion block to the specified torque.

Multiport fuel injected four-cylinder engine

22   Remove the accelerator control splash shield from the cable retainer bracket.

23   Loosen the trunnion bolt on the TV control rod **(see illustration)**.

24   Make sure TV return spring is connected and holding the transaxle TV lever to its idle stop position (lever rotated clockwise as far as it will travel when viewed from the left side of the vehicle).

25   Ensure the accelerator throttle lever is resting on the closed throttle stop (engine at idle speed configuration).

26   Verify that the sliding part of the TV control rod (the middle section with the trunnion bolt) is properly seated by applying a slight downward pressure on the trunnion bolt (not enough to move the TV lever off its idle stop), then tighten the trunnion bolt to the torque listed in this Chapter's Specifications.

27   Check linkage for proper operation (refer to step 6 of this Section).

28   Reinstall accelerator control splash shield.

V6 engine

29   Remove the accelerator control splash shield from the cable retainer bracket.

30   Unsnap the TV cable adjuster locking clip (white clamp) at the upper cable retainer bracket.

31   Hold transaxle TV lever in idle position against idle stop (lever rotated clockwise as far as it will travel when viewed from the left side of the vehicle).

32   Ensure the accelerator throttle lever is resting on the closed throttle stop (engine at idle speed configuration).

33   Position the snap adjuster locking clip (white clamp) against the upper cable retainer bracket so that all cable slack is eliminated and snap the clip into the locked position.

34   Check linkage for proper operation (refer to step 6 this Section).

35   Reinstall the accelerator control splash shield.

---

4   Gearshift linkage - check, adjustment and replacement

Refer to illustrations 4.4, 4.7, 4.12, 4.14, 4.15, 4.16, 4.17, 4.18, 4.25, 4.30, 4.31, 4.32 and 4.35

Check

1   If the engine won't start in Park and/or Neutral, any of the following problems could be the cause:
 a) *The transaxle Neutral safety switch is out of adjustment. Readjust it (refer to Chapter 12).*
 b) *The transaxle cable retainer bracket is loose* **(refer to illustration 4.32)**. *Secure the bracket by tightening the two bolts to specification.*
 c) *The cable bracket attached to the transaxle retainer bracket is loose* **(refer**

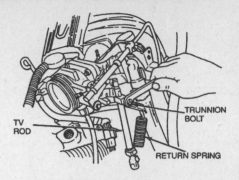

3.23 Loosening the TV control rod trunnion bolt on four-cylinder multiport fuel-injected engines

to illustration 4.32). Tighten it to specifications.
 d) *The shift linkage requires adjustment (refer to Steps 6 through 10).*

2   If the gear position indicator doesn't match the transaxle gear:
 a) *Refer to Steps 1b, 1c, and 1d above.*
 b) *The clip securing the cable to the housing or the clip securing the cable to the lever assembly is loose. Install the clip(s) properly* **(refer to illustration 4.6 and Steps 11 through 16.)**

3   If the gear position indicator doesn't light up:
 a) *The bulb is burned out. Replace the bulb (refer to Chapter 12).*
 b) *The wiring harness is damaged. Repair or replace the harness.*

4   If there's a rattle, noise, buzz, etc.:
 a) *The shift knob is loose. Tighten the locking nut on the upper end of the shift lever* **(refer to illustration 4.25)**.
 b) *The lever and housing assembly is not bolted tightly to the floor pan. Tighten the mounting nuts (refer to Step 19).*
 c) *The park gear lockout spring is not hooked. Attach the spring properly* **(see illustration).**
 d) *The bezel assembly is loose. Tighten the bezel assembly mounting screws* **(refer to illustration 4.14)** .
 e) *The transaxle gear shift lever cable bushing is missing. Install the bushing* **(refer to illustration 4.17)**.
 f) *The transaxle control shift rod clevis bushing is missing. Install the bushing* **(refer to illustration 4.4)**.

5   If water enters the inside of the vehicle:
 a) *The cable assembly grommet is not secured to the floor pan. Secure the grommet to the floor pan* **(refer to illustration 4.35)**.
 b) *The cable assembly grommet is torn. Install a new cable assembly (refer to Steps 28 through 44).*
 c) *The lever and housing assembly is loose. Tighten the bolts that attach the housing to the floor pan (refer to Step 19).*
 d) *The lever and housing assembly seal is missing or torn* **(refer to illustration 4.4)**. *Refer to Step 19.*

1   Shift lever knob
2   Shift rod spring
3   Release button
4   Shift lever assembly
5   Park gear lockout return spring
6   Spacer
7   Shift lever pawl
8   Shift lever sleeve
9   Selector rod
10 Shift lever shaft clevis bushing
11 Housing assembly
12 Seal
13 Pilot bolt
14 Nut
15 Bezel
16 Indicator light
17 Bulb
18 Screw
19 Bolt
20 Nut
21 Cable bracket retainer assembly
22 Cable and bracket assembly
23 Shift lever bushing
24 Retaining pin
25 Brake cable spring lock clip
26 Cable bracket insulator
27 Cable bracket spacer
28 Bolt
29 Shift arm insulator
30 Shift connecting rod
31 Nut
32 Nut and washer

4.4 Automatic transaxle shifter assembly components - exploded view

Adjustment

Note: *The control linkage adjustments must be performed in the order in which they appear. Refer to the exploded view (see illustration 4.4) when necessary for the following adjustment and component replacement procedures.*

6   Position the shift lever on the transaxle in the Drive position, against the rear stop. The shift lever must be held in the rear position while the linkage is being adjusted.

7   Loosen the manual lever-to-control cable retaining nut **(see illustration)**.

8   Move the shift lever inside the vehicle to the Drive position.

9   Tighten the control cable nut to the specified torque.

10 Check the operation of the transaxle in each shift lever position (try to start the engine in each gear-the starter should operate in Park and Neutral only).

Component replacement

Shift lever and housing assembly

11 Place the shift lever in a position (D, 2 or 1) that will incline the lever towards you.

12 To detach the shift knob, grasp it securely, depress the release button and pull up **(see illustration)**. **Note:** *The release button is spring loaded. Make sure that it doesn't pop out of the shift knob and get lost.*

13 Remove the console/consolette assembly (refer to Chapter 11).

14 Remove the four screws from the bezel assembly **(see illustration)**.

15 Lift the bezel assembly slightly, disconnect the indicator light harness **(see illustration overleaf)** and remove the bezel assembly.

16 Remove the cable retaining clips from

7B

4.7 To adjust the control linkage, place the shift lever in Drive, loosen the manual lever-to-control cable retaining nut (arrow), move the transaxle lever to the second detent from the rear position and tighten the nut

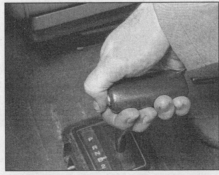

4.12 To remove the knob from the shift lever, put the lever in any gear that places the lever at an angle in line with your forearm, grip the knob firmly, depress the button and pull straight up

4.14 The shift lever bezel housing screws (arrows)

4.15 Unplug the shift indicator light harness connector before attempting to remove the shift lever bezel housing

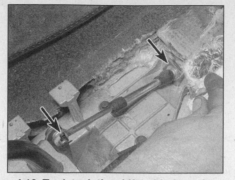

4.16 To detach the shift cable from the shift lever, remove the retaining pin and the clip (arrows)

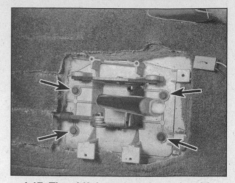

4.17 The shift lever housing assembly mounting bolts (arrows)

the shift lever and the housing assembly **(see illustration)**. Place the control cable assembly and bushing aside. If equipped, remove interlock cable and cable bracket from shift housing.

17   Remove the four bolts which attach the shift lever and lever housing assembly to the floor pan **(see illustration)** and remove the assembly.

18   Remove the selector lever pilot bolt nut, slide the pilot bolt out and separate the lever from the housing. Remove the pilot bolt bushings from the selector lever clevis **(see**

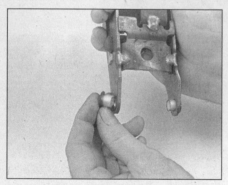

4.18 To get at the shift lever clevis bushings, remove the pilot bolt and nut and pull the lever from the housing - if the bushings are worn or damaged, replace them

illustration) and inspect them for damage and wear. If either bushing is worn or damaged, replace the pair and reassemble the selector lever and housing assembly. Be sure to coat the new bushings with multi-purpose grease to prevent squeaking and wear.

19   Check the selector lever housing seal, then install the lever and housing assembly and secure it with the four bolts. Tighten the bolts securely.

20   Inspect the control cable bushing for wear and damage. Replace it if necessary. Slide the control cable assembly and bushing onto the shaft. Be sure to lubricate the bushing with multi-purpose grease to prevent squeaking and wear.

21   Secure the cable assembly and bushing to the selector lever by installing the retainer pin **(see illustration 4.16).**

22   Position the control cable assembly in the lever and housing assembly and secure it by installing the cable retaining clip **(see illustration 4.16).** If equipped, install the interlock cable and cable bracket to shift housing.

23   Install the bezel assembly over the shift lever, connect the indicator light harness and secure the bezel assembly to the selector housing with the four screws.

24   Install the console on the lever and housing assembly and attach it with the four

screws (refer to Chapter 11 if necessary).

25   Make sure that the locking nut on the upper end of the shift lever is tight **(see illustration).**

26   Assembly the shift knob, spring and button.

27   Hold the shift knob securely and depress the button all the way, then firmly push the shift knob onto the lever until it s seated.

Cable and bracket assembly

28   Remove the shift knob, console, bezel assembly, control cable clip and cable retaining pin (refer to Steps 11 through 18).

29   Raise the vehicle and place it securely on jackstands.

30   Disengage the rubber grommet from the floor pan by pushing it towards the engine compartment **(see illustration).** Be careful not to tear it.

31   Remove the retaining nut and control cable assembly from the transaxle lever **(see illustration).**

32   Remove the control cable assembly bracket bolts **(see illustration).**

33   Pull the cable through the floor pan.

34   Feed the round end of the new control cable assembly through the floor pan.

35   Press the rubber boot on the control cable assembly into the body panel opening **(see illustration).**

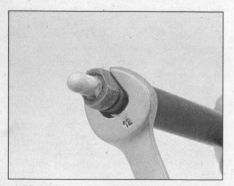

4.25 Make sure the locking nut on top of the shift lever is tight

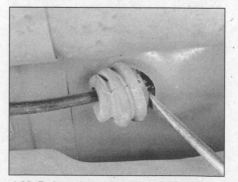

4.30 Before detaching the shift cable, pry the rubber grommet out - if it's worn, cracked or torn, replace it (or water will get into the passenger compartment)

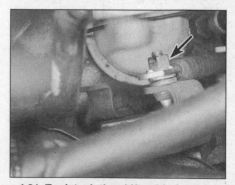

4.31 To detach the shift cable from the transaxle lever, remove the retaining nut (arrow)

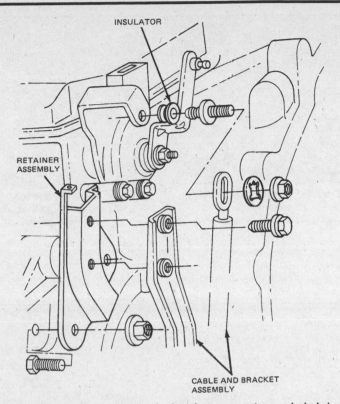

4.32 Shift control cable bracket and related components - exploded view

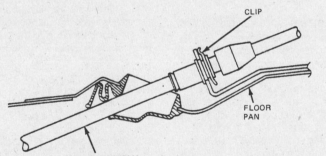

4.35 Be sure the rubber grommet is properly installed in the opening in the floor pan (if it isn't, water may get into the vehicle through the hole)

36   Position the control cable assembly in the selector lever housing assembly and install the spring clip.

37   Install the bushing and control cable assembly on the selector lever and housing assembly shaft and secure it with the retaining pin.

38   Install the bezel assembly, console and shift knob (refer to Steps 19 through 27).

39   Position the shift lever in the Drive position. The lever must be held in this position while attaching the other end of the control cable assembly .

40   Position the control cable bracket on the retainer bracket and secure it with the two bolts, then tighten both bolts to specifications.

41   Shift the transaxle manual lever into Drive (the second detent from the rear position).

42   Place the cable end on the transaxle manual lever stud, using care not to align the flats on the stud with the slot in the cable. Start the attaching nut.

43   Make sure the shift lever hasn't moved from the Drive detent, then tighten the nut securely.

44   Lower the vehicle and make sure the engine starts in Park and Neutral only.

Retainer bracket assembly

45   Raise the vehicle and place it securely on jackstands.

46   Remove the bolts securing the cable bracket to the retainer bracket assembly .

47   Remove the two nuts which attach the retainer bracket assembly to the engine mount bracket. Do not remove the two bolts.

48   Slide the retainer bracket assembly off.

49   Place the retainer bracket assembly on

the engine mount bolts and secure it by installing the two nuts. Tighten to specification.

50   Position the cable assembly bracket on the retainer bracket and install the bolts. Tighten to specifications.

51   Lower the vehicle and check the shift lever operation.

Lever and adapter assembly

52   Remove the shift knob, console and bezel assembly (refer to steps 11 through 15) and disconnect the control cable assembly from the shift lever and housing assemblies (refer to steps 16 and 17).

53   Remove the lever, adapter and housing assemblies (refer to Step 18).

54   Unscrew the lever and adapter assembly pivot nut and remove the pivot bolt.

55   Pull the shift lever assembly out of the selector housing.

56   Remove the pivot bushings from the lever and adapter assembly.

57   Install the pivot bushings in the lever and adapter assembly. Apply silicone grease to the lever assembly park pawl, park pawl slot and the bushings.

58   Insert the lever and adapter assembly into the housing and align the bolt holes.

59   Install the pivot bolt and nut and tighten the nut to specification.

60   Install the lever and housing assembly (refer to steps 20 through 27).

61   Install the control cable assembly, bezel assembly, console and shift knob (refer to Steps 19 through 27)

62   Adjust the control linkage (refer to steps 6 through 10).

5   Fluid and filter change

Refer to illustrations 5.5, 5.8, 5.9 and 5.11
Note: *Periodic fluid and filter changes are not specified by the factory as normal mainte-nance items. However if the vehicle is driven continuously or under severe conditions fluid and filter changes should be done at regular intervals.*

1   Before beginning work, purchase the specified transaxle fluid (see Recommended lubricants and fluids in Chapter 1) and a new filter. The filter will come with a new pan gasket and O-ring.

2   The fluid should be drained immediately after the vehicle has been driven. More sediment and contaminants will be removed with the fluid if it s hot. **Caution:** *Fluid temperature can exceed 350-degrees in a hot transaxle, so wear gloves when draining the fluid.*

3   After the vehicle has been driven to warm up the fluid, raise it and support it on jackstands.

4   Position a drain pan under the transaxle. Be careful not to touch any of the hot exhaust components.

5   Remove all of the pan bolts except for

7B

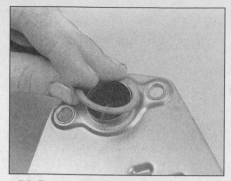

5.5 Remove all but the two rear pan bolts (arrows), then carefully pry the pan loose from the transaxle case - prying too hard will result in a distorted flange that will leak

5.8 The filter is held in place with three bolts

5.9 Be sure to install the new O-ring or gasket before bolting the new filter to the transaxle

the two at the rear corners **(see illustration)**. Unscrew the two remaining bolts several turns, but leave them in place to support the pan.

6   Carefully separate the pan from the transaxle case and allow the fluid to drain out. Try not to splash fluid all over as the gasket seal is broken and the pan is detached. Once the fluid has drained, remove the two bolts and detach the pan.

7   Scrape all traces of the old gasket from the pan and the transaxle case, then clean the pan with solvent and dry it with compressed air - DO NOT use a rag to wipe out the pan (lint from the rag could contaminate the transaxle).

8   Remove the filter bolts **(see illustration)** and detach the filter. Discard the filter and the O-ring.

9   Attach the new O-ring to the new filter **(see illustration)**, then bolt the filter to the transaxle. Tighten to specification.

10   Position the new gasket on the pan, then hold the pan against the transaxle case and install the bolts. Tighten to specifications.

11   Tighten the pan bolts to the specified torque in a criss-cross pattern **(see illustration)**. Work up to the final torque in three steps. **Caution:** *Don t overtighten the bolts or the pan flange could be distorted and leaks could result.*

12   Refill the transaxle with fluid (see Chapter 1 if necessary).

13   Lower the vehicle, drive it for several miles, then recheck the fluid level and look for leaks at the transaxle pan.

6   Automatic transaxle - removal and installation

Note: *The automatic transaxle and engine must be removed as an assembly. If any attempt is made to remove either component separately, damage to the transaxle or to the lower engine compartment structure may result.*

1   Remove the engine/transaxle assembly from the vehicle (refer to Chapter 2, Part C). Note that the driveplate-to-torque converter nuts are removed while the engine/transaxle is still in the vehicle.

2   Remove the transaxle-to-engine bolts and pull the transaxle away from the engine until the two are separated. Rock the transaxle from side-to-side if it doesn't separate from the engine easily.

3   The four studs on the torque converter must be lined up with the four holes in the driveplate during reassembly of the engine and transaxle.

4   Insert an alignment punch through the transaxle-to-engine bolt hole on either side to align the engine and transaxle housings, then push them together. If the engine and transaxle can't quite be mated, then the

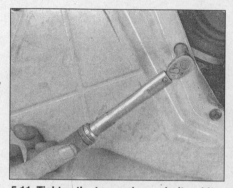

5.11 Tighten the transaxle pan bolts with a torque wrench - follow a criss-cross pattern and work up to the final torque in three steps to avoid warping the pan flange

torque converter studs aren't aligned with the holes in the driveplate. Have an assistant turn the crankshaft pulley slightly until the studs align with the holes and push the two assemblies all the way together.

5   Remove the drift punches, then install the transaxle-to-engine bolts and tighten them to the specified torque.

6   Install the engine/transaxle assembly (refer to Chapter 2, Part C). **Note**: *Although you can install the four torque converter mounting nuts before installing the engine/transaxle assembly it's much easier to do so after the engine/transaxle assembly is installed in the vehicle.*

Chapter 8
Clutch and driveaxles

Contents

Specifications

Torque specifications   Ft-lbs

Pressure plate-to-flywheel bolts	12 to 24
Clutch release lever-to-shaft bolt	30 to 40
Driveaxle/hub nut	180 to 236

1   General information

All models with a manual transaxle have a single dry plate, diaphragm spring type clutch. The clutch plate has a splined hub which allows it to slide along the splines on the input shaft. The clutch and pressure plate are held in contact by spring pressure exerted by the diaphragm spring in the pressure plate.

During gear shifting, the clutch pedal is depressed, which operates a cable, pulling on the release lever so the throwout bearing pushes on the diaphragm spring fingers, disengaging the clutch.

The clutch pedal incorporates a self-adjusting device which compensates for clutch wear. A spring in the clutch pedal arm maintains tension on the cable and the adjuster pawl grabs a ratcheting mechanism when the pedal is depressed and the clutch is released. Consequently the slack is always taken up in the cable, making adjustment unnecessary.

Power from the engine passes though the clutch and transaxle to the front wheels by two driveaxles. The driveaxles are of unequal length. The driveaxles consist of three sections: an inner Constant Velocity (CV) joint which is held in the differential by a spring clip, the axleshaft and the outer CV joint, which is held in the hub by a nut. The CV joints are internally splined and contain ball bearings which allow them to operate at various lengths and angles as the suspension is compressed and extended. The CV joints are lubricated with special grease and are protected by rubber boots which must be inspected periodically for cracks, holes, tears and signs of leakage, which could lead to damage of the joints and failure of the driveaxle.

It should be noted that the terms used in this manual to describe various clutch components may vary somewhat from those used by parts vendors. For example, such terms as the clutch plate, pressure plate and release bearing are used throughout this Chapter. An auto parts store or dealer parts department, however, might use the terms clutch disc, clutch cover and throwout bearing, respectively, for the above parts. The important thing to keep in mind is that the terms are interchangeable - they mean the same thing.

Warning: *Dust produced by clutch wear and deposited on clutch components may contain asbestos, which is hazardous to your health. DO NOT blow it out with compressed air and DO NOT inhale it. DO NOT use gasoline or petroleum-based solvents to remove the dust. Brake system cleaner should be used to flush the dust into a drain pan. After the clutch components are wiped clean with a rag, dispose of the contaminated rags and cleaner in a covered container.*

8

2 Clutch - description and check

1   All models with a manual transmission use a single dry plate, diaphragm spring-type clutch. The clutch disc has a splined hub which allows it to slide along the splines of the transmission input shaft. The clutch and pressure plate are held in contact by pressure exerted by the diaphragm spring in the pressure plate.

2   The mechanical clutch release system used on these models includes the clutch pedal with adjuster mechanism, a clutch cable which actuates the clutch release lever, and the release bearing.

3   When pressure is applied to the clutch pedal to release the clutch, mechanical pressure is exerted against the outer end of the clutch release lever. As the lever pivots the shaft fingers push against the release bearing. The bearing pushes against the fingers of the diaphragm spring of the pressure plate assembly, which in turn releases the clutch plate.

4   Terminology can be a problem when discussing the clutch components because common names are in some cases different from those used by the manufacturer. For example, the driven plate is also called the clutch plate or disc, and the clutch release bearing is sometimes called a throwout bearing.

5   Other than to replace components with obvious damage, some preliminary checks should be performed to diagnose clutch problems.

a) *To check "clutch spin down time," run the engine at normal idle speed with the transmission in Neutral (clutch pedal up - engaged). Disengage the clutch (pedal down), wait several seconds and shift the transmission into Reverse. No grinding noise should be heard. A grinding noise would most likely indicate a problem in the pressure plate or the clutch disc.*

b) *To check for complete clutch release, run the engine (with the parking brake applied to prevent movement) and hold the clutch pedal approximately 1/2-inch from the floor. Shift the transmission between 1st gear and Reverse several times. If the shift is hard or the transmission grinds, component failure is indicated.*

c) *Visually inspect the pivot bushing at the top of the clutch pedal to make sure there is no binding or excessive play.*

d) *A clutch pedal that is difficult to operate is most likely caused by a faulty clutch cable. Check the cable where it enters the housing for frayed wires, rust and other signs of corrosion. If it looks good, lubricate the cable with penetrating oil. If pedal operation improves, the cable is worn out and should be replaced.*

e) *If a whirring or howling sound is heard only when pressure is applied to the clutch pedal, the release (or throwout) bearing is most likely faulty.*

3 Clutch components - removal, inspection and installation

Refer to illustrations 3.4, 3.9 and 3.12
Warning: *Dust produced by clutch wear and deposited on clutch components may contain asbestos, which is hazardous to your health. DO NOT blow it out with compressed air and DO NOT inhale it. DO NOT use gasoline or petroleum-based solvents to remove the dust. Brake system cleaner should be used to flush the dust into a drain pan. After the clutch components are wiped clean with a rag, dispose of the contaminated rags and cleaner in a covered container.*

Removal

1   Remove the engine/transaxle assembly from the vehicle (see Chapter 2, Part C) or simply remove the transaxle (see Chapter 7, Part A). If the entire engine/transaxle assembly was removed, remove the bolts and separate the engine from the transaxle before proceeding.

2   Use a center-punch to mark the position of the pressure plate assembly on the flywheel so it can be installed in the same position. This is only necessary if the same pressure plate is going to be installed.

3   Loosen the pressure plate bolts a little at a time, in a criss-cross pattern, to avoid warping the cover.

4   Remove the bolts and detach the pressure plate and clutch disc from the flywheel **(see illustration).**

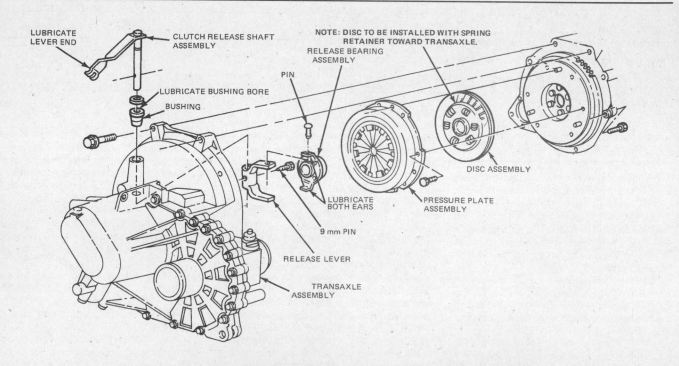

3.4 An exploded view of the clutch assembly and related components

NORMAL FINGER WEAR

EXCESSIVE — WEAR

EXCESSIVE FINGER WEAR

BROKEN OR BENT FINGERS

3.9 Replace the pressure plate if any of these conditions exist

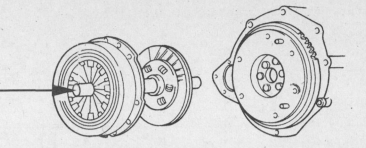

3.12 A special tool (arrow) is needed to align the clutch disc with the transaxle input shaft

5   Handle the clutch carefully, trying not to touch the lining surface, and set it aside.

Inspection

6   Inspect the friction surfaces of the clutch disc, pressure plate and flywheel for signs of uneven contact, indicating improper installation or damaged clutch springs. Also look for score marks, burned areas, deep grooves, cracks and other types of wear and damage. The flywheel should be resurfaced whenever a new clutch disc is installed. See Chapter 2, Part A or B for the flywheel removal procedure.

7   To see how worn the clutch disc is, measure the distance from the rivet heads to the lining surface. There should be at least 1/16-inch of lining above the rivet heads. However, the clutch disc is ordinarily replaced with a new one whenever it s removed for any reason (due to the relatively low cost of the part and the work involved to get to it). Check the lining for contamination by oil or grease and replace the clutch disc with a new one if any is present. **Note:** If the clutch plate is contaminated with oil, be sure to check the rear main oil seal and the transaxle input shaft oil seal for leakage. Check the hub for cracks, blue discolored areas, broken springs and contamination by grease or oil. Slide the clutch disc onto the input shaft to make sure the fit is snug and the splines are not burred or worn.

8   Remove and inspect the release bearing and release lever as described in Section 4.

9   Check the flatness of the pressure plate with a straightedge. Look for signs of overheating, cracks, deep grooves and ridges. The inner end of the diaphragm spring fingers should not show any signs of uneven

wear. Replace the pressure plate with a new one if its condition is in doubt **(see illustration)**.

10   Make sure the pressure plate fits snugly on the flywheel dowels. Replace it with a new one if it fits loosely on the dowels.

Installation

11   Position the clutch disc and pressure plate on the flywheel, and install the bolts finger-tight. Be sure to install the clutch disc properly (most replacement discs will be marked "flywheel side" or something similar).

12   Center the clutch disc by inserting an alignment tool through the splined hub and into the bore in the crankshaft **(see illustration)**. Wiggle the alignment tool up, down or from side-to-side as needed to center the clutch.

13   With the clutch plate held in place by the alignment tool, place the pressure plate in position on the flywheel dowels, aligning it with the marks made at the time of removal.

13   Install the bolts and tighten them in a criss-cross pattern, one or two turns at a time, until they're at the specified torque. Remove the alignment tool.

14   Install the release lever and release bearing (see Section 4).

15   Attach the transaxle to the engine (see Chapter 7, Part A) or reinstall the engine/transaxle assembly (see Chapter 2, Part C), depending on how the teardown was performed.

4   Clutch release bearing and lever - removal, inspection and installation

Refer to illustration 4.2

Warning: *Dust produced by clutch wear and deposited on clutch components may contain asbestos, which is hazardous to your health. DO NOT blow it out with compressed air and DO NOT inhale it. DO NOT use gasoline or petroleum-based solvents to remove the dust. Brake system cleaner should be used to flush the dust into a drain pan. After the clutch components are wiped clean with a rag dispose of the contaminated rags and cleaner in a covered container.*

Removal

1   Remove the engine/transaxle assembly from the vehicle, separate the transaxle from the engine and clean the clutch housing as described in the Warning above.

2   Remove the release bearing retaining pin from the release lever and slide the bearing off the transaxle extension **(see illustration)**.

3   To remove the release lever from the shaft, remove the lever-to-shaft bolt. Pull the shaft up through the clutch housing and lift out the lever **(see illustration 3.4)**.

4   Separate the release bearing from the lever by VERY CAREFULLY removing the nylon pin from the lever and bearing. **Caution:** *Be sure you don't damage the pin, since a new pin may not be included with the new bearing. If the pin is damaged in any way, you'll have to obtain one from a Ford dealer parts department, since the pin is necessary for the bearing to retract properly.*

Inspection

5   Check the lever arms and shaft for excessive wear and galling.

6   Inspect the bearing for damage, wear and cracks. Hold the center of the bearing and spin the outer race. If the bearing doesn't turn smoothly or if it s noisy, replace it with a new one. It s common practice to replace the bearing with a new one whenever a clutch job is performed, to decrease the possibility of a bearing failure in the future.

TRANSAXLE EXTENSION

LUBRICATE BOTH BORES

VIEW Z

4.2 The release bearing rides on the transaxle extension

8

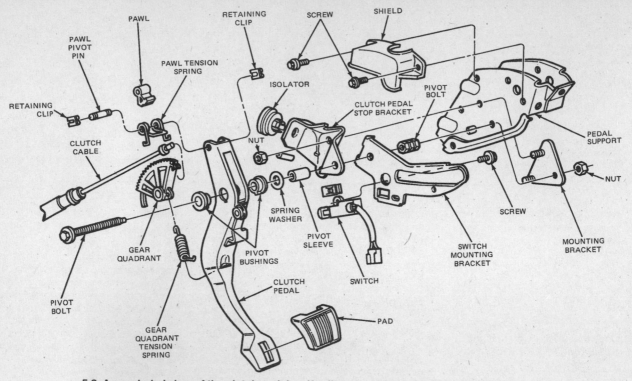

5.2 An exploded view of the clutch pedal, self-adjuster mechanism and related components

Installation

7   Wipe the old grease from the release bearing if the bearing is to be reused. Do not clean it by immersing it in solvent; it's sealed at the factory and would be ruined if solvent got into it. Fill the cavities and coat the inner surface, as well as the transaxle extension, with high-temperature multi-purpose grease.

8   Lubricate the release shaft bushings, position the release lever in the clutch housing and slide the shaft down through the lever and into the bottom bushing. Install the lever-to-shaft bolt and tighten it to the torque listed in this Chapter's Specifications. Lubricate the release lever arms where they contact the bearing with high-temperature multi-purpose grease.

9   Slide the release bearing onto the transaxle extension and position it in the release lever arms with the ears on the bearing straddling the lever arms. Insert the locating pin through the top ear and into the release lever.

10   Work the clutch release shaft lever by hand to verify smooth operation of the release bearing and shaft.

5   Clutch cable - removal and installation

Refer to illustrations 5.2 and 5.3

Removal

1   Remove the left side under dash panel.
2   Using a small screwdriver, disengage the adjuster pawl from the gear quadrant **(see illustration)**.

3   Remove the air cleaner assembly for access to the clutch cable. Pull the clutch cable from the clutch release lever with a pair of pliers. Grab the cable end, not the cable itself **(see illustration)**.

4   Pull the cable and housing through the insulator on the transaxle **(see illustration 5.3)**.

5   Loosen the front clutch pedal shield screw, remove the rear screw and swing the shield up and out of the way. Tighten the front screw to hold the shield up **(see illustration 5.2)**.

6   With the pawl released from the gear quadrant, rotate the quadrant forward and unhook the cable. The quadrant is under spring tension - don't let it snap back into position.

7   Pull the cable from the clutch pedal assembly and push it through the firewall to the engine compartment.

Installation

8   Insert the cable through the firewall from the engine compartment side.

9   Working under the dash, guide the cable through the insulator on the pedal stop bracket **(see illustration 5.2)**. Lift up on the clutch pedal, release the pawl and rotate the quadrant forward. Hook the cable end into the quadrant.

10   Swing the shield back into place and tighten the two screws.

11   Route the cable through the insulator on the transaxle housing.

12   Have an assistant pull back on the clutch pedal and hold it there. Connect the cable to the clutch release lever.

13   Depress the clutch pedal a few times to adjust the cable.

14   Install the under dash panel.

15   Install the air cleaner assembly.

6   Starter/clutch interlock switch - removal and installation

Refer to illustration 6.1

Check

1   Disconnect the electrical connector from the starter/clutch interlock switch **(see illustration)** and connect the leads of an ohmmeter between the two terminals on the switch where the electrical connector was connected. With the clutch pedal released, there should not be continuity (infinite ohms). With the clutch pedal depressed, there should be continuity (zero ohms).

Removal

2   Remove the left side under dash panel.
3   Detach the electrical connector from the interlock switch.
4   Remove the interlock switch-to-bracket screw and rotate the switch down **(see illustration 6.1)**.
5   Compress the barb at the end of the switch rod and remove the switch from the clutch pedal.

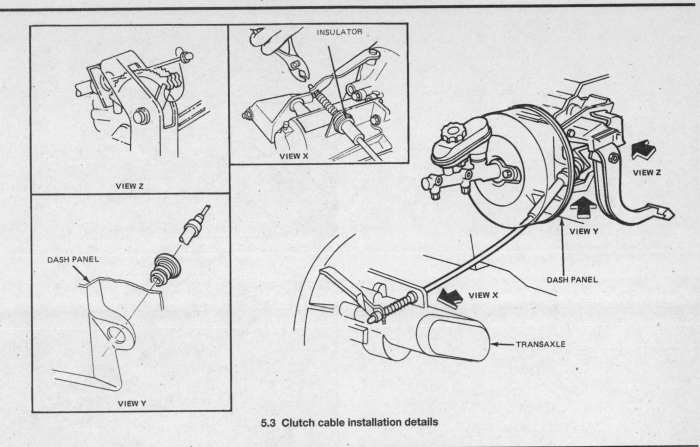

5.3 Clutch cable installation details

Installation

6   Position the adjuster clip approximately 1-inch from the end of the rod .

7   Insert the barbed end of the rod into the bushing on the clutch pedal.

8   With the clutch pedal all the way up, swing the switch up into place. Install the mounting screw and tighten it securely.

9   Push the clutch pedal to the floor to adjust the switch.

10   Install the under dash panel.

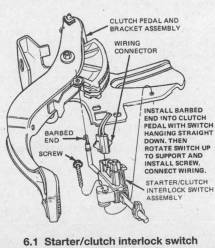

6.1 Starter/clutch interlock switch mounting details

7   Driveaxles, constant velocity (CV) joints and boots - check

1   The driveaxles, CV joints and boots should be inspected periodically and whenever the vehicle is raised for any reason. The most common symptom of driveaxle or CV joint failure is knocking or clicking noises when turning.

2   Raise the vehicle and support it securely on jackstands.

3   Inspect the CV joint boots for cracks, leaks, dimples and broken retaining bands. Dimples can be "popped out" if no other damage is noted by simply grasping the dimple and pulling it in opposite directions. If the dimple returns, try loosening one of the boot clamps to release any possible pressure/vacuum. If lubricant leaks out through a hole or crack in the boot, the CV joint will wear prematurely and require replacement. Replace any damaged boots immediately (Section 9). It's a good idea to disassemble, clean, inspect and repack the CV joint whenever replacing a CV joint boot, to ensure that the joint is not contaminated with moisture or dirt, which would cause premature CV joint failure.

4   Check the entire length of each axle to make sure they aren't cracked, dented, twisted or bent.

5   Grasp each axle and rotate it in both directions while holding the CV joint housings to check for excessive movement, indicating worn splines or loose CV joints.

6   If a boot is damaged or loose, remove the driveaxle as described in Section 8. Disassemble and inspect the CV joint as outlined in Section 9.

Note: *Some auto parts stores carry "split" type replacement boots, which can be installed without removing the driveaxle from the vehicle. This is a convenient alternative; however, it's recommended that the driveaxle be removed and the CV joint disassembled and cleaned to ensure that the joint is free from contaminants such as moisture and dirt, which will accelerate CV joint wear.*

8   Driveaxles - removal and installation

Caution: *Whenever both the right and left driveaxles are removed at the same time, the differential side gears must be supported so they don't fall into the case. A wooden dowel, approximately 15/16-inch in diameter, inserted into each side gear will work. If this precaution is not heeded and the side gears do drop, the differential will have to be removed from the transaxle to realign the gears, which will necessitate towing the vehicle to a Ford dealer service department or other repair shop.*

8

8.6   Use a large screwdriver or prybar (arrow) to carefully pry the CV joint out of the transaxle

8.7   A two-jaw puller can be used to push the driveaxle from the hub – DO NOT hammer on the axle!

8.8   After the driveaxle has been pushed out of the hub, pull out on the strut/knuckle assembly and free the stub shaft from the hub

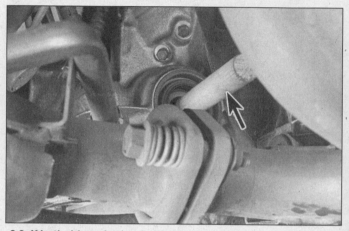
8.9   If both driveaxles are being removed, insert a wooden dowel (arrow) into the differential side gear to keep the gears from falling into the case

Removal

Note: *If the left driveaxle must be removed on a model with an automatic transaxle, it is necessary to remove the right driveaxle first. However, it isn't necessary to remove the right driveaxle completely - you can skip Steps 2 and 3, leaving the outer CV joint attached to the hub.*

Right driveaxle only on models with an automatic transaxle; either driveaxle on models with a manual transaxle

Refer to illustrations 8.6, 8.7, 8.8 and 8.9

1   Loosen the wheel lug nuts, raise the vehicle and support it securely on jackstands. Remove the wheel(s).
2   Remove the caliper and brake disc as outlined in Chapter 9.
3   Remove the hub driveaxle/nut (if you have an automatic transaxle equipped vehicle and both driveaxles are being removed, work on the right one first). Place a prybar between two of the wheel studs to prevent the hub from turning while loosening the nut.

4   Remove the brake hose support bracket-to-strut bolt.
5   Remove the control arm balljoint pinch bolt and separate the control arm from the steering knuckle (see Chapter 10, Section 6).
6   Using a large screwdriver or prybar, pry the inner CV joint assembly from the transaxle **(see illustration)**. Be careful not to damage the case or the oil pan. Suspend the axle with a piece of wire–don't let it hang, or damage to the outer CV joint may occur.
7   Push the driveaxle out of the hub with a two-jaw puller **(see illustration)**.
8   Once the driveaxle is loose from the hub splines, pull out on the strut/knuckle assembly and guide the outer CV joint out of the hub. Remove the support wire and carefully detach the driveaxle from the vehicle **(see illustration)**.
9   If both driveaxles are being removed on a vehicle equipped with a manual transaxle, insert a snug fitting wooden dowel (approximately 15/16-inch in diameter) into the right side differential side gear **(see illustration)**, then repeat the procedure in Steps 1 through 8 to remove the left driveaxle. Support the left side gear also.

Left driveaxle on models with an automatic transaxle

Refer to illustration 8.11

10   Remove the right driveaxle as described in Steps 1 through 8). Also, perform Steps 1 through 5 to the left driveaxle.
11   Using a narrow screwdriver inserted through the right hand differential side gear, drive the left driveaxle stub shaft out of the left differential side gear just far enough to unseat the circlip on the stub shaft from the side gear

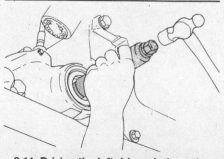
8.11   Driving the left driveaxle from the differential side gear

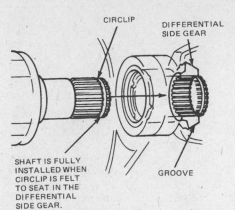

CIRCLIP

DIFFERENTIAL SIDE GEAR

SHAFT IS FULLY INSTALLED WHEN CIRCLIP IS FELT TO SEAT IN THE DIFFERENTIAL SIDE GEAR.

GROOVE

8.14 The inner CV joint stub shaft is completely seated when the circlip on the shaft snaps into the groove in the differential side gear

(see illustration). Insert a snug fitting wooden dowel (15/16-inch diameter) into the right differential side gear to prevent it from falling when the left driveaxle is removed.

12   Follow Steps 7 and 8 to remove the left driveaxle from the vehicle. Insert a wooden dowel into the left side gear.

Installation (both driveaxles)

Refer to illustration 8.14
Note: *If both driveaxles were removed, install one at a time, removing the wooden dowel from each side only when the driveaxle is ready for insertion into the transaxle.*

13   Install a **new** circlip on the inner stub shaft splines.

14   Coat the differential seal lips with multi-purpose grease and insert the stub shaft into the differential side gear until the shaft is seated and the circlip snaps into place **(see illustration)**.

15   Pull out on the strut/knuckle assembly and insert the outer CV joint stub shaft into the hub (make sure the splines are aligned). Push the shaft as far into the hub as possible by hand.

16   Support the outer CV joint housing and carefully tap on the hub, using a soft-faced hammer, until enough threads on the stub shaft are exposed to thread the old driveaxle/hub nut on. **Caution:** *Don't allow*

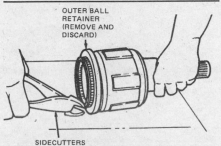

OUTER BALL RETAINER (REMOVE AND DISCARD)

SIDECUTTERS

9.4b If the CV joint is equipped with a "roll crimp" ball retainer, cut the retainer and pry it from the outer race

9.3 Cut the boot clamps off and discard them

any force to be transmitted to the inner portion of the CV joint.

17   Tighten the nut until the stub shaft is pulled completely into the hub, then remove the nut and discard it.

18   Install the driveaxle/hub washer and a **new** nut. Tighten the nut to the torque listed in this Chapter's Specifications while preventing the hub from turning by placing a screwdriver between two wheel studs.

19   Pry down on the control arm and insert the balljoint stud into the steering knuckle. Install a **new** pinch bolt and tighten it to the torque listed in the Chapter 10 Specifications.

20   Install the brake disc and caliper (see Chapter 9).

21   Install the brake hose support bracket bolt.

22   Install the wheel and lug nuts and lower the vehicle. Tighten the lug nuts to the torque listed in the Chapter 1 Specifications.

23   Check the transaxle lubricant level and add, if necessary (see Chapter 1).

9   Driveaxle boot replacement and CV joint overhaul

Inner CV joint and boot

Note: *There are three types of inner CV joints possible, depending on the vehicle and year: one Double Offset type and two Tripod types. The Double Offset type can possibly be found*

9.5 With the retainer removed, the outer race can be pulled off the bearing assembly

9.4a Pry the wire ring from the outer race with a small screwdriver

on any model. Its overhaul will be treated separately. The Tripod types were first introduced in 1992, and can be found on any vehicle since that year. The Tripod CV joint on four-cylinder models is slightly different than on the V6 model; therefore, pay close attention to specific callouts within the Tripod overhaul section. The only way to tell the difference is to remove the boot and inspect the joint.

Double offset type

Disassembly

Refer to illustrations 9.3, 9.4a, 9.4b, 9.5, 9.6, 9.7, 9.9, 9.10 and 9.11

1   Remove the driveaxle from the vehicle (see Section 8).

2   Mount the driveaxle in a vise. The jaws of the vise should be lined with wood or rags to prevent damage to the axleshaft.

3   Cut the boot clamps from the boot and discard them **(see illustration)**.

4   Slide the boot back on the axleshaft and pry the wire ring ball retainer from the outer race **(see illustration)**. Some inner CV joints use a "roll crimp" type ball retainer, which must be cut to remove it **(see illustration)**. A retainer is not necessary for reassembly. The reassembly procedure for the wire ring ball retainer should be followed.

5   Pull the outer race off the inner bearing assembly **(see illustration)**.

6   Remove the stop ring from the groove in the axleshaft with a pair of snap-ring pliers and slide the stop ring back on the axle **(see illustration)**.

8

9.6 Spread the stop ring and slide it back on the unsplined portion of the axleshaft . . .

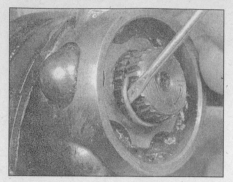

9.7 . . . then push the inner race and cage assembly back and pry the circlip off the shaft

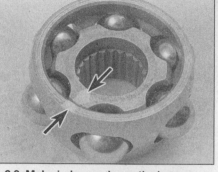

9.9 Make index marks on the inner race and cage so they'll both be facing the same direction when reassembled

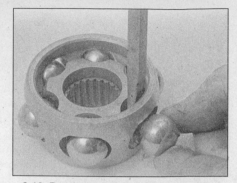

9.10 Pry the balls from the cage with a screwdriver (be careful not to nick or scratch them)

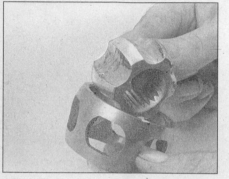

9.11 Tilt the inner race 90-degrees and rotate it out of the cage

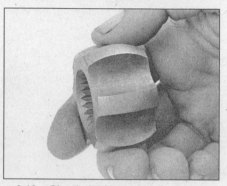

9.12a Check the inner race lands and grooves for pitting and score marks

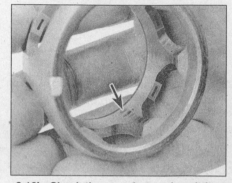

9.12b Check the cage for cracks, pitting and score marks (shiny spots are normal and don't affect operation)

7   Push the inner bearing assembly toward the center of the axleshaft far enough to gain access to the circlip. Remove the circlip with a small screwdriver and discard it (see illustration).

8   Slide the inner bearing assembly off the axleshaft.

9   Mark the inner race and cage to ensure that they are reassembled with the correct sides facing out (see illustration).

10   Using a screwdriver or piece of wood, pry the balls from the cage (see illustration). Be careful not to scratch the inner race, the balls or the cage.

11   Rotate the inner race 90-degrees, align the inner race lands with the cage windows and rotate the race out of the cage (see illustration).

Inspection

Refer to illustrations 9.12a and 9.12b

12   Clean the components with solvent to remove all traces of grease. Inspect the cage and races for pitting, score marks, cracks and other signs of wear and damage. Shiny, polished spots are normal and will not adversely affect CV joint performance (see illustrations).

Reassembly

Refer to illustrations 9.14, 9.15, 9.17, 9.18, 9.19, 9.20, 9.22a, 9.22b, 9.23, 9.24 and 9.25

13   Insert the inner race into the cage.

Verify that the matchmarks are on the same side. However, it's not necessary for them to be in direct alignment with each other.

14   Press the balls into the cage windows with your thumbs (see illustration).

15   Wrap the axleshaft splines with tape to avoid damaging the boot. Slide the small boot clamp and boot onto the axleshaft, then remove the tape (see illustration).

16   Install a new stop ring on the axleshaft. Don't seat it in the groove at this time, but slide it past the splined area.

17   Install the inner race and cage assembly on the axleshaft with the larger diameter side or "bulge" of the cage facing the axleshaft end (see illustration).

9.14 Press the balls into the cage through the windows

9.15 Wrap the splined area of the axle with tape to prevent damage to the boot

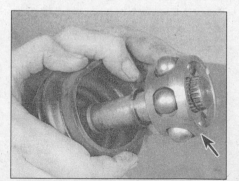

9.17 Install the inner race and cage assembly with the "bulge" (arrow) facing the axleshaft end

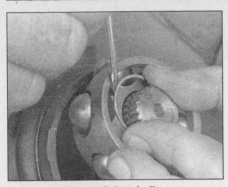

9.18 Install the circlip . . .

9.19 . . . then seat the stop ring in the groove

9.20 Pack grease into the bearing until it's completely full

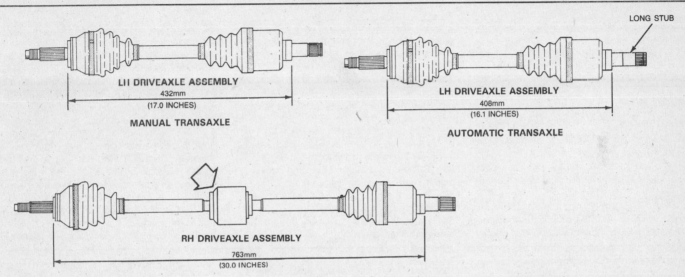

LH DRIVEAXLE ASSEMBLY
432mm
(17.0 INCHES)
MANUAL TRANSAXLE

LONG STUB

LH DRIVEAXLE ASSEMBLY
408mm
(16.1 INCHES)
AUTOMATIC TRANSAXLE

RH DRIVEAXLE ASSEMBLY
763mm
(30.0 INCHES)

9.22a Driveaxle standard length - 1991 and earlier models (note the beveled portion of the damper assembly on the right side driveaxle [arrow] faces toward the outer end)

18   Install the circlip and slide the inner race and cage assembly out until the inner race contacts the circlip **(see illustration)**.
19   Install the stop ring in the groove **(see illustration)**. Make sure it's completely seated by pushing on the inner race and cage assembly.
20   Fill the outer race and boot with CV joint grease (normally included with the new boot kit). Pack the inner race and cage assembly with grease, by hand, until grease is worked completely into the assembly **(see illustration)**.
21   Slide the outer race down onto the inner race and install the wire ring retainer.
22   Wipe any excess grease from the axle boot groove on the outer race. Seat the small diameter of the boot in the recessed area on the axleshaft and install the clamp. Push the other end of the boot onto the outer race and move the race in-or-out to adjust the axle to the proper length **(see illustrations)**.
23   With the axle set to the proper length, equalize the pressure in the boot by inserting a dull screwdriver between the boot and the outer race **(see illustration overleaf)**. Don't damage the boot with the tool.
24   Install the boot clamp. A pair of special clamp-crimping pliers are required. The pliers

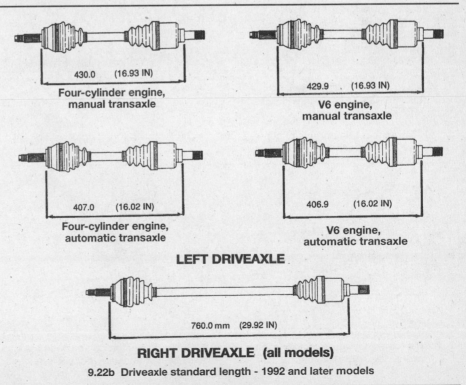

430.0   (16.93 IN)
Four-cylinder engine, manual transaxle

429.9   (16.93 IN)
V6 engine, manual transaxle

407.0   (16.02 IN)
Four-cylinder engine, automatic transaxle

406.9   (16.02 IN)
V6 engine, automatic transaxle

LEFT DRIVEAXLE

760.0 mm   (29.92 IN)

RIGHT DRIVEAXLE (all models)

9.22b Driveaxle standard length - 1992 and later models

8

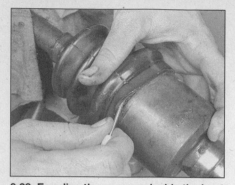

9.23 Equalize the pressure inside the boot by inserting a small screwdriver between the boot and the outer race

9.24 Securing the boot clamp with the special pliers (available at most auto parts stores)

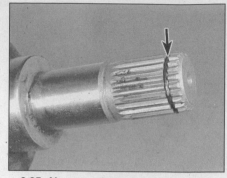

9.25 Always replace the circlip on the inner stub axle

are available at most auto parts stores **(see illustration)**.

25   Install a new clip on the stub axle **(see illustration)** and install the driveaxle as described in Section 8.

Tripod type

Disassembly

Refer to illustrations 9.30, 9.31, 9.32a. 9.32b, 9.33 and 9.34

26   The major difference between the two types of inner Tripod joints is in the method of securing the tripod bearing assembly to the axleshaft. The right Tripod joint on four-cylinder models uses the driveshaft shoulder to prevent inward movement and one snap-

ring to prevent outward movement. Both driveaxles on V6 models and the left driveaxles on four-cylinder models use snap-rings to prevent movement in both directions. The following procedure will specify when the process differs.

27   Remove the driveaxle from the vehicle (see Section 8).

28   Mount the driveaxle in a vise. The jaws of the vise should be lined with wood or rags to prevent damage to the axleshaft.

29   Cut the boot clamps from the boot and discard them **(see illustration 9.3)**.

30   Bend the retaining tabs slightly to allow for tripod removal **(see illustration)**.

31   Remove tripod assembly from outer race **(see illustration)**.

32   On the four-cylinder engine right driveaxle, remove the snap-ring at the end of the driveaxle and remove the Tripod assembly **(see illustrations)**.

33   On the four-cylinder engine left driveaxle and either V6 engine axle, move the inner (exposed) stop ring down the shaft about 1/2-inch **(see illustration)**.

34   On the four-cylinder engine left axle and any V6 engine axle, move the Tripod down the shaft towards the inner snap-ring until the circlip is visible on the end of the driveaxle. Remove the circlip and remove the tripod assembly off the driveaxle **(see illustration)**.

35   No further disassembly of the Tripods is possible. Inspect the tripod rollers, roller bearings and races carefully for damage,

9.30 Bend the retaining tabs to allow Tripod removal

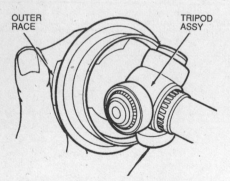

9.31 Removing the Tripod assembly

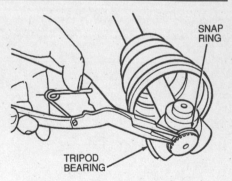

9.32a Removing the snap ring on the four-cylinder engine right axle Tripod

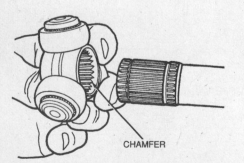

9.32b Removing the four-cylinder engine right axle Tripod assembly

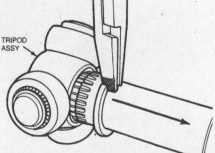

9.33 Move the stop ring down the axle shaft (V6 [either axle] and four-cylinder [left axle])

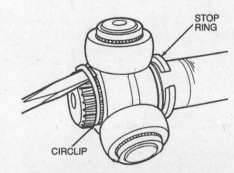

9.34 Remove the circlip and pull off the Tripod assembly (V6 [both axles] and four-cylinder left axle)

worn spots and smooth operation. Damaged or worn Tripods cannot be rebuilt and must be replaced.

36 If new boots will be installed on V6 engine models (either driveaxle) and four-cylinder model (left axle), remove the inner stop ring completely and remove the old boot.

Reassembly

Refer to illustrations 9.41a, 9.41b and 9.42

37 Slide new clamp and inner CV joint boot on the axleshaft (**see illustration 9.15**).

38 On four-cylinder engine left and all V6 engine axles, install a new inner stop ring past the second ring groove about 1/2-inch.

39 Install the Tripod assembly on the driveaxle with the chamfered side inward (**see illustration 9.32b**).

40 On the four-cylinder engine right side axle, install a new snap-ring onto driveaxle end to secure Tripod assembly.

41 On four-cylinder engine left and all V6 engine axles, push the Tripod assembly down the axle far enough to allow circlip installation. Install the new circlip and push the Tripod assembly towards the axle end until the Tripod seats on the circlip and the inner stop ring groove is exposed. Next, move the inner stop ring to its groove to secure the Tripod assembly (**see illustrations**).

42 On all axles, fill the outer race with CV joint grease and spread some on the inside of the boot as well (**see illustration**). The left axle Tripods use about 6.5 oz. of grease and the right axles use about 5 oz on the four-cylinder and about 7 oz. for the V6. Push the Tripod assembly into outer race and bend the six retaining tabs back to their original shape.

43 Wipe any excess grease from the axle boot groove on the outer race. Seat the small diameter of the boot in the recessed area on the axleshaft and install the clamp. Push the other end of the boot onto the outer race and move the race in-or-out to adjust the axle to the proper length (**see illustrations 9.22a and 9.22b**).

44 With the axle set to the proper length, equalize the pressure in the boot by inserting a dull screwdriver between the boot and the outer race (**see illustration 9.23**). Don't damage the boot with the tool.

45 Install the boot clamp. A pair of special clamp-crimping pliers are required (**see illustration 9.24**).

46 Install a new clip on the stub axle (**see illustration 9.25**).

47 Install the driveaxle as described in Section 8.

Outer CV joint and boot

Note: *On 1992 and later models, the outer CV joint is a non-serviceable item and is permanently retained to the driveaxle. If any damage or excessive wear occurs to the axle or the outer CV joint, the entire driveaxle assembly must be replaced (excluding the inner CV joint). Service to the outer CV joints*

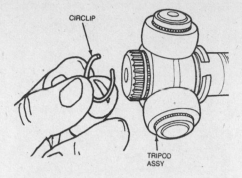

9.41a Installing the Tripod snap ring (V6 [both axles] and four-cylinder left axle)

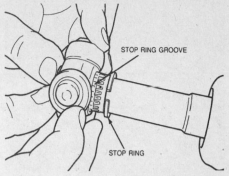

9.41b Push the Tripod assembly toward the axle end (V6 [both axles] and four-cylinder left axle) then install the stop ring in its groove

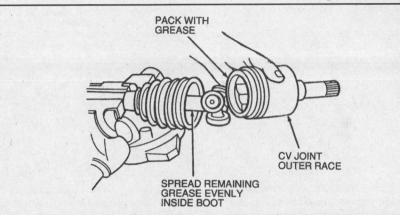

9.42 Apply grease to the outer race and spread some inside the boot

is limited to boot replacement and grease repacking only. Earlier year models use removable Double Offset-type CV joints and procedures for disassembly and reassembly are included in this Section.

Boot replacement (1992 and later models)

48 Remove the driveaxle from the vehicle (Section 8).

49 Mount the driveaxle in a vise. The jaws of the vise should be lined with wood or rags to prevent damage to the axleshaft.

50 Cut the boot clamps from both inner and outer boots and discard them (**see illustration 9.3**).

51 Remove inner CV joint and boot (see Steps 30 through 36).

52 Remove the outer CV joint boot. Wash the outer CV joint assembly in solvent and inspect it, as described in Step 12. Replace the axle assembly if any CV joint components are excessively worn. Install the new, outer boot and clamp onto the axleshaft (**see illustration 9.15**).

53 Repack the outer CV joint with CV joint grease and spread grease inside the new boot as well.

54 Position the outer boot on the CV joint and install new boot clamps, using boot clamp pliers (**see illustration 9.24**).

55 Reassemble the inner CV joint and boot (see Steps 37 through 45).

56 Install a new clip on the inner stub axle (**see illustration 9.25**).

57 Install the driveaxle as described in Section 8.

1991 and earlier models

Disassembly

Refer to illustrations 9.60, 9.62, 9.63, 9.64 and 9.65

58 Remove the driveaxle from the vehicle.

59 Follow the procedure in Steps 2 and 3 of this Section.

60 Slide the boot off the outer race. With a brass drift positioned on the inner race, dislodge the CV joint assembly from the axle (**see illustration**). A lot of force will be

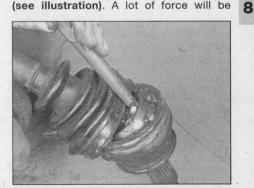

9.60 Dislodge the CV joint assembly with a brass drift and hammer (be careful not to let the joint fall)

8

9.62 Tilt the inner race far enough to allow ball removal - a brass punch can be used if the inner race is difficult to move

9.63 If necessary, pry the balls out with a screwdriver

9.64 Tilt the inner race and cage 90-degrees, then align the windows in the cage with the outer race lands and rotate the inner race up and out of the outer race

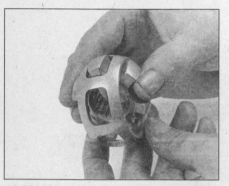

9.65 Align the inner race lands with the cage windows and rotate the inner race out of the cage

9.68 The beveled edge of the inner race (arrow) must face out when assembled

9.69 Align the cage windows and the inner and outer race grooves, then tilt the cage and inner race to insert the balls

required, as the inner race must overcome a circlip on the axleshaft. Do not let the CV joint assembly fall.

61   Mount the assembly in a vise lined with wood or rags.

62   Press down on the inner race far enough to allow a ball to be removed. If it's difficult, tap the inner race with a brass drift and a hammer **(see illustration)**.

63   Pry the balls from the cage, one at a time, with a blunt screwdriver or wooden tool **(see illustration)**.

64   With all of the balls removed from the cage and the cage/inner race assembly tilted 90-degrees, align the cage windows with the outer race lands and remove the assembly from the outer race **(see illustration)**.

65   Remove the inner race from the cage by turning the inner race 90-degrees in the cage, aligning the inner lands with the cage windows and rotating the inner race out of the cage **(see illustration)**.

Inspection

66   Wash all of the parts in solvent. Inspect the components as described in Step 12.

Reassembly

Refer to illustrations 9.68, 9.69, 9.70, and 9.74

67   Install the inner race in the cage by reversing the technique described in Step 65.

68   Install the inner race and cage assembly in the outer race by reversing the removal

method used in Step 64. The beveled edge of the inner race splined area must face out after it's installed in the outer race **(see illustration)**.

69   Press the balls into the cage windows **(see illustration)**.

70   Pack the CV joint assembly with CV joint grease through the inner splined hole. Force the grease into the bearing by inserting a wooden dowel through the splined hole and pushing it to the bottom of the joint. Repeat this procedure until the bearing is completely packed **(see illustration)**.

9.70 Apply grease through the splined hole, then insert a wooden dowel (approximately 15/16-inch diameter) into the hole and push down - the dowel will force the grease into the joint

71   Install the boot on the axleshaft as described in Step 15. Apply a liberal amount of grease to the inside of the boot.

72   Install a new stop ring in the groove in the axleshaft.

73   Install a new circlip on the inner end of the axleshaft.

74   Position the CV joint assembly on the axleshaft, aligning the splines. Using a brass or plastic hammer, drive the CV joint onto the axleshaft until it seats against the stop ring **(see illustration)**.

9.74 Line up the splines of the inner race with the axleshaft splines, then tap the CV joint assembly onto the shaft with a brass or plastic hammer until the inner race is seated against the stop ring

75   Install the boot and clamps **(see illustrations 9.23 and 9.24)**.

76   Install the driveaxle as described in Section 8.

10   Differential seals - replacement

Refer to illustrations 10.2 and 10.3

Caution: *Whenever both the right and left driveaxles are removed at the same time, the differential side gears must be supported so they don't fall into the case. A wooden dowel, approximately 15/16-inch in diameter, inserted into each side gear will work. If this precaution is not heeded and the side gears do drop, the differential will have to be removed from the transaxle to realign the gears (which will necessitate towing the vehicle to a Ford dealer service department or other repair shop).*

1   Refer to Section 8 and remove the driveaxle.

10.2 Carefully pry the old seal from the case with a screwdriver

2   Pry the seal from the transaxle case with a large screwdriver or prybar **(see illustration)**. Be careful not to damage the case.

3   Coat the outer edge of the new seal with oil or grease, then position it in the bore and

10.3 Drive the new seal into the case with a large socket (arrow) or piece of pipe - be careful not to cock the seal in the bore

carefully drive it in with a hammer and large socket (if a socket isn't available, a section of pipe will also work) **(see illustration)**.

4   Lubricate the seal lip with moly-base grease, then install the driveaxle (see Section 8).

8

Notes

Chapter 9 Brakes

Contents

Specifications

Brake fluid type .... See Chapter 1

Disc brakes

Brake disc	
Thickness	
Standard	0.945 inch
Minimum*	0.882 inch
Thickness variation limit (l-inch from edge)	0.0005 inch
Runout limit	0.003 inch
Minimum brake pad thickness	See Chapter 1

Refer to marks stamped on the disc (they supersede information printed here).

Drum brakes

Brake drum	
Diameter	
Standard	
1984 and 1985	8.006 inches
1986 on	8.065 inches
Maximum*	
1984 and 1985	8.065 inches
1988 on	8.124 inches
Out-of-round limit	0.005 inch
Minimum brake lining thickness	See Chapter 1

Refer to marks cast into the drum (they supersede information printed here).

Torque specifications

	Ft-lbs (unless otherwise indicated)
Brake caliper mounting pins	18 to 25
Brake hose-to-caliper bolt	30 to 40
Master cylinder to-booster nuts	13 to 25
Fluid control valve	96 to 120 in-lbs
Pressure control valves	10 to 18
Power brake booster nuts	13 to 15
Wheel cylinder bolts	108 to 156 in-lbs
Wheel lug nuts	See Chapter 1
Rear axle nut	
Step 1 (initial torque)	17 to 25
Step 2	Back off 1/2 turn
Step 3 (final torque)	
1988 and earlier	10 to 15 in-lbs
1989 and later	24 to 28 in-lbs

1   General information

Description

All models are equipped with disc type front and drum type rear brakes which are hydraulically operated and vacuum assisted.

The front brakes feature a single piston, floating caliper design. The rear drum brakes are leading/trailing shoe types with a single pivot.

The front disc brakes automatically compensate for pad wear during usage. The rear drum brakes also feature automatic adjustment.

Front drive vehicles tend to wear the front brake pads at a faster rate than rear drive vehicles. Consequently, it's important to inspect the brake pads frequently to make sure they haven't worn to the point where the disc itself is scored or damaged.

All models are equipped with a cable actuated parking brake which operates the rear brakes.

The hydraulic system is a diagonally-split type with a dual master cylinder. In the event of a brake line or seal failure, half the brake system will still operate. The master cylinder also incorporates two pressure control valves that reduce the pressure to the rear brakes in order to limit rear wheel lockup during hard braking.

Precautions

Use only DOT 3 brake fluid.

The brake pads and linings may contain asbestos fibers, which are hazardous to your health if inhaled. When working on brake system components, carefully clean all parts with brake system cleaner. Don't allow the fine dust to become airborne.

Safety should be paramount when working on brake system components. Don't use parts or fasteners that aren't in perfect condition and be sure that all clearances and torque specifications are adhered to. If you're at all unsure about a certain procedure, seek professional advice. When finished working on the brakes, test them carefully under controlled conditions before driving the vehicle in traffic. If a problem is suspected in the brake system, don't drive the vehicle until the fault is corrected.

2   Front brake pads - replacement

Refer to illustrations 2.4a through 2.4i
Warning: *Disc brake pads must be replaced* on both front wheels at the same time - never replace the pads on only one wheel. Also, the dust created by the brake system contains asbestos, which is harmful to your health. Never blow it out with compressed air and don't inhale any of it. An approved filtering mask should be worn when working on the brakes. Do not, under any circumstances, use petroleum-based solvents to clean brake parts. Use brake system cleaner only! When servicing the disc brakes, use only high quality, nationally recognized brand name pads.

1   Remove about two-thirds of the fluid from the master cylinder reservoir.

2   Loosen the wheel lug nuts, raise the vehicle and support it securely on jackstands. Remove the front wheels.

3   Check the disc carefully as outlined in Section 4. If machining is necessary, follow the procedure in Section 4 to remove the disc.

4   Follow the accompanying photos, beginning with illustration 2.4a, for the actual pad replacement procedure. Be sure to stay in order and read the information in the caption under each illustration.

5   Once the new pads are in place and the caliper pins have been installed and properly tightened, install the wheels and lower the vehicle to the ground. **Note:** *If the brake hose*

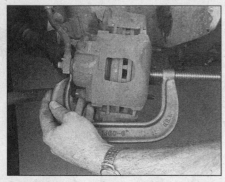

2.4a Using a large C-clamp, push the piston back into the caliper bore - note that one end of the clamp is on the flat area near the brake hose fitting and the other end (screw end) is pressing on the outer pad

2.4b Remove the two caliper mounting pins (this will require a special TORX socket)

2.4c Rotate the bottom of the caliper up and off the brake disc (don't put excessive strain on the brake hose or damage could occur)

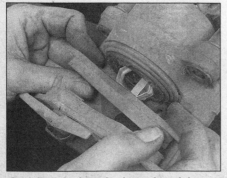

2.4d Pull the inner brake pad straight out of the caliper piston (inspect the piston for cracks and signs of leakage, which will warrant replacement of the caliper)

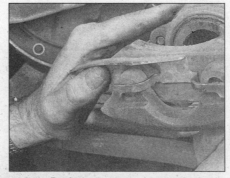

2.4e Push the outer pad towards the piston to dislodge the locating lugs from the caliper frame, then lift out the pad

2.4f Push the piston into the cylinder bore to provide room for the new pads to fit over the disc - use a block of wood and C-clamp; don't use excessive force or damage to the plastic piston will result

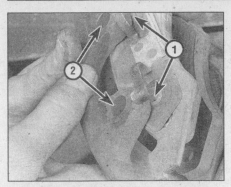

2.4g To install the new pads into the caliper, carefully push the inner pad retaining clips straight into the piston until the brake pad backing plate rests on the piston face - slide the outer pad into the caliper as shown (be sure the locating lugs on the pad [1] seat into the mounting holes in the caliper frames [2])

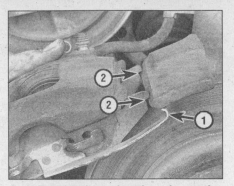

2.4h Position the anti-rattle spring on the outer pad (1) under the upper arm of the steering knuckle with the notches in the upper edge of both pads on the upper arm of the knuckle (2), rotate the caliper down until the notches in the opposite end of the pads seat against the lower arm of the steering knuckle (make sure the brake hose is not twisted)

2.4i Apply silicone grease to the caliper pins and to the inside of the pin insulators and insert the pins through the caliper housing into the steering knuckle arms (tighten them by hand first, then to the torque listed in this Chapter's Specifications)

was disconnected from the caliper for any reason, the brake system must be bled as described in Section 10.

6   Fill the master cylinder reservoir(s) with new brake fluid and slowly pump the brakes a few times to seat the pads against the rotor.

7   Check the fluid level in the master cylinder reservoirs one more time and then road test the vehicle carefully before driving it in traffic.

---

3 Front brake caliper - removal, overhaul and installation

Refer to illustrations 3.2a, 3.2b, 3.6, 3.7, 3.8, 3.9a, 3.9b, 3.11, 3.13, 3.14, 3.15 and 3.16.
Warning: *The dust created by the brake system may contain asbestos, which is hazardous to your health. Don't blow it out with compressed air and don't inhale any of it. An approved filtering mask should be worn when working on the brakes. Do not, under any circumstances, use petroleum-based solvents to clean brake parts. Use brake*

cleaner only! When servicing the disc brakes, use only high quality, nationally recognized brand name pads. **Note:** *If an overhaul is indicated (usually because of fluid leakage), explore all options before beginning the job. New and factory rebuilt calipers are available on an exchange basis, which makes the job easier. If it's decided to rebuild the calipers, make sure a rebuild kit is available before proceeding. Always rebuild the calipers in pairs - never rebuild just one of them.*

Removal

1   Loosen the wheel lug nuts, raise the vehicle and support it securely on jackstands. Remove the wheel.

2   Disconnect the brake hose from the back of the caliper **(see illustration)**. Have a rag handy for fluid spills and wrap a plastic bag around the end of the hose to prevent fluid loss and contamination. Discard the fittings washers - new ones should be used during installation. If the caliper is only being removed to get at the disc, don't detach the hose. Suspend the caliper with a piece of

wire from the strut **(see illustration)**. This will save the trouble of bleeding the brake system.

3   Refer to the first few Steps in Section 2 to separate the caliper from the knuckle and disc - it's part of the brake pad replacement procedure.

Overhaul

4   Refer to Section 2 and remove the brake pads from the caliper.

5   Clean the exterior of the caliper with brake system cleaner. Never use gasoline, kerosene or petroleum-based cleaning solvents. Place the caliper on a clean workbench.

6   Position a wooden block or numerous rags in the caliper as a cushion, then use compressed air to remove the piston from the caliper bore **(see illustration)**. Use only enough air pressure to ease the piston from the caliper. If the piston is blown out, it may be damaged. **Warning:** *Never place your fingers in front of the piston in an attempt to catch or protect it when applying air pressure, as serious injury could result.*

3.2a Removing the brake hose fitting bolt (be sure to use new sealing washers on each side of the fitting to prevent fluid leaks)

3.2b To avoid damage to the brake hose, support the caliper with a piece of wire

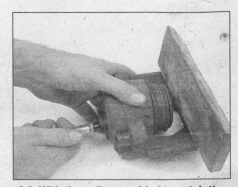

3.6 With the caliper padded to catch the piston, use compressed air to force the piston out of the bore - make sure your fingers are out of the way!

9

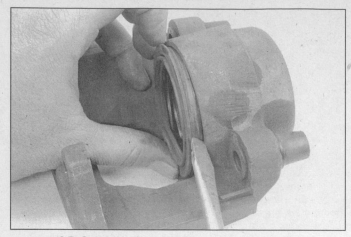

3.7 Carefully pry the dust boot from the caliper

3.8 To avoid damage to the caliper bore or seal groove, remove the seal with a plastic or wooden tool - a pencil works well

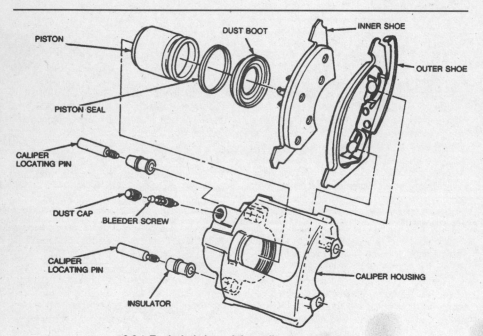

PISTON

DUST BOOT

INNER SHOE

OUTER SHOE

PISTON SEAL

CALIPER LOCATING PIN

DUST CAP

BLEEDER SCREW

CALIPER LOCATING PIN

INSULATOR

CALIPER HOUSING

3.9a Exploded view of the caliper components

7   Carefully pry the dust boot out of the caliper bore and discard it **(see illustration)**.

8   Using a plastic or wooden tool, remove the piston seal from the groove in the caliper bore and discard it **(see illustration)**.

9   Remove the mounting pins and remove and discard the pin insulators from caliper **(see illustrations)**.

10 Clean the remaining parts with brake cleaner or denatured alcohol.

11 Carefully examine the piston for surface irregularities or small chips and cracks **(see illustration)**. Replace piston if damaged.

12 Check the caliper bore for score marks, nicks, loss of plating and burrs. Light polishing of the bore with crocus cloth is permissible to remove light corrosion and stains.

13 When reassembling, lubricate the piston bore and new seal with brake fluid. Position the new piston seal into the caliper bore groove **(see illustration)**.

14 Install a new dust boot in the piston groove, with the flange facing up **(see illustration)**.

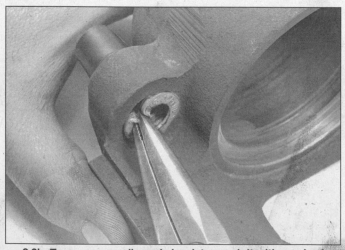

3.9b To remove a caliper pin insulator, grab it with a pair of needle-nose pliers, twist it and push it through the caliper frame

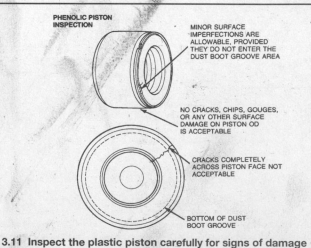

PHENOLIC PISTON INSPECTION

MINOR SURFACE IMPERFECTIONS ARE ALLOWABLE, PROVIDED THEY DO NOT ENTER THE DUST BOOT GROOVE AREA

NO CRACKS, CHIPS, GOUGES, OR ANY OTHER SURFACE DAMAGE ON PISTON OD IS ACCEPTABLE

CRACKS COMPLETELY ACROSS PISTON FACE NOT ACCEPTABLE

BOTTOM OF DUST BOOT GROOVE

3.11 Inspect the plastic piston carefully for signs of damage as shown

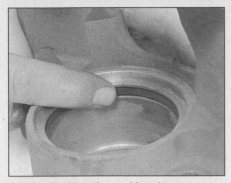

3.13 Position the seal into its groove, making sure it isn't twisted

3.14 Stretch the new boot over the top of the piston, making sure it rests in the piston groove - the flange must be nearest to the top of the piston

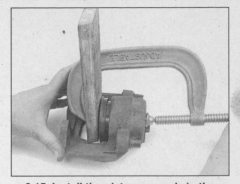

3.15 Install the piston squarely in the caliper bore, then push it in by hand as far as possible (it may be necessary to use a C-clamp and a block of wood to bottom the piston in the bore - work slowly, making sure the piston does not become cocked - it should slide in with very little resistance)

3.16 Use a punch to carefully seat the dust boot

15 Lubricate the piston with brake fluid and insert it squarely into the caliper bore, then push it into the bore with both hands. If it resists, place a wood block or other flat stock (like an old brake pad) over the piston and use a C-clamp to carefully press the piston into its bore until it seats **(see illustration)**. **Caution:** *Never use the C-clamp directly on the piston surface, as damage can result.*

16 Position the dust boot in the caliper bore, then use a punch to seat it **(see illustration)**.

17 Install new insulators in the caliper ears and fill the area inside the insulators with silicone grease.

18 Install the mounting pins through the caliper insulators.

Installation

19 Refer to Section 2 for the caliper installation procedure.

20 After the caliper is reinstalled, reconnect the brake hose (if removed) using new washers on each side of the brake hose fitting bolt. Tighten the bolt to the torque listed in this Chapter's Specifications.

21 Pump the brake pedal several times to bring the pads into contact with the disc.

22 Bleed the brakes as described in Section 10. This isn't necessary if the brake hose was left connected to the caliper (if the caliper was removed for access to other parts).

23 Install the wheel and lower the vehicle.

4   Brake disc - inspection, removal and installation

Refer to illustrations 4.2, 4.3a, 4.3b, 4.4a and 4.4b

Inspection

1 Loosen the wheel lug nuts, raise the vehicle and support it securely on jackstands. Remove the wheel and install two lug nuts to hold the disc in place.

2 Visually inspect the disc surface for score marks and other damage. Light scratches and shallow grooves are normal after use and may not be detrimental to brake operation. Deep score marks - over 0.015-inch - require disc removal and refinishing by an automotive machine shop. Be sure to check both sides of the disc **(see illustration)**.

3 To check disc runout, attach a dial indicator to the brake caliper and locate the stem about 1-inch from the outer edge of the disc **(see illustration)**. Set the indicator to zero and turn the disc. The indicator reading should not exceed the value listed in this Chapter's Specifications. If it does, the disc should be resurfaced by an automotive

machine shop. **Note:** *Professionals recommend resurfacing of brake discs regardless of the dial indicator reading (to produce a smooth, flat surface that will eliminate brake pedal pulsations and other undesirable symptoms related to questionable discs). At the very least, if you elect not to have the discs resurfaced, deglaze the brake pad surface with sandpaper or emery cloth (use a swirling motion to ensure a non-directional finish)* **(see illustration)**.

4.2 The brake pads on this vehicle were obviously neglected, as they were down to the rivets and cut deep grooves into the disc - wear this severe will require replacement of the disc

4.3a With two lug nuts installed to hold the disc in place, check the runout with a dial indicator - if the reading exceeds the maximum allowable runout limit, the disc will have to be machined or replaced

4.3b Using a swirling motion, remove the glaze from the disc with sandpaper or emery cloth.

Check brake operation carefully before driving the vehicle in traffic.

4.4a The minimum allowable thickness is cast into the inside of the disc

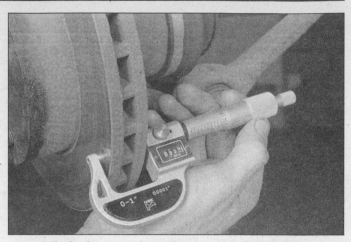

4.4b A micrometer is used to measure disc thickness

4   The disc should never be machined to a thickness under the specified minimum allowable thickness, which is cast into the inside of the disc itself **(see illustration)**. The disc thickness can be checked with a micrometer **(see illustration)**.

Removal and installation

5   Refer to Section 3 and remove the brake caliper. **Warning:** *Don't allow the caliper to hang by the brake hose and don't disconnect the hose from the caliper.*

6   Remove the two lug nuts which were put on to hold the disc in place and detach the disc from the hub.

7   Installation is the reverse of removal.

---

5   Rear brake drum - removal, inspection and installation

Refer to illustrations 5.2, 5.3, 5.6 and 5.9

Removal

1   Loosen the wheel lug nuts, raise the rear of the vehicle and support it securely on jackstands. Block the front wheels, then remove the rear wheel.

2   Remove the grease cap, cotter pin, nut lock and retaining nut **(see illustration)**.

3   Grasp the brake drum and pull it out far enough to dislodge the outer bearing and washer **(see illustration)**. If the drum is stuck, loosen the brake adjuster star wheel as shown in **illustration 6.9a**.

4   Remove the bearing.

5   Pull the hub/drum assembly off the axle.

Inspection

6   Check the drum for cracks, score marks, deep grooves and signs of overheating of the shoe contact surface. If the drums have blue spots, indicating overheated areas, they should be replaced. Also, look for grease or brake fluid on the shoe contact surface. Grease and brake fluid can be removed with denatured alcohol or brake cleaner, but the brake shoes must be replaced if they are contaminated. Surface glazing, which is a glossy, highly polished finish, can be removed with sandpaper or emery cloth **(see illustration)**. **Note:** *Professionals recommend resurfacing the drums whenever a brake job is done. Resurfacing will eliminate the possibility of out-of-round drums. If the drums are worn so much that they can't be surfaced without exceeding the maximum allowable*

diameter (stamped into the drum), then new ones will be required.

Installation

7   While the hub/drum assembly is off the vehicle, it's a good idea to clean, inspect and repack or, if necessary, replace the rear wheel bearings. Refer to Chapter 10 for rear wheel bearing service.

8   Place the hub/drum assembly on the axle, install the outer wheel bearings and washer and push the assembly into place.

9   Install the retaining nut and washer and tighten the nut to the initial specified torque while rotating the drum. Back off the adjusting nut 1/2 turn, then tighten the nut to the final torque **(see illustration)**.

10 Install the nut lock, cotter pin and grease cap. Be careful not to damage the grease cap. Install the wheel, lower the vehicle and tighten the lug nuts to the torque listed in this Chapter's Specifications.

---

6   Brake shoes - replacement

Refer to illustrations 6.5a through 6.5n, 6.8, 6.9a and 6.9b
Warning: *The brake shoes must be replaced on both rear wheels at the same time - never*

5.2 A hammer and chisel can be used to gently tap the grease cap from the hub/drum assembly

5.3 After the cotter pin and nut lock have been removed, pull the drum out to dislodge the bearing - be careful not to drop it

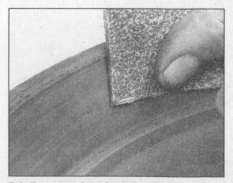

5.6 Remove glaze from the drum surfaces with sandpaper or emery cloth

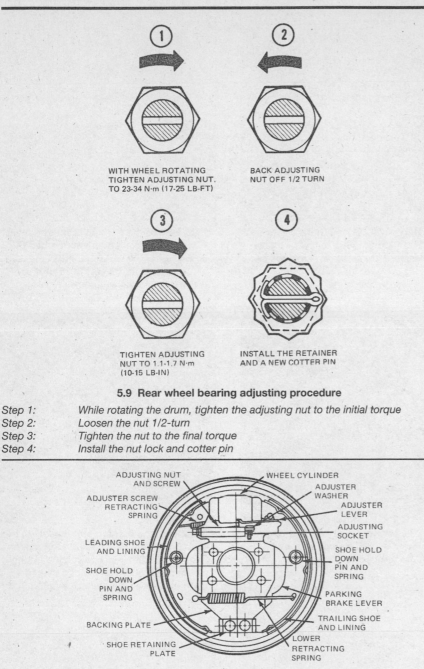

WITH WHEEL ROTATING
TIGHTEN ADJUSTING NUT.
TO 23-34 N·m (17-25 LB-FT)

BACK ADJUSTING
NUT OFF 1/2 TURN

TIGHTEN ADJUSTING
NUT TO 1.1-1.7 N·m
(10-15 LB-IN)

INSTALL THE RETAINER
AND A NEW COTTER PIN

5.9 Rear wheel bearing adjusting procedure

Step 1:   While rotating the drum, tighten the adjusting nut to the initial torque
Step 2:   Loosen the nut 1/2-turn
Step 3:   Tighten the nut to the final torque
Step 4:   Install the nut lock and cotter pin

ADJUSTING NUT
AND SCREW

WHEEL CYLINDER

ADJUSTER SCREW
RETRACTING
SPRING

ADJUSTER
WASHER

ADJUSTER
LEVER

ADJUSTING
SOCKET

LEADING SHOE
AND LINING

SHOE HOLD
DOWN
PIN AND
SPRING

SHOE HOLD
DOWN
PIN AND
SPRING

PARKING
BRAKE LEVER

BACKING PLATE

TRAILING SHOE
AND LINING

LOWER
RETRACTING
SPRING

SHOE RETAINING
PLATE

6.5a Rear drum brake components - left side shown

replace the shoes on only one wheel. Also, brake system dust may contain asbestos, which is harmful to your health. Never blow it out with compressed air and don't inhale any of it. Do not, under any circumstances, use petroleum-based solvents to clean brake parts. Use brake system cleaner only. Whenever the brake shoes are replaced, the return and hold-down springs should also be replaced. Due to the continuous heating/cooling cycle that the springs are subjected to, they lose their tension over a period of time and may allow the shoes to drag on the drum and wear at a much faster rate than normal. When replacing the rear brake shoes, use only high quality, nationally recognized brand-name parts.

1   Remove about two-thirds of the brake fluid from the master cylinder reservoir.

2   Loosen the wheel lug nuts, raise the rear of the vehicle and support it on jackstands. Block the front wheels and remove the rear wheels from the vehicle.

3   Refer to Section 5 and remove the brake drums.

4   Carefully inspect the brake drums as outlined in Section 5. Also inspect the wheel cylinder for fluid leakage as described in Chapter 1.

5   Follow the accompanying photos **(see illustrations 6.5a through 6.5n)** for the

6.5b Before removing any drum brake components, wash them off with brake cleaner and allow them to dry - position a drain pan under the brake to catch the residue - DO NOT USE COMPRESSED AIR TO BLOW THE BRAKE DUST FROM THE PARTS!

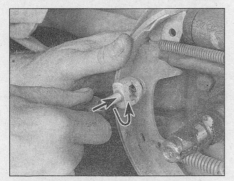

6.5c Depress and turn the spring retainers and remove the hold down springs and pins

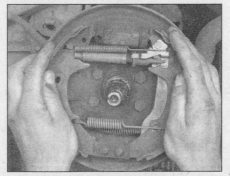

6.5d Slide the entire assembly up and off the shoe retaining plate (be careful not to bend the adjuster lever)

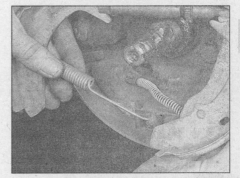

6.5e Unhook the lower retracting spring from the trailing brake shoe . . .

9

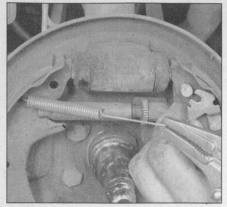

6.5f . . . then remove the adjuster screw retracting spring from the adjuster lever (at which time the adjuster lever, adjuster screw assembly and the leading brake shoe can also be removed)

6.5g Unclip the parking brake cable end from the parking brake lever on the trailing shoe, then remove the shoe and lever assembly

6.5h Spread the parking brake retaining clip with a screwdriver and remove the clip and spring washer (note that the lever mounts to the BACK SIDE of the trailing shoe)

6.5i Attach the parking brake lever to the new shoe, inserting the pivot pin through the front of the shoe, then through the lever - install the spring washer and retaining clip and crimp it closed with a pair of pliers

6.5j Lubricate the brake shoe contact areas (arrows) with high-temperature grease

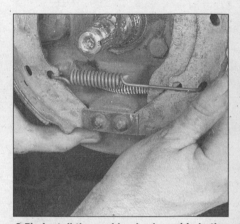

6.5k Install the parking brake cable in the lever, position the shoes on the backing plate, hook the lower retracting spring between the two shoes and slide the shoes down on the shoe retaining plate

6.5l Install the trailing shoe hold-down pin, spring and retainer, then insert the adjuster screw assembly into the trailing shoe as shown (be sure the correct letter is facing up, depending on the side of the vehicle you are working on)

6.5m Position the adjuster lever on the parking brake lever pivot pin . . . .

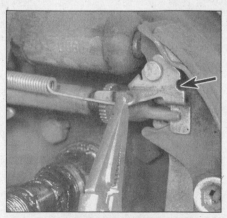

6.5n . . . then install the leading shoe hold-down pin, spring and retainer - stretch the adjuster screw retracting spring, WITH THE STRAIGHT PART OF THE SPRING OVER THE ADJUSTER LEVER , and hook it in the notch on the adjuster lever (arrow)

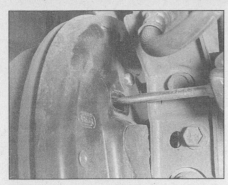

6.8 Turn the star wheel on the adjuster screw until the brake shoes drag on the drum . . .

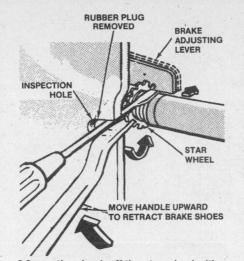

6.9a . . . then back off the star wheel with a brake tool while holding the adjuster lever away from the star wheel until the brake shoes drag just slightly on the drum (the drum must still be able to rotate freely)

6.9b Two screwdrivers may also be used to adjust the brakes

actual shoe replacement procedure. Be sure to stay in order and read the information in the caption under each illustration.

6 Once the new shoes are in place, install the hub/drum assembly as outlined in Section 5.

7 Remove the rubber plug from the brake backing plate.

8 Insert a narrow screwdriver or brake adjusting tool through the adjustment hole and turn the star wheel until the brakes drag slightly as the drum is turned **(see illustration)**.

9 Turn the star wheel in the opposite direction until the drum turns freely. Keep the adjuster lever from contacting the star wheel or it won't turn **(see illustrations)**.

10 Repeat the adjustment on the opposite wheel.

11 Install the plug in the backing plate access holes.

12 Install the wheels and lower the vehicle. Tighten the lug nuts to the torque listed in this Chapter's Specifications.

13 Adjust the parking brake as described in Section 11 of this Chapter.

14 Top off the master cylinder with brake fluid and pump the pedal several times. Lower the vehicle and check brake operation before driving the vehicle in traffic.

7 Wheel cylinder - removal and installation

Refer to illustration 7.3

Note: *If the wheel cylinder is leaking or malfunctioning, replace it with a new or factory rebuilt unit.*

1 Loosen the wheel lug nuts, raise the rear of the vehicle and support it on jackstands, then block the front wheels. Remove the rear wheel(s).

2 Remove the rear hub/drum (see Section 5) and brake shoes (see Section 6).

3 Disconnect the brake line from the back of the wheel cylinder and plug it **(see illustration)**.

4 Unbolt the wheel cylinder and remove it from the backing plate. Clean the backing plate and wheel cylinder mating surfaces.

5 Place the wheel cylinder and foam seal

into position on the backing plate. If the foam seal is damaged, apply RTV-type sealant to the wheel cylinder mating surface of the backing plate. Carefully insert the brake fitting into the cylinder and tighten it by hand.

6 Install the two wheel cylinder mounting bolts and tighten them securely.

7 Tighten the brake line fitting securely.

8 Install the brake shoes and the hub/drum (see Sections 6 and 5).

9 Bleed the brakes (see Section 10).

10 Install the wheels and lower the vehicle. Check the brakes for proper operation before driving the vehicle in traffic.

8 Master cylinder - removal, overhaul and installation

Refer to illustrations 8.2a, 8.2b, 8.4a, 8.4b, 8.9, 8.11

Note: *The master cylinder installed on this vehicle features a plastic reservoir mated to an aluminum body. If service is indicated*

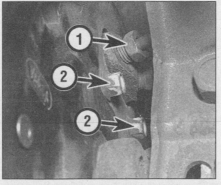

7.3 Unscrew the brake line fitting (1), then remove the two wheel cylinder bolts (2)

(usually because of insufficient pedal resistance or no resistance at all, or external fluid leakage) it's recommended that the master cylinder be replaced rather than attempt to rebuild it. New and factory rebuilt units are available on an exchange basis, which makes this job quite easy and will ensure that the master cylinder is in top condition. If it's decided to rebuild the master cylinder, make sure a rebuild kit is available before proceeding. The factory recommends replacing the piston assemblies (including the seals) as opposed to just the seals alone. In addition, if the plastic reservoir must be removed from the master cylinder, the reservoir must be replaced.

Removal

1 Place rags under the fittings and prepare caps or plastic bags to cover the ends of the lines once they are disconnected. Remove as much fluid as possible with a suction gun before starting this procedure. **Caution:** *Brake fluid will damage paint. Cover all body parts and be careful not to spill fluid during this procedure.*

2 Loosen the fittings at the ends of the brake lines where they enter the master cylinder **(see illustration)**. To prevent rounding off the flats, use a flare-nut wrench, which wraps around the nut. **Note:** *On later models, the lines exit the master cylinder through the bottom and require a back-up wrench to hold the pressure control valves*

8.2a Unscrew the brake line fittings (4) from the master cylinder - a flare nut wrench is recommended

9

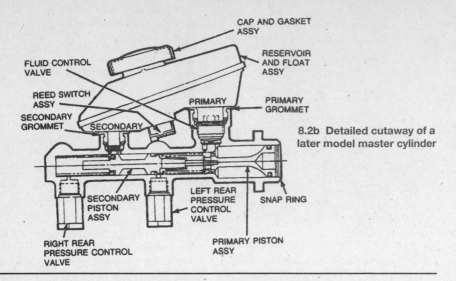

FLUID CONTROL VALVE

REED SWITCH ASSY

SECONDARY GROMMET

SECONDARY

PRIMARY

CAP AND GASKET ASSY

RESERVOIR AND FLOAT ASSY

PRIMARY GROMMET

SECONDARY PISTON ASSY

RIGHT REAR PRESSURE CONTROL VALVE

LEFT REAR PRESSURE CONTROL VALVE

SNAP RING

PRIMARY PISTON ASSY

8.2b Detailed cutaway of a later model master cylinder

while loosening the line fittings **(see illustration)**.

3   Pull the brake lines away from the master cylinder slightly and plug the ends to prevent contamination.

4   Unplug the electrical connector at the master cylinder, then remove the two nuts attaching the master cylinder to the power booster **(see illustrations)**. Pull the master cylinder off the studs and lift it out of the engine compartment. Again, be careful not to spill the fluid as this is done.

Overhaul

5   Mount the master cylinder in a vise. Be sure to line the vise jaws with rags or blocks of wood to prevent damage to the cylinder body.

6   Remove the primary piston snap-ring by depressing the piston and removing the ring with snap-ring pliers.

7   Remove the primary piston assembly from the bore.

8   Remove the secondary piston assembly from the bore. It may be necessary to remove the master cylinder from the vise and invert it, carefully tapping it against a block of wood to expel the piston.

9   If the reservoir grommets have been leaking, pry the reservoir from the master cylinder **(see illustration)**. **Warning:** *If the reservoir is removed, it must be replaced with a new one.*

10   If you removed the reservoir, also remove the sealing grommets from the master cylinder.

11   Using a 12mm socket, remove the fluid control valve from the master cylinder and inspect for contamination under the seal or in the center orifice **(see illustration)**. **Note:** *Other than cleaning, the fluid control valve is not serviceable and must be replaced as an assembly.*

12   On later models, remove the pressure control valves and inspect them for contami-

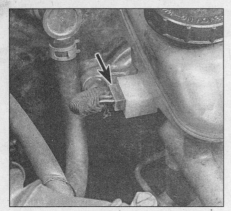

8.4a Unplug the electrical connector from the master cylinder reservoir (dislodge the locking tab on the underside of the connector to allow removal)

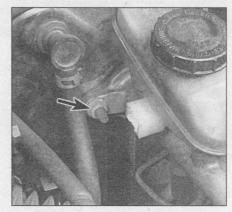

8.4b Remove the two master cylinder mounting nuts and pull the master cylinder off the power booster

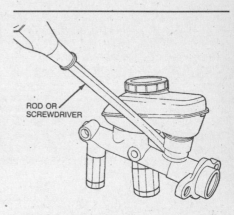

ROD OR SCREWDRIVER

8.9 If it's necessary to remove the fluid reservoir (to replace leaking seals or a broken reservoir), pry it off with a screwdriver

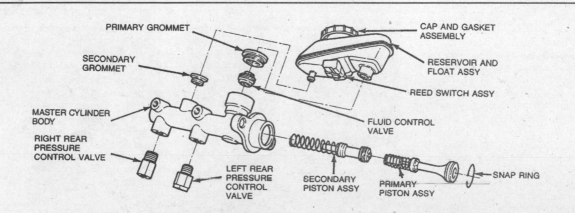

PRIMARY GROMMET

SECONDARY GROMMET

MASTER CYLINDER BODY

RIGHT REAR PRESSURE CONTROL VALVE

LEFT REAR PRESSURE CONTROL VALVE

SECONDARY PISTON ASSY

PRIMARY PISTON ASSY

CAP AND GASKET ASSEMBLY

RESERVOIR AND FLOAT ASSY

REED SWITCH ASSY

FLUID CONTROL VALVE

SNAP RING

8.11 Exploded view of the master cylinder

nation **(see illustration 8.2b).**

13 Clean the master cylinder body, the primary and secondary piston assemblies, fluid control valve, pressure control valves and the reservoir with brake system cleaner. **Warning:** *DO NOT, under any circumstances, use petroleum-based solvents to clean brake parts.*

14 Inspect the master cylinder piston bore for corrosion and score marks. If any corrosion or damage in the bore is evident, replace the master cylinder assembly. Don't use abrasives to try to clean it up.

15 Inspect the reservoir for cracks and distortion. If any damage is evident, replace it.

16 Dip new replacement piston assemblies in clean brake fluid.

17 Lubricate the cylinder bore with clean brake fluid and install the secondary (smaller) piston assembly into the bore, spring end first **(see illustration 8.11).**

18 Install the primary piston assembly in the cylinder bore, spring end first **(see illustration 8.11)**, depress it and install the snap-ring.

19 Install the fluid control valve and tighten it to the torque listed in this Chapter's Specifications.

20 If the reservoir was removed, install new grommets in the master cylinder, lubricating them with brake fluid first.

21 Install a new reservoir if the old one was removed.

22 On later models, reinstall the pressure control valves and tighten them to the torque listed in this Chapter's Specifications.

23 **Note:** *Whenever the master cylinder is removed, the complete hydraulic system must be bled. The time required to bleed the system can be reduced if the master cylinder is filled with fluid and bench bled before it's installed on the vehicle (refer to Steps 24 through 28).*

24 Insert threaded plugs of the correct size into the brake line outlet holes and fill the reservoirs with brake fluid. The master cylinder should be supported so brake fluid won't spill during the bench bleeding procedure.

25 Loosen one plug at a time and push the piston assembly into the bore to force air from the master cylinder. To prevent air from being drawn back in, the appropriate plug must be tightened before allowing the piston to return to its original position.

26 Stroke the piston three or four times for each outlet to ensure that all the air has been expelled.

27 Since high pressure isn't involved in the bench bleeding procedure, there is an alternative to the removal and replacement of the plugs with each stroke of the piston assembly. Before pushing in on the piston assembly, remove one of the plugs completely. Before releasing the piston, however, instead of replacing the plug, simply put your finger tightly over the hole to keep air from being drawn back into the master cylinder. Wait several seconds for the brake fluid to be drawn from the reservoir into the piston bore, then repeat the procedure.

When you push down on the piston it'll force your finger off the hole, allowing the air inside to be expelled. When only brake fluid is being ejected from the hole, replace the plug and go on to the other port.

28 Refill the master cylinder reservoir and install the cap.

Installation

29 Install the master cylinder over the studs on the power brake booster and tighten the nuts only finger tight at this time.

30 Using your fingers, thread the brake line fittings into the master cylinder. Since the master cylinder is still a bit loose, it can be moved slightly in order for the fittings to thread in easily. Don't strip the threads as the fittings are tightened.

31 Tighten the brake line fittings and the two mounting nuts.

32 Fill the master cylinder reservoir with brake fluid. It will be necessary to bleed the master cylinder to remove any air that may be present.

33 Place plenty of rags or newspapers under and around the master cylinder to absorb the brake fluid that will escape during the bleeding process. It is also recommended that eye protection be worn while performing the bleeding procedure.

34 With an assistant seated in the driver's seat, loosen the upper secondary brake line fitting, the one closest to the front of the vehicle, approximately 3/4-turn. Have your assistant push the brake pedal slowly to the floor and hold it there. Tighten the fitting and have the assistant slowly return the pedal to the released position. Wait five seconds, then repeat this operation until the stream of fluid from the loosened fitting is free of air bubbles.

35 Repeat the procedure at the upper primary brake line fitting (the one closest to the power booster). Be sure to keep an eye on the fluid level.

36 Fill the reservoir to the MAX indicator and install the filler cap.

37 Remove the newspapers or rags. Be

careful not to let any brake fluid drip on the vehicle's paint. Rinse the area around the master cylinder with water immediately to wash away residual fluid that will damage the engine compartment paint.

38 Refer to Section 10 for further brake hydraulic system bleeding.

9 Brake hoses and lines - inspection and replacement

Refer to illustration 9.3

Inspection

1 About every six months, with the vehicle raised and supported securely on jackstands. the rubber hoses which connect the steel brake lines with the front and rear brake assemblies should be inspected for cracks, chafing of the outer cover, leaks, blisters and other damage. These are important and vulnerable parts of the brake system and inspection should be complete. A light and mirror will he helpful for a thorough check. If a hose exhibits any of the above conditions, replace it with a new one.

Flexible hose replacement

2 Clean all dirt away from the ends of the hose.

3 Disconnect the brake line from the hose fitting using a back-up wrench on the fitting **(see illustration)**. Be careful not to bend the frame bracket or line. If necessary, soak the connections with penetrating oil.

4 Unbolt the hose bracket from the strut assembly.

5 Remove the U-clip from the female fitting at the bracket **(see illustration 9.3)** and remove the hose from the bracket.

6 Disconnect the hose from the caliper, discarding the copper washers on either side of the fitting block.

7 Using new copper washers, attach the new brake hose to the caliper. Tighten the fluid fitting bolt to the torque listed in this Chapter's Specifications.

8 Pass the female fitting through the frame bracket. With the least amount of twist in the hose, install the fitting in this position (use the stripe on the hose to help determine twist). **Note:** *The weight of the vehicle should be on the suspension, so the vehicle should not be raised while positioning the hose.*

9 Install the U-clip in the female fitting at the frame bracket.

10 Attach the brake line to the hose fitting using a back-up wrench on the fitting.

11 Mount the brake hose bracket to the strut assembly.

12 Carefully check to make sure the suspension or steering components don't make contact with the hose. Have an assistant push on the vehicle and also turn the steering wheel from lock-to-lock during inspection.

13 Bleed the brake system as described in Section 10.

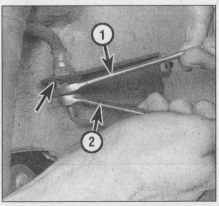

9.3 To disconnect the brake hose from the steel brake line, place a back-up wrench (1) on the hose fitting and loosen the tube nut with a flare nut wrench (2) (the U-clip [arrow] can now be removed)

10.8 When bleeding the brakes, a hose is connected to the bleeder screw and then submerged in brake fluid, - air will be seen as bubbles in the container and the hose (all air must be removed before continuing to the next wheel)

11.5 The center console trim panel must be removed to reveal the parking brake adjusting nut (arrow)

Rigid brake line replacement

14　When replacing brake lines, be sure to use the correct parts. Don't use copper tubing for any brake system components. Purchase steel brake lines from a dealer or auto parts store.

15　Prefabricated brake line, with the tube ends already flared and fittings installed, is available at auto parts stores and dealers. These lines are also bent to the proper shapes. Since brake lines are critical to driving safety, we don't recommend fabricating your own brake lines.

16　Bleed the brake system as outlined in the next Section and test the brakes carefully before driving the vehicle in traffic.

10　Brake hydraulic system - bleeding

Refer to illustration 10.8
Warning: *Wear eye protection when bleeding the brake system. If the fluid comes in contact with your eyes, immediately rinse them with water and seek medical attention.*

1　Bleeding the hydraulic system is necessary to remove any air that manages to find its way into the system as a result of removal and installation of a hose, line, caliper or master cylinder. Use only the specified fluid in this system or extensive damage could result. It will probably he necessary to bleed the system at all four brakes if air has entered the system due to low fluid level, or if the brake lines have been disconnected at the master cylinder.

2　If a brake line was disconnected only at one wheel, then only that caliper (or wheel cylinder) must be bled.

3　If a brake line is disconnected at a fitting located between the master cylinder and any of the brakes, that part of the system served by the disconnected line must be bled.

4　Remove any residual vacuum from the power brake booster by applying the brake several times with the engine off.

5　Remove the master cylinder reservoir cap and fill the reservoir with brake fluid. Reinstall the cap. **Note:** *Check the fluid level often during the bleeding operation and add fluid as necessary to prevent the level from falling low enough to allow air bubbles into the master cylinder.*

6　Have an assistant on hand, as well as a supply of new brake fluid, an empty clear plastic container, a length of 3l16-inch clear plastic or vinyl tubing to fit over the bleeder screw and a wrench to open and close the bleeder screw.

7　Beginning at the right rear wheel, loosen the bleeder screw slightly, then tighten it to a point where it's snug but can still be loosened quickly and easily.

8　Place one end of the tubing over the bleeder screw and submerge the other end in brake fluid in the container **(see illustration)**.

9　Have an assistant pump the brakes a few times to get pressure in the system, then hold the pedal down.

10　While the pedal is held down, open the bleeder screw until brake fluid begins to flow. Watch for air bubbles to exit the submerged end of the tube. When the fluid flow slows after a couple of seconds, tighten the screw and have your assistant release the pedal slowly.

11　Repeat Steps 9 and 10 until no more air is seen leaving the tube, then tighten the bleeder screw and proceed to the left front wheel, the left rear wheel and the right front wheel, in that order, and perform the same procedure. Be sure to check the fluid in the master cylinder reservoir frequently.

12　Never use old brake fluid. It contains moisture which will deteriorate the brake system components. Moisture in the brake fluid can also cause the fluid to boil under heavy braking conditions, which could cause a loss of pressure in the hydraulic system.

13　Refill the master cylinder with fluid at the end of the operation.

14　Check the operation of the brakes. The pedal should feel solid when depressed, with no sponginess. If necessary, repeat the entire process. **Warning**: *Do not operate the vehicle if you are in doubt about the effectiveness of the brake system.*

11　Parking brake - adjustment

Refer to illustration 11.5
Note: *Prior to adjusting the parking brake, verify that the rear brakes are properly adjusted (see Section 6).*

1　Start the engine and firmly depress the brake pedal several times to seat the shoes in the brake drum. Turn off the engine.

2　Raise the rear of the vehicle and support it securely on jackstands. Block the front wheels.

3　Remove the console trim surrounding the parking brake lever (refer to Chapter 11).

4　Pull up on the parking brake lever until the twelfth notch is engaged (listen for the clicks).

5　Tighten the adjusting nut until approximately 1-inch of the threaded adjuster rod is exposed beyond the nut **(see illustration)**.

6　Release the lever and rotate the rear wheels. The wheels should turn freely, but a slight drag is acceptable.

7　If the brake lever travels too far or the parking brake fails to hold the vehicle on a hill, tighten the adjusting nut a little more and recheck the operation of the parking brake.

12　Parking brake cables - removal and installation

Refer to illustrations 12.4 and 12.7

Removal

1　Remove the console trim that surrounds the parking brake lever. Partially apply the parking brake lever to gain access to the adjusting nut. Loosen but do not remove the nut, then return the lever to the released position.

2   Loosen the wheel lug nuts on the side of the vehicle that the cable is to be removed from, raise the rear of the vehicle and support it on jackstands. Block the front wheels.

3   Remove the wheel and the brake drum (see Section 5).

4   Disengage the parking brake cable from the equalizer, located above the exhaust pipe and heat shield in the floor pan tunnel **(see illustration)**. It may be necessary to remove the exhaust pipe and heat shield to gain access to the equalizer (see Chapter 4).

5   Remove the cable retaining clips from the fuel tank support bracket and the screw from the rear tie-rod mounting bracket.

6   Unhook the other cable end from the brake shoe lever. Refer to Section 6 in this Chapter if necessary.

7   Depress the cable housing retention tangs and pull the cable from the backing plate **(see illustration)**.

Installation

8   Push the cable and housing through the backing plate until the retention tangs pop into place. Attach the cable end to the parking brake lever.

9   Attach the cable housing retaining clip to the rear tie-rod mounting bracket.

10 Route the cable around the fuel tank and install the retaining clips.

11 Slip the cable end into the equalizer.

12 Reinstall the brake drum and wheel.

13 Install the heat shield and exhaust pipe if previously removed.

14 Lower the vehicle and adjust the parking brake as outlined in Section 11.

13   Power brake booster - check, removal, installation and adjustment

Refer to illustrations 13.9, 13.15 and 13.19

1   The power brake booster unit requires no special maintenance apart from periodic inspection of the vacuum hose and the case.

2   Dismantling of the brake booster requires special tools and is not ordinarily done by the home mechanic. If a problem develops, install a new or factory rebuilt unit.

Operating check

3   Depress the brake pedal several times with the engine off and make sure that there is no change in the pedal reserve distance.

4   Depress the pedal and start the engine. If the pedal goes down slightly, operation is normal.

Airtightness check

5   Start the engine and turn it off after one or two minutes.

Depress the brake pedal several times slowly. If the pedal goes down farther the first time but gradually rises after the second or third depression, the booster is airtight.

6   Depress the brake pedal while the engine is running, then stop the engine with the pedal depressed. If there is no change in the pedal reserve travel after holding the pedal for 30 seconds, the booster is airtight.

Removal

7   Remove the master cylinder (see Section 8).

8   Disconnect the vacuum hose where it attaches to the power brake booster.

9   Working in the passenger compartment under the steering column, unplug the wiring connector from the brake light switch, then remove the pushrod retaining clip and nylon washer from the brake pedal pin. Slide the pushrod off the pin **(see illustration)**.

10 Also remove the nuts attaching the brake booster to the firewall **(see illustration 13.9)**.

11 Carefully detach the booster from the firewall and lift it out of the engine compartment.

Installation

12 Place the booster into position on the firewall and tighten the mounting nuts. Connect the pushrod and brake light switch to the brake pedal. Install the retaining clip in

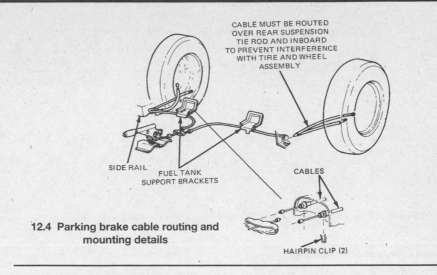

CABLE MUST BE ROUTED OVER REAR SUSPENSION TIE ROD AND INBOARD TO PREVENT INTERFERENCE WITH TIRE AND WHEEL ASSEMBLY

SIDE RAIL

FUEL TANK SUPPORT BRACKETS

CABLES

HAIRPIN CLIP (2)

12.4 Parking brake cable routing and mounting details

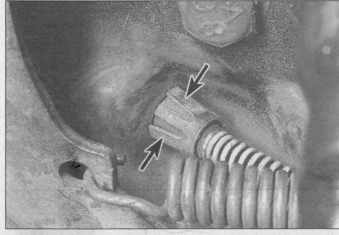

12.7 Depress the retention tangs (arrows) to free the cable and housing from the brake backing plate

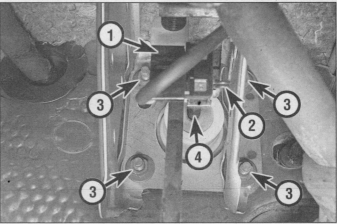

13.9 The following under-dash components must be removed to allow power brake booster removal

1 Brake light switch electrical connector	3 Booster mounting nuts
2 Pushrod retaining clip	4 Pushrod

9

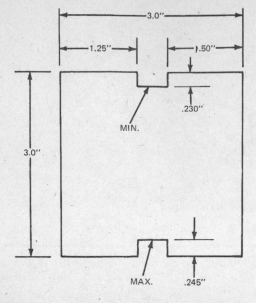

13.15 Power brake booster pushrod gauge template

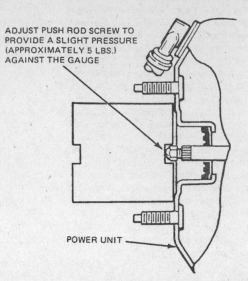

ADJUST PUSH ROD SCREW TO
PROVIDE A SLIGHT PRESSURE
(APPROXIMATELY 5 LBS.)
AGAINST THE GAUGE

POWER UNIT

**13.19 Checking the pushrod length (the pushrod is factory preset
and most likely will never need adjustment)**

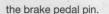

the brake pedal pin.

13 Install the master cylinder and vacuum hose. Refer to Section 8 for the master cylinder bleeding procedure.

14 Carefully check the operation of the brakes before driving the vehicle in traffic.

Adjustment

15 Some boosters features an adjustable pushrod. They are matched to the booster at the factory and most likely will not require adjustment, but if a misadjusted pushrod is suspected, a gauge can be fabricated out of heavy gauge sheet metal using the accompanying template **(see illustration)**.

16 Some common symptoms caused by a misadjusted pushrod include dragging brakes (if the pushrod is too long) or excessive brake pedal travel accompanied by a groaning sound from the brake booster (if

the pushrod is too short).

17 To check the pushrod length, unbolt the master cylinder from the booster and position it to one side. It isn't necessary to disconnect the hydraulic lines, but be careful not to bend them.

18 Block the front wheels, apply the parking brake and place the transaxle in Park or Neutral.

19 Start the engine and place the pushrod gauge against the end of the pushrod, exerting a force of approximately five pounds to seat the pushrod in the power unit **(see illustration)**. The rod measurement should fall somewhere between the minimum and maximum cutouts on the gauge. If it doesn't, adjust it by holding the knurled portion of the pushrod with a pair of pliers and turning the end with a wrench.

20 When the adjustment is complete, reinstall the master cylinder and check for

proper brake operation before driving the vehicle in traffic.

14 Brake light switch - removal and installation

Refer to illustration 14.2

Removal

1 Remove the under dash panel.

2 Locate the switch near the top of the brake pedal and disconnect the electrical connector **(see illustration)**.

3 Remove the pushrod retaining clip and nylon washer from the brake pedal pin and slide the pushrod off far enough for the outer hole of the switch to clear the pin. Now pull up on the switch to remove it.

Installation

4 Position the switch so it straddles the pushrod and the slot on the inner side of the switch rests on the pedal pin. Slide the pushrod and switch back onto the pin, then install the nylon washer and retaining clip.

5 Reconnect the electrical connector.

6 Install the under dash panel.

7 Check the brake lights for proper operation.

15 Brake pedal - removal and installation

Refer to illustration 15.4

Removal

1 Disconnect the cable from the negative terminal of the battery.

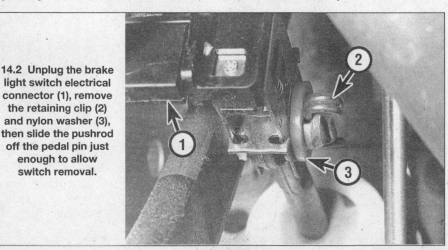

14.2 Unplug the brake light switch electrical connector (1), remove the retaining clip (2) and nylon washer (3), then slide the pushrod off the pedal pin just enough to allow switch removal.

2 Remove the under dash panel and unplug the electrical connector from the brake light switch.

3 Disconnect the brake pedal from the power brake booster pushrod by removing the retaining clip and washer and sliding the pushrod off the pedal pin **(see illustration 14.2)**.

4 Remove the nut and pivot bolt from the top of the pedal **(see illustration)**.

5 The brake pedal, spacer and bushings can now be removed from the bracket.

Installation

6 Use new bushings and lubricate the bushings, spacer, bolt and all friction parts with a light coat of engine oil.

7 Place the pedal, bushings and spacer in position and slide the pivot bolt into place. Note that it should be installed with the head on the left side of the bracket.

8 Tighten the nut and attach the booster pushrod and brake light switch to the pedal.

9 Operate the brake pedal several times to ensure proper operation.

10 Connect the wire harness to the brake light switch and install the under dash cover. Connect the battery.

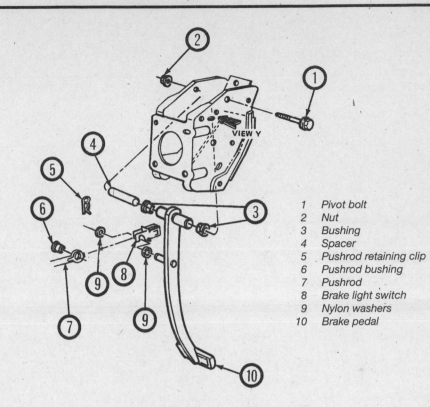

1   Pivot bolt
2   Nut
3   Bushing
4   Spacer
5   Pushrod retaining clip
6   Pushrod bushing
7   Pushrod
8   Brake light switch
9   Nylon washers
10 Brake pedal

15.4 Brake pedal installation details

9

Notes

Chapter 10
Suspension and steering systems

Contents

Specifications

Torque specifications

	Ft-lbs
Front suspension	
Strut-to-shock tower nuts	25 to 30
Strut-to-steering knuckle pinch bolt	68 to 81
Strut damper shaft nut	35 to 46
Control arm-to-body pivot bolt nut	48 to 55
Control arm-to-steering knuckle pinch bolt nut	38 to 45
Stabilizer bar-to-control arm nut	98 to 115
Stabilizer bar U-bracket bolts	66 to 77
Rear suspension	
Strut-to-shock tower nuts	25 to 30
Strut-to-spindle bolts	85 to 96
Strut shaft nut	35 to 46
Control arm-to-spindle bolt/nut	60 to 80
Control arm-to-inner mount bolt/nut	30 to 40
Rear stabilizer bar U-bracket bolts	18 to 22
Rear stabilizer bar to link nuts	6 to 17
Rear stabilizer bar link to strut bracket nuts	6 to 17
Tie-rod-to-spindle nut	46 to 53
Tie-rod-to-body nut	40 to 53
Steering system	
Steering wheel-to-steering shaft	
1984 and 1985 (nut)	30 to 40
1986 and 1987 (bolt)	30 to 35
1988 on (bolt)	25 to 34
Intermediate shaft clamp bolts	20 to 37
Steering gear mounting bracket bolts	
1984 through 1986	48 to 55
1987	55 to 70
1988 on	40 to 55
Tie-rod end-to-steering knuckle*	27 to 32
Wheel lug nuts	See Chapter 1
Power steering pump-to-mounting bracket	15 to 22

* Tighten to the minimum specified torque, then align the next slot in the nut with the cotter pin hole.

10

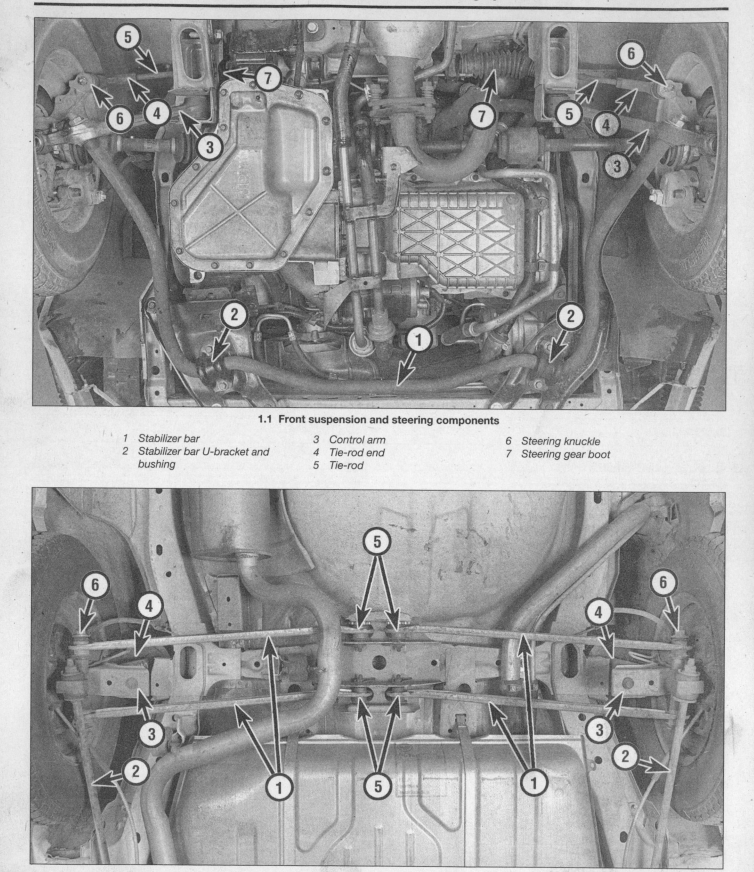

1.1 Front suspension and steering components

1	Stabilizer bar	3	Control arm	6	Steering knuckle
2	Stabilizer bar U-bracket and bushing	4	Tie-rod end	7	Steering gear boot
		5	Tie-rod		

1.2 Rear suspension components

1	Control arm	3	Suspension stop bracket	5	Inner control arm mounts
2	Tie-rod	4	Strut/spring assembly	6	Control arm-to-spindle mounting bolt/nut

1 General information

Refer to illustrations 1.1 and 1.2
Warning: *On models so equipped, whenever working in the vicinity of the front grille/bumper, steering wheel, steering column or other components of the airbag system, the system should be disarmed. To do this, perform the following steps:*

a) *Turn the ignition switch to Off.*
b) *Detach the cable from the negative battery terminal, then detach the positive cable. Wait two minutes for the electronic module backup power supply to be depleted.*

To enable the system

a) *Turn the ignition switch to the Off position.*
b) *Connect the positive battery cable first, then connect the negative cable.*

The front suspension is a MacPherson strut design. The steering knuckle is located by a control arm and both front control arms are connected by a stabilizer bar, which also controls fore-and-aft movement of the control arms **(see illustration).**

The rear suspension also utilizes MacPherson struts. Lateral movement is controlled by two parallel control arms on each side, with longitudinally mounted tie-rods between the body and the rear spindles **(see illustration).**

The rack-and-pinion steering gear is located behind the engine/transaxle assembly on the firewall and actuates the steering arms which are integral with the steering knuckles. Most vehicles are equipped with power steering. The steering column is connected to the steering gear through an articulated intermediate shaft. The steering column is designed to collapse in the event of an accident.

Note: *These vehicles use a combination of standard and metric fasteners on the various suspension and steering components, so it would be a good idea to have both types of tools available when beginning work.*

Warning: *Whenever any of the suspension or steering fasteners are loosened or removed they must be inspected and if necessary, replaced with new ones of the same part number or of original equipment quality and design. Torque specifications must be followed for proper reassembly and component retention.*

2 Front stabilizer bar and bushings - removal and installation

Refer to illustrations 2.2, 2.3a, 2.3b, 2.4 and 2.6

Note: *The stabilizer bar used on this vehicle is unique in that it also serves to prevent longitudinal movement of the control arms.*

Removal

1   Raise the vehicle and support it securely on jackstands. If only the stabilizer bar bushings are being replaced, proceed to Step 4, then to Step 6, as it isn't necessary to unbolt the stabilizer bar from the control arms for bushing replacement.
2   Remove both large stabilizer-to-control arm nuts and concave washers **(see illustration).**
3   Remove the control arm-to-body pivot bolt from one side of the vehicle **(see illustrations).**
4   Remove the four stabilizer bar U-bracket bolts. Support the bar while removing the last two bolts to prevent the stabilizer bar from falling **(see illustration).**

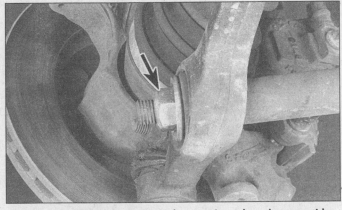

2.2 The stabilizer bar-to-control arm nuts and washers must be removed to separate the bar from the control arms (note how the washer is dished away from the control arm bushing)

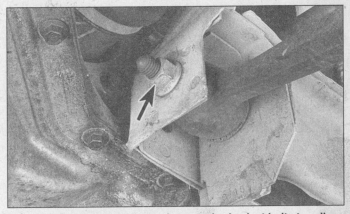

2.3a Remove one of the control arm-to-body pivot bolts to relieve tension on the stabilizer bar

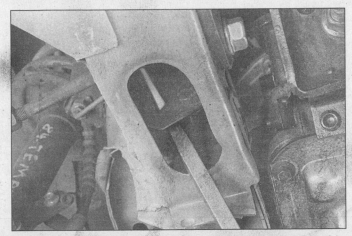

2.3b Pry the control arm pivot bolt from the control arm and body bracket

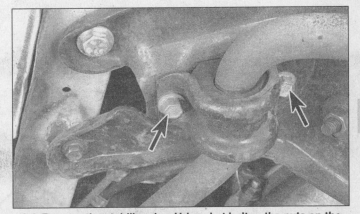

2.4 Remove the stabilizer bar U-bracket bolts - the nuts on the other side of the mounting bracket are pressed into the bracket and don't require a wrench unless they strip out (in which case a wrench must be used to hold them)

10

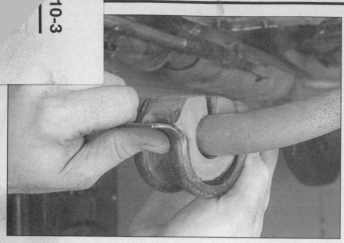

2.6 Use a rocking motion to detach the U-brackets from the bushings

4.4 Remove the balljoint pinch bolt from the steering knuckle - after the nut is removed, a punch may be used to drive the bolt out

5   Separate the stabilizer bar from the control arms (be careful not to lose the stabilizer bar-to-control arm spacers).

Bushing replacement

6   Pull the U-bracket off the stabilizer bar and rubber bushing using a rocking motion **(see illustration).**
7   Remove the rubber bushing from the bar and clean the bushing area with a stiff wire brush to remove any rust or dirt.
8   Lubricate the inside and outside of the new bushing with vegetable oil (used in cooking) to simplify reassembly. **Caution:** *Don't use petroleum or mineral-based lubricants or brake fluid - they will lead to deterioration of the bushing.*
9   Place the new bushing on the stabilizer bar and install the U-bracket, using a rocking motion if resistance is encountered. If only the stabilizer bar bushings were replaced, proceed to Steps 13 and 14.

Installation

10   Push the stabilizer bar-to-control arm spacers into the rubber insulators in the control arm, with the washer end facing the front of the vehicle.
11   Insert the stabilizer bar ends into the control arms, install the concave washers (with the dished portion facing away from the bushing) and the nuts. Start the nuts on the threads by hand, but don't tighten them yet.
12   Attach the control arm to the body. It may be necessary to pry between the body and the stabilizer bar to push the control arm in far enough to insert the pivot bolt through the body and control arm. Tighten the nut to the torque listed in this Chapter's Specifications.
13   Install the stabilizer bar U-bracket bolts, starting all four by hand before tightening any of them.
14   Tighten the U-bracket bolts to the torque listed in this Chapter's Specifications.
15   Tighten the two large stabilizer bar-to-control arm nuts to the torque listed in this Chapter's Specifications. Recheck your work, then lower the vehicle.

3   Balljoints - check and replacement

The balljoints on this vehicle are not replaceable separately. The entire control arm must be replaced if the balljoints are worn out. Refer to the *Steering and suspension check* in Chapter 1 for the checking procedure. Refer to Section 4 in this Chapter for control arm removal and installation.

4   Control arm-removal, inspection and installation

Refer to illustrations 4.4 and 4.6

Removal

1   Loosen the wheel lug nuts on the side to be dismantled, raise the front of the vehicle, support it securely on jackstands and remove the wheel.
2   Remove the stabilizer bar-to-control arm nut and concave washer **(see illustration 2.2).**
3   Remove the bolt and nut from the inner control arm pivot **(see illustrations 2.3a and 2.3b).**
4   Remove the balljoint pinch bolt and nut from the steering knuckle **(see illustration).** Spread the joint slightly with a screwdriver or prybar.
5   Pry the control arm down to separate it from the steering knuckle.
6   Pull the control arm off the stabilizer bar and remove it from the vehicle (be careful not to lose the stabilizer bar spacer) **(see illustration).**

Inspection

7   Check the control arm for distortion and the bushings for wear, damage and deterioration. Replace a damaged or bent control arm with a new one. If the inner pivot bushing or stabilizer bar bushings are worn, take the

4.6 After the balljoint stud has been detached from the knuckle, pull the control arm off the stabilizer bar

control arm assembly to a dealer service department or other repair shop, as special tools are required to replace them. If the balljoint is worn or damaged, the control arm must be replaced.

Installation

8   Place the control arm balljoint stud into the steering knuckle. Note that the notch in the balljoint stud must be aligned with the hole in the knuckle before the pinch bolt is inserted. Insert the bolt from the front of the steering knuckle and tighten the nut to the torque listed in this Chapter's Specifications.
9   Push the stabilizer bar spacer into the rubber insulator in the control arm from the front side. Swing the control arm into position over the stabilizer bar end.
10   Install the control arm pivot bolt and tighten the nut to the torque listed in this Chapter's Specifications. It may be necessary to pry between the body and stabilizer bar to push the control arm in far enough to insert the pivot bolt through the body and control arm.
11   Install the stabilizer bar-to-control arm washer and nut (with the dished portion of the washer facing away from the rubber insulator). Tighten the nut to the torque listed in this Chapter's Specifications.

5.3 Remove the brake hose bracket bolt . . .

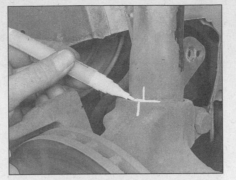

5.4 . . . then mark the relationship of the strut to the steering knuckle

5.5 Remove the strut-to-steering knuckle pinch bolt . . .

12   Install the wheel and lug nuts, lower the vehicle and tighten the lug nuts to the torque listed in the Chapter 1 Specifications.

5   Front strut assembly - removal, inspection, replacement and installation

Refer to illustrations 5.3, 5.4, 5.5, 5.7, 5.8a, 5.8b, 5.9, 5.15, 5.17 and 5.20

Removal

1   Loosen the wheel lug nuts.
2   Raise the vehicle and support it securely on jackstands. Remove the front wheel.
3   Disconnect the brake hose support bracket from the strut **(see illustration)**.
4   Using white paint, a marker or a scribe, mark the strut-to-steering knuckle joint **(see illustration)**. This will help position the strut during reassembly and simplify pinch bolt installation.
5   Remove the strut-to-steering knuckle pinch bolt **(see illustration)**.
6   Apply penetrating oil to the strut where it joins the steering knuckle and allow it to soak for a few minutes.
7   Using a screwdriver or prybar, spread the pinch joint slightly to relieve the pressure on the strut **(see illustration)**.
8   Using a large pry bar positioned between the body and steering knuckle, pry

down until the end of the strut nears the top of the knuckle, then pull out on the strut to disengage it from the knuckle **(see illustrations)**. Be careful not to damage the brake hose.
9   Remove the two upper strut mounting nuts from the shock tower while supporting the strut/spring assembly so it doesn't fall **(see illustration)**.
10   Carefully guide the strut and spring assembly out of the wheel well.

Inspection

11   Checking of the strut assembly is limited to inspection for leaking fluid, dents, damage and corrosion. If the strut damping unit or spring are damaged or known to be worn out, proceed with the operations 12 through 18 for further disassembly. If the strut need not be disassembled, proceed to Step 19.

Strut replacement

Warning: *Disassembling a strut assembly is a potentially dangerous undertaking and utmost attention must be directed to the job, or serious injury may result. Therefore, it is suggested that this work be left to a dealer or other repair shop. However, if after reading the procedure you feel capable, you'll need a spring compressor for this procedure. Spring compressors are available on a daily rental basis at most auto parts stores or equipment yards. Use only a high-quality spring compressor and carefully follow the manufac-*

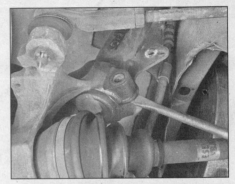

5.7 . . . then apply penetrating oil to the strut/knuckle joint and wedge a screwdriver in the joint to spread it apart

turer's instructions furnished with the tool. After removing the coil spring from the strut assembly, set it aside in a safe, isolated area.
12   If the struts or coil springs exhibit the telltale signs of wear (leaking fluid, loss of damping capability, chipped, sagging or cracked coil springs) explore all options before beginning any work. The struts are not serviceable and must be replaced if a problem develops. However, strut assemblies complete with springs may be available on an exchange basis, which eliminates much time and work. Whichever route you choose to take, check on the cost and availability of parts before disassembling your vehicle.
13   If not already removed, remove the strut

5.8a Pry down on the knuckle until the strut nears the top, . . .

5.8b . . . then pull the strut out of the knuckle

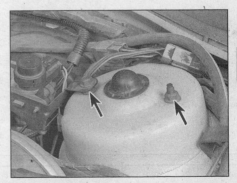

5.9 Remove the upper mounting nuts and detach the strut from the vehicle

10

5.15 A spring compressor is essential for disassembling the strut and coil spring assembly

assembly following Steps 1 through 10 this section.

14   Mount the strut assembly in a vise. Line the vise jaws with wood or rags to prevent damage to the unit and don't tighten the vise excessively.

15   Install the spring compressor in accordance with the manufacturer's instructions **(see illustration)**. Compress the spring until you can wiggle the mount assembly and spring seat.

16   To loosen the damper shaft nut, hold the shaft with a box-end wrench or locking pliers while loosening the shaft nut. **Warning:** *Keep away from the ends of the spring, since the spring compressor could fail and the spring could fly off with great force, causing personal injury.*

17   Disassemble the strut by removing the large washer, top mount, upper insulator, spring, bumper and lower insulator from strut **(see illustration)**.

18   Depending on the nature of the original failure and the variation of replacement parts or assemblies, reassemble the strut in reverse order using the original parts as

required. Be careful not to damage the damper shaft or the strut will leak. When installing the spring, be sure the spring ends are properly seated in their insulators and mounts. Tighten the damper shaft nut to the torque listed in this Chapter's Specifications.

Installation

19   To install the strut, place it in position with the studs extending up through the shock tower. Install the nuts and tighten them finger tight.

20   Prying down on the stabilizer bar, insert the strut into the steering knuckle with the blade on the strut positioned in the joint opening **(see illustration)**. Align the marks that were previously applied to the strut and knuckle.

21   Install the pinch bolt and tighten it to the torque listed in this Chapter's Specifications.

22   Attach the brake hose support bracket to the strut.

23   Tighten the two upper strut-to-shock tower mounting nuts to the torque listed in this Chapter's Specifications.

24   Install the wheel and lower the vehicle. Tighten the lug nuts to the torque listed in this Chapter's Specifications.

6   Steering knuckle and hub - removal and installation

Refer to illustrations 6.5 and 6.10

Warning: *Dust created by the brake system may contain asbestos, which is harmful to your health. Never blow it out with compressed air and don't inhale any of it. Do not, under any circumstances, use petroleum-based solvents to clean brake parts. Use brake system cleaner only.*

Note: *Refer to Chapter 8 and read the driveaxle removal and installation procedure carefully before beginning this operation, to decide whether or not you want to undertake a job of this nature.*

Removal

1   Loosen the wheel lug nuts, raise the vehicle and support it securely on jackstands. Remove the wheel.

2   Remove the brake caliper and support it

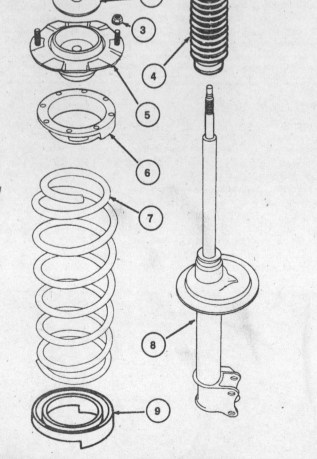

1   Nut
2   Washer
3   Nut
4   Jounce bumper and dust shield
5   Top mount
6   Insulator
7   Rear spring
8   Shock strut
9   Lower insulator

5.17 Typical strut/coil spring assembly - exploded view

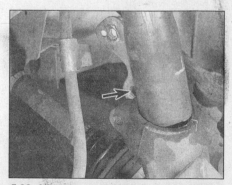

5.20 Align the strut blade (arrow) with the joint and install the strut in the knuckle

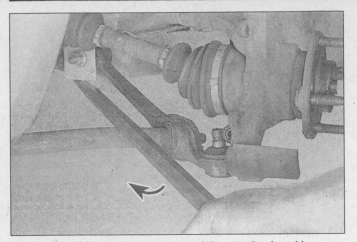

6.5 Pry the balljoint stud out of the steering knuckle

6.10 Using a brass, lead or shot-filled hammer, tap the steering knuckle off the strut

with a piece of wire as described in Chapter 9. Separate the brake disc from the hub.

3   Loosen, but do not remove the strut-to-steering knuckle pinch bolt **(see illustration 5.5).**

4   Separate the tie-rod end from the steering knuckle arm as outlined in Section 16.

5   Remove the balljoint pinch bolt and nut from the steering knuckle **(see illustration 4.4).** Using a large prybar between the lower control arm pivot and the stabilizer bar, pry the balljoint stud from the steering knuckle arm **(see illustration).**

6   Loosen but do not remove the upper strut-to-shock tower nuts.

7   Push the driveaxle from the hub as described in Chapter 8.

8   Mark the relationship of the strut to the steering knuckle **(see illustration 5.4).** This will simplify reassembly.

9   Remove the strut-to-steering knuckle pinch bolt. Apply penetrating oil to the strut-to-knuckle joint. Spread the pinch joint slightly with a screwdriver or pry bar **(see illustration 5.7).**

10   Gently tap the steering knuckle and hub assembly off the strut with a brass, lead or shot-filled hammer, supporting it with your other hand to prevent it from falling when it comes off the strut **(see illustration).**

Installation

11   Position the knuckle and hub assembly on the end of the strut, aligning the blade on the strut with the joint. The previously applied alignment marks can be used to accomplish this.

12   Install the strut-to-steering knuckle pinch bolt. Don't tighten it at this time.

13   Install the driveaxle in the hub (see Chapter 8).

14   Pry down on the stabilizer bar and insert the balljoint stud into the steering knuckle. Note that the notch in the balljoint stud must be aligned with the hole in the knuckle before the pinch bolt is inserted. Install a new pinch bolt from the front and tighten the new nut to

the torque listed in this Chapter's Specifications.

15   Tighten the strut-to-knuckle pinch bolt to the torque listed in this Chapter's Specifications.

16   Tighten the upper strut-to-shock tower nuts to the torque listed in this Chapter's Specifications.

17   Attach the tie-rod end to the steering knuckle arm as described in Section 16.

18   Place the brake disc on the hub and install the caliper as outlined in Chapter 9. Tighten the driveaxle/hub nut to the torque listed in the Chapter 8 Specifications.

19   Install the wheel and lug nuts.

20   Lower the vehicle and tighten the lug nuts to the torque listed in the Chapter 1 Specifications.

---

7   Front hub and bearing assembly - removal and installation

Due to the special tools and expertise required to press the hub and bearing from the steering knuckle, this job should be left to a professional mechanic. However, the steering knuckle and hub may be removed and the assembly taken to a local dealer

service department or other repair shop. Refer to Section 6 for steering knuckle and hub removal.

---

8   Rear control arms - removal and installation

Refer to illustrations 8.2, 8.3 and 8.6

Removal

1   Raise the rear of the vehicle and support it securely on jackstands. Block the front wheels.

2   Remove the control arm-to-spindle bolt and nut **(see illustration).**

3   If one of the rear control arms is being removed, mark the relationship of the toe adjuster wheel to the inner control arm mounting bracket **(see illustration).** This will ensure that the toe adjustment will be returned to the same setting.

4   Remove the inner mounting bolt and nut while supporting the control arm. Be careful- the edges on the stamped control arms are very sharp .

5   Remove the control arm from the vehicle.

10

8.2 Remove the control arm-to-rear wheel spindle nut and bolt (arrow)

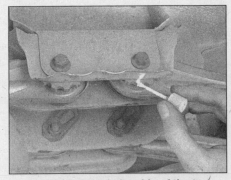

8.3 Mark the relationship of the toe adjuster wheel to the inner mounting bracket if one of the rear control arms must be removed

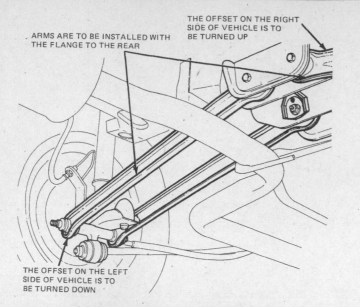

8.6 Rear control arm mounting details

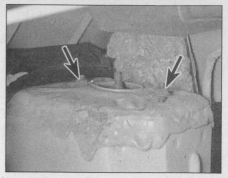

9.1 The upper strut-to-shock tower nuts can be reached from inside the trunk

Installation

6   Position the control arm with the 10 mm hole at the inner mount and the flanged side toward the rear, then install the new inner mounting bolt finger tight **(see illustration)**.

7   Insert a new control arm-to-spindle bolt through the control arms and spindle from the front. Install a new nut and washer and tighten the nut hand tight.

8   Place a jack under the spindle and raise it to simulate normal ride height.

9   Tighten the inner mounting bolt to the torque listed in this Chapter's Specifications.

10   Tighten the outer nut to the torque listed in this Chapter's Specifications.

11   Install the wheel and lug nuts, then lower the vehicle to the ground. Tighten the lug nuts to the torque listed in the Chapter 1 Specifications.

12   Have the rear wheel alignment checked by a dealer service department or an alignment shop.

9   Rear tie-rod - removal and installation

Refer to illustrations 9.1, 9.4, 9.5 and 9.10

Removal

1   From inside the trunk, loosen but don't remove the upper strut-to-shock tower nuts **(see illustration)**.

2   Loosen the wheel lug nuts, raise the vehicle and support it securely on jackstands. Block the front wheels and remove the rear wheel.

3   Remove the large tie-rod-to-spindle nut. Use a wrench on the flat area of the tie-rod to prevent it from turning. Note the washer and bushing arrangement.

4   Remove the large tie-rod-to-body nut, washer and bushing. Again, keep the rod from turning by holding it with a wrench on the flat portion **(see illustration)**. Keep the front bushings separate from the rear bushings-they are different (the rear bushings have indentations in them) .

5   Remove the parking brake cable bracket bolt near the forward tie-rod mount **(see illustration)**.

6   Have an assistant pull the spindle/strut assembly toward the rear of the vehicle. At the same time, pull the tie-rod from the front mount and remove it from the vehicle.

Installation

7   Check the rubber bushings for cracks and wear. Replace them if necessary.

8   Place the concave washers and inner bushings on the ends of the tie-rod, with the dished portion of each washer toward the center.

9   Insert the tie-rod (with inner washers and bushings in place) into the spindle. Have an assistant pull the spindle/strut assembly back and insert the front of the tie-rod into the body mount.

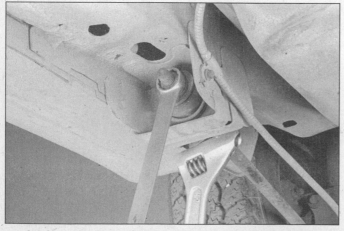

9.4 Use a back-up wrench on the flats of the tie-rod when removing the nuts

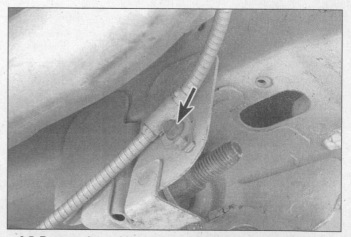

9.5 Remove the parking brake cable bracket bolt to allow the strut/spindle assembly to be pulled to the rear far enough for tie-rod removal

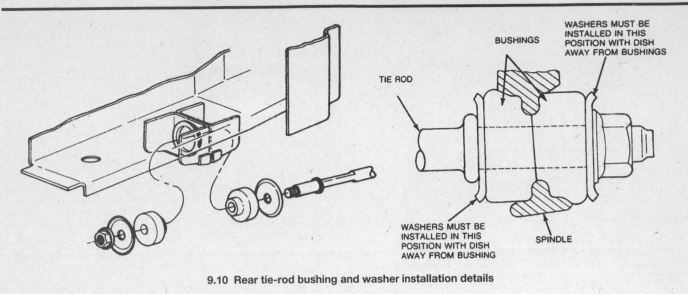

9.10 Rear tie-rod bushing and washer installation details

10   Install the outer bushings, washers and new nuts on the ends of the tie-rod, with the dished portions of the washers facing away from the bushings **(see illustration)**. Raise the spindle with a floor jack to simulate normal ride height, then tighten the nuts to the torque listed in this Chapter's Specifications.

11   Install the wheel and lug nuts and lower the vehicle to the ground. Tighten the lug nuts to the torque listed in the Chapter 1 Specifications.

12   Tighten the strut-to-shock tower nuts to the torque listed in this Chapter's Specifications.

10   Rear hub and wheel bearings - inspection and lubrication

Refer to illustrations 10.7, 10.9, 10.10a, 10.10b, 10.11a and 10.11b

Warning: *Dust created by the brake system may contain asbestos, which is harmful to your health. Never blow it out with compressed air and don't inhale any of it. Do not, under any circumstances, use petroleum-based solvents to clean brake parts. Use brake system cleaner only.*

1   Remove the rear brake drum/hub assembly (see Chapter 9).

2   Check the bearings for proper lubrication and signs that the grease has been contaminated by dirt or water (it will have a gritty feel or a milky-white appearance).

3   Use a screwdriver to pry the grease seal out of the hub (discard the seal).

4   Clean the bearings with solvent and dry them with compressed air.

5   Check the bearings for wear, pitting and scoring of the rollers and cage. Light discoloration of the bearing surfaces is normal, but if the surfaces are badly worn or damaged, replace the bearings with new ones.

6   Clean the hub with solvent and remove the old grease from the hub cavity.

7   Inspect the bearing races for wear, signs of overheating, pitting and corrosion. If the races are worn or damaged, drive them out with a hammer and punch **(see illustration)**.

8   Drive the new races in with a hammer and bearing driver. If a bearing driver isn't available, use the old races as a driver, but be very careful not to damage the new races or get them cocked in the bore.

9   Pack the bearings with high-temperature, multi-purpose EP grease prior to installation. Work generous amounts of grease in from the back of the cage so the grease is forced up through the rollers **(see illustration)** .

10   Add a small amount of grease to the hub cavity and to the center of the spindle **(see illustrations)**.

11   Lubricate the outer edge of the new grease seal, insert the bearing and press the

10.7 The bearing races can be driven out with a hammer and punch (work carefully and don't damage the hub)

10.9 Work the grease completely into the rollers

10.10a Put a small amount of grease into the hub cavity . . .

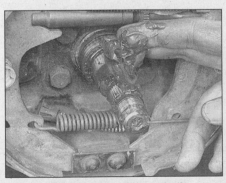

10.10b . . . and on the spindle

10

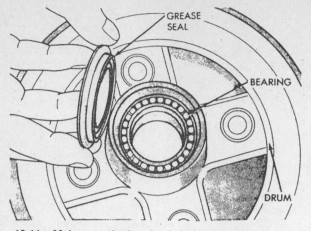

10.11a Make sure the bearing is in place in the hub . . .

10.11b . . . then tap the seal into place with a hammer and block of wood

seal into position with the lip facing in **(see illustration)**. Make sure the seal is seated completely in the hub by tapping it evenly into place using a hammer and block of wood **(see illustration)**. Apply grease to the seal cavity and lip and the polished sections of the spindle.

12   Install the hub and drum assembly as described in Chapter 9.

11   Rear wheel spindle - removal and installation

Refer to illustrations 11.3, 11.4a, 11.4b, 11.5, 11.7 and 11.9

Warning: Dust created by the brake system may contain asbestos, which is harmful to your health. Never blow it out with compressed air and don't inhale any of it. Do not, under any circumstances, use petroleum-based solvents to clean brake parts. Use brake system cleaner only.

Removal

1   Loosen the wheel lug nuts, raise the vehicle and support it on jackstands.

Block the front wheels and remove the rear wheel.

2   Remove the rear brake drum/hub assembly (see Chapter 9).

3   Unbolt the brake hose support bracket from the strut **(see illustration)**.

4   Remove the four bolts that secure the brake backing plate to the spindle. Detach the backing plate and rear brake assembly from the spindle and suspend it with a piece of wire from the spring. It isn't necessary to remove the parking brake

cable from the backing plate **(see illustrations)**.

5   Loosen, but don't remove the strut-to-spindle bolts **(see illustration)**.

6   Remove the control arm-to-spindle bolt, nut and washers **(see illustration 11.5)**.

7   Remove the rear tie-rod nut. Use a wrench on the flats of the rod to prevent it from turning. Remove the washer and rubber bushing **(see illustration)**.

8   Remove the previously loosened strut-

11.3 Remove the bolt and detach the brake hose bracket from the strut

11.4a Remove the brake backing plate bolts (arrows) . . .

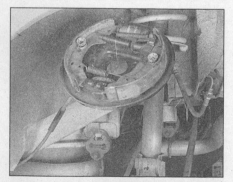

11.4b . . . then carefully slide the backing plate off the spindle and hang it from the strut spring with a piece of wire

11.5 Loosen the strut-to-spindle bolts, then remove the control arm-to-spindle nut and bolt (arrows)

11.7 Use a wrench to grip the flats of the tie-rod to keep it from turning as the large nut is removed

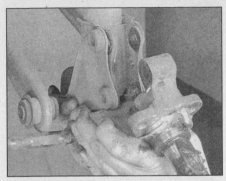

11.9 Pull the spindle straight out from the strut bracket

12.3 Be extremely careful when repositioning the brake hose support bracket or the brake line may be damaged

to-spindle bolts while supporting the spindle so it doesn't fall.

9   Detach the spindle from the strut bracket **(see illustration)**.

Installation

10   Inspect the tie-rod bushings for cracks, deformation and signs of wear. Replace them if necessary.

11   Place the spindle on the tie-rod end, then push it into the strut bracket, aligning the two bolt holes. Insert two new strut-to-spindle bolts and tighten them finger tight.

12   Install the outer tie-rod bushing, washer and a new nut. Don't tighten the nut at this time.

13   Install a new control arm-to-spindle bolt, washer and nut. Tighten the nut by hand.

14   Place a jack under the spindle and raise it to simulate normal ride height.

15   Tighten the strut-to-spindle bolts to the torque listed in this Chapter's Specifications.

16   Tighten the large tie-rod nut to the torque listed in this Chapter's Specifications.

17   Tighten the lower control arm bolt/nut to the torque listed in this Chapter's Specifications.

18   Attach the brake backing plate to the spindle and tighten the four bolts securely.

19   Bolt the brake hose bracket to the strut. Be careful not to damage the line when bending it back into place.

20   Install the rear brake drum/hub assembly (see Chapter 9).

21   Install the wheel and lug nuts. Lower the vehicle and tighten the lug nuts to the torque listed in the Chapter 1 Specifications.

12   Rear strut assembly - removal, inspection, replacement and installation

Refer to illustration 12.3

Removal

1   Loosen but don't remove the two strut-to-shock tower nuts **(see illustration 9.1).**

2   Loosen the wheel lug nuts, raise the vehicle and support it securely on jackstands. Block the front wheels and remove the rear wheel.

3   Unbolt the brake hose support bracket from the strut and very carefully bend the brake line so the bracket is out of the way of the strut-to-spindle bolts. Be careful not to kink the brake line **(see illustration)**.

4   Loosen but don't remove the strut-to-spindle bolts **(see illustration 11.5).**

5   Remove the two strut mounting nuts from the top of the shock tower.

6   Remove the two strut-to-spindle bolts and detach the suspension stop bracket from the strut.

7   Push in on the strut and pull out on the brake backing plate to separate the strut from the spindle. Remove the strut/spring assembly from the vehicle.

Inspection

8   Checking of the strut assembly is limited to inspection for leaking fluid, dents, damage and corrosion. If the strut damping unit or spring are damaged or known to be worn out, proceed with strut replacement instructions for further disassembly. If the strut need not be disassembled, proceed to Step 10.

Strut replacement

9   Refer to Section 5, Steps 12 through 18 for the strut replacement procedure. Be sure to read the Warning that precedes Step 12 in that Section.

Installation

10   Position the strut/spring assembly in place with the upper mounting studs protruding through the holes in the shock tower. Install the nuts on the upper mounting studs. An assistant may be necessary.

11   Place the suspension stop bracket on the strut bracket and align the holes.

12   Insert the spindle into the strut bracket, align the holes and install the new bolts. Tighten the bolts to the torque listed in this Chapter's Specifications.

13   Attach the brake hose bracket to the strut, being careful not to damage the line. Tighten the bolt securely.

14   Install the wheel and lug nuts.

15   Lower the vehicle and tighten the lug nuts to the torque listed in the Chapter 1 Specifications.

16   Tighten the two upper mounting nuts to the torque listed in this Chapter's Specifications.

13   Rear stabilizer bar and bushings - removal and installation

Refer to illustration 13.2

Removal

1   Raise the vehicle and support it securely on jackstands.

2   Remove the stabilizer bar to strut bracket link nuts, washers and all four link bushings on both sides of the bar **(see illustration)**.

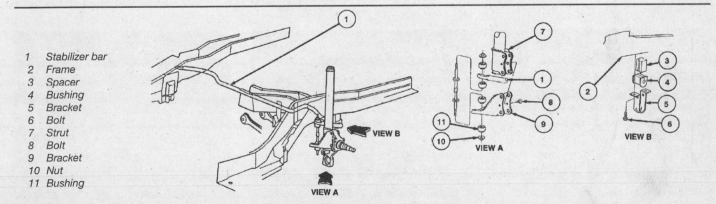

1   Stabilizer bar
2   Frame
3   Spacer
4   Bushing
5   Bracket
6   Bolt
7   Strut
8   Bolt
9   Bracket
10   Nut
11   Bushing

VIEW B

VIEW A

VIEW A

VIEW B

13.2 Rear stabilizer bar installation details

10

3   Remove the four stabilizer bar U-bracket bolts. Support the bar while removing the last two bolts to prevent the stabilizer bar from falling
4   Separate the stabilizer bar from the vehicle

Bushing replacement

5   Pull the U-bracket off the stabilizer bar and rubber bushing using a rocking motion
6   Remove the rubber bushing from the bar and clean the bushing area with a stiff wire brush to remove any rust or dirt.
7   Lubricate the inside and outside of the new bushing with vegetable oil (used in cooking) to simplify reassembly. **Caution:** *Don't use petroleum or mineral-based lubricants or brake fluid- they will lead to deterioration of the bushing.*
8   Place the new bushing on the stabilizer bar and install the U-bracket, using a rocking motion if resistance is encountered.
9   Assemble the stabilizer bar links to the strut brackets using four new lower bushings.
10   Install two of the four new upper link bushings onto the top of the links in preparation for stabilizer bar reinstallation.

Installation

11   Position the ends of the stabilizer bar over the link ends and install new upper bushings.
12   Install new stabilizer bar U-bracket bolts, starting all four by hand before tightening any of them.
13   Tighten the U-bracket bolts securely.
14   Tighten the two upper link nuts securely. Recheck your work, then lower the vehicle.

14   Steering system - general information

All models are equipped with rack-and-pinion steering. Most are power assisted. The steering gear is bolted to the firewall and operates the steering arms via tie-rods. The inner ends of the tie-rods are protected by rubber boots which should be inspected periodically for secure attachment, tears and leaking lubricant.
The power assist system consists of a belt-driven pump and associated lines and hoses. The power steering pump reservoir fluid level should be checked periodically (see Chapter 1).
The steering wheel operates the steering shaft, which actuates the steering gear through universal joints and the intermediate shaft. Looseness in the steering can be caused by wear in the steering shaft universal joints, the steering gear, the tie-rod ends and loose retaining bolts .

15   Steering wheel - removal and installation

Refer to illustrations 15.10, 15.11, 15.12, 15.13 and 15.14

Warning: *Some models are equipped with airbags. Always turn the steering wheel to the straight ahead position, place the ignition switch in the Lock position and disable the airbag system (see Chapter 12) before working in the vicinity of the impact sensors, steering column or instrument panel to avoid the possibility of accidental deployment of the airbag, which could cause personal injury.*

Note: *A new steering wheel retaining bolt must be used. Make sure you have one before beginning the procedure*

Removal (airbag models)

1   Disconnect the negative battery cable, then the positive battery cable and wait two minutes before proceeding. **Note:** *Make sure the wheels of the vehicle are in the straight-ahead position, place the ignition switch in the Lock position and remove the key.*
2   Remove the four nuts that secure the airbag module to the steering wheel. These are accessible from the rear of the wheel.
3   Lift the airbag module carefully away from the steering wheel and disconnect the airbag electrical connectors. Remove the airbag module. **Warning:** *When carrying the airbag module keep the trim side of it facing away from your body, and when you set it down, make sure the trim side is facing up.*
4   Use a ratchet and deep socket to remove the steering wheel bolt. Remove the vibration damper and re-install the bolt loosely.
5   Make two alignment marks to indicate the exact orientation of the steering wheel to the shaft, and use a steering wheel puller (available at most auto parts stores) to remove the wheel.
6   Route the wires through the wheel as it is removed.

Installation (airbag models)

7   Installation is the reverse of removal. Connect the airbag connectors to the back of the airbag module just as it was before steering wheel removal. Use a NEW steering wheel bolt and tighten to the torque listed in this Chapter's specifications.
8   Refer to Chapter 12 for the procedure to enable the airbag system.

Removal (no airbag)

9   Disconnect the negative cable from the battery.
10   Remove the two screws securing the horn pad to the steering wheel. Grasp the pad assembly at the top two corners and pull it straight back off the steering wheel, releasing the clips **(see illustration)**.
11   Unplug the electrical connector and remove the horn pad **(see illustration)** .
12   Remove the steering wheel mounting nut/bolt **(see illustration)**.
13   Use a puller to remove the steering wheel **(see illustration)**. **Caution:** *Don't hammer on the shaft to remove the steering wheel.*

15.10 After removing the screws, pull out on the horn pad to disengage the clips

15.11 Use a small screwdriver to pry off the electrical connector

15.12 Hold the steering wheel with one hand while loosening the nut or bolt

15.13 Remove the wheel from the shaft with puller - DO NOT beat on the shaft

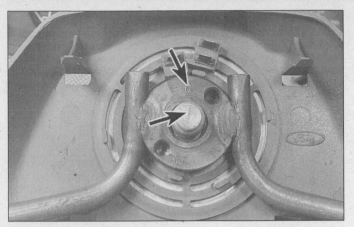

15.14 Align the mark on the steering wheel hub with the mark on the shaft when installing the steering wheel

16.3 Use a two-jaw puller to detach the tie-rod end from the steering knuckle arm

Installation (no airbag)

14   Align the index mark on the steering wheel hub with the mark on the shaft and slip the wheel onto the shaft **(see illustration)**. Install the mounting nut/bolt and tighten it to the torque listed in this Chapter's Specifications.

15   Plug in the electrical connector and install the horn pad.

16   Connect the negative battery cable.

16   Tie-rod ends - removal and installation

Refer to illustrations 16.3, 16.4a, 16.4b and 16.4c

Removal

1   Loosen the wheel lug nuts. Raise the front of the vehicle, support it securely, block the rear wheels and set the parking brake. Remove the front wheel.

2   Remove the cotter pin and loosen the nut on the tie-rod end stud.

3   Disconnect the tie-rod from the steering knuckle arm with a puller **(see illustration)**. Remove the nut and separate the tie-rod.

4   Hold the tie-rod end with a wrench and loosen the jam nut enough to mark the position of the tie-rod end in relation to the threads **(see illustrations)**. Remove the tie-rod end **(see illustration)**.

Installation

5   Thread the tie-rod end on to the marked position and insert the tie-rod stud into the steering knuckle arm. Tighten the jam nut securely.

6   Install a new nut on the stud and tighten it to the torque listed in this Chapter's Specifications. Install a new cotter pin.

7   Install the wheel and lug nuts. Lower the vehicle and tighten the lug nuts to the torque listed in the Chapter 1 Specifications.

8   Have the alignment checked by a dealer service department or an alignment shop.

17   Steering gear boots - replacement

1   Loosen the lug nuts, raise the vehicle and support it securely on jackstands. Remove the wheel.

2   Refer to Section 16 and remove the tie-rod end and jam nut.

3   Remove the steering gear boot clamps and slide the boot off.

4   Before installing the new boot, wrap the threads and serrations on the end of the steering rod with a layer of tape so the small end of the new boot isn't damaged.

5   Slide the new boot into position on the steering gear until it seats in the groove in the steering rod and install new clamps.

6   Remove the tape and install the tie-rod end (see Section 16).

7   Install the wheel and lug nuts. Lower vehicle and tighten the lug nuts to the torque listed in the Chapter 1 Specifications.

18   Steering gear - removal and installation

Refer to illustrations 18.6, 18.7 and 18.14

Warning: *Don't allow the steering shaft to turn with the steering wheel removed. If the shaft turns, the airbag coil assembly (the mechanism which protects the airbag wiring when the steering wheel is turned) will become uncentered, which will cause the airbag harness to break when the vehicle is returned to service. To prevent the shaft from turning, turn the ignition key to the Lock position before beginning work or run the seat belt through the steering wheel and clip the seat belt into place.*

16.4a Loosen the jam nut while holding the tie-rod end with a wrench to prevent it from turning

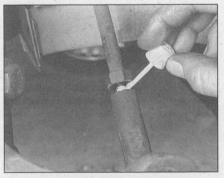

16.4b The relationship of the tie-rod and tie-rod end can be marked with white paint

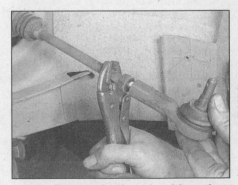

16.4c Remove the tie-rod end from the tie-rod (if necessary, prevent the tie-rod from turning by holding it with a pair of locking pliers positioned directly behind the threads)

10

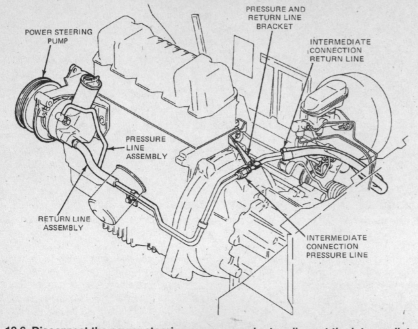

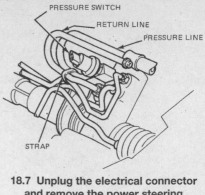

18.7 Unplug the electrical connector and remove the power steering pressure switch

18.6 Disconnect the power steering pressure and return lines at the intermediate connections located above the transaxle housing (have rags and a drain pan ready to catch the fluid)

Note: *The following is a difficult procedure for the home mechanic. It is best performed with a vehicle hoist and specialized (tall and adjustable) jackstands or jacks, because the subframe must be lowered four inches to remove the steering gear.*

Removal

1 Disconnect the cable from the negative battery terminal.
2 Turn the ignition key to the Run position to unlock the steering wheel .
3 Remove the left side under dash panel.
4 On power steering-equipped models, remove the four screws securing the steering column boot to the inside of the firewall. Pull back on the boot to expose the intermediate shaft.
5 Mark the intermediate shaft, the steering gear input shaft and the steering column shaft so they can be reassembled in the same relative positions. Remove the clamp bolts at both ends of the intermediate shaft and spread the clamp joints slightly with a screwdriver.
6 On power steering-equipped models, remove the air cleaner housing (see Chapter 4). Disconnect the pressure and return lines at the fittings located above the transaxle and drain the fluid into a container **(see illustration)**. Remove the pressure line from the support bracket.
7 From above, remove the power steering pressure switch **(see illustration)** .
8 Loosen the lug nuts on both front wheels. Raise the vehicle and support it securely on jackstands. Apply the parking brake and remove the front wheels.
9 Separate the tie-rod ends from the steering knuckle arms (see Section 16).

10 On models with an automatic transaxle, disconnect the speedometer cable at the transaxle.
11 Remove the exhaust system as outlined in Chapter 4.
12 On models with an automatic transaxle, disconnect the shift cable at the transaxle lever, unbolt the cable bracket from the transaxle housing and position it out of the way (see Chapter 7, Part B, for the shift cable removal and installation procedure).
13 Turn the steering wheel to the extreme left so the left tie-rod will be positioned correctly.
14 Unbolt the steering gear mounting brackets from the firewall and remove the rubber insulators from the steering gear. Note that the insulators and brackets are not interchangeable. Mark them if necessary to avoid confusion **(see illustration)**.
15 Gently pull the steering gear assembly forward and down, away from the firewall. while an assistant pulls up on the intermediate shaft from inside the vehicle to dislocate it from the steering gear input shaft.
16 Maneuver the steering gear assembly through the right side opening in the wheel well just far enough to allow the left tie-rod to clear the wheel well opening and other components. Carefully lower the entire assembly down and out while guiding the power steering hoses (if so equipped) out from behind the transaxle.

Installation

17 Rotate the input shaft counterclockwise until it stops.
18 Place the right tie-rod through the opening in the wheel well. Move the assembly to the right, through the opening far

enough so the left tie-rod can be raised up into the opening. Move the assembly up and to the left, into position.
19 Route the power steering hoses into the proper position.
20 Push the steering gear input shaft through the opening in the firewall. Have an assistant guide the intermediate shaft onto the input shaft, aligning the previously applied marks. Install the bolts finger tight into both ends of the intermediate shaft pinch clamps.
21 Install the rubber mounting insulators. Make sure the flat portion of the left insulator is parallel to the firewall.
22 Place the mounting brackets over the insulators and install the bolts. Tighten the left upper bolt half way. Tighten the left lower bolt to the torque listed in this Chapter's Specifications.
23 Tighten the left upper bolt to the torque listed in this Chapter's Specifications.
24 Tighten the two right side bracket bolts to the torque listed in this Chapter's Specifications.
25 Install the tie-rod ends in the steering knuckle arms (see Section 16).
26 On automatic transaxle equipped vehicles, reconnect the shift cable and bracket assembly.
27 Reinstall the speedometer cable if previously removed.
28 Install the exhaust system (see Chapter 4).
29 Install the wheels and lug nuts. Lower the vehicle and tighten the lug nuts to the torque listed in the Chapter 1 Specifications.
30 Tighten the intermediate shaft clamp bolts, beginning with the intermediate shaft-to-input shaft bolt, then the intermediate shaft-to-steering column bolt, to the torque listed in this Chapter's Specifications. Install the steering column boot on power steering equipped models. Install the under dash panel.
31 On power steering equipped models, connect the pressure and return lines and install them in the support bracket. Reinstall the air cleaner assembly.
32 Install the pressure switch.
33 Turn the ignition key Off and connect the negative battery cable.

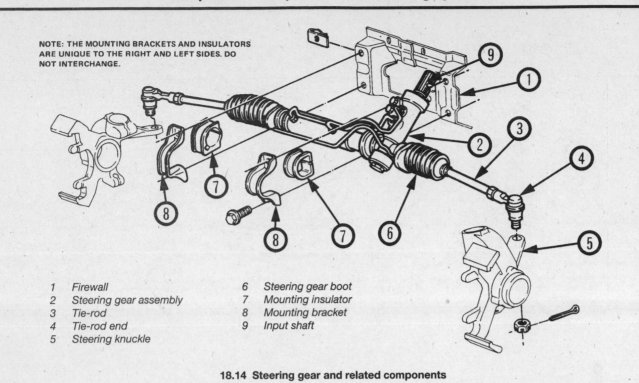

NOTE: THE MOUNTING BRACKETS AND INSULATORS
ARE UNIQUE TO THE RIGHT AND LEFT SIDES. DO
NOT INTERCHANGE.

1   Firewall
2   Steering gear assembly
3   Tie-rod
4   Tie-rod end
5   Steering knuckle

6   Steering gear boot
7   Mounting insulator
8   Mounting bracket
9   Input shaft

18.14 Steering gear and related components

34   On power steering equipped vehicles fill the fluid reservoir with the specified fluid and refer to Section 19 for the power steering bleeding procedure.

35   Have the front end alignment checked by a dealer service department or an alignment shop.

19   Power steering pump - removal and installation

Refer to illustrations 19.7, 19.8, 19.9, 19.10 and 19.13

Note: *On 1992 and later models, the power steering pumps changed from combined pump/reservoir type to a remote reservoir design. However, the following procedures apply to all models unless specified.*

Removal

1   Disconnect the cable from the negative battery terminal.

2   On pre-1992 models, loosen the alternator and remove the belt. Swing the alternator up all the way to gain access to the steering pump (see Chapter 5 if necessary).

3   Remove the coolant reservoir.

4   Remove the serpentine drivebelt (see Chapter 1).

5   Mark the relationship of the pulley to the pump hub, then remove the bolts.

6   Detach the pump pulley.

7   On pre-1992 models, disconnect the pressure and return lines from the pump and allow the fluid to drain into a container **(see illustration)**. Use a back-up wrench on the pressure line fitting to avoid twisting the line. Plug the hoses and pump ports.

8   On 1992 and later models, disconnect the steering gear return line (small line) from the remote reservoir and drain fluid into container **(see illustration)**.

9   On 1992 and later models, disconnect the steering pump pressure line (steel line) and reservoir supply hose from the pump.

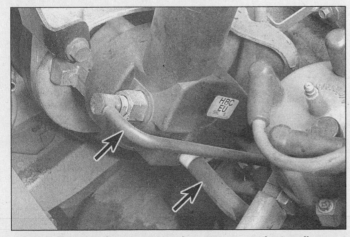

19.7 Remove the power steering pressure and return lines (arrows); use a back-up wrench on the pressure fitting to avoid twisting the line - the return hose is retained by a hose clamp

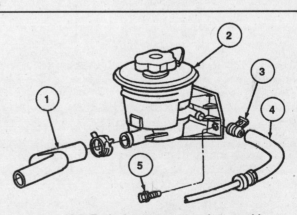

19.8 Typical remote reservoir assembly

1   Hose
2   Reservoir assembly
3   Clamp

4   Hose
5   Bolt

10

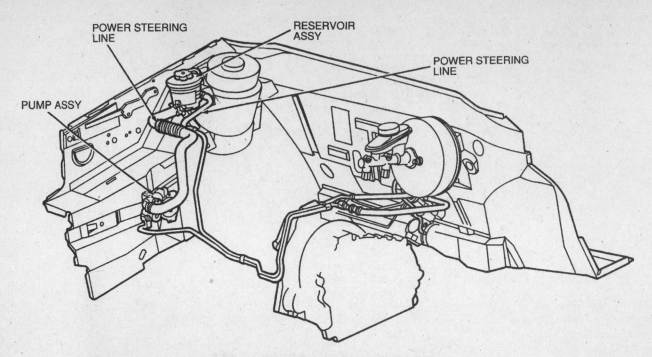

19.9 Power steering pump and remote reservoir layout

Plug all lines to prevent contamination (see illustration).

10   Remove the three pump-to-bracket bolts (two bolts on V6 models and detach the pump (see illustration).

Installation

11   Place the pump in the bracket and install the bolts.

12   Install pump pulleys.

13   Attach the pressure and return/supply lines to the pump.

Note: *On 1992 and later models, replace the plastic seal on the high-pressure tube nut*

fitting (see illustration). *To avoid damage to the new seal, pre-stretch the seal slightly on a tapered center-punch until it is large enough to slip over the fitting threads. The seal will return to it's original shape shortly.*

14   On 1992 and later models, reinstall the steering gear to reservoir return line.

15   Install the serpentine drivebelt (see Chapter 1).

16   Install the alternator drivebelt on pre-1992 models (see Chapter 1).

17   Install the coolant reservoir.

18   Fill the pump reservoir with the specified fluid, bleed the system as described in Section 20 and check the fluid level.

20   Power steering system - bleeding

1   The power steering system must be bled whenever a line is disconnected. Bubbles can be seen in power steering fluid which has air in it and the fluid will often have a tan or milky appearance. On later models, low fluid level can cause air to mix with the fluid, resulting in a noisy pump as well as foaming of the fluid.

2   Open the hood and check the fluid level in the reservoir, adding the specified fluid necessary to bring it up to the proper level (see Chapter 1).

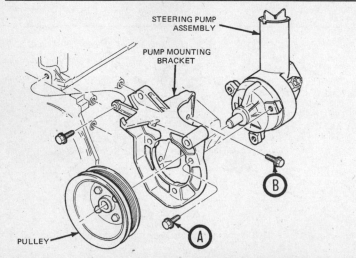

19.10 Power steering pump mounting details (earlier model with pump-mounted reservoir shown, others similar)

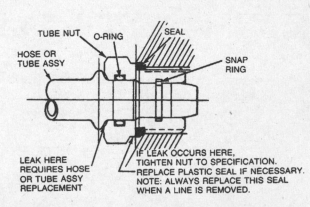

19.13 Replace the seal between the high-pressure fitting and the pump housing on 1992 and later models

3   Start the engine and slowly turn the steering wheel several times from left-to-right and back again. Do not turn the wheel completely from lock-to-lock. Check the fluid level, topping it up as necessary until it remains steady and no more bubbles appear in the reservoir.

21 Wheel alignment - general information

Proper wheel alignment is essential for safe steering and even tire wear. Symptoms of alignment problems are pulling of the steering to one side or the other and uneven tire wear.

If these symptoms are present, check for the following before having the alignment adjusted:

Loose steering gear mounting bolts
Damaged or worn steering gear mounts
Worn or damaged wheel bearings
Bent tie-rods
Worn balljoints
Improper tire pressures
Mixing tires of different construction

Front or rear wheel alignment should be left to a dealer service department or an alignment shop.

22 Wheels and tires- general information

1   Check the tire pressures (cold) weekly (see Chapter 1).
2   Inspect the sidewalls and treads periodically for damage and signs of abnormal or uneven wear.
3   Make sure the wheel lug nuts are properly tightened.
4   Don't mix radial and bias ply tires or tires with different tread patterns on the same axle.
5   Never include the temporary spare in the tire rotation pattern as it's designed for use only until a damaged tire is repaired or replaced.
6   Periodically inspect the wheels for elongated or damaged lug holes, distortion and nicks in the rim. Replace damaged wheels.
7   Clean the wheels inside and out and check for rust and corrosion, which could lead to wheel failure.
8   If the wheel and tire are balanced on the vehicle, one wheel stud and lug hole should be marked whenever the wheel is removed so it can be reinstalled in the original position. If balanced on the vehicle, the wheel should not be moved to a different axle position.

10

Notes

Chapter 11   Body

Contents

1   General information

The Tempo/Topaz has a "unibody" layout, using a floor pan with front and rear frame side rails which support the body components, front and rear suspension systems and other mechanical components. Since it's introduction, the Tempo/Topaz has gone through several styling changes, both on the interior and exterior.

As released, the Tempo/Topaz was equipped with standard formed steel bumpers with bumper extensions (an accordion like trim piece) to comply with the slow speed impact law. In 1986 the formed steel bumpers were replaced with strength-optimized, lightweight steel or aluminum channel bumpers with more aesthetically pleasing impact-resistant plastic "bumper covers". Although the Tempo still used bumper extensions, the Topaz incorporated the same function into the bumper cover by using push connectors that will shear off in the event of a minor accident. The bumper design was changed again in 1988, this time incorporating a lightweight, one piece, integrated bumper and cover unit which is used on all vehicles except for the rear bumper of two-door models.

The interior changes are less technical and are more for convenience and aesthetic appeal. Although many small changes have

occurred over the years, a major change in 1988 resulted in an entirely new dashboard, center console and door panels. Other interior options included power seats, power mirrors and automatic shoulder harnesses.

This Chapter addresses those components that are particularly vulnerable to accident damage and can be unbolted and repaired or replaced. Among these parts are the body moldings, bumpers, the hood and trunk lids and some glass.

Only general body maintenance practices and body panel repair procedures within the scope of the do-it-yourselfer are included in this Chapter.

Warning: *On models so equipped, whenever working in the vicinity of the front grille/bumper, steering wheel, steering column or other components of the airbag system, the system should be disarmed. To do this, perform the following steps:*

a) *Turn the ignition switch to Off.*
b) *Detach the cable from the negative battery terminal, then detach the positive cable. Wait two minutes for the electronic module backup power supply to be depleted.*

To enable the system

a) *Turn the ignition switch to the Off position.*
b) *Connect the positive battery cable first, then connect the negative cable.*

2   Body - maintenance

1   The condition of your vehicle's body is very important, because the resale value depends a great deal on it. It's much more difficult to repair a neglected or damaged body than it is to repair mechanical components. The hidden areas of the body, such as the wheel wells, the frame and the engine compartment, are equally important, although they don't require as frequent attention as the rest of the body.

2   Once a year, or every 12,000 miles, it's a good idea to have the underside of the body steam cleaned. All traces of dirt and oil will be removed and the area can then be inspected carefully for rust, damaged brake lines, frayed electrical wires, damaged cables and other problems. If equipped with the proper fittings, the front suspension components should be greased after completion of this job.

3   At the same time, clean the engine and the engine compartment with a steam cleaner or water soluble degreaser.

4   The wheel wells should be given close attention, since undercoating can peel away and stones and dirt thrown up by the tires can cause the paint to chip and flake, allowing rust to set in. If rust is found, clean down to the bare metal and apply an anti-rust paint.

11

5   The body should be washed about once a week. Wet the vehicle thoroughly to soften the dirt, then wash it down with a soft sponge and plenty of clean soapy water. If the surplus dirt is not washed off very carefully, it can wear down the paint.

6   Spots of tar or asphalt thrown up from the road should be removed with a cloth soaked in solvent.

7   Once every six months, wax the body and chrome trim. If a chrome cleaner is used to remove rust from any of the vehicle's plated parts, remember that the cleaner also removes part of the chrome, so use it sparingly.

3   Vinyl trim - maintenance

1   Don't clean vinyl trim with detergents, caustic soap or petroleum-based cleaners. Plain soap and water works just fine, with a soft brush to clean dirt that may be ingrained. Wash the vinyl as frequently as the rest of the vehicle.

2   After cleaning, application of a high quality rubber and vinyl protection will help prevent oxidation and cracks. The protection can also be applied to weather-stripping, vacuum lines and rubber hoses, which often fail as a result of chemical degradation, and to the tires.

4   Upholstery and carpets - maintenance

1   Every three months remove the carpets or mats and clean the interior of the vehicle (more frequently if necessary). Vacuum the upholstery and carpets to remove loose dirt and dust.

2   Leather upholstery requires special care. Stains should be removed with warm water and a very mild soap solution. Use a clean, damp cloth to remove the soap, then wipe again with a dry cloth. Never use alcohol, gasoline, nail polish remover or thinner to clean leather upholstery.

3   After cleaning, regularly treat leather upholstery with a leather wax. Never use car wax on leather upholstery.

4   In areas where the interior of the vehicle is subject to bright sunlight, cover leather seats with a sheet if the vehicle is to be left out for any length of time.

5   Hinges and locks - maintenance

Once every 3000 miles, or every three months, the hinges, locks and latch assemblies on the doors, hood and trunk should be given a few drops of light oil or lock lubricant. The door latch strikers should also be lubricated with a thin coat of grease to reduce wear and ensure free movement.

6   Body repair - minor damage

See photo sequence

Repair of minor scratches

1   If the scratch is superficial and does not penetrate to the metal of the body, repair is very simple. Lightly rub the scratched area with a fine rubbing compound to remove loose paint and built up wax. Rinse the area with clean water.

2   Apply touch-up paint to the scratch, using a small brush. Continue to apply thin layers of paint until the surface of the paint in the scratch is level with the surrounding paint. Allow the new paint at least two weeks to harden, then blend it into the surrounding paint by rubbing with a very fine rubbing compound. Finally, apply a coat of wax to the scratch area.

3   If the scratch has penetrated the paint and exposed the metal of the body, causing the metal to rust, a different repair technique is required. Remove all loose rust from the bottom of the scratch with a pocket knife, then apply rust inhibiting paint to prevent the formation of rust in the future. Using a rubber or nylon applicator, coat the scratched area with glaze-type filler. If required, the filler can be mixed with thinner to provide a very thin paste, which is ideal for filling narrow scratches. Before the glaze filler in the scratch hardens, wrap a piece of smooth cotton cloth around the tip of a finger. Dip the cloth in thinner and then quickly wipe it along the surface of the scratch. This will ensure that the surface of the filler is slightly hollow. The scratch can now be painted over as described earlier in this section.

Repair of dents

4   When repairing dents, the first job is to pull the dent out until the affected area is as close as possible to its original shape. There is no point in trying to restore the original shape completely as the metal in the damaged area will have stretched on impact and cannot be restored to its original contours. It is better to bring the level of the dent up to a point which is about 1/8-inch below the level of the surrounding metal. In cases where the dent is very shallow, it is not worth trying to pull it out at all.

5   If the back side of the dent is accessible, it can be hammered out gently from behind using a soft-face hammer. While doing this, hold a block of wood firmly against the opposite side of the metal to absorb the hammer blows and prevent the metal from being stretched.

6   If the dent is in a section of the body which has double layers, or some other factor makes it inaccessible from behind, a different technique is required. Drill several small holes through the metal inside the damaged area, particularly in the deeper sections. Screw long, self tapping screws into the holes just enough for them to get a good grip in the

metal. Now the dent can be pulled out by pulling on the protruding heads of the screws with locking pliers.

7   The next stage of repair is the removal of paint from the damaged area and from an inch or so of the surrounding metal. This is easily done with a wire brush or sanding disk in a drill motor, although it can be done just as effectively by hand with sandpaper. To complete the preparation for filling, score the surface of the bare metal with a screwdriver or the tang of a file or drill small holes in the affected area. This will provide a good grip for the filler material. To complete the repair, see the Section on filling and painting.

Repair of rust holes or gashes

8   Remove all paint from the affected area and from an inch or so of the surrounding metal using a sanding disk or wire brush mounted in a drill motor. If these are not available, a few sheets of sandpaper will do the job just as effectively.

9   With the paint removed, you will be able to determine the severity of the corrosion and decide whether to replace the whole panel, if possible, or repair the affected area. New body panels are not as expensive as most people think and it is often quicker to install a new panel than to repair large areas of rust.

10   Remove all trim pieces from the affected area except those which will act as a guide to the original shape of the damaged body, such as headlight shells, etc. Using metal snips or a hacksaw blade, remove all loose metal and any other metal that is badly affected by rust. Hammer the edges of the hole inward to create a slight depression for the filler material.

11   Wire brush the affected area to remove the powdery rust from the surface of the metal. If the back of the rusted area is accessible, treat it with rust inhibiting paint.

12   Before filling is done, block the hole in some way. This can be done with sheet metal riveted or screwed into place, or by stuffing the hole with wire mesh.

13   Once the hole is blocked off, the affected area can be filled and painted. See the following subsection on filling and painting.

Filling and painting

14   Many types of body fillers are available, but generally speaking, body repair kits which contain filler paste and a tube of resin hardener are best for this type of repair work. A wide, flexible plastic or nylon applicator will be necessary for imparting a smooth and contoured finish to the surface of the filler material. Mix up a small amount of filler on a clean piece of wood or cardboard (use the hardener sparingly). Follow the manufacturer's instructions on the package, otherwise the filler will set incorrectly.

15   Using the applicator, apply the filler paste to the prepared area. Draw the applicator across the surface of the filler to achieve the desired contour and to level the

filler surface. As soon as a contour that approximates the original one is achieved, stop working the paste. If you continue, the paste will begin to stick to the applicator. Continue to add thin layers of paste at 20-minute intervals until the level of the filler is just above the surrounding metal.

16   Once the filler has hardened, the excess can be removed with a body file. From then on, progressively finer grades of sandpaper should be used, starting with a 180-grit paper and finishing with 600-grit wet-or-dry paper. Always wrap the sandpaper around a flat rubber or wooden block, otherwise the surface of the filler will not be completely flat. During the sanding of the filler surface, the wet-or-dry paper should be periodically rinsed in water. This will ensure that a very smooth finish is produced in the final stage.

17   At this point, the repair area should be surrounded by a ring of bare metal, which in turn should be encircled by the finely feathered edge of good paint. Rinse the repair area with clean water until all of the dust produced by the sanding operation is gone.

18   Spray the entire area with a light coat of primer. This will reveal any imperfections in the surface of the filler. Repair the imperfections with fresh filler paste or glaze filler and once more smooth the surface with sandpaper. Repeat this spray-and-repair procedure until you are satisfied that the surface of the filler and the feathered edge of the paint are perfect. Rinse the area with clean water and allow it to dry completely.

19   The repair area is now ready for painting. Spray painting must be carried out in a warm, dry, windless and dust free atmosphere. These conditions can be created if you have access to a large indoor work area, but if you are forced to work in the open, you will have to pick the day very carefully. If you are working indoors, dousing the floor in the work area with water will help settle the dust which would otherwise be in the air. If the repair area is confined to one body panel, mask off the surrounding panels. This will help minimize the effects of a slight mismatch in paint color. Trim pieces such as

chrome strips, door handles, etc., will also need to be masked off or removed. Use masking tape and several thicknesses of newspaper for the masking operations.

20   Before spraying, shake the paint can thoroughly, then spray a test area until the spray painting technique is mastered. Cover the repair area with a thick coat of primer. The thickness should be built up using several thin layers of primer rather than one thick one. Using 600-grit wet-or-dry sandpaper, rub down the surface of the primer until it is very smooth. While doing this, the work area should be thoroughly rinsed with water and the wet-or-dry sandpaper periodically rinsed as well. Allow the primer to dry before spraying additional coats.

21   Spray on the top coat, again building up the thickness by using several thin layers of paint. Begin spraying in the center of the repair area and then, using a circular motion, work out until the whole repair area and about two inches of the surrounding original paint is covered. Remove all masking material 10 to 15 minutes after spraying on the final coat of paint. Allow the new paint at least two weeks to harden, then use a very fine rubbing compound to blend the edges of the new paint into the existing paint. Finally, apply a coat of wax.

7   Body repair - major damage

1   Major damage must be repaired by an auto body shop specifically equipped to perform unibody repairs. These shops have available the specialized equipment required to do the job properly.

2   If the damage is extensive, the body must be checked for proper alignment or the

vehicle's handling characteristics may be adversely affected and other components may wear at an accelerated rate.

3   Due to the fact that all of the major body components (hood, fenders, etc.) are separate and replaceable units, any seriously damaged components should be replaced rather than repaired. Sometimes the components can be found in a wrecking yard that specializes in used vehicle components, often at considerable savings over the cost of new parts.

8   Hood - removal, installation and adjustment

Refer to illustrations 8.2 and 8.6
Warning: *If vehicle is equipped with airbags, refer to Chapter 12 to disarm the airbag system prior to performing any work described below.*

1   Open the hood.

2   Scribe or paint alignment marks along the edges of the hood hinge assembly flange **(see illustration).**

3   Disconnect the trouble light connector at hinge and remove the hinge assembly-to-hood mounting bolts.

4   Remove the hood.

5   Installation is the reverse of removal.

6   The hood can be adjusted fore-and-aft and side-to-side by loosening the two hood-to-hinge bolts at each hinge **(see illustration).** Reposition the hood and tighten the bolts.

7   To raise or lower the rear of the hood, loosen the hinge-to-body bolts. Raise or lower the hinge as necessary to make the hood flush with the surrounding panels. Then tighten the hinge-to-body bolts.

8.2 Before loosening the bolts, scribe around the hinges to ensure proper alignment of the hood when it's reinstalled

8.6 Note that the hood hinge upper mounting bolt holes are slotted to allow a slight amount of fore-and-aft movement and the lower mounting holes are similarly designed to permit a small amount of up-and-down adjustability

U-NUT

HOOD ASSEMBLY

HINGE ASSEMBLY

U-NUT

11

These photos illustrate a method of repairing simple dents. They are intended to supplement *Body repair - minor damage* in this Chapter and should not be used as the sole instructions for body repair on these vehicles.

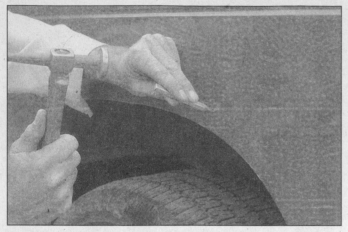

1   If you can't access the backside of the body panel to hammer out the dent, pull it out with a slide-hammer-type dent puller. In the deepest portion of the dent or along the crease line, drill or punch hole(s) at least one inch apart . . .

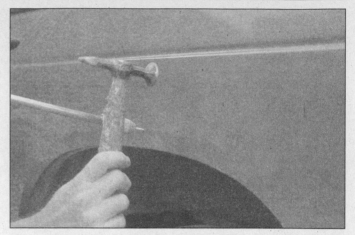

2   . . . then screw the slide-hammer into the hole and operate it. Tap with a hammer near the edge of the dent to help 'pop' the metal back to its original shape. When you're finished, the dent area should be close to its original contour and about 1/8-inch below the surface of the surrounding metal

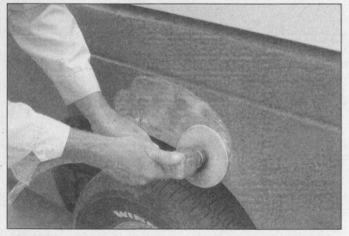

3   Using coarse-grit sandpaper, remove the paint down to the bare metal. Hand sanding works fine, but the disc sander shown here makes the job faster. Use finer (about 320-grit) sandpaper to feather-edge the paint at least one inch around the dent area

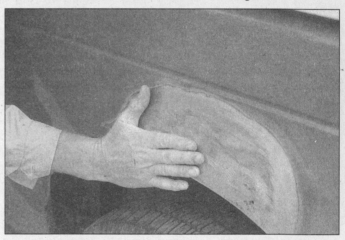

4   When the paint is removed, touch will probably be more helpful than sight for telling if the metal is straight. Hammer down the high spots or raise the low spots as necessary. Clean the repair area with wax/silicone remover

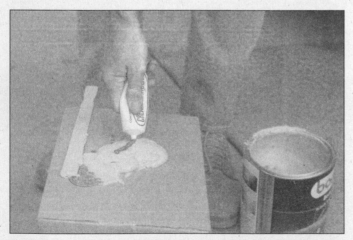

5   Following label instructions, mix up a batch of plastic filler and hardener. The ratio of filler to hardener is critical, and, if you mix it incorrectly, it will either not cure properly or cure too quickly (you won't have time to file and sand it into shape)

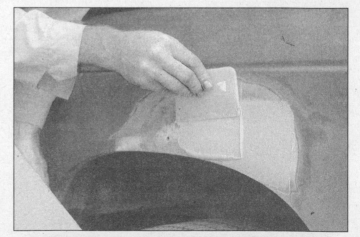

6   Working quickly so the filler doesn't harden, use a plastic applicator to press the body filler firmly into the metal, assuring it bonds completely. Work the filler until it matches the original contour and is slightly above the surrounding metal

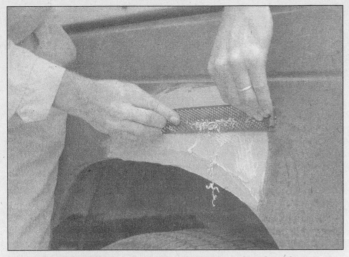

7   Let the filler harden until you can just dent it with your fingernail. Use a body file or Surform tool (shown here) to rough-shape the filler

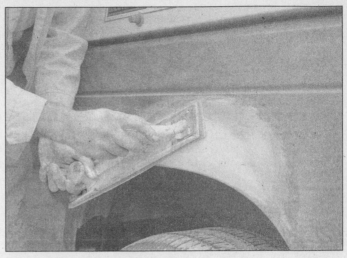

8   Use coarse-grit sandpaper and a sanding board or block to work the filler down until it's smooth and even. Work down to finer grits of sandpaper - always using a board or block - ending up with 360 or 400 grit

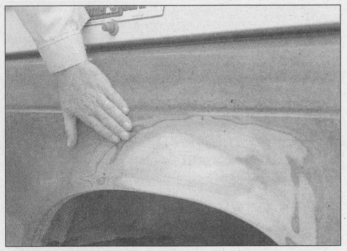

9   You shouldn't be able to feel any ridge at the transition from the filler to the bare metal or from the bare metal to the old paint. As soon as the repair is flat and uniform, remove the dust and mask off the adjacent panels or trim pieces

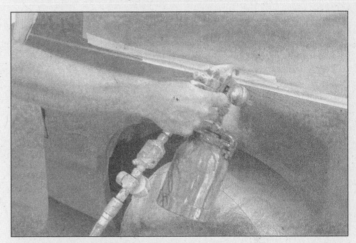

10   Apply several layers of primer to the area. Don't spray the primer on too heavy, so it sags or runs, and make sure each coat is dry before you spray on the next one. A professional-type spray gun is being used here, but aerosol spray primer is available inexpensively from auto parts stores

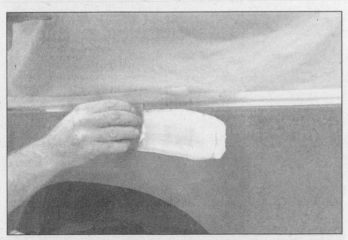

11   The primer will help reveal imperfections or scratches. Fill these with glazing compound. Follow the label instructions and sand it with 360 or 400-grit sandpaper until it's smooth. Repeat the glazing, sanding and respraying until the primer reveals a perfectly smooth surface

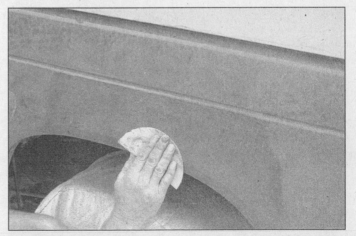

12   Finish sand the primer with very fine sandpaper (400 or 600-grit) to remove the primer overspray. Clean the area with water and allow it to dry. Use a tack rag to remove any dust, then apply the finish coat. Don't attempt to rub out or wax the repair area until the paint has dried completely (at least two weeks)

9   Trunk lid - removal, installation and adjustment

Refer to illustrations 9.2 and 9.6

1   Open the trunk lid.
2   Scribe or paint alignment marks around the trunk lid hinge bolt flanges **(see illustration)**.

9.2 Always scribe or paint alignment marks on the trunk lid mounting flange to ensure correct alignment of the trunk lid when it's reinstalled

3   Disconnect courtesy light connector at hinge and loosen and remove the hinge bolts.
4   Remove the trunk lid.
5   Installation is the reverse of removal.
6   The trunk lid can be shifted fore-and-aft and from side-to-side. The up-and-down adjustment is made by loosening the hinge screws and raising or lowering the trunk lid **(see illustration)**.
7   The trunk lid should be adjusted for an even and parallel fit in the opening. It should also be adjusted up-and-down for a flush fit with the surrounding panels. Care should be taken not to distort or mar the trunk lid or surrounding body panels.

10   Front bumper - removal and installation

Refer to illustrations 10.2, 10.3, 10.6a, 10.6b, 10.7 and 10.12

1984 and 1985 models

1   Raise the vehicle and place it securely on jackstands.
2   Pop the extension assembly retainers loose and remove the mounting stud nuts from both ends of the bumper **(see illustration)**.
3   Remove all four bolts from each isolator and bracket assembly **(see illustration)**.
4   Remove the bumper.
5   Installation is the reverse of removal.

1986 and 1987 models

Note: *These models are equipped with a bumper cover. The design of the bumper covers for Tempo and Topaz models differs somewhat. Tempo covers have extension assemblies, while Topaz covers are a wraparound design.*
6   If your vehicle is a Tempo, remove the nuts attaching the bumper extensions to the front fender. If your vehicle is a Topaz, remove the push retainers attaching the bumper cover assembly to the front fender **(see illustrations)**.
7   Remove the bolts attaching the bumper to the isolator and bracket assemblies and remove the bumper and cover assemblies as a unit (this is easier than trying to separate the bumper and cover assemblies while the bumper is still installed on the vehicle) **(see illustration)**.

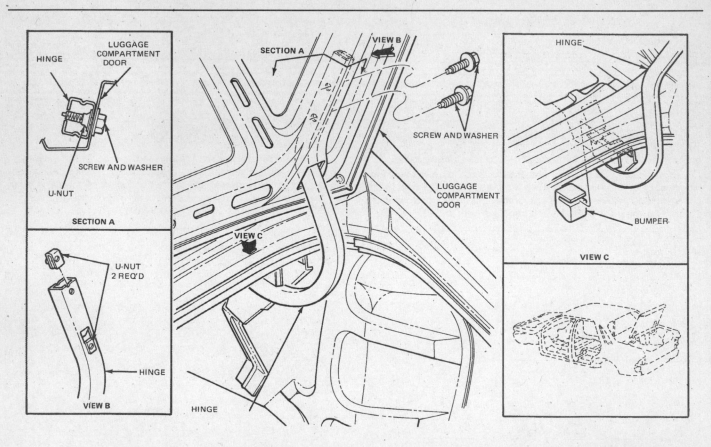

9.6 Note that the U-nuts that accept the trunk lid mounting bolts can be moved slightly to permit proper alignment of the trunk lid with the rear quarter panels

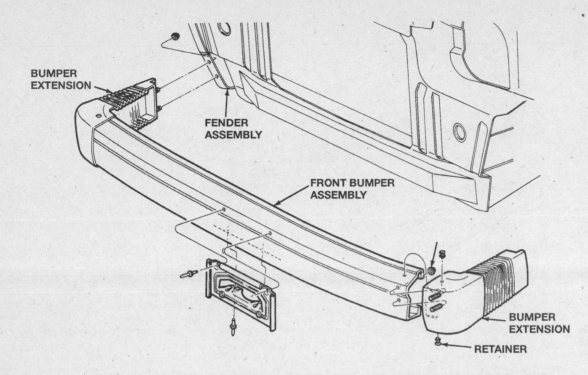

10.2 To detach the bumper extensions from the bumper on 1984 and 1985 models, pop loose and push aside the extension retainers, disconnect the retaining stud nuts and push the studs through the mounting holes in the bumper

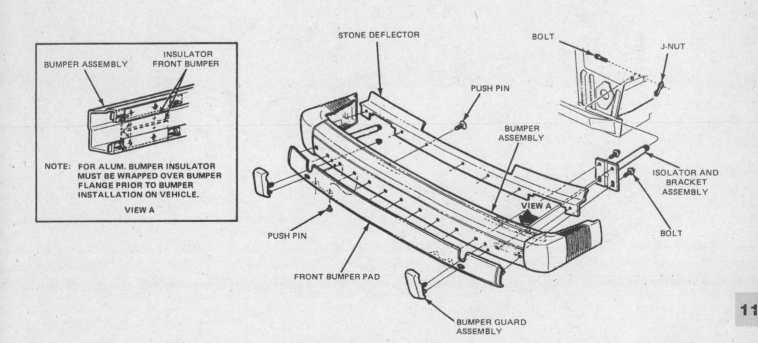

10.3 After detaching the extension assemblies from both ends of the bumper on 1984 and 1985 models, remove all four bolts from each isolator and bracket assembly and detach the bumper

11

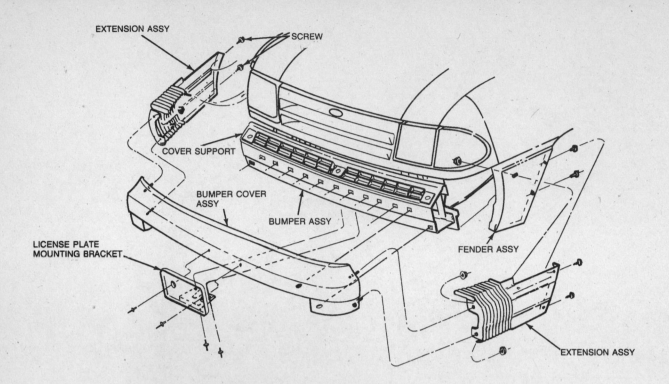

10.6a An exploded view of the Tempo front bumper cover assembly (1986 and 1987 models)

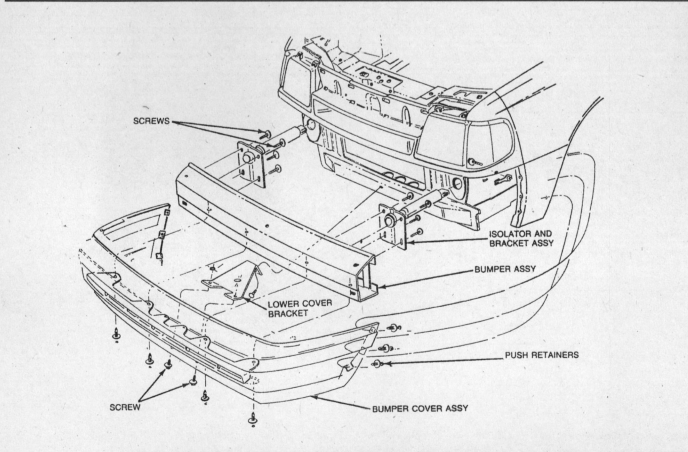

10.6b An exploded view of the Topaz front bumper cover assembly (1986 and 1987 models)

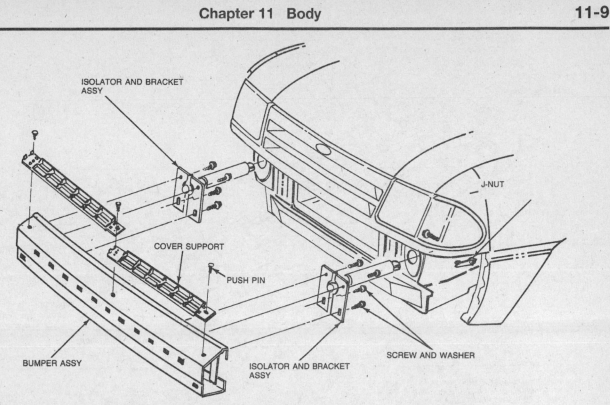

10.7 An exploded view of the Tempo front bumper assembly (1986 and 1987 models)

8   If your vehicle is a Tempo, remove the nuts attaching the bumper cover to the extensions.

9   From the back side of the bumper, squeeze the retaining tabs with a pair of pliers and disengage them from the bumper. Remove the bumper cover.

10   Installation is the reverse of removal.

1988 and later models

Warning: *If vehicle is equipped with airbags, refer to Chapter 12, to disarm the airbag system prior to performing any work described below.*

Note: *These models are equipped with an integrated one-piece bumper and cover.*

11   Remove the fog lamps, if equipped.

12   Remove the four bolts attaching the bumper to the isolators **(see illustration)**.

13   Pull the bumper forward to disengage the right and left slotted retainers.

14   Installation is the reverse of removal.

Note: *If bumper is to be replaced, remove the license plate bracket.*

11   Rear bumper - removal and installation

Refer to illustrations 11.2, 11.6, 11.7, 11.8 and 11.13

1984 and 1985 models

1   Raise the vehicle and support it securely on jackstands.

2   Pop the extension assemblies loose

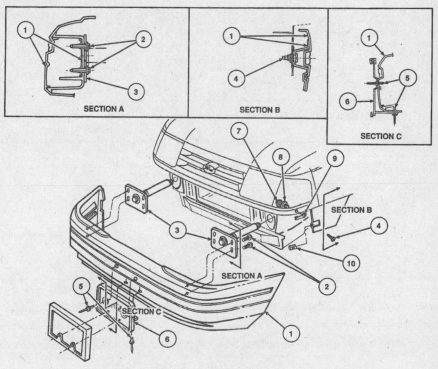

10.12 An exploded view of the Tempo/Topaz front bumper assembly (1988 and later models)

1	Bumper assembly	4	Screw and washer	7	Bolt
2	Screw and washer	5	Rivet	8	Washer
3	Isolator and bracket assembly	6	License plate bracket	9	J-nut
				10	U-nut

11

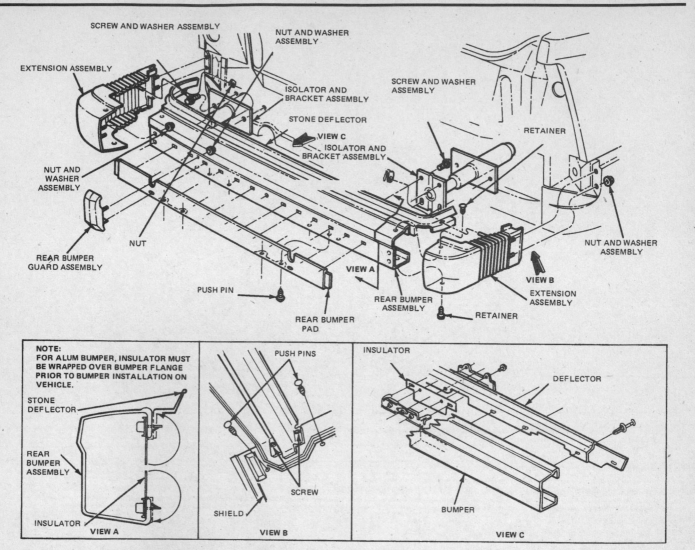

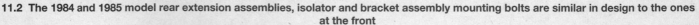

11.2 The 1984 and 1985 model rear extension assemblies, isolator and bracket assembly mounting bolts are similar in design to the ones at the front

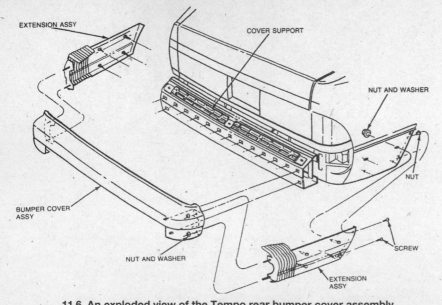

11.6 An exploded view of the Tempo rear bumper cover assembly (1986 and 1987 models)

from both ends of the bumper **(see illustration)**.

3   Remove all four bolts from each isolator and bracket assembly.

4   Remove the bumper.

5   Installation is the reverse of removal.

1986 and 1987 models

Note: *These models are equipped with a rear bumper cover. The design of the bumper covers for Tempo and Topaz models differs somewhat. Tempo covers have extension assemblies, while Topaz covers are a wraparound design.*

6   On Tempo models, remove the nuts attaching the bumper extensions to the rear quarter panel **(see illustration)**.

7   If your vehicle is a Topaz, remove the screws attaching the bumper cover assembly to the rear fender, then remove the four screws from within the trunk and four from the quarter panel reinforcement brackets **(see illustration)**.

8   Remove the bolts attaching the bumper to the isolator and bracket assemblies **(see illustration)** and remove the bumper and

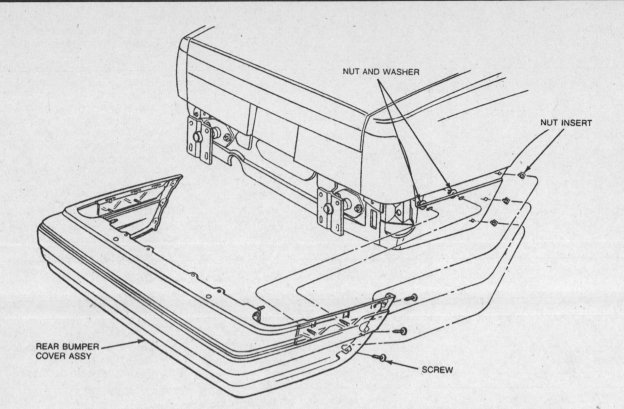

NUT AND WASHER

NUT INSERT

REAR BUMPER
COVER ASSY

SCREW

11.7 To remove the rear Topaz bumper cover on 1986 and 1987 models and on all two-door models 1988 and later, first remove the cover-to-fender screws as shown

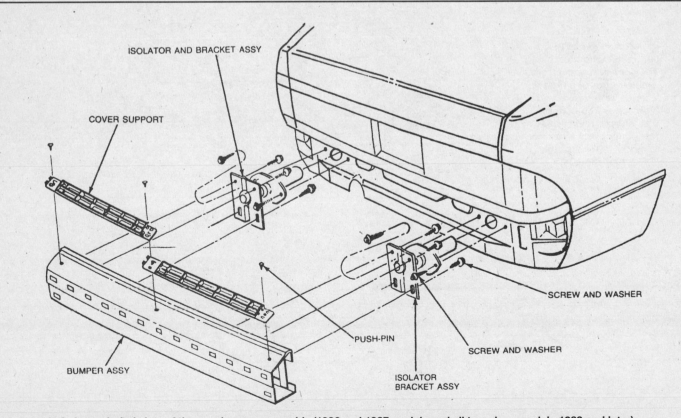

ISOLATOR AND BRACKET ASSY

COVER SUPPORT

SCREW AND WASHER

PUSH-PIN

SCREW AND WASHER

BUMPER ASSY

ISOLATOR
BRACKET ASSY

11.8 An exploded view of the rear bumper assembly (1986 and 1987 models and all two-door models 1988 and later) -
Note: *Topaz does not use cover supports*

11

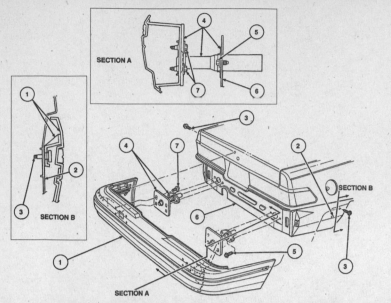

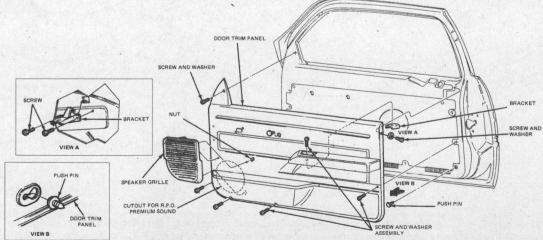

11.13 An exploded view of the Tempo/Topaz rear bumper assembly (1988 and later four-door models)

1	Bumper assembly	4	Isolator and bracket	6	Lower back panel
2	Quarter panel		assembly	7	Bolt and washer
3	Screw and washer	5	Screw and washer		assembly

cover assemblies as a unit (this is easier than trying to separate the bumper and cover assemblies while the bumper is still installed on the vehicle).

9   On Tempo models, remove the nuts attaching the bumper cover to the extensions.

10   To remove the bumper cover from the back side of the bumper, squeeze the retaining tabs with a pair of pliers and disengage them from the bumper, Remove the bumper cover.

11   Installation is the reverse of removal.

1988 and later two-door models

12   This procedure is the same as for the 1986 and 1987 Topaz.

1988 and later four-door models

Note: *Both Tempo and Topaz four-door models are equipped with an integrated one-piece bumper and cover.*

13   Remove the four bolts attaching the bumper to the isolators **(see illustration)**.

14   Pull the bumper forward to disengage the right and left slotted retainers.

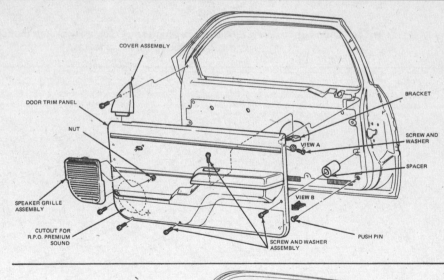

12.1a Refer to this illustration when removing the door trim panel from either door of a high-series Tempo/low and high series Topaz (top) or a low and mid series Tempo (bottom) two-door model (1984 through 1987 models)

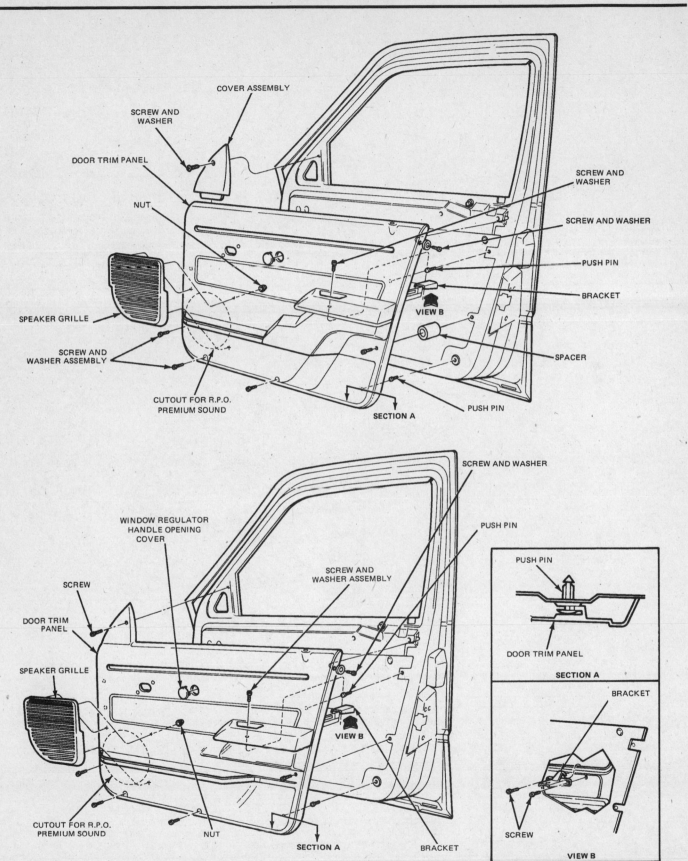

12.1b Refer to this illustration when removing the door trim panel from either front door of a high-series Tempo/low and high series Topaz (top) or a low and mid series Tempo (bottom) four-door model (1984 through 1987 models)

11

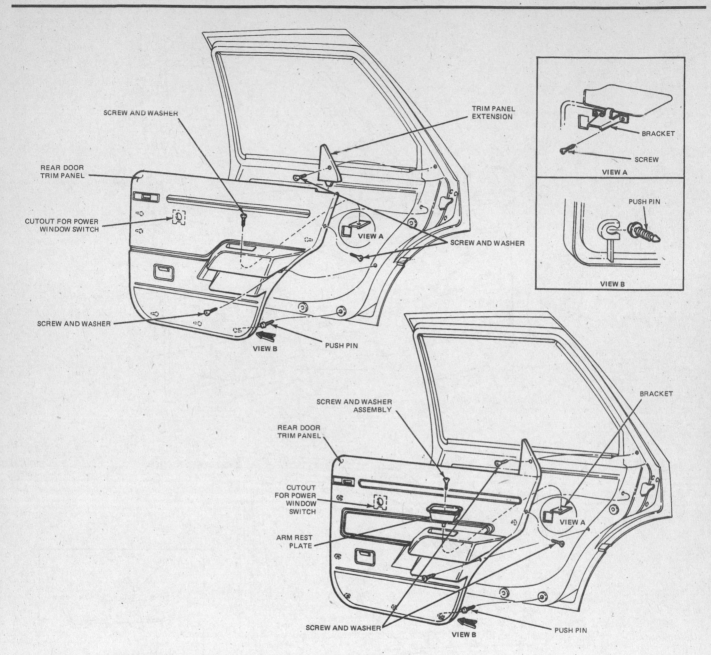

12.1c Refer to this illustration when removing the door trim panel from either rear door of a high series Tempo/low and high series Topaz (top) or a low and mid series Tempo (bottom) four-door model (1984 through 1987 models)

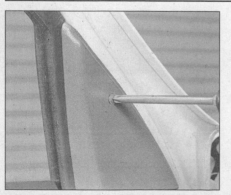

12.1d The cover assembly is held in place with a Phillips screw (early model shown)

15   Installation is the reverse of removal. **Note:** *If the bumper is to be replaced, remove the license plate bracket.*

12   Door trim panel - removal and installation

Refer to illustrations 12.1a, 12.1b, 12.1c, 12.1d, 12.2, 12.3, 12.4, 12.5, 12.6, 12.7, 12.8, 12.9, 12.12a, 12.12b, 12.12c and 12.12d
Note: *The following procedure applies specifically to the front door trim panel of a four-door Tempo/Topaz. However, the procedures for two-door models and for the rear doors on four-door models are similar.*

1984 through 1987 models

1   Remove the Phillips screw from the cover assembly or trim panel extension **(see illustrations).**
2   Remove the Torx screw from the window regulator handle **(see illustration).**
3   Remove the Torx screw from the remote control unit **(see illustration).**
4   Remove the Phillips screw from the armrest **(see illustration).**
5   Remove the Phillips screw from the trim panel just below the armrest **(see illustration).**
6   Remove the Phillips screw from the upper rear edge of the trim panel **(see illustration).**

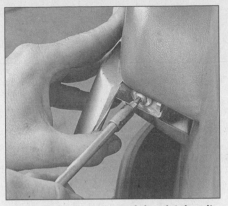

12.2 The window regulator handle is held in place with a Torx screw, which requires a special tool for removal (early model shown)

12.3 The remote control door latch unit can be detached after removing the Torx screw (early model shown)

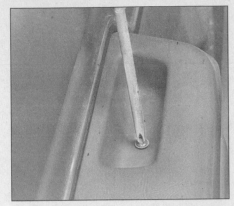

12.4 Remove the Phillips screw from the armrest . . .

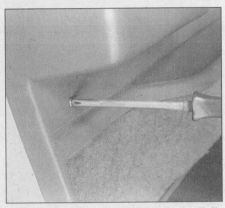

12.5 . . . and the trim panel underneath it

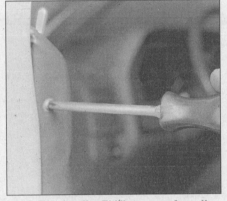

12.6 Remove the Phillips screw from the upper rear edge of the trim panel . . .

12.7 . . . the Allen head screw from the mirror bezel . . .

7 Remove the Allen head screw from the mirror remote control bezel **(see illustration)**.

8 Remove the two screws from the lower edge of the trim panel **(see illustration)**.

9 Using a homemade tool **(see illustration)**, pry the trim panel retaining push pins from the door inner panel and remove the trim panel.

10 If the trim panel is to be replaced, transfer the trim panel retaining push pins to the new panel assembly. Replace any bent, broken or missing push pins.

11 Installation is the reverse of removal.

1988 and later models

12 **Note:** *Although the door trim panels are slightly different on later models, the same general procedures used above apply. Exploded views **(see illustrations)** are included for reference.*

12.8 . . . and the Phillips screws from the lower edge of the trim panel

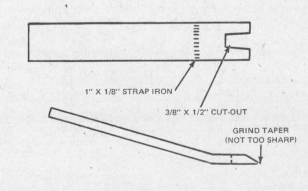

1" X 1/8" STRAP IRON

3/8" X 1/2" CUT-OUT

GRIND TAPER (NOT TOO SHARP)

12.9 A piece of 1-inch by 1/8-inch strap iron bent like this with a 3/8 by 1/2-inch cutout on the tapered end makes a handy trim panel removal tool

11

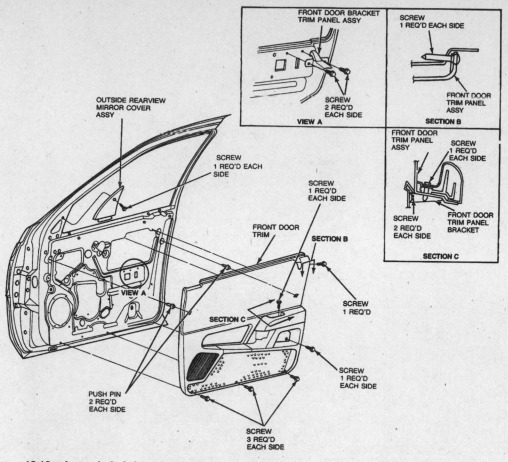

12.12a An exploded view showing later model front door panel details (four-door models)

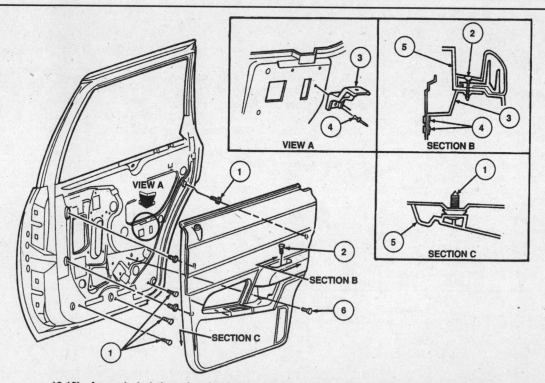

12.12b An exploded view showing later model rear door panel details (four-door models)

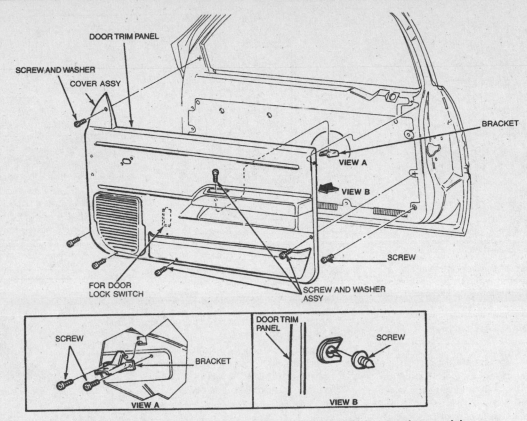

12.12c An exploded view showing later model door panel details for two-door models

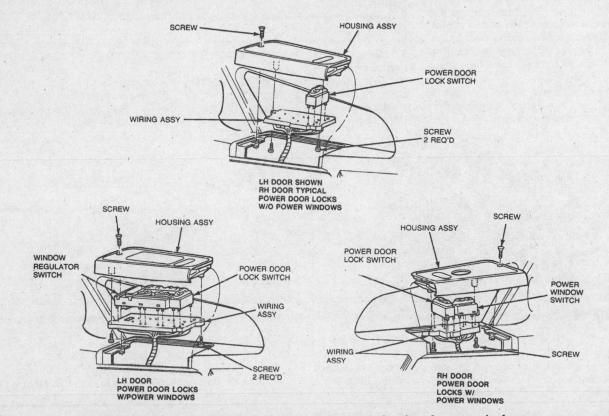

12.12d An exploded view showing later model door-mounted options for removal reference

11

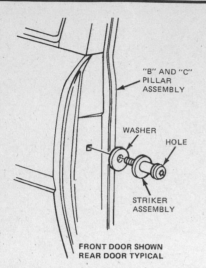

13.1 Because of the eccentric shape of the base plate and washer, the striker can be adjusted both laterally and vertically

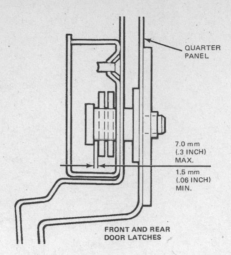

13.2 Striker adjustment details (note the required clearance)

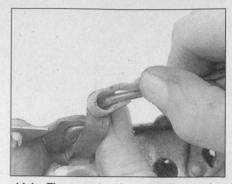

14.4a There are two types of clips on the typical Tempo/Topaz door latch assembly - to disconnect a rod from this type, simply push the elongated portion of the clip aside as shown, twist the rod and pull it out

13   Door striker - adjustment

Refer to illustrations 13.1 and 13.2

1   The striker assembly **(see illustration)** can be adjusted laterally and vertically as well as fore-and-aft. The striker should not, however, be adjusted to correct door sag.

2   The striker should be shimmed to get the clearance shown **(see illustration)** between the striker and the latch. To check the clearance, clean the latch jaws and the striker area. Apply a thin layer of dark grease to the striker. As the door is closed and opened, a definite pattern will result on the latch striker. Use a maximum of two shims under the striker.

3   Move the striker assembly in-or-out to provide a flush fit at the door and pillar or quarter panel. You'll need a no. 50 Torx driver

to loosen and tighten the latch striker. Tighten the striker securely.

14   Door latch and remote controls - removal and installation

Refer to illustrations 14.4a, 14.4b, 14.6a, 14.6b, 14.6c and 14.6d

1   Remove the door trim panel (see Section 12).

2   Remove the three door latch screws so the door latch can be moved around inside the door to disconnect the four link rods.

3   Remove the plastic latch cover from the latch assembly.

4   With the latch disconnected from the door, detach the inside door lock rod, the inside remote handle rod, the key lock cylinder rod and the outside remote door

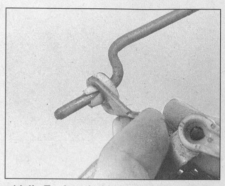

14.4b To detach this type of clip, simply twist the rod and slide it out

handle rod **(see illustrations)**. Note that each rod has a unique shape and that the ends of each rod are shaped differently. Note which end of each rod attaches to the latch mechanism.

5   Remove the latch.

6   Installation is the reverse of removal **(see illustrations)**.

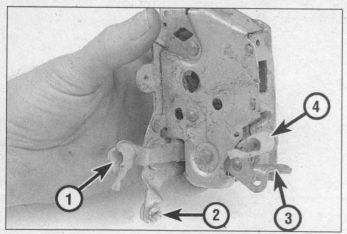

14.6a There are four rod-actuated devices on the front door latch (the rear latch looks the same but doesn't have an outside key lock cylinder)

1   To inside locking knob
2   To inside remote door handle
3   To outside key lock cylinder
4   To outside remote door handle

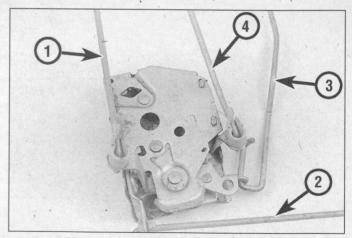

14.6b The four rods attached to the latch mechanism (removed from the door for clarity - they look just like this in place)

1   Inside locking knob rod
2   Inside remote door handle rod
3   Outside key lock cylinder rod
4   Outside remote door handle rod

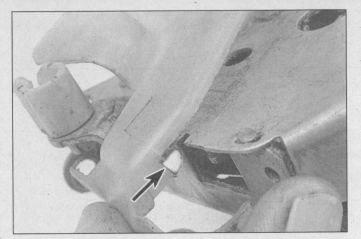

14.6c When installing the plastic cover on the latch assembly, the tab on the cover (arrow) must fit into the slot in the latch . . .

14.6d . . . and the post (arrow) must fit into the hole

15 Outside mirror - removal and installation

Refer to illustrations 15.2a , 15.2b and 15.3

1   Remove the door trim panel (see Section 12).

2   On cable-adjust mirrors, remove the mirror mounting stud nuts **(see illustrations)** and detach the mirror and adjustment cable assembly from the door. Be sure to note the routing of the adjustment cable before removing the mirror.

3   On electrically powered mirrors, remove the mirror electrical connector and remove the trim cover with the control assembly **(see illustration). Note:** *The control assembly is retained to the trim cover with an Allen head set screw.* Remove the mirror mounting stud nuts and detach the mirror. **Note:** *Guide the harness out of the hole while removing the mirror.*

4   Installation is the reverse of removal.

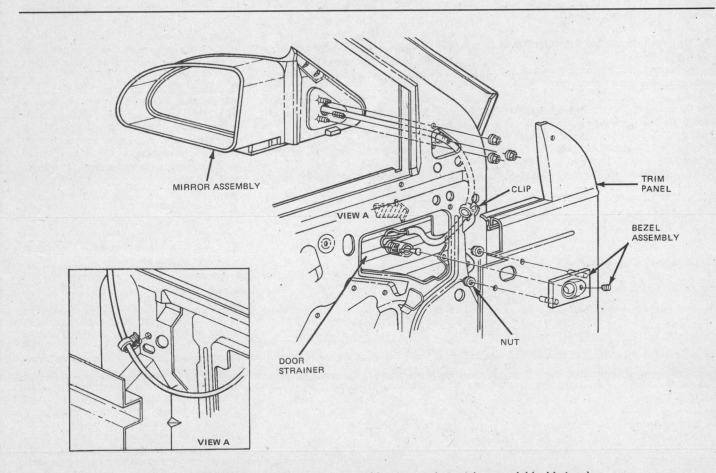

15.2a An exploded view of the mirror assembly on an early two-door model (cable type)

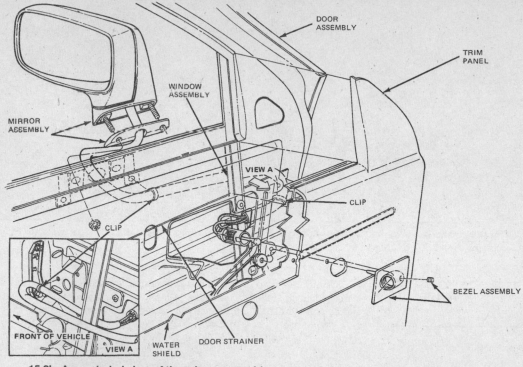

15.2b An exploded view of the mirror assembly on an early four-door model (cable type)

16   Door window glass - removal and installation

Refer to illustration 16.2

1   Remove the front door trim panel and watershield (see Section 12).
2   Remove the two rivets attaching the glass to the run and bracket assembly **(see illustration)**. **Caution:** *Prior to removing the center pins from the rivets, it is recommended that a suitable block support be inserted between the door outer panel and glass bracket to stabilize the glass during rivet removal.* Remove the center pin from each rivet with a drift punch. Using a 1/4-inch diameter drill, drill out the remaining rivets as damage to the plastic glass retainer and spacer could otherwise result.
3   Remove the glass.
4   Remove any debris from the bottom of the door.
5   Snap the plastic retainer and spacer into the two retainer holes in the new glass. Make certain that metal washer in the retainer assembly is on outboard side (towards door skin) of glass.
6   Insert the glass into the door.
7   Position the glass-to-glass bracket and install the two rivets to secure the glass-to-glass bracket. **Note:** *Two 1/4-inch-20 x 1-inch bolts, nuts and washer assemblies may be used as alternates for glass retention. However, torque must not exceed 36 to 61 inch-lbs.*
8   Install the door trim panel and watershield (see Section 12).

17   Door window regulator - removal and installation

Refer to illustration 17.3

Warning: *If the regulator motor or counterbalance spring must be removed or replaced for any reason, ensure that the regulator arms are in a fixed position prior to removal to prevent possible injury during counterspring rewind.*

1   Remove the door trim panel and watershield (see Section 12).
2   Prop the glass in the full-up position.
3   Remove the four rivets (power windows) or three rivets (manual windows) attaching the regulator mounting plate assembly to the door inner panel **(see illustration)**.
4   On models with power windows, detach the electrical connector. Remove the window

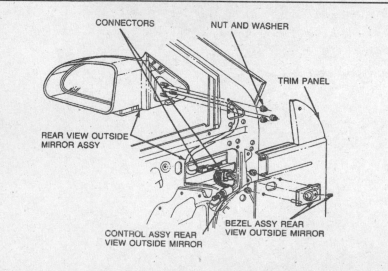

15.3 An exploded view of the power mirror assembly on a later two-door model (four-door similar)

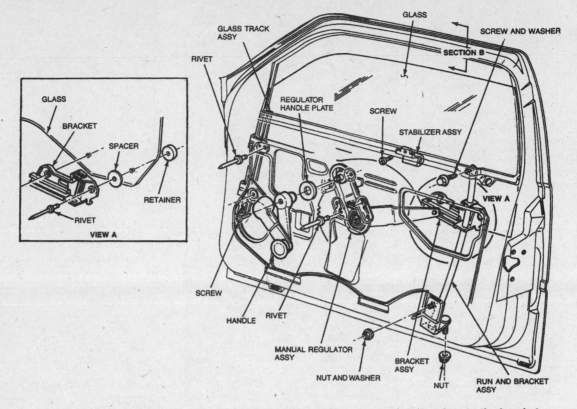

16.2 Door glass attachment details - View A shows how the rivets attach the glass to the bracket

regulator from the door. **Note:** *Use the access hole in the door inner panel for removal and installation.*

5 Install the window regulator through the access hole in the rear of the door and slide the arm roller into the glass bracket C-channel.

6 Install three rivets (manual windows) or four rivets (power windows). **Note:** *As an alternative, use the same quantity of 1/4-inch-20 x 1/2-inch bolts, nuts and washers. Tighten them securely.*

7 On power regulators, reconnect the electrical connector.

8 Raise the glass up and down to check for smooth operation.

9 Install the watershield and door trim panel (see Section 12).

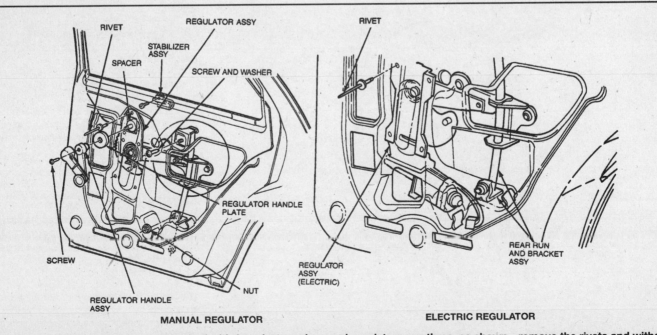

MANUAL REGULATOR

ELECTRIC REGULATOR

17.3 Power window regulators are attached with four rivets and manual regulators use three, as shown - remove the rivets and withdraw the window regulator from the hole in the door

11

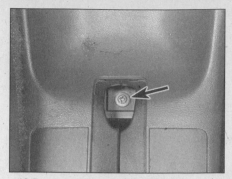

18.3 Remove the two screws from the litter container and lift it out . . .

18.4 . . . then remove the two screws (arrows) from the rear of the center finish panel . . .

18.5 . . . and the screw from the front of the center finish panel to detach the panel

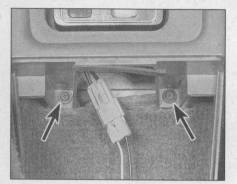

18.6 Remove the two screws from the consolette immediately behind the gear shift lever bezel

18.7 Remove the two screws (arrows) from the rear of the consolette and lift it out

18 Center console - removal and installation

Refer to illustrations 18.3, 18.4, 18.5, 18.6, 18.7, 18.8a, 18.8b, 18.10, 18.24, 18.25a and 18.25b

Warning: *If vehicle is equipped with airbags, refer to Chapter 12, to disarm the airbag system prior to performing any work described below.*

Consolette (1984 through 1987 models)

1   Detach the cable from the negative terminal of the battery.
2   Remove the free standing armrest, if so equipped.
3   Remove the two rear litter container screws **(see illustration)** and detach the litter container.
4   Remove the two center finish panel-to-support bracket rear screws **(see illustration)**.
5   Remove the front screw and detach the center finish panel **(see illustration)**.
6   Remove the front consolette screws **(see illustration)**.
7   Remove the rear consolette-to-support bracket screws **(see illustration)** and detach the consolette assembly.
8   Installation is the reverse of removal. Refer to the accompanying exploded views **(see illustrations)** during reassembly.

Console (1984 through 1987 models)

9   Detach the cable from the negative terminal of the battery.
10   Remove the two console-to-front support bracket screws **(see illustration)**.
11   Remove the two console-to-rear support bracket screws.
12   Open the console door and remove the two console-to-floor bracket screws.
13   Remove the free standing armrest, if so equipped.
14   Pull the parking brake lever all the way to the rear.
15   Remove the three center finish panel screws, lift the panel up and back,

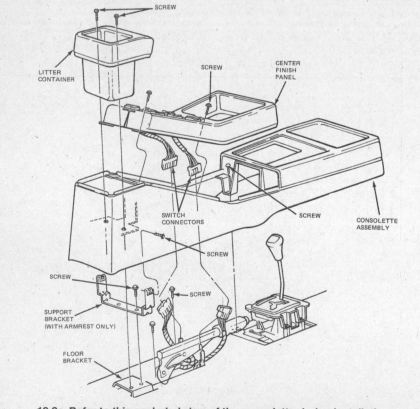

18.8a Refer to this exploded view of the consolette during installation (1984 to 1987 models)

SCREW

LITTER CONTAINER

SCREW

CENTER FINISH PANEL

SWITCH CONNECTORS

SCREW

CONSOLETTE ASSEMBLY

SCREW

SCREW

SCREW

SUPPORT BRACKET (WITH ARMREST ONLY)

FLOOR BRACKET

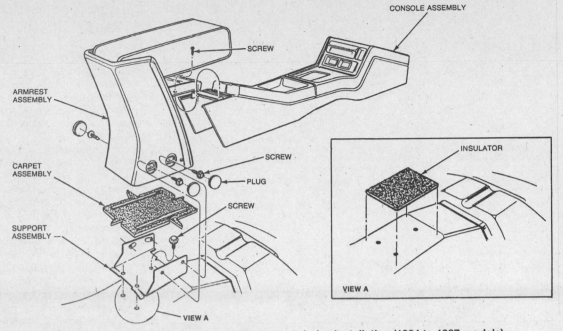

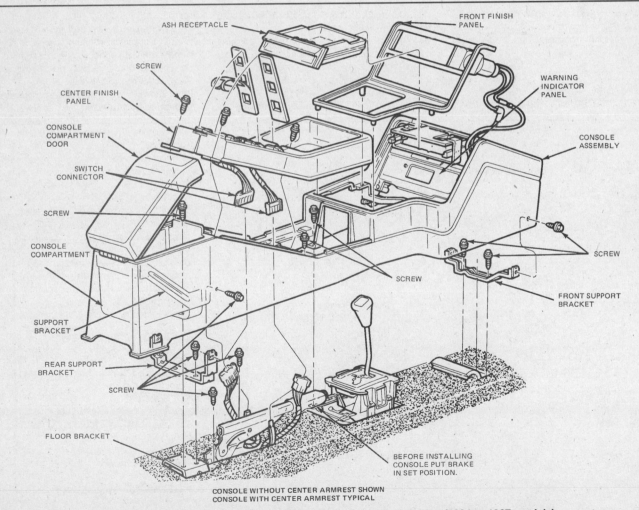

18.8b Refer to this exploded view of the armrest during installation (1984 to 1987 models)

18.10 Refer to this exploded view of the console during installation (1984 to 1987 models)

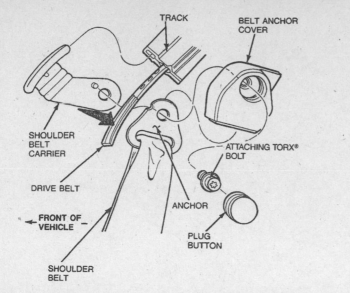

18.24 Remove the upper shoulder belt anchor plug buttons and the bolts - allow the belts to retract into the console as far as possible

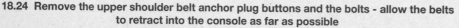

Console (1988 and later models)

24 If the vehicle is equipped with an automatic shoulder harness, cycle the shoulder belts to the A-pillar position. Remove the upper shoulder belt anchor plug buttons and the bolts **(see illustration)**. Allow the belts to retract into the console as far as possible. **Note:** *Anchor bolts require a Torx-type socket.*

25 If the console has no armrest, remove the top rear panel from the console (it snaps out), then remove the one console rear support retaining screw **(see illustrations)**. **Note:** *Refer to illustration 18.25a for trim-to-console hardware and 18.25b for console-to-body hardware.*

26 If the console is equipped with an armrest, snap off the two shoulder belt bezels to gain access to the four armrest retaining screws and remove the screws (two on each side) and the armrest. Remove one console-to-rear support retaining screw.

27 Using a small screwdriver, relieve the pressure on the retaining clip on the underside of both shoulder harness emergency release lever handles and pull the handles off.

28 Remove the two emergency lever finish panel-to-console retaining screws and lift the panel out of console. Remove the two console-to-center support retaining screws located under the finish panel.

29 Remove the drop-in cupholder and the two cassette tray attaching screws. Lift the

disconnect all wires and remove the finish panel.

16 Remove one screw and loosen the other screw from the crossmember in front of the brake lever. Rotate the crossmember forward and out of the way.

17 Remove the two center console-to-floor screws.

18 Remove the ash receptacle.

19 Pry up the bottom edge of the front

finish panel, pull up and back to disengage the two tabs at the top front edge.

20 Disconnect the cigar lighter wires and remove the finish panel.

21 Remove the four graphic display mounting plate screws. Unplug the electrical connectors and remove the graphic display.

22 Lift the console up to clear the shift lever and knob and remove the console.

23 Installation is the reverse of removal.

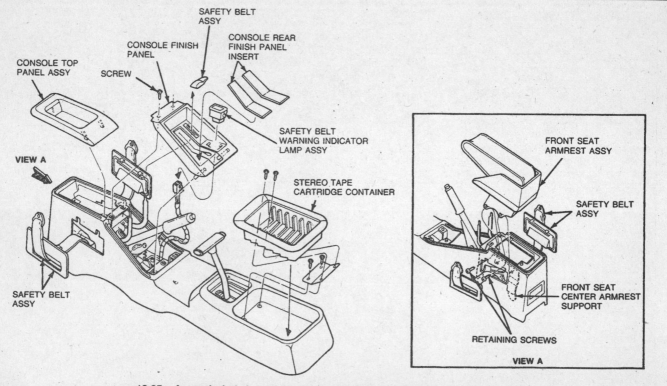

18.25a An exploded view of the console with armrest (1988 and later models)

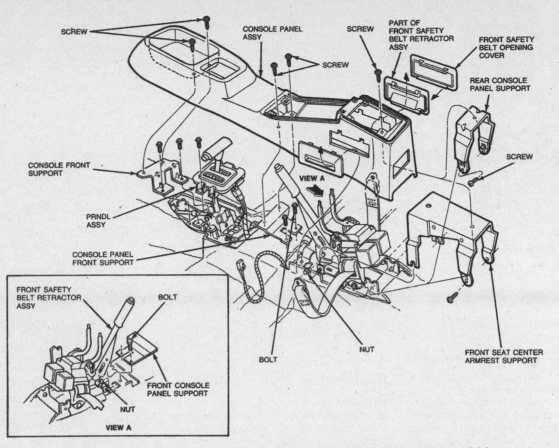

18.25b An exploded view of the console without an armrest (1988 and later models)

cassette tray out to gain access to the two console retaining screws. Remove the two front console retaining screws.

30   If not already done, snap out the two shoulder belt finish bezels from the console. Lift the console up and feed the shoulder belts and bezels through the opening in the console and remove the console.

31   To install, reverse the removal procedure. **Caution**: *Tighten the upper shoulder harness anchor bolts to 12 to 18 ft-lbs and check for proper operation of the automatic shoulder harness system.*

19   Seats - removal and installation

Refer to illustrations 19.1, 19.9 and 19.14

Front seats

1   Seat tracks are attached to the floor pan by studs with nut and washer assemblies and/or bolts (washer head type). All attaching hardware is removed from inside the vehicle **(see illustration)**.

3   Remove the front and rear track assembly trim shields (and side trim on some models) by removing the screws.

4   Remove the front and rear seat track mounting nuts and washers and/or bolts from inside the vehicle.

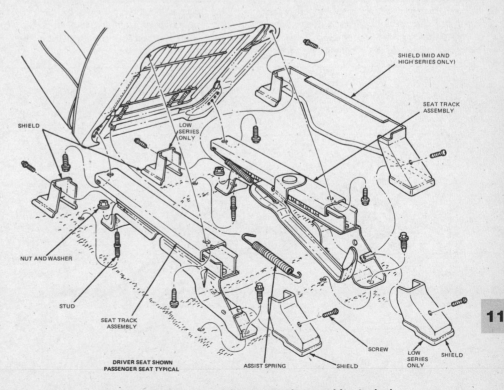

19.1 An exploded view of the seat track assembly - typical

11

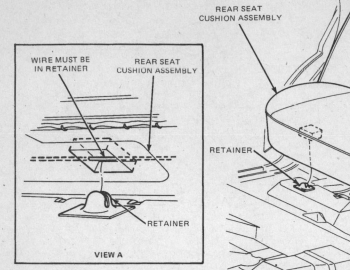

19.9 Rear seat cushion mounting details

5   On non-power seats, lift the seat and track assembly out of the vehicle.

6   On power seats, lift the seat up just enough to disconnect the electrical connector. Remove the seat from the vehicle. **Caution:** *Use care when handling power seats. Dropping them or sitting in them while they're not in the vehicle can damage the track drive mechanism.*

7   If the seat tracks are being replaced, transfer the assist springs and spacers (if any) to the new track assembly.

8   Installation is the reverse of removal.

Rear seat

Cushion

9   Apply knee pressure to the lower portion of the rear seat cushion, then push toward the rear of the vehicle to disengage the seat cushion from the retainers **(see illustration)**.

10   Place the seat cushion assembly in position.

11   Place the seatbelts on top of the cushion.

12   Apply knee pressure to the lower portion of the seat cushion to hook the wire in the retainer.

Seat back

13   Remove the rear seat cushion as described above.

14   Remove the seatbelt assembly bolts **(see illustration)**.

15   Grasp the seat back assembly at the bottom and lift up to disengage the hanger wire from the retainers.

16   Place the seat back in position in the vehicle with the hanger wires engaged in the retainers **(see illustration 19.14)**.

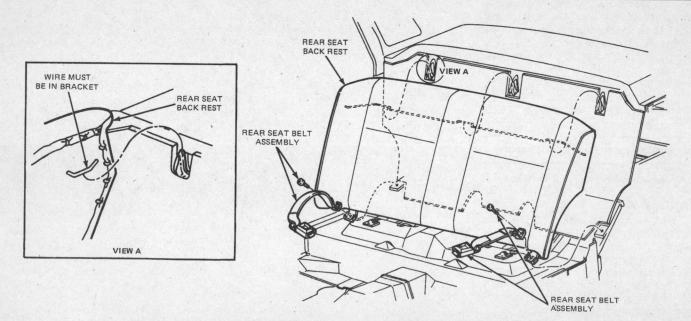

19.14 Rear seat back mounting details

17   Install the seatbelt assemblies and tighten the bolts securely.
18   Install the rear seat cushion.

20   Automatic shoulder harness - general information

Many late-model vehicles are equipped with automatic front seat shoulder harnesses. They are termed automatic because you don't have to buckle them - the shoulder harness automatically positions itself when the door is closed and the key is turned on. An emergency release lever allows the harness to be manually removed for exit in an emergency. **Warning:** *Be sure to fasten the manual (lap) seatbelt as well. The automatic shoulder harness will not work properly unless the lap belt is fastened.*

Most systems have a warning light and buzzer that indicate the emergency release lever has been pulled up, releasing the shoulder harness. Make sure the release lever is down and the light/buzzer are off to ensure proper operation of the automatic shoulder harness.

Also, if you disconnect any wires or remove any automatic shoulder harness components when performing repair procedures on other vehicle components, be sure to reinstall everything and check the harness for proper operation when the repairs are complete.

Since the automatic shoulder harness is operated by several electrical switches and is computer controlled, diagnosis and repair must be done by a dealer service department. Do not jeopardize the safety of front-seat occupants - if the automatic shoulder harness malfunctions, or you have questions regarding the proper use or operation of the system, contact a dealer service department.

21   Windshield and fixed glass - removal and installation

1   Replacement of the windshield and fixed glass requires the use of special fast-setting adhesive/caulk materials. These operations should be left to a dealer or a shop specializing in glass work.
2   Windshield-mounted rear view mirror support removal is also best left to experts, as the bond to the glass also requires special tools and adhesives.

22   Glove box - removal and installation

1   Empty the glove compartment.
2   If the glove box is to be removed completely (as in replacement), remove the two hinge screws from under dashboard.
3   If only access is needed behind the glove box, simply push the sides of the glove compartment liner in, swing the liner down from the opening and let it hang on the hinges.
4   Installation is the reverse of removal.

23   Hood release latch and cable - removal, installation and adjustment

Refer to illustrations 23.2, 23.3 and 23.8

Warning: *If vehicle is equipped with airbags, refer to Chapter 12, to disarm the airbag system prior to performing any work described below.*

Removal and installation

1   Open the hood and position the prop rod.
2   Remove the two screws retaining the latch assembly to the upper radiator support **(see illustration)**.

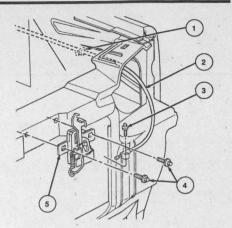

23.2 To remove the hood release latch, remove the two screws retaining the latch assembly to the upper radiator support

3   Remove the screw retaining the cable end to the latch assembly **(see illustration)**.
4   Rotate the cable end out of the latch return spring and remove the latch from the cable.
5   If only the latch is to be removed/replaced, reinstall the latch by reversing the above Steps. If the cable is to be replaced, proceed to the next Step.
6   To facilitate reinstallation of a new cable, fasten a length of mechanic's wire, about 8 feet long, to the cable.
7   From inside the vehicle, locate the release cable coming through the firewall and unseat the sealing grommet towards the release handle.
8   Remove the right side kick panel, then remove the cable mounting bracket retaining screws and carefully pull the cable assembly out **(see illustration)**. **Note:** *Pull the cable out just far enough to clear the end of the mounting bracket. Do not pull the mechanic's wire all the way out.*
9   Install the wire to the new cable and pull the new cable assembly through the retaining wall from the other end, using the mechanic's wire.

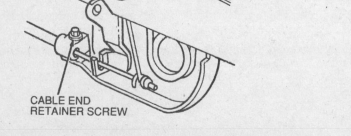

23.3 Remove the release cable end retainer screw and rotate the cable end out of latch return spring

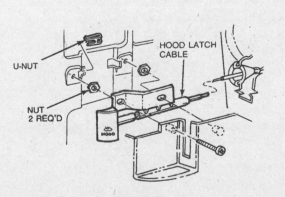

23.8 Remove the right side kick panel, then remove the cable mounting bracket retaining screws and carefully pull the cable assembly out

10   Seat the grommet securely and install the cable mounting bracket retaining screws.

11   Install the terminal end of the cable into the latch return spring, then rotate the cable through the V-slot and install the screw retaining the cable to the latch assembly.

12   Position the latch assembly on the upper radiator support. Install the retaining screws.

13   Check the operation of the hood latch cable before closing the hood. Adjust as outlined below, if necessary.

Adjustment

14   Loosen the hood latch retaining bolts in the radiator support until they are just loose enough to move the latch from side-to-side.

15   Move the latch from side-to-side to align it with the opening in the hood. The hood latch housing should not contact the striker opening.

16   Move the hood latch up or down as required to obtain a flush fit between the top of the hood and the fenders when upward pressure is applied to the front of the hood. If alignment is good, tighten the hood latch retaining bolts.

17   Open and close the hood several times to check operation.

18   If hood closing effort or inside hood release effort are too high, adjust the hood latch assembly upwards and/or adjust the hood bumpers downwards. Secure the latch retaining bolts and hood bumper locknuts.

19   Raise the two hood bumpers to eliminate any looseness at the front of the hood when closed. Secure the hood bumper locknuts.

20   Repeat the alignment and operation checks.

Chapter 12
Chassis electrical system

Contents

Specifications

Blower motor current draw

Low	2.0 amps/5.5 volts
Medium	3.5 amps/8.0 volts
High	7.0 amps/12.9 volts

Torque specifications

Neutral start switch bolts	84 to 108 in-lbs

1   General information

Warning: *To prevent electrical shorts, fires and injury, always disconnect the cable from the negative terminal of the battery before checking, repairing or replacing electrical system components.*

The chassis electrical system of this vehicle is a 12-volt, negative ground type. Power for the lights and all electrical accessories is supplied by a lead/acid-type battery which is charged by the alternator.

This chapter covers repair and service procedures for various chassis (non-engine related) electrical components. For information regarding the engine electrical system components (battery, alternator, distributor and starter motor), see Chapter 5.

Warning: *On models so equipped, whenever working in the vicinity of the front grille/bumper, steering wheel, steering column or other components of the airbag system, the system should be disarmed. To do this, perform the following steps:*

a) *Turn the ignition switch to Off.*
b) *Detach the cable from the negative battery terminal, then detach the positive cable. Wait two minutes for the electronic module backup power supply to be depleted.*

To enable the system
a) *Turn the ignition switch to the Off position.*
b) *Connect the positive battery cable first, then connect the negative cable.*

2   Electrical troubleshooting - general information

A typical electrical circuit consists of an electrical component, any switches, relays, motors, fuses, fusible links or circuit breakers, etc. related to that component and the wiring and connectors that link the component to both the battery and the chassis. To help you pinpoint an electrical circuit problem, wiring diagrams are included at the end of this book.

Before tackling any troublesome electrical circuit, first study the appropriate wiring diagrams to get a complete understanding of what makes up that individual circuit. Trouble spots, for instance, can often be isolated by noting if other components related to that circuit are operating properly. If several components or circuits fail at one time, chances are the problem is in a fuse or ground connection because several circuits are often routed through the same fuse and ground connections.

Electrical problems usually stem from simple causes such as loose or corroded connectors, a blown fuse, a melted fusible link or a bad relay. Visually inspect the condition of all fuses, wires and connectors in a problem circuit before troubleshooting it.

The basic tools needed for electrical troubleshooting include a circuit tester, a high impedance (10 K-ohm) digital voltmeter, a continuity tester and a jumper wire with an inline circuit breaker for bypassing electrical components. Before attempting to locate or define a problem with electrical test instruments, use the wiring diagrams to decide where to make the necessary connections.

Voltage checks

Perform a voltage check first when a circuit is not functioning properly. Connect one lead of a circuit tester to either the negative battery terminal or a known good ground.

Connect the other lead to a connector in the circuit being tested, preferably nearest to the battery or fuse. If the bulb of the tester lights up, voltage is present, which means that the part of the circuit between the connector and the battery is problem free.

Continue checking the rest of the circuit in the same fashion.

12

When you reach a point at which no voltage is present, the problem lies between that point and the last test point with voltage. Most of the time the problem can be traced to a loose connection. **Note:** *Keep in mind that some circuits receive voltage only when the ignition key is in the Accessory or Run position.*

Finding a short circuit

One method of finding shorts in a circuit is to remove the fuse and connect a test light or voltmeter in its place. There should be no voltage present in the circuit. Move the wiring harness from side-to-side while watching the test light. If the bulb goes on, there is a short to ground somewhere in that area, probably where the insulation has rubbed through. The same test can be performed on each component in the circuit, even a switch.

Ground check

Perform a ground test to check whether a component is properly grounded. Disconnect the battery and connect one lead of a self-powered test light, known as a continuity tester, to a known good ground (an ohmmeter can also be used). Connect the other lead to the wire or ground connection being tested. If the bulb goes on, the ground is good. If the bulb does not go on, the ground is not good.

Continuity check

A continuity check determines if there are any breaks in a circuit - if it is conducting electricity properly. With the circuit off (no power in the circuit), a self-powered continuity tester can be used to check the circuit (an ohmmeter can also be used). Connect the test leads to both ends of the circuit, and if the test

light comes on the circuit is passing current properly. If the light doesn't come on, there is a break somewhere in the circuit. The same procedure can be used to test a switch, by connecting the continuity tester to the power in and power out sides of the switch. With the switch turned on, the test light should come on.

Finding an open circuit

When diagnosing for possible open circuits it is often difficult to locate them by sight because oxidation or terminal misalignment are hidden by the connectors. Merely wiggling a connector on a sensor or in the wiring harness may correct the open circuit condition. Remember this if an open circuit is indicated when troubleshooting a circuit. Intermittent problems may also be caused by oxidized or loose connections.

Electrical troubleshooting is simple if

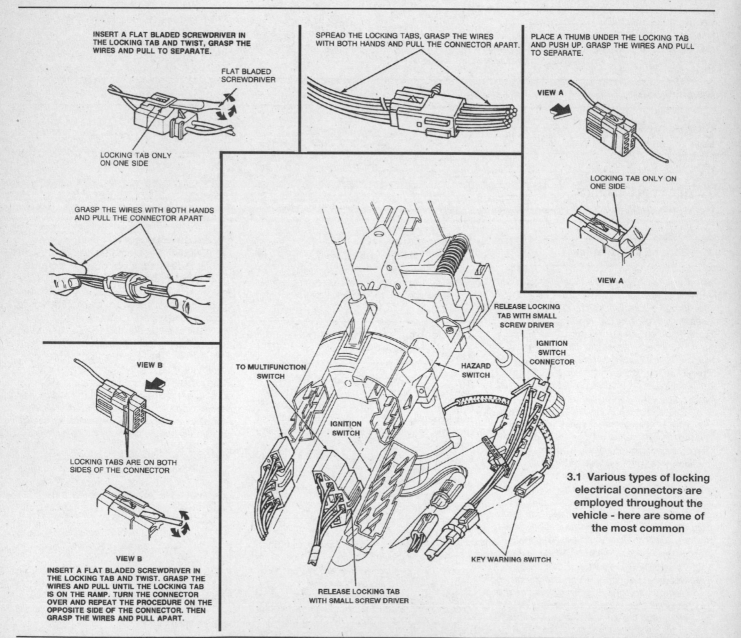

INSERT A FLAT BLADED SCREWDRIVER IN THE LOCKING TAB AND TWIST, GRASP THE WIRES AND PULL TO SEPARATE.

FLAT BLADED SCREWDRIVER

LOCKING TAB ONLY ON ONE SIDE

SPREAD THE LOCKING TABS, GRASP THE WIRES WITH BOTH HANDS AND PULL THE CONNECTOR APART.

PLACE A THUMB UNDER THE LOCKING TAB AND PUSH UP. GRASP THE WIRES AND PULL TO SEPARATE.

VIEW A

LOCKING TAB ONLY ON ONE SIDE

VIEW A

GRASP THE WIRES WITH BOTH HANDS AND PULL THE CONNECTOR APART

VIEW B

LOCKING TABS ARE ON BOTH SIDES OF THE CONNECTOR

VIEW B

INSERT A FLAT BLADED SCREWDRIVER IN THE LOCKING TAB AND TWIST. GRASP THE WIRES AND PULL UNTIL THE LOCKING TAB IS ON THE RAMP. TURN THE CONNECTOR OVER AND REPEAT THE PROCEDURE ON THE OPPOSITE SIDE OF THE CONNECTOR. THEN GRASP THE WIRES AND PULL APART.

TO MULTIFUNCTION SWITCH

IGNITION SWITCH

HAZARD SWITCH

RELEASE LOCKING TAB WITH SMALL SCREW DRIVER

IGNITION SWITCH CONNECTOR

RELEASE LOCKING TAB WITH SMALL SCREW DRIVER

KEY WARNING SWITCH

3.1 Various types of locking electrical connectors are employed throughout the vehicle - here are some of the most common

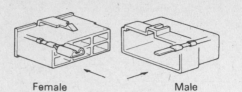

Female   Male

3.2 To distinguish between male and female halves of a connector, look at the terminal pins

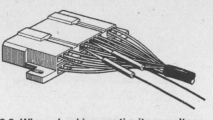

3.3 When checking continuity or voltage with a circuit testing device, insert the test probe from the wire harness side

4.1 The fuse panel is located underneath the left end of the dashboard

you keep in mind that all electrical circuits are basically electricity running from the battery, through the wires, switches. relays, fuses and fusible links to each electrical component (light bulb, motor, etc.) and then to ground, from which it is passed back to the battery. Any electrical problem is an interruption in the flow of electricity to and from the battery.

3 Connectors - general information

Refer to illustrations 3.1, 3.2 and 3.3

1   Always release the lock lever(s) before attempting to unplug inline type connectors. There are a variety of lock lever configurations **(see illustration)**. Although nothing more than a finger is usually necessary to pry

lock levers open, a small pocket screwdriver is effective for hard to-release levers. Once the lock levers are released, try to pull on the connectors themselves, not the wires, when unplugging two connector halves (there are times, however, when this is not possible - use good judgment).

2   It is usually necessary to know which side, male or female, of the connector you're checking. Male connectors are easily distinguished from females by the shape of their internal pins **(see illustration)**.

3   When checking continuity or voltage with a circuit tester, insertion of the test probe into the receptacle may open the fitting of the connector and result in poor contact. Instead, insert the test probe from the wire harness side of the connector **(see illustration)**.

4 Fuses - general information

Refer to illustrations 4.1, 4.2 and 4.6

1   The electrical circuits of this vehicle are protected by a combination of fuses, fusible links and circuit breakers. The fuse panel is located in the left end of the dashboard above the left side kick panel **(see illustration)** .

2   The fuse block is equipped with miniaturized fuses because their compact dimensions and convenient blade-type terminal design allow fingertip removal and installation. Each fuse protects one or more circuits. The protected circuit is identified on the face of

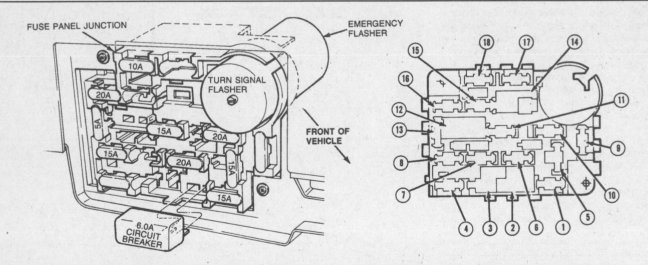

4.2 Typical later model Tempo/Topaz fuse panel (always check the fuse panel guide in your owner's manual when possible)

1   Brake lights, hazard warning lights, shift lock (15 amp fuse)
2   Windshield wiper, windshield washer pump, interval wiper (8.25 amp circuit breaker)
3   Spare (not used)
4   Tail lights, parking lights, side marker lights, cluster illumination light, license light, headlight "on" chime (15 amp fuse)
5   Turn signal lights, back-up lights, rear window defogger switch and relay, heater controls, running light module (15 amp fuse)
6   Power window relay, illuminated entry module (5 amp fuse)
7   Fog lights, fog light indicator (10 amp fuse)
8   Courtesy lights, key warning/chimes, clock, glove compartment light, map light, engine compartment light, deck lid light, radio, illuminated visor, power mirrors, door lock lights, running lights (15 amp fuse)

9   Blower motor (30 amp fuse)
10   Flash-to-pass (20 amp fuse)
11   Radio, tape player, premium sound amplifier (15 amp fuse)
12   Power seats, power door locks, power windows, power lumbar (20 amp circuit breaker)
13   Illumination of instrument cluster (5 amp fuse)
14   Spare (not used)
15   Spare (not used)
16   Horn, cigar lighter, speed control relay, deck lid release (30 amp fuse)
17   A/C clutch, heater control switch (15 amp fuse)
18   Instrument cluster gages, speed control, airbag, passive restraint chime (10 amp fuse)

12

Fuse Value Amps	Color Code
4	Pink
5	Tan
10	Red
15	Light Blue
20	Yellow
25	Natural
30	Light Green

4.6 Each fuse amp value has a corresponding color code

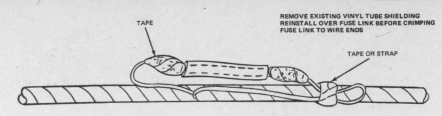

TYPICAL REPAIR USING THE SPECIAL #17 GA. (9.00" LONG-YELLOW) FUSE LINK REQUIRED FOR THE AIR/COND. CIRCUITS (2) # 687E AND #261A LOCATED IN THE ENGINE COMPARTMENT

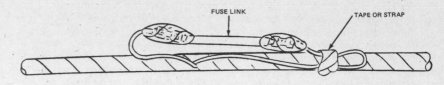

TYPICAL REPAIR FOR ANY IN-LINE FUSE LINK USING THE SPECIFIED GAUGE FUSE LINK FOR THE SPECIFIED CIRCUIT

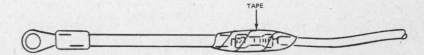

TYPICAL REPAIR USING THE EYELET TERMINAL FUSE LINK OF THE SPECIFIED GAUGE FOR ATTACHMENT TO A CIRCUIT WIRE END

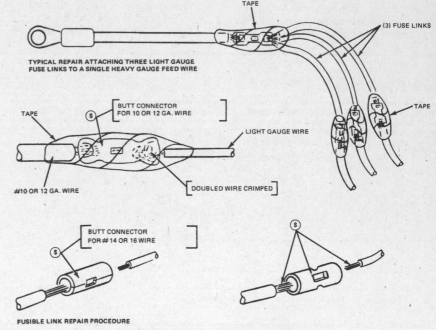

TYPICAL REPAIR ATTACHING THREE LIGHT GAUGE FUSE LINKS TO A SINGLE HEAVY GAUGE FEED WIRE

FUSIBLE LINK REPAIR PROCEDURE

5.1a Fusible link servicing procedures

the fuse panel cover above each fuse. A fuse guide is included here **(see illustration)** but consult your owner's manual - it will have the most accurate guide for your vehicle.

3   If an electrical component fails, always check the fuse first.

4   A blown fuse, which is nothing more than a broken element, is easily identified through the clear plastic body. Visually inspect the element for evidence of damage. If a continuity check is called for, the blade terminal tips are exposed in the fuse body.

5   Remove and insert fuses straight in and out without twisting. Twisting could force the terminals open too far, resulting in a bad connection.

6   Be sure to replace blown fuses with the correct type and amp rating. Fuses of different ratings are physically interchangeable, but replacing a fuse with one of a higher or lower value than specified is not recommended. Each electrical circuit needs a specific amount of protection. The amperage value of each fuse is usually molded into the fuse body. Different colors are also used to denote fuses of various amperage values. The accompanying color code **(see illustration)** shows common amperage values and their corresponding colors. **Caution:** *Always turn off all electrical components and the ignition switch before replacing a fuse. Never bypass a fuse with pieces of metal or foil. Serious damage to the electrical system could result.*

7   If the replacement fuse immediately fails, do not replace it again until the cause of the problem is isolated and corrected. In most cases, this will be a short circuit in the wiring caused by a broken or deteriorated wire .

5   Fusible links - general information

Refer to illustrations 5.1a, 5.1b and 5.2

Some circuits are protected by fusible links. These links are used in circuits which are not ordinarily fused, such as the ignition circuit. If a circuit protected by a fusible link becomes inoperative, inspect for a blown fusible link.

Although fusible links appear to be of heavier gauge than the wire they are protecting, their appearance is due to thicker insulation. All fusible links are several wire gauges smaller than the wire they are designed to protect. The location of the fusible links on your particular vehicle can be

determined by referring to the wiring diagrams at the end of this Chapter.

Fusible links cannot be repaired. If you must replace one, make sure that the new fusible link is a duplicate of the one removed with respect to gauge, length and insulation. Original and Ford replacement fusible links have insulation that is flame proof. Do not fabricate a fusible link from ordinary wire-the insulation may not be flame proof. **Warning:** *Do not mistake a resistor wire for a fusible link. The resistor wire is generally longer and is identified by a "Resistor-don't cut or splice" warning.*

Charging system fusible link

1   To replace the fusible link in the charging system, proceed as follows:

a) *Disconnect the negative cable at the battery.*

b) *Disconnect the fusible link from the wiring harness or the fusible link eyelet terminal from the battery terminal of the starter relay (on some vehicle applications, the fusible link is looped outside the wire harness).*

c) *Cut the damaged fusible link and the splices from the wires to which it is* attached. *Disconnect the feed wire part of the wiring and cut out the damaged portion as closely as possible behind the splice in the harness. If the fusible link wire insulation is burned or opened, disconnect the feed as close as possible behind the splice in the harness. If the damaged fusible link is between two splices (the weld points in the harness), cut out the damaged portion as close as possible to the weld points.*

d) *Strip the insulation back approximately 1/2-inch.*

e) *Splice and solder the new fusible link to the wires from which the old link was cut. Use rosin core solder at each end of the new link to obtain a good solder joint.*

f) *Wrap the splices completely with vinyl electrical tape around the soldered joint. No wires should be exposed* **(see illustration)**.

g) *Securely connect the eyelet terminals (if any) to the battery stud on the starter relay.* **Note:** *Some fusible links* **(see illustration)** *have an eyelet terminal for a 5/16-inch stud on one end. When the terminal is not required, use one of the fusible links shown with the insulation stripped from both ends.*

h) *Install the repaired wiring as before, using existing clips, if provided.*

i) *Connect the battery ground cable.*

j) *Test the circuit for proper operation.*

All other fusible links

2   To service any other blown fusible link, use the following procedure:

a) *Determine which circuit is damaged, its location* **(see illustration)** *and the cause of the open fusible link. If the damaged fusible link is one of three fed by a common 10 or 12 gauge feed wire, determine the specific affected circuit.*

b) *Disconnect the negative battery cable.*

c) *Cut the damaged fusible link from the*

**WIRING ASSEMBLY — FUSE LINK
(WITH INSULATION STRIPPED BOTH ENDS)**

D3AZ—14A526-H   #14 GA. WIRE — 9.00" ± .50 LENGTH
(GREEN INSULATION)

D3AZ—14A526-J   #16 GA. WIRE — 9.00" ± .50 LENGTH
(ORANGE INSULATION) AS REQ D.

D3AZ—14A526-K   #17 GA. WIRE — 9.00" ± .50 LENGTH
(YELLOW INSULATION) AS REQ'D.
(SPECIAL USED WITH AIR CONDITIONING SYSTEM)

D3AZ—14A526-L   #18 GA. WIRE — 9.00" ± .50 LENGTH
(RED INSULATION) AS REQ D.

D3AZ—14A526-M   #20 GA. WIRE — 9.00" ± .50 LENGTH
(BLUE INSULATION) AS REQ D.

**WIRING ASSEMBLY — FUSE LINK
(WITH EYELET TERMINAL AND ONE END STRIPPED)**

D3AZ—14A526-D   #14 GA. WIRE — 9.00" ± .50 LENGTH
(GREEN INSULATION) AS REQ'D.

D3AZ—14A526-E   #16 GA. WIRE — 9.00" ± .50 LENGTH
(ORANGE INSULATION) AS REQ'D.

D3AZ—14A526-F   #18 GA. WIRE — 9.00" ± .50 LENGTH
(RED INSULATION) AS REQ'D.

D3AZ—14A526-G   #20 GA. WIRE — 9.00" ± .50 LENGTH
(BLUE INSULATION) AS REQ'D.

BUTT CONNECTOR — WIRING SPLICE

D3AZ—14488-Y   FOR #10 AND 12 GA. WIRE (LOAD CIRCUIT) AS REQ'D.
D3AZ—14488-Z   FOR #14 AND 16 GA. WIRE (LOAD CIRCUIT) AS REQ'D.

5.1b Fusible link end connector types

Fuse Link Chart

Fuse Link	Gauge	Location
Electric rear window defroster, fuel filter door	18	In wiring assy near starter motor relay
Headlamp feed	16	Engine compartment on starting motor relay
Ignition feed (all)	16	Near starter motor relay
Alternator output	12	In charging circuit near starter motor relay
Fuel pump relay, EEC power relay	20	For PCM relay, A/C controller in wiring assy on starter motor relay, fuel pump relay and PCM
Fan relay	14	For cooling fan relay in wiring assy on starter motor relay
Air bag module	20	Engine compartment near starter motor relay
Passive Restraint Module	20	Engine compartment on starter motor relay
HEGO, A/C Fan Controller	20	Near LH shock tower
Ignition Coil, TFI Module, ECA Relay	20	Near LH shock tower
Alternator	18	In charging circuit near starter motor relay
Powertrain Control Module (PCM) 12B590	18	Near starter motor relay

5.2 Listing, size and location for later model fusible links

12

*wiring harness and discard it. If the
fusible link is one of three circuits fed by
a single wire, cut it out of the harness at
each splice and discard it.*

d) *Identify and procure the proper fusible
link and butt connectors for attaching
the fusible link to the harness.*

3   To service any fusible link in a three-link
group with one feed:

a) *After cutting the open link out of the
harness, cut each of the remaining
undamaged fusible links close to the
feed wire weld.*

b) *Strip approximately 1/2-inch of insulation
from the detached ends of the two good
fusible links. Insert two wire ends into
one end of a Ford butt connector and
carefully push one stripped end of the
replacement fusible link into the same
end of the butt connector and crimp all
three firmly together* **(see illustration
5.1a). Note:** *Be very careful when fitting
the three fusible links into the butt
connector - the internal diameter is a
snug fit for three wires. Be sure to use a
proper crimping tool. Pliers, side cutters,
etc. will not apply the proper crimp to
retain the wires.*

c) *After crimping the butt connector to the
three fusible links, cut the weld portion
from the feed wire and strip about
1/2-inch of insulation from the cut end.
Insert the stripped end into the open
end of the butt connector and crimp
very firmly.*

d) *To attach the remaining end of the
replacement fusible link, strip about
1/2-inch of insulation from the wire end
of the circuit from which the blown
fusible link was removed and firmly
crimp a butt connector to the stripped
wire. Insert the end of the replacement
link into the other end of the butt
connector and crimp firmly.*

e) *Using rosin core solder with a consistency of 60-percent tin and 40-percent
lead, solder the connectors and the
wires at the repairs and insulate with
electrical tape.*

4   To replace any fusible link on a single
circuit in a harness, cut out the damaged
portion, strip about 1/2-inch of insulation
from the two wire ends and attach the appropriate replacement fusible link to the stripped
wire ends with two proper size butt
connectors. Solder the connectors and wires
and insulate with tape.

5   To service any fusible link which has an
eyelet terminal on one end (like the charging
circuit), cut off the open fusible link behind
the weld, strip about 1/2-inch of insulation
from the cut end and attach the appropriate
new eyelet fusible link to the cut stripped wire
with an appropriate size butt connector.
Solder the connectors and wires at the point
of service and insulate with tape.

6   Connect the cable to the negative
terminal of the battery.

7   Test the system for proper operation.

6   Circuit breakers - general information

1   Circuit breakers protect accessories
such as power windows, power door locks,
the windshield wiper, windshield wiper pump,
interval wiper, low washer fluid, etc. Circuit
breakers are located in the fuse box. Refer to
the fuse panel guide in Section 4 and the fuse
panel guide in your owner's manual for the
location of the circuit breakers used in your
vehicle.

2   Because a circuit breaker resets itself
automatically, an electrical overload in a
circuit breaker protected system will cause
the circuit to fail momentarily, then come
back on. If the circuit does not come back
on, check it immediately.

a) *Remove the circuit breaker from the fuse
panel.*

b) *Using an ohmmeter, verify that there is
continuity between both terminals of the
circuit breaker. If there is no continuity,
replace the circuit breaker.*

c) *Install the old or new circuit breaker. If it
continues to cut out, a short circuit is
indicated. Troubleshoot the appropriate
circuit (see the wiring diagrams at the
back of this book) or have the system
checked by a professional mechanic.*

7   Turn signal/hazard/flash-to-pass/dimmer switch (multi-function switch) - check and replacement

*Refer to illustrations 7.3, 7.18, 7.19, 7.20,
7.22 and 7.23*

Check
Mechanical diagnosis

1   Make the following mechanical function
checks before conducting any electrical
tests:

a) *If the turn signal lever will not stay in its
mating hole, either the switch is worn or
damaged or the retaining pin in the
switch is missing. Replace the switch.*

b) *If the headlight will not switch from
bright to dim, or vice versa, the dimmer
switch is binding or jammed. Replace
the switch.*

c) *If the switch will not cancel, the
canceling cam is coming off its shaft, is
out of position or is cracked. Replace
the switch.*

d) *If the lever will not stay in the turn
position, the switch is worn or damaged.
Replace the switch.*

Continuity test

2   Always check the fuse first. If it's blown,
remove the wire harness from the switch
(see illustration 7.22), then test continuity
between ground (the switch casting)
and each corresponding feed circuit to
the switch. Continuity between any
feed circuit and ground indicates that the
switch is shorted and will have to be
replaced.

3   Refer to the appropriate wiring diagrams
at the end of this book and the
accompanying terminal guide **(see illustration)** when performing the following continuity tests. You will also need a circuit or
continuity tester.

4   Prior to testing, make sure that the
hazard knob is pushed in all the way to the
Off position.

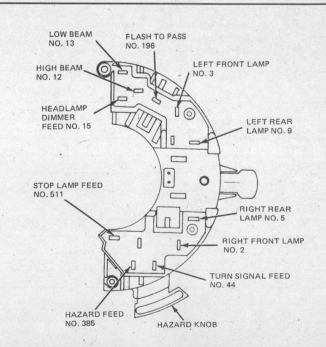

7.3 Turn signal/hazard/dimmer switch continuity check points

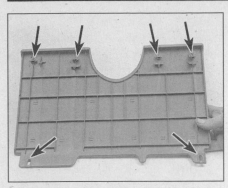

7.18 To remove the dash panel underneath the steering column, remove the two screws from the slotted adjustment holes along the lower edge, then pop the panel fasteners loose from the clips attached to the dashboard along the upper edge of the panel

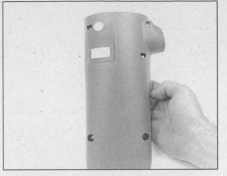

7.19 The two steering column shroud halves are held together by five screws

7.20 To remove the switch lever from the multi-function stalk, pull it straight off

5   With the lever in the Neutral position (and the brake lights inoperative), there should be:
 a) *Continuity between circuit 511 (brake light switch-to-turn signal switch) and circuits 5 (right rear turn signal) and 9 (left rear turn signal).*
 b) *No continuity between 511 and ground (switch casting).*
 c) *No continuity between circuit 44 (turn signal flasher-to-turn signal switch) and 2 (right front turn signal), 3 (left front turn signal), 5 (right rear turn signal) and 9 (left rear turn signal).*

6   Operate the switch from left turn to right turn to Neutral while checking the continuity between circuit 511 and ground. Continuity between 511 and ground in any position indicates a short in the switch.

7   With the lever in the left turn position (and the right brake light inoperative), there should be:
 a) *Continuity between circuits 44, 3 and 9.*
 b) *Continuity between circuits 511 and 5.*
 c) *No continuity between circuit 44 and ground.*
 d) *No continuity between circuits 44 and 5.*

8   With the lever in the right turn position (and the left brake light inoperative), there should be:
 a) *Continuity between circuits 44, 2 and 5.*
 b) *Continuity between circuits 511 and 9.*
 c) *No continuity between circuit 44 and ground.*
 d) *No continuity between circuits 44 and 9.*

9   While operating the switch from left turn to right turn to Neutral, check continuity between circuit 44 and ground. Continuity between 44 and ground in any position indicates a short in the switch.

10   With the emergency warning switch in the On position (and the emergency warning lights inoperative), there should be:
 a) *Continuity between circuits 385 (flasher-to-emergency warning switch) and 2, 3, 5 and 9.*

 b) *Continuity between circuits 511, 2, 3, 5 and 9.*
 c) *No continuity between circuit 385 and ground and circuits 385 and 44.*

11   While operating the hazard switch from On to Off, check the continuity between circuit 385 and ground. Continuity in any position indicates a short in the switch.

12   With the headlight dimmer at the Low beam position (and the low beam inoperative), there should be:
 a) *Continuity between circuits 15 (headlight dimmer switch feed) and 13 (headlight dimmer switch-to-Low beams).*
 b) *No continuity between circuits 15 and 12 (headlight dimmer switch-to-High beams).*
 c) *No continuity between circuits 196 (headlight flash-to-pass switch feed), 13 (headlight dimmer switch-to-Low beams) and 12.*

13   With the headlight dimmer in the High beam position (and the high beam inoperative), there should be:
 a) *Continuity between circuits 15 and 12.*
 b) *No continuity between circuits 15 and 13.*
 c) *No continuity between circuits 196 and 13 and between 196 and 12.*

14   While operating the turn signal lever to both the High and Low beam positions, check continuity between circuit 15 and ground. Continuity in either position indicates a short in the switch.

15   With the lever held up in the flash-to-pass position, there should be:
 a) *Continuity between circuits 196 and 12.*
 b) *No continuity between circuits 196 and 13.*

16   If the multi-function switch fails any of the above tests, replace it.

Replacement

17   Detach the cable from the negative terminal of the battery.

18   Remove the dash panel underneath the steering column by removing the two screws along the bottom edge and popping the upper edge loose from the clips attached to the dashboard **(see illustration)**.

19   Remove all five steering column shroud screws **(see illustration)** and detach the upper and lower halves of the shroud.

20   Remove the multi-function switch lever by pulling it straight off the stalk **(see illustration)**. To facilitate assembly, note that the key on the lever must be aligned with the keyway in the switch.

21   Note the position of the switch cover foam, then carefully peel it from the switch.

22   Unplug the two multi-function switch electrical connectors **(see illustration)**.

23   Remove the two self-tapping screws that attach the switch to the lock cylinder housing **(see illustration)** and disengage the switch from the housing. The screws require a special Torx driver.

24   Installation is the reverse of removal.

7.22 Unplug both electrical connectors (arrows) from the multi-function switch

7.23 Remove both self-tapping screws (arrows) from the multi-function switch to remove the switch

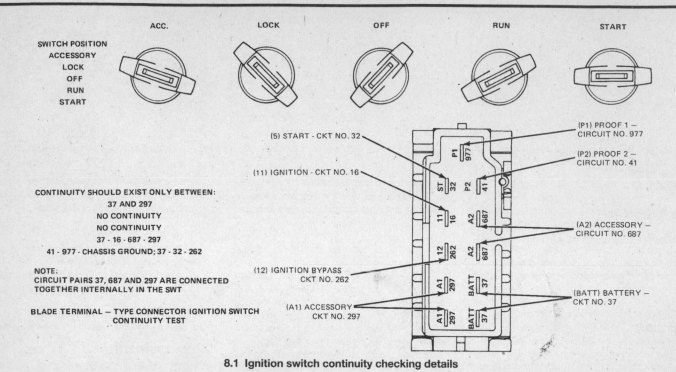

| ACC. | LOCK | OFF | RUN | START |

SWITCH POSITION
ACCESSORY
LOCK
OFF
RUN
START

(5) START - CKT NO. 32

(11) IGNITION - CKT NO. 16

(P1) PROOF 1 — CIRCUIT NO. 977

(P2) PROOF 2 — CIRCUIT NO. 41

CONTINUITY SHOULD EXIST ONLY BETWEEN:
37 AND 297
NO CONTINUITY
NO CONTINUITY
37 - 16 - 687 - 297
41 - 977 - CHASSIS GROUND; 37 - 32 - 262

NOTE:
CIRCUIT PAIRS 37, 687 AND 297 ARE CONNECTED
TOGETHER INTERNALLY IN THE SWT

BLADE TERMINAL — TYPE CONNECTOR IGNITION SWITCH
CONTINUITY TEST

(12) IGNITION BYPASS CKT NO. 262

(A1) ACCESSORY CKT NO. 297

(A2) ACCESSORY — CIRCUIT NO. 687

(BATT) BATTERY — CKT NO. 37

8.1 Ignition switch continuity checking details

8 Ignition switch and key lock cylinder - check and replacement

Refer to illustrations 8.1, 8.8, 8.10 and 8.26
Warning: *If vehicle is equipped with airbags, refer to Section 25 to disarm the airbag system prior to performing any work described below.*

Check

Continuity

1   Disconnect the multiple terminal electrical connector (see the replacement part of this Section) by spreading apart the locking fingers on each end of the connector shell while pulling to disengage from the ignition switch. Connect a self-powered test light, a circuit tester or an ohmmeter between the indicated blade terminals **(see illustration)** and test the switch continuity:

a) With the switch in the Accessory

position, there should be continuity between circuits 37 (battery to load) and 297 (the accessory feed from the ignition switch).
b) With the switch in the Lock position, there should be no continuity between any circuits.
c) With the switch in the Off position, there should be no continuity between any circuits.
d) With the switch in the Run position, there should be continuity between circuits 37, 16 (ignition switch to ignition coil Battery terminal), 687 (accessory feed) and 297.
e) With the switch in the Start position, there should be continuity between circuits 41 (warning light prove out), 977 (brake warning switch-to-indicator light) and chassis ground and between circuits 37 (battery-to-load), 32 (starter control) and 262 (starter motor relay-to-ignition coil "I" terminal).

2   If the ignition switch fails any of the above tests, replace it.
3   If an "engine won't crank'' condition exists, determine if the condition exists with the shift lever in both the Park and Neutral positions before performing the above ignition switch continuity tests. If the "no crank" condition occurs in one shift lever position but not in the other, a more probable cause is the Neutral start switch located on the transaxle (see Section 21).

Key lock cylinder

4   Test the steering column ignition system mechanical operation by rotating the key through all switch positions. The movement should feel smooth with no sticking or binding. The ignition switch should return from the Start position to the Run position without assistance (spring return). If sticking or binding is encountered, remove the lock cylinder assembly and check for burrs on the key and for binding of the lock cylinder. If damage is evident, replace the lock cylinder assembly.

Replacement
Ignition switch

5   Detach the cable from the negative terminal of the battery.
6   Remove the dash panel from underneath the steering column **(see illustration 7.18)**.
7   Remove the five steering column shroud **(see illustration 7.19)**.
8   Unplug the multi-terminal ignition switch electrical connector **(see illustration)**.
9   Turn the ignition key lock cylinder to the On (Run) position.
10   Using a 1/8-inch bit, drill out the shear-head bolts **(see illustration)** that connect the switch to the lock cylinder housing.

8.8 Unplug the multi-terminal electrical connector located under the steering column

8.10 To detach the ignition switch from the lock cylinder housing, drill holes in these two shear head bolts (arrows) with a 1/8-inch drill bit and remove the bolts with a screw extractor tool

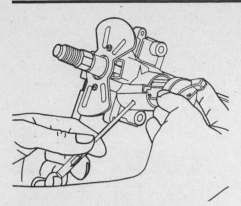

8.26 Insert a 1/8-inch pin punch into the hole in the lock cylinder casting and depress the punch while pulling out on the lock cylinder

11   Remove both bolts with a screw extractor tool.

12   Disengage the ignition switch from the actuator pin.

13   Make sure that the actuator pin slot in the ignition switch is in the Run position. **Note:** *A new replacement switch assembly will be set in the On (Run) position.*

14   Make sure that the ignition key lock cylinder is in the Run position to properly locate the lock actuator pin. The Run position can be located by rotating the key lock cylinder about 90-degrees from the lock position.

15   Install the ignition switch onto the actuator pin. **Note:** *It may be necessary to move it back-and-forth slightly to align the switch mounting holes with the column lock housing threaded holes.*

16   Install new shear-head bolts and tighten them until the heads break off.

17   Connect the electrical connector to the ignition switch.

18   Connect the negative battery cable to the battery terminal.

19   Check the ignition switch for proper operation, including the Start and Acc positions. Also make certain that the steering column is locked when in the Lock position.

20   Install the upper and lower steering column shroud halves. Do not overtighten the five screws or you will strip them out.

Ignition key lock cylinder assembly

Note: *The following procedure pertains only to functional lock cylinders for which keys are available or for which keys can be made the lock cylinder number is known. If the ignition lock is inoperative and the lock cylinder cannot be turned due to a lost or broken lock cylinder key, the key number is not known or the lock cylinder cap is damaged and/or broken to the extent that the lock cylinder cannot be turned, have the lock cylinder assembly replaced by a dealer service department. Replacement will likely involve installation not only of a new lock cylinder but a new lock cylinder housing as well, a procedure that is beyond the scope of the home mechanic.*

21   Detach the cable from the negative terminal of the battery.

22   If your vehicle is equipped with a tilt column, remove the upper extension shroud by unsnapping the shroud from the retaining clip at the 9 o'clock position.

23   Remove the five screws and detach the two steering column trim shroud halves **(see illustration 7.19).**

24   Locate the key warning buzzer electrical lead (the insulated single wire coming out the front of the key lock cylinder housing), trace it back to the pigtail connector near the multi-terminal connector for the ignition switch and unplug it.

25   Turn the lock key to the Run position.

26   Place a 1/8-inch punch in the hole in the casting surrounding the lock cylinder. Depress the punch while pulling out on the lock cylinder to remove it from the column housing **(see illustration)**.

27   Install the lock cylinder by turning it to the Run position and depressing the retaining pin. Insert the lock cylinder into the lock cylinder housing. Make sure that the cylinder is completely seated and aligned in the interlocking washer before turning the key to the Off position. This will permit the retaining pin to extend into the hole.

28   Turn the lock to ensure that the operation is correct in all positions.

29   The remainder of installation is the reverse of removal.

---

9   Windshield wiper/washer switch and motor - description, check and component replacement

Description

Windshield wiper/washer switch

1   The standard wiper/washer switch has three positions: Off, Low and Hi.

2   To activate the Wash function, the wiper switch lever must be in the Low or Hi position for washer operation.

3   With an interval system switch, low and high speed wiper operation is the same as the standard wiper system above.

4   When the wiper control switch is in the interval position, the wipers make single swipes separated by a pause. The duration of the pause is determined by a control knob on the wiper switch assembly. It can vary between 1 and 12 seconds.

5   Washer operation differs from the standard system. If the wiper control switch is in the Off or Int position, the wipers will run as long as the washer switch is activated by the operator. When the washer switch is released, the washers will stop immediately but the wipers will run for 1 to 4 more cycles, then return to the Off position or Interval operation. If the wiper control switch is in the Low or Hi position, the washers will operate with no change in wiper operation.

Windshield wiper motor

6   The two-speed, permanent magnet, three-brush electric motor has a brush rigging that permits a choice of low or high

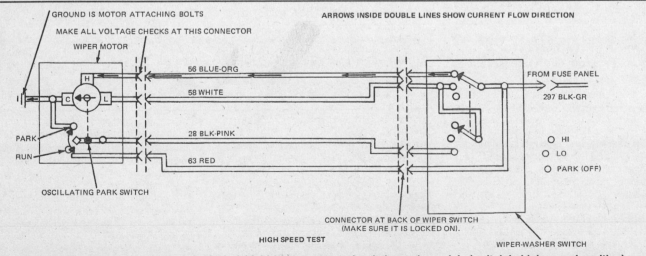

9.7a Wiring diagram for the standard windshield wiper motor and switch - early models (switch in high-speed position)

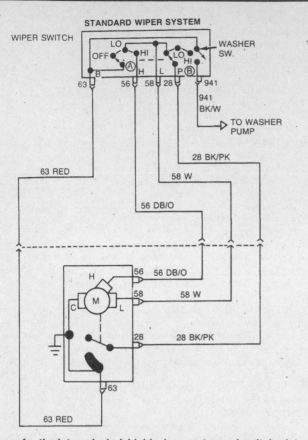

STANDARD WIPER SYSTEM

WIPER SWITCH

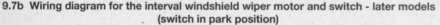

9.7b Wiring diagram for the interval windshield wiper motor and switch - later models (switch in park position)

speed operation. When the control selector is in the Low position, the grounded brush and the white wire brush are used and the motor operates at low speed. When the control selector is in the High position, the grounded brush and the blue/orange wire brush are used. Current bypasses a portion of the armature winding, causing the motor to run faster. When the control selector is moved to the Park position, the motor will continue at low speed until the off switch outer contacts open, stopping the motor in the Park position.

Check

Standard system High speed test

Refer to illustrations 9.7a and 9.7b

7   With the wiper switch in the High position, the current flows from the ignition switch through the wiper switch to the wiper motor high terminal **(see illustrations).**

8   To check high-speed operation, turn the ignition switch to the On position and place the wiper switch in the High position. Unplug the connector at the motor and check for voltage at the circuit 56 pin (blue/orange wire) on the vehicle harness side.

 a) *If no voltage is present, on early steering-column-mounted switch models, check the voltage at the circuit 297 pin (black/green wire) at the wiper switch. On later dash panel-mounted switch*

models, disconnect the electrical connector at the switch and check for voltage at pin 63 on the harness side.

 b) *If voltage is present at circuit 297 (early models) or 63 (later models), but not at 56, replace the wiper switch.*

 c) *If voltage is not present at circuit 297 (early models) or 63 (later models), trace the circuit back to its voltage source to determine the problem.*

 d) *If voltage is present at circuit 56 but the motor does not run, ground the motor case to the body.*

 e) *If the motor runs, repair the ground.*

 f) *If the motor does not run, replace it.*

Standard system Low speed test

9   With the wiper switch in the Low position, current flows from the ignition switch through the wiper switch to the wiper motor low terminal **(see illustrations 9.7a and 9.7b).**

10   To check low-speed operation, turn the ignition switch to the On position and place the wiper switch in the Low position. Unplug the electrical connector at the motor and check for voltage at the circuit 58 pin (white wire) on the vehicle harness side.

 a) *If no voltage is present, perform supply voltage test as defined in Step 8a.*

 b) *If voltage is present at circuit 297 (early models) or 63 (later models), but not at 58, replace the wiper switch.*

 c) *If voltage is not present at circuit 297 (early models) or 63 (later models), trace the circuit back to its voltage source to determine the problem.*

 d) *If voltage is present at circuit 58 but the motor does not run, ground the motor case to the body.*

 e) *If the motor runs, repair the ground.*

 f) *If the motor does not run, replace the motor.*

Standard system Park test

11   With the wiper switch Off, the wipers will complete one cycle through the wiper motor park switch. Current flows from the ignition switch through the wiper switch to the wiper motor oscillating park switch for 9/10ths of a cycle. The low-speed run circuit is from the wiper motor park switch through the wiper switch to the motor low-speed brush, across the armature and out a common brush to ground. At the last 1/10th portion of the cycle, the oscillating park switch moves from the Run position to the Park (ground) position, stopping the motor in the Park position **(see illustrations 9.7a and 9.7b).**

12   To check the Park operation, turn the ignition switch to the On position and place the wiper switch in the Off position. With the electrical connector still plugged into the motor, insert the probe of a voltmeter into the backside of the connector and check for voltage at circuits 58 (white wire), 28 (black/pink dot) and 63 (red) pins at motor. **Note:** *Wiper blades must be in a non-parked position for this test to be valid.*

 a) *If voltage is present on all three circuits, ground the motor case to the body.*

 b) *If the motor parks, repair the motor ground.*

 c) *If the motor does not move to the Park position, replace the wiper motor.*

 d) *If a voltage check shows voltage only at the circuit 63 pin, replace the wiper motor.*

 e) *If a voltage check shows voltage only at circuits 63 and 28, replace the wiper switch.*

 f) *If voltage is still not present at circuit 58, trace circuits 28 and 58 back toward the wiper switch to determine the source of the open circuit problem.*

Interval system High speed test

Refer to illustrations 9.13a and 9.13b

13   With the wiper switch in the High position, current flows from the ignition switch through the wiper switch to the wiper motor to ground **(see illustrations).**

14   The test for this circuit is the same as for the standard wiper motor High speed test (see Step 8).

Interval system Low speed test

15   With the wiper switch in the Low position, current flows from the ignition switch through the wiper switch and energized relay contacts of the governor to the wiper motor **(see illustrations 9.13a and 9.13b).** **Note:** *If the governor relay is inoperative, the wipers*

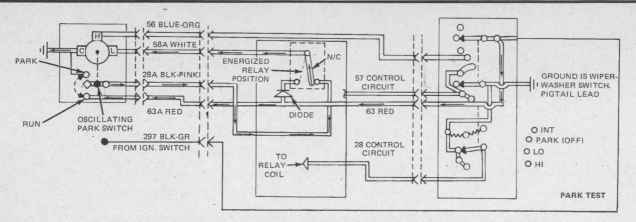

9.13a Wiring diagram for the interval windshield wiper motor - early models (switch in park position)

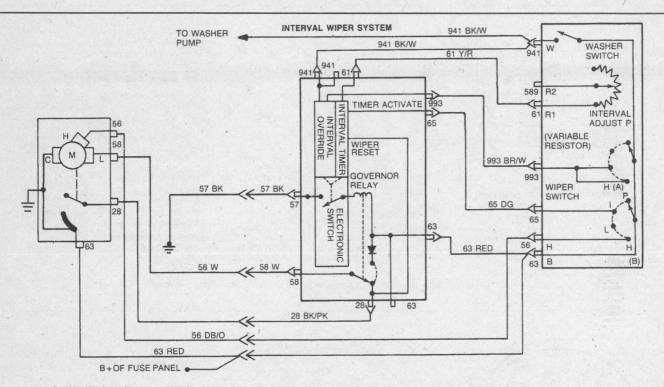

9.13b Wiring diagram for the interval windshield wiper motor and switch - later models (switch in park position)

will only operate in the High-speed and Park modes. Low and interval will not work.

16   To check low-speed operation, place the ignition switch in the On position and the wiper switch in the Low position. Unplug the electrical connector at the motor and check for voltage at the circuit 58 (white wire) pin on the vehicle harness side.

  a) *If voltage is present and the wiper motor does not run, ground the motor case to the body.*

  b) *If motor runs, repair the motor ground.*

  c) *If the motor does not run, replace the motor.*

  d) *If voltage is not present at pin 58, check for voltage at governor connector pins 63 (red), 993 (brown/white) and 58.*

  e) *If voltage is present at all pins, repair the open in circuit 58 from the governor to the motor.*

  f) *If voltage is present at 63 and 993 only, replace the governor.*

  g) *If voltage is not present at 993, replace the switch.*

  h) *If voltage is not present at 63, trace the circuit back to the voltage source to find the problem.*

Interval system Park test

17   When the wiper switch is placed in the Int mode, the park switch contacts are grounded (assuming that the wipers started in the Park position) and the relay is energized. Initially, current flows from the ignition switch through the circuit breaker, the wiper switch, through a diode and energized contacts in the governor to the wiper motor low-speed brush. The motor rotates 1/10th of a cycle, mechanically switching the oscillating park switch contacts within the motor from Park (ground)

to Run (B+). After the partial cycle, the governor de-energizes the interval circuit, and the motor continues to rotate through the remaining 9/10th of one cycle powered by the oscillating Park switch circuit. At the completion of one cycle, the oscillating park switch contacts again touch ground (Park) and the motor parks. The governor electronic circuit delays energizing the interval relay until the circuit times out and the low-speed interval is repeated. The discharge rate of the capacitor in the governor circuit to ground through the wiper switch variable resistor controls the time delay of the system.

18   When the wiper switch is placed in the Off position, the wipers complete one full cycle through the wiper motor park switch. Current flows from the ignition switch across a circuit breaker in the fuse panel to the wiper switch, to the wiper motor oscillating park switch

12

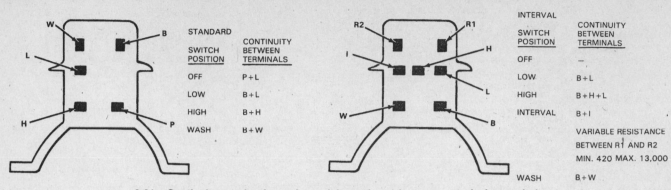

SWITCH POSITION	CONTINUITY BETWEEN TERMINALS
OFF	P + L
LOW	B + L
HIGH	B + H
WASH	B + W

STANDARD

INTERVAL

SWITCH POSITION	CONTINUITY BETWEEN TERMINALS
OFF	—
LOW	B + L
HIGH	B + H + L
INTERVAL	B + I
	VARIABLE RESISTANCE BETWEEN R1 AND R2 MIN. 420 MAX. 13,000
WASH	B + W

9.21a Continuity test for the early model steering column-mounted wiper switch

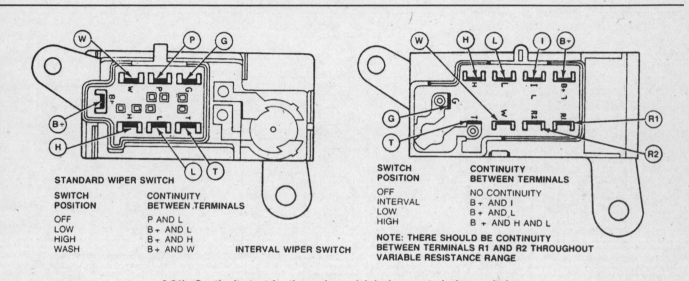

STANDARD WIPER SWITCH

SWITCH POSITION	CONTINUITY BETWEEN TERMINALS
OFF	P AND L
LOW	B + AND L
HIGH	B + AND H
WASH	B + AND W

INTERVAL WIPER SWITCH

SWITCH POSITION	CONTINUITY BETWEEN TERMINALS
OFF	NO CONTINUITY
INTERVAL	B + AND I
LOW	B + AND L
HIGH	B + AND H AND L

NOTE: THERE SHOULD BE CONTINUITY BETWEEN TERMINALS R1 AND R2 THROUGHOUT VARIABLE RESISTANCE RANGE

9.21b Continuity test for the early model dash-mounted wiper switch

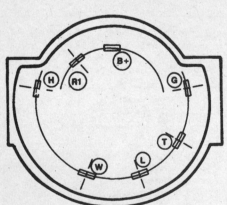

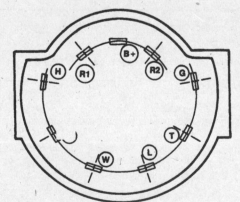

INTERVAL WIPER SWITCH

SWITCH POSITION	CONTINUITY BETWEEN TERMINALS
OFF	NO CONTINUITY
INTERVAL	B+ AND I
LOW	B+ AND L
HIGH	B + AND H AND L
WASH	B + AND W

NOTE: THERE SHOULD BE CONTINUITY BETWEEN TERMINALS R1 AND R2 THROUGHOUT VARIABLE RESISTANCE RANGE (MINIMUM 420 TO 880 OHMS, MAXIMUM 7,000 TO 13,000 OHMS)

T-TERMINAL IS SWITCH ILLUMINATION

STANDARD WIPER SWITCH

SWITCH POSITION	CONTINUITY BETWEEN TERMINALS
OFF	R1 AND L
LOW	B+ AND L
HIGH	B+ AND H
WASH	B+ AND W

NOTE: T-TERMINAL IS SWITCH ILLUMINATION

9.21c 1988 and later model dash-mounted wiper switch continuity test

(Run). From the park switch, the current flows through the normally closed contacts of the governor relay (de-energized) to the wiper motor low speed brush, across the armature and out a common brush to ground for 9/10ths of a cycle. At the last 1/10th of the cycle, the oscillating park switch moves from Run to Park, stopping the motor in the Park position **(see illustrations 9.13a and 9.13b)**.

19 To check the park operation, place the ignition switch in the On position and move the wiper switch from operating mode to the Off position. With the connector still mated to the motor, insert the probe into the back side of the connector and check for the presence of voltage at pins 58, 63 and 28. **Note:** *Wiper blades must be in a non-parked position for this test to be valid.*

 a) *If voltage is present at pin 58 and the motor does not park, ground the wiper motor case to the body.*
 b) *If the motor parks, repair the ground.*
 c) *If the motor does not run, replace the motor.*
 d) *If voltage is present at the pins for circuits 63 and 28, but not at the circuit 58 pin, replace the governor.* **Note:** *Wiper blades must be in a non-parked position for this test to be valid.*
 e) *If there is voltage at the circuit 63 pin but not at the circuit 28 pin, and the motor is not parked, replace the wiper motor.*
 f) *If no voltage is present at pin 63, perform supply voltage test as defined in Step 8a.*
 g) *If voltage is present at circuit 297 (early model), replace the wiper switch.*
 h) *If voltage is present at circuit 63 (later model), trace circuit 63 from switch to motor to correct open circuit.*
 i) *If voltage is not present at circuit 297 (early model) or 63 (later model), trace the circuit back to its voltage source to determine the problem.*

9.26 To remove the steering column-mounted windshield wiper/washer switch, unplug both electrical connectors and remove the two bolts (arrows)

Note: *Before troubleshooting the Interval operating mode, the wiper system must be performing properly in both Low and Park modes. If the wipers run continuously at low speed or the interval delay is excessive with the ignition switch on and the wiper switch in the Int position, remove the wiper switch and check continuity and resistance values (see below). If the switch is okay, replace the governor. Otherwise, replace the wiper switch.*

Circuit breaker

20 The 8.25 amp circuit breaker is located in the fuse panel. Two separate tests are necessary to check the circuit breaker for correct operation, but the instrument required for testing it, a volt-amp alternator, is a specialized tool. If the circuit breaker is suspect, take it to a dealer and have it tested, or replace it.

Wiper switch continuity

Refer to illustrations 9.21a, 9.21b and 9.21c

21 Check the continuity between the switch terminals **(see illustrations)**. Either a self-powered test light or an ohmmeter can be used to test a standard two-speed switch. An ohmmeter must be used to test a switch used with the interval wiper system.

Wiper interval governor

22 If interval operation is unsatisfactory, first check the motor current draw and the control switch and all connecting wires for continuity. If the motor, switch and connecting wires are okay, replace the electronic governor.

Component replacement

Wiper switch (steering-column-mounted)

Refer to illustration 9.26

Note: *The switch handle is an integral part of the switch and cannot be removed separately.*

23 Detach the cable from the negative terminal of the battery.

24 Remove the kick panel underneath the steering column from the dashboard (see the illustrations in Section 7).

25 Remove the steering column shrouds (see the illustrations in Section 7).

26 Unplug the electrical connectors **(see illustration)** from the wiper/washer switch.

27 Remove the two wiper/washer switch attaching bolts and remove the switch.

28 Installation is the reverse of removal.

Wiper switch (dash-mounted, early models)

Refer to illustration 9.30

29 Remove the instrument panel finish panel.

30 Remove the switch housing retaining screws and remove the switch housing from the instrument panel **(see illustration)**.

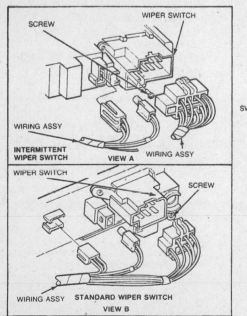

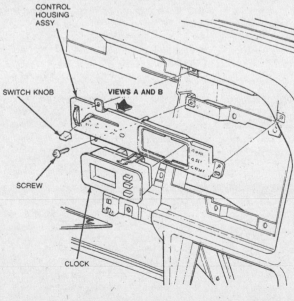

9.30 To remove an early model dash-mounted windshield wiper/washer switch, remove the three housing screws, pull it from the dash and unplug the electrical connector

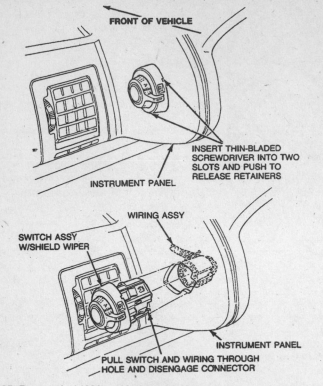

9.35 Removal of 1988 and later model instrument panel-mounted windshield wiper/washer switch

9.48 To remove the electronic governor, unplug the electrical connectors from the fuse panel and remove the governor-to-steering column bracket bolts

31   Pull wiper switch knob off.
32   Disconnect electrical connector from switch assembly.
33   Remove two screws retaining switch to switch housing plate and remove switch.
34   Installation is reverse of removal.

Wiper switch (dash-mounted, later models)

Refer to illustration 9.35

35   Insert a small screwdriver into the small slot on top of the switch bezel **(see illustration).**
36   While pushing down on the screwdriver, work the top part of the switch bezel away from the instrument panel.

37   Insert the screwdriver into the small slot on the bottom of the switch bezel.
38   While pushing up on the screwdriver, work the bottom part of the switch bezel away from the instrument panel.
39   Remove the switch from the instrument panel.
40   Unplug the electrical connector from the switch by holding the switch and carefully pulling on the wires running to the connector.
41   To install the switch, pull the connector and wires through the hole in the instrument panel, then plug in the connector.
42   Insert the switch into the hole in the instrument panel, align the switch so the graphics are in the proper position.
43   Push on the switch until the bezel seats

against the instrument panel and the clips lock into place.

Electronic governor (interval wiper-equipped models only)

Refer to illustration 9.48

44   Detach the cable from the negative terminal of the battery.
45   Remove the kick panel underneath the steering column from the dashboard **(see illustration 7.18).**
46   Remove the steering column shrouds **(see illustration 7.19).**
47   Unplug the governor electrical connectors from the fuse panel.
48   Remove the two attaching screws - one has a ground pigtail under it **(see illustration).**
49   Installation is the reverse of removal.

Windshield wiper motor

Refer to illustrations 9.50a, 9.50b, 9.51, 9.53 and 9.54

50   Detach the cable from the negative terminal of the battery. Remove the rubber molding and the water shield cover from the cowl on the passenger side **(see illustrations).**
51   Unplug the electrical connector from the wiper motor **(see illustration).**
52   Remove the three attaching bolts from the wiper motor and bracket assembly.
53   Pull the motor from its recess in the cowl far enough to get at the wiper arm connecting clip, remove the clip with a small

9.50a To gain access to the windshield wiper motor, peel away the rubber molding from the passenger side of the cowl . . .

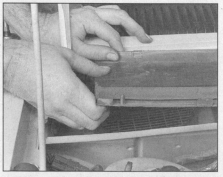

9.50b . . . then pop the water shield clips loose from the cowl and set the shield aside

9.51 To detach the windshield wiper motor from the cowl, unplug the electrical connector and remove the mounting bolts (arrows)

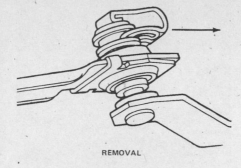

9.53 To detach the wiper linkage drive arm from the motor wiper arm pin, lift and slide the clip off the pin with a small screwdriver

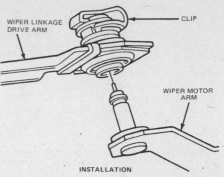

9.54 To attach the wiper linkage drive and motor wiper arm, push the drive arm firmly onto the pin until it's locked in place

9.55 To remove the windshield wiper arm assembly from the pivot shaft, raise the arm off the windshield and pry the latching lever away from the arm with a screwdriver

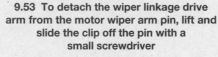

9.57 To install the windshield wiper arm assembly onto the pivot shaft, press the arm head onto the shaft, slide the latching lever in all the way until it locks underneath the shaft, then lower the arm onto the windshield

screwdriver **(see illustration)**, disconnect the wiper arm from the motor and remove the motor.

54   Installation is the reverse of removal. To reattach the wiper arm and the wiper linkage drive arm, push the drive arm firmly onto the wiper arm pin until it's locked firmly into place **(see illustration)**.

Wiper arm assembly

Refer to illustrations 9.55 and 9.57

Note: *Before removing a wiper arm assembly, always note the position of the arm with respect to the cowl and windshield and make sure that you install the new arm in exactly the same position.*

55   Raise the blade end of the arm off the windshield and, with a screwdriver, move the slide latch away from the pivot shaft **(see illustration)**. This unlocks the wiper arm from the pivot shaft and holds the blade end of the arm off the glass at the same time. The wiper arm can now be pulled off the pivot shaft without any tools.

56   To install the wiper arm, push the main arm head over the pivot shaft. Be sure that the pivot shaft is in the Park position and that the blade assembly is positioned correctly.

57   Hold the main arm head on the pivot shaft while raising the blade end of the wiper arm, push the slide latch into the lock under

the pivot shaft **(see illustration)**, then lower the blade to the windshield. If the blade does not touch the windshield, the slide latch is not completely in place.

10 Hazard/turn signal flashers and chime - replacement

Refer to illustrations 10.6, 10.11a and 10.11b

1   Detach the cable from the negative terminal of the battery.
2   The turn signal and hazard flashers are located on the fuse panel, which is in the left underside of the dashboard **(see illustration 4.1)**.

Turn signal flasher

3   If you are replacing the turn signal flasher, unplug it from the fuse panel by pulling it straight out.
4   Install the new flasher unit. Be sure to line up the metal contacts with the slots in the fuse panel, then press the flasher firmly into place.

Hazard flasher

5   If you are replacing the hazard flasher, remove the dash panel under the steering column **(see illustration 7.18)**.

6   Unplug the hazard flasher **(see illustration)** by pulling it straight up.
7   Install the new flasher unit. Be sure to line up the metal contacts with the slots in the fuse panel, then press the flasher firmly into place.
8   The rest of installation is the reverse of removal.

Chime

9   Detach the cable from the negative terminal of the battery.
10   On early models, remove the dash panel under the steering column to gain access to

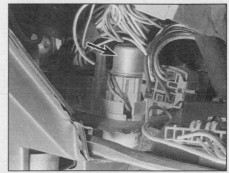

10.6 The hazard flasher unit (arrow) can be removed by pulling it straight up from the panel

12

the chime module **(see illustration 7.18)**. On later models the chime is located on the left side of the radio mounted to a bracket and does not require panel removal for access.

11 Unplug the electrical connector from the chime **(see illustrations)**.

12 Remove the screws from the bracket and detach the chime.

13 Installation is the reverse of removal.

---

11 Headlight control switch and rheostat-check and replacement

Check

1 Before performing any of the following checks, be sure that the battery is fully charged and that all battery cable connections are clean and tight.

2 Visual inspection is an important part of these checks. Look for wires with frayed or damaged insulation, loose connections and improper harness routing. Correct any problems of this type before checking the headlight switch.

Headlight switch

3 If the headlights do not work but the park and tail lights are okay:

a) *The headlight wiring is open or shorted. Check the wiring and connections between the headlight switch and lights (see the wiring diagrams at the end of this Chapter). Repair as necessary.*

b) *There is a poor ground connection. Check (see the wiring diagrams at the end of this Chapter) and repair as necessary.*

c) *The dimmer switch is damaged. Check the dimmer switch and replace it if necessary (see Section 7).*

d) *The headlight switch is damaged. Check the headlight switch and replace if necessary.*

4 If all the exterior lights do not work:

a) *There is an open or a short in the wiring. Check the wiring and connections between the power source and the*

10.11a To replace the chime, unplug the electrical connector and remove the bracket screw (arrows) - early model shown

headlight switch (see the wiring diagrams at the end of this Chapter).

b) *The headlight switch is damaged. Check the switch and replace it if necessary.*

5 If the headlights flash on and off:

a) *There is a shorted circuit. Check the wiring and connections between the headlight switch and the headlights (see the wiring diagrams at the end of this Chapter). Repair as necessary.*

b) *The headlight switch is damaged. Replace the headlight switch.*

6 If the park and tail lights do not work but the headlights are okay:

a) *A fuse is blown. Replace it (see Section 4).*

b) *There is an open in the wiring or a poor ground. Check the wiring and connections between the headlight switch and lights (see the wiring diagrams at the end of this Chapter). Repair as necessary.*

c) *The headlight switch is damaged. Check the switch and replace if necessary.*

7 If the instrument panel lights do not work or will not dim:

a) *A fuse is blown. Replace it (see Section 4).*

b) *There is an open or a short in the wiring. Check the wiring between the headlight switch and lights (see the wiring*

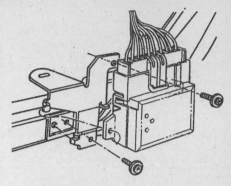

10.11b On later models, the chime module is located on the left side of the center console next to the radio - to replace it, unplug the electrical connector and remove the two bracket screws

diagrams at the end of this Chapter). Repair as necessary.

c) *The headlight switch is damaged. Check the switch and replace it if necessary.*

8 If the dome light will not work:

a) *A fuse is blown. Replace it (see Section 4).*

b) *There is an open or a short in the wiring. Check the wiring between the headlight switch and the dome light and between the headlight switch and the fuse panel (see the wiring diagrams at the end of this Chapter). Repair as necessary.*

c) *The headlight switch is damaged. Check the switch and replace if necessary.*

Headlight switch connector

Refer to illustrations 11.9a, 11.9b and 11.9c

Note: *In the following sequence of switch connector checks, the first set of designated terminals refer to 1984 and 1985 models; the indicated terminals in parentheses refer to 1986 and 1987 models and bracketed terminal designators indicate 1988 and later models. The second terminal designator is assumed good for all models except if indicated.*

9 Connect a 12-volt test light between terminal B1 (B) [B1] and a good ground **(see illustrations)**. The test light should light. If it

---

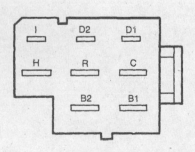

11.9a Headlight switch connector terminals - 1984 and 1985 models

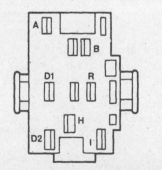

11.9b Headlight switch connector terminals - 1986 and 1987 models

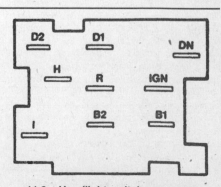

11.9c Headlight switch connector terminals - 1988 and later models

doesn't, trace the circuit back to the fusible link and repair as necessary.

10   Connect a 12-volt test light between terminal B2 (A) [B2] and a good ground. The test light should light. If it doesn't, trace the circuit back to the fuse panel and repair as necessary.

11   Connect a jumper wire between terminals B1 (B) [B1] and H. The headlights should come on.

a) If they don't, trace circuit H back to the headlights and repair it as necessary.

b) If the power circuit is okay, check the ground circuit between the headlights and ground.

12   Connect a jumper wire between terminals B2 (A) [B2] and R. The park lights, rear lights and marker lights should come on.

a) If they don't, trace the R circuit and repair as necessary.

b) If the power circuit is okay, then check the ground circuit from the lights to ground.

13   Connect a jumper wire between terminals B2 (A) [B2] and I. The instrument panel lights should come on full bright. If they don't, trace the I circuit to the instrument panel lights and repair as necessary.

14   Connect a 12-volt test light between [IGN] and a good ground. Turn the ignition switch to the Run position. The test light should light. If not, trace [IGN] circuit back to the ignition switch and repair it. **Note:** *This test is applicable to 1988 and later models only.*

15   Connect a jumper wire between terminals [B2] and [DN]. Only the liquid crystal display lights should light. If not, trace [DN] circuit back to the light s and repair as necessary. If liquid crystal light s light, check the ground circuit from the light to ground. **Note:** *This test is applicable to 1988 and later models only.*

16   Connect a 12-volt test light between [D1] and a good ground. The test light should

light. If not, trace [D1] circuit back to the fuse panel and repair if necessary. **Note:** *This test is applicable to 1988 and later models only.*

17   Connect a jumper wire between terminals [D1] and [D2]. With all of the doors closed, the dome light should light. If not, trace [D2] circuit back to the dome light. If the dome light functions, check the ground circuit from the dome light to ground. **Note:** *This test is applicable to 1988 and later models only.*

Headlight switch continuity check

Refer to illustrations 11.18a, 11.18b and 11.18c

Note: *A self-powered test light or ohmmeter will be required for the following checks.*

18   Refer to the accompanying table and perform continuity checks between the indicated terminals **(see illustrations).**

19   If the headlight switch fails any of the above checks, replace it.

Replacement (toggle-type switch)

Refer to illustrations 11.21, 11.22 and 11.23

20   Detach the cable from the negative terminal of the battery.

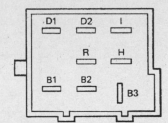

Switch Terminals	Switch Positions		
	Off	Park	Headlamp
B1 to H	No Cont.	No Cont.	Continuity
B1 to R	No Cont.	No Cont.	No Cont.
B1 to B2	No Cont.	No Cont.	No Cont.
B1 to B3	Continuity	Continuity	Continuity
R to H	No Cont.	No Cont.	No Cont.
R to B2	No Cont.	Continuity	Continuity
H to B2	No Cont.	No Cont.	No Cont.
D1 to D2	Continuity should only exist with thumbwheel rotated to extreme right.		
I to R	Continuity should be checked with thumbwheel rotated to extreme right. Then slowly rotate thumbwheel to the left and test lamp should dim.		

11.18a Headlight switch connector terminals and continuity chart - 1984 and 1985 models

Switch Terminals	Switch Positions		
	Off	Park	Headlamp
B to H	No Cont.	No Cont.	Continuity
B to R	No Cont.	No Cont.	No Cont.
B to A	No Cont.	No Cont.	No Cont.
R to H	No Cont.	No Cont.	No Cont.
R to A	No Cont.	Continuity	Continuity
H to A	No Cont.	No Cont.	No Cont.
D to D	Continuity should only exist with rheostat in full counterclockwise position.		
I to R	Continuity should be measured with rheostat in full counterclockwise position. Then slowly rotate rheostat clockwise and test lamp should slowly dim.		

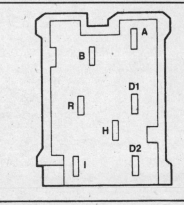

11.18b Headlight switch connector terminals and continuity chart - 1986 and 1987 models

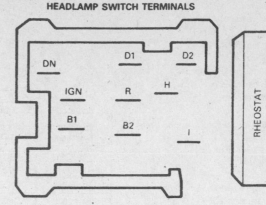

HEADLAMP SWITCH TERMINALS

DN   D1   D2
IGN   R   H
B1   B2   I

RHEOSTAT

HEADLAMP SWITCH TEST

Switch Terminals	Switch Positions		
	Off	Park	Headlamp
B1 to H	No Cont.	No Cont.	Continuity
B2 to R	No Cont.	Continuity	Continuity
DN to IGN	Continuity	No Cont.	No Cont.
DN to I	No Cont.	Continuity	Continuity
R to I	Rotate knob clockwise — ohmmeter will show smoothly increasing resistance.		
D1 to D2	With knob fully counterclockwise (in detent) — Continuity With knob clockwise (out of detent) — No Continuity		

11.18c Headlight switch connector terminals and continuity chart - 1988 and later models

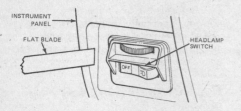

INSTRUMENT PANEL

FLAT BLADE

HEADLAMP SWITCH

OFF   D

11.21 To replace an early model toggle-type headlight switch, insert a thin steel blade on each side to depress the spring clips, then pry out the switch

21   Insert a thin flat blade under the flange at the side of the switch (see illustration) to depress the spring retaining clip. Twist the blade to remove the switch on one side, then insert the blade on the other side of the switch and depress the other spring clip.

22   If you are unable to remove the switch from the dash this way, remove the panel underneath the steering column from the dashboard, then reach around behind the switch, depress the spring clips (see illustration) and pop the switch out through the hole in the dash.

23   Unplug the electrical connector from the switch (see illustration).

24   Installation is the reverse of removal.

Replacement (pull/push-type switch)

Refer to illustrations 11.26 and 11.28

25   Detach the cable from the negative terminal of the battery.

26   On models without air conditioning, remove the left air vent control cable (two

11.22 If you can't depress the spring clips (arrows) far enough to get the headlight switch out of the dashboard with a thin steel blade, remove the kick panel under the steering column, reach around behind the switch and depress the clips with your fingers

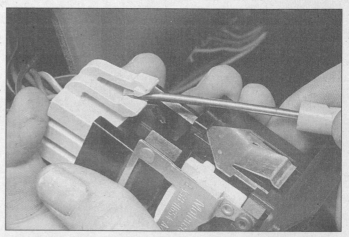

11.23 Once the headlight switch is out of the dash, release the locking lever on the electrical connector and unplug it

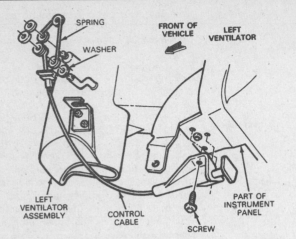

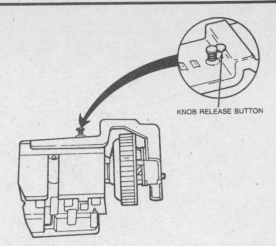

11.26 To gain access to the later model pull/push headlight switch, first remove the air vent control cable assembly if so equipped

11.28 To remove the knob and shaft on a later model pull/push type switch, push the knob release button as shown and pull the shaft out of the switch

retaining screws) and drop the cable and bracket down **(see illustration)**.

27 Remove the fuse panel bracket retaining screws (two) and move the fuse panel assembly aside to gain access to the headlight switch.

28 Pull the headlight knob out to the ON position and depress the headlight knob and shaft retainer button on the headlight switch, then remove the knob and shaft assembly **(see illustration)**.

12.2 To remove an early model sealed beam headlight, first detach this electrical connector from the back of the headlight, then . . .

29 Remove the headlight switch retaining bezel, then disconnect the electrical connector and remove the switch from the instrument panel.

30 Install the headlight switch into the instrument panel and plug in the electrical connector, then install the headlight switch retaining bezel.

31 Install the knob and shaft assembly by inserting the shaft into the switch and gently pushing until the shaft locks into position.

32 The remainder of installation is the reverse of removal.

12 Headlights - removal and installation

Sealed beam headlights

Refer to illustrations 12.2, 12.3 and 12.4

1 Detach the cable from the negative terminal of the battery.

2 Locate the electrical connector on the back of the bad headlight **(see illustration)** and unplug it.

3 From the front of the vehicle, remove the two screws **(see illustration)** from the

headlight trim ring, pry the trim ring tabs from the slots in the headlight molding and remove the trim ring.

4 Remove the four screws from the headlight bezel **(see illustration)**.

5 Remove the headlight.

6 Installation is the reverse of removal. Make sure that the tabs on the bottom of the trim ring are properly seated in the slots in the headlight molding.

Halogen bulb headlights (aerodynamically styled)

Refer to illustration 12.8

Warning: *The replaceable halogen bulb contains gas under pressure. The bulb may shatter if the glass is scratched or the bulb is dropped. Handle the bulb carefully. Grasp the bulb only by it's plastic base to avoid touching glass.*

7 Make sure the headlight switch is in the OFF position. Lift the hood and locate the bulb installed in the rear of the headlight body.

8 Unplug the electrical connector from the bulb holder **(see illustration)**.

9 Remove the bulb retaining ring by rotating it counterclockwise (when viewed

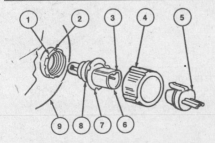

12.8 Halogen headlight bulb details

1 Socket	5 Electrical
2 Locking tab	connector
3 Flat portion of	6 Bulb holder
bulb holder	7 Mounting flange
4 Retaining	8 Bulb
ring	9 Headlight housing

12

12.3 . . . remove the two screws (arrows) from the upper edge of the headlight trim ring and lift it up to detach the tabs on the bottom of the trim ring, then . . .

12.4 . . . remove the four screws (arrows) from the headlight bezel, detach the bezel and remove the headlight

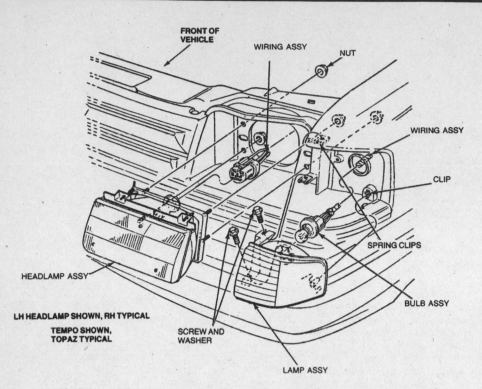

12.15 Headlight housing installation details - 1988 through 1991 models

FRONT OF VEHICLE

WIRING ASSY

NUT

WIRING ASSY

CLIP

SPRING CLIPS

BULB ASSY

HEADLAMP ASSY

LH HEADLAMP SHOWN, RH TYPICAL

TEMPO SHOWN, TOPAZ TYPICAL

SCREW AND WASHER

LAMP ASSY

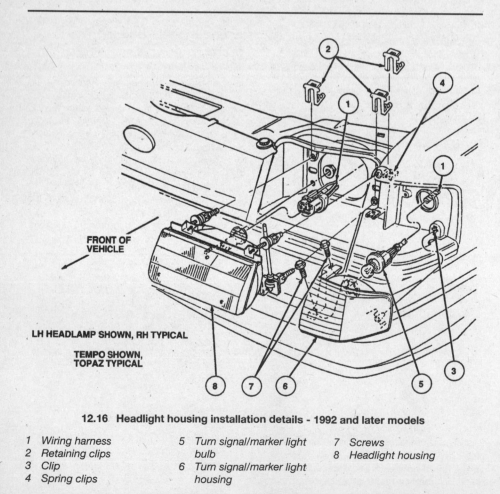

12.16 Headlight housing installation details - 1992 and later models

FRONT OF VEHICLE

LH HEADLAMP SHOWN, RH TYPICAL

TEMPO SHOWN, TOPAZ TYPICAL

1 Wiring harness
2 Retaining clips
3 Clip
4 Spring clips
5 Turn signal/marker light bulb
6 Turn signal/marker light housing
7 Screws
8 Headlight housing

from the rear) about one-eighth turn and sliding the ring off the bulb holder. Keep the ring; it will be used again to retain the new bulb.

10   Carefully remove the headlight bulb assembly from the housing by gently pulling it straight out. Do not rotate the bulb during removal.

11   With the flat side of the bulb holder facing up, insert the bulb and holder into the socket in the headlight housing. Turn the holder slightly to the left or right, if necessary, to align the grooves in the forward part of the holder with its corresponding locating tabs in the socket. When grooves are aligned, push the bulb firmly into the socket until the mounting flange on the base contacts the rear face of the socket.

12   Slip the bulb retaining ring over the rear of the bulb holder. Turn the ring clockwise - a stop will be felt when the ring is fully engaged.

13   Plug in the electrical connector. Turn the headlights on and check for proper operation. **Note:** *A properly aimed headlight normally need not be re-aimed after installation of this bulb. A burned out bulb should not be removed from the headlight housing until just before a replacement bulb is to be installed. Removal of a bulb for an extended period of time may allow contaminants (dust, moisture, smoke) to enter the headlight body and affect the performance of the headlight. When servicing the headlight bulb, energize the bulb only while it is contained within the headlight housing.*

Headlight assembly replacement (aerodynamically styled)

Refer to illustrations 12.15 and 12.16

Warning: *The replaceable halogen bulb contains gas under pressure. The bulb may shatter if the glass is scratched or the bulb is dropped. Handle the bulb carefully. Grasp it only by its plastic base to avoid touching the glass.*

14   Remove the bulb from the rear of the headlight housing as described in Steps 7 through 10.

15   On 1988 through 1991 models, remove the four headlight retaining nuts securing the housing to the vehicle **(see illustration)**.

16   On 1992 and later models, remove the three headlight retaining clips securing the housing to the vehicle **(see illustration)**.

17   Remove the headlight assembly from the vehicle

18   Installation is the reverse of removal.

13 Headlights - adjustment

Note: *It is important that the headlights be aimed correctly. If adjusted incorrectly they could blind the driver of an oncoming vehicle and cause a serious accident or seriously reduce your ability to see the road. The*

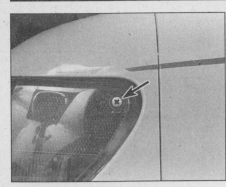

14.3 To remove the side marker/turn signal lens assembly on early models, remove the screw, then . . .

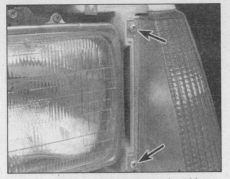

14.4 . . . remove the two turn signal lens screws (arrows)

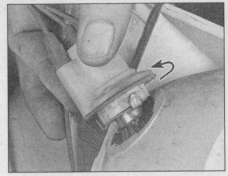

14.5 To remove the bulb holder from the side marker/turn signal lens assembly, turn it counterclockwise and pull it out

headlights should be checked for proper aim every 12 months and any time a new headlight is installed or front end body work is performed. It should be emphasized that the following procedure is only an interim step which will provide temporary adjustment until the headlights can be adjusted by a properly equipped shop.

1   Earlier model sealed beam type headlights have two spring-loaded adjusting screws, one on the top controlling up-and-down movement and one on the side controlling left-and-right movement. Later model halogen headlights utilize two upper adjusting screws for left-and-right movement and one lower corner angle drive mechanism for up-and-down movement.

2   There are several methods of adjusting the headlights. The simplest method requires a blank wall 25 feet in front of the vehicle and a level floor.

3   Position masking tape vertically on the wall in reference to the vehicle centerline and the centerlines of both headlights.

4   Position a horizontal tape line in reference to. the centerline of all the headlights. **Note:** It may be easier to position the tape on the wall with the vehicle parked only a few inches away.

5   Adjustment should be made with the vehicle sitting level, the gas tank half-full and no unusually heavy load in the vehicle.

6   Starting with the low beam adjustment, position the high intensity zone so it is two inches below the horizontal line and two inches to the right of the headlight vertical line. Adjustment is made by turning the appropriate adjusting screw (refer to step 1) to raise or lower the beam or to move the beam left or right.

7   With the high beams on, the high intensity zone should be vertically centered with the exact center just below the horizontal line. **Note:** *It may not be possible to position the headlight aim exactly for both high and low beams. If a compromise must be made, keep in mind that the low beams are the most used and have the greatest effect on driver safety.*

8   Have the headlights adjusted by a dealer service department at the earliest opportunity.

14 Bulb replacement

Refer to illustrations 14.3, 14.4, 14.5, 14.15, 14.19, 14.20, 14,24, 14.30, 14.35, 14.38 and 14.42

Front side marker/turn signal lights (1984 through 1987 models)

1   Detach the cable from the negative terminal of the battery.

2   Remove the headlight trim ring (see Section 12).

3   Remove the screw from the upper rear corner of the side marker lens **(see illustration)**.

4   Remove the two screws from the inside edge of the turn signal lens **(see illustration)**.

5   Pull the side marker/turn signal lens assembly from the headlight molding, turn the bulb holder counterclockwise and pull the holder from the assembly **(see illustration)**.

6   Push down and twist out the bulb.

7   Installation is the reverse of removal.

Front side marker/turn signal lights (1988 and later models)

8   Detach the cable from the negative terminal of the battery.

9   Open the hood and remove the two screws retaining the light housing to the grille

opening panel **(see illustrations 12.15 and 12.16)**.

10   Grasp the housing and pull it straight forward to release the lower outboard hidden fastener. Pull the assembly out far enough to gain access to the bulb socket.

11   Release the bulb socket from the housing by twisting, then remove the bulb from the socket by pushing down and turning it counterclockwise.

12   Installation is the reverse of removal.

Rear turn signal light/back-up lights

Note: *The procedure for the rear turn signal and the back-up light bulbs is the same.*

13   Detach the cable from the negative terminal of the battery.

14   Peel the luggage compartment carpeting from the light housing.

15   Turn the bulb holder counterclockwise and remove it from the light assembly **(see illustration)**.

16   Push down and twist the bulb counterclockwise and remove it.

17   Installation is the reverse of removal.

License plate lights

18   Detach the cable from the negative terminal of the battery.

19   Open the trunk and unscrew the two license plate light mounting screws **(see illustration)**.

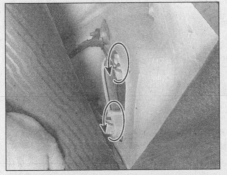

14.15 To remove either the brake or turn signal bulb holders from the rear lens assembly, turn counterclockwise and pull straight out

14.19 To detach the license plate light assembly from the trunk lid, remove the two screws

12

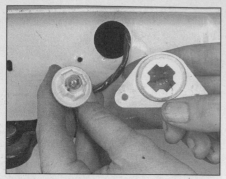

14.20 After detaching the license plate assembly from the trunk lid, separate the lens from the bulb holder, then pull the bulb straight out of the holder

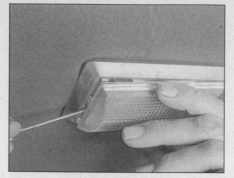

14.24 To replace the dome light bulb, pop the plastic lens loose with a small screwdriver

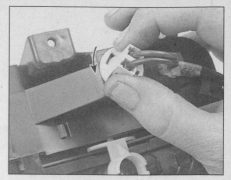

14.30 To replace the gear position indicator bulb rotate the bulb holder counterclockwise, pull it straight out, then push down and twist on the bulb to remove it from the holder

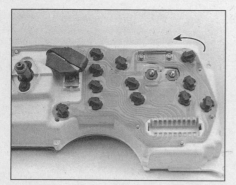

14.35 To replace an instrument panel bulb, remove the instrument panel from the dashboard. turn it over, rotate the holder for the faulty bulb counterclockwise, pull it out of the instrument panel and pull the bulb straight out from the holder (early instrument panel shown, later models similar)

20   Remove the light assembly from the trunk and separate the bulb holder from the bracket **(see illustration).**
21   Pull the bulb out of the holder.
22   Installation is the reverse of removal.

Dome light

23   Detach the cable from the negative terminal of the battery.
24   Pry the dome light lens loose with a small screwdriver **(see illustration).**
25   Pull the bulb straight out from the holder.
26   Installation is the reverse of removal.

Gear position indicator bulb (automatic transaxle models only)

27   Detach the cable from the negative terminal of the battery.

28   Remove the center console (see Chapter 11).
29   Remove the selector lever bezel (see Chapter 7, Part B).
30   Turn the bezel upside down and turn the bulb holder counterclockwise to remove it **(see illustration).**
31   To remove the bulb from the holder, push down and twist.
32   Installation is the reverse of removal.

Instrument panel bulbs

33   Detach the cable from the negative terminal of the battery.
34   Remove the instrument panel (see Section 17).
35   Turn the instrument panel upside down **(see illustration)** and turn the bulb holder counterclockwise to remove it.
36   Installation is the reverse of removal.

High-mounted brake light (two-door models)

37   Locate the wire to the high-mounted brake light under the package tray from the inside of the luggage compartment. Pull the wire loose from its plastic clip.
38   Remove the two beauty caps from the light cover and remove the two screws from the side of the cover **(see illustration).**
39   Pull the assembly toward the front of the vehicle.
40   The bulb sockets can then be removed by turning them counterclockwise.
41   Installation is the reverse of removal.

High-mounted brake light (four-door models)

42   From inside the luggage compartment, twist the socket counterclockwise and remove it from housing **(see illustration).**
43   Remove the bulb from the socket.
44   Installation is the reverse of removal.

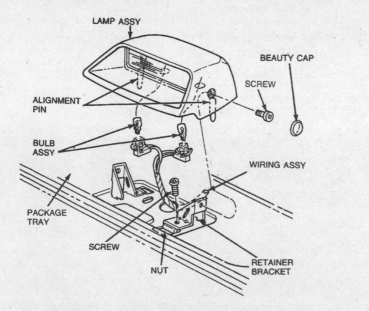

14.38 Exploded view of the high-mount brake light assembly (two-door models)

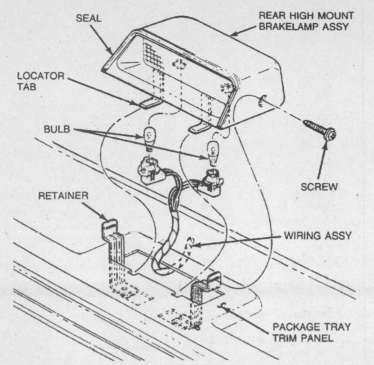

14.42 Exploded view of the high-mount brake light assembly (four-door models)

Labels on diagram: SEAL, REAR HIGH MOUNT BRAKELAMP ASSY, LOCATOR TAB, BULB, SCREW, RETAINER, WIRING ASSY, PACKAGE TRAY TRIM PANEL

15 Radio and speakers - removal and installation

Refer to illustrations 15.2a, 15.2b, 15.2c, 15.3, 15.4, 15.6, 15.10, 15.13, 15.24, 15.29, 15.30, 15.33 and 15.34

AM/FM radio (1984 through 1987 models)

1   Detach the cable from the negative terminal of the battery.

2   Remove the radio trim panel screws, pinch the upper edge trim panel clips **(see illustrations)** together and remove the trim panel from the dashboard.

3   Remove the four radio mounting screws **(see illustration)**.

4   Slide the radio out far enough from the dashboard to unplug the antenna lead and the electrical connectors **(see illustration)**.

5   Remove the radio.

6   Installation is the reverse of removal. Be sure the metal tab on the radio support structure is properly inserted into the clip on the bottom of the radio **(see illustration)** when the radio is pushed back into the dashboard.

15.2a Remove the two screws (arrows) on the underside of the radio trim panel to detach the lower edge of the panel from the dashboard

15.2b To release the upper edge of the trim panel, pinch the spring clips (arrows) together

15.2c The radio trim panel spring clips showing the points (arrows) at which they must be depressed so they will release from the dashboard

15.3 Remove the four screws (arrows) to detach the radio from the dashboard

15.4 After pulling the radio from the dash, unplug the electrical connectors and the antenna lead (arrows)

15.6 When installing the radio, make sure the tab on the metal support structure is properly inserted into the spring clip on the bottom of the radio (arrows)

12

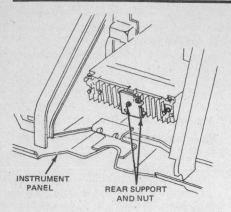

15.10 Pull the radio out and raise the rear so it clears the clip in the back

Electronically-tuned radio/tape player (1984 through 1987 models)

7   Detach the cable from the negative terminal of the battery.

8   Remove the center instrument trim panel (see Chapter 11).

9   Remove the four screws **(see illustration 15.3)** retaining the radio and mounting bracket to the instrument panel.

10   Push the radio to the front and raise the back of the radio slightly so the rear support bracket clears the clip **(see illustration)** in the dashboard, then pull the radio out of the instrument panel.

11   Detach the electrical connectors and the antenna lead.

12   Installation is the reverse of removal.

Electronically-tuned radio/tape player (1988 and later models)

13   The procedure for removal and installation of the radio in 1988 and later models is much simpler than for earlier units. However, you'll have to obtain a pair of special radio removal tools (T87P-19061-A or equivalent - available from a dealer or an automotive radio store) **(see illustration)**.

14   Detach the cable from the negative battery terminal.

15   Pop out the instrument panel radio opening cover **(see illustrations 15.2a and 15.2b)**.

16   Insert the radio removal tools into each side of the radio faceplate. Press them in a full inch to release the radio retaining clips. Pull the radio out of the instrument panel using the tools as handles.

17   Unplug the electrical connectors and antenna lead from the rear of the radio.

18   If you're replacing the radio, switch the rear mounting bracket to the new radio.

19   Attach the electrical connectors and antenna lead to the radio.

20   Slide the radio into the instrument panel. Engage the rear mounting bracket in the track in the instrument panel.

21   Install the dashboard radio opening cover.

22   Attach the cable to the negative battery terminal.

Premium sound amplifier

23   Detach the cable from the negative terminal of the battery.

24   Remove the two nuts retaining the amplifier to the bottom of the package tray in the luggage compartment **(see illustration)**.

25   Lower the amplifier and unplug the two electrical connectors.

26   Installation is the reverse of removal.

Speakers

Front (front doors)

27   Detach the cable from the negative terminal of the battery.

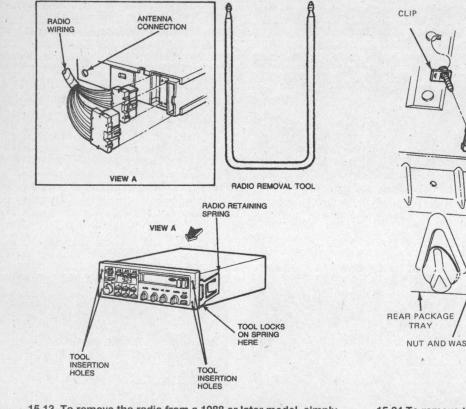

15.13 To remove the radio from a 1988 or later model, simply insert a special radio removal tool (there are two in a set) into the holes at the sides of the radio faceplate, push them in about an inch to release the retaining springs and, using the tools as handles, pull the radio out of the dash far enough to detach the electrical connectors and antenna lead

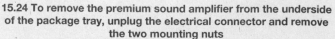

15.24 To remove the premium sound amplifier from the underside of the package tray, unplug the electrical connector and remove the two mounting nuts

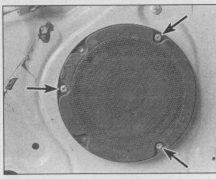

15.29 After removing the door trim panel, remove the three screws (arrows) and pull the speaker out

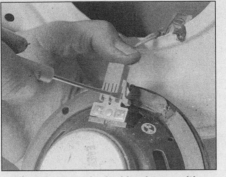

15.30 Release the locking levers with a small screwdriver and unplug the electrical connector from the speaker

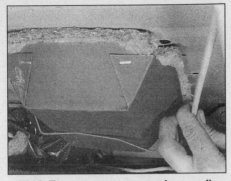

15.33 To remove a rear speaker, unclip one end of the wire retaining clip from the underside of the package tray in the luggage compartment and remove the protective enclosure

28 Remove the door trim panel (see Chapter 11).

29 Remove the three speaker mounting screws **(see illustration)**.

30 Pull the speaker from the mounting recess in the door and unplug the electrical connector **(see illustration)**.

31 Installation is the reverse of removal.

Rear (package tray)

32 Detach the cable from the negative terminal of the battery.

33 Remove the wire retaining clip and the protective speaker enclosure from the underside of the package tray in the luggage compartment **(see illustration)**.

34 Unplug the electrical connector, detach the rubber restraining strap **(see illustration)** and remove the speaker.

35 Installation is the reverse of removal.

---

16 Radio antenna - check and replacement

Refer to illustrations 16.1, 16.3, 16.6, 16.7a, 16.7b, 16.7c, 16.9, 16.10 and 16.11

Note: *If you are replacing a broken antenna mast, unscrew the old mast and install a new one. If, however, reception is poor even though the antenna looks okay, perform the following tests and, if the antenna assembly fails either test, refer to the replacement part of this Section and replace the entire antenna base and cable assembly.*

Resistance check

Antenna cable-to-mast

1 With the antenna cable installed on the vehicle and the cable unplugged from the radio, check the resistance between the cable and the mast with an ohmmeter by contacting the antenna assembly at the indicated points **(see illustration)**.

2 If the indicated readings are as specified, the antenna is okay. If they're not, check the antenna cable and base.

Antenna cable-to-base

3 With the antenna cable unplugged from the radio, check the resistance between the cable and the base with an ohmmeter by contacting the antenna assembly at the indicated points **(see illustration)**.

15.34 Unplug the electrical connector (arrow), detach the retaining strap (arrow) from its hook and remove the speaker

4 If the indicated readings are as specified, the cable is okay. If they're not, replace the antenna cable and base assembly.

Replacement

5 Push in the sides of the glovebox door and allow the door to swing to its fully open position, then reach around behind the right end of the radio and detach the antenna cable. If you are unable to disconnect the

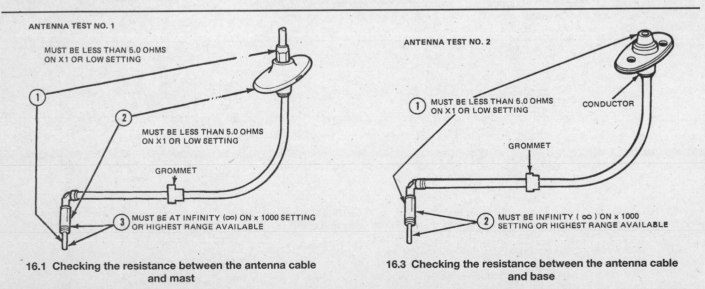

16.1 Checking the resistance between the antenna cable and mast

16.3 Checking the resistance between the antenna cable and base

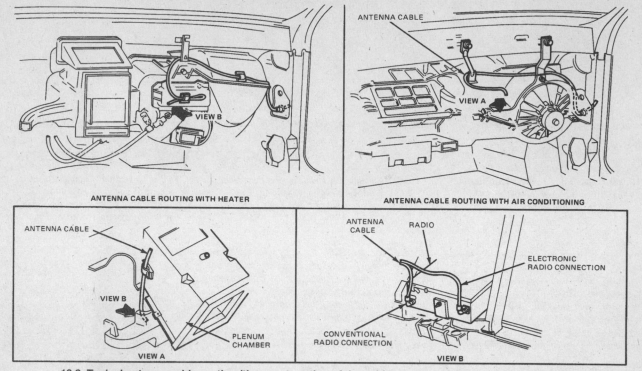

ANTENNA CABLE ROUTING WITH HEATER

ANTENNA CABLE ROUTING WITH AIR CONDITIONING

16.6 Typical antenna cable routing (the exact routing of the cable on your vehicle may vary somewhat)

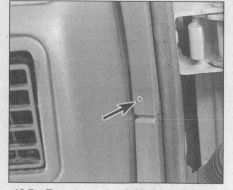

16.7a To remove the right side cowl trim panel, remove the screw which attaches the windshield garnish side molding and cowl trim panel to the windshield pillar . . .

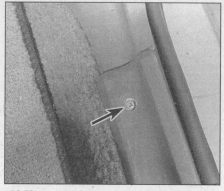

16.7b . . . and the screw which attaches the scuff plate and cowl trim panel to the lower edge of the door opening . . .

cable this way, pull the radio out of the dashboard and disconnect the antenna cable from the back of the radio (see Section 15).

6   Looking through the open glove box recess with a flashlight, note the routing of the antenna cable, then detach it from all clips on the heater and/or air conditioning assemblies **(see illustration).**

7   Remove the right cowl side trim panel screws and the single pop fastener **(see illustrations)**, then remove the trim panel.

8   Unscrew the antenna mast.

9   Pry the cap loose with a small screwdriver **(see illustration).**

10   Remove the base attaching screws **(see illustration).**

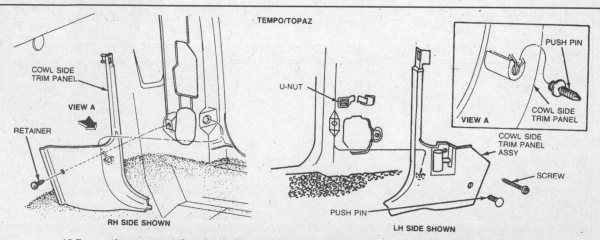

16.7c . . . then pop out the plastic fastener located underneath the right end of the dashboard

16.9 Pry the antenna base cap loose with a small screwdriver . . .

16.10 . . . then remove the screws from the antenna base

pulling the cable through the hole from inside the vehicle.

15 Route the new antenna cable exactly like the old one.

16 Connect the cable to the radio.

17 Attach the cable retaining clips.

18 Install the right side cowl trim panel.

19 Push in on the sides of the glovebox and close it.

17 Instrument cluster and clock - removal and installation

Refer to illustrations 17.2a, 17.2b, 17.2c, 17.3, 17.5, 17.10, 17.11, 17.15 and 17.22

Warning: *If vehicle is equipped with airbags, refer to Section 25, to disarm the airbag system prior to performing any work described below.*

Instrument cluster (1984 through 1987 models)

1 Remove the kick panel under the steering column from the dashboard.

11 Pull the antenna cable through the hole in the door hinge pillar and fender. The grommet in the front body lower pillar **(see illustration)** should come free. If it doesn't, pry it loose with a small screwdriver. Remove the antenna base and cable assembly from the vehicle.

12 With the front right door open, put the gasket in position on the antenna, place the antenna base and cable assembly into position in the fender opening and install the antenna base to the fender.

13 Install the antenna base cap and screw in the antenna mast.

14 Pull the antenna lead through the door hinge pillar opening. Seat the grommet by

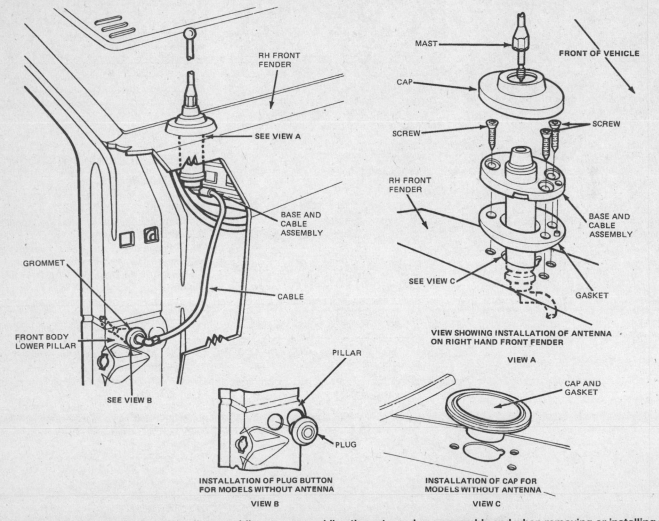

16.11 Refer to this illustration when disassembling or reassembling the antenna base assembly and when removing or installing the cable between the base and the grommet in the front body lower pillar

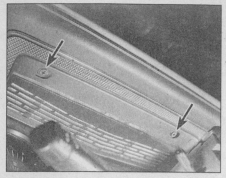

17.2a To remove the instrument cluster finish panel from the dashboard, remove the two screws from the upper left edge of the instrument cluster finish panel

17.2b Remove the two screws from the tabs on the lower left edge of the panel after first removing the kick panel under the steering column

17.2c Remove the screw from the upper right corner of the recess for the digital clock

17.3 To detach the instrument cluster from the dashboard, remove the four mounting screws (arrows)

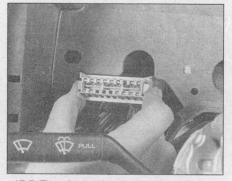

17.5 To release the electrical connector from the socket in the back side of the instrument cluster, depress the two locking levers and pull on the connector

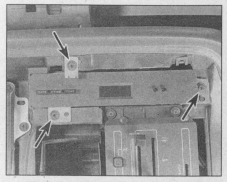

17.10 To detach the clock from the dashboard, remove the three mounting screws (arrows)

2   Remove the screws from the instrument cluster finish panel **(see illustrations)** and remove the panel.
3   Remove the screws from the instrument cluster **(see illustration)**.
4   Pull the cluster away from the dash slightly, reach around behind it and detach the speedometer cable by pressing on the flat surface of the plastic connector.
5   Pull the cluster from the dash far enough to unplug the electrical connector. To unplug the connector, depress the two locking levers on either side of the plug **(see illustration)**.

6   Remove the cluster.
7   Installation is the reverse of removal.

Clock

8   Detach the cable from the negative terminal of the battery.
9   Remove the instrument cluster finish panel.
10   Remove the three clock mounting screws **(see illustration)**.
11   Pull the clock out and unplug the electrical connector **(see illustration)**.
12   Remove the clock.
13   Installation is the reverse of removal.

Instrument cluster (1988 and later models)

Removal

14   Detach the cable from the negative battery terminal.
15   Remove the two retaining screws at the bottom of the steering column opening and snap the column cover out **(see illustration)**.
16   Remove the steering column shroud **(see illustration 7.19)**.
17   Remove the lower cluster finish panels.
18   Remove the four cluster opening finish panel retaining screws.
19   Detach the speedometer cable at the transaxle.
20   Remove the four screws which retain the cluster and carefully pull the cluster out far enough to disengage the speedometer cable.
21   Carefully pull the cluster away from the instrument panel. Detach the cluster feed plugs from the printed circuit.

Installation

22   When you install the cluster back in the dash, insert the left corner into position first **(see illustration)**.

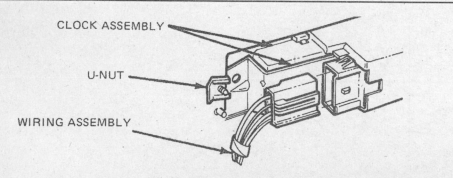

CLOCK ASSEMBLY
U-NUT
WIRING ASSEMBLY

17.11 After pulling the clock from the opening in the dashboard, unplug the electrical connector

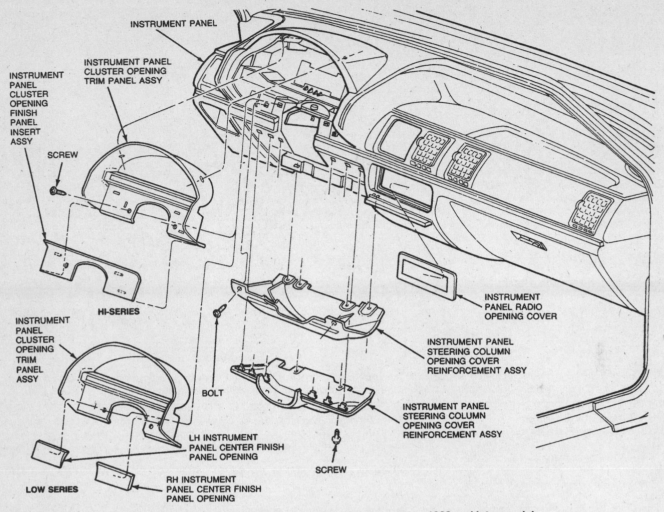

INSTRUMENT PANEL

INSTRUMENT PANEL CLUSTER OPENING TRIM PANEL ASSY

INSTRUMENT PANEL CLUSTER OPENING FINISH PANEL INSERT ASSY

SCREW

HI-SERIES

INSTRUMENT PANEL CLUSTER OPENING TRIM PANEL ASSY

LOW SERIES

BOLT

LH INSTRUMENT PANEL CENTER FINISH PANEL OPENING

RH INSTRUMENT PANEL CENTER FINISH PANEL OPENING

SCREW

INSTRUMENT PANEL RADIO OPENING COVER

INSTRUMENT PANEL STEERING COLUMN OPENING COVER REINFORCEMENT ASSY

INSTRUMENT PANEL STEERING COLUMN OPENING COVER REINFORCEMENT ASSY

17.15 Exploded view of the instrument panel components - 1988 and later models

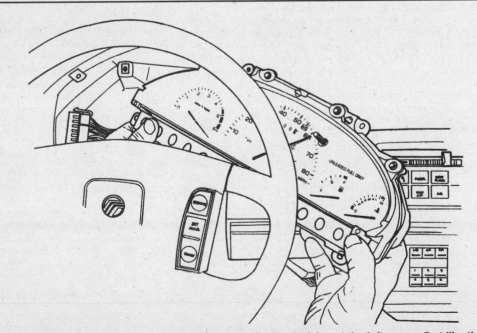

17.22 When installing the instrument cluster in the dash insert the left corner first like this

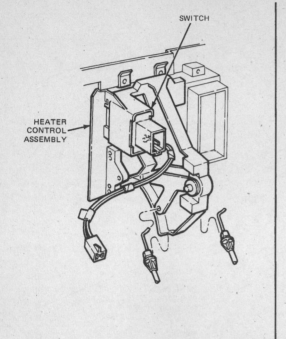

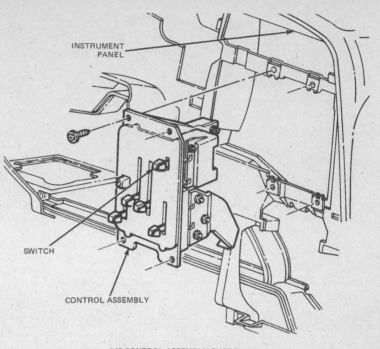

A/C CONTROL ASSEMBLY SHOWN
HEATER CONTROL ASSEMBLY TYPICAL

18.1 The rear window defogger switch is located in the upper right corner of the heater and air conditioner control assembly on early models - to check and/or replace it, first remove the control assembly from the dashboard

23   Place the cluster in position.
24   Attach the speedometer cable to the cluster.
25   Plug in the electrical connectors to the printed circuit.
26   Attach the speedometer cable to the transaxle.
27   Install the four cluster retaining screws.
28   Install the cluster opening finish panel and the four retaining screws.
29   Install the snap-in lower cluster finish panels.
30   Install the steering column trim shroud.
31   Install the steering column cover and two retaining screws.
32   Attach the battery ground cable.

18   Rear window defogger - check and repair

Refer to illustrations 18.1, 18.2, 18.10, 18.13, 18.26 and 18.36

Defogger switch (1984 through 1987 models)

1   The rear window defogger switch is located in the upper right corner of the air conditioner/heater control assembly. To check it, detach the air conditioner/heater control assembly from the dashboard (see Chapter 3), turn the control assembly around so the back is facing you and locate the electrical connector for the defogger switch **(see illustration)**.
2   Referring to the accompanying terminal

guide **(see illustration)**, ground pin G, connect a jumper wire between pins I and B and connect a 12-volt test light between pin L and ground.
3   Apply power to pin B. The test light should not light.
4   Momentarily put the switch in the On position. The test light should come on and stay on after the control returns to the Normal position.
5   The test light should go off under the following conditions:
   a) *If the switch is moved to the Off position.*
   b) *If the power to the ignition Acc terminal is removed or approximately ten minutes have elapsed.*
6   If the switch fails any of the above checks, replace it.
7   To replace the switch, unplug the

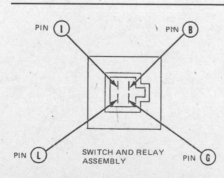

18.2 Refer to this terminal guide when checking the rear window defogger switch

electrical connector and remove the switch from the control assembly.
8   Installation is the reverse of removal.

Defogger switch (1988 and later models)

9   The rear window defogger switch is located in the heater control panel assembly. To check it, detach the control assembly from the dashboard (see Chapter 3), turn the control assembly around so that the back is facing you and locate the electrical connector for the defogger switch.
10   Referring to the accompanying terminal guide **(see illustration)**, check for voltage at

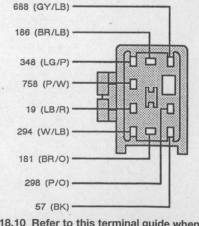

688 (GY/LB)
186 (BR/LB)
348 (LG/P)
758 (P/W)
19 (LB/R)
294 (W/LB)
181 (BR/O)
298 (P/O)
57 (BK)

18.10 Refer to this terminal guide when checking the rear window defogger at the heater control assembly (1988 and later models)

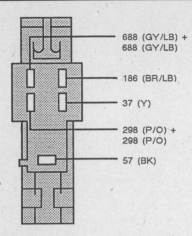

18.13 Refer to this terminal guide when checking the rear window defogger at the defrost relay/timer (1988 and later models)

- 688 (GY/LB) +
- 688 (GY/LB)
- 186 (BR/LB)
- 37 (Y)
- 298 (P/O) +
- 298 (P/O)
- 57 (BK)

pin 298 (working from the back side of the connector) with the ignition switch in the Run position. If no voltage is present, trace the circuit back to the fuse panel (fuse 5) and repair as required.

11   If voltage is present, insert probe into pin 186 from the back side of the connector. With ignition switch in the Run position, press the rear defrost button and check for a momentary voltage spike as the button is depressed. If no momentary voltage is present, replace the switch.

Rear window defogger relay/timer (1988 and later models)

12   The rear window defogger relay is located on the left side of the center console next to the warning chime module.

13   Referring to the accompanying terminal guide **(see illustration)**, check for voltage at pin 298 (from the back side of the connector) with the ignition switch in the Run position. If no voltage is present, trace the circuit back to the fuse panel (fuse 5) and repair as required.

14   If voltage is present, insert the probe into pin 186 (from the back side of the connector). With the ignition switch in the Run position, press the rear defrost button and check for a momentary voltage spike as the button is depressed. If no momentary voltage is present, trace the circuit back to the defogger switch and repair as required.

15   From the back side of the connector, check for voltage at pin 37. If no voltage is present, repair the fusible link to the starter relay terminal.

16   From the backside of the connector, check for voltage at pin 688 with the ignition switch in the Run position and after depressing defrost button. The test light should come on and stay on after the control returns to the Normal position. The test light should go off under the following conditions:

a) *If the switch is moved to the Off position.*

b) *If the power to the ignition Acc terminal is removed or approximately ten minutes have elapsed.*

17   If no voltage is present or the circuit remains energized for significantly less or more then ten minutes, replace the relay.

Rear window defogger grid wire

Check

18   Use a strong light inside the vehicle. Visually inspect the wire grid from the outside. A broken grid wire will appear as a brown spot.

19   Run the engine at idle. Set the control switch to On. The indicator light should come on.

20   Working inside the vehicle with a voltmeter, contact the broad red brown strips (the "bus") on the sides of the rear window. The meter should read 10-to-13 volts. A lower voltage reading indicates a loose ground wire (pigtail) connection at the grounded side of the glass.

21   Contact a good ground point with the negative lead of the meter. The voltage reading should not change.

22   With the negative lead of the meter grounded, touch each grid line of the heated rear window at its midpoint with the positive lead:

a) *A reading of approximately 6-volts indicates that the line is good.*

b) *A reading of 0-volts indicates that the line is broken between the mid-point and the positive side of the grid line.*

c) *A reading of 12-volts indicates that the circuit is broken between the mid-point of the grid and ground.*

Repair

Note: *Any break in the grid longer than one inch cannot be repaired. The rear window must be replaced. For breaks less than one inch in length, use the following procedure. You will need to obtain grid repair compound and brown touch-up paint from a Ford dealer service department or an auto parts store.*

23   Bring the vehicle inside and allow it to reach room temperature, which should be 60-degrees F or above.

24   Clean the entire grid line repair area with glass cleaner or a suitable cleaning solvent. Remove all dirt, wax, grease, oil or other foreign matter. The repair area must be clean and dry.

25   Mark the location of the break on the outside of the window.

26   Using cellulose tape, mask off the area directly above and below the grid break. The break area should be at the center of the mask and the tape gap must be no wider than the existing grid line **(see illustration)**.

27   If both the brown and silver layers of the grid are broken or missing, apply a coating of the brown touch-up paint across the break area first. Two coats may be necessary to obtain the proper color. Allow the touch-up paint to dry.

28   Apply three coats of the silver grid repair compound. Allow three to five minutes drying time between coats. The coating of the silver grid repair compound should extend at least 1/4-inch on both sides of the break. **Note**: *If the brown layer of the grid is not broken or missing, apply only the silver grid repair compound to the break. Allow the compound to dry for five minutes, then remove the mask.*

29   After removing the mask, check the outside appearance of the grid repair. If the silver repair compound is visible above or below the grid, this excess should be removed. This can be done by placing a

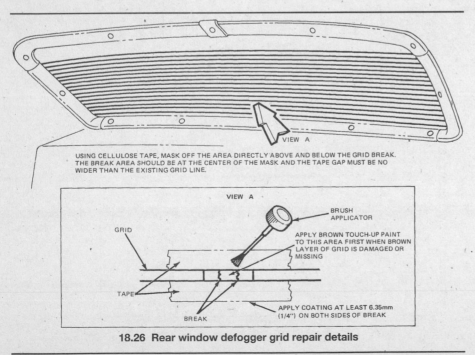

USING CELLULOSE TAPE, MASK OFF THE AREA DIRECTLY ABOVE AND BELOW THE GRID BREAK. THE BREAK AREA SHOULD BE AT THE CENTER OF THE MASK AND THE TAPE GAP MUST BE NO WIDER THAN THE EXISTING GRID LINE.

VIEW A

GRID

TAPE

BRUSH APPLICATOR

APPLY BROWN TOUCH-UP PAINT TO THIS AREA FIRST WHEN BROWN LAYER OF GRID IS DAMAGED OR MISSING

BREAK

APPLY COATING AT LEAST 6.35mm (1/4") ON BOTH SIDES OF BREAK

18.26 Rear window defogger grid repair details

12

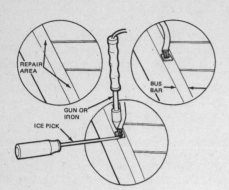

18.36 Position the terminal on the bus bar in the area that was tinned and hold it in place with an ice pick or screwdriver

single edge razor blade on the glass parallel to the grid and scraping gently towards the grid. **Caution:** *Be careful not to damage the gridline with the razor blade.*

30   The repair coating will air dry in about one minute and can be energized within three to five minutes. Optimum hardness and adhesion occurs after approximately 24 hours. At that time, the repair area may be cleaned with a mild window cleaner.

Lead wire terminal service

31   Allow the rear window to warm up to room temperature for a half-hour to an hour.
32   Clean the bus bar in the area to be repaired using fine steel wool (3/0 to 4/0 grade).
33   Restore the area where the bus bar terminal was originally attached by applying three coats of grid repair compound. Allow approximately ten minutes drying time between coats.

34   Working as quickly as possible to avoid overheating the glass, tin the bus bar with solder in the area where the terminal will be reattached.
35   Using a heat gun or heat lamp, pre-heat the glass in the solder area to between 120 and 150-degrees F just prior to soldering the terminal on.
36   Position the terminal on the bus bar in the area that was tinned and hold it in place with an ice pick or screwdriver **(see illustration).**
37   Apply soldering heat to the pad of the terminal until the solder flows. **Caution:** *To avoid damaging the bus bar, remove the soldering gun or iron as soon as the solder flows.*
38   Start the vehicle, turn the heated rear window on and leave it on for five minutes.

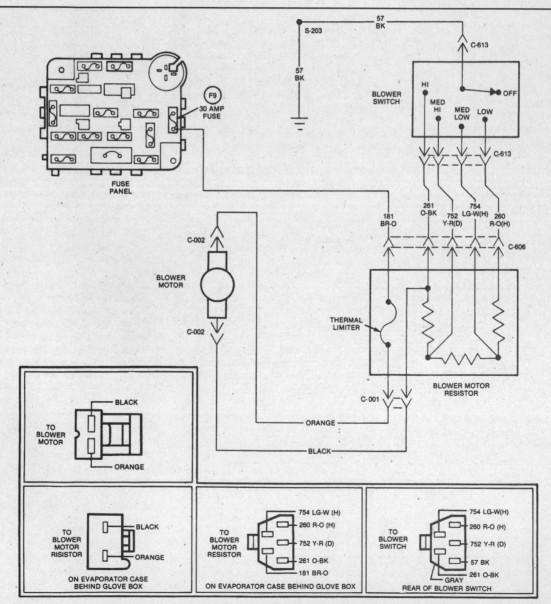

19.1a Refer to this wiring diagram and terminal guide when checking the blower motor circuit on 1984 through 1987 models

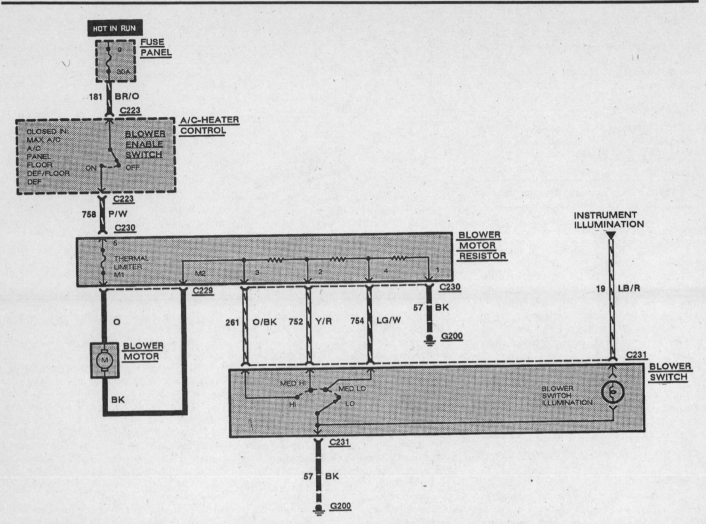

19.1b Refer to this wiring diagram and terminal guide when checking the blower motor circuit on 1988 and later models

19 Heater electrical components - check and replacement

Refer to illustrations 19.1a, 19.1b, 19.1c and 19.4

Blower switch continuity check

Note: *The blower switch on 1984 through 1987 models is located in the heater control*

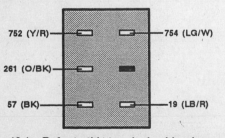

19.1c Refer to this terminal guide when checking blower motor switch continuity on 1988 and later models

panel while on 1988 and later models the switch is mounted separately on the right side of the instrument panel. Refer to Chapter 3 for the removal procedure.

1 Refer to the accompanying heater system wiring diagrams **(see illustrations)**. On 1984 through 1987 models, check switch terminal continuity between pin 57 (BK) and pins 261 (HI), 752 (MED HI), 754 (MED LOW) and 260 (LOW) with the switch at the correct speed position. On 1988 and later models check switch terminal continuity between pin 57 (BK) and pins 261 (HI), 752 (MED HI), 754 (MED LOW) with the switch at the correct speed position. **Note:** 1988 and later models LOW speed operation is controlled by the blower enable switch within the heater control assembly.

   a) *The test light should go on for each connected pair of terminals.*

   b) *There should be no continuity between any terminal and the switch case.*

2 On all electrical circuits, continuity must exist from the source of power (the battery) to the unit where the power is used, and back to

ground. A check at each connection in a circuit, beginning at the battery, will locate an open circuit or will show that the circuit is complete.

3 An ohmmeter or self-powered test light connected at any two points of circuit with the power removed from the circuit will show if the circuit between the two connections is open or complete:

   a) *If the meter does not move or has a light movement (high resistance), the circuit may have a poor connection or broken wire.*

   b) *If the test light does not light, the circuit is open.*

   c) *If the meter movement is great or full (low resistance), the circuit is complete.*

   d) *If the test light lights, the circuit is complete.*

Heater blower motor current draw check

4 This in-vehicle test will determine if the blower motor is operating properly. Connect a 0 to 30 amp ammeter as shown **(see illus-**

12

tration). Ground the negative side of the blower motor connector with a 10 gauge or larger jumper wire and measure the motor current draw. If the current draw is not as shown in the Specifications, replace the blower motor.

Replacement

5   If the heater/air conditioning control assembly, blower motor or resistor require replacement, refer to Chapter 3.

20 Horn - removal and installation

1   Detach the cable from the negative terminal of the battery.
2   Raise the front of the vehicle and place it securely on jackstands.
3   From underneath the right front corner of the vehicle, locate the horn between the right front wheel housing and the bumper.
4   Unplug the electrical connector.
5   Remove the nut from the stud that attaches the horn to its mounting bracket and remove the horn.
6   Installation is the reverse of removal.

21 Neutral start switch - check, adjustment and replacement

Refer to illustrations 21.2, 21.3 and 21.9

Check

1   Models equipped with an automatic transaxle have a neutral start switch in the starter control circuit which prevents operation of the starter unless the selector lever is in Neutral or Park.
2   If the vehicle will not start in Neutral or Park, check the switch by unplugging the electrical connector and attaching the probes of a circuit or continuity tester to the outside terminal blades of the switch terminal **(see illustration)**. There should be continuity between these blades in Neutral and Park.

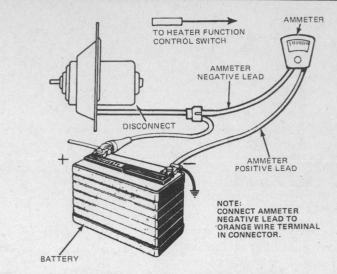

19.4 Blower motor current draw test

a) If there is no continuity between these terminals in Neutral and Park, adjust the switch.
b) If there is continuity between the outside terminals in any other gears, replace the switch.

Adjustment

3   To adjust the switch, place the selector lever in Neutral, loosen the two mounting bolts, insert a No. 43 drill bit (0.089-inch) into the adjustment hole **(see illustration)** and tighten the bolts to the torque listed in this Chapter's Specifications. Note that the drill bit cannot be inserted as far into the adjustment hole in any other gear as it can in Neutral.
4   The vehicle should now start in Park and Neutral. If it still doesn't start in Park and Neutral, or starts in any position other than Park or Neutral, replace the switch.

Replacement

5   Place the gear selector lever in Neutral. Disconnect the cable from the negative terminal of the battery.

6   Unplug the neutral start switch electrical connector.
7   Remove the nut that secures the lever to the lever shaft and separate the lever from the shaft. Note that the sides of the shaft are flattened so that it is impossible to install the lever improperly.
8   Remove the two neutral start switch attaching bolts.
9   Remove the Neutral start switch. Note the position of the two raised ridges on the inside of the plastic collar that fits over the lever shaft **(see illustration)**. The bushing on the new switch should be in this position when the switch is installed.
10   Install the new switch on the lever shaft.
11   Adjust the switch in accordance with the procedure outlined above.
12   Plug in the neutral start switch electrical connector.
13   Connect the cable to the negative terminal of the battery.
14   Start the engine in both Park and Neutral to verify that the switch is properly adjusted. If it isn't, readjust the switch until the engine starts in both ranges.

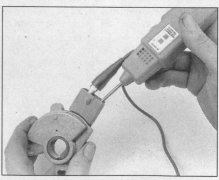

21.2 To check the Neutral start switch, touch the probes of a continuity tester or ohmmeter to the outside terminal blades (the switch is removed from the transaxle in this photo for clarity but this check can be performed with the switch installed)

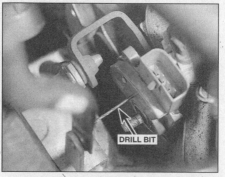

21.3 To adjust the Neutral start switch, loosen the bolts, place the lever in the Neutral position and insert a No. 43 (0.089-inch) drill bit into the adjustment hole, then tighten the bolts

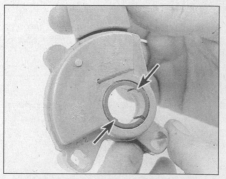

21.9 Note the position of the ridges (arrows) on the inside of the Neutral switch collar that fits over the manual lever shaft when the transaxle is in Neutral - make sure that the ridges are in this position when you install the switch

22 Cruise control - general information

Because of the complexity of the cruise control system and the special tools and techniques required for diagnosis, and the considerations of safety, repair should be left to a dealer service department or other repair shop. However, it is possible for the home mechanic to make simple checks of the wiring and vacuum connections for minor faults which can be easily repaired. These include:

a) Inspect the cruise control actuating switches for broken wires and loose connections.
b) Check the cruise control fuse.
c) The cruise control system is operated by vacuum so it's critical that all vacuum switches, hoses and connections are secure. Check the hoses in the engine compartment for tight connections, cracks and obvious vacuum leaks.

23 Power door lock system - general information

The power door lock system operates the door lock actuators mounted in each door. The system consists of the switches, actuators and the associated wiring. Diagnosis can usually be limited to simple checks of the wiring connections and actuators for minor faults which can be easily repaired. These include:

a) Checking the system fuse and/or circuit breaker.
b) Checking the switch wiring for damage or loose connections.
c) Checking the switches for continuity.
d) Removing the door panels(s) and checking the actuator electrical connections for looseness or damage. Inspect the actuator rods (if equipped) to make sure that they are not bent, damaged or binding. The actuator can be checked by applying battery power momentarily. A solid click indicates the solenoid is operating properly.

24 Power windows - general information

The power window system operates the electric motors mounted in the doors which lower and raise the windows. The system consists of the control switches, the motors (regulators), glass mechanisms and associated wiring.

Diagnosis can usually be limited to simple checks of the wiring connections and motors for minor faults which can be easily repaired. These include:

a) Inspect the power window actuating switches for broken wires and loose connections.
b) Check the power window fuse/and or circuit breaker.
c) Remove the door panel(s) and check the power window motor wires to see if they're loose or damaged. Inspect the glass mechanisms for damage which could cause binding.

25 Airbag - general information

Some models are equipped with an airbag system. This is designed to protect the driver and, on later models, the front seat passenger from serious injury in frontal collisions. The system consists of an airbag contained in the center of the steering wheel to protect the driver; a similar passenger airbag on the right side of the instrument panel (on models so equipped); crash sensors located at the radiator center, in the center console area, and behind the right side kick panel, in the airbag diagnostic monitor; and an airbag warning indicator on the instrument panel. Crash sensors may also be located along the top of each inner fender panel, behind each kick panel, and, on some models there might only be one (located inside the electronic diagnostic monitor).

Each of the airbag modules contains a housing incorporating the airbag, an igniter and an inflator, The inflator is activated when an electrical signal from any of the sensors is sent to the the igniter, which inflates the bag.

Electronic diagnostic monitor

The electronic diagnostic monitor supplies the current to the airbag system in the event of the collision, even if battery power is cut off. It checks this system every time the vehicle is started, causing the "AIR BAG" light to go on then off, if the system is operating properly. If there is a fault in the system, the light will go on and stay on, flash, or the dash will make a beeping sound. If this happens, the vehicle should be taken to your dealer immediately for service.

Disabling the system

Whenever working in the vicinity of the steering wheel, steering column or near other components of the airbag system, the system should be disarmed. To do this, perform the following steps:

a) Turn the ignition switch to Off.
b) Detach the cable from the negative battery terminal, then detach the positive cable. Wait two minutes for the electronic module backup power supply to be depleted.

Enabling the system

a) Turn the ignition switch to the Off position.
b) Connect the positive battery cable first, then connect the negative cable.

26 Wiring diagrams - general information

Since it isn't possible to include all wiring diagrams for every model covered by this manual, the following diagrams are those that are typical and most commonly needed.

Prior to troubleshooting any circuits, check the fuse and circuit breakers (if equipped) to make sure they're in good condition. Make sure the battery is properly charged and has clean, tight cable connections (Chapter 1).

When checking the wiring, make sure all connectors are clean, with no broken or loose pins. When unplugging a connector, don't pull on the wires, only on the connector housings themselves.

Wiring color code

When referring to the wiring diagrams, use the following alphabetical code to determine the color of the wires you are checking:

B = Black
BR = Brown
DB = Dark blue
DG = Dark green
GY = Gray
LB = Light blue
LG = Light green
N = Natural
O = Orange
P = Purple
PK = Pink
R = Red
T = Tan
W = White
Y = Yellow
(H) = Hash*
(D) = Dot*

Note: The presence of a tracer on the wire is indicated by a secondary color followed by a "H" for hash or a "D" for dot. A stripe is understood if no letter follows.

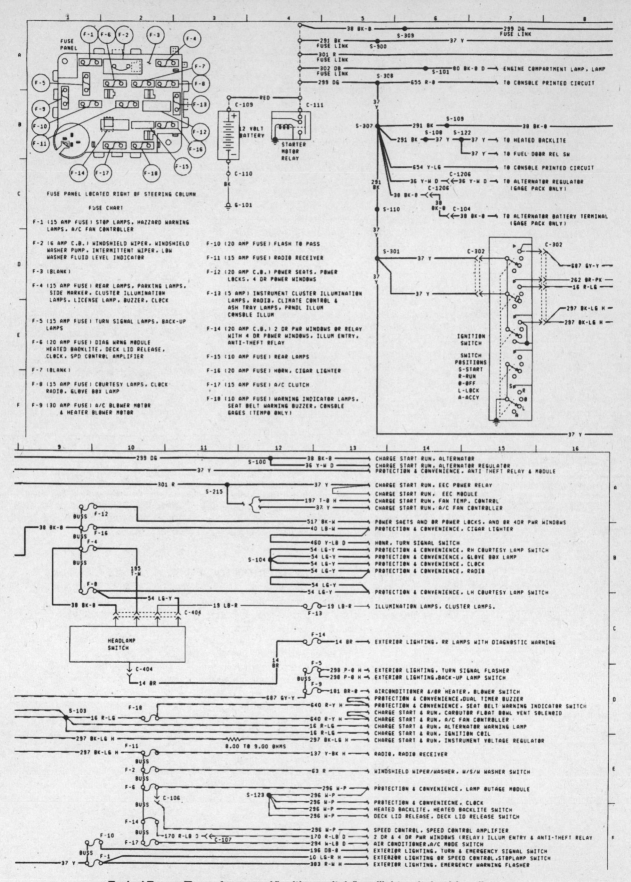

Typical Tempo/Topaz fuse panel/ignition switch/headlight switch wiring diagram

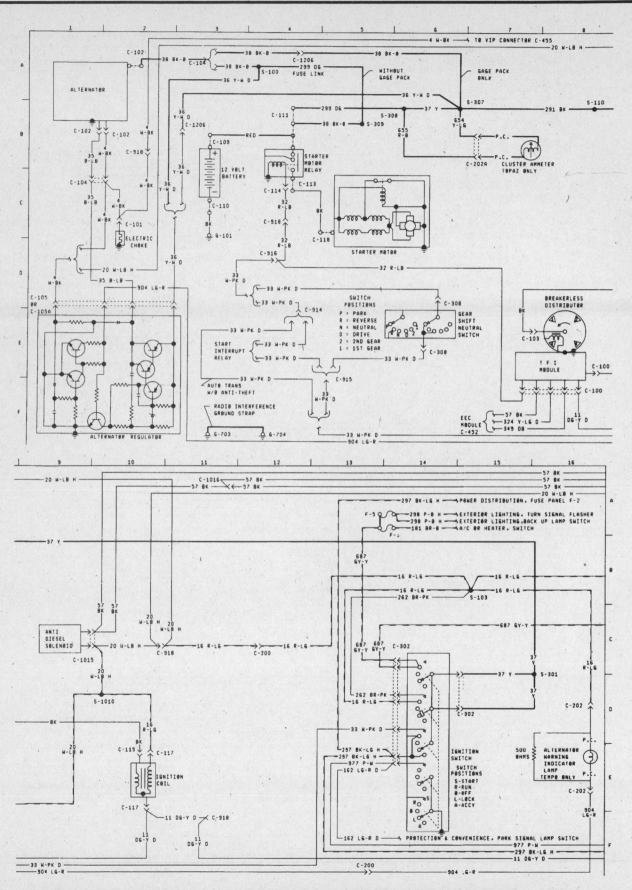

Typical underhood component and dash panel wiring diagram (1984 US and 1984 to 1987 Canadian models

12

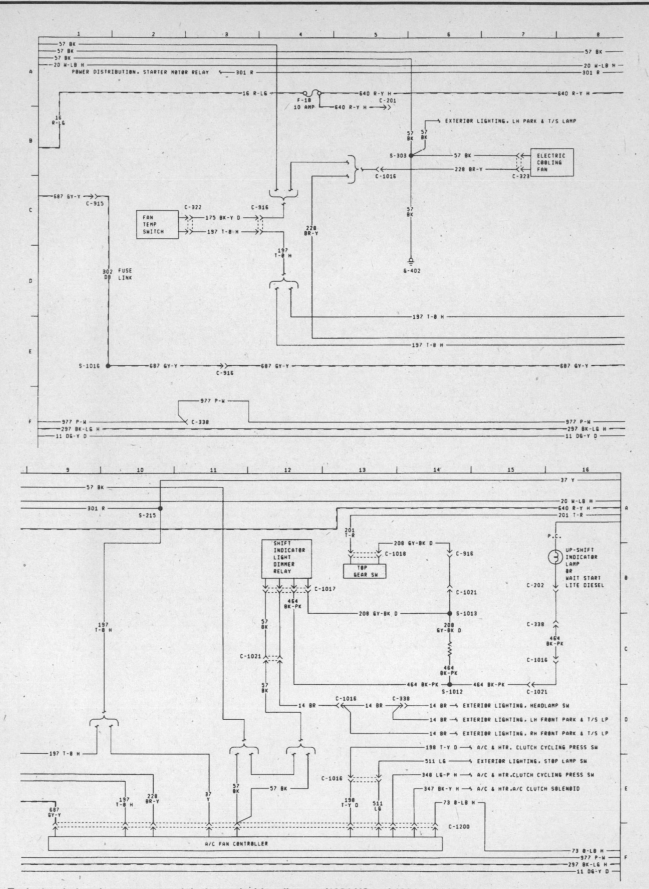

Typical underhood component and dash panel wiring diagram (1984 US and 1984 to 1987 Canadian models) - continued

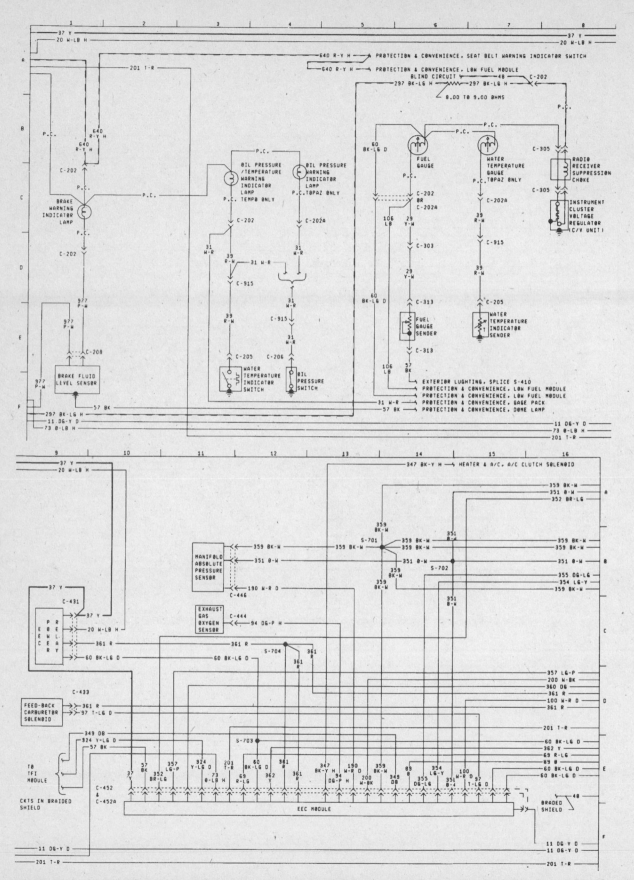

Typical underhood component and dash panel wiring diagram (1984 US and 1984 to 1987 Canadian models) - continued

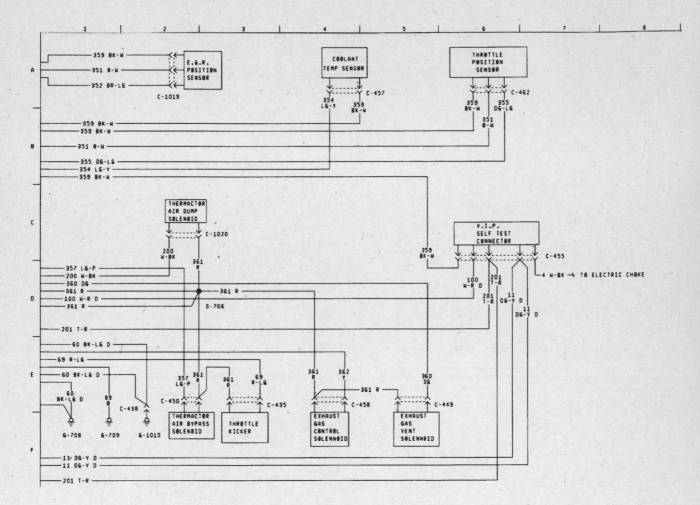

Typical underhood component wiring diagram (1984 US and 1984 to 1987 Canadian models)

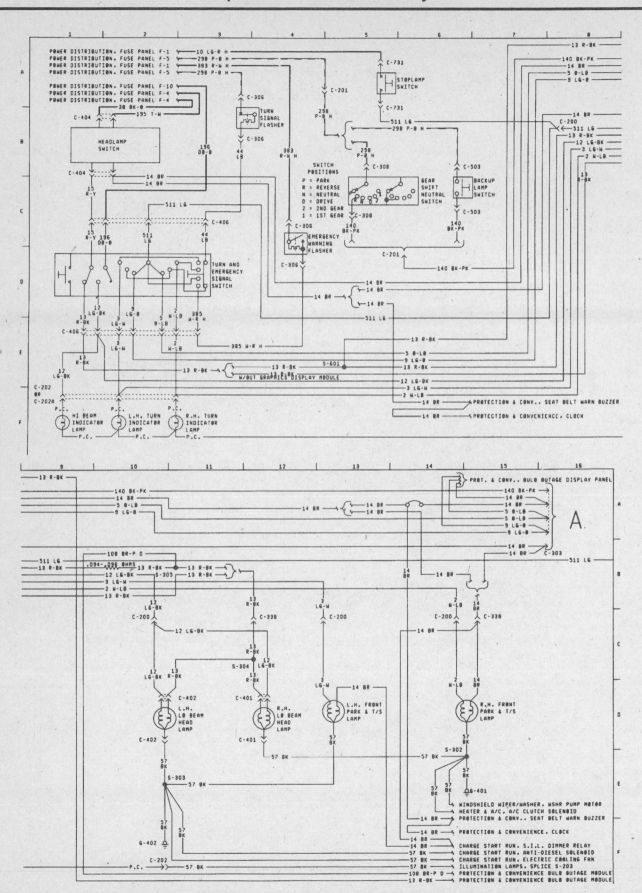

Typical front exterior lights/light switches wiring diagram (1984 to 1987 Canadian models)

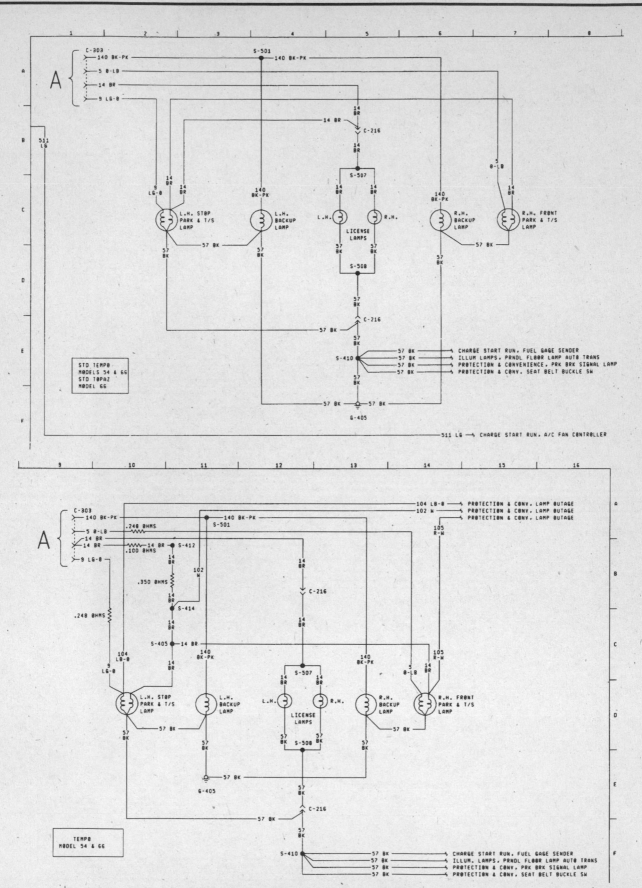

Typical rear exterior light wiring diagram (1984 US and 1984 to 1987 Canadian models) - Tempo model 54 and 66, Topaz model 66

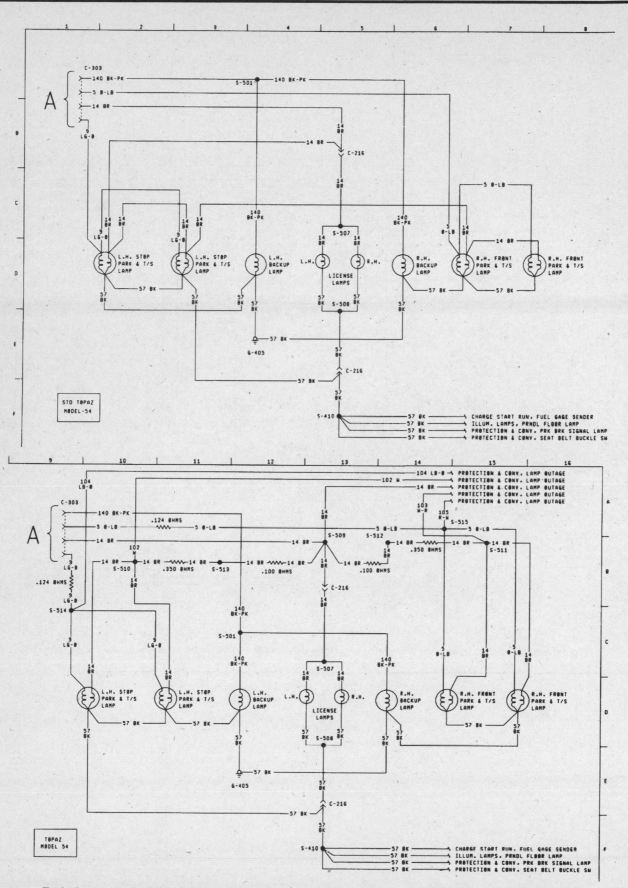

Typical rear exterior light wiring diagram (1984 US and 1984 to 1987 Canadian models) - Topaz model 54

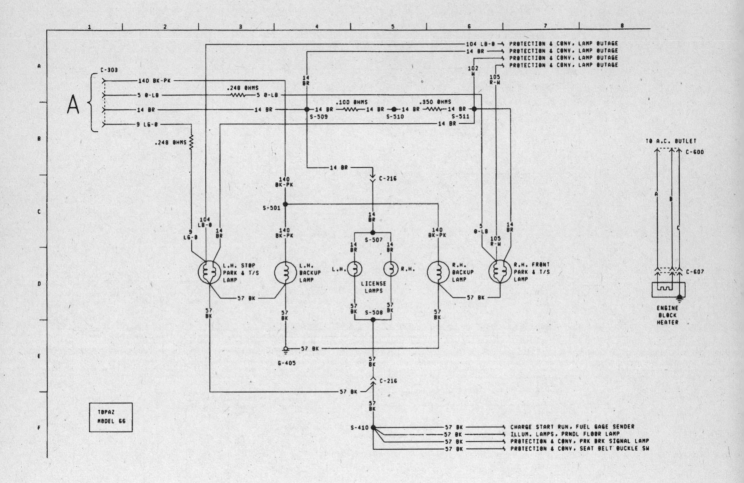

Typical rear exterior exterior light wiring diagram (1984 US and 1984 to 1987 Canadian models) - Topaz model 66

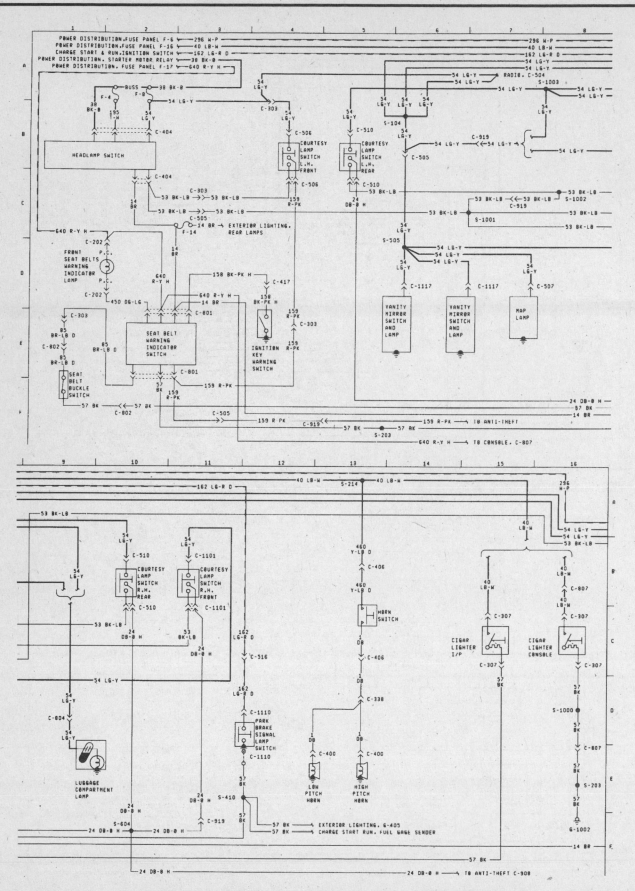

Typical interior light wiring diagram (1984 US and 1984 to 1987 Canadian models)

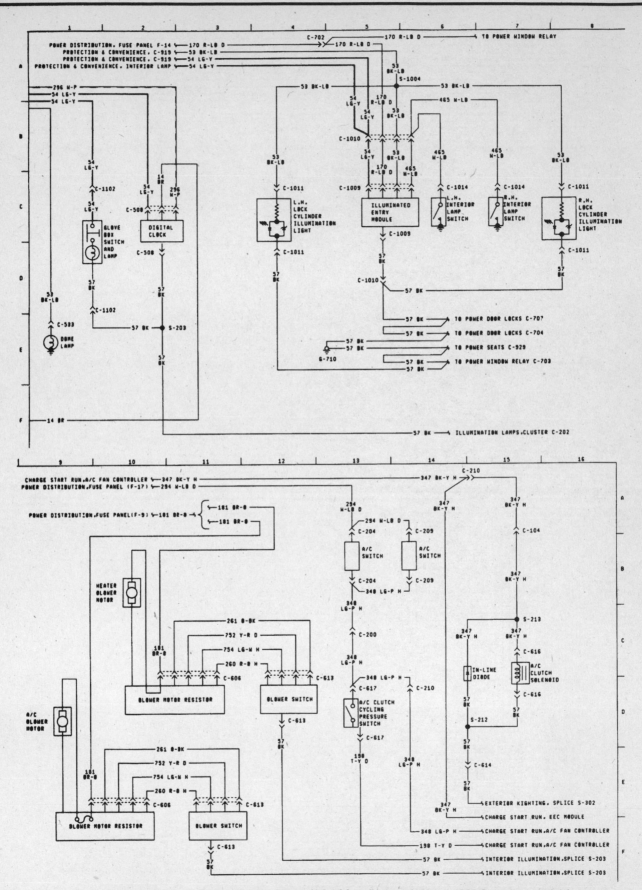

Typical interior light/power distribution/heater/AC wiring diagram (1984 to 1987 Canadian models)

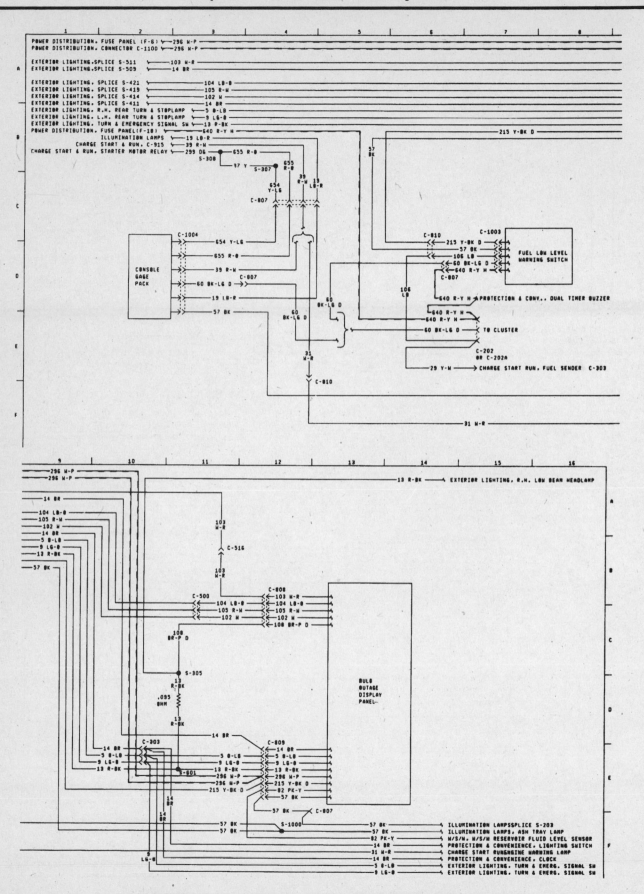

Typical dash panel/console wiring diagram (1984 to 1987 Canadian models)

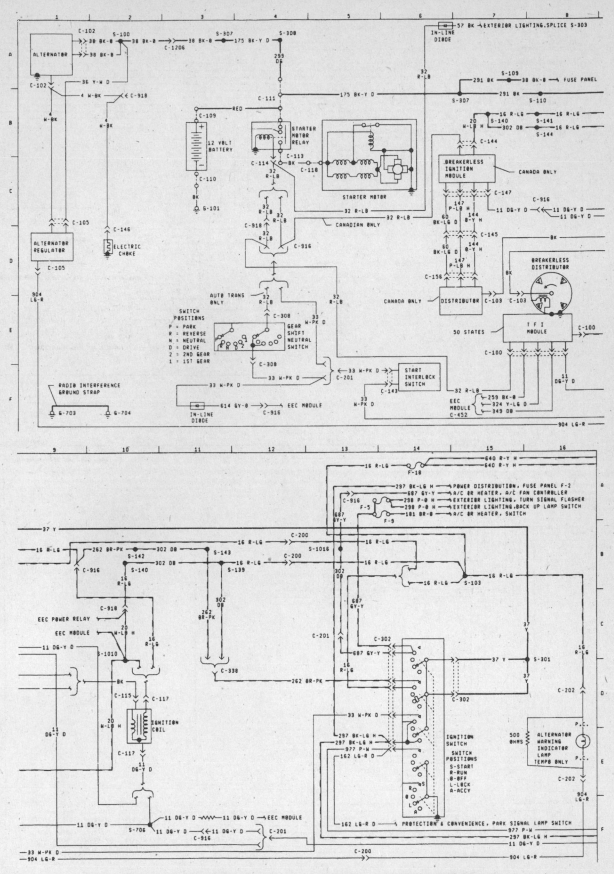

Typical underhood component and dash panel wiring diagram (1985 to 1987 US models)

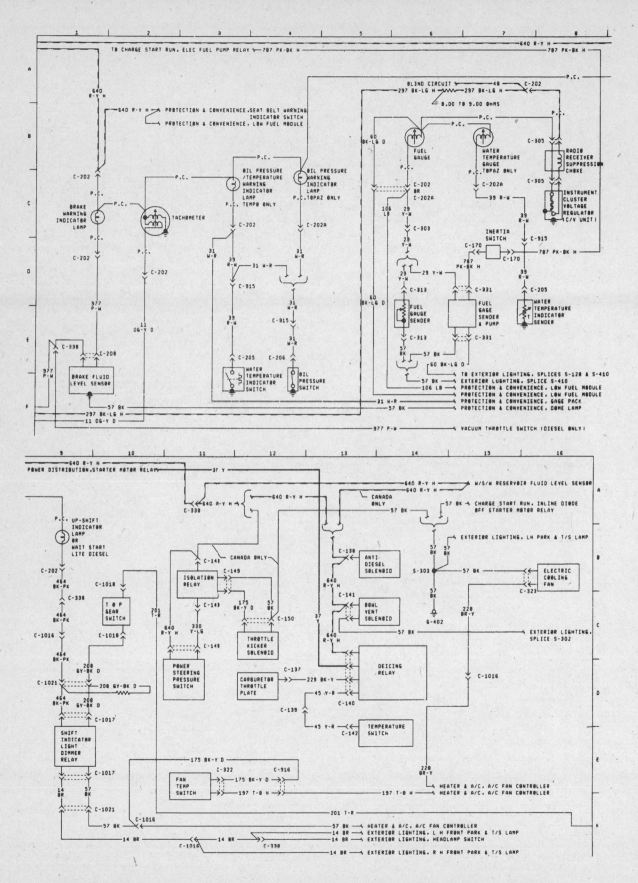

Typical underhood component and dash panel wiring diagram (1985 to 1987 US models) - continued

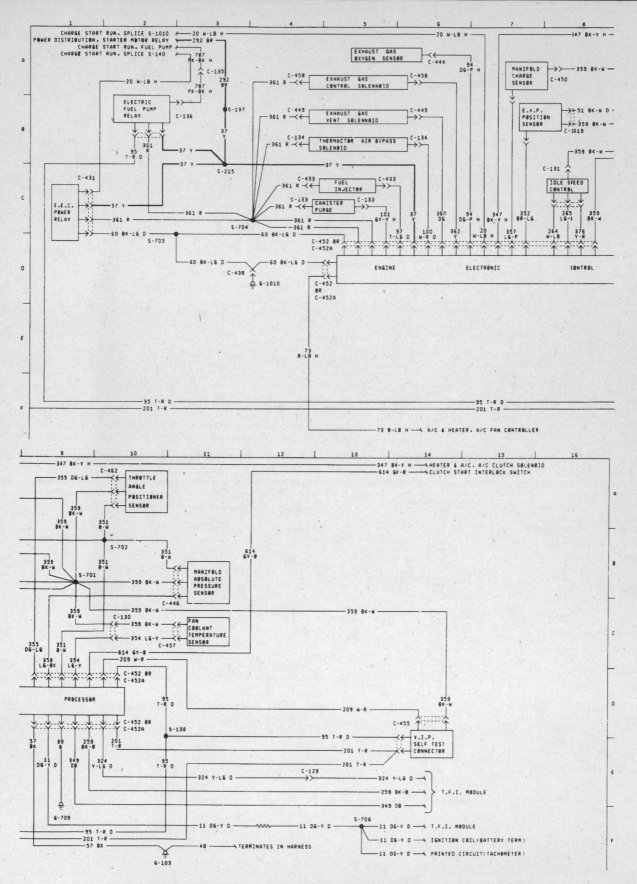

Typical underhood component wiring diagram (1985 to 1987 US models) - continued

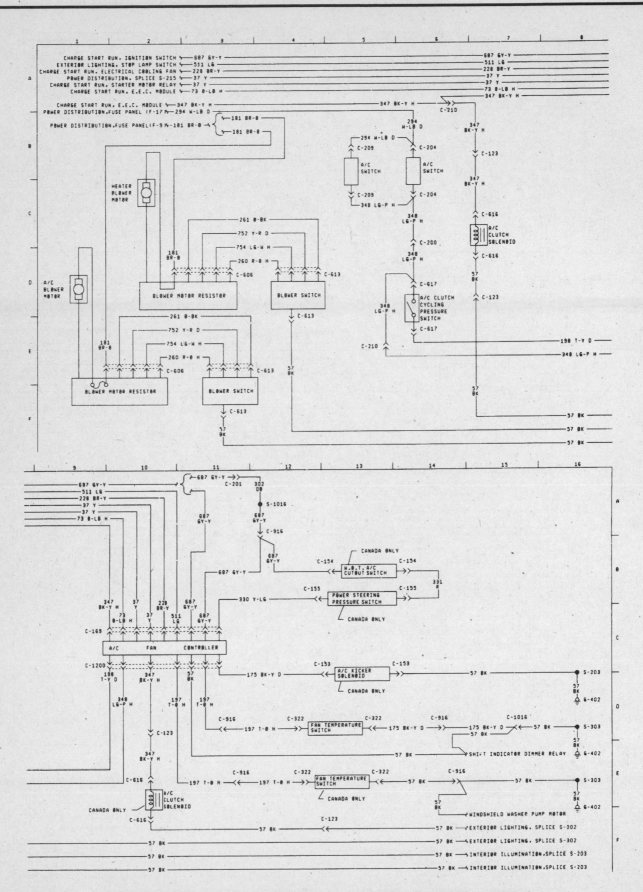

Typical underhood component wiring diagram (1985 to 1987 US models) - continued

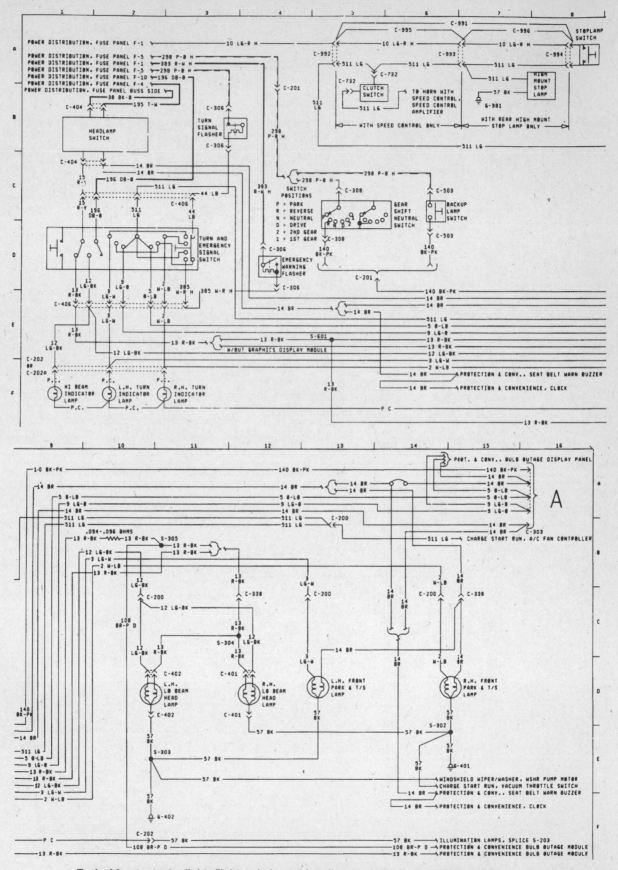

Typical front exterior lights/light switches wiring diagram (1985 to 1987 US models)

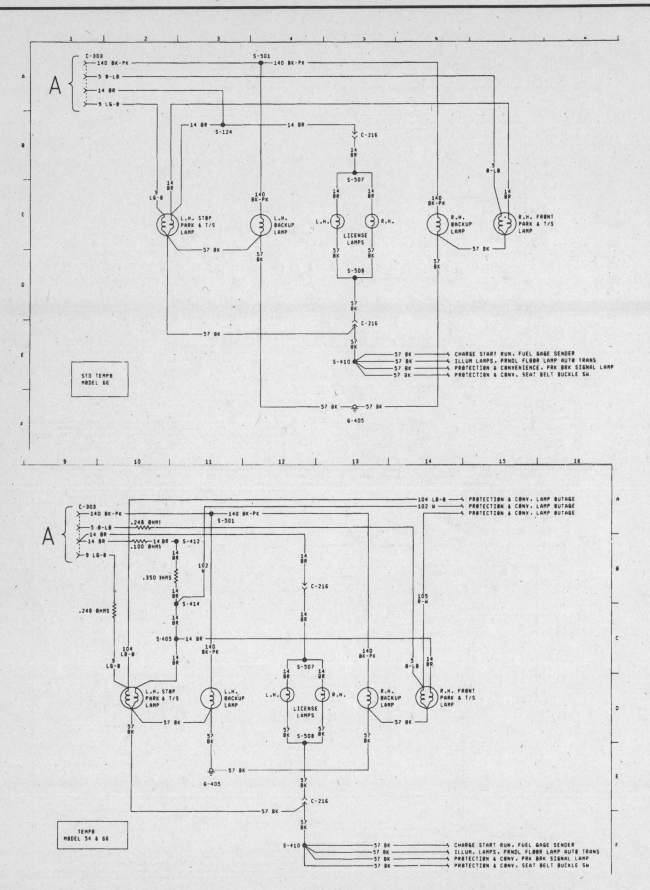

Typical rear exterior light wiring diagram (1985 to 1987 US models) - Tempo models 54 and 66

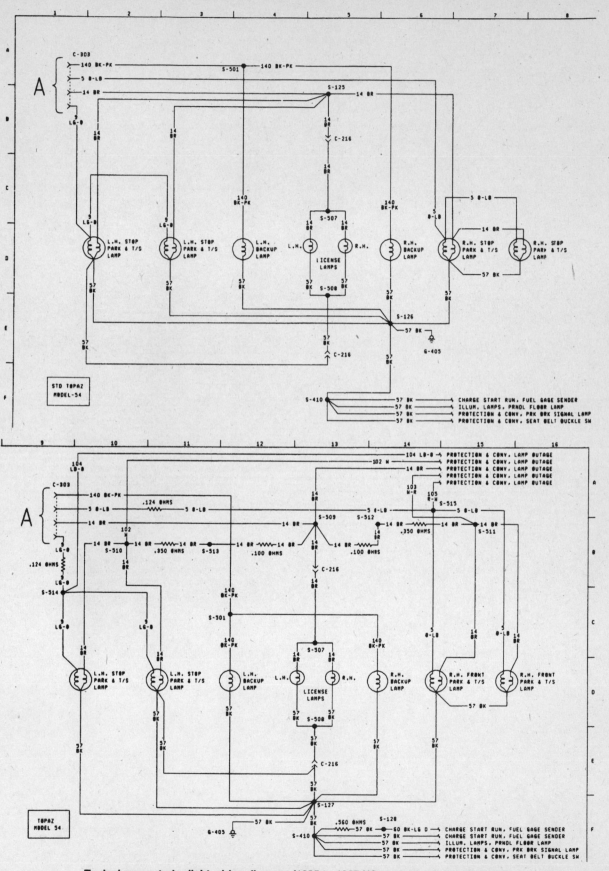

Typical rear exterior light wiring diagram (1985 to 1987 US models) - Topaz model 54

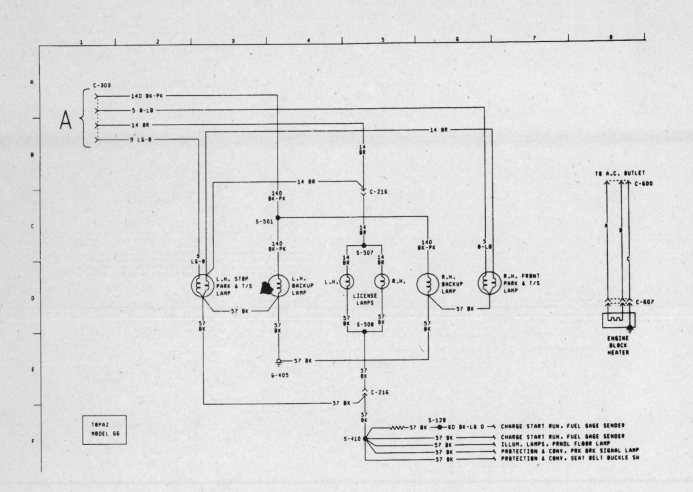

Typical rear exterior light wiring diagram (1985 to 1987 models) - Topaz model 66

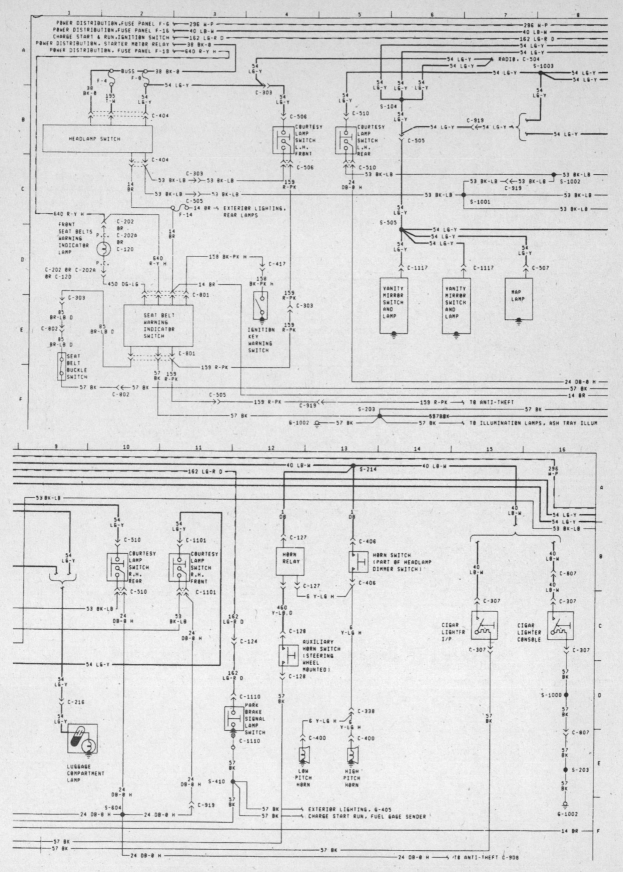

Typical interior light wiring diagram (1985 to 1987 US models)

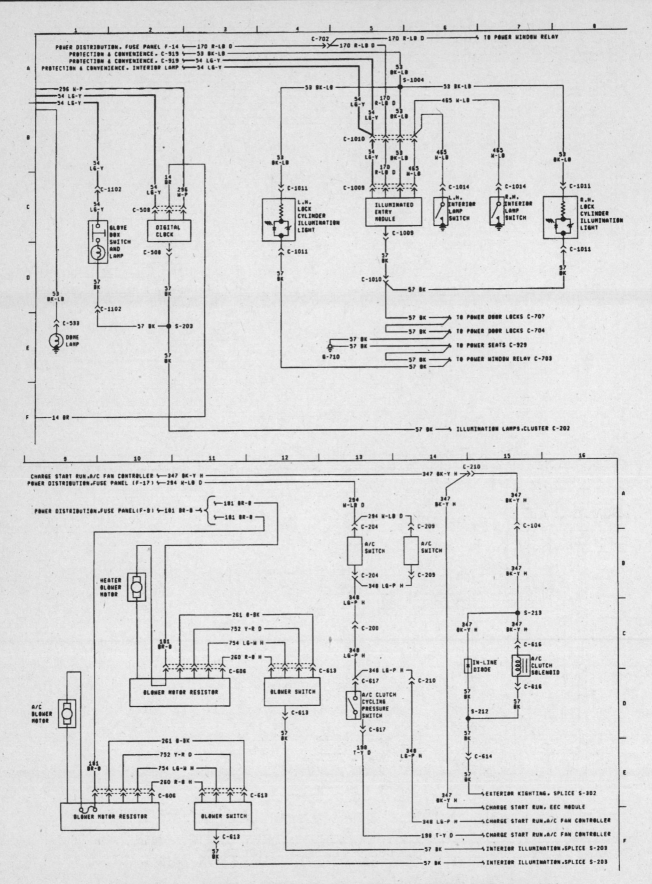

Typical interior light/power distribution/heater/AC wiring diagram (1985 to 1987 US models)

12

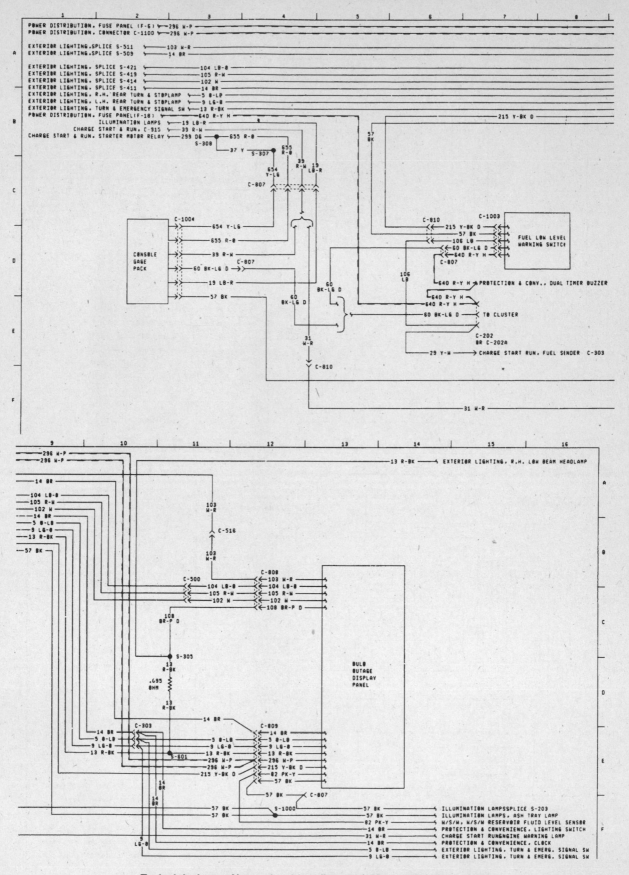

Typical dash panel/console wiring diagram (1985 to 1987 US models)

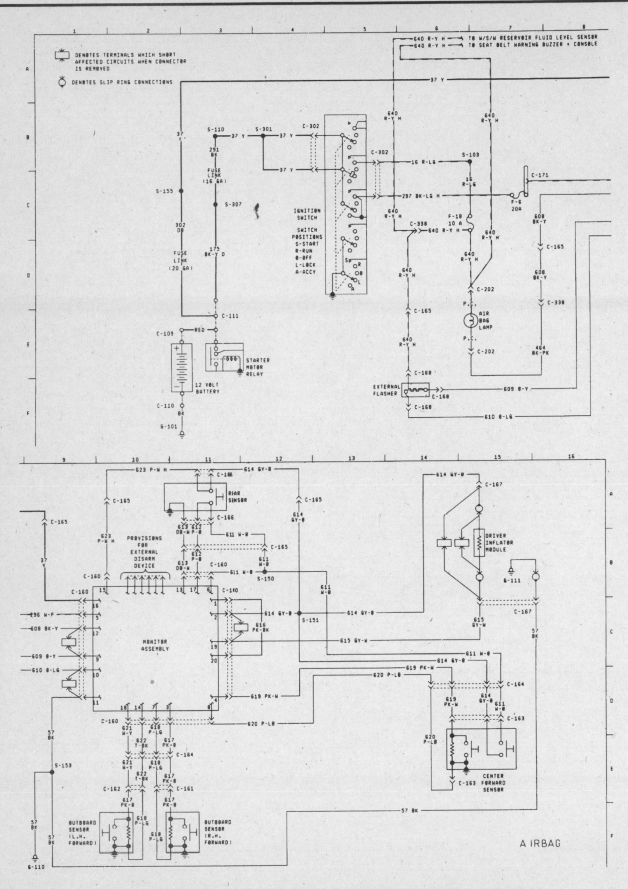

Typical dash panel/console wiring diagram (1985 to 1987 US models) - continued

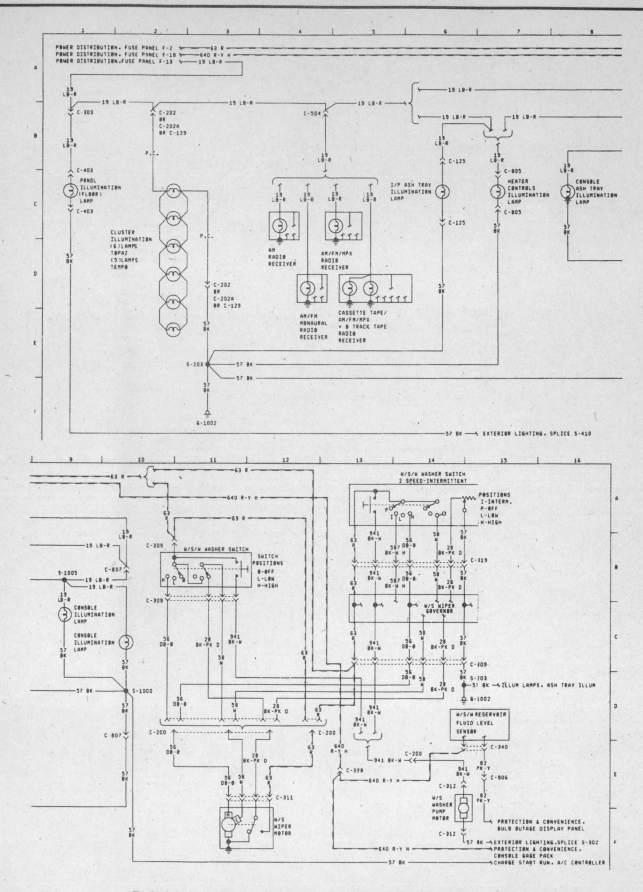

Typical dash panel/console wiring diagram (1985 to 1987 US models) - continued

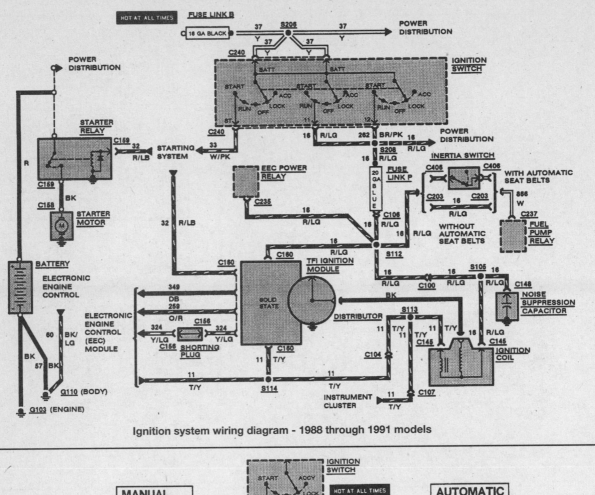

Ignition system wiring diagram - 1988 through 1991 models

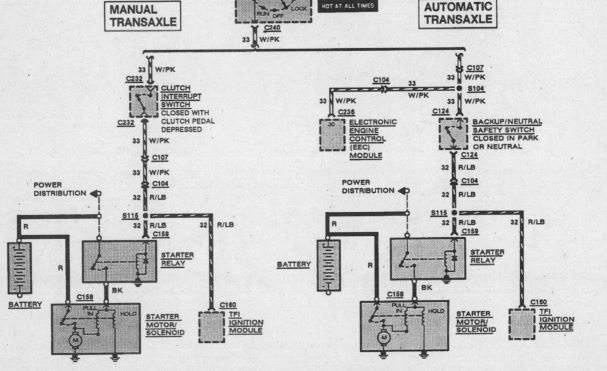

Starting system wiring diagram - 1988 and later models

12

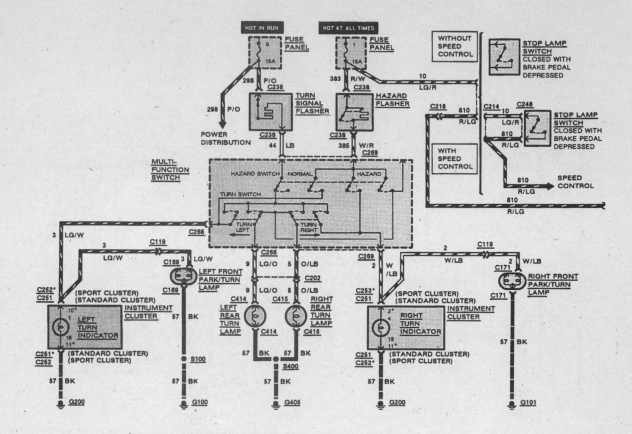

Turn/stop/hazard lamps - 1988 and later models

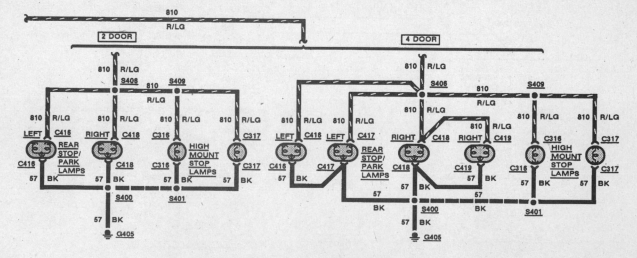

Turn/stop/hazard lamps - 1988 and later models

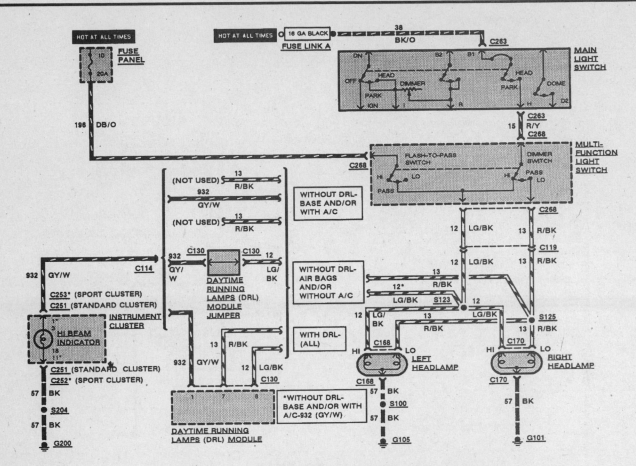

Headlight wiring diagram - 1988 through 1993 shown, 1994 similar

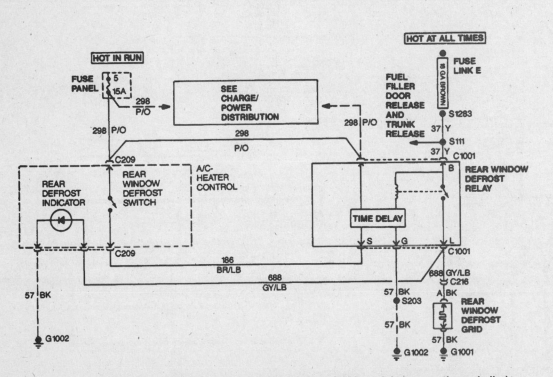

Typical rear window defroster wiring diagram (1992 model shown, others similar)

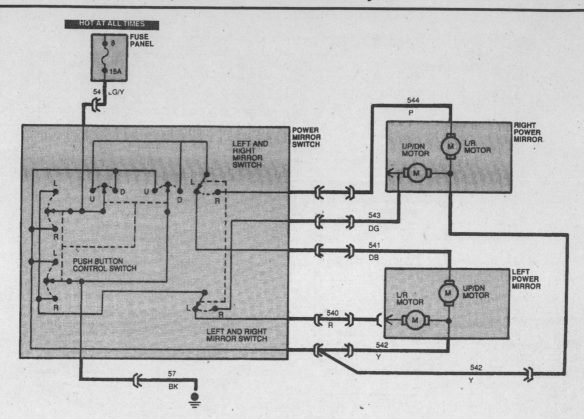

Typical power mirror wiring diagram (1993 model shown, others similar)

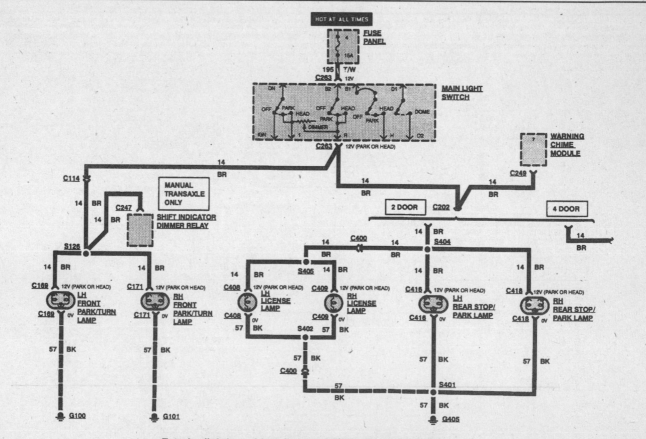

Exterior lighting wiring diagram (1988 and later models)

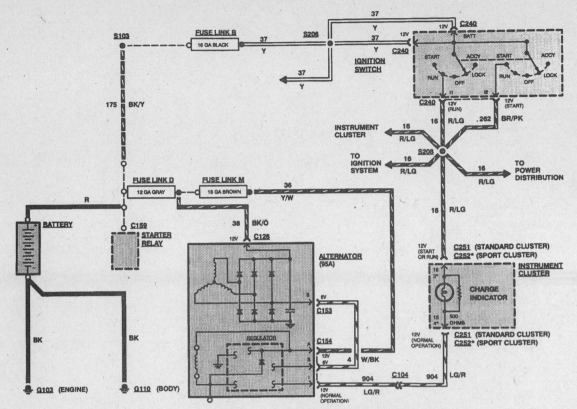

Charging system wiring diagram - 1988 and later four-cylinder models

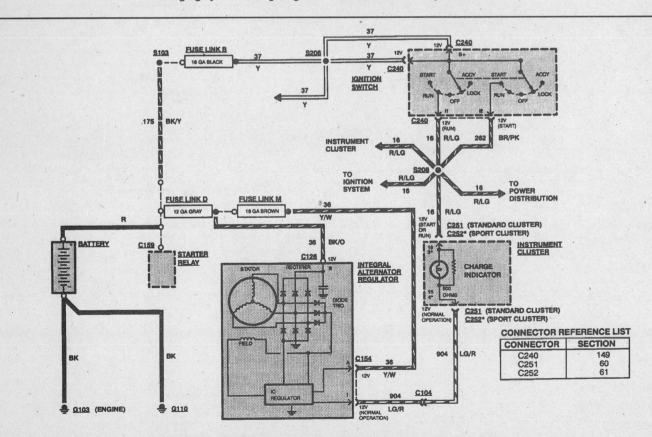

Charging system wiring diagram - 1992 and later six-cylinder models

CONNECTOR REFERENCE LIST	
CONNECTOR	SECTION
C240	149
C251	60
C252	61

12

Notes

Index

A

B

Haynes Automotive Manuals

NOTE: New manuals are added to this list on a periodic basis. If you do not see a listing for your vehicle, consult your local Haynes dealer for the latest product information.

ACURA
- **12020** Integra '86 thru '89 & Legend '86 thru '90
- **12021** Integra '90 thru '93 & Legend '91 thru '95

AMC
- Jeep CJ - see JEEP (50020)
- **14020** Mid-size models '70 thru '83
- **14025** (Renault) Alliance & Encore '83 thru '87

AUDI
- **15020** 4000 all models '80 thru '87
- **15025** 5000 all models '77 thru '83
- **15026** 5000 all models '84 thru '88

AUSTIN-HEALEY
- Sprite - see MG Midget (66015)

BMW
- *18020** 3/5 Series not including diesel or all-wheel drive models '82 thru '92
- *18021** 3-Series incl. Z3 models '92 thru '98
- **18025** 320i all 4 cyl models '75 thru '83
- **18050** 1500 thru 2002 except Turbo '59 thru '77

BUICK
- Century (front-wheel drive) - see GM (38005)
- *19020** Buick, Oldsmobile & Pontiac Full-size (Front-wheel drive) all models '85 thru '00 Buick Electra, LeSabre and Park Avenue; Oldsmobile Delta 88 Royale, Ninety Eight and Regency; Pontiac Bonneville
- **19025** Buick Oldsmobile & Pontiac Full-size (Rear wheel drive) Buick Estate '70 thru '90, Electra'70 thru '84, LeSabre '70 thru '85, Limited '74 thru '79 Oldsmobile Custom Cruiser '70 thru '90, Delta 88 '70 thru '85,Ninety-eight '70 thru '84 Pontiac Bonneville '70 thru '81, Catalina '70 thru '81, Grandville '70 thru '75, Parisienne '83 thru '86
- **19030** Mid-size Regal & Century all rear-drive models with V6, V8 and Turbo '74 thru '87
- Regal - see GENERAL MOTORS (38010)
- Riviera - see GENERAL MOTORS (38030)
- Roadmaster - see CHEVROLET (24046)
- Skyhawk - see GENERAL MOTORS (38015)
- Skylark - see GM (38020, 38025)
- Somerset - see GENERAL MOTORS (38025)

CADILLAC
- **21030** Cadillac Rear Wheel Drive all gasoline models '70 thru '93
- Cimarron - see GENERAL MOTORS (38015)
- Deville - see GENERAL MOTORS (38031)
- Eldorado - see GM (38030 & 38031)
- Fleetwood - see GM (38031)
- Seville - see GM (38030 & 38031)

CHEVROLET
- *24010** Astro & GMC Safari Mini-vans '85 thru '98
- **24015** Camaro V8 all models '70 thru '81
- **24016** Camaro all models '82 thru '92
- *24017** Camaro & Firebird '93 thru '00
- Cavalier - see GENERAL MOTORS (38016)
- Celebrity - see GENERAL MOTORS (38005)
- **24020** Chevelle, Malibu & El Camino '69 thru '87
- **24024** Chevette & Pontiac T1000 '76 thru '87
- Citation - see GENERAL MOTORS (38020)
- **24032** Corsica/Beretta all models '87 thru '96
- **24040** Corvette all V8 models '68 thru '82
- *24041** Corvette all models '84 thru '96
- **10305** Chevrolet Engine Overhaul Manual
- **24045** Full-size Sedans Caprice, Impala, Biscayne, Bel Air & Wagons '69 thru '90
- **24046** Impala SS & Caprice and Buick Roadmaster '91 thru '96
- Impala - see LUMINA (24048)
- Lumina '90 thru '94 - see GM (38010)
- *24048** Lumina & Monte Carlo '95 thru '01
- Lumina APV - see GM (38035)
- **24050** Luv Pick-up all 2WD & 4WD '72 thru '82
- Malibu '97 thru '00 - see GM (38026)

- **24055** Monte Carlo all models '70 thru '88
- Monte Carlo '95 thru '01 - see LUMINA (24048)
- **24059** Nova all V8 models '69 thru '79
- **24060** Nova and Geo Prizm '85 thru '92
- **24064** Pick-ups '67 thru '87 - Chevrolet & GMC, all V8 & in-line 6 cyl, 2WD & 4WD '67 thru '87; Suburbans, Blazers & Jimmys '67 thru '91
- **24065** Pick-ups '88 thru '98 - Chevrolet & GMC, full-size pick-ups '88 thru '98, C/K Classic '99 & '00, Blazer & Jimmy '92 thru '94; Suburban '92 thru '99; Tahoe & Yukon '95 thru '99
- *24066** Pick-ups '99 thru '01 - Chevrolet Silverado & GMC Sierra full-size pick-ups '99 thru '01, Suburban/Tahoe/Yukon/Yukon XL '00 thru '01
- **24070** S-10 & S-15 Pick-ups '82 thru '93, Blazer & Jimmy '83 thru '94,
- *24071** S-10 & S-15 Pick-ups '94 thru '01, Blazer & Jimmy '95 thru '01, Hombre '96 thru '01
- *24075** Sprint & Geo Metro '85 thru '94
- *24080** Vans - Chevrolet & GMC '68 thru '96

CHRYSLER
- **25015** Chrysler Cirrus, Dodge Stratus, Plymouth Breeze '95 thru '00
- **10310** Chrysler Engine Overhaul Manual
- **25020** Full-size Front-Wheel Drive '88 thru '93
- K-Cars - see DODGE Aries (30008)
- Laser - see DODGE Daytona (30030)
- **25025** Chrysler LHS, Concorde, New Yorker, Dodge Intrepid, Eagle Vision, '93 thru '97
- *25026** Chrysler LHS, Concorde, 300M, Dodge Intrepid, '98 thru '01
- **25030** Chrysler & Plymouth Mid-size front wheel drive '82 thru '95
- Rear-wheel Drive - see Dodge (30050)
- *25040** Chrysler Sebring, Dodge Avenger '95 thru '02

DATSUN
- **28005** 200SX all models '80 thru '83
- **28007** B-210 all models '73 thru '78
- **28009** 210 all models '79 thru '82
- **28012** 240Z, 260Z & 280Z Coupe '70 thru '78
- **28014** 280ZX Coupe & 2+2 '79 thru '83
- 300ZX - see NISSAN (72010)
- **28016** 310 all models '78 thru '82
- **28018** 510 & PL521 Pick-up '68 thru '73
- **28020** 510 all models '78 thru '81
- **28022** 620 Series Pick-up all models '73 thru '79
- 720 Series Pick-up - see NISSAN (72030)
- **28025** 810/Maxima all gasoline models, '77 thru '84

DODGE
- 400 & 600 - see CHRYSLER (25030)
- **30008** Aries & Plymouth Reliant '81 thru '89
- **30010** Caravan & Plymouth Voyager '84 thru '95
- *30011** Caravan & Plymouth Voyager '96 thru '99
- **30012** Challenger/Plymouth Saporro '78 thru '83
- **30016** Colt & Plymouth Champ '78 thru '87
- **30020** Dakota Pick-ups all models '87 thru '96
- *30021** Durango '98 & '99, Dakota '97 thru '99
- **30025** Dart, Demon, Plymouth Barracuda, Duster & Valiant 6 cyl models '67 thru '76
- **30030** Daytona & Chrysler Laser '84 thru '89
- Intrepid - see CHRYSLER (25025, 25026)
- *30034** Neon all models '95 thru '99
- **30035** Omni & Plymouth Horizon '78 thru '90
- **30040** Pick-ups all full-size models '74 thru '93
- *30041** Pick-ups all full-size models '94 thru '01
- **30045** Ram 50/D50 Pick-ups & Raider and Plymouth Arrow Pick-ups '79 thru '93
- **30050** Dodge/Plymouth/Chrysler RWD '71 thru '89
- **30055** Shadow & Plymouth Sundance '87 thru '94
- **30060** Spirit & Plymouth Acclaim '89 thru '95
- *30065** Vans - Dodge & Plymouth '71 thru '99

EAGLE
- Talon - see MITSUBISHI (68030, 68031)
- Vision - see CHRYSLER (25025)

FIAT
- **34010** 124 Sport Coupe & Spider '68 thru '78
- **34025** X1/9 all models '74 thru '80

FORD
- **10355** Ford Automatic Transmission Overhaul
- **36004** Aerostar Mini-vans all models '86 thru '97
- **36006** Contour & Mercury Mystique '95 thru '00
- **36008** Courier Pick-up all models '72 thru '82
- *36012** Crown Victoria & Mercury Grand Marquis '88 thru '00
- **10320** Ford Engine Overhaul Manual
- **36016** Escort/Mercury Lynx all models '81 thru '90
- **36020** Escort/Mercury Tracer '91 thru '00
- **36024** Explorer & Mazda Navajo '91 thru '01
- **36028** Fairmont & Mercury Zephyr '78 thru '83
- **36030** Festiva & Aspire '88 thru '97
- **36032** Fiesta all models '77 thru '80
- *36034** Focus all models '00 and '01
- **36036** Ford & Mercury Full-size '75 thru '87
- **36040** Granada & Mercury Monarch '75 thru '80
- **36044** Ford & Mercury Mid-size '75 thru '86
- **36048** Mustang V8 all models '64-1/2 thru '73
- **36049** Mustang II 4 cyl, V6 & V8 models '74 thru '78
- **36050** Mustang & Mercury Capri all models Mustang, '79 thru '93; Capri, '79 thru '86
- *36051** Mustang all models '94 thru '00
- **36054** Pick-ups & Bronco '73 thru '79
- **36058** Pick-ups & Bronco '80 thru '96
- *36059** Pick-ups, Expedition & Mercury Navigator '97 thru '99
- *36060** Super Duty Pick-ups, Excursion '97 thru '02
- **36062** Pinto & Mercury Bobcat '75 thru '80
- **36066** Probe all models '89 thru '92
- **36070** Ranger/Bronco II gasoline models '83 thru '92
- *36071** Ranger '93 thru '00 & Mazda Pick-ups '94 thru '00
- **36074** Taurus & Mercury Sable '86 thru '95
- *36075** Taurus & Mercury Sable '96 thru '01
- **36078** Tempo & Mercury Topaz '84 thru '94
- **36082** Thunderbird/Mercury Cougar '83 thru '88
- **36086** Thunderbird/Mercury Cougar '89 and '97
- **36090** Vans all V8 Econoline models '69 thru '91
- *36094** Vans full size '92 thru '01
- *36097** Windstar Mini-van '95 thru '01

GENERAL MOTORS
- **10360** GM Automatic Transmission Overhaul
- **38005** Buick Century, Chevrolet Celebrity, Oldsmobile Cutlass Ciera & Pontiac 6000 all models '82 thru '96
- *38010** Buick Regal, Chevrolet Lumina, Oldsmobile Cutlass Supreme & Pontiac Grand Prix (FWD) '88 thru '99
- **38015** Buick Skyhawk, Cadillac Cimarron, Chevrolet Cavalier, Oldsmobile Firenza & Pontiac J-2000 & Sunbird '82 thru '94
- *38016** Chevrolet Cavalier & Pontiac Sunfire '95 thru '00
- **38020** Buick Skylark, Chevrolet Citation, Olds Omega, Pontiac Phoenix '80 thru '85
- **38025** Buick Skylark & Somerset, Oldsmobile Achieva & Calais and Pontiac Grand Am all models '85 thru '98
- *38026** Chevrolet Malibu, Olds Alero & Cutlass, Pontiac Grand Am '97 thru '00
- **38030** Cadillac Eldorado '71 thru '85, Seville '80 thru '85, Oldsmobile Toronado '71 thru '85, Buick Riviera '79 thru '85
- *38031** Cadillac Eldorado & Seville '86 thru '91, Deville '86 thru '93, Fleetwood & Olds Toronado '86 thru '92, Buick Riviera '86 thru '93
- *38035** Chevrolet Lumina APV, Olds Silhouette & Pontiac Trans Sport all models '90 thru '95
- *38036** Chevrolet Venture, Olds Silhouette, Pontiac Trans Sport & Montana '97 thru '01
- General Motors Full-size Rear-wheel Drive - see BUICK (19025)

GEO
- Metro - see CHEVROLET Sprint (24075)
- Prizm - '85 thru '92 see CHEVY (24060), '93 thru '96 see TOYOTA Corolla (92036)
- **40030** Storm all models '90 thru '93
- Tracker - see SUZUKI Samurai (90010)

(Continued on other side)

---

* Listings shown with an asterisk (*) indicate model coverage as of this printing. These titles will be periodically updated to include later model years - consult your Haynes dealer for more information.

Haynes North America, Inc., 861 Lawrence Drive, Newbury Park, CA 91320-1514 • (805) 498-6703

Haynes Automotive Manuals (continued)

GMC
Vans & Pick-ups - see CHEVROLET

HONDA
42010 **Accord CVCC** all models '76 thru '83
42011 **Accord** all models '84 thru '89
42012 **Accord** all models '90 thru '93
42013 **Accord** all models '94 thru '97
*42014 **Accord** all models '98 and '99
42020 **Civic 1200** all models '73 thru '79
42021 **Civic 1300 & 1500 CVCC** '80 thru '83
42022 **Civic 1500 CVCC** all models '75 thru '79
42023 **Civic** all models '84 thru '91
42024 **Civic & del Sol** '92 thru '95
*42025 **Civic** '96 thru '00, **CR-V** '97 thru '00, **Acura Integra** '94 thru '00
42040 **Prelude CVCC** all models '79 thru '89

HYUNDAI
*43010 **Elantra** all models '96 thru '01
43015 **Excel & Accent** all models '86 thru '98

ISUZU
Hombre - see CHEVROLET S-10 (24071)
*47017 **Rodeo** '91 thru '97; **Amigo** '89 thru '94; **Honda Passport** '95 thru '97
47020 **Trooper & Pick-up** '81 thru '93

JAGUAR
49010 **XJ6** all 6 cyl models '68 thru '86
49011 **XJ6** all models '88 thru '94
49015 **XJ12 & XJS** all 12 cyl models '72 thru '85

JEEP
50010 **Cherokee, Comanche & Wagoneer Limited** all models '84 thru '00
50020 **CJ** all models '49 thru '86
*50025 **Grand Cherokee** all models '93 thru '00
50029 **Grand Wagoneer & Pick-up** '72 thru '91 Grand Wagoneer '84 thru '91, Cherokee & Wagoneer '72 thru '83, Pick-up '72 thru '88
*50030 **Wrangler** all models '87 thru '00

LEXUS
ES 300 - see TOYOTA Camry (92007)

LINCOLN
Navigator - see FORD Pick-up (36059)
*59010 **Rear-Wheel Drive** all models '70 thru '01

MAZDA
61010 **GLC Hatchback (rear-wheel drive)** '77 thru '83
61011 **GLC (front-wheel drive)** '81 thru '85
*61015 **323 & Protegé** '90 thru '00
*61016 **MX-5 Miata** '90 thru '97
61020 **MPV** all models '89 thru '94
Navajo - see Ford Explorer (36024)
61030 **Pick-ups** '72 thru '93 Pick-ups '94 thru '00 - see Ford Ranger (36071)
61035 **RX-7** all models '79 thru '85
61036 **RX-7** all models '86 thru '91
61040 **626 (rear-wheel drive)** all models '79 thru '82
*61041 **626/MX-6 (front-wheel drive)** '83 thru '91
*61042 **626** '93 thru '01, **MX-6/Ford Probe** '93 thru '97

MERCEDES-BENZ
63012 **123 Series Diesel** '76 thru '85
63015 **190 Series** four-cyl gas models, '84 thru '88
63020 **230/250/280** 6 cyl sohc models '68 thru '72
63025 **280 123 Series** gasoline models '77 thru '81
63030 **350 & 450** all models '71 thru '80

MERCURY
64200 **Villager & Nissan Quest** '93 thru '01
All other titles, see FORD Listing.

MG
66010 **MGB** Roadster & GT Coupe '62 thru '80
66015 **MG Midget, Austin Healey Sprite** '58 thru '80

MITSUBISHI
68020 **Cordia, Tredia, Galant, Precis & Mirage** '83 thru '93
68030 **Eclipse, Eagle Talon & Ply. Laser** '90 thru '94
*68031 **Eclipse** '95 thru '01, **Eagle Talon** '95 thru '98
68040 **Pick-up** '83 thru '96 & **Montero** '83 thru '93

NISSAN
72010 **300ZX** all models including Turbo '84 thru '89
72015 **Altima** all models '93 thru '01
72020 **Maxima** all models '85 thru '92
*72021 **Maxima** all models '93 thru '01
72030 **Pick-ups** '80 thru '97 **Pathfinder** '87 thru '95
*72031 **Frontier Pick-up** '98 thru '01, **Xterra** '00 & '01, **Pathfinder** '96 thru '01
72040 **Pulsar** all models '83 thru '86
Quest - see MERCURY Villager (64200)
72050 **Sentra** all models '82 thru '94
72051 **Sentra & 200SX** all models '95 thru '99
72060 **Stanza** all models '82 thru '90

OLDSMOBILE
73015 **Cutlass** V6 & V8 gas models '74 thru '88
For other OLDSMOBILE titles, see BUICK, CHEVROLET or GENERAL MOTORS listing.

PLYMOUTH
For PLYMOUTH titles, see DODGE listing.

PONTIAC
79008 **Fiero** all models '84 thru '88
79018 **Firebird** V8 models except Turbo '70 thru '81
79019 **Firebird** all models '82 thru '92
79040 **Mid-size Rear-wheel Drive** '70 thru '87
For other PONTIAC titles, see BUICK, CHEVROLET or GENERAL MOTORS listing.

PORSCHE
80020 **911** except Turbo & Carrera 4 '65 '89
80025 **914** all 4 cyl models '69 thru '76
80030 **924** all models including Turbo '76 thru '82
80035 **944** all models including Turbo '83 thru '89

RENAULT
Alliance & Encore - see AMC (14020)

SAAB
*84010 **900** all models including Turbo '79 thru '88

SATURN
*87010 **Saturn** all models '91 thru '99

SUBARU
89002 **1100, 1300, 1400 & 1600** '71 thru '79
89003 **1600 & 1800** 2WD & 4WD '80 thru '94

SUZUKI
*90010 **Samurai/Sidekick & Geo Tracker** '86 thru '01

TOYOTA
92005 **Camry** all models '83 thru '91
92006 **Camry** all models '92 thru '96
*92007 **Camry, Avalon, Solara, Lexus ES 300** '97 thru '01
92015 **Celica Rear Wheel Drive** '71 thru '85
92020 **Celica Front Wheel Drive** '86 thru '99
92025 **Celica Supra** all models '79 thru '92
92030 **Corolla** all models '75 thru '79
92032 **Corolla** all rear wheel drive models '80 thru '87
92035 **Corolla** all front wheel drive models '84 thru '92
*92036 **Corolla & Geo Prizm** '93 thru '01
92040 **Corolla Tercel** all models '80 thru '82
92045 **Corona** all models '74 thru '82
92050 **Cressida** all models '78 thru '82
92055 **Land Cruiser** FJ40, 43, 45, 55 '68 thru '82
*92056 **Land Cruiser** FJ60, 62, 80, FZJ80 '80 thru '96
92065 **MR2** all models '85 thru '87
92070 **Pick-up** all models '69 thru '78
92075 **Pick-up** all models '79 thru '95
*92076 **Tacoma** '95 thru '00, **4Runner** '96 thru '00, & **T100** '93 thru '98
92080 **Previa** all models '91 thru '95

*92082 **RAV4** all models '96 thru '02
92085 **Tercel** all models '87 thru '94

TRIUMPH
94007 **Spitfire** all models '62 thru '81
94010 **TR7** all models '75 thru '81

VW
96008 **Beetle & Karmann Ghia** '54 thru '79
*96009 **New Beetle** '98 thru '00
96016 **Rabbit, Jetta, Scirocco, & Pick-up** gas models '74 thru '91 & Convertible '80 thru '92
96017 **Golf & Jetta** all models '93 thru '97
*96018 **Golf & Jetta** all models '98 thru '01
96020 **Rabbit, Jetta & Pick-up** diesel '77 thru '84
*96023 **Passat** '98 thru '01, **Audi A4** '96 thru '01
96030 **Transporter 1600** all models '68 thru '79
96035 **Transporter 1700, 1800 & 2000** '72 thru '79
96040 **Type 3 1500 & 1600** all models '63 thru '73
96045 **Vanagon** all air-cooled models '80 thru '83

VOLVO
97010 **120, 130 Series & 1800 Sports** '61 thru '73
97015 **140 Series** all models '66 thru '74
97020 **240 Series** all models '76 thru '93
97040 **740 & 760 Series** all models '82 thru '88
97050 **850 Series** all models '93 thru '97

TECHBOOK MANUALS
10205 **Automotive Computer Codes**
10210 **Automotive Emissions Control Manual**
10215 **Fuel Injection Manual, 1978 thru 1985**
10220 **Fuel Injection Manual, 1986 thru 1999**
10225 **Holley Carburetor Manual**
10230 **Rochester Carburetor Manual**
10240 **Weber/Zenith/Stromberg/SU Carburetors**
10305 **Chevrolet Engine Overhaul Manual**
10310 **Chrysler Engine Overhaul Manual**
10320 **Ford Engine Overhaul Manual**
10330 **GM and Ford Diesel Engine Repair Manual**
10340 **Small Engine Repair Manual, 5 HP & Less**
10341 **Small Engine Repair Manual, 5.5 - 20 HP**
10345 **Suspension, Steering & Driveline Manual**
10355 **Ford Automatic Transmission Overhaul**
10360 **GM Automatic Transmission Overhaul**
10405 **Automotive Body Repair & Painting**
10410 **Automotive Brake Manual**
10411 **Automotive Anti-lock Brake (ABS) Systems**
10415 **Automotive Detaling Manual**
10420 **Automotive Eelectrical Manual**
10425 **Automotive Heating & Air Conditioning**
10430 **Automotive Reference Manual & Dictionary**
10435 **Automotive Tools Manual**
10440 **Used Car Buying Guide**
10445 **Welding Manual**
10450 **ATV Basics**

SPANISH MANUALS
98903 **Reparación de Carrocería & Pintura**
98905 **Códigos Automotrices de la Computadora**
98910 **Frenos Automotriz**
98915 **Inyección de Combustible 1986 al 1999**
99040 **Chevrolet & GMC Camionetas** '67 al '87 Incluye Suburban, Blazer & Jimmy '67 al '91
99041 **Chevrolet & GMC Camionetas** '88 al '98 Incluye Suburban '92 al '98, Blazer & Jimmy '92 al '94, Tahoe y Yukon '95 al '98
99042 **Chevrolet & GMC Camionetas Cerradas** '68 al '95
99055 **Dodge Caravan & Plymouth Voyager** '84 al '95
99075 **Ford Camionetas y Bronco** '80 al '94
99077 **Ford Camionetas Cerradas** '69 al '91
99083 **Ford Modelos de Tamaño Grande** '75 al '87
99088 **Ford Modelos de Tamaño Mediano** '75 al '86
99091 **Ford Taurus & Mercury Sable** '86 al '95
99095 **GM Modelos de Tamaño Grande** '70 al '90
99100 **GM Modelos de Tamaño Mediano** '70 al '88
99110 **Nissan Camioneta** '80 al '96, **Pathfinder** '87 al '95
99118 **Nissan Sentra** '82 al '94
99125 **Toyota Camionetas y 4Runner** '79 al '95

Haynes North America, Inc., 861 Lawrence Drive, Newbury Park, CA 91320-1514 • (805) 498-6703